"This book will become a standard in the field of ethics for years to come. The depth and breadth of the research is magisterial. The footnotes alone are worth the price of the book! Regardless of one's religious tradition, Daniel Heimbach's *Fundamental Christian Ethics* should be required reading for anyone seeking to grasp this important field of study."

—**Daniel L. Akin**, president and professor of preaching and theology, Southeastern Baptist Theological Seminary

"Daniel Heimbach always careful, clear, biblical, and thorough. Beginning from a thoughtful exploration of the theological foundations and the history of ethical and moral thinking, he explores the whole range of personal, sexual, and social ethical issues, both classic and contemporary. In this outstanding resource, Heimbach helps us think and live well in the complexities of our world."

—**Gerry Breshears**, professor of theology, Western Seminary

"Daniel Heimbach has written from within the world, without being of the world. *Fundamental Christian Ethics* begins by educating and guiding the reader in a wide range of biblical, theological, historical, and philosophical fundamentals of ethics. Heimbach then practices what he preaches, directly engaging a remarkable range of ethical issues, from assisted reproduction, gambling, and pornography to wealth and poverty, religious liberty, and racism, and many more. This is a work of both depth and breadth, worthy of a correspondingly thoughtful and wide reading."

—**W. David Buschart**, professor of theological and historical studies, Denver Seminary

"The challenge of living faithfully in a pluralistic world demands a new level of engagement in the study of Christian ethics. This monumental work provides an enormous storehouse of food for thought on that subject. It combines an uncompromising call to return to the authority and supremacy of God's Word with a careful exploration of the complex, subtle, nuanced and even paradoxical nature of what we actually find when we open God's Word, and when we strive to apply it in our challenging world."

—**Greg Forster**, director, Oikonomia Network

"This exceptionally valuable resource is a remarkable achievement. It reveals a broad and deep knowledge of the field of ethics which could only be the result of a lifetime of academic research and teaching. While firmly anchored in the teachings of Scripture, Heimbach enriches his analysis with a mature understanding of philosophical ethics and of the development of Christian ethical teaching throughout church history. The bibliographical information in each section is extensive, and where there are differences among evangelical writers on certain topics, he accurately summarizes the different positions and makes reference to the best defenders of each position."

—**Wayne A. Grudem**, distinguished research professor of
theology and biblical studies, Phoenix Seminary

"Encyclopedic in scope, rich in its treasury depths, faithful to the historic Christian faith, and timely, timely, timely, Daniel Heimbach's book is the ideal go-to book for all of us negotiating the ever-bombarding issues of our harried modern fast-life."

—**Os Guinness**, senior fellow, Oxford Center for Christian Apologetics

"Comprehensive, thorough, articulate, timely, and faithful. These are just a few words that describe Daniel Heimbach's *magnum opus*. Heimbach's vast experience, careful scholarship, and mature reflection will make *Fundamental Christian Ethics* a standard work in Christian ethics for decades to come."

—**C. Ben Mitchell**, Graves Professor of Moral Philosophy, Union University

"The entire concept of Christian ethics has been confused in our secularizing age. Daniel Heimbach's *Fundamental Christian Ethics* is a massive antidote to that confusion. Here is a work that is genuinely biblical, deeply theological, consistently thoughtful, and truly Evangelical. Heimbach helps the Christian to know how to think, not just what to think, when it comes to the urgent ethical issues of our day. This book is a great contribution to Christian ethics, and it arrives on the scene just as evangelical Christians face ethical challenges from every direction at once."

—**R. Albert Mohler, Jr.**, president and Centennial Professor of Christian
Theology, The Southern Baptist Theological Seminary

Fundamental
CHRISTIAN
ETHICS

Fundamental
CHRISTIAN
ETHICS

Daniel R. Heimbach

B&H
ACADEMIC
NASHVILLE, TENNESSEE

"Let everyone who calls on the name of the Lord
turn away from wickedness" (2 Tim 2:19).

"For I have often told you, and now say again with tears,
that many live as enemies of the cross of Christ.
Their end is destruction; their god is their stomach;
their glory is in their shame" (Phil 3:18–19).

To Tong, whose life and untimely death
moved me to love the light more than the
darkness (John 3:19) and to open my
heart to Jesus (Rev 3:20) as he did.

This work is the fruit of a long journey
that started in a jungle village, took me
to the pinnacles of power, led me into
the halls of learning, and leaves me in
awe of the majesty and wonder of
God's perfections. It is my prayer
readers will perceive that tone
underlies all they read here
from start to finish.

CONTENTS

FOREWORD

Daniel R. Heimbach, Senior Research Professor of Christian Ethics at Southeastern Baptist Theological Seminary, was not always Professor Heimbach. He was Danny to his parents, Dan to his siblings, and "Doc" to his Naval Academy classmates because of the initials D. R. on his uniform nametag. He was Sir to sailors in the Navy and Lieutenant to other officers, and he became Doctor after earning his PhD. He was Professor Heimbach to me while I was a student, and he mentored me in Christian ethics. But he is Dan to me now since we have become colleagues and friends pursuing the same calling.

I remember when Dan Heimbach first told me of a book he was writing that now is *Fundamental Christian Ethics*. It was a Spring day, and I had stopped by his office on a return visit to Southeastern Baptist Theological Seminary where I had been privileged in years prior to sit under his teaching and mentorship in master's and doctoral studies. Greetings were exchanged, and for the next hour he sketched out for me what he was working on. As he did, I remember thinking, if anyone could bring a book like this to fruition, it was he. I now will share some biographical details gleaned over two decades of association in order to help readers understand the author and what makes this book the excellent resource it is.

I have encountered many over five decades of living but few with life stories in which God's leading is so evident or revealed in as fascinating a way as in Dan's life. Born of Christian missionary parents serving in remote inland China during the Communist revolution, he arrived six weeks prematurely in the middle of the night in a small Chinese inn with Communist soldiers occupying every inch of floor space in the hall outside his parents' room and a shoot-on-sight curfew outside. He was delivered by his father, who had no medical training, and without surgical instruments, sterilization, or medical assistance of any kind. When the Maoists expelled foreign missionaries in the 1950s, the Heimbach family initially relocated to Singapore and then moved into the jungles of northern Thailand where Dan's parents pioneered a work of first-contact cross-cultural evangelism, church planting, language development, and Bible translation among the Hmong, a tribal people then unreached by the gospel. The first genuine convert was a boy named Tong, and he and Danny (called "Dahnli" by the Hmong) became fast friends. Danny was not yet a Christian himself, and Tong's faith clashed with how he behaved. But Tong's tragic death drove the young Danny Heimbach to turn his life over to Jesus as truly and completely as his childhood friend who had "gone to be with Jesus." Seven decades later, God's work in Tong still impacts the mature Professor Heimbach (see this book's dedication page), and its ripple effect now extends to readers of *Basic Christian Ethics*. This book takes a path not often travelled in the genre largely because its author is a first-rate scholar who nevertheless makes unapologetic reliance on the Word of God paramount to ethical understanding and analysis.

By Heimbach's account, his parents, Ernie and Mertie, were ordinary people whose fidelity was used by God to reveal his reality and power in extraordinary ways. In a 2014 article in Southeastern's *Great Commission Magazine*, Heimbach told how seven young Hmong men evangelized, discipled, and mentored by his father, Ernie, spearheaded a mass turning of Hmong to faith in Jesus Christ. This occurred after Ernie Heimbach was assigned by the Overseas Missionary Fellowship (formerly the China Inland Mission) to broader areas of responsibility, and God used this people movement to rescue thousands of Hmong—individuals, families, and whole villages—from bondage to evil spirits and powers of spiritual darkness.

It happened also to occur just as Communist insurgents from China were starting to infiltrate the northern regions of Thailand. Thus, sinners were saved from God's wrath, but the movement also had political and national security ramifications benefiting Thailand and the world beyond. The Christian Hmong in northern Thailand—alerted by Ernie to how Communism clashes with human nature and biblical truth—would not accept the insurgent ideology. So, after Communist insurgencies succeeded in Laos, Cambodia, and Vietnam, the spread of Communism in Southeast Asia stopped in northern Thailand; and with the Christian Hmong constituting a buffer, Thailand and nations to the south remained free of

Communist domination. As the Hmong of northern Thailand bore witness, Christian faith affects everything in life, not just spiritually but materially, and not only touches personal life but also politics. Heimbach's parents were gospel missionaries, not political organizers. But as a Hmong leader told Heimbach much later, "Your father taught us how to think."

Vocational missionary service runs deep in the Heimbach family. His maternal grandparents were missionaries in what became North Korea, an uncle and aunt and many cousins have been or are career missionaries in Sudan, Tanzania, Kenya, the Czech Republic, and Mexico, and his sister, Ruthi, followed in their parents' footsteps as a career missionary in Thailand. As for Dan himself, the missionary call took a different trajectory. His sense of mission was influenced by Francis A. Schaeffer, the pastor, theologian, cultural critic, and founder of L'Abri Fellowship, who drew searching souls from around the world to a chalet in the Swiss Alps during the turbulent 1960s and 1970s. Schaeffer inspired young people searching for meaning and truth to reject the nihilism and irrational sensualism rising in Western culture and instead to embrace "the God who is there" and live by "true truth" revealed in the Word of God. In a 2014 article celebrating the gift of Schaeffer's personal library to Southeastern's L. Russ Bush Center for Faith and Culture, Heimbach summarized what Schaeffer did as engaging contemporary culture in prophetic moral witness and not only doing it in a manner faithful to what God says but also delivering God's truth "without ugliness or harshness." Heimbach now exemplifies Schaeffer's mission and approach in *Fundamental Christian Ethics*. It is there throughout the book but is especially apparent in how the book tackles hot-button issues in the last few chapters.

Schaeffer was active with the pen, releasing many influential books, beginning in 1968 with *The God Who Is There* and *Escape from Reason*. Heimbach relates how reading the latter in high school led him to view Schaeffer as a person "keenly in tune with my questions." Then at the US Naval Academy and through five years of commissioned service, including combat in the Vietnam War on a guided missile light cruiser in the Tonkin Gulf, Heimbach devoured every new book Schaeffer released. And then following an honorable discharge in 1977, he, too, made his way to Switzerland and L'Abri to meet and learn from Schaeffer directly.

In Schaeffer, Heimbach found a deep-thinking, love-impelled role model who connected biblical revelation with knowledge of history, the arts, and culture to engage questions of the day in ways that were relevant and yet completely true to the Word of God. Heimbach believed God was calling him to do the same, and that led him to pursue higher education. He first went to Trinity Evangelical Divinity School near Chicago, Illinois, where he earned

MDiv (Theology) and MA (Philosophy of Religion) degrees. At Trinity, Heimbach studied under several highly respected Evangelical figures, including Wayne Grudem, Harold O. J. Brown, Paul Feinberg, Norm Geisler, William Lane Craig, Gleeson Archer, John Woodbridge, and Walter C. Kaiser. Then from Trinity, Heimbach went to Drew University where he earned MPhil and PhD degrees in Law, Politics, and Christian Ethics. At Drew, he was schooled by academic specialists in Christian ethics who had themselves been schooled by H. Richard Niebuhr or had worked with Paul Ramsey.

Under mentoring by Edward L. Long, Jr., Heimbach's dissertation explored the intersection of religion, law, and morality with a superb critique of legal philosopher H. L. A. Hart's concept of law. His passion for the subject never faded and, of several courses I later took with him, the course Heimbach taught in religion, law, and morality was a favorite that even now significantly impacts work I do in bioethics. Heimbach's expertise in this cross discipline is uncommon among scholars in the field, and in *Basic Christian Ethics* it shows up in penetrating analyses Heimbach provides on issues dealt with in Chapters 9–12.

While still working on his doctoral dissertation, Heimbach joined the staff of US Senator Richard Lugar in Washington, DC, and there covered a range of volatile issues with enormous ethical implications, such as abortion, parenting free of government interference, fetal tissue research, drug use, and religious liberty. This experience led to four years at the highest levels of public policy and governing responsibility when Heimbach joined the George H. W. Bush Administration in 1989, first serving two years at the White House as Deputy Executive Secretary of the Domestic Policy Council and then serving two years at the Pentagon as Deputy Assistant Secretary of the Navy for Active Duty Manpower (DASNM).

Heimbach specialized in the ethics of war and peace in doctoral studies at Drew, and this became strategic when he was authorized to write a memorandum for the president laying out moral principles to guide and justify liberating Kuwait from occupation by Iraqi forces led by Saddam Hussein in 1991. From that point on, Bush countered pacifist objections to what he did in the Persian Gulf using just war principles commended by Heimbach. That, in turn, resurrected application of just war ethics in the modern world. The tradition had been dismissed as out-of-date and irrelevant since the advent of nuclear weapons. But President Bush's reliance on just war principles, based on Heimbach's memo, not only guided American actions in the Persian Gulf War but also spawned a flurry of new attention to just war ethics among contemporary scholars that continues today.

Following Bush's defeat in 1992, Heimbach briefly headed the nonpartisan Defense Readiness Council (DRC) and then joined the faculty at Southeastern Baptist Theological Seminary where, for twenty-eight years, he has taught and developed courses, developed degrees, and led in building one of the most highly regarded programs in Christian ethics anywhere in the world. Heimbach's professional leadership in Christian ethics extends beyond Southeastern to include founding and leading the Christian Ethics Section within the Evangelical Theological Society, teaching adjunctively at other colleges and seminaries, lecturing at the Marine Corps Command and Staff College, training instructors at the Naval Academy, lecturing at the Defense Intelligence Agency, training military chaplains, doing radio interviews, and providing expert testimony to the United States Congress.

Heimbach's expertise in Christian ethics has led to influencing public understanding of matters troubling the culture at large as occurred, for example, when the issue of torture in prisoner interrogation grabbed national headlines during the administration of President George W. Bush (see Appendix E). But, while prominent on war and peace, Heimbach is not a single-issue ethicist. Search his *curriculum vitae* and you will find numerous publications, invited lectures, doctoral seminars, and debates covering a wide range of subdisciplines that include historical ethics, methodology in ethics, and sexual ethics. Heimbach's work across all aspects of the field can be seen in *Basic Christian Ethics* and especially in the excellent chapters he provides surveying the history of Christian ethics from the first century to the present.

In everything, Heimbach's goal, echoing Schaeffer, has been to "promote God's truth in a culture that is rejecting it." In *Basic Christian Ethics*, Heimbach provides a resource to help present and future Christians understand, navigate, and address challenges in biblical, theological, historical, philosophical, personal, and social ethics that trouble the Church, darken the culture, and oppose the witness God wants Christians to have in the world.

Readers studied in theology, philosophy, and ethics will recognize in *Fundamental Christian Ethics* the marks of a serious student of the Bible and well-read scholar influenced by giants in the field, such as C. S. Lewis, Reinhold Niebuhr, Carl F. H. Henry, and Oliver O'Donovan, to name a few. The book's subtitle alone—announcing it introduces "the entire field"—signals the author has significant academic standing. But, while that most certainly is true in Heimbach's case, first-year seminarians, youth ministers, and interested laypeople, including parents and teenagers, need to know this book is for them as well. The author's style of communicating and passion for equipping others enable him to present profound truth in ways that make it widely accessible.

In seminary libraries one finds many textbooks claiming to introduce "Christian ethics." Most of them do it partially, only academically, or treat moral truth as nothing more than human minds reflecting upon human intuitions, human experiences, or human traditions. Philosophy cloaked in theological jargon typifies most work in the field, and that produces books that tend to be deadening, corrupted, or without much relevance. With no "thus says the Lord," scholars discussing right and wrong, good and bad, or what is virtuous and vicious leave readers swimming in uncertainty.

Yet, God truly has spoken and graciously provided in Scripture everything needed for "training in righteousness" and "equip[ping] for every good work" (2 Tim 3:16–17). *Fundamental Christian Ethics* differs from typical scholarship in the field because it treats the Word of God as foundational, and the difference this makes is increasingly evident as the book progresses. No other text introduces the field with such breadth or clarity. No other text covers the history of Christian ethics past the Social Gospel movement. No other text does more to include Evangelical figures and movements in Christian ethics. No other text better enables readers to understand how nonbiblical approaches corrupt Christian ethical understanding and produce results contrary to God's ethical reality. And, by addressing emerging issues like transgenderism, human trafficking, gene therapy, using technology, terrorism, same-sex marriage, and global warming, *Fundamental Christian Ethics* delivers a degree of contemporary relevance absent in most texts presently available.

Fundamental Christian Ethics is an extraordinary work from an extraordinary scholar. Since Dan first shared with me what he was doing in this book, I have prayed for its completion first because it is a huge undertaking and second because it is so needed. Now reading through the final draft five years later, I remain convinced on both counts. I thank God for what he has done in the life of my mentor and friend Dan Heimbach. It started years ago in the jungles of northern Thailand and results now in *Fundamental Christian Ethics*.

Beyond that, I thank him for being faithful and staying focused on what counts long term over temporary gains and so, by God's grace, finishing this part of the mission he has from God. It is the result of a lifetime, the result of learning but also of maturity tested by fire, the result of research but also of teaching, the result of application but also of time alone with God, and it is the result not only of one life but of awareness that we stand on the shoulders of those who went before—of understanding and continuing in fidelity to how God has led faithful believers from the beginning—and therefore respecting how the future depends on passing truth from one generation to the next. That pleases God and pleases me as well.

Erik Clary
Stillwater, Oklahoma

ACKNOWLEDGMENTS

This book has taken years to write—too many perhaps—but the time taken has enabled much reflection and interaction with others, and those supporting and contributing to these pages deserve recognition.

My able administrative assistant, Billie Goodenough, has been through the whole writing and production process with me and has labored to ensure its formatting, grammatical accuracy, and readability. She has pored over every word, suggested improvements, and at times kept me out of trouble. She is more than a secretary but a friend and colleague who shares the mission and understands the subject nearly as well as I do.

Erik Clary, who contributes the foreward, not only emulates the spirit of godliness promoted in this book but also is one of the smartest people I know. Erik is a former student and now a friend and professional colleague. I mentored Erik's doctoral study in the field of Christian ethics, both guiding and being challenged by him in the process, and besides composing the foreward, Erik has helped edit major portions of this book.

Many of my students at Southeastern Baptist Theological Seminary have read draft chapters and, in doing so, have encouraged me and offered helpful suggestions. Brian Waidmann, a long-time friend from my government days, has read and helped improve sections relating to his areas of expertise. I much appreciate the regular influence, interest, and support of faculty colleagues at Southeastern Baptist Theological Seminary and wish, especially, to recognize President Daniel Akin, provosts Bruce Ashford and Keith Whitfield, and my Christian ethics faculty peers Mark Liederbach, David Jones, and Seth Bible. And I am grateful to the publishing staff at B&H Academic and especially thank Jim Baird, Madison Trammel, Chris Cowan, Chris Thompson, Audrey Greeson, Jessi Wallace, and Michael McEwen for their dedication, patience, and hard work.

I am grateful to my parents, Ernie and Mertie Heimbach, for raising me in the fear of God and for being examples of Christian ethics lived before me as a child. Both were writers. My father was a visionary linguist who reduced the Hmong language to writing, translated Scripture into Hmong, started their hymnology, and composed the Hmong-English dictionary published by the US State Department, and my mother wrote short books about our family and missionaries she knew. At this writing, my mother is over 102 and can no longer see to read. But she bathed this project in prayer all through her nineties, which means more to me than words can say.

I cannot credit my wife, Anna, and sons and daughters-in-law, Jonathan and Nikki, and Joel and Shea, enough for their love, support, prayers, and encouragement. Conversations at home have often started with, "Dad, how's the book going?" And Anna has often compared my writing with childbirth, noting always that she took less time to deliver results than I was taking. This book could not have been written without their backing.

I am most grateful of all, however, to the unseen God who commissioned this book and enabled and guided the whole process. This book is about him, is for him, and is through him. If he does not exist or has not spoken, this book is trash. But he does and has. And that fixes the reality, truth, and importance of what this book is about.

INTRODUCTION

This book is written to resource Christians engaging our culture and the world in moral witness at a time when most are "suppressing the truth" (Rom 1:18) and substituting "darkness for light and light for darkness" (Isa 5:20). We live in days when contesting ethical authority and ethical truth, as well as framing ethical thought, are critical challenges. These all have been contested since our first parents sinned in the Garden of Eden (Gen 3:1–6). But the intensity of ethical conflict rises and falls, and we live at a time when hostility toward ethical reality framed by God is on the rise and the difference it makes is getting more and more obvious. This is a textbook for courses preparing Christian scholars, teachers, and future ministers to understand and apply God's norms, cultivate and inspire godly character, and interpret and teach God's ethical reality. But it is written not just for scholars, teachers, and ministers. It embodies academic rigor but presents content in a manner making it accessible to any interested reader.

Christian ethics is a matter of faith (Heb 11:6), and the biggest challenge to getting it right is, "Did God really say?" (Gen 3:1). Reason and experience are involved, but not as authorities. Reason and experience do not set the compass we live by. They facilitate understanding but do not determine what is ethical. Christian ethical understanding starts with God, depends on God, and ends with God. It requires believing God exists, is the source and measure of good, and is holding us accountable.

Without faith in the one true God who exists, there is no Christian ethics. Christian ethics requires believing in something "unseen" (Heb 11:1) and then viewing what is "seen" in view of something "unseen." A God we do not see determines what is or is not ethical, what is or is not good or bad, what is or is not pure or sinful, and what is or is not righteous or wicked. This unseen God has spoken, and the greatest ethical challenge we have is not intellectual, practical, or scientific but taking the unseen God at his Word—believing and trusting what the unseen God reveals in the Bible. When we doubt the Word of God, we doubt God, and when we trust something else, the moral compass orienting our desires, understanding, and actions changes. If that happens, the ethics we follow can no longer be truly "Christian." Scholars may call it "Christian," and we may call it "Christian." But it is not Christian in the sense of aligning with God and his ethical reality.

This book is the product of a lifetime. It is not entirely sufficient and is not inerrant. No human author achieves that unless inspired by God to write Scripture. This book is not Scripture. But it is the product of much reading, studying, teaching, and thinking. And, considering the subject, it is important to say it also results from much prayer, contemplation, and meditation on the Word of God. It is not lightly considered, not written in a flash, and not compiled just to pass minimal standards. It is the product of a lifetime walking with the Savior through times of testing and growth, along with academic learning and a lot of teaching experience.

The book is dedicated to Tong, my childhood best friend, because it results in a way from the impact he had on me, an impact that set me on a course connected now with this book. The book serves a life mission, or sense of calling, that started with Tong back when both of us were very young. It is not written to climb a professional ladder because it comes at the end of a full and satisfying career when advancing professional credentials is irrelevant. It is written voluntarily and for no reason other than to serve something God is doing, to complete something God has commissioned me to do, and to fulfill something owed my friend Tong. So, what happened?

My parents were first-contact missionaries to the White Hmong of northern Thailand, and I grew up in the jungle with them. Even though only about five or six years old, Tong was the first truly serious Hmong convert, and we became best childhood friends. I was the "mish-kid" who knew about Jesus and the gospel but did not take it seriously. Tong did. He was a true Christian, and I was not. He took it seriously and tried his best to get me to as well. Then he died in a way God used to communicate his reality and power over evil spirits who kept the Hmong in fear. Tong's death shook me into taking God seriously as he had. Tong was the "good one" and I was not. He did not deserve to die, and I did. But he had been ready to die and was with Jesus, whereas if I died, I was not ready and would not be where he was. That is when I became a true Christian. Tong had wanted nothing other than to live for Christ, and on coming to faith I felt, in a sense, that my life needed to count in place of the one he gave up. I know God deals with us individually. But it inspired me to live on God's terms rather than my own. God took Tong early and left me, and I have wanted to serve God as he would have. That led to the mission I have to engage in moral witness, led to a career in Christian ethics, and led to writing this resource to equip others God calls to pursue the same mission.

Because we live in a fallen world, there is a difference between Christian ethics as a divine discipline and Christian ethics as an academic discipline. There is a difference between what Christian ethics means to God and what scholars do with it. We are not God, and anyone writing on Christian ethics is a finite fallen creature. But neither are we limited to imagining what Christian ethics means to God because he has gone to great lengths to reveal that to us as opposed to what humans fabricate.

If there really is a God, we cannot make things up and call it "Christian ethics" without upsetting God. Some do that because they do not believe God exists or do not care if he does. People like that are not Christian. At least they are not Christian in the way Scripture defines it. Nothing anyone makes up on his or her own is real Christian ethics in the divine-discipline sense, and people claiming otherwise should not be listened to. Real Christian ethics in the divine-discipline sense starts with fearing the God revealed in the Bible, and anything else is a sham. It is not the real thing. Christian ethics in the divine-discipline sense is a matter of discovering things that are real and not simply a matter of smart people making things up. It includes some speculating. But even that is not the same as making things up out of thin air because it starts with revealed truth and follows implications.

Speculating based on nothing more than making things up can never be real Christian ethics in the divine-discipline sense even if done by professing Christians. Everything Christians say and do is not necessarily Christian and, if Christians make things up based on nothing more than imagining, it is not Christian ethics in the divine-discipline sense even if that person is a Christian. Christian ethics in the divine-discipline sense starts with something God says, and interpretation is restrained by fearing to take it any way other than God intends.

So, there is a difference between Christian ethics in the academic-discipline sense and Christian ethics in the divine-discipline sense. There is a difference between Christian ethics as scholarship and Christian ethics that pleases God. This is an academic textbook, so it must introduce readers to Christian ethics in the academic-discipline sense. But it also is written to help people who want to live lives that are holy and pleasing to God. So, while introducing Christian ethics in the academic-discipline sense, the book also clarifies and encourages Christian ethics in the God-pleasing divine-discipline sense. And, of these, the second counts more than the first. The first is academically necessary, but the second is spiritually necessary as well. The first concerns scholarship, but the second concerns godliness as well. The first addresses human understanding, but the second addresses pleasing God as well. And it turns out faith is essential to Christian ethics in both cases. Faith enables us to distinguish what is or is not true while studying Christian ethics academically, and faith is the prerequisite to living lives that are holy and pleasing to God.

This book tries to be comprehensive, balanced, historical, up-to-date, and faithful. Comprehensive treatments are not always balanced, historical treatments are not always up-to-date, up-to-date treatments often skip what came before, and libraries are filled with treatments deviating from the Word of God. This book attempts all these at the same time. It also combines scholarship with regular appeal, analysis with common associations, principles with application, and truth with real life. Academics often write in ways that go over the heads of regular readers, and popular writers often assume regular readers cannot be reached without sacrificing academic rigor. I do not agree. When it comes to important things like Christian ethics, the best approach is one appealing to common imagination while addressing profound ideas. Moral truth should not be obscured by argot (specialized vocabulary known only to insiders). The book also tries to be accurate, clear, and concise. It is easy to be dense in the name of accuracy, lengthy in the name of clarity, and imprecise in the name of brevity. This book tries to be accurate, clear, and concise all at the same time.

Writing this way aims at combining the academic rigor of Oliver O'Donovan with the rhetorical skills of C. S. Lewis. Christ is preeminent when it comes to revealing, interpreting, and explaining what Christian ethics should be. But my less than perfect human models for scholarship and style are O'Donovan and Lewis. What truth this book communicates stands on the shoulders of countless teachers before me. The ultimate source of that truth is God himself; any errors or omissions are mine, and what readers do with it depends on them.

"Pray . . . that I may make it known as I should."
Colossians 4:3–4

CHAPTER 1

IMPORTANCE, MEANING & DISTINCTIVES

The greatest challenge in our age, both to the life and witness of the Church and the to survival of surrounding culture, is widespread denial of moral authority, leading to a range of nefarious effects caused by postmodern rejection of objectively fixed truth, secularization of public life, pluralization of worldviews, and privatization of religion.[1] Sadly, one of these effects is the growing hostility toward anything Christian, and fidelity to objectively fixed moral reality is now more openly and seriously contested by surrounding culture than any other area of Christian faith and witness.[2]

---

[1] Joseph Ratzinger, before becoming Pope Benedict XVI, observed in 1984 that "mankind today . . . is in danger of being ruined from within by his own moral decay. But instead of struggling against this life-threatening disease, he stares as though hypnotized at the external danger (i.e., at problems such as war, crime, poverty, economic collapse, rebellion, drug-trafficking, slavery, prostitution, pornography, teen-pregnancy, or single-parenting) which is only a byproduct of his own inner moral disease." Joseph Ratzinger, "Bishops, Theologians and Morality," *Origins* 13 (March 15, 1984): 657.

[2] Carl F. H. Henry observed in 1957 that "Christianity's millennium-long barricade against a resurging paganism is weakening before the onslaughts of iniquity. Powerful forces aim to alter, to discredit, (and) even to replace it . . . moral earnestness almost everywhere halts indecisively at the

Revolutionary movements bent on redefining justice and truth are deconstructing essential institutions in order to justify embracing sensuality, elevating lifestyle over the value of innocent human life, stealing what others have fairly acquired or inherited, overturning the rule of law to pursue impossible ideals, covering the pleas of needy neighbors with a din of lavish self-indulgence, and abandoning lifelong duties for the distractions of passing pleasure. These trends all reject the Judeo-Christian base on which the institutions of Western civilization were erected and without which they cannot endure. Institutions such as marriage, property ownership, free-market enterprise, justice, law, education, and national security cannot maintain themselves and will collapse when loosed from their moral moorings.[3]

Never in the history of the Church or of Western civilization has there been more need for renewing serious study, instruction, and application of Christian ethics in ways that equip Christian men and women to engage surrounding culture in prophetic moral witness. And this should be done not merely to preserve religious freedom or merely to assure personal flourishing, but rather to glorify God by securing the common good on which every man, woman and child relies whether religious or secular, Christian or non-Christian. That is because the foundations on which cohesive social order relies are essentially moral, and preserving the moral order on which social strength and stability rely not only preserves freedom to promote the gospel of Jesus Christ but also assures the survival of civilization.[4]

This means that, even though it insults the spirit of our age, God calls Christians to promote respect for, and compliance with, the objectively fixed reality and universal relevance of God's true moral truth—what Francis Schaeffer called "true truth"—in contrast to other

---

Christian-pagan crossroads." Carl F. H. Henry, *Christian Personal Ethics* (Grand Rapids: Eerdmans, 1957), 13. What Henry saw over fifty years ago has only grown to be far more intense today.

[3] On this, George Washington, first president of the United States, famously declared that "of all the dispositions and habits, which lead to political prosperity, Religion and Morality are indispensable supports. . . . A volume could not trace all their connexions with private and public felicity. . . . And let us with caution indulge the supposition, that morality can be maintained without religion . . . . reason and experience both forbid us to expect, that national morality can prevail in exclusion of religious principle." George Washington, "Farewell Address to the People of the United States" (Philadelphia, 1796), paragraph 27.

[4] Henry claimed, "Ethics is the incisive and universal requisite for survival," and so believed today's "crises in ethics will determine both the continuance of present-day civilization and the destiny of individuals within our culture." Henry, *Christian Personal Ethics*, 13.

moral claims that are ultimately distorted or false.[5] We must resist moral corrosion and, at the same time, strive to make positive gains in the enormous moral war tearing through our surrounding culture and tormenting the Church.

Reinhold Niebuhr observed that "confused and tormented by cataclysmic events in contemporary history, the *modern mind* faces the disintegration of its civilization in alternate moods of fear and hope." He held that because contemporary culture is "the artifact of modern civilization . . . it is therefore not surprising that its minarets of the spirit should fall when the material foundations of its civilization begin to crumble." Yet, Niebuhr did not despair and rather saw this as giving Christians a prime opportunity to redirect our morally rebellious culture back toward God-honoring truth. For Niebuhr, the very darkness of our times means that Christian ethics characterized by "a faith which claims to have a light, *the same yesterday, today, and forever* might conceivably become (once more) a source of illumination to its age."[6] Similarly, Carl F. H. Henry once said, "Either we shall witness the dissolving of all our duties into mere conventions, or we shall mature afresh to the conviction that Hebrew-Christian ethical realities alone can lift the Western world from the mires of paganism."[7] Christians must not curse the darkness but resolve all the more to make a positive moral difference, and for that we must know and understand the meaning and resources of Christian ethics.

In Ephesians 5:15–17, Paul, led by the Holy Spirit, addressed Christians living in "evil days" such as those we now face. Without a doubt, we live in a day of moral relativism, a day of false ideology, a day when right is declared "wrong" and wrong is declared "right," a day when our families, culture, and nation are sinking into moral chaos. The day when most cultural and civic leaders expressed automatic public respect (however insincerely) for Judeo-Christian values is over. Biblical morality is now openly despised, even ridiculed, by cultural trendsetters, and we are seeing the logical effects.

Nevertheless, these disturbing trends are not inevitable. They can be resisted, slowed, and even reversed. But for that to occur, our culture must be infused by a renewal of godly character, moral clarity, and convictional leadership, and the chance we have of moving that

---

[5] Francis A. Schaeffer, *Escape from Reason*, in *The Complete Works of Francis A. Schaeffer: A Christian Worldview*, vol. 1, *A Christian View of Philosophy and Culture* (Wheaton, IL: Crossway, 1982), 218.

[6] Reinhold Niebuhr, *An Interpretation of Christian Ethics* (San Francisco: Harper & Row, 1935), 1. Niebuhr was writing in 1935, but he could have said those words today.

[7] Henry, *Christian Personal Ethics*, 15.

direction will not last much longer. We have a window of opportunity, but that window is closing. Thus, we live in a day when Christian moral witness is no longer one of several equally important segments of a larger mission but has become the pivot on which the dual tasks of fulfilling the Great Commission and of preserving our nation are both turning.

God's message in Ephesians 5:15–17 not only warns that evil days will come but also urges Christians living at such times to make the most of the opportunities they have. This urgent need is exactly what Henry expressed when he said,

> In an age when accepted standards of right and wrong are scorned, when absolutes are demeaned as a return to the superseded past, when doubt threatens to evaporate great national beliefs and political principles and weakens inherited guidelines, when new conceptions degrade the minds and corrupt the lives of the newly emerging generations, those who refuse to abandon history to the forces of decadence must speak out.[8]

The United States Constitution guarantees freedom of religion, freedom of speech, and freedom of peaceful assembly. But despite those legal guarantees, the ground under our feet is moving and moving rather fast. Our political, social, and religious circumstances are changing, and these legally assured political freedoms are eroding. For now, we are free in the eyes of contemporary law to influence, advise, warn, criticize, and vote in ways that translate and apply the measures of God's moral ordering to all areas of life—from raising families, educating children, running businesses, and leading our nation. But we must not take these freedoms for granted and are obligated to use our freedoms to make a God-honoring, neighbor-loving, character-building, marriage-affirming, life-promoting, family-strengthening, economy-saving, justice-assuring, civilization-preserving difference in our own lives and the lives of others living around us.

---

[8] Carl F. H. Henry. *Has Democracy Had Its Day?* (Nashville: ERLC, 1996), 23. In the same work, Henry also says that "to exhibit again the truths and ethical absolutes of revealed religion—not the least of all that Jesus Christ is *the truth*—and define the public behavior this implies for a secular culture that has reached a moral dead end, and to do so compatibly with democratic principles, is now our demanding task." Henry, 62.

Why Be Ethical?

The first question to consider when starting a study of ethics is, "Why be ethical?" Why care about living a morally worthy life? It is a question we must consider even before clarifying exactly what "ethics" means, and that is because answering the question is what gets us to begin. It is the question that grabs our attention enough to generate interest in wanting to understand and pursue ethics. Why should we be interested in being morally good? Why even bother in the first place? The question matters because people who think caring to be moral is trivial or irrelevant never take any further steps. They never start the journey.

Plato began his treatment of ethics with this question and gave two answers that have characterized philosophical speculation on ethics ever since.[9] In Plato's *Republic*, Socrates debated two brothers, Glaucon and Adeimantus, who identified two contrary ways to answer the question, "Why be moral?" Socrates accepted the possibilities they offer but defended one of these two ways, while the brothers defended the other. The brothers, Glaucon and Adeimantus, argued that people only are moral for its desirable effects, and Socrates argued that some do that, but some also choose to be moral for its own value.

To illustrate the difference, Glaucon told the *Ring of Gyges* story, in which a magic ring allows wearers to become invisible at will, thus rendering them free to behave however they most desire without facing negative consequences. If that were so, Glaucon claimed that everyone would use the chance to act immorally, and that, he said, goes to show that people are moral only because they fear or prefer effects caused by a power imposing what is obligatory despite their own free will. Against this view, Socrates instead argued that while being moral does have effects that should be desired,[10] that is not the only reason to be moral, and that besides having desirable effects, being moral is also desirable for its own sake. In other words, Socrates held that being moral is still worth desiring even when it has no desirable effects.

---

[9] Plato, *The Republic* II.357–68. Scott Rae mentions this briefly in *Moral Choices: An Introduction to Ethics*, 4th ed. (Grand Rapids: Zondervan, 2018), 11. For a more in-depth treatment, see William C. Mattison, III, *Introducing Moral Theology: True Happiness and the Virtues* (Grand Rapids: Brazos, 2008), 21–28.

[10] The "morality of happiness" view is argued here by Socrates. But because the book is by Plato, and most believe Plato agreed with Socrates on this point, it, therefore, is likely Plato was using the mouth of Socrates to defend his own view from the position taken by Glaucon and Adeimantus.

To summarize, the "the people choose to be moral only for desirable effects" view (defended by Glaucon and Adeimantus) holds that morality is something we choose only so long as we prefer its desirable effects and would not choose if we thought we could get away with it. They held that immorality generally is more profitable for individuals than morality, and as individuals, people agree to be moral only because they are not powerful enough to get away with being immoral. It is not being able to get away with immorality without negative consequences that forces people to prefer morality, not because morality is inherently worth it, but only because they want to gain the positive benefits of a moral reputation and to avoid the impairment of a bad reputation. And, in Socrates's view, morality is something we choose not just for desirable effects but also and primarily because doing what morality requires is a good and desirable thing all by itself, and therefore, people are immoral only when ignorant of their own true happiness. With this, Socrates concluded, even if being moral has no good effects, and even if doing the right thing produces unpleasant results, people will choose to be moral if they simply know how good it is independent of whatever effects occur.

These two answers given to "Why be moral?" have divided philosophers throughout history. But what does God say? The Bible has much to say on this topic, and there are points at which God's answers are similar to what philosophers have said. For instance, we can see places where the Bible stresses the inherent value of living a morally worthy life and even stresses the intrinsic value of moral rules themselves (Ps 119), and we can see where it says that godly men and women must want to obey God even when everything on earth goes wrong (Job 13:15). Thus, we can see that the Bible aligns with Socrates in some way. But on further examination, we discover places where the Bible stresses desirable rewards that follow doing the right thing (Deut 28:1–14), discourages immorality because it produces bad results (Deut 28:15–68), and comforts righteous people who suffer by assuring them that ultimate results will make it all worthwhile (Ps 73; 2 Cor 4:17). Thus, we can see the Bible, also in some way, aligns with Glaucon and Adeimantus.

God's moral revelation is a lot more complex than most philosophers suppose, and while things in the Bible may align with what one or another philosopher says, there also are many differences that separate what the Bible reveals from all that philosophers say. Not only does the Bible give more answers to the question than Plato imagined, but it also gives answers that are categorically different. While human philosophers give answers that are speculative, theoretical, and impersonal, the Bible gives answers that are dogmatic,[11] verified by the Word of God, and personal in nature. Biblical answers are dogmatic and verified because they are given by the moral ruler of the universe himself and are not generated by fallible human thinkers and maintained by nothing more than human tradition. Biblical answers also are personal in nature because moral obligation in the Bible is to God who is himself personal and no mere theory, rule, or philosophy.

The Bible gives at least twelve motivations that should arouse desire to pursue moral purity. There could be still more, but these are enough to show that God offers many more answers to the "Why be ethical?" question than all human philosophers combined. In the Bible, motives to be ethical include: (1) to be holy as God is holy (Lev 19:2; 1 Pet 1:15–16; 1 John 3:3); (2) to please and glorify God in all we think, say, and do (Prov 16:7; Isa 56:4–5; John 8:29; Rom 12:1–2; 1 Cor 6:20; 1 Thess 4:1; 2 Tim 2:4); (3) to serve and protect God's reputation in the world (Ps 20:7; Matt 5:16; 1 Cor 10:31; Phil 2:14–15; 2 Thess 1:11–12; 1 Pet 2:12); (4) to earn a good reputation for ourselves before others (Prov 10:7; 22:1; Eccl 7:1); (5) to receive God's blessings of provision and protection (Ps 1:6; 34:8–10; Prov 18:10; Matt 6:33); (6) to keep from angering or offending God (Prov 8:13; 1 Cor 6:15; 1 Pet 1:17); (7) to access wisdom and knowledge hidden in Christ (Col 2:2–3); (8) to show gratitude for God's gift of salvation (Heb 10:28–29); (9) to be a good influence on children and others following our example (Prov 14:26–27; Matt 5:13–15; Eph 6:4; Heb 12:11); (10) to cooperate with God's work and presence in our lives (1 Cor 3:16; 6:19–20; Phil 2:12–13); (11) to fulfill God's good purposes (Phil 2:16; 1 Tim 1:5); and (12) to earn a reward in heaven (Matt 5:10; 16:27; Luke 6:35; 1 Cor 3:14–15; Eph 6:8; Rev 22:12).

Of these, God's promise to reward ethical behavior is subject to more criticism than other biblical motives mainly because of how it seems to mix Christian ethics with mercenary self-interest. This concern comes from the influence of Stoic philosophers who insisted moral

---

[11] By saying the Bible gives "dogmatic" answers, I mean they are declared with authority and are not just surmised or conjectured. When God answers the "Why be moral?" question, he states what is factually true and is not guessing. Obviously, I do not mean the Bible ever speaks with blind prejudice or groundless opinion.

good must be desired for its own sake and "not because of any hope or fear or any external incentive"[12] and from Immanuel Kant, who claimed being ethical needs no "incentive other than the (moral) law itself."[13] C. S. Lewis addresses this criticism, saying,

> If there lurks in most modern minds the notion that to desire our own good and earnestly to hope for the enjoyment of it is a bad thing, I submit that this notion has crept in from Kant and the Stoics and is no part of the Christian faith. Indeed, if we consider the unblushing promises of reward and the staggering nature of the rewards promised in the Gospels, it would seem that Our Lord finds our desires not too strong but too weak. We are half-hearted creatures, fooling about with drink and sex and ambition when infinite joy is offered us, like an ignorant child who wants to go on making mud pies in a slum because he cannot imagine what is meant by the offer of a holiday at the sea. We are too easily pleased.
>
> We must not be troubled by unbelievers when they say that this promise of reward makes the Christian life a mercenary affair. There are different kinds of rewards. There is the reward which has no natural connection with the things you do to earn it and is quite foreign to the desires that ought to accompany those things. Money is not the natural reward for love; that is why we call a man mercenary if he marries a woman for the sake of her money. But marriage is the proper reward for a real lover, and he is not mercenary for desiring it.[14]

How the Meaning of "Ethics" Has Evolved

Understanding what *ethics* means requires starting with how the word began and tracing how its use has evolved over time. Human beings have been concerned with right and wrong and with worthy living since before recorded history. But our word *ethics* originated with three Greek words: ἠθικός (*ēthikos*, characteristic, customary, habitual), ἦθος (*ēthos*, character, custom, habit, habitat), and ἔθος (*ethos*, custom, habit, habitat), that came to be linked with this

[12] Diogenes Laërtius, *Lives of the Eminent Philosophers*, 7.89.
[13] Immanuel Kant, *Religion within the Limits of Reason Alone*, trans. T. M. Greene and H. H. Hudson (New York: Harper and Row, 1960), 3.
[14] C. S. Lewis, *The Weight of Glory* (New York: HarperCollins, 2001), 26–27.

ancient interest. What these words meant changed over time even among the Greeks, and after the term *ethics* was adopted by English speakers, what it meant continued to evolve so that it covers more now than it did earlier.

Our word *ethics* began with the Greek word ἠθικός (*ēthikos*), which is an adjective coming from the noun ἦθος (*ēthos*),[15] which in turn is a slightly more emphatic form of the noun ἔθος (*ethos*). Except for the difference between adjectives and nouns, all three words had approximately the same original meaning and thus share the same interesting history.[16] Before Aristotle, these words had no philosophical or theological significance and only referred to customary conduct or contexts (habits and habitats). And yet, even at this early stage, they treated internal disposition and external behavior as one thing because, to the ancients, these were inseparable realities. These terms addressed a "way of living," and because that assumes particular values sustaining particular "ways of living," these terms were used for distinguishing one sort of creature or "way of living" from other sorts. Paul captures this early pre-philosophical meaning of *ethics* when quoting an old Greek proverb that says, "Bad company corrupts good morals" (1 Cor 15:33). Here the word ἤθη (*ēthē*), translated "morals," refers to habits a creature lives by and does not yet carry the latter sense of dogma, philosophy, or even a set of established rules. In other words, the Greek proverb originally meant something more like "bad associations erode good habits."

Aristotle (384–322 BC) was the first on record to connect ἠθικός (*ēthikos*), ἦθος (*ēthos*), and ἔθος (*ethos*) with trying to understand right (as opposed to morally evil) living. He was not the first to examine good and evil or to contemplate living well, but he was the first to connect these particular words with doing that. The ancient Hebrews and early Greeks both were

---

[15] Aristotle, *The Nicomachean Ethics*, Penguin Classics edition, translated by J. A. K. Thompson (London: Penguin Books, 2004), 30n2.

[16] Douma claims that a distinction between ἔθος (*ethos*) and ἦθος (*ēthos*) "is rarely visible" and that scholars should accept "that both senses merge." Jochem Douma, *Responsible Conduct: Principles of Christian Ethics*, trans. Nelson D. Kloosterman (Phillipsburg, NJ: P&R, 2003), 3. But Aristotle indicates that he himself saw a slight variation in what the words meant, saying, "character (ἠθική), on the one hand, is the result of habits (ἤθους, *ēthous*), from which it has actually got its name, being a slight modification of ἤθους (*ethous*)." Aristotle, *Nicomachean Ethics* 1103.a.16–19. In other words, while acknowledging a close connection between the words in both meaning and form, he nevertheless treats ἠθική (*ēthikē*) as able to indicate something (character) produced by ἤθους (*ethous*) not fully present in what the word meant as it was (habit).

interested in these topics, but they used different words. Plato (427–347 BC) dealt extensively with moral reasoning in his *Republic* but used the word δικαιοσύνη (*dikaiosunē*, rightness, justice), not ἠθικός (*ēthikos*).[17] And the ancient Hebrews dealt extensively with good and evil, right and wrong, and living a worthy life, but used words like: (1) דֶּרֶךְ (*derek*, way, manner, custom) as in Deuteronomy 10:12, 2 Samuel 22:31, Psalm 86:11, Proverbs 3:6, Proverbs 16:25, Isaiah 55:8, and Hosea 14:9; (2) חֻקּוֹת (*huqot*, custom, practice, manner) as in Leviticus 18:30, Leviticus 20:23, and 2 Kings 17:8; and (3) אֹרַח (*'orah*, path, way of life) as in Psalm 27:11, Psalm 119:9, Proverbs 2:8, Proverbs 4:14, and Isaiah 26:8. The point is that what *ethics* now means refers to something people were addressing long before Aristotle connected using the word with what it was they were addressing. Therefore, it is inaccurate to suggest the subject to which *ethics* now refers all started with Aristotle as if no one thought or cared about right and wrong or worthy living before he came along.[18]

When it comes to understanding the words ἠθικός (*ēthikos*), ἦθος (*ēthos*), and ἔθος (*ethos*), from which our word *ethics* comes, it is illuminating to note that before they were used for examining right and wrong, and even before they were connected with human conduct, they had to do with the "haunts" or "abodes" of wild animals living in their natural surroundings or "habitats."[19] They first had to do with the customary habits and habitats

---

[17] Plato's *Republic* opens with Socrates requesting a definition of δικαιοσύνη (*dikaiosunē*), with which he launches into a discourse on what we now call "ethics." Plato, *Republic* 331.c.

[18] For example, some take Raziel Abelson's relatively true statement that "Ethical philosophy began in the fifth century BC, with the appearance of Socrates" to be expressing the false notion that "ethics" as a matter of human concern only began with and did not exist prior to the Greeks. Of course, dealing with this claim depends on how much "philosophy" covers and to what "ethics" refers. I will argue that if "philosophy" only concerns human speculation, then "ethics" entails more than "philosophy." Accordingly, "ethics" in the full sense began with man's handling of God's first moral command in the Garden of Eden (Gen 2:17; 3:1–6). See Raziel Abelson and Kai Nielsen, "Ethics, History of," *The Encyclopedia of Philosophy*, vol 3 (New York: Macmillan, 1967), 82.

[19] For example, the Greek historian Herodotus (c. 484–c. 425 BC) used ἤθεα (*ēthea*) to reference "dens" where lions lived in the wild. Herodotus, *The Histories* 7.125. In this regard, Birch and Rasmussen are right about ἦθος (*ēthos*) originally referring to animal dwellings (habitats) but are wrong then to associate the word with human provision of "stability" for domestic animals in artificially constructed "stables." All ancient references are to haunts of wild animals in their customary surroundings, and there is no etymological connection to the words "stable" or "stability." Bruce C. Birch and Larry L. Rasmussen, *Bible and Ethics in the Christian Life* (Minneapolis: Augsburg, 1989), 38.

of animals, and then later were used for a "way of life" sustaining the well-being of men. At this early stage, these words did not yet include the idea of having one proper way of judging right and wrong that applied to everyone, but they did include the idea of standards to which life should conform from the start. Their meaning built on the deep significance customary habits and habitats have for keeping life ordered, secure, and coherent. They had to do with life as it should be. And even though "what should be" varied from one thing to another, they assumed a "larger scheme of things" in reference to which one could assess the way animals and people ought to live. What was customary for lions was different from fish, and both were different from people. But no living creature simply made this all up for themselves.

What Aristotle did was to take the words ἠθικός (*ēthikos*), ἦθος (*ēthos*), and ἔθος (*ethos*), which until he came along only referred to the natural habits and habitats of animals and people, and to begin using them for the study of morally worthy living. Animals live by instinct, but Aristotle saw that when it came to human beings, customary habits needed to be justified. They had to be based on more than selfish ambition or blind prejudice. There had to be a good reason that made some behaviors right and others wrong. Aristotle decided the explanation for this was to be found in qualities of character underlying the ways people behave, and he used ἠθικός (*ēthikos*), ἦθος (*ēthos*), and ἔθος (*ethos*) for examining what these qualities were. For Aristotle, *ethics* only meant examining personal character or the study of virtue and vice and did not include examining the goods of common living (politics), of practical experience (wisdom), of divine revelation (theology), of aligning life with natural purposes (natural law), or of social discipline (human law). *Ethics* for Aristotle only had to do with studying traits of individual character, and other words were needed for the rest.

Aristotle lived four centuries before the New Testament, and his ideas were familiar to all educated people in the first-century Roman world. But the new meaning Aristotle gave to ἠθικός (*ēthikos*) still was so narrowly applied that the term never appears in the New Testament, and the words ἦθος (*ēthos*), and ἔθος (*ethos*) were used by New Testament writers only in their pre-Aristotelian non-philosophical sense of custom or habit.[20] Where writers of the New

---

[20] These words appear in the New Testament in the following forms: ἤθη (1 Cor 15:33); ἔθος (Luke 1:9; 2:42; 22:39; John 19:40; Acts 25:16; Heb 10:25); ἔθη (Acts 6:14; 16:21); ἔθει (Acts 15:1); ἐθῶν (Acts 26:3); ἔθεσι(ν) (Acts 21:21; 28:17); and εἰωθὸς (an obsolete form of ἔθος, Luke 4:16; Acts 17:2).

Testament do refer to what *ethics* means today, they use the word ἀναστροφή (*anastrophē*), manner of life, way of conduct, values by which people live.[21]

After Aristotle, the term *ethics* was for a long time used only for human-centered speculation about worthy living, and even then, only concerned analyzing individual character (virtues). This limited what the word *ethics* meant all the way into the nineteenth century, when the British philosopher Henry Sidgwick (1838–1900), in his early writing, still limited *ethics* to examining attributes of character. But over his career, Sidgwick started using the term in a way that also included studying right and wrong beyond individual character, and what Sidgwick did influenced others. Since the way Sidgwick used the term changed over his career, what he says in one place does not always agree with what he says in another. For example, he first says, "I have taken pains to keep Ethics as separate as I conveniently could from Theology and Metaphysics, and also from Politics,"[22] but then later he says, "Ethics is sometimes considered as an investigation of the true Moral laws or rational precepts of Conduct; (and) sometimes as an inquiry into the nature of the Ultimate End of reasonable human action."[23] In the first place, he follows Aristotle by limiting *ethics* to studying nothing more than individual character (virtue), but in the second he expands what *ethics* means to include examining right and wrong actions and goals as well.

By the end of his career, Sidgwick had enlarged the word *ethics* to mean speculating about right and wrong, not only in relation to character but also in relation to actions and goals, and not only as it concerns individuals but communities and groups as well (politics). And yet, while Sidgwick expanded the meaning of *ethics* to cover more than before, the word at that time still only concerned what is human (not divine), speculative (not dogmatic), mundane (not transcendent), formal (not substantive), theoretical (not practical), and rational (not relational, existential, or personal). It was restricted to human-generated, human-centered philosophical speculation and did not include moral revelation from God. It also did not include real standards of right and wrong by which people should live and only involved speculating what these standards might be. This realization explains why William Wilberforce

---

[21] As, for example, in 2 Corinthians 1:12; 1 Timothy 3:15; Hebrews 13:18; 1 Peter 1:17; 3:2; 2 Peter 3:11.

[22] Henry Sidgwick, *Outlines of the History of Ethics* (London: Macmillan, 1892), vi.

[23] Henry Sidgwick, *The Methods of Ethics* (London: Macmillan, 1901), 2–3.

(1759–1833), when speaking of his aim to reform the ethics of English culture, used the word *manners* instead of *ethics*.[24] Wilberforce sought to reform the way people were behaving, setting goals, and making value judgments, but he lived at a time when the word *ethics* meant less than it does now.[25] For Wilberforce, *manners* covered all aspects of right and wrong, including what actually governs the real world, and the word *ethics* did not yet cover that.

Expansion of what the word *ethics* means to include all aspects of moral understanding and practice did not occur until the middle of the twentieth century when Karl Barth (1886–1968) and others stressed how God not only has revealed much about right and wrong in the real world but also judges us by standards of good and bad that have applied all along. The Bible contains God's moral law, and theologians have been studying what it says for centuries.[26] So if *ethics* had to do with real standards to which human beings must actually conform to live worthy lives, then *ethics* in this sense had to include moral theology.

In fact, Barth realized that *ethics* was coming to be used for everything and anything to do with the understanding and practice of right and wrong, and if so, that means what God

---

[24] On October 28, 1787, Wilberforce wrote in his diary, "God Almighty has set before me two great objects, the suppression of the slave trade and the reformation of manners." Cited from Robert Isaac and Samuel Wilberforce, *The Life of William Wilberforce*, vol. 1 (London: John Murray, 1838), 149. Of Wilberforce's Second Great Object, one biographer writes, "The goal of the reformation of manners was to turn the tide of immorality in Britain. The profligacy and moral decay that marked the Regency era (when Wilberforce first entered public life) gave way to the moral integrity and concern for the welfare of others that was the hallmark of the Victorian era (which began in 1837, just a few years after his death). Wilberforce and his fellow philanthropists were salt and light in their generation, and set on foot an incredible array of charitable initiatives. Their legacy offers the best model we have for turning around a society and culture." Kevin Belmonte, *Hero for Humanity: A Biography of William Wilberforce* (Colorado Springs: NavPress, 2002), 151.

[25] That Wilberforce's plan for "the reformation of manners" addressed what the term *ethics* means today is evident from the fact that his efforts centered on a royally issued document titled *The Proclamation for the Encouragement of Piety and Virtue and for the Preventing of Vice, Profaneness and Immorality*. Eric Metaxas, *Amazing Grace: William Wilberforce and the Heroic Campaign to End Slavery* (New York: HarperCollins, 2007), 81. Notice how this public policy document issued by the King of England concerns the public importance of "immorality" generally and is not limited only to personal disposition or private sentiment.

[26] Barth said that "theology in general includes from the very first and at every point the problem of ethics." Karl Barth, *Ethics*, ed. Dietrich Braun, trans. Geoffrey W. Bromley (New York: Seabury, 1981), 13, originally as *Ethik* in Zürich by Theologischer Verlag, 1928.

reveals and applies is the only real "ethics."[27] If *ethics* concerns real right and wrong and not just speculating, then God's moral revelation is not just part of ethics but turns out to be the whole thing.[28] Of course, this meant Barth was saying the whole tradition of man-centered philosophizing since Aristotle and the early Greeks was all nothing more than fallible human guesswork. In fact, he saw that if *ethics* has to do with real right and wrong, then all human philosophizing about ethics is either unreal (because fabricated), distorted (because man-centered), incomplete (because unable to reach transcendence), or idolatrous (if it presumes a false transcendence to define what is universally true about the meaning and purpose of life, or subordinates God to human beings by using human-generated categories to evaluate divine revelation).[29]

Not everyone has agreed with Barth on this, but even secular philosophers now use the word *ethics* in the much larger sense (compared to previous usage) of having to do with everything connected with the understanding and application of right and wrong—not only virtues, and not only just adding politics and economics, but adding theology and religious understanding and practice as well. These days *ethics* means everything involved with understanding why beliefs about right or wrong should be considered "valid" or "invalid," what moral authority consists of and where it comes from, and how value judgments should be made and put into practice. All ethical views presuppose a source of valuing authority, be it God, reason, or feeling. But, while philosophical ethics never goes beyond speculating as to the nature of moral valuing as conceived and developed by human intellect, theological ethics exposits what God reveals to be right or wrong and applies God's real norms and principles to real life.

In tracing how the meaning of *ethics* has changed and grown over time, we must take care at the same time to deny that the reality to which the term *ethics* refers is anything new. Real right and wrong and human interest in its understanding and practice are both as old as

---

[27] Barth held that "ethics is not possible as an independent discipline alongside dogmatics. Not just in general, but also in particular, the concern of ethics is a proper concern of dogmatics." Barth, 16.

[28] Barth held that "on the field of ethical deliberation . . . (theological Christian ethics) advances the claim that it is the one that with its investigation has the last word which absorbs all others." Barth, *Ethics*, 19–20.

[29] Barth said, "Philosophy cannot . . . go beyond the Word of God, . . . if it is not to become (a false) theology." Barth, 44.

history itself. And although the way people use the word has changed, the reality to which the word now refers has been there all along. The word *ethics* now means something much bigger than it did previously, but character and conduct have always mattered, living a worthy life has always mattered, and the reality of right and wrong was real even when people used other words for it. So, while the meaning of the word *ethics* did not earlier include all it does today, the reality to which the term now refers existed at Creation, applied in the Garden of Eden, and relates to the regency of God since time began.

What *Ethics* Means Now

The meaning of *ethics* today covers everything having to do with discerning, accepting, and applying a right as opposed to wrong way of valuing and behaving, where the standards used for such valuing are, not so much a matter of ordering data accurately (mathematics) or a skill at connecting means with ends (fabricating), as it is a matter of learning to recognize and live according to the true nature or purpose of something (living a worthy life). In other words, *ethics* has mostly to do with a sort of valuing that assesses material life by something more than material things or experiences themselves. It judges life in the body by something more than bodies, and measures the worth of human feelings, actions, and aspirations by more than human desires, experiences, and achievements as they are. It is a matter of appraising what is by what should be and not limiting what should be to what is.

Within this very broad understanding, the term *ethics* is used in three more specific yet related ways.[30] First, *ethics* can be used for a general pattern of living or "way of life;" second, for a "moral code" or specific set of rules governing how to behave; or third, for analyzing the first two, that is, for using reason to examine ways of living and rules of conduct. These uses, while somewhat different, are not entirely distinct and are more shifts of focus than of kind. We have the first in view when speaking of Christian or Buddhist *ethics*, where the word references a worldview guiding all we do. We have the second in view when speaking of the professional *ethics* of physicians, where the word refers to rules governing members of an identifiable group. And we have the third in view when discussing *ethics* as a branch of philosophy or

---

[30] I am following the treatment of Abelson in the *Encyclopedia of Philosophy*. Abelson and Nielsen, "Ethics, History of," 81–82.

theology. That these are variations of focus and not three completely different things is evident on realizing Christian ethics not only is a "way of life" but also involves both "rules to live by" and "examination" of God's moral revelation.

It is typical to define *ethics* as "the science concerning the *right* and *wrong* of human action"[31] or as "the science of morals" that does research to discover and clarify "principles of human conduct."[32] But, while ethics does involve research into how things work (i.e., it involves science), it also involves much more. Ethics is not only a science but also an art, meaning it involves learning to exercise good judgment as well as researching evidence.[33] And it is not just a science and art but also a skill, meaning it also involves practicing to get better and better at doing things the best way possible. But even these categories are not enough to capture all that ethics involves because ethics is also a cultivation of the soul, a service under the regency of God, a fulfillment of personal and corporate destiny, and a matter of worship that entails pleasing the God who made us. Ethics in these last several classifications is as much a matter of mission as of knowledge, judgment, and character.[34] And it is a matter of all four at once—not just one or the other, or even all four one at a time. Ethics always is a matter of mission, knowledge, judgment, and character and never just one or the other.

It is typical as well to say that ethics is "the study" of normative behavior, character, and goals, or of opinions about these topics, or of which opinions about these topics are valid or invalid.[35] But, while "studying" right and wrong is very important to ethics, we need also to realize it is not only a matter of "study" but also of "living." It includes practice as well as information and includes accepting and doing as well as thinking and analyzing. Van Til (1895–1987) rightly argued that ethics deals primarily with the human will and only secondarily with

[31] Michael Boylan, *Basic Ethics* (Upper Saddle River, NJ: Prentice Hall, 2000), 2.

[32] "Ethics," *Oxford English Dictionary*, 2nd ed. (1989).

[33] Scott B. Rae, *Moral Choices: An Introduction to Ethics*, 4th ed. (Grand Rapids: Zondervan, 2000), 20. Here note Aristotle also says, "The virtues are acquired by first exercising them, just as happens in the arts." Aristotle, *Nicomachean Ethics* 1103.a.32–33.

[34] Here I agree with Christopher Wright's case for the missional nature of divine ethics. See his treatment in chapter 11, in Christopher J. H. Wright, *The Mission of God: Unlocking the Bible's Grand Narrative* (Downers Grove, IL: InterVarsity, 2006), 357–392.

[35] Dennis P. Hollinger, *The Meaning of Sex: Christian Ethics and the Moral Life* (Grand Rapids: Baker, 2009), 16 and John Finnis, *Fundamentals of Ethics* (Washington, DC: Georgetown University Press, 1983), 1.

human intellect and emotions.[36] What we human beings know and feel is important to ethics, but aligning the values we live by to a higher, more worthy authority than ourselves is even more important. In fact, nothing is more essential to worthy living than aligning everything we think and do with the authority running the universe. So it is that ethics involves not only "knowing" the difference between good and evil but also "wanting" good more than evil and then "following" good instead of evil.

This all means that ethics is not just a matter of theory but is a matter of practice as well. It is a "way of living" and not just a matter of collecting ideas about various alleged possibilities. It is a practical as well as speculative discipline. In the end, one studies ethics properly if and only if it is in order to conduct one's life properly. The aim of "doing ethics" is not just to collect great thoughts but to live a great life. If ethics is only something we study and never do, if it makes no real difference, then what we merely think should not be called "ethics." It is only a sham and not the real thing.

This insistence on linking theory with practice recaptures Aristotle, who believed that moral goodness, ἦθος (*ēthos*), is not just a matter of knowledge but must be made a habit, ἔθος (*ethos*), through cultivation and practice.[37] It also captures what the Bible teaches in declaring that "the hearers of the law are not righteous before God, but (only) the doers of the law will be declared righteous" (Rom 2:13) and is in line with the biblical exhortation to "be doers of the word and not hearers only, deceiving yourselves," because it "is not a forgetful hearer but a doer who . . . will be blessed in what he does" (Jas 1:22, 25).

Ethics vs. Morality

While the term *ethics* comes from the Greek word ἠθικός (*ēthikos*), meaning characteristic, customary or habitual, the term *morality* comes from the Latin word *mōrālis*, meaning the same thing, and both words came later to be associated with worthy as opposed to unworthy character, behavior, and goals. In other words, *ethics* and *morality* started as two words meaning the same thing, differing only in their language of origin. But, while these terms have the same origin and are often used interchangeably, they are not strictly synonymous, and that is

---

[36] Cornelius Van Til, *Christian Theistic Ethics* (Kingsburg, CA: Dulk Christian Foundation, 1974), 1.

[37] Aristotle, *Nicomachean Ethics* 1103.a.14–27.

because when the term *ethics* began to be used for studying the meaning and nature of right and wrong, the term *morality* did not come along. Thus, when precision is required, *morality* concerns particular standards that specific people actually follow, and *ethics* is used more broadly to cover all *morality* covers and theoretical reflection on "the whole domain of morality" as well.[38] It therefore is typical for scholars to say that ethics is the "study of morality" or is "the task of investigating morality."[39] But no one ever says that morality studies ethics,[40] and that is because the terms are not exactly the same and cannot be reversed.[41]

When speaking generally, I will sometimes use *ethics* and *morality* interchangeably. But when precision matters, it will be understood that the term *morality* refers to norms people live by while *ethics* also includes belief systems that ground moral judgment. It will be understood that *morality* only addresses "what" while *ethics* also addresses "why"; that *morality* only applies rules, while *ethics* also looks for reasons; that *morality* only considers principles, while *ethics* also considers perspectives; and that, while *morality* stops at requirements, *ethics* may include resources as well.[42] The difference distinguishing the larger sense of *ethics* from the

---

[38] Louis P. Pojman, *Ethics: Discovering Right and Wrong*, 5th ed. (London: Thomson Wadsworth, 2006), 2. Similarly, Douma, *Responsible Conduct*, 3, 113; Birch and Rasmussen, *Bible and Ethics*, 39; John S. Feinberg and Paul D. Feinberg, *Ethics for a Brave New World* (Wheaton, IL: Crossway, 1993), 18; Rae, *Moral Choices*, 15; Stanley J. Grenz and Jay T. Smith, *Pocket Dictionary of Ethics: Over 300 Terms & Ideas Clearly & Concisely Defined* (Downers Grove, IL: InterVarsity, 2003), 77; and J.P. Moreland and William Lane Craig, *Philosophical Foundations for a Christian Worldview* (Downers Grove, IL: InterVarsity, 2003), 393.

[39] Moreland and Craig, *Philosophical Foundations*, 393; Birch and Rasmussen, *Bible and Ethics*, 39.

[40] *Ethics* carries a broader metaphysical sense that *morality* never does. So, while *ethics* can substitute for the particular meaning of *morality*, the term *morality* cannot substitute for the general meaning of *ethics*.

[41] This explains the difference between the title of Alasdair MacIntyre's book, *A Short History of Ethics*, and the title of my book, *True Sexual Morality*. Alasdair MacIntyre, *A Short History of Ethics* (Notre Dame: University of Notre Dame, 1998); Daniel R. Heimbach, *True Sexual Morality: Recovering Biblical Standards for a Culture in Crisis* (Wheaton, IL: Crossway Books, 2004). MacIntyre used the term *ethics* for dealing with the way moral right and wrong have been studied, and I used the term *morality* for presenting standards by which Christians must actually live.

[42] This last distinction only pertains to Christian ethics. No ethical approach other than what God reveals in the Bible provides life-transforming empowerment through God's indwelling Holy Spirit. But that empowerment goes beyond just having standards to live by and therefore is a matter of "ethics" rather than "morality."

more narrow sense of *morality* can be seen in the Bible by contrasting God's message to Israel in Isaiah 28:9–13 with what he later says in Micah 6:8. In the first passage, God condemns the immaturity of people who never grow beyond the level of simple morality, those who never grow beyond living for "Law after law, law after law, line after line, line after line, a little here, a little there" (Isa 28:10). And in the second passage God explains how ethics goes beyond mere rule-following morality to include understanding what guides moral judgment and distinguishes right from wrong, saying, "Mankind, He has told you what is good and what it is the LORD requires of you: (which is) to act justly, to love faithfulness, and to walk humbly with your God" (Mic 6:8).

What *Christian Ethics* Means

There was a time when scholars denied that theological treatment of moral matters qualified as ethics.[43] That is no longer the case,[44] but there is still a lot of disagreement as to what *Christian ethics* means. Non-Christian and theologically liberal scholars are in a way excused for lacking clarity because, as Stanley Hauerwas explains, they are "less and less clear [on] . . . what it means to be Christian" in the first place.[45] But Evangelical Christians have no excuse because clarity on what it means to be Christian is what defines us. This section will survey and criticize seven views published in scholarly literature ranging from very bad to rather good but nevertheless incomplete definitions and then will discuss how *Christian ethics* will be understood in this book, using a definition we believe not only is most faithful to the Word of God but also follows the best Christian scholarship on this subject.[46]

---

[43] For the first, see Sidgwick, *Outlines*, vi.

[44] For the second, see Abelson and Nielsen, "Ethics, History of," 81–82.

[45] Stanley Hauerwas, *The Hauerwas Reader*, eds., John Berkman and Michael Cartwright (Durham, NC: Duke University, 2001), 43.

[46] For a longer version of material covered in this section, readers are referred to Daniel R. Heimbach, "Toward Defining Christian Ethics," *Global Journal of Classical Theology*, 8/3 (January 2011), http://www.phc.edu/gj_toc8_3.php. For this book, I have decided not to include two further definitions covered in that article. That is because I am trying to be concise and because these two treatments may be viewed as arising more from differences in focus than in conception.

A First Very Bad Definition

Robin Lovin, in *Christian Ethics: An Essential Guide*, offers a bad definition that treats Christian ethics as nothing more than using human philosophy to make moral choices.[47] Lovin denies God or the Bible provide any "set answers to be learned" and alleges Christian ethics must follow an "Aristotelian understanding" in place of any sort of religious understanding.[48] This definition attracts non-Christians who deny God exists and do not accept the Bible as the Word of God. But it cannot be reconciled with historic Christianity.

A Second Bad Definition

Edward LeRoy Long, Jr., in *A Survey of Christian Ethics*, and Jochem Douma, in *Responsible Conduct*, view Christian ethics as a matter of using human moral philosophy to determine what moral messages in the Bible are acceptable or not.[49] These scholars use the Bible but do not consider it authoritative. For Long, Christian ethics so relies on human moral philosophy it "cannot be understood" without it,[50] and Douma believes, while "the Bible provides building blocks, the Bible itself provides no ethics that we can simply adopt as our own."[51] Thus, for Long and Douma, Christian ethics starts with philosophers like Aristotle, Kant, Bentham, and Mill and then accept from the Bible what corresponds to what they say. This attracts people who deny transcendence, but it defines Christian ethics in a way that clashes with moral revelation and historic Christian faith.

A Third Rather Poor Definition

Lewis Smedes, in *Choices: Making Right Decisions in a Complex World*, and Kerby Anderson, in *Christian Ethics in Plain Language*, offer a less bad but still rather poor definition that views

---

[47] Robin W. Lovin, *Christian Ethics: An Essential Guide* (Nashville: Abingdon, 2000), 16.

[48] Lovin, 7, 17.

[49] Edward LeRoy Long, Jr., *A Survey of Christian Ethics* (New York: Oxford University, 1967); Jochem Douma, *Responsible Conduct*. Douma's work was first published in Dutch as *Verantwoord Handelen: Inleiding in de Christelijke Ethiek* by Kok Voorhoeve, Kampen, 1997.

[50] Long, *Survey*, 3.

[51] Douma, *Responsible Conduct*, 19–25, 30.

Christian ethics as a matter of combining an overall biblical worldview with ideas and prin-ciples collected from human moral philosophy.[52] This definition goes beyond just picking a few preferred statements out of the Bible to using a generally biblical worldview for assessing what philosophical materials are acceptable. But other than starting with a biblical worldview, this definition assumes Christian ethics requires human philosophy for everything else.

Smedes starts out claiming "to let the biblical message control my reasoning" but then never mentions God or the Bible anywhere else in his book,[53] and Anderson claims the philo-sophical ideas he accepts are limited by a "biblical worldview" but then treats Christian ethics as applying philosophy and only using Scripture in a backup manner. He sees the Bible as "the foundation and the filter" for assessing the outer limits of human philosophy but does not think it provides all we must know to live worthy lives.[54] Thus, he thinks the Bible offers a good start but is not sufficient. This definition respects the Bible but does not think the Bible is enough to make Christian ethics a fully operational system of thinking, deciding, and behaving.

A Fourth Slightly Better Inadequate Definition

A fourth slightly better but still inadequate definition views Christian ethics as a matter of divinely revealed moral truth that needs to be interpreted using categories taken from human moral philosophy. This definition sees the Bible as good for more than just setting worldview limits but still treats human philosophy as necessary to understanding Christian ethics. This approach has been followed by some Evangelicals, including Norman Geisler in *Christian Ethics*, John Jefferson Davis in *Evangelical Ethics*, John and Paul Feinberg in *Ethics for a Brave New World*, Joe Trull in *Walking the Way*, and Scott Rae in *Moral Choices*.[55]

---

[52] Lewis Smedes, *Choices: Making Right Decisions in a Complex World* (New York: HarperSanFrancisco, 1991); Kerby Anderson, *Christian Ethics in Plain Language* (Nashville: Thomas Nelson, 2005).

[53] Smedes, *Choices*, xii.

[54] Anderson, *Plain Language*, 20.

[55] Norman L. Geisler, *Christian Ethics: Options and Issues* (Grand Rapids: Baker, 1989); John Jefferson Davis, *Evangelical Ethics: Issues Facing the Church Today*, 3rd ed. (Phillipsburg, NJ: Presbyterian and Reformed, 2004, originally in 1985); Feinberg and Feinberg, *Brave New World*; Joe E. Trull,

Geisler uses the Bible heavily but thinks God's moral revelation has no understandable structure without human philosophy. In fact, this so controls how Geisler interprets the Bible that he overlooks all it says about character, love, wisdom, and virtue in order to claim Christian ethics is a version of what philosophers call "deontological" ethics.[56] Davis, the Feinbergs, and Trull all do much the same,[57] and Rae even says the Bible's moral message needs to borrow structural concepts from philosophers to become "a fully developed biblical ethic."[58]

This fourth definition relies on the Bible more fully than previous definitions, but it still assumes human moral philosophy is necessary to gain a better, more complete understanding of ethics than the Bible provides on its own. This definition assumes God's moral revelation needs human help to fully communicate what he means.

A Fifth Decent but Still Less Than Adequate Definition

Henlee Barnette in *Introducing Christian Ethics*, Terence Anderson in *Walking the Way*,[59] and Dennis Hollinger in two books, *Choosing the Good* and *The Meaning of Sex*,[60] offer a fifth somewhat better but still less than adequate definition that views Christian ethics as a matter

---

Walking in the Way: An Introduction to Christian Ethics (Nashville: Broadman and Holman, 1997); Rae, *Moral Choices*.

[56] Geisler, *Christian Ethics*, 24.

[57] Davis, *Evangelical Ethics*, 16; Feinberg and Feinberg, *Brave New World*, 30; Trull, *Walking in the Way*, 17.

[58] Rae, *Moral Choices: An Introduction to Ethics*, 2nd ed. (Grand Rapids: Zondervan, 2000), 19. In later editions, Rae revises this to claim Scripture itself affirms the notion of supplementing special revelation with natural law. But, since Rae never distinguishes man-centered, humanly devised, natural law "philosophy" (which Scripture never affirms) from God-centered, divinely revealed, natural law "theology" (which it does affirm), Rae's later editions continue to promote thinking Christian ethical thought is not "fully developed" without some mixing with anthropocentric, humanly devised philosophical speculation, and that is something I dispute in chapter 7.

[59] Terence Anderson must not be confused with Kerby Anderson mentioned earlier. Kerby Anderson is the national director of Probe Ministries International. Terence Anderson serves as professor of Christian Ethics at the Vancouver School of Theology.

[60] Henlee H. Barnette, *Introducing Christian Ethics* (Nashville: Broadman, 1961); Terence R. Anderson, *Walking the Way: Christian Ethics as a Guide* (Toronto, ON: The United Church, 1993); Dennis P. Hollinger, *Choosing the Good: Christian Ethics in a Complex World* (Grand Rapids: Baker, 2002); Hollinger, *The Meaning of Sex*.

of divinely revealed moral truth combined with aspects of human moral philosophy that go beyond but do not conflict with anything the Bible says. This view not only uses the Bible to reject biblically incompatible philosophical ideas and to supply moral content by which Christians must live but also uses the Bible to frame Christian moral understanding. This view structures Christian ethics theologically, not philosophically, but still assumes Christian ethics is not as good as it can be made until humanly conceived philosophical ideas are added to things God says in the Bible.

After claiming Christian ethics is "a systematic explanation of the moral example and teaching of Jesus applied to the total life of the individual in society," Barnette goes on to insist it also requires considering "philosophical insights which contribute to an understanding of these problems."[61] Terence Anderson says that while the Bible is our "most authoritative source," Christian ethics must also go beyond what the Bible reveals by learning from other sources as well.[62] And Hollinger thinks that, while the Bible guides Christian moral understanding, Christian ethics can be improved using philosophical theories that "match up to biblical teachings and a Christian understanding of reality."[63]

This definition has worthy qualities but continues to rely too much on humanity and too little on God. It respects God and the Bible more than previous definitions but does not affirm God's claim to have provided in the Bible enough "training in righteousness" for Christians to be completely "equipped for every good work" (2 Tim 3:16–17), and it does not consider God's warning "that no one takes you captive through philosophy and empty deceit based on human tradition, based on the elements (στοιχεῖα, *stoicheia*, foundational presumptions, framing ideas) of the world, rather than Christ" (Col 2:8).

A Sixth Problematic Definition

Stanley Hauerwas, in *The Peaceable Kingdom*, and Wyndy Reuschling, in *Reviving Evangelical Ethics*,[64] offer a definition that views Christian ethics as a matter of human speculating on

---

[61] Barnette, *Introducing Christian Ethics*, 3.
[62] Anderson, *Walking the Way*, 229.
[63] Hollinger, *Meaning of Sex*, 24.
[64] Stanley Hauerwas, *The Peaceable Kingdom: A Primer in Christian Ethics* (Notre Dame, IN: University of Notre Dame, 1983); Wyndy Corbin Reuschling, *Reviving Evangelical Ethics: The Promises*

what Christians say comes from God that, while not classified as philosophy, arrives at similar conclusions. Hauerwas and Reuschling both insist Christian ethics always is theological and not philosophical. But they both reconceive what *theology* means in human rather than divine terms. What they offer begins with man, not God, and is speculative, not dogmatic, which means it really is philosophy despite being labeled "theology." Their version of "theology" is theological only in the sense of using "god-words" to express their own human ideas and does not mean they are discussing Christian ethics in a way that includes anything actually transcendent or that actually comes from God. Neither believes God truly exists (except as something imagined) and both simply are engaging in "god-talk." So, while Hauerwas and Reuschling claim to define Christian ethics theologically, what they in fact say is just philosophical.

Hauerwas claims to define Christian ethics theologically and not philosophically. But he views it as an "activity relative to particular times, places, and communities" with no fixed reality applying to everyone,[65] which does not come from divine revelation but rather from his own imagination. Reuschling also claims to define Christian ethics theologically and not philosophically. But she reduces theology to humanistic speculation.[66] So, while this last approach alleges to define Christian ethics theologically, it denies transcendence and so merely relabels philosophy, calling it "theology" instead. This definition, while theological, must be rejected because it conflicts with the reality of God, with trusting moral revelation, with historic Christian faith and practice, and with treating the Bible as God's Word.

A Seventh Very Good but Incomplete Definition

Wayne Grudem, in *Christian Ethics: An Introduction to Biblical Moral Reasoning,*[67] views Christian ethics as biblical ethics and nothing else. He defines what Christian ethics means as a field of academic study to be nothing more than studying Bible passages and relating them to moral issues. This sounds very good and is better than all the previous definitions because

---

and Pitfalls of Classic Models of Morality (Grand Rapids: Brazos, 2008).

    [65] Hauerwas, 1.

    [66] Reuschling, *Reviving Evangelical Ethics,* 169.

    [67] Wayne Grudem, *Christian Ethics: An Introduction to Biblical Moral Reasoning* (Wheaton, IL: Crossway, 2018).

doing that truly is a most important part of what Christian ethics does and even can be a valid approach to how everything in the field is evaluated. But is studying Bible passages on moral issues just part of what the academic field covers, or is it the whole thing? Is it a valid and very fruitful approach scholars can study, compare with, or use alongside other approaches, or is it the only valid approach scholars have for studying anything in the whole field, leaving no other approaches with which to compare or use it? The problem is this definition views the academic field in a way that excludes large bodies of theological, historical, and philosophical scholarship and cannot even include debating anyone conceiving Christian ethics in ways with which we disagree. That is, it excludes work debating what we see as misconceptions of Christian ethics even though the academic field consists of scholarly examination and debate. Finally, even if used as the only right way of approaching issues, this definition leaves out discussing these same issues in theological, historical, philosophical, and biblical terms.

The Best Definition

This brings us to what most leaders in the field have considered the best definition, which is understanding Christian ethics to be a matter of divinely revealed moral truth, studied and applied by human minds, under the guidance of the Holy Spirit, relying only on what God reveals by his own authority and initiative, and which therefore evaluates but never submits to, depends on, or combines with human philosophy or anything else arising from human reason, feelings, or experiences apart from God. We acknowledge that not everyone agrees with this definition. But it has the advantage not only of being the definition I think is most faithful to Scripture, but of following the best Christian scholarship on this subject as well.[68] And so, for these reasons, that is what Christian ethics will be taken to mean in this book.

By this definition, Christian ethics is entirely theological and is neither reducible to philosophical categories nor something that can be mixed with humanly conceived ideas without compromising or distorting what it means. The definition rejects thinking God's moral

---

[68] I do not dispute the integrity of colleagues preferring other definitions, but I am saying they diverge from the main tradition. Of course, which is correct depends in the end on fidelity to the Word of God, and readers must examine that for themselves. Whatever one concludes, it cannot be disputed that lack of consensus indicates that contrary influences have affected Christian as well as non-Christian understanding of the subject.

revelation is incomplete and needs supplementing from ideas people have starting with nothing but their own minds apart from God. It denies God's moral revelation needs improving from sources other than the Word of God. This definition insists Christian ethics is something transcendent, dogmatic, theistic, theocentric, revealed, and supernaturally ordered and is not something speculative, mundane, naturalistic, anthropocentric, or humanly generated. It is a definition that insists Christian ethics has a vantage point superior to all human thinking and holds that from this vantage point, Christian ethics judges and interprets human philosophy—never the other way around.

We cannot mention here every significant Christian scholar taking this approach, but the list includes Barth in *Ethics* and in *The Christian Life* (volume 4 of his *Church Dogmatics*), Niebuhr in *An Interpretation of Christian Ethics*, Dietrich Bonhoeffer in *Ethics*, Paul Ramsey in *Basic Christian Ethics*, Georgia Harkness in *Christian Ethics*, Henry in *Christian Personal Ethics*, Helmut Thielicke in *Foundations*, Jacques Ellul in *The Ethics of Freedom*, Cornelius Van Til in *Christian Theistic Ethics*, Francis Schaeffer in *How Should We Then Live?*, R. E. O. White in *Christian Ethics: The Historical Development* and in *Biblical Ethics*, Oliver O'Donovan in *Resurrection and Moral Order*, and John Frame in *The Doctrine of the Christian Life*.[69]

Karl Barth insisted Christian ethics could not be distinguished from theology because allowing that denied something truly essential. Christian ethics is itself "a theological discipline . . . in which an answer is sought in the Word of God to the question of the goodness

---

[69] Barth, *Ethics*; Karl Barth, *The Christian Life*, trans. Geoffrey W. Bromiley, titled "Lecture Fragments" in *Church Dogmatics*, volume 4, part 4 (Grand Rapids: Eerdmans, 1981); Niebuhr, *An Interpretation of Christian Ethics*; Dietrich Bonhoeffer, *Ethics* (New York: Macmillan, 1955; Simon & Schuster, 1995); Paul Ramsey, *Basic Christian Ethics* (Louisville: Westminster/John Knox, 1950); Georgia Harkness, *Christian Ethics* (New York: Abingdon, 1957); Henry, *Christian Personal Ethics*; Helmut Thielicke, *Theological Ethics*, vol. 1, *Foundations*, ed. William H. Lazareth (Grand Rapids: Eerdmans, 1979, earlier by Fortress in 1966 and by Mohr in 1958); Jacques Ellul, *The Ethics of Freedom*, trans. and ed. Geoffrey W. Bromiley (Grand Rapids: Eerdmans, 1976, originally 1973), also as *Ethique de la Liberté* (Genève: Editions Labor et Fides, 1973–1974); R. E. O. White, *Christian Ethics: The Historical Development* (Atlanta, GA: John Knox, 1981); Van Til, *Christian Theistic Ethics*; Francis A. Schaeffer, *How Should We Then Live?* (Westchester, IL: InterVarsity, 1972); R. E. O. White, *Biblical Ethics* (Atlanta, GA: John Knox, 1979); Oliver O'Donovan, *Resurrection and Moral Order: An Outline for Evangelical Ethics* (Grand Rapids: Eerdmans, 1986); and John M. Frame, *The Doctrine of the Christian Life: A Theology of Lordship* (Phillipsburg, NJ: Presbyterian and Reformed, 2008).

of human conduct."[70] It could not be separated from theology because "theology in general includes from the very first and at every point the problem of ethics," and, as a Christian, he knew "the goodness of human conduct can be sought only in the goodness of the Word addressed to man."[71]

Barth criticized "the philosopher who really thinks he knows a higher principle by which to ask and answer the question of the whence and whither, and who thinks he can meet the theological as a judge in the question of truth."[72] Philosophers, he said, have no standing from which they may allege ways to improve "the Word of God itself," and for that reason they have no basis for asserting ultimate claims, moral or otherwise. If they do, their attempts are idolatrous because they turn philosophizing into false theology.[73] For Barth, not only is Christian ethics theological but nothing else qualifies. The only truly real ethics, the only ethics that matters in the end, is moral truth revealed on God's terms, in God's way, in the Word of God. This means that Christian ethics makes an ownership claim *vis-à-vis* all human thought on moral matters. Thus, Barth said, in the field of ethical deliberation, Christian ethics "advances the claim that it is the one that with its investigation has the last word which absorbs all others."[74]

Niebuhr believed that "a Christianity which leans unduly on or borrows excessively from naturalistic (philosophical) idealism . . . is really betrayed into dependence upon corruptions of its own ethos and culture."[75]

Dietrich Bonhoeffer observed that "no man can look with undivided vision at God and at the world of reality so long as God and the world are torn asunder. Try as he may, he can only let his eyes wander distractedly from one to the other. But there is a place at which God and the cosmic reality are reconciled. . . . This place does not lie somewhere out beyond reality in the realm of (philosophical) ideas. It lies in the midst of history as a divine miracle. It lies in Jesus Christ, the Reconciler of the world."[76]

---

[70] Barth, *Ethics*, 3.

[71] Barth, 13, 15.

[72] Barth, 22.

[73] Barth, 44.

[74] Barth, 20.

[75] Niebuhr, *An Interpretation of Christian Ethics*, 12.

[76] Bonhoeffer, *Ethics*, 8.

Paul Ramsey taught that Christian ethics is "the continuing conversation among us by which we commend to one another the bearing Jesus Christ has for our ethical thought" and so "rejected the idea that there need be any *necessarily permanent* coalition between Christian ethics and any other school of ethics founded on philosophical insight or the findings of social science."[77]

Carl F. H. Henry warned that "every proposal to arrive at the content of Christian ethics by a synthesis of speculative morality and revealed morality minimizes the extent to which secular ethics is forged from the standpoint of revolt, and is over-optimistic about the precise continuity between speculative systems and the Hebrew-Christian world and life view," and therefore "every attempt to explain Christian ethics as being merely a more complex development of the insights of general (philosophical) ethics either conceals or minimizes the basis that it has in special revelation."[78]

Helmut Thielicke held that "evangelical ethics is completely different from all natural or philosophical ethics," that these "must be sharply differentiated from one another, however much the theme of *obedience* may be common to both," and that "the task of Christian ethics must consist exclusively in putting questions to the secular understanding of reality, in demanding responsibility from it, and in showing it to be a system by means of which man hopes to protect himself against the divine attack."[79]

Cornelius Van Til said, "It is true that we should make our theology and our ethics wide enough to include man's moral relationships to the whole universe. But it is not true that any ethical question that deals with man's place in nature can be interpreted rightly without the light of Scripture."[80] And Francis Schaeffer, following Van Til, believed that because "humanistic philosophers tried to make ethics independent of biblical teaching," it has led, in our culture and even parts of the Church, to "the loss of humanness on every level" and made "ethics equal to no ethics."[81]

Oliver O'Donovan has argued more recently that exploring "Christian moral concepts must always in the first place, be the work of theology," that "Christian ethics must arise from

---

[77] Ramsey, *Basic Christian Ethics*, xxiv, 344.

[78] Henry, *Christian Personal Ethics*, 148, 146.

[79] Thielicke, *Theological Ethics*, 51, 38

[80] Van Til, *Christian Theistic Ethics*, 16.

[81] Francis A. Schaeffer, *Whatever Happened to the Human Race?* In *The Complete Works of Francis A. Schaeffer*, vol. 5 (Wheaton, IL: Crossway, 1982), 290.

the gospel of Jesus Christ. Otherwise, it could not be *Christian* ethics," and that "a belief in Christian ethics is a belief that certain ethical and moral judgments belong to the gospel itself."[82] And lastly, John Frame insists "all ethics is religious, even when it tries hard to be secular," because all ethics "requires allegiance to someone or something that demands devotion and governs all thinking." Thus, Frame joins Barth and others in maintaining Christian ethics is the only real ethics and all "non-Christian ethics is flawed, not only in its conclusions, but also in its initial understanding of its task."[83]

This shows that most leading scholars in the field have agreed with Barth's view of what Christian ethics means. Niebuhr followed Barth, as did Bonhoeffer, as did Ramsey, as did Harkness, as did Van Til, as did Henry, as did Thielicke, as did Schaeffer (following Van Til), as did Jacques Ellul, as did R. E. O. White, and as do O'Donovan and Frame currently. These are not minor figures but represent the most respected minds in the field. This book follows their lead regarding the priority of God's Word over human speculation. It does not treat Christian ethics as something new, speculative, or evolving that builds on philosophers like Aristotle or Kant and only uses God's Word to confirm their ideas. Rather, it treats Christian ethics as something ancient, fixed, universal, transcendent, and dogmatic, based on which the work of philosophers like Aristotle and Kant is evaluated, but never submits to their categories or judgment apart from the one unified moral truth applied to all in the person and work of Jesus Christ.

What Are "Judeo-Christian Values"?

The term *Judeo-Christian values* refers to something so general it cannot be identified by just offering a list of rules. There are rules typically associated with the term, but the term itself more concerns a way of thinking about moral truth than merely listing what it requires. And yet, while the term cannot be reduced to a set of rules, it can be clarified by essential characteristics. First, the term concerns "values," which means it concerns a way of framing moral judgment. This requires a source of moral authority, an application of moral norms, a formation of moral character, a pursuit of moral goals, and an execution of moral accountability.

---

[82] O'Donovan, *Resurrection and Moral Order*, 8, 11, 12.
[83] Frame, *Doctrine of the Christian Life*, 5, 10.

Second, the term concerns values that are "Judeo-Christian," meaning the way it frames moral judgment has to do not only with Jews but also with Christians, and not only with Christians but also with Jews. It is something most Jews and Christians hold in common, which means it does not include matters of moral judgment held by Jews but very few Christians or held by Christians but very few Jews.

So far, this sets limits to what the term *Judeo-Christian values* means, but it does not yet say much about what this commonly held way of framing moral truth actually includes. Even at this point, just because Jews and Christians accept and follow the same moral ruler of the universe, we know enough already to understand that *Judeo-Christian values* means taking an approach to moral thinking that opposes most contemporary ways of valuing. That is, because it necessarily treats God (not man) as being the ultimate source of moral truth and authority; it necessarily treats main principles of moral right and wrong as being fixed (not changing), universal (not limited by culture or place), and timeless (not depending on time and circumstance); it necessarily treats the structuring of moral reality as being objective (beyond human control); it necessarily measures human desires and behavior by norms transcending human volition and ability; and it necessarily relies on enforcement (accountability) from a source that, while governing human life, also transcends human power and perception.

We have said Judeo-Christian values are more a way of thinking than of listing rules, but there are a number of behavioral norms typically associated with the term. Here, it is important to understand that these norms result from what the term generally means, and it is wrong to think they can be used in reverse to define the general term. Thinking so is not just wrong but perverts understanding of what the general term means. It would be like defining *womanhood* by starting with a list of the chores one woman does in her day. The chores she may do in a given day (like cooking food or washing clothes) do not define her, much less every other female, even if they rise out of a relationship she has with a man. She defines her chores; they do not define her. In the same way, Judeo-Christian values define certain norms. But the norms, however typical, do not define Judeo-Christian values.

There is more to Judeo-Christian values than behavioral rules, but the valuing system commonly shared by Jews and Christians does involve honoring and applying the ten commands God issued to Israel at Sinai, and that is because these identify ten categories of moral obligation revealed to be essential for living a morally worthy life. These categories set boundaries for human behavior, but Judeo-Christian values go beyond this to developing good character, learning to exercise wise judgment, and pursuing worthy goals. And even that does not cover all that Judeo-Christian values entail. We have so far only addressed the behavior, character, and goals of individuals, and the moral ordering shared by Jews and Christians includes community as well as individual life. In other words, it includes the right ordering, evaluating, and judging of families, societies, nations, civilizations, and the entire human race—as well as of persons considered individually.

In summary, the term *Judeo-Christian values* refers to an approach to moral truth that requires following rules, developing character, and pursuing purposes that apply to everyone because they come from the one Creator-God. More particularly, *Judeo-Christian values* refers to an approach to moral thinking and living revealed by God to Israel in the Old Testament, applied to Christians in the New Testament, and believed to be true and authoritative by Jews and Christians alike.

Christian Ethics & Apologetics

How does Christian ethics relate to apologetics? These are often confused because people assume they are either totally different or completely the same. Neither is correct. They are related but not the same, and avoiding confusion requires understanding exactly how. "Christian ethics" and "apologetics" relate the way "finance" relates to "saving" or "aesthetics" relates to "painting." They have something in common but connect with it in different ways. Christian ethics is a subject area having to do with the study, practice, and promotion of God's moral revelation, and apologetics is the function of defending what God reveals to be true. So, just as "finance" is a subject area and "saving" is a function, both relating to money, and just as "aesthetics" is a subject area and "painting" is a function, both relating to art, in a similar way "Christian ethics" is a subject area and "apologetics" is a function, both relating to God's revealed truth.

This can be taken further by observing that, just as the function of "saving" can refer to saving time or energy as well as to saving money, and just as the function of "painting" can refer to covering the plaster walls of your house as well as to producing a Rembrandt masterpiece, so also the function of "apologetics" can defend other areas of God's truth besides his moral revelation. And just as the subject area of "finance" includes functions like investing, lending, and accounting besides just saving money, and just as the subject area of "aesthetics" includes functions like acting, drawing, and poetry besides just painting pictures, so also "Christian ethics" is a subject area including other functions like Bible exposition, historical research, character formation, discipleship, and rational analysis besides just defending God's moral revelation.

Practicing apologetics falls into two categories—one legitimate and the other not. Legitimate apologetics, though tasked with defending everything the Word of God reveals, ends up mostly defending God's moral revelation without giving up anything God says is true and without compromising a Christian worldview. And that portion of apologetics is, of course, a function within the field of Christian ethics. It is true, though, that apologetics more broadly understood sometimes defends more than God's moral truth, as it does for example when defending the existence of God. Because Christian ethics studies, applies, and defends God's moral revelation all the while assuming God really does exist, this means arguing for God's existence lies beyond Christian ethics, even though doing so strengthens and supports the Christian ethics subject area. But while apologetics legitimately defends more than God's moral revelation, it mostly, these days, ends up defending Christian ethics, and that is because we live at a time when God's moral truth is being forcefully excluded from public and private spheres. For this reason, legitimate apologetics presently defends Christian ethics more than anything else, which makes contemporary work in apologetics mostly a component (and only just one component) of the larger field of Christian ethics.

That is when apologetics does its job correctly. But scholars doing apologetics sometimes attempt doing something else—something different than defending what God says on biblical terms—and if so, the apologetic task runs into trouble of two sorts. First, it runs into trouble if it uses man-centered speculative thinking to defend God-centered dogmatic revelation. This makes apologetics guilty of trying to frame transcendent reality in mundane terms or of reducing God's reality to what human minds make up or accept on their own terms. This subordinates theology to philosophy rather than the other way around and inevitably places human speculation over the Word of God. And, as Barth explains, the problem with this kind of apologetics is with how it attempts "to establish and justify theological thinking in the context of . . . nontheological thinking," tries "to justify Christian ethics at the bar of philosophical ethics," and measures "theological ethics by philosophical ethics as its appointed judge."[84]

---

[84] Barth, *Ethics*, 21–22.

The second way apologetics can flounder is by shifting focus away from defending God's truth and toward promoting human ideas instead. This occurs when scholars become greater proponents of this or that philosophical system than of what God says, or if they focus more on philosophical ideas than on revealed truth. There is much value in understanding how human philosophies challenge the Word of God. But teaching human philosophy does not defend God's truth on its own any more than going on a foreign tour stops enemy soldiers from invading your country. Knowing where enemy soldiers are from can help us understand how and why they attack but does not substitute for using your own weapons when meeting them in battle. When soldiers fight, the enemy never surrenders just because you may have visited their homeland.

Conclusion

This chapter introduced readers to the importance, meaning, and distinctives of Christian ethics as a field of study situated at the nexus joining Christian belief with Christian action, Christian orthodoxy with Christian orthopraxy, and Christian faith with Christian living. We considered the need to be ethical, learned how the term *ethics* has evolved linguistically, and clarified how the term is used now. Then we covered different ways *Christian ethics* has been defined, arriving at how it should be used by Evangelicals, and lastly, we discussed how Christian ethics relates to apologetics. But Christian ethics is a large and complex field, and we are not yet finished with introducing the field in a general way. The next chapter will finish introducing readers in a general way to this exciting and most relevant field of study.

CHAPTER 2

PARTS, CATEGORIES & FEATURES

We are presently dealing with general matters affecting what we understand Christian ethics to mean, both in the positive sense of defining what it truly is and in the negative sense of clarifying what it is not. The last chapter focused on terms and vocabulary. We did not cover all relevant terms, but rather only those most needed for exploring the territory ahead.[1] In this chapter, we will continue dealing with general matters but will move on to discuss the sort of things studied, subcategories within the field, and features that together make it possible to distinguish Christian ethics from other views and traditions.[2]

---

[1] For glossaries listing ethical terms, see Mark D. Liederbach and Evan Lenow, *Ethics as Worship: Moral Discipleship to the Glory of God* (Phillipsburg, NJ: Presbyterian and Reformed, 2021), 689–702; Grudem, *Christian Ethics*, 1235–46 (see chap. 1, n. 67); David W. Jones, *An Introduction to Biblical Ethics* (B&H Academic, 2013), 205–9; Frame, *The Doctrine of the Christian Life*, 8–18 (see chap. 1, n. 69); Pojman, *Ethics*, 263–69 (see chap. 1, n. 38); Grenz and Smith, *Pocket Dictionary of Ethics* (see chap. 1, n. 38); Trull, *Walking in the Way*, 287–293 (see chap. 1, n. 55); and Geisler, *Christian Ethics*, 311–14 (see chap. 1, n. 55).

[2] The most significant literature treating Christian ethics generally or introducing Christian ethics as a field of study includes J. Elliot Ross, *Christian Ethics: The Book of Right Living* (New York: Devin-Adair, 1923); Niebuhr, *An Interpretation of Christian Ethics*, (see chap. 1, n. 6); John C. Bennett, *Christian Ethics and Social Policy* (New York: Scribner's Sons, 1946); Ramsey, *Basic Christian Ethics* (see chap. 1, n. 69); Barnette, *Introducing Christian Ethics* (see chap. 1, n. 60); D. J. B.

Three Parts to Ethical Thinking

Ethics is a large subject. All ethics concerns understanding and living a morally worthy life, but the next questions after that head in three directions.[3] As commonly experienced, most start asking, "How must we act?" But that leads to asking, "What sort of persons should we be?" And then to help answer those two questions, we end up asking, "What should we live for?" The first concerns conduct, the second concerns character, and the third concerns goals.[4]

Hawkins, *Christian Ethics* (New York: Hawthorn, 1963); Long, *A Survey of Christian Ethics* (see chap. 1, n. 49); David H. C. Read, *Christian Ethics* (Philadelphia: Lippincott, 1969); Perry C. Cotham, ed. *Christian Social Ethics: Perspectives and Problems* (Grand Rapids: Baker, 1979); David C. Cook, *The Moral Maze: A Way of Exploring Christian Ethics* (London: SPCK, 1983); William M. Tillman, *Christian Ethics: A Primer* (Nashville: Broadman, 1986); William M. Tillman, ed., *Understanding Christian Ethics: An Interpretive Approach* (Nashville: Broadman, 1988); Geisler, *Christian Ethics*; Anderson, *Walking the Way* (see chap. 1, n. 60); Feinberg and Feinberg, *Brave New World* (see chap. 1, n. 38); Douma, *Responsible Conduct* (see chap. 1, n. 16); Trull, *Walking in the Way*; John M. Frame, *Perspectives on the Word of God: An Introduction to Christian Ethics* (Eugene, OR: Wipf and Stock, 1999); Lovin, *Christian Ethics* (see chap. 1, n. 47); Rae, *Moral Choices* (see chap. 1, n. 9); Hollinger, *Choosing the Good* (see chap. 1, n. 60); David M. McCarthy, *The Good Life: Genuine Christianity for the Middle Class* (Grand Rapids: Baker, 2004); Kerby Anderson, *Christian Ethics in Plain Language* (see chap. 1, n. 52); D. Stephen Long, *Christian Ethics: A Very Short Introduction* (Oxford: Oxford University, 2010); Samuel Wells and Ben Quash, *Introducing Christian Ethics* (West Sussex, UK: Wiley-Blackwell, 2010); Kent Van Til, *The Moral Disciple: An Introduction to Christian Ethics* (Grand Rapids: Eerdmans, 2012); C. Ben Mitchell, *Ethics and Moral Reasoning: A Student's Guide* (Wheaton, IL: Crossway, 2013); Davis, *Evangelical Ethics* (see chap. 1, n. 55); Ken Magnuson, *Invitation to Christian Ethics: Moral Reasoning and Contemporary Issues* (Grand Rapids: Kregel, 2020); and Liederbach and Lenow, *Ethics as Worship*.

[3] Dennis Hollinger identifies two rather than three "broad dimensions of Christian experience: the internal and the external." But Hollinger's external dimension includes seeking the right goals as well as right behavioral norms of Christian life. See Hollinger, *Choosing the Good*, 11.

[4] This three-part division of ethical understanding is broadly followed by most scholars. A noted example is O'Donovan, who divides Christian ethics into a treatment of "the objective order" (dealing with conduct), "the subjective order" (dealing with character), and "the form of the moral life," which includes dealing with "the end of the moral life." O'Donovan, *Resurrection and Moral Order*, 5 (see chap. 1, n. 69). Others using this three-part approach to ethics include C. S. Lewis, *Mere Christianity* (New York: Macmillan, 1980), 69–73; David Clyde Jones, *Biblical Christian Ethics* (Grand Rapids: Baker, 1994), 11–16; Van Til, *Christian Theistic Ethics*, 3 (see chap. 1, n. 36); and many others. In a similar way, Frame identifies "goal, motive, and standard" as "three categories" constituting a full treatment of Christian ethics and from that develops "three perspectives" on ethical thought. But,

Lewis elaborates, noting that there are three ways things go wrong, morally speaking. The first "is when human individuals drift apart from one another, or else collide with one another and do one another damage, by cheating or bullying"; the second "is when things go wrong inside the individual—when the different parts of him (his different faculties and desires and so on) either drift apart or interfere with one another," and the third is when people pursue goals leading them astray.[5] The first problem is like ships colliding with each other; the second is like ships losing seaworthiness and sinking; and the third is like ships using the wrong chart, or using the right chart the wrong way, and thus setting off in directions that run them into rocks or will never reach their destinations.

These different ways that things go wrong indicate three parts to ethical thinking that together make up a fully operational system. They help us to see that ethics, as a whole, involves not only assessing conduct but character and not only involves assessing conduct and character but goals as well. Putting the sailing analogy Lewis employs into positive terms, the first part of ethical thinking is like ships sailing in formation to avoid collisions; the second is like keeping ships in seaworthy condition to avoid sinking; and the third is like using the right chart the right way to reach the right destination. Thus, Lewis concludes, "if we are to think about morality, we must think of all three departments: relations between man and man; things inside each man; and relations between man and the power that made him."[6]

Thinking about the right and wrong of conduct, character and goals can be conceptually distinguished because they have to do with different aspects of ethical thinking. But in real life, these different aspects always operate together and cannot be separated. They are not unrelated things merely listed together but are parts of a larger whole that does not work unless each part functions properly in relation to each other part. These parts all affect each other, and none can function alone. In other words, ethics involves a complex valuing system with different aspects that work together or not at all. It involves doing good, being good, and serving good all at the same time, and if one part goes wrong, the others do as well.

---

while Frame's three categories align nicely with distinguishing conduct, character, and goals, his three perspectives do not and so cannot be viewed as equivalent. See Frame, *The Doctrine of the Christian Life*, 33–37.

[5] Lewis, *Mere Christianity*, 70–71.

[6] Lewis, 73.

The way conduct, character, and goals work together, or are properly integrated, is much debated. Even reaching agreement on what each part entails gets more difficult moving from conduct, to character, to goals. Agreeing that stealing is wrong is hard enough, getting people to stop envying what others have is harder, and agreeing on why no one should is harder still. Lewis notes that "almost all people at all times have agreed (in theory) that human beings ought to be honest and kind and helpful to one another." But, when we get to how "different beliefs about the universe lead to different behavior," reaching agreement is much harder to achieve. It is like everyone agreeing we should keep ships from running into rocks but then arguing over what chart we should use for setting the right course. Dealing with the way the parts of ethical thinking go together affects how closely Christians are able to work with others on moral issues within secular or religiously diverse surroundings. On this, Lewis says that what usually happens is, "We can all co-operate in the first one. Disagreements begin with the second and (then) become serious with the third."[7] Understanding this progression explains why handling the third element of ethical thinking—the one dealing with setting the right course using the right chart—is what mainly separates Christian ethics from other ways of thinking.

This leads us to ask how this ordering of ethical thinking into conduct, character, and goals relates to the Bible. Is it just a human idea or does it come from God? While human reason and experience affirm it, the idea comes from the mind of God. The questions setting up these parts can be phrased theologically as asking: "What does God want us to do?" "What does God want us to be?" And "What does God want us to achieve?" These questions are all addressed very clearly in Scripture. The Bible is filled with God's revelation concerning worthy conduct (John 14:21; Jas 1:22), worthy character (Rom 8:29, 13:14; Col 3:12–15; 2 Pet 1:5–7), and worthy goals (Matt 6:33; 1 Cor 10:31; Col 3:23); and the Bible also treats these aspects as together comprising treatment of God's moral revelation as a whole.

This can be seen where Micah writes, "He has told each of you what is good and what it is the LORD requires of you: to act justly, to love faithfulness, and to walk humbly with your God" (Mic 6:8). In this verse, the phrase "has told you what is good" refers to God's entire ethical system, which Micah then shows to have three parts. The phrase "act justly" refers to moral conduct, the phrase "love faithfulness" refers to moral character, and the phrase "walk

---

[7] Lewis, 72.

humbly with your God" refers to moving in the right moral direction. This tripartite way of summarizing God's treatment of ethical thinking can also be seen where Paul prays that Christians in Philippi will "be pure and blameless in the day of Christ, filled with the fruit of righteousness that comes through Jesus Christ to the glory and praise of God" (Phil 1:10–11). Here the phrase "fruit of righteousness" refers to moral conduct, the phrase "be pure and blameless" refers to moral character, and the phrase "to the glory and praise of God" refers to the moral goal ultimately guiding the course of human life. By using these together, the Holy Spirit through Micah and Paul reveals how these three aspects together cover God's framing of ethical thinking as a whole.

A third less obvious but nevertheless important place this tripartite ordering of ethics can be seen in the Bible is where Paul tells Christians in Rome, "Do not be conformed to this age, but be transformed by the renewing of your mind, so that you may discern what is the good, pleasing, and perfect will of God" (Rom 12:2).[8] After explaining that all wrong ethical thinking comes from being "conformed to this age," Paul goes on to say that getting human ethical thinking on track requires total mental transformation—not a few adjustments around the edges but a completely new way of thinking. Paul then indicates that this transformed system of ethical thinking has three fundamental characteristics. It is first "good" (ἀγαθός, *agathos*), meaning it is objectively sound. This first term mainly concerns rightly ordered relations or conduct. It is second "pleasing" (εὐάρεστος, *euarestos*). This term addresses internal worthiness, and Paul uses it in a way that refers as much to our finding out God's will aligns with what our desires really should be as it does to God being pleased when our desires conform to his. This second term addresses character in a manner consistent with God's command to "be holy, because I am holy" (Lev 11:44; 1 Pet 1:16). Third, Paul says this radically transformed approach to ethical thinking is "perfect" (τέλειος, *teleios*), a term that references the goal for human life, the purpose for which God made us, the reason we all exist. Thus, the Bible again treats ethical thinking as a whole by referencing conduct, character, and goals.

The most important thing here is not just to realize how ordering ethical thought into three interrelated parts involving conduct, character, and goals fits nicely with some verses in the Bible. It does that, of course. But we must come to see something bigger. The important

---

[8] Jones treats Paul's tripartite reference in this verse more thoroughly than I do here. See Jones, *Biblical Christian Ethics*, 12–14.

thing is to notice that these three parts to ethical thinking already frame the moral reality God reveals to humanity. They already comprise the way God thinks and have not been added to the Word of God.

Categories of Academic Specialization

The field of Christian ethics is divided into five categories of academic specialization. This regards a different way of dividing the ethical task than covered above. We saw earlier how ethical thinking deals with conduct, character, and goals. But these aspects all can be studied in different ways, and these different ways have led to separate academic categories. It is that sort of difference to which we turn now. The difference from which the academic categories arise is more practical than theoretical. Each category addresses all three aspects of moral living (conduct, character, and goals), and each assumes (or should assume) biblical authority and a Christian worldview. These categories only differ in academic focus, and they are biblical Christian ethics, theological Christian ethics, historical Christian ethics, philosophical Christian ethics, and applied Christian ethics.

Biblical Christian Ethics

The first category of academic specialization within the larger field of Christian ethics is biblical Christian ethics. This is the essential core on which all worthy scholarship in the larger field most depends. As an academic category, biblical Christian ethics refers to examining ethical principles, standards, judgments, and ideals present in the Bible. Work in this area is exegetically based and is usually organized in a way framed by how moral teaching appears in the Bible. The focal question for this academic category is, "What does this or that text in the Bible say about moral conduct, character, or goals?" When used for a category of academic specialization, the term *biblical* does not mean that what a scholar says is necessarily faithful to the Bible, only that it concerns the Bible, and the term does not mean that work in other categories is not biblically reliable. Rather, when used this way, the term *biblical* only refers to a focus of academic study and says nothing about a scholar's worldview or whether he should be trusted. Examples of scholarship in this category include examining Old Testament ethics, New Testament ethics, the ethical teaching of Jesus, the ethical teaching of Paul, the structure and content of the Levitical Holiness Code, Old Testament wisdom literature, and debates on whether or on what grounds Jesus allowed morally permissible divorce.

Theological Christian Ethics

A second academic category, referred to either as "theological ethics" or as "moral theology,"[9] involves efforts to systematically organize and explain Christian teaching on moral life. Work in this area starts with the Bible but then uses reason to evaluate what it means or implies—doing so while open to guidance from the Holy Spirit and guidance through experience and tradition, as well as remaining subject to the final authority of God's written revelation. Scholarship in this category focuses on asking, "What does the Bible mean where it addresses this or that ethical subject?" or "Why did God require this and prohibit that?" or "How does all God reveals on this or that subject fit together?" When done properly, theological Christian ethics builds on scholarship in biblical Christian ethics. But that is not always the case and, if not, then we should wonder if what a scholar says might be philosophical speculation rather than theological examination of God's revealed truth.[10] Scholarship in theological Christian ethics may include such things as examining the ethics of created order; Reformed ethics; covenantal ethics; dispensational ethics; the ethical meaning of justification; the ethical meaning of sanctification; the ethical meaning of glorification; and themes, such as the nature and significance of eschatological judgment, the nature and purpose of marriage, the difference (if any at all) between civil and Christian marriage, the relation of natural theology to natural law, Christian discipleship, Christian conscience, the spiritual disciplines, the ethics of Christian hope, the relation of forgiveness to moral responsibility, and how moral law relates to the Gospel of Jesus Christ.

Historical Christian Ethics

A third academic category studies what Christians have believed or taught about moral living over time. Work in historical Christian ethics builds on how Christians have interpreted

---

[9] Catholic scholars have traditionally preferred using the term *moral theology*, while Protestant scholars usually prefer *theological ethics*.

[10] This is how I dealt with the work of Stanley Hauerwas in chapter 1.

God's moral revelation in the Bible and goes on also to examine how Christians have developed various ethical doctrines. Scholarship in historical Christian ethics differs from biblical and theological Christian ethics by asking, "What have Christians in the past thought or taught about this or that ethical subject?" or "How did what Christians believe at this or that time affect how they chose to live?" Study in this category might focus on how Christians dealt with a moral issue at a particular time or changed how they dealt with that issue over time. It might also address what influential figures in Church history taught on moral topics or what moral themes characterized different Christian movements. Examples of work in this area include examining the ethical teachings of the early Church; the ethical teaching of Augustine, Calvin, Luther, or Wesley; the history of Baptist teaching on religious liberty; how various views on the ethics of usury (lending money for interest) affected what different groups did during the Protestant Reformation; or how the ethics of monasticism compared with Puritan ethics.

Philosophical Christian Ethics

A fourth area of academic specialization covers much the same ground as theological Christian ethics but starts from a human perspective that can only speculate on ethical matters rather than from a divine perspective that has authority based on what God says. Work in philosophical Christian ethics involves examining and interacting with various humanly devised theories about the meaning, nature, and source of ethical truth, doing it from a distinctly Christian point of view, and interacting with these theories mainly to evaluate and criticize them. This area of scholarship uses human experience and human reason to evaluate human ideas. But it ought always to respect and never contradict anything God obviously says in the Bible. Some scholars do this more faithfully than others, and some claim even to be doing "philosophical Christian ethics" when pursuing ideas and methods incompatible with the Bible. If that happens, we should ask if that work really is "Christian" and must remember philosophical Christian ethics does not include just anything professing Christians happen to say based on philosophical notions used on their own terms unrelated to Christianity. Examples of work in this area include evaluating deontological, teleological, or relational ethics from a Christian point of view; evaluating positions such as hierarchicalism, conflicting absolutism, or generalism; and comparing Aristotelian notions of virtue with what Paul says in the New Testament.

Applied Christian Ethics

Finally, a fifth category of academic specialization in the field of Christian ethics is referred to as "applied Christian ethics" and is divided into Christian personal ethics and Christian social ethics. This specialization is at times also referred to as Christian social ethics or practical Christian ethics. But these other terms should be avoided; the first because it uses *social* differently than meant when referring to issues involving social dynamics, and the second because it can suggest utilitarian thought. This is the most widely known specialization in the field because more is written about "issues" than anything else. There is a logical progression from biblical, to theological, to applied ethical analysis, and the applied component would not exist if not able to draw from and build on the preceding categories. Beyond this, historical and philosophical scholarship supplement understanding how Christian ethics applies to issues but are not always essential. Applying Christian ethics to issues requires understanding biblical and theological thought and is helped by historical and philosophical considerations. It does not merely focus on the particulars of that issue. Work in this specialization asks questions like, "How should Christians deal with this or that moral problem?" It deals with practical concerns and draws on the other academic specializations when needing to settle questions about theory and authority. Examples of scholarship in this category include evaluating how Christians should deal with issues like abortion, euthanasia, capital punishment, birth control, homosexuality, divorce and remarriage, racial prejudice, or nations going to war. It also includes dealing with how Christians should address wealth distribution, to what degree Christians should get politically involved, and what dressing modestly requires.

Features of Christian Ethics

The last major thing to cover as we introduce Christian ethics as a whole regards how one recognizes when we are dealing with the real thing as opposed to counterfeits, and that requires learning to distinguish Christian ethics not only from views that openly reject Christianity but also from views that claim to be "Christian" but are not the genuine article. We need to know what distinguishes Christian ethics from other views and traditions, and for that we must identify "features" of the discipline. A feature is a characteristic essential to something and thus useful in distinguishing it from other similar things. Just as the shape of a person's nose or chin, or a person's height, weight, or body type help in distinguishing one person from another, so there are features that together set Christian ethics apart from other approaches used for judging right from wrong. Just as unique features are more useful in distinguishing one thing from another than features shared by more than one thing, so also features completely unique to Christian ethics are more useful in distinguishing it from other views than features common to more than one ethical view or tradition.

The features we will address do not simply characterize Christian ethics but together serve to distinguish Christian ethics from all other ways of approaching moral truth. We cannot compile an exhaustive list of features because Christian ethics studies an infinite source that cannot be exhausted. But we can identify its most essential characteristics, and the more we do, the easier it will be to recognize false claims and avoid confusing them with the real thing.

The main features of Christian ethics fall into one of four general classifications we will label: (1) complexity, (2) dogma, (3) actuality, and (4) paradox.[11] We will use these classifications to order and clarify, but they also are distinguishing features in their own right. In other words, Christian ethics is complex (is not one undifferentiated thing), and therefore trying to reduce all Christian ethics to one simple thing perverts the whole enterprise; Christian ethics is dogmatic (is not speculative, imaginary, mundane or anthropocentric), and therefore including non-dogmatic elements turns it into something else; Christian ethics is actual (is not a matter of ideas disconnected from reality), and therefore abstractions have no place in the discipline; and Christian ethics is paradoxical (is not what anyone expects), and therefore shaping it to what most people do or desire is both wrong and irrelevant.

Christian Ethics Features Complexity

Christian ethics has a single source, which is the holiness of God (Lev 19:2; Eph 1:4; 1 Pet 1:15–16); a single aim, which is the glory of God (Isa 43:6–7; John 15:8; 1 Cor 10:31); and a single motive, which is the love of God (John 14:23; 1 Cor 13:2; Gal 5:6; Eph 5:2). But while Christian ethics is unified, being from God, by God, and for God, it is at the same time

---

[11] These categories are my own but result from cataloging a wide range of features addressed by various scholars and trying then to order them along lines suggested by the features themselves. While ordering the many features of Christian ethics into classifications is unique, the nature of each classification is generally accepted.

very complex, having many different aspects, facets, and dimensions, making it impossible to reduce all Christian ethics down to a single philosophical classification, ground norm, rule, or virtue.[12] As Paul says writing to the Romans, "Oh, the depth of the riches both of the wisdom and of the knowledge of God! How unsearchable his judgments and untraceable his ways! For who has known the mind of the Lord? Or who has been his counselor?" (Rom 11:33–34).

Christian ethics is all a matter of obeying, loving, and serving God. But the God we obey, love, and serve is highly complex because,[13] even though the Divine Being is undivided, indivisible, and entirely self-consistent, his ways always will be "higher than our ways" (Isa 55:9) and his greatness always will be "unsearchable" (Ps 145:3).[14] God is infinite in all aspects of his

---

[12] I differ here with a much respected former teacher, Norman Geisler, who categorically states that "Christian ethics is deontological" (Geisler, *Christian Ethics*, 24). I differ with Geisler for two reasons: first, because, being of God, Christian ethics cannot be reduced to speculative categories without distortion, and second, because, though Christian ethics includes obligatory behavioral norms, it also includes nonobligatory heroism, nonbehavioral virtues, future (impossible now to achieve) ideals, and wisdom of a sort requiring situational assessment (like Paul's discussion of whether it is right or wrong to eat meat offered to idols in 1 Cor 8:1–13). On this second point, I think Geisler makes the *dicto simpliciter* mistake of assuming what is true for a part is true for the whole.

[13] Here I am not using the term *complex* in connection with ethics in the same way Dennis Hollinger uses it in *Choosing the Good*. Hollinger uses *complex* in discussing the way human finitude and depravity cloud ethical understanding with confusion, inconsistency, and conflict, whereas Hollinger (and I here) use *complex* to indicate something of the fundamental nature of Christian ethics, not as perceived or practiced by imperfect human beings, but as established and revealed by God. See Hollinger, *Choosing the Good*, 17–20.

[14] Theologians have in the past used *simplicity* to affirm God's unified essence and self-consistency even though he has many attributes, facets, and dimensions. For example, see Thomas Aquinas, *Summa Theologica*, trans. Fathers of the Dominican Province (Westminster, MD: Christian Classics, 1981), pt. 1, q. 3, art. 7. Theologians doing this have sometimes used *complexity* in referring to the heresy of supposing God is composed of parts (is "composite") or is not entirely self-consistent; see Wayne Grudem, *Systematic Theology: An Introduction to Biblical Doctrine* (Grand Rapids: Zondervan, 1994), 177. But the English language has changed, and the words *simplicity* and *complexity* are no longer used in these ways in contemporary speech, which is why Louis Berkhof notes that, "In recent works on theology the simplicity of God is seldom mentioned." Berkhof, *Systematic Theology* (Grand Rapids: Eerdmans, 1941), 62. This shift in the way these words are used generates a two-fold problem. First, continuing to use *simplicity* and *complexity* archaically risks misunderstanding when addressing contemporary English speakers. Second, avoiding the contemporary use of these words interferes with communicating truly and with best effect. I have chosen, for sake of clarity, to use *complexity* in contemporary fashion simply to mean "multidimensional" or "multifaceted." But I also want readers who understand what these

nature, and because Christian ethics reveals and expresses God's infinite character, it studies a reality that never ends and draws from a source of truth that is never exhausted. We can know what is truly true but there is always more to learn, and this affects the fundamental nature of Christian ethics. Millard Erickson indicates something of this in saying we must "think of Jesus as a very *complex* person."[15] He explains that,

> Of the people whom we know, some are relatively simple. This is not a reference to their level of intelligence, but rather to the straightforwardness of their personality. One comes to know them fairly quickly, and they may therefore be quite predictable. Other persons, on the other hand, have much more complex personalities. They may have a wider range of experience, a more varied educational background, or a more complex emotional makeup. There are many facets to their personalities. When we think we know them quite well, another dimension of their lives appears, a dimension which we did not previously know existed. Now if we imagine complexity expanded to an infinite degree, then we have a bit of a glimpse into the "personality of Jesus" as it were.[16]

The complexity of Christian ethics reflecting the complexity of God himself (his personality and character, not the Divine Being) becomes increasingly evident the more we examine his moral revelation.[17] Christian ethics is timeless and yet centers on God's mission to rescue

---

words meant historically to know that I do not deny the historic doctrine and that I do in fact strongly affirm the *unitas simplicitatis* of the Divine Being. The being of God is undivided and indivisible, but God is not "simple" in the sense of being easy to fully comprehend or limited to only a few attributes. Furthermore, God always is entirely self-consistent, but he is at the same time highly "complex" in the sense of being full of surprises and having a limitless variety of experiences, plans, thoughts, emotions, relations, and perhaps dimensions as well.

[15] Emphasis mine.

[16] Millard J. Erickson, *Christian Theology* (Grand Rapids: Baker, 1983), 738.

[17] The enigma of affirming divine "complexity" in the sense used here (and as Erickson uses the term in *Christian Theology*) while also affirming the historic view of divine "simplicity" can be resolved only by denying these terms are necessarily exclusive. There is a sense in which these terms are not compatible, but I am using them in a way that does not presume they must be opposed. Both are possible without contradiction when using *complexity* to indicate something "multifaceted" without saying anything about components. But resolving these terms is assisted as well by the notion of "simplicity" that led Steve Jobs to revolutionize computers, movies, music, communication, and publishing, and that he

sinners "from the domain of darkness" and transfer them "into the kingdom of the Son he loves" (Col 1:13). Christian ethics is universal and yet concerns forming a new community that is "a chosen race, a royal priesthood, a holy nation, a people for his possession" (1 Pet 2:9).[18] O'Donovan observes that "Christian moral judgments in principle address every man" even though to be "Christian" they "must arise from the gospel of Jesus Christ."[19] Christian ethics is objective and transcendent, placing it beyond human manipulation, determination, or control, and yet it is personal and, for that reason, relevant to all persons bearing the image of God (Isa 57:15). Christian ethics distinguishes internal faculties from external behavior but treats them as a whole, never allowing them to be addressed separately. Jesus declared this to be essential, saying, "The one who has my commands and keeps them is the one who loves me" (John 14:21), and Paul reaffirmed it, saying, "Everything that is not from faith is sin" (Rom 14:23).

Christian ethics is more complex than other views or traditions because it concerns the past, the present, and the future all at once (Isa 51:7–8).[20] It is eternal but always timely and never archaic; it is unchanging but always applicable and never irrelevant; it is historic but

---

had in mind when declaring, "Simplicity is the ultimate sophistication." Walter Isaacson observes that what set Apple apart while Jobs led the company was how he thought about the way "simplicity" relates to "complexity." Of Apple, Isaacson says, "Its guiding tenet was simplicity—not merely the shallow simplicity that comes from an uncluttered look and feel and surface of a product, but the deep simplicity that comes from knowing the essence of every product, (along with) the complexities of its engineering." Jony Ive, who understood Jobs better than most, explains what drove him, saying, "As you bring order to complexity, you find a way to make the product defer to you. Simplicity isn't just a visual style. It's not just minimalism or the absence of clutter. It involves digging through the depth of the complexity. To be truly simple, you have to go really deep." Walter Isaacson, "Keep It Simple," *Smithsonian* (September 2012): 45, 48. If "deep simplicity" controls "complexity" by ordering multiple aspects to a single essence in a manner that best utilizes that "complexity" without erasing it in the process, then perhaps we could say it is God's "deep simplicity" that unifies and controls God's "complexity" without confusion, without components, and without erasing it in the process of affirming divine "simplicity."

[18] See St. Augustine, *The City of God*; Karl Barth, *Christengemeinde und Bürgergemeinde* (Zollinkon-Zurich: Evangelischer Verlag, 1948). Also see Oliver O'Donovan, *Common Objects of Love: Moral Reflection and the Shaping of Community* (Grand Rapids: Eerdmans, 2002).

[19] O'Donovan, *Resurrection and Moral Order.* This compares what O'Donovan says on p. 17 with what he says on p. 11.

[20] O'Donovan says Christian morality looks "not only back to the created order which is vindicated, but forwards to our eschatological participation in that order" *(Resurrection and Moral Order,* 22).

always contemporary and never out-of-date; it is for this world and yet looks forward to a world to come. Christian ethics cannot be improved, superseded, or replaced even though our human understanding of God's moral reality never stops growing and is never complete. Like the divine character it reveals, Christian ethics "is the same yesterday, today and forever" (Heb 13:8) even though there is always more to learn and discover.[21]

Lewis expresses this, saying, "The further up and further in you go, the bigger everything gets."[22] He was describing heaven, but that includes God's moral reality. What Lewis says of heaven can be said of Christian ethics because, like heaven, Christian ethics involves ever learning more and more about an infinite reality that never changes. Like Aslan in *The Last Battle*, Jesus calls us to "Come further in! Come further up!"[23] And we find as we do, while God's moral reality does not change, it also is the case that the more we discover, the more we find there is to discover. The more we learn, the more we find there is to learn. It is part of what Lewis calls "the Great Story . . . which goes on forever: in which every chapter is better than the one before."[24]

Another factor complicating Christian ethics is its *translucence*, a term meaning it is partly clear and partly not. We just considered how Christian ethics is unchanging even though there is always more to learn, but this concerns how Christian ethics can be easy to begin with but then gets hard to grasp even when staring you in the face. It starts with things everyone knows without being told but then also includes things that seem foolish to sinners and that no one knows on their own. This makes Christian ethics both lucid and opaque.[25]

---

[21] Geisler explains that "Christian ethics is based on God's will, but God never wills anything contrary to his unchanging moral character" (Geisler, *Christian Ethics*, 22).

[22] C. S. Lewis, *The Last Battle* (New York: Macmillan, 1980), 180.

[23] Lewis, 158.

[24] Lewis, 184.

[25] O'Donovan holds that "together with man's essential involvement in created order and his rebellious discontent with it, we must reckon also upon the opacity and obscurity of that order to the human mind which has rejected the knowledge of its Creator." On the one side "there is the created order and there is natural knowledge," and on the other "there is the new creation and there is revelation in Christ." This, he says, "has encouraged a confusion of the ontological and the epistemological in much modern theology, so that we are constantly presented with the unacceptable polarized choice between an ethic that is revealed and has no ontological grounding and an ethic that is based on creation and so is naturally known." I agree with O'Donovan's rejection of both options because, while all have a degree of "natural knowledge" as "a part of man's created endowment . . . only in Christ do we apprehend that

It is partly plain and partly hidden and is ever so.[26] Paul says Gentiles who "do what the law demands . . . even though they do not have the law" show they have God's moral law "written on their hearts" with enough clarity that their thoughts will "either accuse them or even excuse them on the day when God judges" (Rom 2:14–16). And yet Paul also says, "God's hidden wisdom" (1 Cor 2:7) comes only "by the Spirit," who alone "searches everything, even the depths of God" (1 Cor 2:10). Christian ethics is lucid enough to say God judges everyone by known standards and is yet, at the same time, opaque enough to require the working of God's Spirit to rightly comprehend.

Jesus had this feature of translucence in mind when speaking to crowds in parables. When his disciples asked why, Jesus explained it was because

> to you it has been given to know the secrets of the kingdom of heaven, but to them it has not been given. For to the one who holds on (to what he has), more will be given, and he will have abundance, but from the one who does not hold on (to what he has), even what he (originally) has (or holds) will be taken away. (Matt 13:11–12, my translation)[27]

Jesus tells us here that God is himself keeping his moral truth partly lucid and partly opaque so that those who accept what they have will get more and those who do not will lose what they start with.

Finally, because Christian ethics reflects the limitless perfection of our infinite God, we should not be surprised to find it more complex than can be fully explained to human minds. It is reasonable without being based on what we consider reasonable, desirable without being based on what we desire, worth preferring without being based on what we prefer,

---

order in which we stand and that knowledge of it with which we have been endowed" (O'Donovan, *Resurrection and Moral Order*, 19–20).

[26] Since Christian ethics is included in what Paul says about the Spirit of God revealing "even the depths of God" (1 Cor 2:10), Christian ethics will never be completely understood until God is completely understood. But since God never will be fully disclosed, neither will human beings ever fully fathom Christian ethics.

[27] The Greek verb ἔχω (*echō*) includes the idea of "hanging onto" or "keeping" something already possessed that is not included in how English speakers use the verb *have*. I have translated what Jesus said to bring out the "holding onto" sense, which I think better expresses what Jesus was telling his disciples.

embodied without being based on our flesh, felt without being based on our feelings, experienced without being based on our experiences, creational without being based on anything in creation, natural without being based on nature, supernatural without being based on merely rejecting nature, spiritual without being based on merely affirming spirituality, analyzable without being based on our analysis, and missional without being based on missionizing as if once accomplished the whole thing would be over.[28] Christian ethics is very complex, having many interconnected aspects, facets, and dimensions but is all from God, by God, and for God (Col 1:17).

Christian Ethics Features Dogma

A second class of features characterizing Christian ethics concerns the way Christian ethics is dogmatic, not speculative. Christian ethics deals with moral matters, starting with assurance that truth is known, final authority is settled, and everyone is accountable to that authority for that truth whether they like it or not. There is room in Christian ethics for asking questions, analyzing answers, and debating interpretations. But there is no room for thinking ethics is just a way to express personal feelings, or for thinking everyone gets to make up whatever applies to them, or for saying ethics is nothing more than guessing about things no one knows for sure. That is because Christian ethics is revealed and is not something Christians have made up. It involves individuals but is not just a matter of individual preference, and it involves community but is more than community traditions. That is because Christian ethics is not humanly generated, humanly imagined, or humanly imposed, but rather comes from and reflects the character of the only God who truly exists and communicates with his creatures. Saying this is not just a way Christians like to talk but refers to how things really are, not just for Christians but for everyone. God is real; he has spoken; and Christian ethics examines, declares, and applies the Word of God (Isa 30:21; Ps 33:4; 119:9, 105; Heb 4:12).

---

[28] I agree with Christopher Wright where he asserts that the ethics of God revealed in Scripture are missional. See Wright, *The Mission of God*, 357–96 (see chap. 1, n. 34). However, I do not accept his subordination of the ethics of God to the mission of God, nor do I accept his shaping the ethics of God by the mission of God. Were that so, the ethics of God would cease (become irrelevant) in heaven, as God's moral perfection would no longer matter to the eternal union of Christ with his bride. The mission of God arises out of and is shaped by the ethics of God, not the other way around.

I agree with Barth, who held that because "the theme of dogmatics is simply the Word of God . . . [and because] the theme of the Word of God is simply human existence, life, or conduct," Christian ethics must therefore be dogmatic.[29] I agree also with O'Donovan, who insists "Christian ethics must arise from the gospel of Jesus Christ. Otherwise it could not be *Christian* ethics,"[30] and with Frame, who says, "the point of Christian ethics is . . . to be as biblical as we can be," both of whom are saying in different ways that Christian ethics involves understanding and obeying divine dogma (God's revealed truth) and is not merely a system of human thought.[31] And I agree with Henry, who said,

> The first emphasis of Hebrew-Christian ethics must always be the absolute uniqueness of its revealed character. Every attempt to explain Christian ethics as being merely a more complex development of the insights of general [humanly devised] ethics either conceals or minimizes the basis that it has in special revelation.[32]

Christian ethics is dogmatic, but what it declares dogmatically is not just any dogma from any source of authority. Rather, it only concerns the will, nature, and standards of the only God who reveals himself in the Word of God. This makes Christian ethics "theistic," meaning it comes from God the Father (John 6:38, 7:16, 12:49; Eph 1:17–18), focuses on God the Son (Eph 1:22; Col 1:17–20), and is confirmed, clarified, and guided by God the Holy Spirit (John 14:26, 16:7–14; 1 Cor 2:10–13).[33]

---

[29] Barth held that "not just in general, but also in particular, the concern of ethics is a proper concern of dogmatics" and also maintained that, because "ethics inquires into the goodness of human action and dogmatics . . . aims at the statement that human action is good in so far as God sanctifies it, this point of coincidence is of very special significance to both parts." For Barth, Christian ethics is dogmatic because "the theme of dogmatics is simply the Word of God . . . (and) the theme of the Word of God is simply human existence, life, or conduct." Barth, *Ethics*, 16 (see chap. 1, n. 26).

[30] O'Donovan, *Resurrection and Moral Order*, 11.

[31] Frame, *Doctrine of the Christian Life*, 6.

[32] Henry, *Christian Personal Ethics*, 146 (see chap. 1, n. 2).

[33] Frank R. Barry says, "The vision of God's holy love . . . mediated by his Spirit is the differentia of the Christian ethic." Frank R. Barry, *The Relevance of Christianity: An Approach to Christian Ethics* (London: Nisbet), 102. Barnette includes a whole chapter on the Holy Spirit claiming it is the Holy Spirit's role in Christian morality that "contributes to its unique and distinct nature" (Barnette, *Introducing Christian Ethics*, 87); and Joe Trull insists that "as Christ provides the pattern for Christian living, so the Spirit provides the enabling power" (Trull, *Walking in the Way*, 79).

In *Resurrection and Moral Order*, O'Donovan argues that Christian ethics is not just God-centered but Christ-centered, is not just Christ-centered but gospel-centered (centered on the mission Jesus came to accomplish), and is not just gospel-centered but centered especially on the resurrection of Jesus Christ from the dead.[34] O'Donovan understands that other possibilities could be suggested—possibilities such as the death of Christ (Col 2:20) or his ascension to heaven (Eph 4:8)—and does not deny "the richness of the New Testament ethical appeal." But he concentrates on "the resurrection as our starting point because it tells us of God's vindication of his creation, and also of our created life."[35] He sees this confirmed where Paul says, "if you have been raised with Christ, seek the things above, where Christ is, seated at the right hand of God" (Col 3:1) and where Peter says God "has given us a new birth into a living hope *through the resurrection* of Jesus Christ from the dead" (1 Pet 1:3, emphasis mine).

Christian ethics is divinely framed, biblically based, revelationally promulgated, creationally ordered, eschatologically directed, and resurrectionally centered, all because it starts with God the Father, is fulfilled by God the Son, and is guided by God the Holy Spirit. It all comes together where the Bible says,

> But as it is, Christ has been raised from the dead, the firstfruits of those who have fallen asleep. For since death came through a man, the resurrection of the dead also comes through a man . . . . But each in his own order: Christ, the firstfruits; afterward, at his coming, those who belong to Christ. Then comes the end, when he hands over the kingdom to God the Father, when he abolishes all rule and all authority and power . . . . God has put everything under his feet. Now when it says "everything" is put under him, it is obvious that he who puts everything under him is the exception. When everything is subject to Christ, then the Son himself will also be subject to the one who subjected everything to him, so that God may be all in all. (1 Cor 15:20–28)

Three more features need mentioning in connection with the dogmatic nature of Christian ethics, which are that Christian ethics also features transcendence, personhood, and holiness. Christian ethics features transcendence because, being from God, it involves norms beyond

---

[34] This is the *onus probandi* of (assertion proven in) O'Donovan's first chapter (O'Donovan, *Resurrection and Moral Order*, 11–27).

[35] O'Donovan, 13.

human control. These norms not only come from a source beyond us but also apply whether or not we like them or cannot live up to them. We might wonder how norms so different from us can be relevant. But they are because, while coming from a transcendent source, Christian moral norms are nevertheless personal because God is personal. And because God is personal, his standards apply to us as persons even though beyond our control and power to fulfill.

Christian moral norms do not only feature God's transcendence and personhood but his holiness as well. They do not just come from God but reflect his moral character. In both the Old and New Testaments, God commands human beings made in his image to "be holy as I am holy" (Lev 11:44–45; 19:2; 20:7; 1 Pet 1:16). Put another way, this means that "as the one who called you is holy, you also are to be holy in all your conduct" (1 Pet 1:15). Human beings will never be God, but we must live lives consistent with God's moral perfection. We must be holy in the same way and to the same degree our infinitely perfect God is holy. It is not realistic but is totally relevant. It is not possible without atoning for sin and transforming human nature in a way we cannot do on our own. It does not fit life as we know it but does fit what life is for. It does not fit who we are but fits who we someday will be.

Christian Ethics Features Actuality

A third set of features characterizing Christian ethics concerns the fact that Christian ethics is actual and not abstract. Christian ethics deals with the truly real and is not just a matter of theory about things that do not exist. Francis Schaeffer explains,

> *The truth of Christianity is that it is true to what is there.* You can go to the end of the world and you never need to be afraid, as were the ancients that you will fall off the end and the dragons will eat you up. You can carry out your intellectual discussion to the end of the game, because Christianity is not only true to the dogmas, it is not only true to what God has said in the Bible, but it is also true to what is there, and you will never fall off the end of the world! It is not just an approximate model; it really is true to what is there.[36]

---

[36] Francis Schaeffer, *He Is There and He Is Not Silent* (Wheaton, IL: Tyndale House, 1972), 17. Also in *The Complete Works of Francis A. Schaeffer: A Christian Worldview*, 5 vols. (Wheaton, IL: Crossway,

What Christian ethics studies is something "actual." But this actuality has nonmaterial as well as material aspects, meaning Christian ethics deals not only with things we can see and touch but also with things that exist though impossible to examine with physical senses (2 Cor 4:18). For this, Christian ethics requires faith in God's revelation about nonmaterial existence as well as what can be examined empirically. The Bible says, "faith is the reality (KJV: *substance*)[37] of what is hoped for, the proof (KJV: *evidence*)[38] of what is not seen" (Heb 11:1); and it concerns Christian ethics as surely as salvation by faith in Jesus Christ. Revelation and science both concern actuality, but when moral issues involve both, Christian ethics judges science by God's Word—never the other way around. God understands moral reality far better than we do, and he understands all dimensions of that reality far better than human scientists who can only examine what they see.

Christian ethics deals with how unseen things affect what we see and how seen things affect what we cannot see. While these are different, they are not two realities but one single reality with dimensions that are seen and not seen. Because it is one moral reality, what occurs in one part affects the whole, just like squeezing a rubber ball to change its height changes its width as well. Christian ethics studies how faith in a God we do not see governs life in the world we do see and how the way we live in the world we see has eternal consequences with a God we do not see. And it turns out this interconnection of moral reality occurs as it does precisely because the unseen part truly exists and is not a collection of imaginings lacking actuality in their own right.

Since Christian ethics studies what is actual, it has features making it a science. But since it also concerns unseen realities by which the seen world is measured but with which, it can

---

1982), 1:290. Emphasis is in the original and removed from reproduction in Schaeffer's collected works.

[37] English translators must interpret ὑπόστασις (*hupostasis*), which in the first sense—as defined by Bauer—means "substantial nature," "actual being," or "reality," in contrast to just seeming to be the case. Thus, the KJV translates using the term *substance* and the CSB translates using the term *reality*. But these terms mean the same thing, both referring to a thing that truly exists. On this, see Walter Bauer, *A Greek-English Lexicon of the New Testament and Other Early Christian Literature*, trans. W. F. Arndt and F. W. Gingrich (Chicago: University of Chicago, 1957), 854.

[38] The Greek term ἔλεγχος (*elengchos*) refers to being completely convinced or being sure something is genuinely the case. It does not so much regard the quality of evidence presented (pace KJV) as it does accept some claim actually to be the case. Bauer, 248.

never (or cannot yet) fully comply, Christian ethics also has features making it an art.[39] This might seem like mixing water and oil, but there is no incompatibility because the actuality concerned is the same in both cases. As a science, Christian ethics studies something real whether people like it or not, and as an art, it moves us to want what God wants. What God wants is not hypothetical but rather is perfectly consistent with how things were created. As a science, Christian ethics seeks to know and understand God's moral reality, and as an art, it tries to express it. As a science, Christian ethics aims never to deny that reality, and as an art, it aims never to distort it. As a science, Christian ethics is something to study, test, and discover, and as an art, Christian ethics is something to celebrate, enjoy, and pursue.

Because Christian ethics concerns actuality, it has related features such as beauty, coherence, objectivity, universality, and permanence. Christian ethics is beautiful because it reveals the beauty of God's moral law (Ps 119:129), which itself manifests the beauty of his mind (Rom 11:33–34) and character (Ps 29:2; 96:9).[40] Lewis says, "The Order of the Divine mind, embodied in the Divine Law, is beautiful."[41] Like polishing a brass lamp, Christian ethics exposes the beauty of God's moral truth, while sin hides it under a tarnish of perversion.[42] Christian ethics is coherent, not chaotic, because God is self-consistent and all he

---

[39] I agree with Scott Rae where he insists that "ethics is both an art and a science" because "it does involve some precision like the sciences, but like art, it is an inexact and sometimes intuitive discipline" (Rae, *Moral Choices*, 20). I also agree with Aristotle where he says that "the virtues are acquired by first exercising them, just as happens in the arts" (*The Nicomachean Ethics* 1103.a.32–33). But I differ here with a widely held view that regards Christian ethics to be a matter of science and nothing more. For example, see Barnette, *Introducing Christian Ethics*, 3; Leander S. Keyser, *A Manual of Christian Ethics* (Burlington, IA: Lutheran Literary Board, 1926), 10; and Emil Brunner, *The Divine Imperative,* trans. Olive Wyon (Philadelphia: Westminster, 1947), 86. I agree that Christian ethics includes scientific features but do not agree that Christian ethics can be reduced to scientific inquiry. There is more to love than hormones, more to a rose than botany, more to music than sound, and more to Christian ethics than examining patterns of human behavior.

[40] On beauty and Christian ethics see Richard Harris, *Art and the Beauty of God: A Christian Understanding* (New York: Mowbray, 1994); Nancy Pearcey, *Saving Leonardo: A Call to Resist the Secular Assault on Mind, Morals, and Meaning* (Nashville: B&H, 2010); and John Milbank, Graham Ward, and Edith Wyschogood, *Theological Perspectives on God and Beauty* (Harrisburg, PA: Trinity Press International, 2003).

[41] C. S. Lewis, *Reflections on the Psalms* (San Diego: Harcourt, 1986), 59.

[42] The Bible treats beauty as a property intrinsic to things, such as God's moral law. It may be perceived but exists whether perceived or not. Philosophers have debated the meaning of beauty, however,

does expresses his perfection and purposes (Ps 18:30; 119:96; 1 John 1:5). Christian ethics is objective because it concerns an order that exists and applies no matter what anyone happens to think, want, or prefer (1 John 1:8). While Christian ethics studies and applies an objective moral order, it includes subjective aspects, such as cultivating desire to please God (Ps 119:37). But the objective order with which Christian ethics deals controls its subjective aspects, never the other way around.[43] Personal satisfaction does not make anything morally right or wrong, but living God's way produces great satisfaction (Ps 19:10; 119:72, 127).[44] Christian ethics is universal, not parochial, because it is established by the one who made all things (Col 1:16) and measures all by the same moral reality regardless of culture, religion, or locality (Ps 11:4; 47:2; 103:19; 119:91). Christian ethics is permanent (Ps 119:89, 144, 160; Isa 40:8; 2 Cor 4:18) because it manifests the character of one who never changes (1 Sam 15:29; Ps 33:11; 119:89; Mal 3:6; Heb 1:12; 13:8; Jas 1:17). I, therefore, agree with O'Donovan when he says,

> The order of things that God has made is *there*. It is objective, and mankind has a place within it. Christian ethics, therefore, has an objective reference because it is concerned with man's life in accordance with this order. The summons to live in it is addressed to all mankind, because the good news that we *may* live in it is addressed to all mankind. Thus Christian moral judgments in principle address every man. They

---

with some arguing it has intrinsic reality and others denying that it does. The biblical view aligns with Plato's treatment that regards beauty as an objectively real quality essential to moral goodness, making it something possible to perceive but not depending on perception. Plato, *Philebus*, 64e–65a. Lewis argued that "if our minds are totally alien to reality then all our thoughts, including this thought, are worthless. We must, then, grant logic to the reality (by which we exist); we must, if we are to have any moral standards, grant it (the reality by which we exist) moral standards too. And there is no reason why we should not do the same about standards of beauty." C. S. Lewis, *Christian Reflections* (Grand Rapids: Eerdmans, 1994), 71.

[43] O'Donovan connects the subjective with the objective in Christian ethics, explaining, "Love is the overall shape of Christian ethics, the form of the human participation in created order. It is itself ordered and shaped in accordance with the order that it discovers in its object, and this ordering of love it is the task of substantive Christian ethics to trace." O'Donovan, *Resurrection and Moral Order*, 25–26.

[44] On this see Augustine, *The City of God*, 22.30; David K. Naugle, *Reordered Love, Reordered Lives: Learning the Deep Meaning of Happiness* (Grand Rapids: Eerdmans, 2008); O'Donovan, *Common Objects of Love*; and chapter 11 in my book, *True Sexual Morality*, 225–50 (see chap. 1, n. 41).

are not something which the Christian opted into and which he might as well, quite as sensibly, have opted out of. They are founded on reality as God has given it.[45]

Christian Ethics Features Paradox

A fourth and final class of features characterizing Christian ethics—one that more than all the others makes Christian ethics truly extraordinary and much different than everything else—is pervasive paradox. No other ethical view or tradition is like this at all. Some share features from one or two of the other categories—for example the philosophy of Immanuel Kant is complex and the ethics of Islam is dogmatic—but no other view or tradition is paradoxical. All other approaches fit what most prefer or think makes sense, but Christian ethics is filled from start to finish with things no one expects or thinks reasonable under present circumstances. Lewis says, when it comes to Christian ethical thought, "the principle" of paradox "runs through all life from top to bottom,"[46] giving Christianity what he calls its "blessedly two-edged character."[47]

To say something features paradox or is paradoxical means it involves something that seems contradictory by going against expectations but that is true (not contradictory) despite those expectations because it reveals something deeper than first assumed. A paradox is not really contradictory (does not involve incompatible truth claims), even though it can seem that way, and many wrongly suppose it really is.[48]

---

[45] O'Donovan, *Resurrection and Moral Order*, 17. Emphasis in the original.

[46] Lewis, *Mere Christianity*, 191.

[47] C. S. Lewis, "Some Thoughts," in *God in the Dock: Essays on Theology and Ethics*, ed. Walter Hooper (Grand Rapids: Eerdmans, 1970), 147.

[48] *The Random House College Dictionary*, ed. Jess Stein (New York: Random House, 1984), 964 (first definition); *The American Heritage Dictionary of the English Language*, ed. William Morris (Boston: Houghton-Mifflin, 1980), 950 (first definition); and *The American College Dictionary*, ed. E. L. Barnhart (New York: Random House, 1964), 878 (first definition). Similarly, *The Oxford English Dictionary* (1913 ed.) 7:450; *The Concise Oxford Dictionary* (Oxford: Clarendon, 1981), 742; and *The Chambers Twentieth Century Dictionary* (Edinburgh: W&R Chambers, 1972), 780. These all note that *paradox* also has been used by some less commonly to mean "contradiction." I am using *paradox* in its primary and most common sense. For more, see Wayne Grudem's extended footnote comments in *Systematic Theology*, 34–35.

In God's moral reality, living is dying and dying is living (Mark 8:35; John 12:24; Rom 8:13; 1 Cor 15:36). Try saving your life on your own terms and you will lose it, but lose your life for God's sake and you will save it (Matt 10:39). The best sort of self-love and the only sort that really counts is not self-centered (Matt 6:33; Mark 12:29–31), and the best sort of neighbor love is not neighbor centered (Matt 22:37–39). To be effective in the long run without one destroying the other, both must be God-centered, and what results is far better than focusing all attention on ourselves at the expense of others or on others at expense to ourselves. Loving yourself requires denying yourself (Luke 9:23; 1 Cor 10:24), a fact Lewis expresses when he says, "Until you have given up your self to Him you will not have a real self."[49]

There is honor in shame and joy in persecution (Matt 5:12; Heb 12:2; Jas 1:2). Seek happiness and you will never find it, but seek God and you will (Matt 10:39; 16:26). Please God and you will have pleasures forevermore (Ps 16:11; Matt 6:33), but insist on pleasing yourself and you will never be satisfied (Prov 27:20; 30:15; Eccl 5:10). Exaltation requires humbling yourself (Ezek 21:26; Luke 14:8–9; 1 Pet 5:6) because the way up is down, and promoting yourself over others leads to humiliation (Ezek 21:26; Matt 23:12) because the way down is up. Having is giving and giving is having (Eccl 11:1; Mark 4:24; Luke 6:38), which leads Lewis to say, "The only things we can keep are the things we freely give to God. What we try to keep for ourselves is just what we are sure to lose."[50] Reward comes from expecting nothing (Luke 6:35). Payment comes from those not able to pay you in return (Luke 14:13–14). Money cannot buy what good living most requires (Isa 55:1).

A full life requires pouring it out (Luke 1:53; Phil 2:6–10). Emptiness comes from trying to fill yourself (Luke 1:53; Col 2:8). Those the world considers wise are foolish, and those the world considers foolish are wise (1 Cor 1:27–28; 3:18–20). Unsophisticated, uneducated children are smarter than sophisticated, educated adults (Matt 11:25). This is why Lewis says that in Christianity, "The learned and the adult have no advantage over the simple and the child."[51] The least are greatest, and the greatest are least (Mark 5:30–32; Luke 22:26). The poor are rich, and the rich are poor (Jas 1:9–10). Less is more, and more is less (Mark 12:43–44). The last shall be first, and the first shall be last (Matt 19:30; Mark 9:35). Leading requires serving

---

[49] Lewis, *Mere Christianity*, 190.

[50] Lewis, 181.

[51] C. S. Lewis, *The Problem of Pain* (London: Centenary Press, 1940), 67.

(Mark 10:42–44; Luke 22:25–27). Weakness is strength, and strength is weakness (2 Cor 12:9–10). Lewis concludes that "man approaches God most nearly when he is in one sense least like God. For what can be more unlike than fullness and need, sovereignty and humility, righteousness and penitence, limitless power and a cry for help?"[52]

Winners lose and losers win (Mark 8:36; Phil 3:8). What seems hard is easy and what seems easy is hard (Matt 11:29–30). Freedom is slavery, and slavery is freedom (Rom 6:18–19; 1 Cor 9:19). Your will is not yours until given to God (Luke 22:42; Matt 10:38). As C. S. Lewis puts it, "The more we get what we now call *ourselves* out of the way and let Him take us over, the more truly ourselves we become,"[53] and that is because "those Divine demands which sound to our natural ears most like those of a despot and least like those of a lover, in fact marshal us where we should want to go if we knew what we wanted."[54] We must love those who hate us and hate those we love most (Matt 5:44; 19:29; Luke 14:26). We must respond to insults with blessing (Matt 5:11). Seek heaven and you will get earth in the bargain (Matt 6:33), but seek earth and you will get neither (Matt 16:26; Mark 8:36; Luke 9:25). We must struggle to be good even though God does all the work (Phil 2:12–13). And lastly, we are told that "whoever has, more will be given to him, and he will have more than enough; but whoever does not have, even what he has will be taken away from him" (Matt 13:12).[55]

C. S. Lewis & Reinhold Niebuhr

Lewis and Niebuhr both considered the paradoxical nature of Christian ethics, and although they never collaborated, their treatment developed the subject more thoroughly than previous Christian thinkers. Lewis touched the subject many times throughout his writing but addressed it at most length in a chapter discussing what changes in men and women transformed by Jesus Christ (Rom 12:2). Using a biblical term (2 Cor 5:17; Gal 6:15; Eph 4:24; Col 3:10), Lewis says they become "new men" and summarizes their lives (their ethics) in paradoxical terms, saying,

---

[52] C. S. Lewis, *The Four Loves* (New York: Harcourt-Brace, 1960), 4.
[53] Lewis, *Mere Christianity*, 190.
[54] Lewis, *Problem of Pain*, 41.
[55] See my discussion of this at chapter 2, footnote 26.

Give up your self, and you will find your real self. Lose your life and you will save it. Submit to death, death of your ambitions and favourite wishes every day and death of your whole body in the end: submit with every fibre of your being, and you will find eternal life. Keep back nothing. Nothing that you have not given away will ever be really yours. Nothing in you that has not died will ever be raised from the dead. Look for yourself, and you will find in the long run only hatred, loneliness, despair, rage, ruin, and decay. But look for Christ and you will find Him, and with Him everything else thrown in.[56]

Niebuhr also discussed the paradoxical nature of Christianity, but did so mainly by way of evaluating what he called "the relevance of an impossible ethical ideal" found in the ethics of Jesus.[57] Niebuhr coined this phrase to reference how God requires perfection (Ps 19:7; Matt 5:48) of imperfect people who can never reach perfection no matter how hard we try (Isa 53:6; 64:6; Rom 3:10, 23; 8:7). He noted that in most situations and cultures the "common currency" of moral living consists of balancing "the relatively good" with "the relatively evil." But Christianity approaches ethics in radically different terms. In Niebuhr's words,

[It] demands the impossible; and by that very demand emphasizes the impotence and corruption of human nature . . . . [Therefore its practice] tends to disintegrate into two contrasting types of [false] religion. The one inclines to deny the relevance of the ideal of love, to the ordinary problems of existence, certain that the tragedy of human life must be resolved by something more than moral achievement. The other tries to prove the relevance of the religious ideal to the problems of everyday existence by reducing it to conformity with the prudential rules of conduct which the common sense of many generations and the experience of the ages have elaborated . . . [But] it is the genius and the task of prophetic religion [i.e., Christian ethics] to insist on the organic relation between historic human existence and that which is both the ground and the fulfillment of this existence, the transcendent.[58]

---

[56] Lewis, *Mere Christianity*, 191.

[57] Niebuhr uses this expression for the title he gives to chapter 4 in *An Interpretation of Christian Ethics*. But he deals with paradox in Christian ethics most extensively in chapter 2, which is titled "The Ethic of Jesus." Niebuhr, *An Interpretation of Christian Ethics* (see ch. 1, n. 6), 22–38, 62–83.

[58] Niebuhr, 62–63.

But if an impossible ethical ideal is relevant—if God's perfect standards really do apply even though no one could ever meet them—would this not be the largest, toughest, most impossible to reconcile ethical paradox of them all? And beyond that, what does this say about the justice of God and his worthiness to be worshipped and obeyed? How fair is it for God to judge imperfect creatures by standards we have no hope of achieving? It seems very unreasonable, terribly harsh, and perhaps even cruel. Niebuhr dealt with this paradox in both practical and spiritual terms. Practically, he stressed we must pursue ideals we cannot achieve for two reasons: first, because it keeps us from succumbing to moral complacency; and second, because we can always improve on existing conditions, and ideals show us the direction to go even if we cannot go the whole distance. So, even knowing we cannot reach perfection, Niebuhr says we must seek it not because we will ever get there but just because we can always make things better than they are.[59]

Niebuhr's practical case might be true enough. But even if it is, what he calls the relevance of "impossible possibility" still only expects nothing more than what everyone can do on his or her own without assistance from God. It does not include God's judgment for failing to meet standards we cannot meet and does not address the fairness question that results. As to this fairness question, Niebuhr responded spiritually (not practically) by appealing strictly to faith, saying, when it comes to fulfilling "the transcendent" within imperfect human existence,

> Obligation to support and enhance it can . . . only arise and maintain itself upon the basis of faith that it is the partial fruit of a deeper unity and the promise of a more perfect harmony than is revealed in any immediate situation. If a lesser faith than this prompts moral action, it results in precisely those types of moral fanaticism which impart unqualified worth to qualified values and thereby destroy even their qualified worth. The prophetic faith in a God who is both the ground and the ultimate fulfillment of existence, who is both the creator and the judge of the world, is thus involved in every moral situation.[60]

---

[59] I do not think what Niebuhr says concerning the paradoxical relevance of an impossible possibility can be dismissed as therefore disconnecting the ethical teaching of Jesus from real life. Niebuhr was making the opposite point, which is that standards of ethical perfection cannot be ignored precisely because they pertain to the real situation despite human inability to achieve.

[60] Niebuhr, *An Interpretation of Christian Ethics*, 63–64.

Niebuhr understood, and I agree, that this ultimate paradox in Christian ethics relies more on faith than on human reasoning ability. We can analyze it but never wholly explain it within the limits of human reason and present circumstances. It requires trusting the fairness of a moral mind superior to ours and a power controlling far more than we control when considering our own interpretations. All other ethical systems and traditions either lower moral standards to what human beings can achieve as we are or assume moral perfections are within our ability to achieve—if only we give the right people enough power, redistribute wealth the right way, pass the right laws, require the right education, build a master race of just the right people, or cleanse the world of bad people. God's answer to the fairness paradox is the work and person of Jesus Christ:

> No condemnation now exists for those in Christ Jesus, because the Spirit's law of life in Christ Jesus has set you free from the law of sin and of death. What the law could not do since it was limited by the flesh, God did. He condemned sin in the flesh by sending His own Son in flesh like ours under sin's domain, and as a sin offering, in order that the law's requirement would be accomplished in us who do not walk according to the flesh but according to the Spirit. (Rom 8:1–4)

God does judge imperfect people by standards no one can achieve on his or her own. The good news is that Jesus has bridged the difference and will credit unearned moral perfection to morally imperfect people who accept his terms (2 Cor 5:19). The bad news is there is no other way of solving this problem, and those who refuse those terms must bear the consequences.

Marks of Transcendence

We have seen how Christian ethics features paradox but have not yet considered why this is the case. Why should Christian ethics feature paradox? God does not have to explain anything he does, and when Job insisted, God answered by saying, "Would you really challenge my justice? Would you declare me guilty to justify yourself?" (Job 40:8). If God offers no answer to the questions we ask, we must learn to trust him and go on. But Scripture also commands us to "love the Lord your God with all your . . . mind" (Matt 22:37), and with that shows God wants us to use our minds—not to challenge but to please him—by trying to better understand his character and intentions. The Bible does not answer the "Why filled with paradox?" question directly. But it does give enough information for us to reach at least one good answer, and that is that pervasive paradox not only sets Christian ethics apart but also proves its validity more surely and clearly than anything else. The paradoxes featured in Christian ethics are what I call "marks of transcendence" because their presence proves we are dealing with something that truly is what it claims to be.

If Christian ethics studies something revealed by God, we should not be surprised but ought to expect what God reveals to be complex, dogmatic, actual, and paradoxical. We should expect divinely revealed truth to be multifaceted, marked with certainty, truly real, and different from what human beings make up. Of the four classifications into which we have ordered characteristic features, the one truly setting Christian ethics apart is paradox. Other views and traditions may share aspects of complexity, dogma, and actuality, but none features paradox other than Christian ethics. But there is more. The paradoxical nature of Christian ethics not only best proves we are dealing with something unique but also is what best proves we are dealing with something valid. It is what most proves that Christian ethics studies what Schaeffer called "true truth."[61] It is what best proves we are studying something given to finite minds by an infinite mind about a reality that includes us but is vastly greater than all we know or will know.[62]

Pervasive paradox confirms the validity of Christian ethics in two ways: first, by showing effects of deep simplicity, and second, by showing effects of transition from infinity to finitude. By saying it manifests effects of deep simplicity confirming the validity of Christian ethics, I mean that examining the presence of paradox leads to perceiving a deep consistency running through the entire moral universe, and then on seeing that it leads to realizing a moral power is not just coordinating one thing with another but is moving everything at all levels toward one grand integrating purpose.

The power of deep simplicity is something Steve Jobs, who launched the computer industry, discovered and used to revolutionize business, movies, music, phones, and publishing around the world. It is not the same as being "simplistic," which refers to something shallow. Rather, it refers to a single idea or power that at a deep level moves everything in a complex system toward one unifying purpose. Jobs found that once he knew what that was, it became

---

[61] Schaeffer, *Escape from Reason*, 218 (see chap. 1, n. 5).

[62] I mean here that, even when living in a sinless state in the new Jerusalem (Rev 21:10–27), we will remain finite creatures with limited knowledge and power as compared to God's infinite knowledge and power. What we will know will be vastly superior to what we know now. But, even though what we know of God's moral reality will grow forever, it will never arrive at everything God knows.

possible to arrange everything else properly and to separate what was essential from what was not. He expressed this by saying "simplicity is the ultimate sophistication" and made it Apple's design mantra.[63] Jony Ive, who led the design team at Apple under Jobs, explained that "to be truly simple, you have to go really deep . . . . You have to deeply understand the essence (of a thing) in order to be able to get rid of the parts that are not essential."[64]

I mention this because what Jobs discovered with material things applies to moral things as well. God runs everything both moral and material, and as looking for deep simplicity exposes the way material things operate, so it is that studying paradox in Christian ethics exposes a powerful moral unity working on a far deeper level than we expect. It may seem from what we see that evil is winning or that God's rules are outdated, but the presence of paradox shows there is more going on. There is a unifying power out of our control that is running things at a very deep level. Niebuhr says the paradoxical nature of Christian ethics reveals "a more transcendent source of unity than any discoverable in the natural world" and "produces a morality which implies that every moral value and standard is grounded in and points toward an ultimate perfection of unity and harmony, not realizable in any historic situation."[65]

The Bible calls this the "hand of God" (Ps 139:7–10; 1 Pet 5:6) and tells us that "all things work together for the good of those who love God, who are called according to his purpose" (Rom 8:28). The "all things" in this verse means God is working everything, even the bad and unfair things, together with things we understand and like, toward a good end. And he is doing this, not in the Buddhist sense of denying there is any ultimate difference distinguishing good and evil, and not in the Muslim sense of reducing moral unity to what humans achieve under present circumstances, but rather in the transcendent biblical sense of moving moral reality as a whole toward a unifying conclusion that assures the ultimate triumph of good over evil. The Bible says this deep simplicity manifesting paradox in Christian ethics is the power and person of Jesus Christ himself, not only because "all things have been created through him and for him," but also because he is even now holding all things together (Col 1:16–17). This very deep moral unity leaves nothing out, whether it is sparrows dying, the number of hairs on your head, or a

---

[63] Walter Isaacson, *Steve Jobs* (New York: Simon & Schuster, 2011), 127, 343.

[64] Isaacson, 343.

[65] Niebuhr, *An Interpretation of Christian Ethics*, 64, 69. Niebuhr here was treating the ethic of Jesus but considered it to be the same as interpreting the nature of Christian ethics.

cup of water given to a child (Matt 10:29–30, 42); and paradoxes, like the reversal of first and last, of life and death, of rich and poor, and of simple and sophisticated, show there is something very deep by which a single unifying power is working everything toward a single moral goal.[66]

By noticing how effects of deep simplicity serve to validate Christian ethics, I mean that examining the presence of paradox in Christian ethics leads to perceiving a deep consistency running through the entire moral universe and then realizing how a moral power is not just coordinating one thing with another but is moving everything at all levels toward one grand integrating purpose.

The second way paradox marks the presence of transcendence, confirming the validity of Christian ethics, is by showing effects of transition from infinity to finitude. The paradoxical nature of God's moral revelation is what proves that Christian ethics studies something from an infinite, non-human, non-material, non-earthly source communicated to finite beings— beings who, left to themselves, only see reality in terms limited by their finitude. Left to itself, no human mind would ever devise a view of ethics featuring paradox. It is not what we naturally expect because what we expect is what we think makes sense. It is what we think if left to our own devices. And people, left as they are, never want to be judged by standards they cannot meet, take away what they have, or reverse every advantage they have worked to achieve. Put differently, the absence of paradox in ethics proves you are dealing with something devised by human beings, and the presence of paradox proves the opposite. If an ethic fits what human minds expect, that proves human minds made it up. But if an ethic does not fit what human minds expect, that proves it had to come from a higher, non-human source.

The idea of paradox confirming the validity of Christian ethics by manifesting effects of transition from infinity to finitude—of an infinite mind communicating with finite minds— is affirmed where the Bible says, "There is a way that seems right to a person, but its end is the way to death" (Prov 14:12); where God warns us to realize, "My thoughts are not your thoughts, and your ways are not my ways . . . . For as heaven is higher than earth, so my ways are higher than your ways, and my thoughts than your thoughts" (Isa 55:8–9); and where Jesus rebukes moral teachers saying, "You are the ones who justify yourselves in the sight of others, but . . . what is highly admired by people is revolting in God's sight" (Luke 16:15).

---

[66] Allen Verhey has written an entire book on this theme. See Allen Verhey, *The Great Reversal: Ethics and the New Testament* (Grand Rapids: Eerdmans, 1984).

The features of Christian ethics all fall into one of four general categories: complexity, dogma, actuality, and paradox. Of these categories, it is the pervasive presence of paradox that makes Christian ethics truly extraordinary, not only setting Christian ethics apart from all other views, but also distinguishing Christian ethics as the only body of ethical truth not made up by men but revealed by God.

Conclusion

The first two chapters have introduced readers in a general way to Christian ethics viewed as a whole. The first chapter introduced readers to the importance, meaning, and distinctives of Christian ethics, and this chapter introduced readers to its major parts, categories, and features. In this second chapter, we learned how ethical thinking has three parts with each addressing a different yet interconnected aspect of worthy living: the study of worthy conduct, character, and goals. Then we saw how scholarship in the field divides into five subcategories, these being biblical Christian ethics, theological Christian ethics, historical Christian ethics, philosophical Christian ethics, and applied Christian ethics. Finally, we discussed features that distinguish Christian understanding of ethical truth from other approaches both religious and philosophical.

I now have finished introducing readers in a general way to Christian ethics as a whole, and in the following chapters, I will give readers a closer look at five subcategories composing the field. I will focus now on introducing readers more fully to the distinctives and particularities of biblical Christian ethics, theological Christian ethics, historical Christian ethics, philosophical Christian ethics, and applied Christian ethics. Even though each of these covers only part of something larger, each still covers an enormous range of ethical truth that has engendered large though different bodies of scholarly literature. Readers must not think any of the remaining chapters covers portions of the field entirely and should not imagine they contain everything worth saying. Rather, readers should keep in mind that in these chapters, I am only introducing large sections of an even larger whole. In what follows, we will cover what is most important to each subcategory and do so in a manner that is both comprehensible and true. Some subcategories of the field will be treated in one chapter and others will require more. Each will be treated distinctly even though they are interconnected, starting with biblical and ending with applied.

CHAPTER 3

BIBLE, LAW & STRUCTURE

This chapter introduces readers to biblical ethics as an academic subcategory within the larger field of Christian ethics. As mentioned in the previous chapter, all Christian ethics should be "biblical" in the sense of being consistent with the Bible, based on the Bible, and centered on the Bible. But readers are cautioned to understand that when scholars refer to "biblical ethics," they mean something else. In academic terms, *biblical ethics* indicates a focus of research and does not assure fidelity to biblical truth. We should want that to be so, but readers must realize not all academic work classified as "biblical ethics" is "biblical" in the sense of affirming the inerrancy of Scripture and agreeing with what the Bible really says.

If ethics deals with assessing morally worthy conduct, character, and goals, then biblical ethics deals with assessing morally worthy conduct, character, and goals as given in the Bible by the God who reveals himself in the Bible.[1] Christians are people of "the Book," and biblical

---

[1] There is a vast amount of literature dealing with biblical ethics, but the most noteworthy volumes on this subject as a whole include Ramsey, *Basic Christian Ethics* (see chap. 1, n. 69); John Murray, *Principles of Conduct: Aspects of Biblical Ethics* (Grand Rapids: Eerdmans, 1957, reprinted 1991); Barnette, *Introducing Christian Ethics* (see chap. 1, n. 60); T. B. Maston, *Biblical Ethics* (Macon, GA: Mercer, 1967); Bruce Kaye and Gordon D. Wenham, eds., *Law, Morality and the Bible* (Downers Grove, IL: InterVarsity, 1978); White, *Biblical Ethics* (see chap. 1, n. 69); Stephen Charles Mott, *Biblical Ethics and Social Change* (New York: Oxford, 1982); Jones, *Biblical Christian Ethics* (see chap. 2, n. 88);

ethics is what comes from analyzing how the Bible addresses ethical topics and answers ethical questions. Biblical ethics approaches the study of ethical conduct, character, and goals by seeking to understand what God calls people to be and do in and through his written Word—the Bible. According to John Murray,

> The biblical ethic is that manner of life which is consonant with, and demanded by, the biblical revelation. Our attention must be focused upon divine demand, not upon human achievement, upon the revelation of God's will for man, not upon human behaviour. In the biblical ethic we are concerned with the norms, or canons, or standards of behaviour which are enunciated in the Bible for the creation, direction, and regulation of thought, life, and behaviour consonant with the will of God.[2]

Biblical ethics differs from philosophical ethics, sometimes called speculative ethics,[3] because it is based on assuming the Bible is of God and is the ultimate source of ethical authority for us.[4] The biblical writers do not treat ethics in a mundane, naturalistic way as

---

Trull, *Walking in the Way* (see chap. 1, n. 55); Douma, *Responsible Conduct* (see chap. 1, n. 16); David W. Gill, *Doing Right: Practicing Ethical Principles* (Downers Grove, IL: InterVarsity, 2004); Frame, *The Doctrine of the Christian Life* (see chap. 1, n. 69); Jones, *An Introduction to Biblical Ethics* (see chap. 2, n. 85); and Grudem, *Christian Ethics* (see chap. 1, n. 67). Besides works dealing with biblical ethics as a whole, there are many that focus more narrowly, and of these, some of the most noteworthy include Walter C. Kaiser, Jr., *Toward Old Testament Ethics* (Grand Rapids: Zondervan, 1983); Christopher J. H. Wright, *Walking in the Ways of the LORD: The Ethical Authority of the Old Testament* (Downers Grove, IL: InterVarsity, 1995); Wolfgang Schrage, *The Ethics of the New Testament*, trans. David E. Green (Philadelphia: Fortress, 1982); Richard N. Longenecker, *New Testament Social Ethics for Today* (Grand Rapids: Eerdmans, 1984); and Frank J. Matera, *New Testament Ethics: The Legacies of Jesus and Paul* (Louisville: Westminster John Knox, 1996). The works listed here do not all align with Evangelical Christian hermeneutics. But all take the Bible seriously and so represent the most significant literature with whom others should engage.

[2] Murray, *Principles of Conduct*, 14.

[3] For example, Henry defines all secular philosophical ethics as a matter of "speculative ethics." Henry, *Christian Personal Ethics*, 22 (see chap. 1, n. 2).

[4] This does not mean Christians should have nothing to do with philosophical ethics, but it does mean Christians should not rely on man-generated philosophical speculation to explain, frame, or delimit ethical truth revealed in the Word of God. Reasoned analysis building on a biblical worldview, or speculating on moral truth revealed in the Word of God, is a matter of theological, not philosophical, ethics. Christians should seek to understand and engage man-centered philosophical speculation about ethics. But engaging man-generated philosophical ethics should not be confused with using

something rooted in human aspirations or experience, arising out of social or economic conditions, or generated by human imagination or volition. Rather, they treat ethics in a transcendent supernatural way as rooted in the character of God, authorized by the authority of God, initiated by the will of God, promulgated by acts of God, and fulfilling the purposes of God. Thus, for the biblical writers, how human beings relate to God is not just something affected by ethics but is central to the nature and meaning of ethics itself.

The Bible & Ethics

Biblical ethics studies the structure, content, and application of moral truth in the Bible. But to what degree is the Bible concerned with revealing and interpreting moral truth? The answer is that the Bible addresses ethics on every page and in nearly every verse. Biblical interest in promulgating, explaining, applying, judging, and upholding God's view of ethical truth is "pervasive," meaning God's view of ethical truth is addressed in everything the Bible covers from start to finish. There is nothing in the Bible not related to biblical ethics in some fashion. Everything God addresses in the Bible concerns ethics. Creation has an ethical purpose. Sin is an ethical problem. Salvation is an ethical solution. Righteousness is a matter of ethical purity. Wickedness is a matter of ethical impurity. God's laws set ethical standards. God's wisdom provides ethical guidelines. God's holiness defines ethical character. God's love defines ethical motive. God's glory is the ethical goal of all there is. God's blessings express ethical approval. God's curses express ethical disapproval. God's judgment applies ethical accountability. God's punishment is an ethical sanction. God's reward is an ethical incentive. Hell is a place of ethical torment. Heaven is a place of ethical perfection. Man is a moral agent. Angels are messengers of moral truth. Demons are agents of moral deception. The Devil is a moral enemy. And God is the standard of moral truth, source of moral authority, and judge of moral accountability.

Even if the Bible deals with ethics pervasively, how sufficient is the Bible as a book of ethical instruction? Is it something to which other sources of knowledge and instruction must

---

man-generated philosophical ethics to explain, frame, or delimit biblical truth. Biblical truth should be used to order our view of the world, not the other way around, and biblical truth should be used to order what we think of philosophical ethics, not the other way around.

be added before developing a fully adequate grasp of ethics? Could it be that the Bible is an important source of ethical instruction—perhaps even the most important—and yet is not enough taken alone to give a complete view of ethics? Could it be that ethical instruction in the Bible is something to respect but still needs to be supplemented with material from other sources, such as philosophy, practical experience, or history? The answer to these questions is that the Bible not only deals with ethics pervasively but also deals with ethics sufficiently. This does not mean the Bible directly addresses every question humans will ever think to ask, nor does it mean the Bible speaks directly to every circumstance that ever has, or ever will, arise in human experience. But the Bible is our all-sufficient rule for faith and practice, meaning it provides all we need, or ever will need, to live lives that are holy and pleasing to God. That is because "all Scripture is inspired by God and is profitable for teaching, for rebuking, for correcting, for training in righteousness, so that the man of God may be complete, equipped for every good work" (2 Tim 3:16–17). Because of this, we should agree with the nineteenth-century British theologian J. C. Ryle, who wrote,

> Let the Bible, the whole Bible, and nothing but the Bible, be the rule of our faith and practice. Holding this principle, we travel upon the king's highway. The road may sometimes seem narrow, and our faith may be severely tried, but we shall not be allowed greatly to err. Departing from this principle we enter on a pathless wilderness. There is no telling what we may be led to believe or do. Forever let us bear this in mind. Here let us cast anchor. Here let us abide.[5]

We know that science advances, cultures change, technologies improve, and the sum of human knowledge increases over time. We know, as well, the biblical cannon closed centuries ago and much has taken place since. There is nothing in the Bible that directly addresses things like Communism, same-sex marriage, cloning, or human-animal hybrids. Does this mean we need to supplement the Word of God in Scripture with other sources of ethical instruction? The answer is we do not, or at least the answer is we do not need other sources for assessing right and wrong. This affirms the ethical sufficiency of the Bible, which means we believe God already has provided all we need to frame ethical judgments no matter how the

---

[5] J. C. Ryle, *Expository Thoughts on the Gospels: St. Luke* (New York: Robert Carter and Brothers, 1860), 371.

world changes, no matter how human knowledge increases, no matter what scientists discover, and no matter what technologies are invented.

Changes outside the Bible expand the range of situations and circumstances to which ethical judgments apply but do not, and can never, change ethical meaning, ethical authority, or ethical accountability. The Bible does not give every detail for every ethical application that might ever come along. But it does give us all we will ever need to address anything that will ever come along.[6] The Bible does not provide exhaustive truth, but it provides a sufficient amount of what Schaeffer called "true truth" for us to assess and handle the ethics

---

[6] The position I take here on the "sufficiency" of the Bible for ethical framing is historically orthodox but differs from what many now say, and not just liberals who reject the divine origin of Scripture but even some well-meaning Evangelicals. Barnette claims that without "the insights of philosophy, history, and the social sciences," Christians cannot "make moral norms relevant to contemporary moral decisions" (*Introducing Christian Ethics*, 4). Long assumes Christian ethics cannot be understood "without some appreciation of philosophical ways of dealing with moral issues" (*A Survey of Christian Ethics*, 3 [see chap. 1, n. 49]). Douma says that understanding the Bible "is not enough in many situations" to formulate ethical judgment (*Responsible Conduct*, 75). Rae believes "the Bible is not the only source of ethical inquiry." *Moral Choices: An Introduction to Ethics*, 3rd ed. (Grand Rapids: Zondervan, 2009), 14. Jack T. Sanders alleges we cannot start with Jesus or the Bible "if we wish to develop coherent ethical positions." *Ethics in the New Testament: Change and Development* (Philadelphia: Fortress, 1975), 130. Mott says the Bible must be interpreted "with knowledge of sociological, economic, and ethical categories employed elsewhere (in order) to understand socio-economic structures and conflicts" (*Biblical Ethics and Social Change*, ix). Cook, after affirming "the Bible is a source of Christian moral principles," goes on to say, "Scripture alone, however, is not the only source of Christian moral teaching" (*The Moral Maze*, 46, 58 [see chap. 2, n. 86]). Davis says that, while the Bible serves as a bottom line, "the natural and social sciences may aid moral reflection" (*Evangelical Ethics*, 9 [see chap. 1, n. 55]). Bruce Birch and Larry Rasmussen reject using the contemporary authority of the Bible entirely, saying, "it is certainly clear that the Bible is not authoritative for Christian ethics at the point of making ethical decisions for us." (*Bible & Ethics in the Christian Life* (Minneapolis: Augsburg, 1989), 141. Trull says that he believes Christians "can turn to many resources for discovering God's will in human relationships" even though the Bible is "the major moral compass" (*Walking in the Way*, 7, 5). Paul Jersild says, "the ethical witness of the Bible is neither sufficiently clear nor consistent to give it a blanket hermeneutical primacy." *Spirit Ethics: Scripture and the Moral Life* (Minneapolis: Fortress, 2000), 80. And Van Til maintains the Bible is not a sufficient ethical source because he thinks that "there is not just one biblical ethic" and that "in the Bible, moral norms, virtues, and desired consequences develop over time" (*The Moral Disciple*, 19 [see chap. 2, n. 86]). These, all in different ways, deny that the Bible really is the Christian's "all sufficient" rule for faith and practice.

of any situation that will ever arise.[7] So, even though the Bible does not mention surrogate mothering, we can be sure it provides everything needed to answer ethical questions about surrogate mothering.

Christian Ethics & Biblical Ethics

We saw in the previous chapter that, as a field of academic study, Christian ethics is divided into five subcategories, with biblical ethics being one.[8] Academically speaking, the terms *Christian ethics* and *biblical ethics* do not refer to the same thing, but they are closely related. The difference is more a matter of scope and focus than of kind. One field (biblical ethics) is included in the other (Christian ethics), so they do not, or at least should not, conflict. Christian ethics addresses the wider question, "What is the distinctly Christian understanding of, or approach to, matters of ethical right and wrong?" Biblical ethics addresses the narrower question, "What is the manner of life and behavior which the Bible requires and which faith in the biblical God produces?"[9]

All Christian ethics ought to be biblical in the sense of being submitted to biblical authority, faithful to biblical revelation, and compatible with how the Bible frames ethical reality and defines ethical truth. But biblical ethics is distinct in that it just focuses on studying what the Bible says and means, whereas Christian ethics not only studies what the Bible says and means but also uses what it says and means to address everything else. So, while Christian ethics includes biblical ethics and should center on biblical ethics and depend on biblical ethics, the fields have different academic boundaries.[10] As an academic discipline, Christian ethics

---

[7] Francis Schaeffer, *The Complete Works of Francis A. Schaeffer*, vol. 1 (Wheaton, IL: Crossway, 1982), 218–219.

[8] Besides biblical Christian ethics, the other subcategories within the larger field of Christian ethics are theological Christian ethics, historical Christian ethics, philosophical Christian ethics, and applied Christian ethics.

[9] This phrasing follows Murray, *Principles of Conduct*, 6.

[10] This understanding of Christian ethics has been challenged in recent work by Grudem (*Christian Ethics*, 37–40). Considering Christian ethics (the study of Christian moral understanding) to be an academic pursuit that includes, centers on, builds upon, and requires biblical ethics (which only examines the moral meaning of Bible passages), but that nevertheless as a larger discipline (or field of study) incorporates more than biblical ethics alone, is the long established view held by nearly all faithful

deals with more than biblical ethics, but it cannot do anything properly without relying on the included discipline of biblical ethics.

Christian ethics is a larger field because it addresses philosophical thinking, theological doctrines, historical movements, and applying God's ethical norms to new and changing circumstances—as well as examining what the Bible requires and how it frames ethical judgment. Christian ethics starts with biblical ethics but goes on to engage opposing systems and competing truth claims. Christian ethics uses what biblical ethics produces to interpret, affirm, or criticize the truth of morally relevant facts and theories coming from other fields of study, such as philosophy, economics, medicine, politics, sociology, anthropology, physics, and psychology.

Although Christian ethics covers more, it should never either cover less or reject what biblical ethics produces. For either to be true, both must affirm something Jones captures by saying,

> The controlling purpose of the Christian life is the glory of God; the impelling motive of the Christian life is love for God; and the directing principle of the Christian life is the will of God as revealed in Christ and the holy Scriptures.[11]

Christian ethics utilizes reason—but only as a tool and never as a source of truth competing with the Word of God. And Christian ethics considers human experience and culture and science—but only to apply what the Bible intends and never to undo or redefine the framing of biblical ethics.[12] Valid Christian ethics is never far removed from the Bible because that is the only place ethical truth is revealed to everyone for all time by the will and authority of God Himself.

Before finishing this section, we must acknowledge that what distinguishes biblical from Christian ethics is not always understood and sometimes has been confused by distinguished

---

Christian teachers and theologians throughout Christian history. Wayne Grudem questions this tradition, claiming the entire field should be viewed as including nothing other than studying the moral meaning of Bible passages and for this reason Christian ethics must be considered indistinguishable from biblical ethics.

[11] Jones, *Biblical Christian Ethics*, 16.

[12] Van Til and Hollinger say the same. See Van Til, *Christian Theistic Ethics*, 16 (see chap. 1, n. 36) and Hollinger, *Choosing the Good*, 16 (see chap. 1, n. 60).

scholars writing books on these topics. For example, Ramsey, Trull, and Grudem have produced texts treating biblical ethics with titles classifying them as "Christian ethics,"[13] and Rae has written a work on Christian ethics in which he asks readers to consider it "biblical ethics."[14] The point is that, while Christian ethics and biblical ethics are conceptually distinct, they are not always treated that way. To avoid confusing them, readers must rely on content more than terms a writer uses, and latitude must be granted when authors are not precise.

What Biblical Ethics Is & Is Not

Biblical ethics is not the same as just using the Bible when discussing ethics because the first assumes a degree of authority and coherence the second often ignores and might even deny.[15] Scholars who deny the authority and coherence of the Bible may still mention the Bible for background, may go through it for ideas, or may use it as a foil. But just mentioning the Bible like this does not qualify as biblical ethics because biblical ethics not only mentions the Bible but also analyzes the text in some way. Done properly, biblical ethics analyzes what the Bible says is right or wrong, is righteous or wicked, or is commendable or blameworthy in ways that rely on the Bible, derive from the Bible, are framed by the Bible, and are viewed as consistent with what the Bible says—not just in places but as a whole and not just as a way of starting off but as the source of moral truth.[16] This does not mean all scholarship in the field of biblical ethics is without error or beyond disputing. All human interpreters are fallible and

---

[13] Ramsey's classic work in biblical ethics is titled *Basic Christian Ethics*; Trull's work in biblical ethics is subtitled *An Introduction to Christian Ethics* (Trull, *Walking in the Way*) and Grudem's work in biblical ethics is titled *Christian Ethics*.

[14] Rae, *Moral Choices*, 14.

[15] This follows James F. Childress, who says, "We should not confuse biblical ethics with the use of the Bible in ethics." "Scripture and Christian Ethics: Some Reflections on the Role of Scripture in Moral Deliberation and Justification," *Interpretation: A Journal of Bible and Theology* 34 (October 1980): 376.

[16] David Kelsey observes that "to call a set of writings 'scripture' is to say that they ought to be used in certain normative and rulish ways in the common life of the church." *The Uses of Scripture in Recent Theology* (Philadelphia, Fortress Press, 1975), 164. Allen Verhey says that biblical ethics views Scripture as the final word for the "perspective" one takes on moral matters and that this perspective then "limits, corroborates, and transforms appeals to natural morality on other levels of moral discourse." "The Use of Scripture in Ethics," *Religious Studies Review* 4 (January 1978): 35.

must be scrutinized. This does mean, however, that biblical ethics done properly presumes a high view of Scripture and is different than using the Bible to supplement moral discussion really based on something else.[17]

While biblical ethics can be distinguished within the larger field of Christian ethics,[18] the two are so entwined that distinctives marking one are the same as for the other. This makes sense because authentic Christian ethics begins with, centers on, and builds upon biblical ethics such that anything less lacks validity and ends up perverting the study of Christian ethics. It is not possible to be authentically Christian without trusting the Word of God. Distinctives marking both biblical and Christian ethics include the objective reality of moral standards, ideals, and norms; the alignment of subjective components of our inner lives (especially including what the Bible calls "the heart") with that objective reality; a combination of affectional, volitional, and rational aspects with divine revelation; a combination of transcendent authority with personal relevance; striving for perfection united with imputed perfection through grace that reconciles what we are with what we should be; the belief that human perfection is a matter of conforming to the image of God; a reckoning with a perfection that surpasses all we are or ever could do for ourselves; participation in an order that presently exists but is heading toward something better; tension between social ideals and social reality; tension between a fixed reality that is universal and timeless and relative judgments affected by changing circumstances; a coherence by which external reality limits and directs internal reality; conviction that, while human finitudes of knowledge and ability affect what we do, the human moral problem stems from depravity and not from ignorance or socio-economic conditions; an accounting that covers both individuals and communities because it is both personal and political; and an interconnectedness of conduct, character, and goals according to the will of God, the holiness of God, and the character of God.[19]

---

[17] I side here with Van Til, who cautions the phrase "using the Bible . . . might give the impression that we stand at some distance from the Bible" and only consult the Bible "now and again for bits of moral guidance" (*The Moral Disciple*, 17). Cook is less cautious and vulnerable to criticism at this point. Cook not only fails to distinguish biblical ethics from using the Bible in ethics but also only considers the Bible to be one of several sources from which Christians derive moral principles (*The Moral Maze*, 45–46).

[18] The previous section discusses this in more detail.

[19] Different listings of distinctives have been suggested, with some distinctives appearing on one list and not on others, and with some lists claiming to recognize distinctives that many others dispute. Jones

Biblical ethics is not the same as philosophical ethics. Although these disciplines are not usually confused, what distinguishes one from the other often is. The difference between philosophical and biblical ethics is not a matter of reason versus faith, nor is it a matter of denying the supernatural versus accepting it. Philosophical ethics sometimes accepts the supernatural, and biblical ethics includes loving God with the mind as well as with the heart, soul, and strength (Luke 10:27; Mark 12:30; Matt 22:37).[20] The only truly essential difference separating biblical from philosophical ethics is the question of ultimate authority.[21] As Barnette explains, "In contrast to philosophical ethics," biblical ethics starts by assuming "biblical revelation sets forth the will of God as the ethical goal of man" and then "by means of biblical exegesis and interpretation . . . seeks to determine the nature and purpose of God's will

---

(*An Introduction to Biblical Ethics*, 2–5) lists five distinctives, including an objective, theistic worldview; imputed righteousness; participation in God's moral order; immorality stemmed from human depravity; and incorporation of conduct, character, and goals. Murray (*Principles of Conduct*, 12–13) lists four, including a concern for the heart out of which issues of life arise, a coherence that orders actions into a unifying pattern, an accounting for the behavior not only of individuals but of groups, and a reckoning with a perfection that surpasses everyone on earth. And Jones (*Biblical Christian Ethics*, 11–16) lists ten or more, including a focus on God's salvific call; salvation made possible by divine grace; a combination of affectional, volitional, and rational aspects; immorality arising from fallen human nature; the good pursued as something revealed by God; a view that perfection is conforming to the image of God; objective, normative, and never changing values; the belief that God's glory is the purpose of life; the conviction that God's love is the motive of life; and the view that God's will is the principle of life. Geisler (*Christian Ethics*, 22–25 [see chap. 1, n. 55]) lists five, including classification as a form of divine command theory; obligations being absolute (never situational or discretionary); requirements being revealed (never reasoned or interpreted); righteousness being a matter of legal prescription (with no place for wisdom); and ethics being a matter of doing one's duty (with no place for love, volition, or desire). Most Evangelicals in biblical ethics now object to Geisler's distinctives either because they claim too much, do not claim enough, or force biblical ethics into philosophical categories. In making my own list, I have tried to be comprehensive without losing coherence.

[20] Matthew does not list "with all your strength," but all three passages include loving God with our minds.

[21] Brunner maintained that the main difference distinguishing philosophical from Christian (including biblical) ethics is what each presumes from the start to be the source of ultimate authority, with one looking to man and the other looking to God (Brunner, *The Divine Imperative*, 86 [see chap. 2, n. 123]); and Van Til held that "Christian (including biblical) ethics does not differ from other (i.e., philosophical) ethics in that it seeks to answer different questions than other ethical theories do, but it differs from other ethical theories in that it answers these questions differently" (*Christian Theistic Ethics*, 18).

for human action."[22] Although biblical ethics may dispute matters of interpretation or application, it always starts with the Bible, always assumes divine revelation, and always acknowledges the supremacy of scriptural authority. By comparison, philosophical ethics never starts with the Bible, never assumes divine revelation, and never acknowledges the supremacy of scriptural authority.

There is a sense in which biblical ethics is what some call "bifocal," meaning it keeps one eye on the Bible and another on the world. But this can be taken the wrong way.[23] Biblical ethics does examine the world to understand circumstances and situations to which God's truth applies.[24] But it never looks to the world for moral authority. Biblical ethics evaluates the world by what the Word of God says, but never evaluates the Word of God by what the world says. It studies the changing ways people and cultures address moral issues—changes Jesus referred to as "signs of the times" (Matt 16:3)—but never adapts God's moral standards to accommodate such changes.[25] In summary, biblical ethics looks to the Bible in order to understand the source, nature, and standards of unchanging moral authority and studies the world to understand the many changing circumstances and situations subject to and needing to be aligned with that unchanging moral authority.

There is general agreement among Evangelical Christians that the Bible is the Word of God, and because of this, we maintain that the Bible is both morally authoritative and without error in the original manuscripts. But while Evangelicals agree "that" the Bible is essential to ethics, there is disagreement even among inerrantist Evangelical Christians over "how" biblical moral revelation applies or should be interpreted. This leads to problem areas Christians must

---

[22] Barnette, *Introducing Christian Ethics*, 4.

[23] This term is employed by Barnette who elaborates by saying that biblical ethics looks "to other disciplines (outside the Bible) for factual data for intellectual action" (*Introducing Christian Ethics*, 4). But while this often is the case, I also believe Barnette goes too far. The Bible makes factual as well as valuative claims, and should scientists or historians make claims of fact opposing what the Bible says, then biblical ethics must rely on what God says over what scientists may claim is the case. We need to remember that human scientists are fallible, while the Creator never is.

[24] Here I differ slightly from Van Til who held that biblical ethics only focuses on biblical content and that one crosses into Christian ethics when considering other sources of information bearing on moral life—even if only for the purpose of application (*Christian Theistic Ethics*, 15–16).

[25] For a whole book on this subject, see Francis A. Schaeffer, *The Great Evangelical Disaster* (Wheaton, IL: Crossway, 1984).

be humble enough to acknowledge even while zealous for the moral relevance of Scripture. Christians must learn to "live . . . on every word that comes from the mouth of the LORD" (Deut 8:3). But in doing so, we must not mistake human for divine authority because that leads to misinterpreting and misusing God's moral revelation.

Many ethical rules, standards, and principles treated in the Bible are revealed clearly, but not all. For example, we know that committing acts of murder and adultery are both absolutely wrong (Exod 20:13–14). But how should Bible believing Christians interpret what Paul says about women not wearing gold, pearls, or expensive jewelry (1 Tim 2:9)? What about God's command that witches (Lev 20:27) and rebellious children (Deut 21:18–21) be stoned to death? What about keeping the Sabbath on the first day of the week when God ordered it be kept on the seventh day (Deut 5:14)? What about God ordering builders to install railings around the roofs of new houses (Deut 22:8)? What about God commanding no one eat pork (Lev 11:7), clams, or oysters (Lev 11:10)? What about serving in the military and going to war when Jesus called followers to pursue peace (Matt 5:9)? And what about God ordering wars in which "you must not let any living thing survive," not just men, but also women, children, the elderly, and the infirmed (Deut 20:16)?[26]

Even though Evangelicals believe God's moral revelation in Scripture is inerrant, coherent, and consistent, this does not mean we can take every command in the Bible and apply it without modification.[27] Of course, we may not set ourselves over Scripture by only accepting portions we like while discarding the rest. But doing biblical ethics cannot avoid interpreting the meaning, intention, and relevance of Scripture even for Evangelicals who submit to the authority of Scripture. This involves hermeneutics—the science of biblical interpretation—and Evangelicals doing biblical ethics must decide how much and in what ways the Bible guides us "along the right paths for his name's sake" (Ps 23:3).

---

[26] For a treatment of this question maintaining an Evangelical view of the Bible, see Daniel R. Heimbach, "Crusade in the Old Testament and Today," in *Holy War in the Bible: Christian Morality and an Old Testament Problem*, Heath A. Thomas, Jeremy Evans, and Paul Copan, eds. (Downers Grove, IL: InterVarsity, 2013), 179–200.

[27] Feinberg and Feinberg say, "The Bible presents a perspective on ethics, but that does not mean every biblical teaching can be applied to modern times without modification. The Evangelical must decide which rules as stated in Scripture apply to our own day, and he must know how to decide which apply" (*Brave New World*, 33 [see chap. 1, n. 38]).

There is a vast literature on hermeneutics, all relevant to interpreting what God's moral revelation in Scripture requires of us today.[28] We cannot cover all that here, but I will mention a few questions to illustrate the sort of things Evangelicals doing biblical ethics may ask in search of moral truth revealed in the Bible. These questions do not challenge but rather assume the ethical authority of Scripture. They aim at understanding how God wants us to live and not to justify natural passions. They submit to the Word of God rather than resist it in favor of something else. Such questions might include: Does the Bible itself make this something God wants everyone to follow, or is it something unique to the relationship God had with ancient Israel? Does the Bible itself indicate this is something God meant to apply for all time, or is it something he issued only for a certain period and later discontinued? Does the Bible itself distinguish between moral law, ceremonial law, and civil law, and if so, how might this affect what matters now? Did ceremonial and civil laws issued by God to Israel in the Old Testament ever apply to others, and do they have any connection with life today? Even if ceremonial and civil laws no longer apply directly, might they reflect principles that still do

---

[28] Some of the most noteworthy literature dealing with biblical hermeneutics include: E. D. Hirsh, Jr., *Validity in Interpretation* (New Haven, CT: Yale, 1967); George B. Caird, *The Language and Imagery of the Bible* (Philadelphia: Westminster, 1980); William W. Klein, Craig L. Blomberg, and Robert L. Hubbard, *Introduction to Biblical Interpretation* (Dallas: Word, 1993); Donald A. Carson, *Exegetical Fallacies*, 2nd ed. (Grand Rapids: Baker, 1996); Gordon D. Fee and Douglas Stuart, *How to Read the Bible for All Its Worth* (Grand Rapids: Zondervan, 2003); J. Scott Duvall and J. Daniel Hayes, *Grasping God's Word: A Hands-On Approach to Reading, Interpreting, and Applying the Bible* (Grand Rapids: Zondervan, 2005); Grant R. Osborn, *The Hermeneutical Spiral: A Contemporary Introduction to Biblical Interpretation* (Downers Grove, IL: InterVarsity, 2006); Graeme Goldsworthy, *Gospel-Centered Hermeneutics: Foundations and Principles of Evangelical Biblical Interpretation* (Downers Grove, IL: InterVarsity, 2007); Howard G. Hendricks and William D. Hendricks, *Living by the Book: The Art and Science of Reading the Bible* (Chicago: Moody, 2007); Walter C. Kaiser, Jr. and Moisés Silva, *Introduction to Biblical Hermeneutics: The Search for Meaning* (Grand Rapids: Zondervan, 2007); Anthony C. Thiselton, *Hermeneutics: An Introduction* (Grand Rapids: Eerdmans, 2009); Robert L. Plummer, *40 Questions about Interpreting the Bible*, ed. Benjamin L. Merkle (Grand Rapids: Kregel, 2010); Andreas J. Köstenberger and Richard D. Patterson, *Invitation to Biblical Interpretation: Exploring the Hermeneutical Triad of History, Literature, and Theology* (Grand Rapids: Kregel, 2011); Stanley E. Porter and Jason C. Robinson, *Hermeneutics: An Introduction to Interpretive Theory* (Grand Rapids: Eerdmans, 2001); Nicholas T. Wright, *Scripture and the Authority of God: How to Read the Bible Today* (New York: HarperOne, 2011); and Stanley E. Porter Jr. and Beth M. Stovell, eds., *Biblical Hermeneutics: Five Views* (Downers Grove, IL: InterVarsity, 2012).

apply? Do moral laws in the Old Testament apply to Christians if not specifically reaffirmed in the New Testament? Does the Bible itself indicate this is something essential to conforming life to the character of God that never changes, or is it something merely symbolizing God's character in a way that changes depending on time, circumstance, or the transition between the Old and New Testament worship systems?

Since the character of God never changes (Num 23:19; Ps 102:27; Mal 3:6; Heb 1:12; 3:8; Jas 1:17), we know everything addressed in God's mandate to "Be holy because I, the LORD your God am holy" (Lev 19:2; see also 1 Pet 1:15–16) must be fixed and unchanging. But God also issued requirements in the Bible symbolizing moral purity in his relations with Israel in ways that never were meant for others to follow (Lev 20:26), and some of these applied to Israel only for a time and were later discontinued (Acts 10:11–16). All this must be considered properly and in context to ascertain how commands, requirements, and standards issued in the Bible apply to us now.[29] Not everything in the Bible still pertains as it did, and, while we should never dismiss anything in God's moral law, neither should we take everything in the Bible as included in it.

Continuity and Discontinuity of Biblical Law

One of the most far-reaching challenges biblical ethics must address when interpreting Scripture concerns the way ethics in the Old Testament relates to ethics in the New.[30] This

---

[29] The Feinbergs list four hermeneutical principles that biblical ethicists ought to employ, these being (1) distinguishing between general commands and specific applications of those commands; (2) considering commands in light of their original social, political, and religious context; (3) discerning the reason motivating a biblical command; and (4) deciding how the work of Jesus in the New Testament does or does not affect Old Testament law (*Brave New World*, 33–34). But, while these principles are helpful to consider, they should not be viewed as exhausting the interpretive task. Trull offers a yet longer list of general principles that he thinks must be used to ensure biblical ethics is interpreted correctly (*Walking in the Way*, 46–50). But again, while helpful, even these do not exhaust the interpretive task.

[30] Some noteworthy works on this subject include: Carl F. H. Henry, "The Biblical Particularization of the Moral Life: The Old Testament," chapter 11 in *Christian Personal Ethics* (Grand Rapids: Eerdmans, 1957), 264–77; Oliver O'Donovan, "Towards an Interpretation of Biblical Ethics" *Tyndale Bulletin* 27 (1976): 54–78; Daniel P. Fuller, *Gospel and Law: Contrast or Continuum? The Hermeneutics of Dispensational and Covenant Theology* (Grand Rapids: Eerdmans, 1980); Kaiser, *Toward Old*

is especially important to Evangelicals who hold to and defend the inerrancy of God's Word and the unchanging nature of God's character in all the Bible teachings on every topic. When Scripture is properly interpreted, Evangelicals know there can be no ethical contradictions. Of course, human interpreters are fallible and sin compromises moral purity, but God never sins and never makes mistakes. He is morally perfect, and his moral perfection never changes. God neither is corrupt, nor can he be corrupted. God is ever the same and that means he is never inconsistent and never contradicts himself. All this is included where James says God "does not change like shifting shadows" (Jas 1:17). Which leads us to ask, if God never changes and if God in the New Testament is the same as God in the Old, how then do the many rules, standards, and practices issued or approved by God in the Old Testament relate to the ethics of Jesus, Paul, and of other writers of Scripture in the New Testament?

Evangelical theologians can be found defending a variety of positions on how the Old and New Testaments relate, ranging from almost total continuity to complete discontinuity with a number of mixed positions in between.[31] Continuity is often associated with Covenant

---

Testament Ethics; Christopher J. H. Wright, *An Eye for an Eye: The Place of Old Testament Ethics Today* (Downers Grove, IL: InterVarsity, 1983); John S. Feinberg, ed., *Continuity and Discontinuity: Perspectives on the Relationship between the Old and New Testaments* (Westchester, IL: Crossway, 1988); Reynald E. Showers, *There Really Is a Difference! A Comparison of Covenant and Dispensational Theology* (Bellmawr, NJ: The Friends of Israel Gospel Ministry, 1990); John Goldingay, *Approaches to Old Testament Interpretation*, 2nd ed. (Downers Grove, IL: InterVarsity, 1990); Vern S. Poythress, *The Shadow of Christ in the Law of Moses* (Phillipsburg, NJ: Presbyterian and Reformed, 1991); David A. Dorsey, "The Law of Moses and the Christian: A Compromise," *Journal of the Evangelical Theological Society* 34/3 (September 1991): 322–24; Walter C. Kaiser, Jr., "New Approaches to Old Testament Ethics," *Journal of the Evangelical Theological Society* 35/3 (1992): 289–97; Stephen Westerholm, *Israel's Law and the Ways of the Lord: The Ethical Authority of the Old Testament* (Downers Grove, IL: InterVarsity, 1995); Wright, *Walking in the Ways*; Wayne G. Strickland, ed., *Five Views on Law and Gospel* (Grand Rapids: Zondervan, 1999); J. Daniel Hayes, "Applying the Old Testament Law Today," *Bibliotheca Sacra* 158 (January–March 2001): 21–35; and Joe M. Sprinkle, *Biblical Law and Its Relevance: A Christian Understanding and Ethical Application for Today of the Mosaic Regulations* (Lanham, MD: University Press of America, 2006).

[31] Douglas Moo claims, "The straightforward alternatives *continuity* and *discontinuity* are much too boldly drawn. (Because) In reality, it is a matter of emphasis, with positions ranging along a wide spectrum of alternatives." "The Law of Moses or the Law of Christ," in *Continuity and Discontinuity: Perspectives on the Relationship between the Old and New Testaments*, ed. John S. Feinberg (Westchester, IL: Crossway, 1988), 204.

Theology and discontinuity with Dispensationalism.[32] But this is not fair for two reasons: first, because most Covenant theologians also affirm some discontinuity and most Dispensational theologians also affirm some continuity and second, because the dominant teaching of the Church through history has always maintained continuity on some things and discontinuity on others. For example, Augustine famously said, "The New Testament is in the Old concealed, the Old is in the New revealed" (*Novum Testamentum in Vetere latet, Vetus Testamentum in Novo patet*),[33] and by this showed he thought that while the Old and New Testaments are different (there is discontinuity), they constitute a unified whole (there is continuity). Augustine held there is unity in their diversity and diversity in their unity, and if that is correct, we ought never to focus so much on one that we end up denying either continuity or discontinuity. Both are essential, and the question is how much there is of each. More especially, for biblical ethics, the question is how much of God's moral law revealed in the Old Testament pertains after the advent of Christ in the New.

Although many have written on the subject and articulated various views, no one has yet categorized the full range of positions defended by Evangelicals. It is easy to identify extremes and then to label other positions as "moderate." As it is, several quite different positions have been taken along the continuum between opposing extremes, and these should not be confused nor even be considered "moderate" in all cases. So, to clarify the range of Evangelical thinking on this issue, I identify seven different positions—three favoring continuity, three favoring discontinuity, and one that balances both about equally. These positions are: (1) *hard continuity*, (2) *moderately hard continuity*, (3) *mild continuity*, (4) *hard discontinuity*, (5) *moderately hard discontinuity*, (6) *mild discontinuity*, and (7) *complete moral continuity mixed with complete ceremonial and civil discontinuity*.

Hard Continuity

The *hard continuity* position is easy to understand even though no one has held the position for a long time. *Hard continuity* is thinking nothing of real consequence changed between

---

[32] Feinberg, *Continuity and Discontinuity*, xii.

[33] Saint Augustine, *Questions Concerning the First Seven Books of the Bible* 2, 73: PL 34, 623. Written in AD 419 or 420.

the Old and New Testaments and that laws issued by God in the Old all apply in the New, no matter what they concern. The position argues that Christ in the New Testament lived up to, but did not discontinue, the reason or relevance for any law in the Old. Although no one holds this position today, it was defended by a group of first generation Christians called "Judaizers" who grew to be quite influential in the Jerusalem church (Acts 11:2–3; 15:1; Gal 2:12). These Judaizers disrupted life in the early Church by hindering Gentile converts (Gal 2:15–16) and threatening Church unity (Acts 15:1–2). The position remained influential until officially rejected by the First Church Council in about AD 50,[34] the actions of which are recorded in Acts 15:1–41. No one takes this position now—not even those defending the strongest continuity view held today. But it did affect the Church and must be included for reference.

Moderately Hard Continuity

The *moderately hard continuity* position argues for continuity between the Old and New Testaments with respect to moral and civil law, while agreeing that ceremonial requirements of the Old Testament law have been discontinued. Those taking this position see that Christ in the New Testament instituted a different worship system than God gave Israel in the Old, and they agree that, with this transition, rules issued for the old worship system no longer apply. For Greg Bahnsen, Christ never abrogated the meaning or intention of Old Testament ritual ordinances, but he has made "their old manner of *observation* irrelevant."[35] Van Til thought that what distinguishes biblical law in the Old Testament from biblical law in the New "is merely that of stages of development of the same redemptive principle."[36] And Knox Chamberlin argues that the Law of Christ in the New Testament "is *not a different law* from the Law of Moses" and that Paul in the New Testament "speaks not of gospel replacing law, nor of a new law, but of a new and more personal administration of the ancient law." But then

---

[34] Holger Zeigan, *The Apostle Meeting in Jerusalem* (Leipzig: Evangelische Verlagsanstalt, 2005).

[35] Greg Bahnsen, *Theonomy in Christian Ethics* (Phillipsburg, NJ: Presbyterian and Reformed, 1977), 210.

[36] Van Til, *Christian Theistic Ethics*, 15.

after stressing continuity so strongly, Chamberlin goes on to say that "with respect to redemption, there is *discontinuity*."[37]

Mild Continuity

Mild continuity goes beyond the *moderately hard continuity* position by allowing that some discontinuity might possibly affect any classification of Old Testament law, not just ceremonial laws but possibly affecting moral and civil laws as well. This remains a continuity position because it argues we should assume all that the Old Testament requires remains in force unless the New Testament says otherwise. The general principle by which this position operates is that "whatever is true and binding during OT times still applies for the NT era, *unless the NT either explicitly or implicitly abrogates it*."[38]

Hard Discontinuity

The *hard discontinuity* position argues that nothing in the Old Testament has any direct bearing on believers after Calvary in the New. For believers today, the Old Testament is just historical background because the work and teaching of Christ in the New Testament supersedes everything God did earlier and does so at all levels. God's moral law present at creation, or as delivered to Moses, is discontinued, having been replaced by grace and internal leading of the Holy Spirit.[39]

---

[37] Knox Chamberlin, "The Law of Moses and the Law of Christ," in *Continuity and Discontinuity: Perspectives on the Relationship between the Old and New Testaments*, ed. John S. Feinberg (Westchester, IL: Crossway, 1988), 182, 192, 195.

[38] Feinberg and Feinberg, *Brave New World*, 36. Although I use this quote, I do not think the Feinbergs are right in saying this principle fits better with taking a discontinuity rather than continuity position. The idea that continuity is normal and discontinuity is not most certainly functions as a mildly continuous position whatever others may say. The Feinbergs simply are inconsistent to affirm this principle (on page 36) and then to deny it by saying "none of the OT law (even parts not specifically abrogated) applies today" (on page 39).

[39] This view interprets what Paul says in Romans 6:14 and Galatians 5:18 in ways theologians have disputed throughout Church history.

Early proponents of Dispensationalism thought this way. For example, C. I. Scofield held that God's moral law revealed to Moses on Mount Sinai (the Ten Commandments) did not need to be distinguished from ceremonial law because "the believer does not come to that mount at all."[40] For Scofield, "the law . . . given by Moses . . . dominates, characterizes, the time (from Sinai to Calvary); just as grace dominates, or gives its peculiar character to, the dispensation which begins at Calvary," and he insisted "it is of the most vital moment to observe that Scripture never, in *any* dispensation, *mingles* these two principles."[41] Scofield thought that the New Testament doctrine of grace makes God's moral law in the Old Testament irrelevant for believers today. Similarly, Charles Ryrie completely separated what God requires in the New Testament from what he required in the Old, saying, "God may add or even change in one era what He had given in another."[42] For Scofield and Ryrie both, what changed between the Old and New Testaments includes moral as well as ceremonial and civil law.

William McGrath demonstrates the same hardline view of discontinuity when explaining the way Amish and Mennonite Christians are able to reject moral standards implemented in the Old Testament without denying the inerrancy of Scripture. It is because they believe "Christ sets aside the temporary permissive will of God in effect during the Mosaic dispensation."[43] By this, he means they believe the New replaces the Old entirely and nothing God revealed to Moses still applies. Every Old Testament law is superseded, and there is no continuity even when it comes to how God measures ethical right and wrong. McGrath is thus able to claim some things that were ethically right for Old Testament saints are now ethically wrong for New Testament Christians, and some things that would have been ethically wrong before have become ethically right now.

Moderately Hard Discontinuity

The *moderately hard discontinuity* position argues for general discontinuity separating the Old and New Testaments and affecting all categories of law, while recognizing that many moral

---

[40] Cyrus I. Schofield, *Rightly Dividing the Word of Truth* (Westwood, NJ: Revell, 1896), 44.

[41] Schofield, 34.

[42] Charles C. Ryrie, *Basic Theology* (Wheaton, IL: Victor Books, 1986), 114.

[43] William R. McGrath, *Why We Are Conscientious Objectors to War* (Carrollton, OH: Amish Mennonite, 1980), 21.

norms in the Old Testament law are found again in the new order established in the New Testament. Those taking this position deny there is any direct connection making any Old Testament law part of what guides New Testament believers because, since Calvary, we are guided by a totally new valuing system known as the Law of Christ or the Law of Love. But while any direct continuity is denied linking the Old with the New, those taking this position nevertheless see that what the Law of Christ requires turns out to include many things very similar to what we find in the Old Testament. Thus, they argue, while nothing in the Old still applies just because it did before, we should not be surprised that God has included some of the same things in the new system that applies to us now.

Herman Ridderbos takes this position in claiming Christ fulfills the law to such a degree that "the church no longer has to do with the law in any other way than in Christ and thus is *ennomos Christou*,"[44] by which he means we are governed by the Law of Christ and nothing else. And Douglas Moo says that "no commandment, even the Decalogue, is binding simply because it is part of the Mosaic Law," and that "the Christian is no longer bound to the Mosaic Law (because) Christ has brought its fulfillment."[45] Nevertheless, Moo claims New Testament believers are not antinomian for two reasons: first, because Christians are bound to Christ's law in which "some Mosaic commandments are taken up and reapplied to the New Covenant people of God," and second, because "the power of God's Spirit" now indwells every believer.[46]

Mild Discontinuity

Mild discontinuity goes beyond the *moderately hard discontinuity* position by allowing a small degree of direct continuity linking parts of God's law in the Old Testament with what regulates life for believers in the New, and it differs from the *mild continuity* position by reversing that approach. While *mild continuity* says we must assume all the Old Testament requires remains in force unless the New Testament says otherwise, it also holds we should assume God's grace frees New Testament believers from all that the Old Testament requires unless specific exception is made somewhere in the New Testament itself. The general principle by which *mild*

---

[44] Herman Ridderbos, *Paul: An Outline of His Theology* (Grand Rapids: Eerdmans, 1974), 282.
[45] Moo, "The Law of Moses or the Law of Christ," 217.
[46] Moo, 217–18.

discontinuity operates is "unless the NT repeats an OT law, it is no longer in force."[47] But then it adds that "where the content of the Mosaic Law . . . and the Law of Christ overlap, appeal to the OT is proper" and may even "give fuller explanation to a principle and God's reasoning for it than one finds in the NT."[48]

Observe, however, that while *mild continuity* and *mild discontinuity* are opposites with each reversing how the other addresses the same issue, both positions allow that, in moving from the Old Testament to the New, God may change moral as well as ceremonial and civil laws, and both positions also allow that God may preserve not only moral but ceremonial and civil laws as well. For *mild continuity*, all that matters is whether an Old Testament law is specifically abrogated in the New, and, for *mild discontinuity*, all that matters is whether an Old Testament law is specifically repeated in the New. Neither position looks at how differences distinguishing moral, ceremonial, and civil law might affect the question, and neither position looks at how God's unchanging character and everlasting holiness restrict the answers given. For that, we must turn to a seventh and altogether different position on the degree to which God's moral law in the Old Testament applies today.

Complete Moral Continuity Mixed with Complete Ceremonial and Civil Discontinuity

The *complete moral continuity mixed with complete ceremonial and civil discontinuity* position refers to an approach most Christians have taken throughout Church history, not only early on in declaring the teaching of Marcion to be heretical,[49] but especially since the Reformation, which Rodney Petersen says gave "the moral laws and precepts of the OT . . . added weight as guides to the Christian life."[50] Although terms like ceremonial and civil law were not used

---

[47] Feinberg and Feinberg, *Brave New World*, 36.

[48] Feinberg and Feinberg, 39.

[49] Marcion of Pontus (d. c. AD 160) taught that nothing in the Old Testament, moral or otherwise, has any bearing on the way New Testament believers live their lives. Wright says Marcion believed "the Hebrew Bible had no relevance or authority for Christians and should be regarded as having no place in Christian Scripture" (*Walking in the Ways*, 69–70).

[50] Rodney Petersen, "Continuity and Discontinuity: The Debate throughout Church History," in *Continuity and Discontinuity*, ed. John S. Feinberg (Westchester, IL: Crossway, 1988), 27. Also see, O'Donovan, "Towards an Interpretation," 58–60.

early on, most Christians have always taken Old Testament moral stipulations to be eternally applicable while denying other Old Testament stipulations still apply.[51]

The problem with viewing Old Testament law as a whole from a discontinuity stance is that it leads to denying the biblical doctrine of divine immutability. God acts and reacts, he is pleased and grieved by human conduct, and he rewards and punishes all we do and say. But God's character never changes (Num 23:19; Ps 102:27; Mal 3:6; Heb 1:12; 13:8; Jas 1:17). He is "the same yesterday, today, and forever" (Heb 13:8). Since the Old Testament moral law reveals God's unchanging character and what living in conformity to God's character requires, this can only mean when the New Testament reminds Christians God still requires them to "be holy, because I am holy" (1 Pet 1:15–16) that Old Testament moral law still applies—not in pieces or parts, but entirely.[52]

The harder discontinuity positions deny this more obviously, but even mild discontinuity runs afoul of the immutability of God's moral character. That is because *mild discontinuity* argues any moral law not repeated in the New Testament no longer remains in force, which, to be consistent, would mean that since the Old Testament prohibition of sex with animals (Exod 22:19; Lev 18:23; Deut 27:21) is not repeated in the New, God's character has changed to allow it. No one arguing *mild discontinuity* ever says this, but it follows from what the principle governing that position requires.

Problems also arise from viewing Old Testament law as a whole from a continuity stance for two reasons: first, because the New Testament so clearly discontinues some aspects of Old Testament law and, second, because continuity positions all operate on a principle that does not sufficiently distinguish one sort of law from another. Every view dealing with Old Testament law as a whole from a continuity stance assumes any law, in any category, still applies if not explicitly abrogated. While this is more obvious with the harder continuity positions, it remains problematic for *mild continuity* as well because even *mild continuity* argues that any Old Testament law, in any category, stays in force unless explicitly abrogated in the New. To be consistent, this would mean because Old Testament architectural stipulations are

---

[51] For more on this, see O'Donovan, 58–60.

[52] Kaiser also observes that "to restrict our source of moral and ethical directions to the NT would be to form a canon within the canon and to run squarely into the face of what the NT taught—namely, that the OT was 'profitable' for just such moral and ethical instruction (2 Tim 3:15–16)" (Kaiser, "New Approaches," 292).

not explicitly abrogated in the New, we must, therefore, still construct railings around the roofs of new houses (Deut 22:8), and, because the Old Testament death penalty for rebellious children (Deut 21:18–21) is not explicitly abrogated in the New, we should, therefore, execute such children today. Again, no one arguing *mild continuity* ever says this, but it follows from what the principle governing that position requires.

The main problem with the first six positions comes from thinking a single interpretive principle determines the relevance of all laws in the Old Testament such that every one either is continuous or discontinuous, and all for the same reason, unless an exception is found that justifies modifying that single interpretive principle. The solution is to do what most Christians have through history, which is to recognize that the Old Testament includes different sorts of law and then to interpret these different sorts by different principles. This treats all Old Testament laws neither as continuous nor as discontinuous. Rather, it treats different sorts of law differently while at the same time treating all laws in the same classification the same without resorting to exceptions. In this way, the *complete moral continuity mixed with complete ceremonial and civil discontinuity* position treats God's moral law in the Old Testament—including the Decalogue, principles revealed in wisdom literature, and injunctions to love God and neighbors—as universal, timeless, and unchanging, and thus completely continuous, while at the same time it treats other sorts of Old Testament law as never universal and always timebound, subject to change, and completely discontinuous in the New Testament.

Carl Henry, Walter Kaiser, Christopher Wright, and Oliver O'Donovan all argue,[53] as I am here, that viewing moral law revealed in the Old Testament as eternally relevant while denying the ongoing relevance of other sorts of Old Testament law is something disclosed in the Bible itself and does not come from reading things into the Bible not present in the text itself.[54] God is self-consistent and never contradicts himself, and thus we affirm the Bible, as the written Word of God, is entirely consistent. But affirming this brings a challenge we must not overlook, which is that the New Testament offers two different views on how Christians

---

[53] Henry, *Christian Personal Ethics*, 267–269; Kaiser, *Toward Old Testament Ethics*, 312; Wright, *Walking in the Ways*, 93; O'Donovan, "Towards an Interpretation," 59.

[54] Henry says, "The Old Testament disclosure itself requires from the outset a distinction within revealed ethics between perpetual obligations and temporary obligations. Some great principles of obedience are of perpetual obligation, and others are binding at one period and abolished in another" (Henry, *Christian Personal Ethics*, 267).

stand in relation to Old Testament laws. We will look first at what the New Testament says and then at how it is properly interpreted.

On the one hand, the Jerusalem council denied that Gentile believers needed to be circumcised or commanded "to keep the law of Moses" (Acts 15:5); Paul exhorted new Christians, saying, "Don't let anyone judge you in regard to food and drink or in the matter of a festival or a new moon or a Sabbath day" (Col 2:16); and in Hebrews, believers are told Old Testament laws were "a symbol for the present time" and no more than "physical regulations" imposed for a limited period (Heb 9:9–10). On the other hand, Jesus announced he was not discontinuing "the Law or the Prophets" and assured his disciples that "until heaven and earth pass away, not the smallest letter or one stroke of a letter will pass from the law" (Matt 5:17–18).[55] Paul also insisted the laws of ancient Israel remain "holy and just and good" (Rom 7:12), were issued not only for Old Testament saints but "for our sake" (1 Cor 9:10), and are profitable for "training in righteousness" (2 Tim 3:16). Paul denied that salvation "by grace through faith" (Eph 2:8) renders the Old Testament law irrelevant, insisting, "Do we then nullify the law through faith? Absolutely not! On the contrary, we uphold the law" (Rom 3:31).

How should this be interpreted? The only options are either to assume biblical ethics is incoherent, inconsistent, and self-contradictory, or to assume biblical ethics is consistent, which leads to distinguishing different sorts of Old Testament law and applying different principles of interpretation. If the Bible is self-consistent, the New Testament must be saying different things about different things and not saying conflicting things about one thing. Thus, we conclude the New Testament teaches two things: first, that nothing revealed as moral law in the Old Testament ever changes and thus applies now the same as always and, second, that other Old Testament stipulations do not apply since they are not moral in nature, never were meant to last, and never were for everyone.[56] Different principles of interpretation govern

---

[55] The Greek word καταλῦσαι (*katalusai*) is often rendered "destroy," but "discontinue" is legitimate here, not only because it is lexically permitted, but more especially because Jesus uses the term in contrast to the continuing existence of heaven and earth.

[56] I agree with and recommend six hermeneutical assumptions Wright says are revealed in Scripture and apply to how we interpret the relevance and authority of Old Testament laws. These are (1) that Old Testament laws are part of the Scriptures, which, being God-breathed, remain ethically relevant; (2) that what God required of Israel ethically must yet apply because Christians have been made members of the same people of God to which the ancient Israelites belonged; (3) that Old Testament laws never were given to save but served rather to reveal humanity's need for grace; (4) that God's commitment

different sorts of biblical law—one principle governs moral law and another governs other classifications. God's moral law is completely continuous without exception and other Old Testament stipulations are completely discontinuous also without exception.[57]

Types of Biblical Law

Identifying different categories of Old Testament law and treating their relevance and continuity differently solves many problems that arise in biblical ethics, but not everyone agrees. Dorsey claims, "The categorizing of certain selected laws as 'moral' is methodologically questionable."[58] Wenham says, "The three-fold division of the law is in my view arbitrary and artificial."[59] Wilson believes that in some places the moral, ceremonial, and civil aspects of Old Testament law are so entwined they cannot be distinguished,[60] and Moo rejects ethical distinctions, alleging "the NT does not approach the matter this way."[61] Nevertheless, most Christians throughout history have believed that differentiating categories within Old Testament law is not only true to Scripture but also easier to determine than detractors allege. I think distinguishing one category from another is easier and less problematic than what one must do if not accepting the trifold division of Old Testament law. In that case, one is forced either to maintain that all Old Testament laws remain in full force (which no one distinguishing the Old and New Testaments can say) or must construct a new and different ethical system

---

to Israel served a more ancient, higher commitment to humanity as a whole and what God required of Israel ethically and requires of all today serves a common purpose; (5) that God appointed Israel to display and teach his moral law to others; and (6) that moral law in the Old Testament always had a relevance and application beyond the historical and cultural borders of Israel (Wright, *Walking in the Ways*, 111–14).

[57] Kaiser says, "The moral law, as revealed in the Old Testament, was the recognized standard of holiness that remained authoritative for Christ, the apostles, and the early church *because it was written* . . . . we believers are finished with the law in its ceremonial (and civil) demands and ceremonial (and civil) sanctions, but . . . the moral law continues to function as one of Scripture's formal teachers on what is right and wrong in conduct" (Kaiser, *Toward Old Testament Ethics*, 312).

[58] Dorsey, "The Law of Moses and the Christian," 330.

[59] Gordon J. Wenham, *The Book of Leviticus* (Grand Rapids: Eerdmans, 1979), 32.

[60] R. R. Wilson, "Approaches to Old Testament Ethics," in *Canon, Theology and Old Testament Interpretation*, ed. G. M. Tucker, D. L. Peterson, and R. R. Wilson (Philadelphia: Fortress, 1988), 66–67.

[61] Moo, "The Law of Moses or the Law of Christ," 218.

from New Testament material alone—starting with a few statements from Jesus, adding a few more from Paul, and then filling in the rest based on sensations judged to come from what Moo calls "union with Christ" or "God's Spirit operative in the believer."[62] But while "union with Christ" sounds pious, once severed from God's enduring moral law revealed in the Old Testament, sensations become nearly impossible to separate from subjective feelings, and passions of the flesh are all too easily mistaken for movements of the Holy Spirit. This does not answer the methodological question, but it should caution against dismissing the trifold division of biblical law too quickly and call for serious examination instead.

Everyone knows that Old Testament law includes more than moral stipulations because it so obviously includes ceremonial regulations and civil requirements. For this reason, no treatment of ethics in the Old Testament can avoid making distinctions of some sort. All biblical law comes from God and concerns standards God wants people to follow. But some Old Testament laws concern Israel alone, while others concern everyone; some laws are procedural and administrative, while others are essential; and some laws are rescinded later by God, while others stand forever. We see as well that, while various categories of law differ, they also interrelate, and while they interrelate, they yet have different functions. So, while we affirm different categories within Old Testament law, we also affirm they are connected, and while affirming their connection, we also affirm they have fixed distinctions—not as to origin but as to purpose and not as to how or by whom they are enforced but as to their nature, endurance, and scope.

Some argue that, if the old rabbis did not divide God's law into categories, then neither should we.[63] But here I agree with O'Donovan, who explains how this objection comes from confusing description with analysis. Dividing Old Testament law into moral, ceremonial, and

---

[62] Moo, 218.

[63] For example, see Dorsey, "The Law of Moses and the Christian," 329–30. I do not agree with Dorsey's claim that rabbinic tradition never divided the law into categories and mean here only to say that distinguishing categories of biblical law does not depend on whether they did or did not do so. A strong case can be made that distinguishing categories of law is discernible in the Bible itself (as for example at the first Church council recorded in Acts 15), and I agree also with Dalman, Montefiore, and Kaiser, who contend that ancient rabbis did in fact recognize categorical distinctions in the law. See Gustaf Dalman, *Jesus-Jeshua: Studies in the Gospels*, trans. Paul P. Levertoff (London: SPCK, 1929); C. G. Montefiore, *Rabbinic Literature and Gospel Teaching* (London: Macmillan, 1930), 316–17; and Kaiser, *Toward Old Testament Ethics*, 44–48.

civil categories does not come from how ancient Israelites interpreted their obligations but rather comes from "an attempt to analyze from a Christian point of view what the constituent elements of those obligations were."[64] It is the same thing scholars do when detecting different literary genres (like history, wisdom, poetry, prophesy, gospel, epistles, and apocalyptic) in the Bible and should not be confused with schools of rabbinic interpretation. So, while categorical designators like "moral," "ceremonial," and "civil" are not in the biblical text, using them does not introduce something foreign to the text. They identify something already present in the way God framed biblical law and are equivalent to how Scripture reveals the triune nature of God, even though the term *Trinity* appears nowhere in the text.

Now we may ask, if God's moral revelation in the Old Testament still applies after the advent of Christ in the New, and if Old Testament law is not all a matter of moral law, and if affirming three categories of Old Testament law is needed to distinguish what is moral from the rest, how then can we tell one from the other, and can this be done without forcing biblical revelation to fit categories not in the text itself? This can be done, but not without paying close attention to distinguishing features. If we know what features distinguish a dog from a cat, then we can tell one from the other even in a room full of dogs and cats. Similarly, if we know what features distinguish moral, ceremonial, and civil law, then we can tell one from the other even in passages where they might be mixed.

Moral Law

Old Testament moral law is divine because it comes from God. But moral law is divine for a second still more important reason, and that is because it reveals the nature and character of God more immediately and completely than other categories of law in the Bible. God's moral law, and only God's moral law, is in view where he orders people, in both the Old and New Testaments, to "be holy because I, the LORD your God am holy" (Lev 19:2; see also 1 Pet 1:15–16). God's moral law is central to all biblical law because, while other categories line up with God's character, only the moral law defines or provides actual expression of God's holiness (Lev 19:2; 1 Pet 1:15), love (Exod 20:6; 1 John 4:8), and glory (Isa 43:6–7; 1 Cor 10:31). The moral law, and only the moral law, reveals what conforming in actuality

---

[64] O'Donovan, "Towards an Interpretation," 60.

to the immediate reality of God's holiness, love, and glory requires in relationships we have with God, with each other, and with the world. The moral law consists of rules having to do with securing, maintaining, or expressing moral purity, and is both universal and timeless. It applies to everyone forever because the character of God never changes (Num 23:19; Mal 3:6; Heb 13:8; Jas 1:17).

Ceremonial Law

Old Testament ceremonial law is divine as well because it too comes from God. But ceremonial law relates to the nature and character of God less immediately, less completely, and less permanently than moral law because it deals with matters one step removed from actually conforming to God himself. Ceremonial law relates to God's moral law but serves a different purpose. Old Testament ceremonial law portrays or displays God's holiness, love, and glory, but always in representational ways distinct from the reality they portray. What the ceremonial law requires presents a model or pattern (תַּבְנִית, *taḇenît*) of something else and is never more than representative (here compare Exod 25:9 with Heb 9:11). In Hebrews, we are told that Old Testament ceremonial laws were "only a shadow of the good things to come, and not the reality itself of those things" (Heb 10:1). They served to symbolize God's holiness, love, and glory and involved rules regarding sacrifices, rituals, days and seasons, clean or unclean foods, religious clothing, and tithing.[65] What the Old Testament ceremonial law required never was universal or timeless. They applied just to ancient Israel and never were thought to

---

[65] I take the Old Testament tithing requirement to be a matter of ceremonial law based on passages like Deuteronomy 12:6. In doing so, I follow the hermeneutical approach detailed by Kaiser and Silva in *Introduction to Biblical Hermeneutics*, 235–37, as opposed to Arthur W. Pink and Elmer B. Steward who argue that tithing is a matter of continuing moral law. Pink, *Tithing in the Scripture* (Grand Rapids: Christian Classics, 2007) and Steward *The Tithe* (Chicago: Winona, 1903). I disagree as well with two others who, though denying the continuing nature of the Old Testament tithing requirement, reach this conclusion based on what I think are wrong reasons. I disagree with Russell E. Kelly, in *Should the Church Teach Tithing?* (New York: Writers Club, 2001) who dismisses tithing based on denying that any Old Testament law, not even moral law, has any continuing force, because I believe moral law remains applicable for all. And I disagree with Elliot Miller, in "Tithing," *Christian Research Journal* 26/3 (2003), who dismisses tithing based on identifying it as a matter of civil law, because I think it more accurate to connect the Old Testament tithing requirement with ceremonial stipulations regulating religious life (see Deut 12:6).

be eternally adequate (Deut 18:15–19; Jer 31:31–34; Heb 10:18) or effective in themselves (Ps 51:16–17; Heb 10:4).

Civil Law

Like moral and ceremonial law, Old Testament civil law too is divine because it came from God. Old Testament civil law is compatible with God's character in the sense of not contradicting or compromising his holiness. But, like the ceremonial law, the civil law too deals with matters less directly related to God's immediate character as compared to moral law and could be yet further removed than ceremonial law. Consistency with God and distance from God are different things, and while civil and ceremonial law both came from God and so were consistent with his character, civil law dealt with matters still less immediately related to God as compared to the kind of thing with which ceremonial law was concerned. While moral law provides and ceremonial law portrays, Old Testament civil law functions only to protect or defend God's holiness, love, and glory, doing it in terms that, while guarding respect for moral norms, are themselves subject to changing circumstances, cultural variation, and developments in technology.

Civil law secures or stabilizes outward behavioral conformity to God's nature, character, and purposes in a fallen world. But guarding conformity must not be confused with what it guards. How something is guarded can be revised or replaced without changing what is guarded, just as guard duty at the Tomb of the Unknown Soldier in Washington, DC, passes from soldier to soldier even though nothing changes in the tomb itself. Old Testament civil law consists of rules regarding boundaries, architectural standards, trial procedures, cities of refuge, and punishments prescribed for various offenses; and, like ceremonial rules, civil rules were never universal or timeless. They were given only to the nation of Israel and just for a time—not to everyone for all time.

While Old Testament civil laws were never for everyone for all time, they deserve respect and should not be demeaned. We must not forget that the civil laws of ancient Israel came directly from God, which means even though their relevance is limited, we ought yet to consider them astute and judicious. We must not view civil death penalties for adultery (Lev 20:10), for homosexual activity (Lev 20:13), or for witchcraft (Lev 20:27) as undeserved, disproportionate, or cruel; we should respect the value of building codes that reduced foreseeable dangers even if we no longer have houses that need railings on their roofs (Deut 22:8); and we should admire the wisdom of resting crop land every seven years even if not legally required (Lev 25:3–5).

Although I think it is fairly easy to distinguish one category of Old Testament law from another and although I think it is usually fairly easy to decide which category a particular law belongs to, I nevertheless acknowledge some cases are not easy to resolve. The status of a few Old Testament stipulations is not that clear, as is the case with prohibiting sex in marriage during menstruation (Lev 18:19) and prohibiting the eating of blood (Lev 17:10–12). The first appears twice in Leviticus, first on a list of ceremonial requirements (Lev 15:19–24) but then on a list of moral offenses (Lev 18:6–23). While the second shows up in a ceremonial passage in Leviticus dealing with animal sacrifices (Lev 17:10–12), it also appears in God's covenant with Noah, where it is listed parallel to a moral rule prohibiting murder (Gen 9:4–6), and in the New Testament, where it is again listed parallel to moral requirements (Acts 15:20). Should these be viewed as moral laws applying to everyone forever or as ceremonial laws that once applied to ancient Israel but are no longer relevant? When deadlocks emerge, I agree with advice R. C. Sproul offers on handling problems that sometimes occur when trying to distinguish what is permanent in the Bible from what is relative:

> What if after careful consideration of a biblical mandate, we remain uncertain as to the question of its character as principle or custom? If we must decide to treat it one way or the other but have no conclusive means to make the decision, what can we do? Here the biblical principle of humility can be helpful. The issue is simply—would it be better to treat a possible custom as a principle and be guilty of being over-scrupulous in our design to obey God; or would it be better to treat a possible principle as a custom and be guilty of being unscrupulous in demoting a transcendent requirement of God to the level of a mere human convention? I hope the answer is obvious.[66]

---

[66] Robert C. Sproul, "Controversy at Culture Gap," *Eternity* 27/5 (May 1976): 40. When it comes to applying this "humility principle," Sproul also cautions against treating it as a "right to legislate the conscience of Christians where God has left them free." It is, he says, only "a guideline of last resort" that must not be used to short-circuit the arduous labor of responsible exegesis.

Sproul's advice on problems with distinguishing what is permanent from what is not applies also to handling problems with trying to distinguish moral from ceremonial from civil laws in the Bible. If certainty is beyond reach, it is better to err on the side of humility than pride. It is better to risk complying with something unnecessary than to risk a cavalier attitude toward "him who has authority to throw people into hell" (Luke 12:5).

The Structure of Biblical Ethics

We turn now to one last topic that should be covered in a chapter surveying biblical ethics—how moral revelation in Scripture is structured by God. Structure concerns the way something is ordered. It concerns the way individually different pieces fit with other individually different pieces to compose a coherent, well working whole. Paul, in Ephesians, speaks of the Church being a "whole body" comprised of individually different parts that all are "fitted and knit together" in a way that "build(s) up itself in love by the proper working of each individual part" (Eph 4:16). This ordering of the Church is something God does by assigning gifts and talents that vary from individual to individual (1 Cor 12:4–7) but, when used in cooperation, enable the Christian community to serve a unifying purpose the way that bodies function best when their many parts all fulfill their assigned roles (1 Cor 12:14–25). God is not a God of disorder and chaos (1 Cor 14:33) but rather of order and purpose. Nothing he does is random or confused. We must, therefore, assume that, like his ordering of the Church, God's moral law is ordered as well.

The Bible contains hundreds of individual laws,[67] but they are not like a mess of old toys, furniture, and clothing left in an attic in hope that someone someday will get them into some sensible kind of order. Rather than a mess of old items in the attic, biblical law is more like a nuclear powered aircraft carrier, with every moving part in proper working order, every fuel tank full, every chart up-to-date, and every member of the crew trained and ready to deploy. Biblical law is not only consistent but also coherent and not only coherent but also well ordered. Moreover, this coherent orderliness is something already there. Biblical law has no

---

[67] Jewish tradition usually maintains that the Torah includes 613 individual commands. This follows a counting method credited to Maimonides. See Moses Maimonides, *The Book of Divine Commandments*, trans. Charles Ber Chavel and Moses ibn Tibbon (London: Soncino, 1940).

need to be ordered by anything external to the Word of God.[68] It has sense and makes sense as it is, which means it already has some kind of discernibly ordered structure. If so, then we should be able to find that structure, and on finding that structure, should be able to examine it, and then on examining it, be able to interpret it without turning to non-biblical sources like human philosophy. The structure by which biblical ethics makes sense must be in the text because it all comes from an orderly God, who arranges all he disposes on orderly lines and reveals all he reveals in a fashion ordered by a unifying purpose. Since this characterizes biblical law in general, it certainly must be the case for God's revelation of moral law in particular. What then has God revealed about the structure of biblical ethics?

One Heart and Center of Biblical Ethics

The first structural level in biblical ethics is that it all begins with, comes from, and centers on God himself alone,[69] and this one fact distinguishes biblical ethics from all other ethical views both philosophical and religious.[70] In the Old Testament, the entire human race is told

---

[68] I am building here on O'Donovan's groundbreaking work in which he declared that he would "describe the shape of Christian moral thought theologically." *Resurrection and Moral Order*, 26 (see chap. 1, n. 69). In this work, O'Donovan breaks ranks with an academy that widely assumes making ordered sense of God's moral revelation must rely on human philosophy and also assumes that without philosophical structuring, moral teachings in the Bible are just a random collection of commands, standards, principles, goals, heroic stories, and proverbs. I affirm with O'Donovan that moral truth in the Bible owes not just its content but its form to God. I also assume biblical ethics is not just from God but ordered by God, is not just spoken by God but structured by God, and is delivered to us, not in a jumbled mess, but arranged in a form that is both sensible and beautiful and thus worth examining in its own right.

[69] Others saying much the same thing include Barth, *Ethics*, 117–18 (see chap. 1, n. 26); Barth, *The Christian Life*, 3 (see chap. 1, n. 69); Ellul, *The Ethics of Freedom*, 7 (see chap. 1, n. 69); Murray, *Principles of Conduct*, 14; Rae, *Moral Choices*, 24; and Jones, *An Introduction to Biblical Ethics*, 2–4.

[70] Philosophical views of ethics inevitably start with an ultimate ideal or *Grundnorm* (most basic principle) from which all other standards, rules, virtues, or values derive meaning, validity, and authority, while religious views of ethics tend to rely more on human enforcement than coherence. Given the truth of Scripture, both sorts are by nature and function anthropocentric as compared to biblical ethics, which alone is genuinely theocentric on all levels. Although philosophers allege a sort of transcendence in declaring universal truths, and while religions not having the one true Word of God claim divine authority for themselves, neither philosophies nor false religions truly rise past mundane limitations.

that "what is good" reduces to "what it is the LORD requires of you" (Mic 6:8), and Israel (and through Israel all humanity) is urged to "do what is right and good in the LORD's sight" (Deut 6:18) and "to fear the LORD your God by walking in all his ways" (Deut 10:12). Then in the New Testament, Jesus urges everyone to "be perfect, therefore, as your heavenly Father is perfect" (Matt 5:48); Paul urges all to "be imitators of God" (Eph 5:1); and James explains that "every good and perfect gift is from above, coming down from the Father of lights" (Jas 1:17). Furthermore, because biblical ethics all begins with, comes from, and centers on God, this means, conversely, that "everything that is not from faith is sin" (Rom 14:23).

This makes biblical ethics something fundamentally personal and yet transcendent at the same time. While ethical norms apply fairly to personal beings made in the image of God, they also cannot be altered or controlled by them. Other ethical views either treat impossible ideals as if they can be reached with enough effort or treat moral norms as nothing more than whatever people choose. Only biblical ethics treats moral norms as both relevant and beyond manipulation, and that is because biblical ethics alone begins with, comes from, and centers on the only God who truly exists rather than man-centered thoughts or experiences.

Three Facets of Biblical Ethics

The second structural level in biblical ethics is that moral living as a whole is characterized in three different yet related ways—the holiness of God, the love of God, and the glory of God.

The Holiness of God

Man is made in God's image (Gen 1:27; 9:6), and God orders all bearing the *imago Dei* to "be holy, because I, the LORD your God, am holy" (Lev 19:2). We exist only for him, and our own reality is ordered by his, for "he chose us in him, before the foundation of the world, to be holy and blameless in love before him" (Eph 1:4). Holiness is such an important way of summarizing all biblical ethics and requires that "without it no one will see the Lord" (Heb

---

Only biblical ethics derives meaning, validity, and authority from the only source truly outside human control yet applicable to human life, and only biblical ethics is judged and enforced by a power both personal and transcendent.

12:14).[71] But, while conforming to the holiness of God is one way we find what moral living requires as a whole summarized in the Bible, it does not stand alone and is not the only way of doing so.

The Love of God

A second but equally important way Scripture characterizes moral living as a whole puts it in terms of what a certain sort of love requires. Israel is told to "love the LORD your God with all your heart, with all your soul, and with all your strength" (Deut 6:5); Jesus commands His disciples to "remain in My love" after explaining that he has loved them "as the Father has loved me" (John 15:9). Paul declares not only that "love . . . is the fulfillment of the law" (Rom 13:10) but that "in Christ Jesus neither circumcision nor uncircumcision accomplishes anything" and "what matters is faith working through love" (Gal 5:6). These very broad statements put all that biblical ethics requires in terms of love. But I agree here with Murray that such statements do not mean "love is allowed to discover its own standards or patterns of conduct" or can be "conceived of as an autonomous, self-acting agency which of itself, apart from any extraneous prescription or regulation, defines its own norms of behaviour."[72] Life ordering love in the Bible does not free our fancies to allow things contrary to the moral law revealing God's holiness. Biblical love is no law to itself apart from God but rather is an orientation inclining hearts to please him voluntarily. It is not a self-validating, self-defined sort of love but rather a love that is God-validated and God-defined.

The Glory of God

A third equally important way we find that Scripture characterizes moral living as a whole is promoting God's glory. In Hebrew, references to the glory of God (כָּבוֹד, *kābôd*) indicate manifestations of his stunning holiness (Isa 6:3),[73] and references in Greek to God's glory (δόξα, *doxa*) indicate not only his matchless power (Col 1:11) but his righteous perfection as

---

[71] I differ here with Kaiser and Rae, who both treat holiness as sufficient by itself to summarize God's entire moral revelation. Kaiser claims God's holiness alone "is most decisive for Old Testament ethics" (*Toward Old Testament Ethics*, 6), and Rae calls holiness "the central concept that unifies Old Testament ethics" (*Moral Choices*, 32).

[72] Murray, *Principles of Conduct*, 24.

[73] R. Laird Harris, ed., *Theological Wordbook of the Old Testament*, vol.1 (Chicago: Moody, 1980), 427.

well (Rom 3:23).[74] In both the Old and New Testaments, passages referring to the glory of God indicate his moral excellence in connection especially with its disclosure to, and fulfillment in, God's relation to humanity (Num 14:21; Ps 72:19; 86:9; Hab 2:14). God declares that every human being is "created for my glory" (Isa 43:7) and promises a day will come when sinners "will be righteous . . . so that I may be glorified" (Isa 60:21). Worthy behavior in this life aims to "glorify God with your body" (1 Cor 6:20), can be summarized as a matter of doing "whatever you do . . . for the glory of God" (1 Cor 10:31), and serves to "bring praise to his glory" (Eph 1:12). These all show that promoting the glory of God characterizes biblical ethics as a whole in regard to its one overriding purpose.

The holiness of God, the love of God, and the glory of God are not parts but facets of biblical ethics because each, in a different way, characterizes biblical ethics as a whole.[75] They are not like sections of a pie that must be added one to the other before having a whole thing to look at but are like different facets of a well cut diamond that each offer a view of something totally there all the time. The holiness of God is the ultimate objective measure of biblical ethics as a whole. The love of God—that not only binds (Col 3:14) but also reciprocates (Rom 11:36)—is the ultimate subjective disposition of biblical ethics as a whole, and the glory of God is the ultimate aim, purpose, or goal of biblical ethics as a whole.[76]

---

[74] Baur, *A Greek-English Lexicon*, 202–203 (see chap. 2, n. 121).

[75] I differ here in some degree with Ellul who, in *The Ethics of Freedom*, connects the ethics of holiness, the ethics of freedom, and the ethics of love with the theological virtues of faith, hope, and love. Ellul may be right to connect the virtue of faith with an ethics of holiness, and the virtue of love with an ethics of relationship. But if so, I think the virtue of hope should connect with an ethics of God's glory and not with an ethics of freedom (though Ellul views freedom not as license but as something rather like God's glory filling the earth). I agree where Ellul says "holiness in isolation is inadequate" because "it demands relationship." But if the theological virtues connect with how the holiness, love, and glory of God each frame biblical treatment of moral living as a whole, then Ellul must be wrong to suppose each corresponds to a different "sector of Christian life." These are not sectors but facets in the same sense that being faithful to my wife, loving my wife, and enjoying my wife are facets of one thing all the time rather than different things that occur at different times.

[76] This is similar but not identical to Jones, who says, "The controlling purpose of the Christian life is the glory of God; the impelling motive of the Christian life is love for God; and the directing principle of the Christian life is the will of God as revealed in Christ and the holy Scriptures" (*Biblical Christian Ethics*, 16). I differ with Jones only because I believe the Bible teaches that God's will, although sovereign in relation to all outside himself, is subject nevertheless to his own moral character. I therefore would revise his statement to say, "The directing principle of the Christian life is the

Two Dimensions of Biblical Ethics

The third structural level in biblical ethics is that all moral law has two fundamental dimensions—a vertical dimension relating life to God and a horizontal dimension relating life to other people. When some Pharisees asked Jesus, "Which command in the law is the greatest?" (Matt 22:36), he replied it was to "love the Lord your God with all your heart, with all your soul, and with all your mind" (Matt 22:37; see Deut 6:5), but then he went beyond their question, adding that the second greatest command was to "love your neighbor as yourself" (Matt 22:39; see Lev 19:18). He was expected only to identify one commandment, but he mentioned two. Why was that? It was to explain that "all the Law and the Prophets depend (hang, NIV) on these two commands" (Matt 22:40). The verb used is a structural term,[77] and Jesus went beyond the original question to reveal how these commands together serve to frame God's entire law. They are not just two among hundreds of other commands, and they are not just the first and second most important commands. Rather, Jesus showed how these commands together define two dimensions structuring all the rest.

In presenting the vertical and horizontal dimensions of biblical ethics, Jesus gave both in terms of love, and some have interpreted this to mean Jesus taught a new ethic they see as superior and even contrary to ethics in the Old Testament. Those doing this suppose that, while the Old Testament teaches an ethic of holiness, the New Testament teaches an ethic of love.[78] But this overlooks how, in structuring God's moral law in terms of loving God and neighbors, Jesus relied on the Old Testament (Deut 6:5; Lev 19:18) without revising what it said. Jesus also firmly denied teaching a new and different ethic, saying, "Don't assume that I came to destroy the Law or the Prophets," and, "I assure you: Until heaven and earth pass away, not the smallest letter or one stroke of a letter will pass from the law" (Matt 5:17–18).

---

holiness of God's fixed character revealed truly but partially in the Old Testament and more perfectly and fully in Christ as presented in the New Testament Scriptures."

[77] Jesus was speaking his native language, and the Greek κρέμαται (krematai) in Matthew 22:40 most likely translates the Hebrew שָׁעֵנוּ (šā'ěnû).

[78] Barnette takes this approach in dismissing Old Testament ethics as "for a people at an early state of religious development" now superseded by "the higher ethics of Christ" (*Introducing Christian Ethics*, 16); as does David Gushee, who now says, "The Bible is a human book," offering a sadly deficient ethical vision in the Old Testament at odds with an extraordinary vision proclaimed in the New. *The Sacredness of Human Life* (Grand Rapids: Eerdmans, 2013), 9.

The love ethic in the New does not replace Old Testament moral law but rather clarifies and strengthens what holy living requires and always has required—not just externally but internally. Paul says that love "is the fulfillment of the law" (Rom 13:10). But while love fulfills the law, love does not determine (much less change) what biblical ethics requires. Love refers to something directional as well as emotional. Love refers to a sentiment impelling action but also to a path along which action is taken. Both aspects have a place in biblical ethics but should not be confused. Emotional love is a self-located internal feeling, while directional love is an other-located orientation aiming for something (not self) that draws one's self toward an object outside and beyond the inner self.[79] Emotional love impels us to obey God willingly and with joy rather than grudgingly out of duty, while directional love accepts God on his terms and so aligning all we are (heart, soul, and mind) to what he requires.

These work together to effect what God's moral law requires. Love in biblical ethics does not rival holiness and does not replace objective standards with subjective feelings. God's moral law is neither an impersonal system nor an abstract theory. It is structured rather by dimensions of love aligned by, to, and through a personal God (Rom 11:36) for persons made to express his image in their manner of life (Eph 2:10). Biblical ethics goes beyond conforming to external standards by also insisting on hearts that delight to please God (Ps 40:8; Heb 12:2) and follow his example in relating to others (John 13:34–35). When this happens, a level of integration results that is not only holy and serves the glory of God but also is powerfully uniting and cohesive (John 17:22–23; Col 3:14). Self-centered sentiments do not do this, but God-centered love joining emotion to direction does. When it does, love pursues holiness to the glory of God.

Ten Categories of Obligation within Biblical Ethics

The fourth structural level in biblical ethics regards the fact that God's ordering of moral law involves ten categories of moral obligation. After starting with the character, initiative, and authority of God himself, then seeing how God's holiness, love, and glory permeate moral reality as a whole, and then realizing how moral truth has vertical and horizontal dimensions,

---

[79] I am indebted here to Murray without using his terms (*Principles of Conduct*, 22). Murray distinguishes "emotive" from "motive" love. But these do not express what he means as clearly as may be done.

we then find God is concerned with ten distinguishable yet interconnected categories of moral obligation ordered by the Decalogue, or Ten Commandments (Exod 20:1–17; Deut 5:6–21).[80] On careful examination, the Ten Commandments turn out to be more than just simple rules. Though stated briefly at Sinai, each one is expounded in growing detail throughout the rest of God's Word, not only through the prophets and wisdom literature of the Old Testament but through the teaching of Jesus and others in the New Testament as well.

The Ten Commandments were issued by God to Israel at Sinai to govern his covenant relationship with the nation. Their reality predates that occasion, and their relevance was not limited only to that purpose. Rather, their reality goes back to creation, and their relevance was universal from the beginning. This can be seen not only in the way God punishes Cain for murder (Gen 4:11) but also in the way God tells Moses that Israel's fidelity to his moral law must serve to inform and convict all nations (Deut 4:6–8) and in the way Romans 2:21–24 treats the Ten Commandments as affirming norms by which God judges the whole world. I, thus, agree with B. B. Warfield, who said, "There is no duty imposed upon the Israelite in

---

[80] Many books have been written concerning the Ten Commandments, with some focusing on interpretation and others on application. Some of the best include but are not limited to B. H. Carroll, *The Ten Commandments* (Nashville: Broadman, 1938); Emmet Fox, *The Ten Commandments: The Master Key to Life* (New York: Harper and Row, 1953); Terence J. Finlay, *The Ten Commandments* (New York: Scribner, 1961); Charles L. Allen, *The Ten Commandments: An Introduction* (Westwood, NJ: Revell, 1965); Ronald S. Wallace, *The Ten Commandments: A Study in Ethical Freedom* (Grand Rapids: Eerdmans, 1965); William Barclay, *The Ten Commandments for Today* (Grand Rapids: Eerdmans, 1973); G. Campbell Morgan, *The Ten Commandments* (Grand Rapids: Baker, 1974); Jan M. Lockman, *Signposts to Freedom: The Ten Commandments and Christian Ethics* (Minneapolis: Augsburg, 1982); Joy Davidman, *Smoke on the Mountain: An Interpretation of the Ten Commandments* (Philadelphia: Westminster, 1985); Ben-Zion Segal, ed., *The Ten Commandments in History and Tradition* (Jerusalem: Magnes, 1990); Calum M. Carmichael, *The Origins of Biblical Law: The Decalogues and the Book of the Covenant* (Ithaca, NY: Cornell, 1992); Jochem Douma, *The Ten Commandments: A Manual for the Christian Life*, trans. Nelson D. Kloosterman (Phillipsburg, NJ: P&R, 1992); Brian H. Edwards, *The Ten Commandments for Today* (Epson, Surrey, UK: DanOne, 2002); William J. Doorly, *The Laws of Yahweh: A Handbook of Biblical Law* (New York: Paulist, 2002); John C. Holbert, *The Ten Commandments* (Nashville: Abingdon, 2002); Philip G. Ryken, *Written in Stone: The Ten Commandments and Today's Moral Crisis* (Wheaton, IL: Crossway, 2003); Alistair Begg, *Pathway to Freedom: How God's Laws Guide Our Lives* (Chicago: Moody, 2003); Gill, *Doing Right*; Albert R. Mohler, *Words from the Fire* (Chicago: Moody, 2009); Mark F. Rooker, *The Ten Commandments: Ethics for the Twenty-First Century* (Nashville: B&H, 2010); and Henning Graf Reventlow and Yair Hoffman, eds., *The Decalogue in Jewish and Christian Tradition* (London: T&T Clark, 2011).

the Ten Commandments which is not equally incumbent upon all men, everywhere. These commandments are but the positive publication to Israel of the universal human duties, the common morality of mankind."[81]

No one denies that the Ten Commandments are basic to God's moral law. But in what way should they be regarded so? They must be basic in some way that involves more than merely considering them a little more important than other stipulations. They are important, but it must be in a way that also requires listing them in a carefully ordered manner and explains why taking them together should be viewed as a suitable way of summarizing everything God's moral law requires (Matt 19:17–19). Observations like these suggest that the Ten Commandments must have a degree of structural importance for God's moral law as a whole, and if so, this structural importance must regard something other than what led Jesus to say loving God and loving neighbors is so critical: "All the Law and the Prophets depend on these two commands" (Matt 22:40). The answer is that the Ten Commandments are basic not because they reveal dimensions to God's moral law but rather because they list categories of obligation that together add up to everything of which God's moral law consists.[82]

While the Ten Commandments serve a different structural role, they do align with and reaffirm the dimensions Jesus affirms in Matt 22:40. This can be seen by how the first three commandments (1–3) line up along the vertical dimension in God's moral law having to do with relating rightly to God; the last six commandments (5–10) line up along the horizontal dimension having to do with relating rightly to other people; and the fourth commandment appears at the juncture where the vertical and horizontal dimensions meet,

---

[81] Benjamin B. Warfield, *Selected Shorter Writings of Benjamin B. Warfield*, ed. John E. Meeter, 2 vols. (Nutley, NJ: Presbyterian and Reformed, 1970–1973), 1:213.

[82] Although the Ten Commandments were used in the early Church to order categories in God's moral law (see Robert M. Grant, "The Decalogue in Early Christianity," *Harvard Theological Review* 40 [1947]: 1–17), their use in this way predates Christian practice. Philo Judaeus of Alexandria (20 BC to AD 50) is well known for using the Ten Commandments as organizing principles ordering the rest of God's moral legislation. Philo, *On the Decalogue, On the Special Laws, On the Virtues*, trans. F. H. Colson, in *The Loeb Classical Library*, ed. E. H. Warmington (Cambridge: Harvard, 1933–1939). Contemporary Christian examples include Frame in Part Four of *Doctrine of the Christian Life*, 385–849; Gill, in Part Two of *Doing Right*, 79–321; and Jones in Chapter 5 of *An Introduction to Biblical Ethics*, 107–21.

having as much to do with relating rightly to God as with relating rightly to other people.[83] On this, Maston observes,

> There are (within the Ten Commandments) two major divisions. The first deals with right relation to God, and the second with right relation to the human community or to one's fellow man. Here . . . there is a balancing of the vertical and the horizontal. It should be noted that right relation to God or the vertical comes first, followed by right relation to one's fellow man . . . . It should never be forgotten, however, that these two belong together: to be right with God means to be right with one's neighbor.[84]

I should add, however, that while the vertical and horizontal dimensions structuring the Ten Commandments cannot be separated, neither can they be reversed. Relating rightly to God not only demands treating one's neighbor the right way but also defines what relating the right way to one's neighbor requires regardless of what a neighbor happens to prefer, and just accommodating everything a neighbor likes, desires, or chooses will never guarantee that we are pleasing God by doing so.

The Ten Commandments can be summarized as follows: (1) do not have other gods; (2) do not make idols; (3) do not misuse God's name; (4) keep the Sabbath day holy; (5) honor your

---

[83] I differ here with Henry, Frame, and Rae, all of whom assign the fourth command strictly to the vertical dimension and by that suppose it only concerns what Henry calls duties "directed especially to God" (Henry, *Christian Personal Ethics*, 271–72). This causes Henry to think the fifth command could be "the transition . . . (that) in some respects may be attached either to the first or second table" (Henry, 271–72). Frame and Rae also assign the fourth command to the vertical alone but then see no other command as transitional. Frame just says that the last six commands all concern "our relationships to one another" (Frame, 849), and Rae claims that after the fourth, the rest all deal with "moral responsibilities to others" (Rae, *Moral Choices*, 31). Deciding where and how to divide the Ten Commandments is much disputed, but four reasons lead me to believe the fourth command is transitional and connects the vertical with the horizontal dimension in God's law. These are (1) because a natural reading of this command tends to view time management as relating as much to others as to God; (2) because the biblical text specifically mentions relating to others as well as to God; (3) because the command's form is the second of three positive statements which, if taken as structural markers, distinguishes the fourth command from those set off by the first in Exodus 20:2 as well as those set off by the third in Exodus 20:12; and (4) because the Masoretic scribes used a reading marker called a *Parashah* (meaning "portion" and represented by the Hebrew letter פ), which introduced a breathing pause like a paragraph division that separates the fourth command from those read before.

[84] Maston, *Biblical Ethics*, 18.

parents; (6) do not murder; (7) do not commit adultery; (8) do not steal; (9) do not give false testimony; and (10) do not covet. Naming categories of obligation addressed by each of these ten commands requires interpretation. God's words are stated without error but how we interpret their meaning is fallible. My best effort to accurately describe the ethical categories structured by God's ten commands is: (1) the sanctity of allegiance to ultimate authority; (2) the sanctity of perceiving ultimate authority; (3) the sanctity of applying ultimate authority; (4) the sanctity of managing time, work, and rest; (5) the sanctity of human governing relations; (6) the sanctity of human life; (7) the sanctity of relational intimacy[85]; (8) the sanctity of property; (9) the sanctity of communication[86]; and (10) the sanctity of desires, motives, and intentions.

1. The first commandment concerns the sanctity of allegiance to ultimate authority because it asserts the supremacy of God over all with no exceptions allowed. It is the first and most important category of obligation because ethical thinking, whether religious or not, always starts with choosing where to start, and choosing where to start is an act of worship. Worship is an act by which one submits to whatever authority will be used for evaluating everything else, and the first command requires that ethical judgment always start with recognizing the ultimate authority of the one true God over everything else.

2. The second commandment concerns the sanctity of perceiving ultimate authority because the only true source of ultimate authority can be denied as effectively through perversion as by rejection. The second command forbids trying to represent God to ourselves and then focusing on representations in place of God himself. Although people doing so may claim to follow the same source of authority, it always distorts how they perceive it, and that in turn distorts ethical judgment all down the line.

3. The third commandment concerns the sanctity of applying ultimate authority because it prohibits misusing God's name, a term referring to God's ethical authority

---

[85] While "sex and marriage" could be used here, I agree with Jones in preferring "relational intimacy" to cover all this ethical category seems to address (*An Introduction to Biblical Ethics*, 171).

[86] Jones uses "material stewardship" and "truth" for what the eighth and ninth commands address (*An Introduction to Biblical Ethics*). While these are accurate, I prefer using "property" for the eighth and "communication" for the ninth because I believe these terms express the categories of obligation these commands address a little more clearly.

(Exod 23:21), ethical character (Exod 34:5–6), ethical standards (Deut 28:58), ethical approval (Num 6:27), ethical presence (Exod 20:24), ethical judgment (Jer 25:29), and ethical reputation (Exod 9:16). While it forbids demeaning God's authority, the third command also addresses all ways that men claim divine sanction for what they approve or disapprove.

4.   The fourth commandment concerns the sanctity of managing time, work, and rest, which deals with using the time we have for God's glory and in ways God knows are best, both for ourselves and for those affected by the way we balance time spent working with time spent resting. The fourth command renews proper ethical alignment by requiring us to refocus periodically on how all life (whether spiritual or material) depends more on God than on us and guards against oppression that comes from desiring and depending on material things too much.

5.   The fifth commandment concerns the sanctity of governing relationships or governing institutions because all institutions governing human interrelatedness grow out of, and continue to rely on, the integrity, strength, and stability of the nuclear family. Both functionally and historically, the ethics of teacher-student relations in education, of military and police relations in national security, of disciplinary and penal relations in courts of law, of employer-employee relations in the workplace, and of ruler-citizen relations in politics all grow from the ethics of parent-child relations in the family.

6.   The sixth commandment concerns the sanctity of human life, which in particular guards against offending the *imago Dei* by which men and women are distinguished from everything else in space-time-material creation. The Bible does not elevate human life to the point at which nothing is higher. Some things are worth dying for and others worth killing for. The sixth commandment does not prohibit killing in justified wars or to punish crimes that forfeit a perpetrator's claim on God's gift of life, and it guards something unique to human beings that animals do not share.[87] But the sixth command also does more than prohibit indiscriminate slaughter and using force

---

[87] The King James Version translates the Hebrew רָצַח (*rāṣḥ*) in Exodus 20:13 as "kill." But that is too broad, and modern versions like the Christian Standard Bible translate using "murder." See R. Laird Harris, Gleason J. Archer, Jr., and Bruce K. Waltke, eds, *Theological Wordbook of the Old Testament*, vol. 2 (Chicago: Moody, 1980), 860.

disproportionately because Jesus showed it even forbids words insulting the value of another person's life (Matt 5:21–22).

7. The seventh commandment concerns the sanctity of relational intimacy, which involves sexual identity, is expressed most intimately through male-female union, and is rightly ordered by the institution of marriage. In prohibiting sexual intimacy outside marriage (adultery), the seventh command secures family life, which relies on marital fidelity, and that in turn secures social stability and survival. But in limiting sexual intimacy to male-female union in marriage, the seventh command also orders how gendered people relate one to the other, not just in marriage, but beyond marriage. Humans are gendered beings all the time in all circumstances, and no human relationship can flourish without honoring rightly ordered marriage and respecting proper gender associations. The seventh commandment does more than prohibit actions harming sexual intimacy because Jesus showed it also forbids wanting to even if never acted upon (Matt 5:27–28).

8. The eighth commandment concerns the sanctity of property because it affirms private ownership of material assets and regulates their use in relation to others. The eighth command absolutely prohibits taking property owned by others (stealing) but also incentivizes honest work and undergirds respect for industry, frugality, and saving. The command also encourages generosity, which requires accumulating assets from which one then can share with those in need. Property in the Bible is a stewardship trust, and stealing not only disobeys God but also shows lack of faith in his ability to provide.

9. The ninth commandment concerns the sanctity of communication, which means it encourages candor, hinders shadiness, and absolutely prohibits calling on God to validate false testimony. But while the ninth command promotes integrity at all times in all places, it also anticipates complexities generated by innuendo, insinuation, ambiguity, unstated assumptions, and mixed messages often used to harm others without misstating facts directly. The command qualifies candor in most situations by limiting obligation to what fearing God requires (Prov 8:13) and forbids qualifying candor only when testifying in God's name under oath.[88] In issuing the ninth command,

---

[88] This is where we get the court tradition of swearing in witnesses by asking, "Do you solemnly swear or affirm that you will tell the truth, the whole truth, and nothing but the truth, so help you God?"

God used technical vocabulary particular to adjudicating disputes through appeal to his authority, judgment, and character (as in courts of law). But, with it, God also prevented false accusation, slander, gossip, vilification, character assassination, flattery, and all other forms of miscommunicating that threaten human welfare, justice, and social stability.

10. The tenth commandment concerns the sanctity of desires, motives, and intentions and as such focuses on the inner life standing behind and expressed outwardly through actions. There is a sense in which the last command is redundant. Desiring murder already is prohibited by the sixth (Matt 5:21–22) and desiring adultery already is forbidden by the seventh (Matt 5:27–28), and that is because each of the Ten Commandments already has both internal and external components. The last thus secures the rest by ensuring none is reduced to regulating external behavior alone.[89] There is a sense also in which the last command sets a category of obligation separate to itself, and that is because God's moral order not only is self-consistent but also reveals what is truly true and aligns God's moral order to its overall purpose. We must ultimately desire what God desires we ultimately desire, and "coveting" refers to getting it wrong. The last command forbids wrong desires of every kind, whether desiring something bad (desiring wrongly), desiring to obtain something good in a bad way (having wrong intentions), or desiring anything good or bad for bad reasons (having wrong motives). It exposes the sinfulness of wanting to sin based on considering sin to be something worthwhile or enjoyable. The tenth command shows that, when properly understood, human thriving requires not just behaving ethically but wanting to as well.

The Ten Commandments present us with the most strategically important ethical standards by which God judges all desire and behavior, and that means they cover everything we think, feel, and do. They are not manmade yet apply to men. They are perfect yet not merely ideal. They set standards that apply now and are not just aspirations toward which men aim but need not actually reach. They were delivered by God to Israel yet never were limited to

---

[89] According to Henry, "That the Decalogue itself has in view the interior life of motive and thought, and not merely external conduct, is brought to the fore especially in the last commandment" (*Christian Personal Ethics*, 275).

one people and always have applied to everyone everywhere. They are comprehensive yet particular. They are eternal yet apply in time. And though put succinctly, they are more than rules but also define categories of ethical obligation.

Conclusion

This chapter introduced readers to biblical ethics as an academic subcategory within the larger field of Christian ethics. We learned biblical ethics is a specialization that is foundational to all the other academic subcategories but uses "biblical" only to indicate a subject and not to assure fidelity to the text. We learned how biblical ethics studies the structure, content, and application of ethical revelation in the Bible, how ethical revelation is on every page and in nearly every verse of the Bible, and how, while ethical revelation in the Bible is trustworthy and sufficient, it is not exhaustive. It supplies all we need to live lives pleasing to God but does not answer all questions and so requires trusting that God is good and knows what he is doing even if we do not understand what he is doing. We examined what biblical ethics is and is not, as well as what distinguishes biblical ethics from speculating on similar topics. We surveyed positions dividing Evangelical scholars over how relevant moral law in the Old Testament is for New Testament Christians, considered what distinguishes and yet connects moral law with other sorts of biblical law, and learned how ethical revelation in the Bible is ordered by God in a way that combines many pieces in a single, perfectly consistent, well-working whole.

Layout of Biblical Ethics within Biblical Law

Level 1
Source

GOD

Level 2
Aspects

HOLY
LOVE
GLORY

Level 3
Dimensions

LOVE GOD ↔ LOVE OTHERS

Level 4
Categories

Sanctity of allegiance
Sanctity of perception
Sanctity of application
Sanctity of time, work, and rest
Sanctity of government
Sanctity of human life
Sanctity of intimacy
Sanctity of property
Sanctity of communication
Sanctity of desires

Level 5
Moral Law

MORAL LAW

Level 6
Biblical Law

CIVIL LAW
CEREMONIAL LAW
MORAL LAW

CHAPTER 4

THEOLOGY, REVELATION & REASON

This chapter introduces readers to theological ethics as an academic subcategory within the larger field of Christian ethics. Theological ethics builds on, but also moves beyond, the range of biblical ethics, using God-given reasoning ability to study and explain the nature, meaning, organizational themes, and ultimate aim of ethical truth ordered by the Word of God.[1] While biblical ethics focuses on what the Bible says about living an ethically worthy life,

---

[1] The most significant literature in theological ethics includes Augustine, *The City of God*, trans. Marcus Dods (New York: Random House, 1950); Augustine, *Concerning the Nature of Good*, in *Basic Writings of Saint Augustine*, trans. A. H. Newman, ed. Whitney J. Oates (New York: Random House, 1948); Augustine, *The Enchiridion on Faith, Hope and Love*, ed. Henry Paolucci (Chicago: Henry Regnery, 1961); Augustine, *On the Morals of the Catholic Church*, trans. Richard Stothert and Albert H. Newman, in *St. Augustine: The Writings Against the Manicheans and Against the Donatists*, vol. 4 of *The Nicene and Post-Nicene Fathers*, ed. Philip Schaff (Grand Rapids: Eerdmans, 1974); Aquinas, *Summa theologica* (see chap. 2, n. 14); John Calvin, *Institutes of the Christian Religion*, 2 vols., trans. Ford Lewis Battles, ed. John T. McNeill (Philadelphia: Westminster, 1960); Martin Luther, *The Christian Society*, trans. W. A. Lambert, ed. James Atkinson, vol. 44, *Works of Martin Luther*, ed. Helmut T. Lehmann (Philadelphia: Fortress, 1966); Barth, *Ethics* (see chap. 1, n. 26); Barth, *The Christian Life* (see chap. 1, n. 69); Ramsey, *Basic Christian Ethics* (see chap. 1,

theological ethics builds on what the Bible says by applying reason to address further questions, such as: "What does the Bible mean when addressing this or that ethical topic?" "How

n. 69); John Ryle, *Holiness: It Nature, Hindrances, Difficulties, and Roots* (London: James Clark, 1952); Anders Nygren, *Agape and Eros*, trans. Philip S. Watson (Philadelphia: Westminster, 1953); Bonhoeffer, *Ethics*, (see chap. 1, n. 76); Henry, *Christian Personal Ethics* (see chap. 1, n. 2); Carl F. H. Henry, *Evangelical Responsibility in Contemporary Theology* (Grand Rapids: Eerdmans, 1957); Paul Tillich, *Love, Power and Justice: Ontological Analysis and Ethical Applications* (New York: Oxford, 1960); Niebuhr, *An Interpretation of Christian Ethics* (see chap. 2, n. 57); John Howard Yoder, *The Christian Witness to the State* (Newton, KA: Faith & Life, 1964); Dietrich Bonhoeffer, *Christ the Center*, trans. John Bowden (New York: Harper & Row, 1966); Thielicke, *Theological Ethics* (see chap. 1, n. 69); Ernst Käsemann, *Jesus Means Freedom*, trans. Frank Clark (Philadelphia: Fortress, 1970); Paul Althaus, *The Ethics of Martin Luther*, trans. Robert C. Schultz (Philadelphia: Fortress, 1972); Van Til, *Christian Theistic Ethics* (see chap. 1, n. 36); Ellul, *The Ethics of Freedom* (see chap. 1, n. 69); Charles E. Curran, *Themes in Fundamental Moral Theology* (Notre Dame, IN: University of Notre Dame, 1977); James M. Gustafson, *Christian Ethics and the Community* (New York: Pilgrim, 1979); James M. Gustafson, *Ethics from a Theocentric Perspective*, 2 vols. (Chicago: University of Chicago, 1981); Stanley Hauerwas, *The Community of Character* (Notre Dame, IN: University of Notre Dame, 1981); Wolfhart Pannenberg, *Ethics*, trans. Keith Crim (Philadelphia: Westminster, 1981); Charles E. Curran, *Moral Theology: A Continuing Journey* (Notre Dame, IN: University of Notre Dame, 1982); Stanley Hauerwas, *The Peaceable Kingdom* (see chap. 1, n. 64); Joseph L. Allen, *Love and Conflict: A Covenantal Model of Christian Ethics* (Nashville: Abingdon, 1984); Dermot Lane, *Foundations for a Social Theology: Praxis, Process and Salvation* (New York: Paulist, 1984); Alasdair MacIntyre, *After Virtue: A Study in Moral Theory*, 2nd ed. (Notre Dame, IN: University of Notre Dame, 1984); Jürgen Moltmann, *On Human Dignity: Political Theology and Ethics*, trans. M. Douglas Meek (Philadelphia: Fortress, 1984); Charles E. Curran, *Directions in Moral Theology* (Notre Dame, IN: University of Notre Dame, 1985); James William McClendon, *Ethics: Systematic Theology*, vol. 1 (Nashville: Abingdon, 1986); O'Donovan, *Resurrection and Moral Order* (see chap. 1, n. 69); Timothy F. Sedgwick, *Sacramental Ethics: Paschal Identity and the Christian Life* (Philadelphia: Fortress, 1987); J. Philip Wogaman, *Christian Moral Judgment* (Louisville: Westminster/John Knox, 1989); L. Gregory Jones, *Transformed Judgment: Toward a Trinitarian Account of the Moral Life* (Notre Dame, IN: University of Notre Dame, 1990); J. I. Packer, *A Quest for Godliness: The Puritan Vision of the Christian Life* (Wheaton, IL: Crossway, 1990); Anderson, *Walking the Way* (see chap. 1, n. 60); Stanley J. Grenz, *The Moral Quest: Foundations of Christian Ethics* (Downers Grove, IL: InterVarsity, 1997); Donald L. Alexander, *The Pursuit of Godliness: Sanctification in Christological Perspective* (New York: University Press of America, 1999); Hollinger, *Choosing the Good* (see chap. 1, n. 60); Glen H. Stassen and David P. Gushee, *Kingdom Ethics* (Downers Grove, IL: InterVarsity, 2003); Willard M. Swartley, *Covenant of Peace* (Grand Rapids: Eerdmans, 2006); Mattison, *Introducing Moral Theology* (see chap. 1, n. 9); John Howard Yoder, *The War of the Lamb: The Ethics of Nonviolence and Peacemaking*, ed. Glen Stassen et al. (Grand Rapids: Baker, 2009); and Gushee, *Sacredness* (see chap. 3, n. 78). This listing includes works representing different faith traditions, meaning they are not

does biblical revelation on ethical topics fit together?" "What principle unifies God's moral ordering of reality?" And "What structural themes are used in the Bible to reveal God's moral ordering of reality?" In general, work in theological ethics obeys the injunction Jesus gave to love God "with all your mind" (Matt 22:37; Mark 12:30; Luke 10:27), and that should presume accepting the authority of Scripture and seeking guidance from the Holy Spirit while trying to properly understand God's revelation of moral order.[2] It is also a matter of heeding Paul's admonition to eschew "childish . . . thinking" and rather to become "adult in your thinking" (1 Cor 14:20).

According to the Karl Barth, "Ethics as a theological discipline is the auxiliary science in which an answer is sought in the Word of God to the question of the goodness of human conduct . . . . [And] as a special elucidation of the doctrine of sanctification, it is reflection on how far the Word of God proclaimed and accepted in Christian preaching effects a definite claiming of man."[3] But theological ethics goes on also to consider how human existence and interactions are ordered by God and studies Scripture to find revealed categories structuring God's moral ordering of human lives.[4] Most Evangelical theologians believe God orders human life using four relational categories: first, by treating us as creatures made by God, in the image of God, for a unique relationship with God; second, by treating us as sinners both judged and pardoned by God; third, by treating us as children loved by God and called into family intimacy with God; and fourth, by treating us as heirs entitled by God to share future

---

consistent one with the other and do not all align with the Bible or with historic Christian faith. But all must be engaged because they have influenced many.

[2] Some theologians list experience and tradition with reason as three equally important tools men have for evaluating biblical truth. But I do not include experience and tradition here because, when it comes to theological comprehension, I do not think experience and tradition are able to analyze and understand the meaning of Scripture without depending on reason the way reason can be used sometimes to analyze and understand the meaning of Scripture without depending on either experience or tradition.

[3] Barth, *Ethics*, 3.

[4] Evangelical Christian theologians do not agree with Long, who believes "Theological ethics pursues its work in relation to many other disciplines and cannot be understood apart from them," and who then goes as far as to claim theological ethics cannot be understood (rightly or fully) without "at least a bird's-eye view of ethical discourse as found in moral philosophy and the social sciences." *A Survey of Christian Ethics*, 3 (see chap. 1, n. 49).

regency with God in the eternal kingdom of God.[5] Sometimes, these four categories structuring ethical life in theological terms are referred to more briefly as "creation," "fall," "redemption," and "consummation."[6] Each of these four theologically structured categories ordering ethical life will be discussed in more detail later in this chapter.

Ethics & Dogmatics

Theological ethics is ethics in the sphere of theology, and if theology presents reality as God directs through his Word, then theological ethics presents God's ethical ordering of reality as directed to man by God through his Word. It is a practical, as well as cognitive, discipline that concerns the sanctifying work of God in human lives, which means theological ethics operates (or should) in a manner that conforms human life to ethical reality as directed by and aligned to God himself. Since "dogmatics" studies truth revealed by God, theological ethics is the part within theological dogmatics that inquires into the goodness of human behavior, character, and goals as God directs them. This means ethics is theological ethics to the extent, and only to the extent, that it starts with divine truth, illuminates divine will, obeys divine authority, conforms to divine character, serves divine goals, loves the divine persons, and loves others here on earth in the way divine love requires. In other words, ethics is theological ethics to the extent, and only to the extent, that it is dogmatic. So, if one inquires into the goodness of human behavior, character, and goals based on moral ordering revealed by God in his Word, then one pursues ethics as a matter of theological dogmatics.

Theological ethics conceives moral goodness as a matter of conforming life to God and goes on to claim moral goodness never is truly understood any other way. Theological ethics understands that every worthy act we perform and every worthy thought or feeling we have are as much works of God as of man, and it understands that the human side of God's kingdom is positioned within the larger scope of his all-encompassing regency. It understands no one thinks, speaks, or draws a single breath without doing it in relation to God's moral

---

[5] My ordering varies from Barth's theological subcategories in that I do not use the unnecessary and essentially non-theological category with which Bart begins and have added the theologically significant child/family category frequently used in the ethical teaching of Jesus but overlooked in Barth's ordering. To compare, see Barth, *Ethics*, 45–61.

[6] For example, Hollinger, *Choosing the Good*, 86.

order, which means true answers to ethical questions must and can only be formulated in ways that are dogmatic.[7] There is no easy way to get around this. We can recognize the theological nature of presuppositions framing the way we answer ethical questions, or we can sacrifice truth by hiding or denying this reality. But there is no non-theological starting point from which to begin assessing ethical reality because the act of deciding where and how to begin answering ethical questions (the very act itself) is theological and, therefore, dogmatic in nature.

The first emphasis for biblical Christians doing theological ethics always must be the uniqueness of its revealed character, and here I agree where Henry says, "Every attempt to explain a theological version of ethical truth as being merely another perhaps more complex formulation of the insights common to non-theological versions either conceals or minimizes the basis that it has in Divine revelation."[8] The way we as Christians view ethical reality builds upon a coherent and self-consistent revelation of ethical truth that operates on distinctive assumptions and controlling ideas not shared with other systems of thought. In fact, these distinctive assumptions and controlling ideas are such that without them other attempts to understand or explain ethics are deficient (not complete), perverted (not rightly aligned), or sometimes both at the same time.

Theological ethics explores and gives answers to the question of human goodness within, and never outside or even partly outside, the boundaries of what God reveals ethical reality to be. Theological ethics never ceases believing that God exists and reveals himself through his Word, and for this reason, it insists that God and human goodness are coordinate and inseparable. Not only are devotion to God and to the good of others compatible (they do not compete one against the other), it is also not possible to truly understand or rightly practice one without the other. Because it relies on divine revelation so completely, theological ethics cannot unite with or submit to any treatment of ethics elevating itself over the uniquely coherent moral truth applied to everyone for all time by the One Creator God through the person

---

[7] Here, I take a stand with which some do not agree. But I am not alone. Barth holds that "the goodness of human conduct can be sought only in the goodness of the Word addressed to man" (Barth, *Ethics*, 15); and Thielicke maintains that "in an ultimate sense—*coram Deo* [before God]—there is no such thing as autonomy of the various spheres of life" *(Theological Ethics, 36).*

[8] Henry, *Christian Personal Ethics,* 146.

and work of Jesus Christ. This means it cannot be reduced to any system of ethical thought that originates in human imagination independent of God's moral revelation.

This last point leads to considering how reason relates to doing theological ethics. If theological ethics relies on revelation so thoroughly, how then does human reasoning ability relate to the study and evaluation of revealed ethics? Revelation provides reason with its only secure source of presuppositions. Revelation does not make reason irrelevant. Rather, it unveils realities, and humans then use reason to explore and analyze. Revelation does not oppose reason, but it does insist on keeping the way we use reason subordinate to what God says. On this, Henry says,

> Hebrew-Christian ethics is not content simply to take the broken fragments of discordant morality (views formulated by reason apart from revelation) and to blend them into an eclectic whole. Rather, it transcends the antinomies of the speculative systems. It transcends them, not by abandoning the enduring need of man for a coherent grasp of the form and content of morality, but by exhibiting that form and content in such a way as to do justice to all the legitimate claims of the ethical life and neglecting none.[9]

Furthermore, John Stott commends the value of using reason submitted to revelation in pursuing theological ethics, pointing out that:

> (1) It glorifies God, because he has made us rational beings in his own image and has given us in Scripture a rational revelation which he intends us to study. (2) It enriches us, because every aspect of our Christian discipleship (e.g., our worship, faith and obedience) depends for its maturing on our reflection, respectively, upon God's glory, faithfulness and will. [And] (3) It strengthens our witness in the world, because we are called like the apostles not only to "preach" the gospel, but also to "defend" and "argue" it and so "persuade" people of its truth (e.g., Acts 17:2f.; 19:8; 2 Corinthians 5:11; Philippians 1:7).[10]

---

[9] Henry, 165.

[10] John Stott, *Issues Facing Christians Today*, 4th ed. (Grand Rapids: Zondervan, 1984).

While theological ethics employs human reasoning ability as rigorously as any philosopher or social scientist speculating on what ethics is or requires, it does so based on a reliable foundation for analyzing ethical reality that reason does not have apart from revelation. Moreover, this foundation is so unique it is not, and never can be, shared with any other system of ethical thought. What sets theological ethics apart from philosophy or science is not the degree to which it uses reason but what Pannenberg calls "the exclusive nature of its ethical foundation."[11] Tension can, and often does, arise between reason used to analyze what God reveals and what reason used apart from revelation comes up with to explain what ethics is and requires. But, when tension arises, it mainly comes not from Christians embracing the irrational but from non-believers objecting to what the Word of God reveals despite its rationality, or from believers refusing to treat man-centered speculations as the ethics of God's kingdom rule.

Theological Methods in Conflict

The most important structural task that any work in theological ethics must address is to identify what principle unifies God's ethical ordering of reality. God is not random, incoherent, or arbitrary but is ordered, coherent, and purposeful. If so, then God's ethical ordering of reality is structured, and, if structured, it must have an ordering principle. All works in theological ethics identify or assume an ordering principle by which God's moral revelation coheres as a whole and is made self-consistent as to its logical force and implications. But to date, there is no agreement among theologians as to what this ordering principle—referred to as a theologian's "method"—might be. All agree there must be a unifying principle or method, or else God would not be consistent and ethical reality would be disordered. With few exceptions, nearly everyone contributing to theological ethics has so far proposed something different:

---

[11] Pannenberg, *Ethics*, 57. Agreeing with Pannenberg at this point means I do not agree with Van Til's claim that "for Christians the difference between theological and philosophical ethics can be no more than one of emphasis" (Van Til, *Theistic Ethics*, 5). For, by using "emphasis" to define the distinction, Van Til indicates that the difference between what God reveals and what others say is nothing more than a matter of stress or focus. That is, Van Til assumes there is no real difference other than variations explained by which part of the same reality is in view. That, I believe, is both wrong and dangerous. What distinguishes revealed ethics from what men imagine is foundational, not focal, and is a matter of supremacy, not stress.

- Augustine of Hippo used the method of living as citizens of two cities (heavenly and earthly) ordered by opposing loves.[12]

- Thomas Aquinas used the method of citizens living under four kinds of law (eternal, divine, natural, and human).[13]

- Martin Luther used the method of living between two kingdoms (of God and of man) that exclude one another.[14]

- John Calvin used the method of affirming God's sovereign rule over all things.[15]

- J. C. Ryle used the method of centering on the holiness of God's character.[16]

- Walter Rauschenbusch and Joseph Fletcher both used the method of pursuing neighbor love in human-centered terms.[17]

- Reinhold Niebuhr used the method of dialectical tension between love and justice.[18]

- Karl Barth and Dietrich Bonhoeffer used the method of living in obedience under the kingdom rule of God centered on Christ.[19]

- James Gustafson used the method of building on a man-centered experience of dependence upon ultimate power.[20]

- Paul Ramsey used the method of correlating God's love, righteousness, and reign.[21]

---

[12] Augustine, *The City of God*, 1.preface, and 19.24.

[13] Aquinas, *Summa*, Q94a2.

[14] Luther, *Works of Martin Luther*, vol. 3, 225–73.

[15] Calvin, *Institutes*, 1.16.3 and 4.20.1–6.

[16] Ryle, *Holiness*, ch. 3.

[17] For Rauschenbusch, see *A Theology for the Social Gospel* (New York: Macmillan, 1917). For Fletcher, see *Situation Ethics: The New Morality* (Philadelphia: Westminster, 1966).

[18] Niebuhr, *An Interpretation of Christian Ethics*, 22–38 (see chap. 2, n. 141). This also is the major theme of Niebuhr's compendium of essays published as *Love and Justice*, ed., D. B. Robertson (Philadelphia: Westminster, 1957), and readers should especially note the essay "Justice and Love," on pages 27–29.

[19] For Barth, see *Ethics*, vii and *Christian Life*, 74.2. For Bonhoeffer, see "Christ, Reality and Good" in *Ethics*, 186–210 and also *Christ the Center*, 12. For a good treatment of both, see Robin W. Lovin, *Christian Faith and Public Choices: The Social Ethics of Barth, Brunner, and Bonhoeffer* (Philadelphia: Fortress, 1984).

[20] Gustafson, *Ethics from a Theocentric Perspective*, 1:158, 327, 342 but also *Christian Ethics and the Community*, 264.

[21] Ramsey, *Basic Christian Ethics*, especially 1–35.

- John Howard Yoder used the method of two-kingdom peacemaking that distinguishes peace in the kingdom of Christ the Son from peace in the kingdom of God the Father (thus devising a realist eschatological peacemaking ethic).[22]

- Stanley Hauerwas and Willard Swartley use the method of nonviolent peacemaking in man-centered terms (thus devising an idealist present world peacemaking ethic).[23]

- Charles E. Curran uses the method of applying four relational categories (God, neighbor, the world, and self).[24]

- James McClendon and Stanley Grenz used, and Richard Hays uses, the method of sharing desire to build Christian community in man-centered terms.[25]

- Helmut Thielicke and Jacques Ellul used the method of pursuing Christ-centered freedom.[26]

- Carl F. H. Henry used the method of bringing life into conformity with God-centered character (the *imago Dei*) through Christ as revealed in the Bible.[27]

- John Frame uses the method of starting with philosophical perspectives (the normative, the situational, and the existential) and redefining them theologically.[28]

- Glen Stassen and David Gushee use the method of affirming the reign of God in man-centered terms (thus devising an idealist present world, just peacemaking, sanctity of human life ethic)[29]

---

[22] Yoder, *Christian Witness*, 9–15.

[23] For Hauerwas, see *Peaceable Kingdom*, xvi–xviii, 16, 54. For Swartley, see *Covenant of Peace*, 8–10.

[24] Curran, *Directions*, 12–14.

[25] For McClendon, see *Ethics*, 41–46. For Grenz, see *Moral Quest*, 205–6, 227–39, 257. For Hays, see *The Moral Vision of the New Testament* (San Francisco: HarperSanFrancisco, 1996), 196–200, 343–44, 374–76, 400–403, 438–41, 457–60.

[26] For Ellul, see *The Ethics of Freedom*, 51–75, 94–100. For Thielicke, see *Theological Ethics*, 455–64.

[27] Henry, *Christian Personal Ethics*, 145–160, 239–61.

[28] Frame, *Doctrine of the Christian Life*, See "Part Three: Christian Ethical Methodology," 127–382 (see chap. 1, n. 69).

[29] Stassen and Gushee, *Kingdom*, 19–31, 99–24. Also note Gushee, *Sacredness*, 9, where Gushee indicates that his theological ethic does not affirm the plenary inspiration of Scripture and does not accept the biblical text as inerrant. Gushee's theological method views the Bible as "a human book" that merely "bears witness to . . . hearing and heeding God's word." As such, Gushee's method never rises above his own man-centered efforts to pick between parts of the Bible he thinks "offer moments

- Christopher Wright uses the method of centering on the mission of God.[30]
- Oliver O'Donovan and N. T. Wright use the method of ethical reality being framed by God's intention to bring all things in heaven and earth together in Christ centering on, held together, explained by, and made possible through the resurrection of Jesus Christ from the dead.[31]

The point of listing all these ways theologians have explained what unifies God's ethical ordering of reality is to illustrate the degree of confusion and disagreement there is on this subject. But, having pointed this out, we are left with needing to decide which if any of these options to follow, and we cannot approach it like a smorgasbord where diners select items based on personal taste. We are dealing here with a matter of ultimate importance affecting everyone, in every way, for eternity, and we have only two ways to go. Since we know God's ethical ordering of reality is not chaotic, we must choose either to accept one of the options already suggested, or to look for something new and not yet suggested. In this case, I believe we should accept one of the previously suggested options based on two reasons: first, because it is faithful to Scripture and, second, because it illuminates God's strategy for ordering reality to his character more powerfully than the rest. That option, I believe, is the one argued by O'Donovan and added to later by Wright. I think these two British Evangelicals have been right to suggest that ethical reality for everyone (not just for Christians or the Church) for all time (not just starting with the life of Christ on earth) is framed by God's intention to bring all things in heaven and earth together in Christ, centering on, held together, explained by, and made possible through the resurrection of Jesus Christ from the dead.

This does not mean I think we should reject everything others have said, and I especially do not want to discard what Augustine, Calvin, Ryle, Barth, Bonhoeffer, Thielicke, Ellul, or Henry had to offer. Many of the methods suggested are incompatible with one another, but

---

of extraordinarily profound proclamation" and other moments in which he thinks "the written words or narrated events of Scripture fall considerably short."

[30] Wright, *The Mission of God*, 33–69 (see chap. 1, n. 34).

[31] For O'Donovan, see *Resurrection and Moral Order*, 11–75. For Wright, see *After You Believe* (New York: HarperCollins, 2010), ix and *Surprised by Hope: Rethinking Heaven, the Resurrection, and the Mission of the Church* (New York: HarperCollins, 2008), 104–6, 189–205.

several are compatible and seem related, producing increasing clarity and understanding of God's moral truth.

Thus, I would say Augustine was right to realize how, in a general way, God's ethical ordering of reality faces resistance that generates opposing communities ordered by opposing loves. Calvin was right then to add how there is no reality to be ordered apart from the one ordered by God; therefore, authorities on earth are always accountable to God and must either submit to or be judged by God's ultimate sovereignty. Ryle was right then to stress how God's character governs his ethical ordering of reality. Barth and Bonhoeffer were right then to realize how reality is ethically ordered, not just by centering on God in general, but by centering specifically on the person and work of Christ. Thielicke and Ellul were right then to realize beyond that how ethical reality centers on the person and work of Christ in a way that aims at an amazing destiny by which men are freed to be and enjoy all God has ever intended they be and enjoy. Henry was right then to clarify how the ethical centering of reality on Christ involves privileges and duties having to do with our being assigned to bear the image of God and how that links ethics in the old, created order corrupted by the fall with ethics in a new, perfected creation that will endure forever. Lastly, and with the most clarity of all, O'Donovan and Wright have been right to point out how God's ethical ordering of reality centers not only on Christ and not only more narrowly on what Christ came to do and will achieve but also on the resurrection of Jesus Christ and how it affects our own present and future lives.

Following the passage in 1 Peter 1:3–4 that tells us ethical transformation from the old order marred by sin into a new "imperishable, uncorrupted, and unfading" order is achieved "through the resurrection of Jesus Christ from the dead," O'Donovan says this reveals that the resurrection of Christ must play the key role in God's ethical ordering of reality and is the one thing that most explains its coherence (interconnection and consistency) over time. Building on 1 Peter 1:3–4, O'Donovan maintains that the resurrection of Christ unifies God's ethical ordering of reality for two theological reasons: first, "because it tells us of God's vindication of his creation, and so our created life," and, second, because by it we are changed in a way that anticipates our own eschatological participation in a new creation wherein we shall be glorified and the kingdom of God perfected.[32] In agreement with O'Donovan, Wright observes how "the final hope of Christians is not simply 'going to heaven,' but resurrection into God's

---

[32] O'Donovan, *Resurrection and Moral Order*, 13, 22, 26, 31, 56, 58.

new creation, the 'new heaven and new earth,'" to which he adds, "the promise and hope of resurrection, in other words, is the thing that has both reshaped how virtue works and also given it fresh moral content."[33]

The Trinitarian Principle in Theological Ethics

In this chapter introducing theological ethics, we turn now to consider a trinitarian principle that occurs so often as to suggest it is more than coincidental and reflects something truly significant. I refer here to the frequent occurrence in theological ethics of things appearing in groups of three, and I use the term *trinitarian* over *triadic* to suggest it connects in some way to God's Trinitarian nature. When capitalized, the term *Trinitarian* indicates something related to the being of God consisting in three persons—Father, Son, and Holy Spirit. When not capitalized the term can indicate things that appear in groups of three. In this second noncapitalized sense, *trinitarian* is synonymous with *triadic*. But, to avoid confusion, it is conventional to use the term *triadic* in places where no association with God's Trinitarian nature is intended. Understanding this, I prefer employing the term *Trinitarian* over *triadic* in referencing the phenomenon considered here because I do actually mean to suggest a connection exists between the frequent recurrence of "three-ness" in theological ethics and the Trinitarian nature of the One Being at the center of, and who disposes, the ethical ordering of reality.

We have seen something of this earlier. We have noted already that God's ordering of ethical reality involves three component parts comprising ethical living, three facets presenting ethical reality, and three categories of biblical law. In Chapter 2, while introducing Christian ethics as a whole, we saw how the Bible presents ethical living as having three component parts, these being right conduct (Jas 1:22), right character (Rom 8:29), and right goals (Col 3:23). Then in Chapter 3, when introducing biblical ethics, we encountered two further triads. First, we saw how law in the Bible falls into three subclassifications, which are ceremonial law that changes from the Old Testament to the New (Heb 10:1), civil law that only concerned governing ancient Israel and never was meant for others (Lev 25:3–5), and moral law that lasts forever (Heb 13:8; Jas 1:17). Then we saw how God's ethical ordering in the Bible involves three facets that each present ethical reality in a different way—all we are and do must

---

[33] Wright, *After You Believe*, ix, 186.

be holy as God is holy (Lev 19:2; 1 Pet 1:16), all we are and do must remain in God's love (John 15:10; 1 John 4:12), and all we are and do must be for the glory of God (1 Cor 10:31).

These three different sets of "three-ness" all relate to God's ordering of ethical life, and considered together, are enough to indicate there is more going on than happenstance. These three different sets of three cannot be coincidental and together reveal a recurring presence of "three-ness" in God's ordering of ethical reality. But what we have observed to this point in turn hints at something larger and far more profound, which is that God's ordering of ethical reality involves multiple triads all reflecting a Trinitarian principle. Besides those covered already, other triads reflecting this Trinitarian principle include the following:

- There is Trinitarian ordering in three things required for Israel to stay in right relation with God, which are for them "to fear the LORD your God by walking in all his ways, to love him, and to worship the LORD your God" (Deut 10:12).
- There is Trinitarian ordering in three things required for anyone to stay in right relation with God, which are "to act justly, to love faithfulness, and to walk humbly with your God" (Mic 6:8).
- There is Trinitarian ordering in three things Jesus required of disciples, which are to "love Me" (John 14:15, 21, 23–24), "keep My commands" (John 14:15, 21, 23–24), and "remain in Me" (John 15:4–6).
- There is Trinitarian ordering in three motifs used for ethical revelation in the Old Testament. Christopher Wright, in analyzing Old Testament ethics, discerns three structural themes, one focusing on God as a king ruling all nations while forming and preserving an elect people, a second focusing on Israel as a people chosen for a relationship with God they never earned and do not deserve, and a third focusing on the Promised Land as a place where God blesses Israel while using them to bless others.[34]
- There is Trinitarian ordering in three motifs in the ethical teaching of Jesus. White, in analyzing the ethics of Jesus, identifies three structural themes, which are the "family" theme, portraying ethics as living a "life of sonship" relating to God as a Father; the "kingdom" theme, portraying ethics as living a "life of obedience" relating to God as

---

[34] Christopher J. H. Wright, *Old Testament Ethics for the People of God* (Downers Grove, IL: InterVarsity, 2004), 17–20. Also note Wright's discussion of "A Structure for Old Testament Ethics" in chapters 1–3.

a King; and the "discipleship" theme, portraying ethics as living a "life of imitation" relating to Jesus as a role model.[35]

- There is Trinitarian ordering in three motifs in the ethical teaching of Paul. Hays, in analyzing the ethics of Paul, identifies three structural themes, which are becoming a "counter community" by which the Church resists the influences of surrounding culture, bearing "the cross" by which the death of Jesus is the model for costly fidelity in a hostile world, and living as "new creations" by which Christians live in the present fallen world in view of a new world to come.[36]

- There is Trinitarian ordering in three ways for portraying the character of God. Theologians have found the Bible typically portrays the character of God in one of three ways, and sometimes in all three ways together: first, as a matter of holiness, second, as a matter of righteousness, and third, as a matter of love. Ryle and Jerry Bridges portray God's character only in terms of holiness;[37] Van Til portrays it only in terms of righteousness;[38] and Niebuhr and O'Donovan portray it mainly in terms of love.[39] Ramsey and Henry move beyond this in portraying the divine character as uniting God's righteousness with His love.[40] But Hollinger and Geoffrey Bromiley view it in triadic terms, suggesting, "Christians should think of God as the ground of ethics, the norm of ethics, and the power for ethical living,"[41] so as to integrate God's holiness, righteousness, and love in ways that lead not just to believing in but also to living out the grace and presence of God in our lives.

- There is Trinitarian ordering in three ways of assessing godliness in Christian conduct, which are growing in holiness (2 Cor 1:12), in righteousness (Rom 2:13), and in blamelessness (Phil 2:14–15); and Paul mentions all three together where he says,

---

[35] White, *Biblical Ethics*, chapters 4, 5, and 6 (see chap. 1, n. 69).

[36] Hays, *Moral Vision*, 196–200.

[37] Ryle, *Holiness*, 34–50. Jerry Bridges, *The Pursuit of Holiness* (Colorado Springs: NavPress, 1976), 21–30.

[38] Van Til, *Theistic Ethics*, 46–47.

[39] Niebuhr, *An Interpretation of Christian Ethics*, chs. 2, 5–6; O'Donovan, *Resurrection*, chs. 9–12 (see chap. 1, n. 69). Also note O'Donovan, *Common Objects of Love* (see chap. 2, n. 18).

[40] Ramsey, *Basic Christian Ethics*, 2–24. Henry, *Christian Personal Ethics*, chs. 8–9.

[41] Hollinger, *Choosing the Good*, 64. Geoffrey Bromiley, "Ethics and Dogmatics," in *International Standard Biblical Encyclopedia*, vol. 2 (Grand Rapids: Eerdmans, 1982), 186–90.

"You are witnesses, and God also, how holy and righteous and blameless was our conduct toward you believers" (1 Thess 2:10, ESV).

- There is Trinitarian ordering in the commanding roles God takes in relation to humanity. Barth discerns three mutually reinforcing roles that together structure God's ethical ordering of reality, and these are the commanding of "God as creator," the commanding of "God as reconciler," and the commanding of "God as redeemer."[42] The first addresses men as creatures of God. The second addresses them as sinners pardoned by God, and the third addresses them as heirs of the kingdom of God.[43]

- There is Trinitarian ordering in three virtues essential to living the Christian life, which are faith, hope, and love (Rom 5:2–5; 1 Cor 13:13; Gal 5:5–6; Col 1:4–5; 1 Thess 1:3; 1 Thess 5:8; Heb 6:10–12; Heb 10:22–24; 1 Pet 1:3–8; 1 Pet 1:21–22). The New Testament elevates these three virtues over all others, indicating they are in some way more essential than all others. Paul thus commends believers in Thessalonica for "your work produced by faith, labor motivated by love, and your endurance inspired by hope in our Lord Jesus Christ" (1 Thess 1:3). Aquinas insists faith, hope, and love are greater than the cardinal virtues recognized by the early Greeks and especially Aristotle,[44] and Lewis uses them to explain what makes Christian ethics especially unique.[45]

- There is Trinitarian ordering in three stages of salvation. Theologians analyzing the doctrine of salvation note how the biblical text employs the term "salvation" (σωτηρίαν, *sōtērian*) in three ways and so use three different terms to distinguish one from the other. *Justification* (Eph 2:8) refers to salvation past (how we have been cleansed once for all and declared righteous by the work of Christ), *sanctification* (Phil 2:12) refers to salvation present (how we now should be growing in greater and greater moral conformity to Christ), and *glorification* (1 Pet 1:5) refers to salvation future (how someday we shall be perfected).[46]

---

[42] Barth, *Ethics*, chs. 2–4.

[43] Barth, 45.

[44] Aquinas, *Summa theologica*, q. 62, "Of the Theological Virtues."

[45] Lewis, *Mere Christianity*, III.9–12 (see chap. 2, n. 4).

[46] Grudem, *Systematic Theology*, chs. 36, 38, 42 (see chap. 2, n. 14); Erickson, *Christian Theology*, 954–961, 967–974, 997–1002 (see chap. 2, n. 16); John Theodore Mueller, *Christian Dogmatics* (St. Louis: Concordia, 1955), 367–83, 384–435, 639–44. Also see David Pawson,

- There is Trinitarian ordering in three functions of moral law. Calvin, in considering uses of God's moral law revealed in the Bible, found "it consists of three parts," which led to a tripartite analogy.[47] The first use of God's moral law is like a mirror revealing sin for what it is (Rom 3:20; 7:7); its second use is like a bridle restraining sinful behavior for fear of punishment (Gal 3:23–24; 1 Tim 1:9–11); and its third use is like a lamp revealing the path of righteousness to those wishing to please God and obey him (Ps 119:105; Prov 6:23).[48]

- There is Trinitarian ordering in three classifications of Old Testament Scripture, which are the Law (תּוֹרָה, *tôrāh*), consisting of the books of Moses; the Prophets (נְבִיאִם, *neḇî'îm*), consisting of all the prophets; and the Writings, (כְּתוּבִים, *keṯûḇîm*) consisting of the rest which, in the Jewish order, started with the book of Psalms.[49] This threefold division of what Rabbis call the Tanakh (תַּנַךְ, *tanak*) was confirmed and used by Jesus in Luke 24:44.[50]

- There is Trinitarian ordering in three components of the moral self. While Evangelicals do not all agree,[51] I am convinced that in 1 Thessalonians 5:23, God reveals the moral self has three components: a spiritual self (τὸ πνεῦμα, *to pneuma*), a mental self (ἡ

"Justification, Sanctification, Glorification," *Youtube*, uploaded September 12, 2010, *www.youtube.com /watch?v=ye-5h5FapKg.*

[47] Calvin, *Institutes*, 2.7.6.

[48] Calvin, 2.7.6–12. Martin Luther considered uses (functions) of God's moral law prior to Calvin but never saw what Calvin identified as its third use (function). See Martin Luther, *A Commentary on St. Paul's Epistle to the Galatians*, ed. Philip S. Watson (London: T&T Clark, 1952), 298–302. Readers should note that Luther's first use (function) aligns with Calvin's second, and Luther's second use (function) aligns with Calvin's first. Although Calvin surpassed Luther by identifying a third use (function) of moral law, he was not alone in doing so because Melanchthon did as well. See Philipp Melanchthon, *Commonplaces*, ed. H. Engelland, in *A Selection of Melanchthon's Works*, ed. R. Stupperich (1535 and later editions), II.i.122.

[49] *Biblia Rabbinica* or *The Rabbinic Bible*, Felix Pratenis, ed. (Venice: Daniel Bomberg, 1516–1517). Also Mordochai ben-Tziyyon, "The 24 Books of the Hebrew Scriptures" (Jerusalem: University of Ha'ivrit), http://mordochai.tripod.com/tanach.html#top.

[50] In Luke 24:44, Jesus refers to "the Law of Moses, the Prophets, and the Psalms," here naming the first book in the third Rabbinic division in place of what is otherwise referred to as "the Writings" (כְּתוּבִים, *keṯûḇîm*).

[51] To review this debate, see Grudem, *Systematic Theology*, 472–78; and Erickson, *Christian Theology*, 524–27.

ψυχὴ, *hē psuchē*), and a physical self (τὸ σῶμα, *to sōma*).[52] Evangelicals who do not accept this believe when the Bible refers to mental (ἡ ψυχὴ) and spiritual (τὸ πνεῦμα) selves, it uses two terms for a single thing that cannot be divided. But that overlooks Hebrews 4:12, which says these are things the Word of God is able to separate the way a "double-edged sword" is able to separate "joints and marrow."

- There is Trinitarian ordering in three ways we must love God. God revealed through Moses, and then Jesus reaffirmed, that we are to "love the Lord your God with all your heart, with all your soul, and with all your strength" (Deut 6:5) or "mind" (Matt 22:37).[53]

- There is Trinitarian ordering in three factors sustaining ethical life, which are that it must come "from a pure heart, a good conscience, and a sincere faith" (1 Tim 1:5).

- There is Trinitarian ordering in three parts to the moral mission of the Holy Spirit. Jesus, before going to the cross, explained the future mission of the Holy Spirit, which would be to "convict the world about sin, righteousness, and judgment" (John 16:8–11). This meant it would be the role of the Holy Spirit to remind the world: (1) of what makes things ethically wrong, (2) of what makes things ethically right, and (3) of the difference it makes in the end.

- There is Trinitarian ordering in three ways the Devil tried to pervert Jesus Christ. After Christ fasted forty days and forty nights in the wilderness, the Devil tempted him in three ways: (1) to satisfy the flesh separate from his Father, (2) to interpret Scripture separate from his Father, and (3) to pursue his mission separate from his

---

[52] The position taken here is called "trichotomy," and the opposing positions are that human selves have two parts, which is a view called "dichotomy," or that human selves have only one element, which is a view called "monism." Evangelical theologians either hold to trichotomy or dichotomy, while monism lies outside the realm of Evangelical thought. For a defense of trichotomy, see Franz Delitzsch, *A System of Biblical Psychology*, trans. R. E. Wallis, 2nd ed. (Grand Rapids: Baker, 1966) and Anthony A. Hoekema, *Created in God's Image* (Grand Rapids: Eerdmans, 1994).

[53] Jesus was discussing interpretation of the Mosaic law with a legal expert, and in quoting Deuteronomy 6:5, Jesus would have spoken the Hebrew word מְאֹד (*mᵉʾōḏ*), meaning "strength" or "driving focus." Matthew translates what he heard Jesus say using the Greek word διανοία (*dianoia*), which means "mind" but also "intellectual focus" (Matt 22:37). Furthermore, when the expert in Mosaic law then answered a question Jesus posed back to him, Luke suggests he may have responded using two Greek words (ἰσχύϊ, or *ischui*, and διανοία, or *dianoia*) to more accurately express the broader range of meaning conveyed by the Hebrew text under discussion (Luke 10:27).

Father (Matt 4:1–11; Luke 4:1–13). The Devil is not an ethical role model, but the strategy by which the Devil tried to pervert Christ reveals (in reverse) what is needed to secure and maintain ethical fidelity, which is to satisfy appetites, interpret Scripture, and fulfill God's mission only on God's terms and not our own.

• There is Trinitarian ordering in three things that turn men away from loving God, which are the lust of the flesh, the lust of the eyes, and the pride of life (1 John 2:16).

Trinitarian Ordering in Theological Ethics

	The PERSON of God— sets the normative facet—defines who is in charge	The PEOPLE of God— sets the relational facet—defines our identity	The PLACE of God— sets the directional facet—defines our goal
The Ordering of OT Ethics Discussed by Christopher Wright in *Old Testament Ethics for the People of God*	**God** The "imitation/ conformity" aspect	**Israel** The "corporate/ social" aspect	**Land** The "ruling/ purposive" aspect
The Ordering of Ethics by Jesus Discussed by R. E. O. White in *Biblical Ethics*	**Discipleship** The "imitation/ conformity" aspect	**Family of God** The "corporate/ social" aspect	**Kingdom of God** The "ruling/ purposive" aspect
The Ordering of Ethics by Paul Discussed by Richard Hays in *The Moral Vision of the New Testament*	**Cross** The "imitation/ conformity" aspect	**Community** The "corporate/ social" aspect	**New Creation** The "ruling/ purposive" aspect
The Ordering of Revealed Ethics Overall	**Holiness** The "imitation/ conformity" aspect	**Love** The "corporate/ social" aspect	**Glory** The "ruling/ purposive" aspect

I have two reasons for listing all these triads. The first is to underscore how many triads there are in God's ordering of ethical reality, and the second is to underscore the question, "Why?" Why should there be so many triads in God's ordering of reality? God never does anything without purpose, so we cannot suppose there is no reason at all. Something repeated to this extent cannot be arbitrary, incidental, or insignificant. It cannot be coincidental. The presence of so many triadic structures embedded in moral revelation reflect something deeper, something very theologically and ethically significant, and that leads me to suppose it must connect with the Trinitarian nature of God himself. It must be that a "Trinitarian principle" runs through God's ethical ordering of reality because God is Trinitarian. It must be that God's ethical ordering of reality aligns not only with his holiness but with his Trinitarian nature as well.

Creation as a Theme in Theological Ethics

The business of theological ethics is to analyze God's ethical ordering of reality, and most theologians understand this ethical ordering in terms of four structural themes—"creation," "sin," "redemption," and "consummation." We will look now at each of these, starting with the theme of creation. The doctrine of creation is important because it establishes where we come from, why we exist, and what O'Donovan refers to as "the reality of a divinely-given order of things in which human nature is located."[54] By the doctrine of creation, we know that everything exists under the ordering rule of God and there is nothing real outside that reality. It is that by which we know any ordering at all relates to God and is subject to God and that we are creatures made to align with God's character, live by his rules, and pursue his purposes.

Creation of the space-time-material universe by God means the reality in which we exist is neither random nor meaningless and is already ordered according to structures and values by which we are defined, measured, and judged, whether we like it or not. The term *creation* not only refers to the raw material of which things are composed but also supposes a reason for everything, a purpose for which everything was made, a goal toward which everything is headed, and a principle by which everything holds together and works as it does (Col 1:16–17). There is balance, relationship, intricacy, and beauty to the way things fit together

---

[54] O'Donovan, *Resurrection and Moral Order*, 17.

and work as they do, and this is ethically significant because living within God's ordering of creation is ethically good, and opposing it is ethically bad.

The doctrine of creation informs theological ethics in four ways.[55] First, it tells us we are made rational and moral beings able to understand and respond to what our Creator commands and are thus obligated to obey his rules and fulfill his purposes. Second, it tells us we are made to serve a responsible role under our Creator and are thus obligated to exercise dominion over the rest of creation. Third, it tells us we are made social and relational beings able to love and be loved and are thus obligated to love our Creator and to love everything else in ways that harmonize with loving him. Fourth, it tells us we are made embodied spirits able to coordinate material life with spiritual life and are thus obligated to seek fulfillment by relating to and enjoying our Creator in a fashion transcending how we relate to everything else, and this fourth component includes understanding that we are made to worship our Creator, can be fulfilled no other way, and are obligated to be faithful to him in all we do, say, think, or desire.

The command of God as Creator and the obedience we owe him as creatures are together linked to the notion of divine likeness called the *imago Dei*, a doctrine within the general doctrine of creation that sets revelational ethics (both Jewish and Christian) apart from every other ethical system or tradition. That is because living worthy lives depends on knowing from whence we are (the basis of our own reality), and the Word of God reveals we are what we are only because God made us beings "in the image of God" (Gen 1:27; 5:1; 9:6). What distinguishes the ethical value of human life from everything else in the space-time-material universe is the *imago Dei*, not the Stoic notion of men each possessing pieces of God,[56] not Aristotle's notion of reason separating men from animals,[57] and not Kant's notion of having good will.[58] These notions are each theologically deficient because, while they distinguish men from nature, they do not distinguish men from God and so do not fit with God saying, "As

---

[55] I am indebted here to the work of John Stott. See Stott, *Issues*, 62.

[56] Epictetus, Ἐπικτήτοθ διατριβαί (*Discourses of Epictetus*), bk. II, ch. 8 (Loeb Classical Library, vol. I, 263).

[57] Aristotle, Τῶν περὶ ζῷα ἱστοριῶν (*History of Animals*), 2.1–2.

[58] Immanuel Kant, *Groundwork for the Metaphysics of Morals* (1785), ak. 4:393. Also Immanuel Kant, *Groundwork for the Metaphysics of Morals*, ed. and trans. Allen W. Wood (New Haven, CT: Yale, 2002), 9.

heaven is higher than earth, so my ways are higher than your ways, and my thoughts than your thoughts" (Isa 55:8–9).

While everyone knows it is very important, theologians are divided on how to interpret the *imago Dei*, with some identifying it with capacities (like reason, conscience, or freedom), some with functions (like dominion, cultivation, or generation), and some with the sort of relationship God designed men to have with himself. I prefer a version of the relational view first argued by Augustine and then affirmed by others like Barth, Ramsey, Thielicke, and O'Donovan.[59] That is, I think the *imago Dei* is more something we reflect like an image seen in a mirror than a capacity or function. It is something the presence of which is derivative and ever depends on relating to God—not merely as creatures but as beings positioned to reflect God's nature and character to the rest of creation.

The *imago Dei* inheres in every human to the same degree regardless of wealth, health, or maturity, but it can be clouded or distorted. It uses capacities like reason (Aristotle) and good will (Kant). But it does not consist of these capacities because it remains when such capacities are diminished, or even absent, as with those with learning disabilities or just forming in the womb. For this reason, Augustine said, "The image and likeness of God [in man] . . . is not preserved except it be in relation to Him by whom it is impressed."[60] As a reflection is more than just a matter of distance and direction but includes something seen, so the *imago Dei* involves something seen in us caused by the position we have before God but that is more than positioning alone. Although related to capacities and functions, it is more than either. Capacities enable and functions direct, but the *imago Dei* also grounds the valuing of human life in a way that stays the same however weak we become or poorly we perform. As light shines the same on multiple mirrors even though what is seen varies a great deal, so the ethical value of human life from creation comes from something that shines the same on all regardless of how well or poorly it is reflected.

The Bible refers to both an old and a new creation (Isa 65:17; 66:22; Rom 8:19–21; 2 Pet 3:10; 3:13; Rev 21:1) and to both an old man perverted by sin and a new man (Eph 4:24;

---

[59] For summaries of these different views, see Erickson, *Christian Theology*, 498–510; Ramsey, *Basic Christian Ethics*, 250–64; Thielicke, *Theological Ethics*, 147–70; and R. Hugh McLean, *In His Image: The Reflection of God in You* (Greenville, SC: The Other Hand Ministry, 2013).

[60] Augustine, *On the Trinity*, XII, 11.

2 Cor 5:17) predestined to conform to the likeness of Christ (Rom 8:29; 1 Cor 15:49; 2 Cor 3:18; Col 3:9–10; 1 John 3:2). Here, I think we should heed O'Donovan, who warns the old and new creations must not be viewed as "polarized options."[61] It is not a case of replacing one thing with something completely different but rather of fixing something damaged in a way that fulfills something started but left unfinished. God's new creation in and through Christ does not exclude his original ordering of creation but rather enables us to apprehend the ordering for which we were made not only as it is but also as it will be. We know this for two reasons: first, because God's new creation reaffirms the old and second, because the old aims toward the new. But then we also know that ethical reality cannot change because God's character and goals remain constant (Num 23:19; Ps 102:27; Mal 3:6; Heb 13:8; Jas 1:17). In fact, the old and new creations operate on a single ethic and differ only in setting and circumstance. The image (ethical likeness) of God revealed in Christ and marking his new creation harkens back to God's original creation, and the ethical likeness of God in which man was originally created points toward and is fulfilled in God's new creation achieved through Christ as intended all along.

Sin as a Theme in Theological Ethics

The second structural theme used to analyze God's ethical ordering of reality concerns understanding we are sinners under righteous condemnation. The doctrine of sin covers what God reveals to be ethically wrong and subject to judgment. It deals with the negative side of ethical truth and explains why we have moral problems, not just with others but within ourselves, and not just in this world but beyond it with God. The one who made us is judging all that we do, say, think, and desire. Our Creator is our Judge.

Sin alienates man from God, which means it alienates us from the origin, measure, and ground of all good. For this reason, sin also distorts our own natural ability to perceive what is good, even in our own best interest. It is the one most fundamental problem from which all others arise, and to deal with it, we first must admit that we have a problem and then come to view it properly. The greatest ethical problem we have is our own fallen nature, not external circumstances. As Ellul points out, this deepest of ethical problems is not "merely a kind of

---

[61] O'Donovan, *Resurrection and Moral Order*, 19.

external condition which is added to a good nature" but one that "applies to the totality of man's being and existence."[62] We have become slaves to sin alienated from ethical perfection, not by finitude but by rebellion, and we are indeed slaves to sin, not because we are failing to try hard enough to break free of sin, but because we do not want to. Our passions cling to corruption over purity.

We are made in God's image but are spiritually and ethically fallen. Human sentiments have been distorted, and human character has become self-centered and defensive. Claims of ethical autonomy are rooted in self-deluded rebellion against the one being on whom all existence depends. But despite such claims, we are not ethically autonomous. As Henry observes, even though sin alienates man from God,

> He remains morally accountable in sin. He does not, even at his worst, degenerate to a state of animalism in which all ethical distinctions are lost. But man is a sinner who [in this state] erects spurious alternatives to the Divine moral law which enable him in self-delusion to "justify himself" by works. Or he raises humanistic standards for himself while the genuine claim of the Divine is dismissed as myth. Man demonstrates his sinfulness by this thought and behavior. But he is not done with ethics nor with God.[63]

We, individually and as a whole humanity, now define ethical goodness over and against God rather than under and aligned with God. We no longer love God with our whole being but have become hostile, viewing him as enemy, not as friend.

Thus, God promulgates law by which he informs us he is in charge and we are not. God's law overcomes human ignorance by clarifying directions and standards, but it also reveals we are sinners "because the knowledge of sin comes through the law" (Rom 3:20). God's law goes beyond merely establishing the existence of ethical authority and what that authority requires to also reveal we are in grave peril. We are creatures under God's ethical authority who are guilty of usurping his administration of good and evil. We are objects of God's righteous wrath condemned by his judgment with no hope of saving ourselves. For those being judged,

---

[62] Ellul, *The Ethics of Freedom*, 47.
[63] Henry, *Personal Ethics*, 150.

condemnation by God magnifies his ethical perfection while stressing the inadequacy of all efforts to justify ourselves.

For Frame, God's judgment is what shows "that God will not be mocked, that his standards will prevail."[64] For Barth it is what forces all to realize "every moment of life . . . is measured and judged and set under an eternal determination."[65] For Thielicke, God's law in a fallen world "corresponds to man as sinner" just as God's "command of creation corresponds to the *imago Dei*."[66] Niebuhr links the doctrine of creation to the doctrine of sin, saying, "The dominant attitudes of prophetic faith are gratitude and contrition; gratitude for Creation and contrition before judgment; or in other words, confidence that life is good in spite of its evil and that it is evil in spite of its good."[67]

Redemption as a Theme in Theological Ethics

The third structural theme used to analyze God's ethical ordering of reality concerns changing doomed sinners into beloved children. While the doctrine of creation identifies the nature and source of ethical authority and the doctrine of sin reveals the ethical problem we have, the doctrine of redemption deals with solving that ethical problem. It reveals God is not only Creator and Judge but Savior, and it includes other constituent doctrines such as the gospel, atonement, regeneration, and adoption.

The Christian gospel proclaims to sinners doomed by God's justice a way they may escape deserved punishment and enter a favorable relationship with the very one by whom they are condemned. The gospel of Jesus Christ opposes what God's law demands, not by replacing it with a different ethic but by overcoming the inability of fallen humanity to meet God's standards (Acts 13:39; Rom 8:3–4). Those who repent are no longer condemned because another pays their debt. The ethics of God applies to everyone alike. No one is exempt. His moral law is universal. But God spares believers and does not spare unbelievers because for the one, their sin is atoned, while for the other, it is not.

---

[64] Frame, *Doctrine of the Christian Life*, 274.
[65] Barth, *Ethics*, 89.
[66] Thielicke, *Theological Ethics*, 151.
[67] Niebuhr, *An Interpretation of Christian Ethics*, 64.

Atoning for sin is what enables God to forgive those who repent without compromising his justice or his holiness. The debt owed for falling short of God's perfection is paid by a sinless substitute who bears the penalty in place of those who deserve it (2 Cor 5:21). The nineteenth century theologian Johannes Ebrard explained this, saying, "Guilt . . . can be removed only by punishment. Either the sinner himself must bear the punishment, or a substitute must be provided to assume the guilt, and bear the punishment, and thus freedom from guilt, or righteousness, is secured for the offender."[68] The penalty we deserve was paid by Christ (Rom 6:23). This does not set aside the verdict against evil but applies it. Redemption does not change ethical reality but rather preserves God's righteousness in a way that allows him to save by grace those unable to save themselves (Eph 2:8–9).

God's redemption offers good news achieved by atonement but also goes beyond just sparing the punishment sinners deserve. It also regenerates. Sinners are "born again" (John 3:3, 7), made "a new creation" (2 Cor 5:17), and morally transformed with power to grow in conformity with the character of God. Here, I agree with Henry, who says,

> Regeneration imparts to man a new character, in which God stands at the center of his motives, decisions, and acts. It does not give him a new metaphysical substance. Man did not cease to be man in the fall, nor does he become a superman through redemption. He becomes partaker of the Divine nature (2 Pet. 1:4), not by an infusion of the essence of God . . . but by living a spiritual and moral life in organic union with Christ.[69]

Yet, even regeneration does not exhaust the good news, for beyond just being forgiven and transformed, former rebels will be adopted. They not only are made new creatures but also are raised to relational favor and intimacy with God at a level surpassing everything else in all of creation (Ps 8:4–6; Eph 2:6–7). Former enemies become children of God (1 John 3:1). Former rebels become brothers and sisters of Christ (Heb 2:11). In justification, God gives right standing before his law. In regeneration, God transforms human nature. But in adoption, God makes us family: "When the time came to completion, God sent his Son, born of a

---

[68] Translated from Johannes Heinrich August Ebrard, *Christian Dogmatics*, vol. 2 (Königsbert: Unzer, 1852), §401, 159.

[69] Ebrard, 389.

woman, born under the law, to redeem those under the law, so that we might receive *adoption as sons*" (Gal 4:4–5, emphasis mine).

Consummation as a Theme in Theological Ethics

The fourth structural theme used to analyze God's ordering of ethical reality concerns realizing that forgiven sinners, made children of God, also become "coheirs with Christ" (Rom 8:17) who someday will rule with him in a kingdom that lasts forever (Luke 1:33) and includes "all things in every way" (Eph 1:22–23). The doctrine of consummation is important because it identifies the ethical destination toward which all things are directed.[70] As the doctrine of creation establishes the source and nature of ethical authority, the doctrine of sin establishes the source of ethical wrong, and the doctrine of redemption establishes how ethical wrong can be corrected, so the doctrine of consummation establishes the ultimate end and purpose of ethical existence. The ethics of God is fixed but not static. It does not change but has direction. It moves toward a goal, aims toward objectives, and seeks specified results. God is not only Creator, Judge, and Savior, but also Benefactor.

At conversion, God immediately credits saved sinners with the righteousness of Christ, and yet it is clear that neither the world as it is nor we ourselves are all that we should be. But that will change. One day all things will be pure and perfect. "We wait for the new heavens and a new earth, where *righteousness* will dwell" (2 Pet 3:13, emphasis mine), and when that day comes, sinners perfected through Christ will receive a glorious inheritance (Eph 1:18; Col 1:12) that includes not just riches in heaven (1 Pet 1:3) but a new earth (Matt 5:5; Rev 21:1–7), and not just a new earth but a completely renewed creation as well (Rom 8:19–21; 2 Pet 3:12–13). We will be perfect people, living in perfect community, in a perfect world:

---

[70] Here, I use consummation only to refer to the final ethical state toward which all things are headed, including ourselves. This means I agree with Stott (*Issues*, 64) and Hollinger (*Choosing the Good*, 83–86) and do not agree with Frame, who treats consummation as equivalent to the eschaton as a whole, claiming it consists of the return of Christ and the final judgment, as well as to the eternal state (*Doctrine of the Christian Life*, 279). Etymologically, the word refers to perfection or completion. That is, it refers to a final state, which generally does not include events or conditions leading up to but not part of the finally perfected state itself.

"When he appears, *we will be like him*" (1 John 3:2, emphasis mine). A "crown of righteousness" will be given "to all those who have loved his appearing" (2 Tim 4:8), "the creation itself will . . . be set free from the bondage to decay" (Rom 8:21), and "*the righteous* will shine like the sun in their Father's kingdom" (Matt 13:43, emphasis mine).

In and through the resurrection of Jesus Christ, "humanity is elevated to that which it has never enjoyed before, the seat at God's right hand which belongs to the Son,"[71] and in our final state we will reign with Christ forever (Eph 2:6–7); "The holy ones of the Most High will receive the kingdom and possess it forever, yes, forever and ever" (Dan 7:18); "If we endure, we will also reign with him" (2 Tim 2:12). Those redeemed by the Lamb "will reign forever and ever" (Rev 22:5), and coheirs seated with Christ in his glory (Rom 8:16–17; Eph 2:6; Col 3:1) will share "authority over the nations" (Rev 2:26) and even judge angels (1 Cor 6:3). Humans will become what we were made for. We will assume lordship of the cosmos (under Christ) and thus fulfill a role we could not realize while alienated from God (Col 1:21) and spiritually dead in "trespasses and sins" (Eph 2:1; see also Col 2:13).[72]

This will fulfill, and not negate, the ethics of God. But in what sense will the ethics of God be fulfilled? We will reign with Christ to be sure, but what will that achieve? Theologians have answered this in two ways: ultimate peace and ultimate freedom. Looking toward our perfect future, God promised that of Christ's "government and of *peace* there will be no end" (Isa 9:7, ESV, emphasis mine) and "the result of righteousness will be *peace . . .* forever" (Isa 32:17, emphasis mine). We have been promised that "the *peace* of God, which surpasses all understanding, will guard your hearts and minds in Christ Jesus" (Phil 4:7, emphasis mine), which in our perfection will last forever. "Perfect *peace*" (Isa 26:3, emphasis mine) will arrive "in days to come" when "Israel will blossom and bloom and fill the whole world with fruit" (Isa 27:6). This is so worth anticipating that some theologians, impatient to escape present circumstances, are tempted to misinterpret God's promise. Peace with God is reduced to peace with men, ultimate peace in future circumstances is confused with present reality, spiritual tranquility is confused with political tranquility, and sinless conditions are treated as an achievement sinners can reach on their own—and not just individually but perhaps

---

[71] O'Donovan, *Resurrection and Moral Order*, 57.

[72] O'Donovan, 54.

worldwide.[73] At this point, most Evangelicals agree with Pannenberg, who says, "Truthfulness requires us to acknowledge that the peace of God about which the New Testament speaks is not identical with world peace."[74] While peace on earth must be distinguished from peace with God, neither are they unrelated. A time will come when they merge, but that will not occur before Christ inaugurates the political rule of God "on earth as it is in heaven" (Matt 6:10). When that happens, perfect peace on earth no longer will be just a vision of things to come. When all sin is erased, the distinction separating present circumstances from the future will be erased as well. Heaven will descend (Rev 21:2) and Christ will reign on a throne located with his people on earth (Ezek 37:27–28, 43:7; Rev 21:3, 22:3).

The other feature that will characterize our consummated state is freedom. We look forward, not only to ethically perfect relationships, but to perfect freedom of ethical action as well. We will be free to flourish as the majestic beings God always had in mind. We will be most truly fulfilled, most truly complete, and most truly ourselves. God created us to be ethically free in an ethically perfect world, but then sin interfered. When we are perfected in a perfect world, we will be back in circumstances for which we were designed and then will be freer than ever before. We will be free to be our own true selves, free to interact with everything and everyone as intended, and because our desires will be free of corruption, we also will be ethically free to do all we most desire.

Van Til says the ethical freedom for which Christians hope "implies that man's freedom consists of doing of his own accord the will of God."[75] Ellul explains such freedom is not license but rather is freedom to do as we should,[76] and Henry adds, "Regenerate man becomes an agent of the Divine will and by his acts of obedience . . . shares creatively in the unfolding plan of God for the age of grace."[77] Lastly, we can expect the ethical freedom anticipated in our

---

[73] Theologians on this path include John Howard Yoder, Stanley Hauerwas, Richard Hays, and Willard Swartley. See Yoder, *The Politics of Jesus* (Grand Rapids: Eerdmans, 1972), *The Christian Witness to the State*, and *The War of the Lamb*; Hauerwas, *The Peaceable Kingdom*; Hays, *Moral Vision*, and Swartley, *Covenant of Peace*.

[74] Pannenberg, *Ethics*, 151.

[75] Van Til, *Theistic Ethics*, 48.

[76] Ellul, *The Ethics of Freedom*, 198.

[77] Henry, *Personal Ethics*, 168.

consummated state to grow and keep on growing forever—it will not be boring or static—and that is because

> if man . . . develops his swiftness and stability of reaction to the will of God, he develops momentum for the doing of the will of God. . . . [Thus] the capacity for doing more for the realization of the kingdom of God would be increased, and therewith man would be given an ever new freedom to do the will of God in areas formerly unknown to him. He [then] would be free indeed.[78]

The Already-and-Not-Yet in Theological Ethics

As Christians, we understand that, while a perfect world is coming, it has not yet arrived. Jesus announced the kingdom of God "has come near" (Matt 4:17; 10:7; Mark 1:15; Luke 10:9) and already "is in your midst" (Luke 17:21). But its perfection remains future (Matt 6:10; Luke 22:18; 1 Cor 15:25). God's ethical rule already governs believers but will not impose social ideals until Jesus reigns on a visible throne in Jerusalem. This sets up an already-and-not-yet tension in the way Christians view ethics. It sets up what Ellul calls an "inextricable and insoluble paradox" formed by "the tension between the Already and the Not Yet, between the new life which has already been given and the resurrection which we await with sure and certain hope, between salvation by grace and working out our salvation with fear and trembling."[79]

For now, we live in a tension that cannot be resolved either by refusing to cooperate with anything less than perfection here and now or by insisting all is hopeless and just waiting for the end of history. Neither extreme is faithful to the Word of God, and both are simplistic. Christ did not pray that the Father should take us "out of the world" (John 17:15) but only that he protect us from "the evil one" (John 17:15) in fallen surroundings. We are not "of the world" yet are sent "into the world" (John 17:16, 18). And the reverse holds as well, for although we are left in corrupt surroundings, neither are we to favor or ignore them. We struggle against sin (Heb 12:4) but must accept its continuing power and presence in the world.

---

[78] Van Til, *Theistic Ethics*, 50.
[79] Ellul, *The Ethics of Freedom*, 11.

Explaining this, Gilbert Meilaender observes that Christian ethics involves an inescapable tension between the demands of the gospel and the limits of human finitude and fallenness. We must seek God's kingdom here and now and yet must realize that perfect peace and justice are beyond human ability.[80] We are redeemed for a community transcending nature and history but must, for now, live in a world filled with sin. Because we are called to love others (and not just for self-interest), Christians try to better social conditions, but we must not demand social perfection. We address social problems but never expect to overcome them entirely. Because of this, Meilaender says, "tensions created by that duality in our nature are the stuff of much that is most troubling in the moral life."[81]

God's ethical standards never change because God never changes (Heb 13:8; Jas 1:17). But the manner in which the perfect world for which Christians hope affects human relationships is different now than will be the case after "the first heaven and the first earth" pass away (Rev 21:1). Fallen human nature, and not merely limited resources, lack of political will, or inadequate planning, presently limits the degree to which social interactions can be improved in ways that will not pertain after Christ banishes all sin and only sinless beings remain (Rev 21:5–8). In saying Christian theological ethics is already-and-not-yet, we are not saying God in the future will shift from one ethic to another, but rather circumstances will change affecting the manner in which we apply the same unchanging ethic as governs life now. New circumstances will remove limits that currently prevent achieving social ideals for which we already hope.

The already-and-not-yet in theological ethics must not be confused with the twentieth century interim-ethics school associated with Johannes Weiss and Albert Schweitzer. This school of thought claimed the ethics of Jesus was meant only for a very brief period of end-of-the-world transition to a perfect universe, never meant for life in the world as it is, and proven invalid when the world did not end in a matter of months. Interim-ethics theologians claimed Jesus misread history and did not offer ethical teaching meant to operate in the world as it is.

---

[80] Gilbert Meilaender, *Faith and Faithfulness: Basic Themes in Christian Ethics* (Notre Dame, IN: University of Notre Dame, 1991), 127, 138.

[81] Gilbert Meilaender, *The Limits of Love: Some Theological Explorations* (University Park, PA: Pennsylvania State University, 1987), 9.

For them, ethics in the present old world and coming new world could not be the same,[82] but the Bible does not set God's ethics for now in opposition to God's ethics to come.

We live between a present age and an age to come (Mark 10:30; Eph 2:7) but not between different ethical orders involving different sources of authority, standards of good and evil, paths to ethical recovery, or views of perfection. We do not criticize the interim-ethics school of thought for affirming the eschatological theme in the ethics of Jesus, for thinking this made his teaching invalid, or for supposing Jesus misinterpreted history. Instead, writes Henry, we should say, "The whole of Christ's ethics is eschatological in the sense that it has final judgment as its premise. And the whole is non-eschatological in the sense that its validity is not suspended at any point upon the immediate end of the historical order."[83]

The already-and-not-yet nature of biblically grounded theological ethics leads to asking two important questions, both having to do with living by an ethical ordering that will not be perfectly realized until Christ returns. The first asks how we should live in a fallen world that cannot reach perfection while sin remains, and the second asks how perfections that cannot be reached while sin remains should nevertheless make a difference to life in the world before Christ returns. Bonhoeffer addressed the first and Niebuhr addressed the second.

The Relevance of the Penultimate in Theological Ethics

As Hitler was rising to power in prewar Germany, Bonhoeffer thought deeply about the way present circumstances affect Christian hope for perfect circumstances that will not be fully realized until Jesus returns, and he used the term *penultimate* to distinguish present possibilities from what God promises ultimately will be realized in the future. The penultimate, he said, "is everything that precedes the ultimate."[84] It is what leads up to God's perfect future

---

[82] For Johannes Weiss, see *Jesus' Proclamation of the Kingdom of God*, trans. and ed. Richard H. Hiers and D. Larrimore Holland (Philadelphia: Fortress, 1971). For Albert Schweitzer, see *The Quest for the Historical Jesus* (New York: Macmillan, 1968) and *The Mystery of the Kingdom of God: the Secret of Jesus' Messiahship and Passion* (London: Adam and C. Black, 1950). For criticism of the interim ethic movement, see J. I. H. McDonald, *Biblical Interpretation and Christian Ethics* (Cambridge: University of Cambridge, 1993), 75–95; and Henry, *Personal Ethics*, 292–95.

[83] Henry, *Personal Ethics*, 295.

[84] Bonhoeffer, *Ethics*, 133.

in the time between receiving the promise and before it arrives—between inaugurating the kingdom of God internally within individual hearts and its social-political-economic arrival in external fullness—between swearing allegiance to God among sinners in a fallen world and celebrating the rule of God among saints in a sinless world.

"As for the question before the last," Bonhoeffer says, "the Christian life means neither a destruction nor a sanctioning of the penultimate."[85] The penultimate is not destroyed because it is the best we can do for now—hungry people need feeding, poor people need assisting, wicked people need punishing, and weak people need defending. But in a perfect world, there will be no hunger, poverty, wickedness, or insecurity, and when perfection arrives, we will discard ethically penultimate efforts to serve the needy, warn the foolish, and restrain evildoers. This difference is not a question of shifting from one ethic to another, but of a fallen world giving way to a sinless world. For now, economics must presume limited resources, but then resources will be limitless. For now, justice demands retribution, but then retribution will be irrelevant. For now, security requires strong defenses, but then defenses will not be needed. For now, freedom magnifies risk, but then freedom will grow with no risk at all.

The difference between the ethically penultimate and ethically ultimate is not a question of shifting from one ethic to another but of replacing present circumstances with transformed circumstances (2 Pet 3:13; Rev 21:1). And it is as inconsistent with the ethics of God to ignore how sin limits possibilities in the present world as it would be to assume the presence and power of sin in the world to come. Bonhoeffer cautioned that tension between what is and what is hoped for cannot be resolved except through Christ: "In Him alone lies the solution for the problem of the relation between the ultimate and the penultimate."[86] Christ transforms sinners in the world as it is (2 Cor 5:17), but he will not replace our fallen world with a new and ethically perfect world until he comes again (2 Pet 3:13).

The Relevance of Impossible Ideals in Theological Ethics

Niebuhr considered the other question following from the already-and-not-yet nature of God's ethical ordering. If the ethically ultimate is future and nothing in the present world is

---

[85] Bonhoeffer, 132.
[86] Bonhoeffer, 130.

or can be ethically perfect, how then can the ethically ultimate make any difference here and now? Would it not then be irrelevant? But, since God never changes, that means the ethic he applies in the future must apply now, in which case there must be some way by which presently impossible ideals make a difference in the world as it is. Niebuhr maintained that what Christians believe to be ultimately future and presently impossible is nevertheless relevant here and now, and he did this without denying fallen human nature, without ignoring the present power of sin, and without divorcing ethics now from ethics in the world to come. For this, Niebuhr discussed a notion he called the relevance of the "impossible possibility."

"There is," Niebuhr said, "no problem of history and no point in society from which one may not observe that the same man who touches the fringes of the infinite in his moral life remains imbedded in finiteness, that he increases the evil in his life if he tries to overcome it without regard to his limitations," and so, he thought, "it is as important to know what is impossible as what is possible in the moral demands under which all human beings stand."[87] He argued it is essential for sinful men and women, no matter how much they long for perfection, to realize they cannot reach complete perfection of anything here and now and only make things worse by imagining they might possibly produce perfect conditions given enough power over others. Two reasons make reaching perfect conditions impossible in the present world, first because men are finite (we are not all-knowing or all-powerful) and second because human nature is morally compromised (we are not perfectly virtuous). Even though Christians are credited with the perfection of Christ, we are not as yet fully conformed to his character, and we struggle with a divided nature (Rom 7:18–24). We look forward to perfection, but we remain sinners compromised by a fallen nature in a fallen world.

To this point, Niebuhr says nothing more than Bonhoeffer, but he went on to criticize those tempted to use the impossibility of achieving perfections here and now to excuse accommodating evil, to stop resisting corruption, or to make no effort toward improving social conditions.[88] Niebuhr pointed out that, even though ideal conditions cannot be reached

---

[87] Niebuhr, *Interpretation of Christian Ethics*, 83.

[88] I do not agree with Hollinger's claim that Niebuhr divorced the ethics of Jesus from application to social ethics. Although Niebuhr warns against perfectionist expectations that overlook the compromised state of human nature, he takes a position quite contrary to Hollinger's interpretation of his thought. Hollinger misjudges Niebuhr by mistaking a position Niebuhr refutes for one he defends. Hollinger quotes Niebuhr saying, "Surely this (the ethics of Jesus) is not an ethic which can give us

among sinners in a fallen world, one can always do better. He held, "The ideal in its perfect form lies beyond the capacities of human nature" but also insisted "no absolute limit can be placed upon the degree to which human society may yet approximate the ideal."[89] Ethical ideals may be impossible to reach in this life, but we must try to approximate them by improving what we can in imperfect circumstances. Reaching ethical ideals in their perfection awaits a new and perfect world, but they are relevant now by serving as guides that direct and motivate efforts to make things better than they are—both in regard to improving personal discipline despite still struggling against a sinful nature and improving social conditions in a fallen world filled with sinners.

Conclusion

This chapter introduced readers to theological ethics as a subcategory within the larger field of Christian ethics and explained how theological ethics builds on but also goes beyond the range of biblical ethics by using God-given reason to analyze the nature, meaning, organizational themes, and ultimate aim of ethical truth ordered by the Word of God. We learned how Christian ethics is rooted in the nature, plans, and purposes of the Triune God, who defines reality and created all things. This makes theological ethics both dogmatic and theocentric. But truth revealed by God must be interpreted, and that requires adopting a suitable method for doing so. We reviewed how this has been debated and concluded that, from a theological perspective, ethical reality is framed by God's intention to center the ordering of all things in heaven and earth on Christ and what was achieved through the resurrection of Jesus Christ from the dead. Thus, in the end, theological ethics is not just theocentric but Christocentric and not just Christocentric but resurrectionally transformative.

---

specific guidance in the detailed problems of social morality" (Hollinger, *Choosing the Good*, 206–7; quoting Niebuhr, *Interpretation of Christian Ethics*, 31). But at the place Hollinger quotes him, Niebuhr is paraphrasing Karl Barth on something with which Niebuhr himself disagrees because, pace Barth, Niebuhr rejects thinking the ethical teaching of Jesus "is not applicable to the problems of contemporary society nor yet to any conceivable society." From that point, Niebuhr goes on to discuss an element in the ethics of Jesus that "brings it into a position of relevance with a social and prudential ethic" so that "actions which flow from its demands must be in harmony and not in conflict with reality" (Niebuhr, 33–34).

[89] Niebuhr, 67.

We learned how theological ethics analyzes God's ethical ordering of reality. Ethical goodness is defined by, flows from, and is judged by God and encompasses the foundational doctrines of creation, sin, redemption, and consummation. An ethically good God created an ethically good universe with human beings bearing his image at the apex of that universe. But men and women rebelled against God's ethical ordering of reality and their assigned role within it, and by so doing, infected the originally good universe with ethical corruption caused by sin affecting all aspects. The ethically good God who created all things then launched a process of redemption culminating in Jesus Christ, the innocent Son of God, dying and rising from the dead. This opened a way to overcome the ethical problem of sin. Now ethical rebels who repent can be restored to a reconciled relationship with their ethically good Creator and restored as well to fulfilling the ethical role in creation for which they were made. But complete renewal in the lives of restored image bearers and realizing ethically perfect social conditions in an ethically perfect world awaits the final consummation of God's ethical rule. Then Christ shall be King of Kings and Lord of Lords, and we shall be ethically perfect children of the ethically perfect God ruling as coheirs with Christ in ethically perfect conditions over an ethically perfect universe. That is the heart of the gospel and the heart of theological ethics.

CHAPTER 5

HISTORY, FIGURES
& MOVEMENTS
EARLY CHURCH TO PIETISM

This is the first of two chapters that introduce readers to historical Christian ethics as an academic subcategory within the larger field of Christian ethics. This chapter starts at the beginning of the Church age, following the New Testament era,[1] and surveys the history of Christian ethical thought up through the ethics of Pietism, a movement that

---

[1] Chapter 1 discussed how the meaning of the term *ethics* has evolved from first referring merely to natural habits or habitats, then evolving to indicate studies of personal character, then evolving to indicate theories seeking to explain right and wrong as a whole, and finally expanding to indicate examining any view of right and wrong, whether theoretical or dogmatic, which is how most use the term *ethics* today and is how we are using it here. But, because the meaning of the term *ethics* has changed over time, early figures in the history of Christian "ethics" did not use the term for what they taught and wrote about. In this chapter, we are using the term *ethics* for what early figures taught and wrote about because that is the word used now for what they did even though they did not use that same term back then. They were doing the same category of thing and so must be included in a history of Christian "ethics." It is only the vocabulary, and not the category, that has changed.

started in Germany at the end of the seventeenth century and spread to affect Protestants all over the world.

Historical Christian ethics studies how Christians in the past have interpreted the ethical teachings of the Bible and applied it to specific questions and circumstances.[2] Even though one sometimes influences the other, studying the history of Christian ethics is not the same as studying the history of philosophical ethics. Readers should know that some scholars do not see much difference between analyzing divinely revealed truth and human-centered speculating on the same subject and, therefore, confuse one with the other.[3] These really are very

---

[2] The most significant literature in historical Christian ethics includes Waldo Beach and H. Richard Niebuhr, *Christian Ethics: Sources of the Living Tradition* (New York: John Wiley and Sons, 1955); Wayne Boulton, Thomas Kennedy, and Allen Verhey, eds., *From Christ to the World* (Grand Rapids: Eerdmans, 1994); C. J. Cadoux, *The Early Church and the World* (Edinburgh: T&T Clark, 1925); Charles Curran and Richard McCormick, *The Historical Development of Fundamental Moral Theology in the United States* (New York: Paulist, 1999); Everett Ferguson, *Christian Life: Ethics, Morality and Discipline in the Early Church* (New York: Garland, 1993); George W. Forell, ed., *Christian Social Teachings: A Reader in Christian Social Ethics from the Bible to the Present* (Minneapolis: Augsburg, 1966); George W. Forell, *History of Christian Ethics*, vol. 1, *From the New Testament to Augustine* (Philadelphia: Augsburg, 1979); John Gallagher, *Time Past, Time Future: An Historical Study of Catholic Moral Theology* (New York: Paulist, 1990); Harry J. Huebner, *An Introduction to Christian Ethics: History, Movements, People* (Waco, TX: Baylor, 2012); Michael Keeling, *The Foundations of Christian Ethics* (Edinburgh: T&T Clark, 1990); Christian E. Luthardt, *History of Christian Ethics* (London: T&T Clark, 1889); Wayne Meeks, *The Moral World of the First Christians* (Philadelphia: Westminster, 1986); Wayne Meeks, *The Origins of Christian Morality* (New Haven, CT: Yale, 1993); Oliver O'Donovan and Joan Lockwood O'Donovan, eds., *From Irenaeus to Grotius: A Sourcebook in Christian Political Thought* (Grand Rapids: Eerdmans, 1999); Ernst Troeltsch, *The Social Teaching of the Christian Church*, 2 vols., trans. Olive Wyon (Louisville: Westminster/John Knox, 1992); Edward Westermarck, *Christianity and Morals* (Freeport, NY: Books for Libraries, 1939); White, *Christian Ethics* (see chap. 1, n. 69); R. E. O. White, *The Insights of History*, in *Christian Ethics* (Macon, GA: Mercer, 1994); J. Philip Wogaman, *Christian Ethics: A Historical Introduction* (Philadelphia: Westminster/John Knox, 1993); and J. Philip Wogaman and Douglas M. Strong, eds., *Readings in Christian Ethics: A Historical Sourcebook* (Philadelphia: Westminster/John Knox, 1996).

[3] Scholars who do not confuse the history of Christian ethics with the history of philosophical speculating include Beach and Niebuhr, *Christian Ethics*; Boulton, Kennedy, and Verhey, *Christ to the World*; Forell, *History of Christian Ethics*; Huebner, *Introduction to Christian Ethics*; and White, *Christian Ethics*. Scholars who do confuse them include Wogaman, *Christian Ethics*; Long, *Christian Ethics* (see chap. 2, n. 86); and Mitchell, *Ethics and Moral Reasoning* (see chap. 2, n. 2).

different things, and we will distinguish them even when discussing points of interaction and when reviewing persons and movements that have mixed or conflated the two.

Historical Christian ethics ignores less significant figures, events, and movements and focuses on those that have made large differences to ethical understanding in the institutional church, or at least within major segments of established Christianity. Cults merely alleging to be "Christian," movements that do not accept divine revelation, and figures rejecting the deity of Christ usually are not included except perhaps to illustrate how Christian ethics is corrupted when the Word of God is forsaken and the faith is redefined (Gal 1:6; Jude 3–4). Biblical ethics addresses what the Bible says, theological ethics addresses the way God orders moral revelation, and historical Christian ethics addresses what Christians have believed, taught, or done through history regarding living to please God and bearing witness to his values, standards, and goals.

Ethics of the Early Church (70–300)

Most Christians in the early Church engaged the world in ethical terms despite hostility. Some withdrew, but most lived by a vibrantly different ethic while remaining engaged with pagan friends and neighbors. Most Christians in the New Testament were Jews, but by the second century, most were Gentiles living in Gentile surroundings, and this affected how they approached Christian ethics. They initially stressed fidelity to God against the world, disciplining physical appetites, and serving neighbors in need. But over time, early Christian ethics tended toward moralism and asceticism.

Scholars dispute whether early Christians ever were predominantly pacifist or opposed serving in government. Some did, but these were a minority, and their views never characterized the main body. Tertullian of Carthage (155–220), the earliest known apologist for Christian pacifism, testifies that in his day, so many Christians served in the army the empire would collapse if they left—a situation that could not have arisen if most early Christians had considered it sinful.[4] The early Church also could not have opposed holding government positions, not only because the Church always included a few highly placed government servants (Luke 8:3; Phil 4:22), but also because Ambrose of Milan (340–397) was made bishop while

---

[4] Tertullian, *Apology for the Christians*, 37.

yet serving as a Roman governor.[5] Ambrose himself explains how he was "snatched into the priesthood from the magistrate's tribunal."[6]

The earliest ethics instruction of the post-apostolic Church is found in a work called the *Didache* (circa 100) written to educate new believers in following the "Way of Life" and avoiding the "Way of Death." It lists sins to avoid and worthy acts to perform. But after issuing an ethical standard, the *Didache* sometimes settles for partial fulfillment: "If you can bear the Lord's full yoke, you will be perfect. But if you cannot, then do what you can."[7]

Tertullian was a strict legalist, claiming Christians should observe the Old Testament law more strictly than even the Pharisees. He believed Christians should avoid secular amusements, women should not wear jewelry and should wear veils in public, the unmarried are more virtuous than those who marry, and second marriages are a form of adultery. Tertullian's famous opposition to engaging surrounding culture was not normative;[8] he was never widely trusted and ultimately favored Montanism—a heretical sect that practiced very strict asceticism.

Clement (150–215) and Origen (182–254), both of Alexandria, were known for mixing Greek philosophy with Christian ethics more than most other Christians accepted. Clement laid the groundwork for Christian humanism as the first to treat philosophy as "handmaid" to theology.[9] But, in doing so, Clement emptied God of emotion and thus denied the centrality of God's love in Christian ethics. Origen so mixed Christian ethics with Greek philosophy that a contemporary pagan once observed that although Origen was a Christian, "In his opinions about material things and the Deity he played the Greek."[10] Origen taught that men move up and down a Platonic scale of being through a process of ethical education: "On earth by means

---

[5] Walter A. Elwell, "Ambrose," in *Evangelical Dictionary of Theology*, 2nd ed. (Grand Rapids: Baker, 2001), 50; P. de Labriolle, *The Life and Times of St. Ambrose* (St. Louis: Herder, 1928), v–vi; Dudden F. Homes, *The Life and Times of St. Ambrose*, vol. 1 (Oxford: Clarendon, 1935), 66–68; and Neil B. McLynn, *Ambrose of Milan* (Berkeley: University of California, 1994), 1–3.

[6] Ambrose, *On Duties of the Clergy* 1.4.

[7] *Didascalia apostolorum* 6.2.

[8] See Tertullian, *Prescription against Heretics*, 7.36. According to C. P. Slater and T. W. Whitlam, "Tertullian's famous cry, 'What has Athens to do with Jerusalem?' did not reflect the general consensus" in R. K. Harrison, ed., *Encyclopedia of Biblical & Christian Ethics* (Nashville: Thomas Nelson, 1992), 63.

[9] Clement of Alexandria, *Stromata* I.V.

[10] Attributed to Porphyry in Eusebius, *The Ecclesiastical History*, trans. J. E. L. Oulton, *Loeb Classical Library* (London: Heinemann, 1932), 6.19, 2:57–58.

of virtue souls grow wings and soar aloft, but when in heaven their wings fall off through evil and they sink down and become earthbound and are mingled with the gross nature of matter."[11]

Other early teachers were more orthodox but had their own peculiarities. Basil the Great (330-379), bishop of Caesarea of Cappadocia, insisted Christian ethics must come from the Bible, not Greek philosophy, and was famous for acts of charity. But Basil interpreted Scripture through a Neoplatonic lens that led him to claim Christian morality is empowered by the sacraments and is otherwise impotent. He also took an extreme view on material assets, insisting Christians must keep nothing for themselves beyond the minimum required for subsistence and, because he thought moral purity results from pursuing the disciplines of poverty and chastity, he concluded Christians can best transform the world by withdrawing from it.[12] John Chrysostom (347-407) also stressed relying on the Bible over Greek thought, yet he too was skewed by Neoplatonism. Chrysostom exalted virginity over marriage, believed widows should not remarry, and urged Christians to abstain from physical pleasures. He also held that Christian ethics would change the world into heaven on earth and took such a negative view of possessions he thought that private property was sinful, that desiring private property was the root of all evil, that private wealth could only arise from wrongdoing, and that removing wealth disparities will erase all wickedness.[13]

Ethics of Augustine (354–430)

Apart from God himself and writers of the Bible, Augustine (354–430) is likely the most influential figure in the history of Christian ethics. He is the one most responsible for formulating the normative lines of Christian ethics, and his views on good, evil, the will, sin, love, virtue, personal character, material wealth, society, just war, and how the Church interacts with human government were so pivotal that now most theological movements claiming orthodoxy take their stand in the Augustinian tradition.

---

[11] Origen, *On First Principles*, trans. G. W. Butterworth (London: SPCK, 1936), 73.

[12] R. Larry Shelton, "Perfection, Perfectionism," in Walter A. Elwell, ed., *Evangelical Dictionary of Theology*, 2nd ed. (Grand Rapids: Baker, 2001), 904.

[13] Forell, *History of Christian Ethics*, 129–53; R. K. Harrison, ed., *Encyclopedia of Biblical & Christian Ethics* (Nashville: Thomas Nelson, 1992), 359; James F. Childress and John Macquarrie, eds., *Westminster Dictionary of Christian Ethics* (Philadelphia: Westminster, 1986), 456.

For Augustine, God is both absolute being and absolute good, and all creation depends on God for being and goodness: "The perfection of all good things, our perfect good, is God. We must neither come short of this, nor go beyond it; the one is dangerous, the other impossible."[14] God is good in himself, and we are good only as we depend on him both intellectually and ontologically. We rely on God not only for enlightenment but also for enablement. He works in us "both to will and to work" (Phil 2:13) what is good and right. Humans are created "with a nature midway between angels and beasts,"[15] not just with a mind to comprehend God's truth, but more significantly with a will (*voluntas*) designed to love and obey God and his truth.

Augustine did not blame the evil things humans do on ignorance, bad reasoning, or wealth disparities, but on misaligned will, that is, on will directed inward and down toward self and the flesh (*cupiditas*) rather than outward and up toward God and his truth (*caritas*). The cause of sin proceeds "from the soul not from the flesh,"[16] and is a matter of pride.[17] The ethical problem is that humans have "free" will but not a "freed" will. The will we have is free of external constraint. But, since the fall, our will is self-corrupted and now is free only to express its corrupt nature.[18] Augustine held that "appetite (*cupiditas*) reigns where the love (*caritas*) of God does not."[19] The will of humanity is free. But unless the will we have is realigned, we destroy ourselves.

The view Augustine held of humans having free will only to express self-corruption would be entirely negative except for his view of grace. The grace of God, he believed, is "that by which alone men are delivered from evil, and without which they do absolutely no good thing."[20] We have no hope in and of ourselves. But the grace of God offers a remedy for evil that grants not just enlightenment but pardon, and not just pardon but favor, and not just favor but power to live righteously. For Augustine, God's moral law in the Old Testament

---

[14] Augustine, *On the Catholic and the Manichean Ways of Life*, VIII.

[15] Augustine, *The City of God*, XII.22.

[16] Augustine, XIV.3.

[17] Augustine, XIV.13.

[18] Augustine, *Against Two Letters of the Pelagians*, 1.2.

[19] Augustine, *Handbook on Faith, Hope, and Love*, XXXI.

[20] Augustine, *On Admonition and Grace*, II.3.

enables us to distinguish right from wrong, but only the grace of God enables us to shun evil and do what is good.[21]

Ethics for Augustine is driven by love, something he viewed as a will-orienting power and not mere sentimentality. A person is as he loves. He is good, as good love (*caritas*) turns his will toward God, thus rightly aligning all things with God and by that with everything else as well; and a person is evil, as bad love (*cupiditas*) turns his or her will toward anything else over God, thus wrongly aligning all things not just with God but everything else as well.[22] "Scripture," he said, "enjoins nothing but good love (*caritas*) and condemns nothing but bad love (*cupiditas*) and in that way fashions the lives of men."[23] He also once famously said, "Love, and do what you want."[24] But this must not be misinterpreted. Augustine was no libertarian and only meant that rightly aligned love leads to rightly aligned behavior.

In *The City of God,* Augustine held that life in community is shaped by an integrating principle—what he conceived as its common love and today we might refer to as what frames its ethical thinking. With this in mind, Augustine supposed a fundamental division between contrary ethical communities that runs through history regardless of culture or circumstance: "There have arisen no more than two classes, as it were, of human society . . . . a city of men who choose to live carnally, and another of those who choose to live spiritually, each aiming at its own kind of peace."[25] These "have been formed by two loves: the earthly by the love of self, even to the contempt of God; (and) the heavenly by the love of God, even to the contempt of self."[26] They generate opposing ethical systems, one true and one false. Augustine's two cities are not the same as church and state because they are internally, not externally, determined. Godly ethics may influence a state, and earthly ethics may infiltrate the Church. No church is entirely good, and no state is entirely bad; that is because Augustine's cities—each formed by a different integrating principle—compete with one another even within individual hearts. Throughout history, the Church may express Godly ethics more nearly than the state, and the state may express the other more nearly than

---

[21] Augustine, I.2.

[22] Augustine, *The City of God,* XIV.7.

[23] Augustine, *On Christian Teaching,* III.10.

[24] Augustine, *Tractates on the First Letter of John,* 7.8.

[25] Augustine, *The City of God,* XIV.1.

[26] Augustine, XIV.28.

the church. But Augustine does not expect social perfection before Christ returns because the opposing ethical systems he identifies will remain intermixed at every level until the end of the world when separated at the last judgment.[27]

We have to this point described Augustine's metaethics, but he addressed applied issues as well. Although he knew sex in marriage was of God and to be honored, he also considered virginity morally superior to marriage and struggled to explain this in biblical terms.[28] The way he interpreted Scripture on sex was skewed by Platonism infiltrating Christian thought, and while he did not originate early Christian denigration of sex in marriage, he boosted it into the Middle Ages by urging clergy to avoid marriage for reasons still influencing Catholics today. Augustine did not oppose wealth disparities but admired common ownership and warned that desiring wealth for its own sake was idolatrous. He thought Christians should try to improve government but also held that they should respect whatever rulers they have, however bad, and expected them to endure what cannot be changed. Augustine did not originate the just war ethical tradition as some claim,[29] nor was he the first theologian to discuss just war in Christian terms.[30] But he did advance just war thinking in a manner that influenced later generations.

Ethics of Medieval Monasticism (300–1500)

As Christianity grew to be more accepted and became a state religion, some devout laymen, influenced by the Greek ideals of solitude and privation, reacted by isolating themselves and depriving their bodies, all to better renounce the world and achieve personal holiness.[31] The

---

[27] Augustine, *On Catechizing the Uninstructed*, 21.37.

[28] See Augustine, *On Holy Virginity*.

[29] For examples wrongly claiming Augustine originated classical just war theory, see Paul Ramsey, *War and the Christian Conscience* (Durham, NC: Duke University Press, 1961), 15; Jean Bethke Elshtain, *Just War against Terror* (New York: Basic Books, 2003), 49; and Yskander Arquimides Saucedo, "St. Augustine's Just War Theory" (posted August 1, 2017), accessible at: https://dogmadoctrineblog .org/2017/08/01/st-augustines-just-war-theory/. The truth is just war theory arose from early Greek and biblical roots. For biblical origins, see Deuteronomy 20 and Amos 1. For early Greek sources, see "The Classical Origins of the Just War," chapter 2 in Roland H. Bainton, *Christian Attitudes toward War and Peace* (Nashville: Abingdon, 1960).

[30] Ambrose, bishop of Milan, articulated a just war ethic in Christian terms prior to Augustine.

[31] Howard A. Tepker says, "a more legalistic and outward type of asceticism entered the Christian church because of Hellenistic influences," which "tended to distort the Christian concept of self-denial,

first monks were individual hermits like Saint Anthony of Egypt (251–356), who is often called the "Father of Monasticism." But the movement did not remain solitary, and monks, especially in Western Europe, began forming communities separated from life in the world.

The ethics of monasticism demanded absolute poverty; prohibited marriage and private ownership; and pursued cleansing by physical pain (flagellation), deprivation, humiliation, and rigid obedience not only to God but also to an abbot who ruled each monastic community. A monk's chastity marked renunciation of the flesh, his poverty marked renunciation of the world, and his obedience marked renunciation of self-will. The monk's view of personal holiness stressed self-effort and judgment over grace and mercy and tended to measure spirituality in physical terms. Monasticism has been criticized for retreating from reality and replacing salvation through Christ with self-saving practices, but it can be admired for taking self-discipline seriously. It suppressed the body as a way to achieve moral (and even spiritual) purity, but it limited ethics to heroism while looking down upon life at home or at work as worldly and corrupt.

Ethics of Medieval Mysticism (1000–1300)

Monasticism was not meant as an end in itself. But rules stressing outward compliance led many to overlook the inner life, and this led others to stress inwardness in mystical terms. Mysticism arose as a reform movement within monasticism, and like the ethics of monasticism, the ethics of medieval mysticism struggled with the tension between renouncing the world and serving the world, between solitude and society, and between denying self and perfecting self. Whereas monasticism generally balanced renouncing the world with performing acts of charity, mysticism focused so strongly on receiving goodness passively that charity was nearly eclipsed.[32] Whereas monasticism tended toward external practices, mysticism probed human affection and tried to approach God by denying everything not God and seeking nothing but God. The mystics replaced grace in Christian ethics with melting into God in a

---

teaching contempt for the material world, abstinence from marriage, and a severe moralism which denied all forgiveness for certain sins." Howard W. Tepker, "Asceticism," in Carl F. H. Henry, ed., *Baker's Dictionary of Christian Ethics* (Grand Rapids: Baker, 1973), 41.

[32] The mystics did not erase charity entirely but affirmed neighbor love only as a step toward reaching personal perfection in mystical terms.

manner crossing into pantheism. So, while medieval mystics never rejected Christianity, their ethical teaching was more Stoic than Christian and more Buddhist than biblical.[33]

Bernard of Clairvaux (1090–1153) taught that purity is more a matter of absorption into God than of understanding and obeying him,[34] and Meister Eckhart (c. 1260–c. 1328) said a mystic's goal was to gaze at God in a state "unconscious of the knowing-process, or love, or anything else."[35] Eckhart held that by willing nothing, desiring nothing, and knowing nothing, humans can reach a state he believed to be the highest of virtues, even surpassing the virtues of faith, hope, and love in the Bible.[36] But in 1329, Pope John XXII charged Eckhart with pantheism and condemned his teaching as heretical.[37]

Ethics of the Medieval Papacy (500–1500)

When pagans ruled the Roman Empire, emperors claimed divine, as well as political, power, and religion was subservient to the state. This relation was reversed during the Middle Ages. The papacy did not question mixing political with religious power and only switched their priority, and this affected Christian ethics profoundly. The ethics of the medieval papacy is a story of codification, corruption, and abuse. Moral duties were codified to better enforce them. But these were corrupted by assuming totalitarian authority that in turn led to enormous abuses of power.

Ecclesial discipline underwent astonishing expansion, and behavioral norms took the form of "canon law."[38] Canon law was viewed as applying God's moral law to daily life, and was, therefore, a system of applied Christian ethics. Practicing canon law led to a sort of moral

---

[33] I do not suggest there was any direct Buddhist connection and only mean it was very similar. Others have said the same. See John H. Kromminga, "Mysticism" in *Baker's Dictionary of Christian Ethics,* ed. Carl F. H. Henry (Grand Rapids: Baker, 1973), 440.

[34] See Bernard of Clairvaux, *The Twelve Steps of Humility and Pride*, chap. xv.

[35] *Meister Eckhart: A Modern Translation*, trans. R. B. Blakney (New York: Harper, 1941), 79.

[36] *Meister Eckhart*, 82–91.

[37] David G. Dunbar, "Meister Eckhart," in *Evangelical Dictionary of Theology*, 2nd ed., ed. Walter A. Elwell (Grand Rapids: Baker, 2001), 755.

[38] Final codification came with papal centralization in the eleventh century and was compiled in writing mainly by Gratian in the *Concordance of Discordant Canons*, used by the Roman Catholic Church until 1918.

reasoning known as "casuistry." Lists were compiled specifying the permissibility or culpability of every action in every conceivable situation. Casuistry addressed the way circumstances sometimes alter accountability to excuse normally wrong actions after considering results, possible exceptions, or even good intentions. Casuistry could be niggling to the point of absurdity and tended to erode ethical responsibility.

Although Christian princes were not allowed to war among themselves, and although the medieval "Truce of God" (*Treuga Dei*) tradition severely limited times when battles could be fought, medieval orthodoxy held that restrictions limiting war did not apply to fighting people declared to be heathen or heretical. Fighting infidels became a spiritual discipline along with fasting, penitential acts, visiting shrines, and almsgiving, and was considered to have such merit it could assure eternal salvation all by itself. Thinking unbelief justified going to war transformed the Church into a military power. The medieval popes—especially Gregory VII (1020–1085), Urban II (1042–1099), and Innocent III (1160–1216)—replaced Augustine's regret about needing to permit war in self-defense with a zeal for combat at odds with neighbor love and the Great Commission. The militant spirit unleashed by popes using God to sanction their human lust for power led to slaughtering thousands for whom Christ died. In declaring holy war on Muslims who held Jerusalem, they reduced spiritual power to military power, confused the kingdom of heaven with the kingdom of men, redefined salvation from reconciling sinners to God to slaughtering them in the name of God, and baptized an ethic of bloodshed contrary not only to the teaching of Christ, the Apostles, and Augustine but also to fundamental Christianity. It perverted Christian ethics and blackened the history of Christian evangelism.

Os Guinness notes the terrible irony by which this occurred. The medieval papacy was made vulnerable to corruption by its successful accumulation of immense power and wealth. Centralizing all spiritual and civil power in a single human institution, led by a single person, left leaders of the Church with no way to correct outbreaks of pride, evil, and hypocrisy within their own ranks. Thus, Guinness says, out of this "great age of faith" came "not only magnificent learning, architecture, art and music, but the worst evils ever perpetrated on the world by the Christian church."[39]

---

[39] Os Guinness, *Renaissance: The Power of the Gospel However Dark the Times* (Downers Grove, IL: InterVarsity, 2014), 128.

Ethics of Medieval Scholasticism (1050–1350)

Scholasticism was a form of thinking developed in the Middle Ages by mixing Greek and Roman philosophy with Christian theology, and while some limited this to what the Bible allows, others changed the Word of God to fit philosophical preferences. Albert the Great (1193–1280) was in the first category. For while he mixed the two, he trusted revelation over speculation and believed true knowing can never oppose what God says. Other scholastics were not so careful and regarded philosophy as not only equal to, but even superior to, the Bible.

Peter Abelard (1079–1142) was the first to break with biblical truth by opposing the whole notion of fixed ethical standards and placing ethics on a subjective basis instead. He flatly denied Augustine's assertion that virtue depends on loving God and disregarded prior Christian teaching by saying he thought "the old philosophers came very near to apostolic perfection."[40] Abelard believed no action is right or wrong in itself but is made so by intention alone—a view that denies ethics has any fixed basis and leaves each to judge his or her own behavior.

John Duns Scotus (1266–1308) and William of Ockham (1280–1348) carried on the ethical revolution Abelard began. Prior to these, everyone thought that since God created everything, he must, therefore, exist in a different way than other things. Scotus changed this by putting existence above God, whom Scotus reduced to participating in reality in the same manner as everything else. This had enormous repercussions, for it meant ethical reality could be apprehended in itself without God. In other words, Scotus supposed ethics could be real whether God was real or not and could be understood apart from revelation. Scotus and Ockham proposed that God could, if he wants, declare falsehood, killing the innocent, or even hating God, to be good rather than bad. Christians, both before and after Scotus and Ockham, have held that God's character limits his moral will so that ethical standards are universal, unchanging, and coherent. But these scholastics preferred philosophical ideas over affirming God's unchanging holiness and self-consistency.

---

[40] Peter Abelard, *Christian Theology*, ii.

Ethics of Thomas Aquinas (1225–1274)

Thomas Aquinas (1225–1274) was the greatest of the medieval scholastics who used ancient philosophy to shape moral theology.[41] Using Aristotle's philosophy based on human reason apart from Scripture, Aquinas broke with Augustine to introduce big changes in the way Catholics have regarded Christian ethics ever since.[42] Scholastics were already challenging the Augustinian tradition before Aquinas came along, but he wrote so persuasively he redirected Catholic ethics and fostered divisions that erupted in the Reformation.

Of the elements Aquinas took from Aristotle to revise Christian ethics, the most important were a teleological view of reality, an optimistic view of human rationality, a golden mean view of virtue, a eudaemonistic (personal happiness) view of the good, and a natural law view of the universe. Aquinas agreed with Aristotle that the supreme goal of rational beings is happiness (*eudaimonia*), but where Aristotle located this within nature, Aquinas located it beyond nature, conceiving it in terms of the beatific vision notion developed by the mystics.[43] Ethics for Aquinas was a matter of aligning each thing to one overriding goal (*telos*) and assessing actions as good or bad based on how they served attaining (or failing to attain) that goal. Like Aristotle, Aquinas also defined virtues as habits inclining the will to pursue worthy ends. He adopted Aristotle's classifications of "intellectual" and "moral" virtues but went on to postulate a third category beyond Aristotle's classifications, which he called "theological" virtues. These, he said, are beyond the reach of reason, are known only by divine revelation, and are needed to attain man's supernatural end.

Aquinas viewed ethical life as set in a well-ordered universe governed by four kinds of law, of which two came from Aristotle (natural and human) and two from Scripture (eternal and divine). The ultimate pattern for right and wrong located in the mind of God, where It is in Itself beyond human knowing, he identified as "eternal law." The expression of eternal

---

[41] It is common to say Aquinas produced a "synthesis of Aristotelian philosophy and Christian theology" (Beach and Niebuhr, *Christian Ethics*, 202). But this supposes the ordering of God's Word is subordinate to philosophical categories, and that is something with which I do not think we should agree.

[42] In 1879, Pope Leo XIII (1810–1903) declared Thomas the official teacher of the Church and required seminaries and universities to base all Catholic education on Thomas.

[43] Aquinas, *Summa theologica*, II.I, q. 2, viii.

law reflected in creation Aquinas defined as "natural law," and this, he claimed, is open to the reason of all, whether they be regenerate or not. "Human law" he viewed to be applications of natural law made by men to particular situations and communities, and "divine law" referred to standards revealed in the Bible, part of which overlaps natural law and regards material life and part of which goes beyond natural law and regards spiritual life.

Interpreters disagree on how the virtue theory of Aquinas relates to his natural law theory.[44] Most give his natural law theory priority and so treat his view of virtue as subsumed within his natural law ethic. But others give his virtue theory priority and so treat his view of natural law as subsumed within his virtue ethic.[45] Aquinas never explained how these went together, however, and most likely followed Aristotle, who treated virtue and natural law as separate things, with neither being a system including the other.

The philosophical ideas Aquinas embraced affected his approach to applied questions. He allowed a poor man to steal because the teleological analysis he used supposed "in cases of need all things are common property."[46] He believed charging interest on loans was immoral because it did not fit within his view of natural law, even though Christ allowed doing so (Luke 19:23).[47] And he relied on Aristotle's view of tyranny to justify rebellion even though Paul condemns it in Romans 13:2.[48] Aquinas also continued the devaluation of sex and marriage that began in the early Church, was affirmed by Augustine, and then was institutionalized by monasticism, but he did this in a different way than before. Applying Aristotle's natural law teleology, Aquinas judged that sex has just one natural purpose and that could only be to produce children. He thus concluded that sex for any other reason, even between a husband and wife in marriage, was both unnatural and immoral.[49] Based on this, he insisted husbands and wives must stop having sex after menopause and held that continuing was against nature (*contra naturam*) and so was immoral for the same reason as having sex with

---

[44] For more on this see, Huebner, *Introduction to Christian Ethics*, 87.

[45] For example, see Daniel Mark Nelson, *Priority of Prudence: Virtue and Natural Law in Thomas Aquinas and the Implications for Modern Ethics* (University Park: Pennsylvania University, 1992). Others suggesting this alternative reading of Aquinas include Karl Rahner, Alasdair MacIntyre, and Stanley Hauerwas.

[46] Aquinas, *Summa theologica* II.II, q. 66, vii.

[47] Aquinas, II.II, q. 78, i.

[48] Thomas Aquinas, *On Kingship*, ch. 11, 80–81.

[49] Thomas Aquinas, *Summa contra gentiles* III, cc. 122–26.

animals. But the reasoning by which Aquinas justified stealing and rebelling, and prohibited charging interest and sex after menopause, all came from philosophical speculation and had little to do with Scripture.

Ethics of Late Medieval Christian Humanism (1480–1540)

In the late Middle Ages, a spirit of intellectual ferment called "humanism" arose opposing ecclesial authority. While it was mostly secular and anticlerical, the movement included some who wanted to restore the Church rather than destroy it. These Christian humanists rejected the two-tiered approach to ethics fostered by monasticism and believed in freeing Christian ethics from the perversions of scholasticism, canon law, and casuistry. But unlike others of their day, the Christian humanists did not want to divide the Church.

Desiderius Erasmus of Rotterdam (1466–1536), the best known Christian humanist, reset Christian ethics along lines very different from medieval piety, returning to Scripture and the imitation of Christ rather than trusting popes and philosophers. Erasmus despised scholastics who regarded philosophy as equal to, or even superior to, theology. He supplemented Scripture with experience and reason but never questioned the Word of God and never used philosophy to frame theological truth.[50] He subjected contemporary practices to withering criticism, and his *The Praise of Folly* uses satire to promote ethical reform. Erasmus focused less on theory than on practice and addressed a wide range of applied issues.

He shocked the status quo by treating marriage as no less worthy than virginity[51] and opposed canon law, which allowed no divorce, by arguing Christians could divorce on the basis of adultery, cruelty, or mutual hatred.[52] He broke with early Church teaching on divorce as well by arguing Christians who get divorced on moral grounds may also remarry without sin.[53]

---

[50] I think Wogaman is wrong to say Erasmus held an "optimistic" view of human nature that relied on "the capacities . . . of universal human reason" (Wogaman, *Christian Ethics*, 129). Erasmus relied on Christ and Scripture over natural reason, and while he used reason and experience to strengthen and explain, he never trusted any human capacity left to itself, including universal human reason.

[51] Desiderius Erasmus, *The Institution of Marriage*.

[52] Desiderius Erasmus, *Annotations on the New Testament*.

[53] Desiderius Erasmus, *Commentary of Erasmus on the New Testament*. For relation to the early Church, see V. Norskoy Olsen, *The New Testament Logia on Divorce: A Study of their Interpretation from Erasmus to Milton* (Tübingen: Mohr, 1971), 2–42.

Erasmus criticized asceticism but distrusted affluence holding "there is nothing wrong with having money" so long as one does not love it. But he also did not think anyone "who passes most of his life heaping riches together" could be "a very good Christian."[54] Erasmus criticized the crusades, saying, "It is neither right nor proper to call ourselves Christian . . . if we dispatch thousands of heathen people to hell rather than convert them."[55] He opposed war most strongly but was not entirely consistent, maintaining that some wars are just and necessary, but then also deploring even the most justified wars and claiming Christ and the Apostles never allowed them.[56]

Another Christian humanist, Sir Thomas More of England (1478–1535), also sought ethical reform without dividing the Church. Unlike Erasmus, More tried renewing Christian ethics without ever referring to Christ or the Bible.[57] More imagined a form of socio-economic communism in which "all things being there common, every man hath abundance of everything."[58] He upheld marriage but challenged gender roles by envisioning women's ordination.[59] And he opposed capital punishment, proposed something equivalent to universal healthcare, and suggested using assassins to kill enemy kings in place of full-scale war.[60] Wogaman notes that More's views were "a remarkable anticipation of nineteenth- and twentieth-century political liberalism and economic socialism."[61] More did not return to Scripture like Erasmus and did not even mix philosophy with theology like Aquinas. Rather, More took a different path, addressing Christian ethics in sentimental terms that included God only as an afterthought. He disconnected Christian ethics from the Bible and theology, but his work can be viewed as a link between the revelation-based ethics of early Christianity and the secularized sentimental ethics of liberal Christianity in the modern world.

---

[54] Desiderius Erasmus, *Handbook of a Christian Soldier*, XXXIV.265.

[55] Erasmus, intro ltr.8.

[56] For allowing justified wars, see Desiderius Erasmus, *The Complaint of Peace*, 44, also Desiderius Erasmus, *Education of a Christian Prince*, 249. For opposing the most justified wars, see Erasmus, *Complaint of Peace*, 66. For Christ and the Apostles never allowing war, see Erasmus, *Christian Prince*, 252.

[57] Huebner, *Introduction to Christian Ethics*, 97.

[58] Thomas More, *Utopia*, Harvard Classics, vol. 36 (New York: Collier & Son, 1938), 167.

[59] More, 231.

[60] More, 143, 130, 132.

[61] Wogaman, *Christian Ethics*, 131.

Ethics of Martin Luther (1483–1546)

Martin Luther (1483–1546) was the most important early leader of the Protestant Reformation, which marked the end of medieval Christianity and the beginning of modernity. Teaching Aristotle's *Nicomachean Ethics* at the University of Wittenberg set Luther on a course that began with rejecting the influence Aristotle had on Christian ethics and ended with widespread theological reform. Luther criticized the respect Aquinas and the scholastics accorded Aristotle, calling Aristotle "damned, conceited, rascally heathen," the scholastics "swine theologians," and Aquinas "the source and foundation of all heresy, error and obliteration of the Gospel."[62] He went on to criticize the ethics of medieval monasticism as well, claiming it was based more on fearing God than on loving him and focused more on self-improvement than on loving others. Luther's marriage in 1525 did for Christian ethics what nailing his theses on the door of the church in Wittenberg did for theology.[63] These events were connected, not only because both were dramatic, but because both flowed from fidelity to Scripture and expressed a radical change of course that rocked the world.

Ethical interest runs throughout all Luther wrote, but for him, ethics was a matter of theology and not a discipline to itself. For moral authority, Luther returned to relying on Scripture alone at a time when that was considered revolutionary. He is often credited with teaching an ethic of love and liberty, which is only partly correct. Luther also stressed an ethic of obligation to obey commands emanating from God and from human authorities as well. Turning back to the Bible, Luther saw Christian ethics as expressing God's grace toward sinful humanity and believed worthy living only came through faith in Christ. Since Christians are called to live in the world without being of the world, he saw a tension that he solved by supposing we live in two ethically independent realms. On the one hand, Luther held that Christians among themselves live by an ethic of love and freedom, while on the other, everyone, including Christians, live by an ethic of obligation and coercion needed to restrain chaos in a wicked world.[64]

---

[62] Denis R. Janz, *Luther and Late Medieval Thomism: A Study in Theological Anthropology* (Waterloo, ON: Wilfrid Laurier, 1983), 3.

[63] I am indebted for this insight to William H. Lazareth, *Luther on the Christian Home: An Application of the Social Ethics of the Reformation* (Philadelphia: Muhlenberg, 1960), 1.

[64] How far Luther took this dualism is expressed in a striking passage where he says, "A prince may very well be a Christian, but as a Christian he is not to rule; and insofar as he rules he is called not a Christian, but a prince. The person is a Christian, but the office or princeship has nothing to do with

Luther saw no positive use for moral law. He understood it only in negative terms and gave it no role after the redeemed are justified. Moral law was good only for two things: first, to "bind the Devil's hands" by restraining the bad behavior of bad people,[65] and second, "to reveal to man his sin," which includes exposing the depth of human depravity, the impossibility of men saving themselves, and their need for God's grace.[66] But of these, the main purpose of moral law, Luther thought, was to humble man before God or, as Hare puts it, "to bring us to our knees."[67] God's moral law is good. But it cannot save and only leads men to despair and to realize they need help. But a justified man, Luther thought, no longer needs moral law and pleases God out of love without any obligation whatsoever. For a Christian, Luther said, "his faith suffices for everything . . . . He has no need . . . of the law," but rather is "free from the law."[68]

With this, Luther taught that Christians live between coexisting eons, each operating on a completely different ethical system. These systems do not conflict because God rules both. One is new and will last forever, while the other is old and will pass away when Jesus returns. So, where medieval Christianity had one ethic for saints who withdraw from the world and another for people living in it, Luther had one ethic for Christians relating to each other and another for everyone living together. In Luther's kingdom of the world, God uses law and moral obligation to restrain the behavior of wicked men, but in Luther's kingdom of justified saints, God rules by love, without coercion or obligation, on a completely voluntary basis.[69] This led Luther to think Christians should not try to change society and politics in the unredeemed world, even though he believed Christians should love their unredeemed neighbors. So, although Luther helped needy individuals, he opposed social change. He hallowed work,

---

his Christianity." Martin Luther, *Commentary on the Sermon on the Mount* (1532), in vol. 43 of *Luther's Works*, ed. Jaroslav Pelikan and Helmut T. Lehmann (Philadelphia: Muhlenberg, 1955–1973).

[65] Luther, *A Commentary on St. Paul's Epistle to the Galatians*, 302 (see chap. 4, n. 48).

[66] Luther, 298–99.

[67] John E. Hare, "History of Christian Ethics," in *New Dictionary of Christian Ethics & Pastoral Theology*, ed. David J. Atkinson, David F. Field, Arthur Holmes, Oliver O'Donovan (Downers Grove, IL: InterVarsity, 1995), 36.

[68] Martin Luther, *Concerning Christian Liberty*, included in *Luther's Works*, ed. Jaroslav Pelikan and Helmut T. Lehmann, 55 vols. (Philadelphia: Muhlenberg, 1955–1973), 57: 63.25; 57: 105.21.

[69] Martin Luther, *Secular Authority: To What Extent It Should Be Obeyed*, in *Works of Martin Luther*, vol. III (Philadelphia: Holman and Castle, 1930), 236–37.

started schools, fed the hungry, exalted the dignity of marriage, and returned moral development to the family rather than centering it in monasteries and convents, but he did all this while also resisting widespread social reform and political change.

Despite the good he achieved, Luther's legacy was mixed and left Christian ethics with serious problems. He returned to relying on Scripture alone, but his ethical dualism left social ethics with little Christian influence. He stopped Christians from leading religious wars but left political ethics with nothing to achieve. He limited positive (aspirational) ethics to Christians interacting with each other and relegated negative (obligational) ethics to life in the world, which left both incomplete and gave Christians no incentive for social reform. Since Luther thought moral law became irrelevant after salvation, his ethic for Christians jumps straight from justification to glorification and seemingly skips the doctrine of sanctification altogether. Luther treated transformation by faith with such optimism that he denied the redeemed have obligations of any sort, which has led some to wonder if he may have erased Christian ethics altogether.[70]

As a result, Luther's understanding of how faith, love, and grace affect Christian ethics has fostered very little social action and has more often fostered blind acceptance of existing systems. Luther was horrified when serfs demanded universal human equality because he thought this confused the ethic for Christians with the ethic for life in the world.[71] When peasants turned violent in the name of Christian freedom, he urged princes to suppress them without remorse, saying, "Let no one have mercy, but let everyone, as he is able, hew, stab, slay, lay about him as though among mad dogs."[72] And when Luther got frustrated with Jews who refused to convert, he urged authorities to "set fire to their synagogues or schools," have their homes "razed and destroyed," have their rabbis "forbidden to teach on pain of death," and have "all cash and treasure of silver and gold . . . taken from them."[73] Sentiments like this have embarrassed Christians ever since, and Luther's religious anti-Semitism left Christians in Germany vulnerable to Hitler's racial anti-Semitism four centuries later.

---

[70] On this, see Gerhard O. Forde, *A More Radical Gospel* (Grand Rapids: Eerdmans, 2004), 138.

[71] Luther, *Luther's Works*, 18:327.

[72] Martin Luther, *An Open Letter Concerning the Hard Book against the Peasants* (1525).

[73] Martin Luther, *On the Jews and Their Lies* (1543).

Ethics of John Calvin (1509–1564)

John Calvin (1509–1564) led the Protestant reformers a generation after Luther and came to influence Protestant ethics to a degree rivaled only by Augustine.[74] Like Luther, Calvin, too, insisted Scripture is the only reliable source of moral authority, but he went further to correct what he considered problems in Luther's ethical teaching.[75] Calvin's ethics differed with Luther by centering on the sovereignty of God rather than on his forgiveness; by making worthy living something for which we strive after justification rather than something achieved by justification; by insisting Christian ethics is unified, universal, and timeless; by extending the ethical mission from life only among Christians to life as a whole; and by interpreting moral law in a positive as well as negative light.

Calvin saw Christian ethics as combining self-discipline with fashioning a sanctified society. God requires absolute obedience and men are totally depraved, but God shows grace toward those he elects in forgiving their sins and transforming their desires. All men are obligated, first, to obey God themselves and, second, to produce, in harmony with others, what most glorifies God. Calvin combined Luther's doctrine of justification with a robust view of sanctification, claimed God has one unchanging ethic that applies to everyone,[76] and, while agreeing with Luther that moral law convicts men of sin and restrains bad behavior, held that it also reveals right and wrong to those who care about how they should live.[77]

While Calvin viewed moral law more favorably than Luther, he did not think Christians should be satisfied only with moral law. "The conscience of believers," he said, "should rise above and advance beyond the law" and should focus away from ourselves "and look only to

---

[74] Calvin was born in the town of Noyon, France, located fifty-eight miles northeast of Paris and named Jean Cauvin by his parents, Gerard and Jeanne le Franc Cauvin. This French name was then anglicized as "John Calvin."

[75] Although Lutherans eventually separated from Calvinists over differences in theology, Calvin always downplayed the differences he had with Luther. But he never denied having differences with Luther, and Beach and Niebuhr are not correct in saying Calvin merely "systematized and related to concrete action the ideas that Luther had propounded" (Beach and Niebuhr, *Christian Ethics*, 267).

[76] Calvin, *Institutes*, II. viii. 7 (see chap. 4, n. 1).

[77] Calvin, II. vii. 6, 10, 12. Calvin's first use of the law (conviction of sin) is Luther's second use, and Calvin's second use of the law (deterring wrong behavior) is Luther's first.

Christ."[78] Moral law is relevant for Christians, but we cannot stop there. Christians aspire not just to meet minimal requirements but to conform to the image of Christ, and that is something sought not out of duty but out of love and pursued not just minimally but as much as possible.[79]

Where Luther tolerated the world, Calvin sought to master it.[80] But unlike the papacy, Calvin sought mastery in organic terms by adhering to a unifying ethic, not in organizational terms by adhering to a unifying institution. Calvin addressed politics but not for the sake of power, economics but not for the sake of wealth, and society but not for the sake of happiness. The overriding aim of Calvin's sociopolitical ethic is to glorify God by forming a holy community that visibly demonstrates God's election of those he saves.

Calvin held that marriage and having children are not just blessings but duties. Marriage "is a good and holy ordinance of God" but not something controlled by the Church and limited just to Christians,[81] and he warned couples preparing for marriage "not to pollute it with uncontrolled and dissolute lust."[82] Calvin combined monastic emphasis on industry and denying luxury with Luther's elevation of secular work to form an economic ethic, later called "intramundane asceticism" or the "Protestant work ethic."[83] And Calvin taught that fallen human nature requires men to be governed.[84] Since human government is composed of men who themselves need restraining, Calvin thought governing power should be divided and so influenced the rise of constitutional government.[85]

---

[78] Calvin, III. xix. 2.

[79] Calvin, III. vi–x.

[80] I do not think Troeltsch is right to claim Calvin produced "for the first time in the history of the Christian ethic . . . a Christian Church whose social influence . . . was completely comprehensive" (Troeltsch, *Social Teaching*, vol. 2, 622). Calvin's teaching was significant, but the way Augustine and Aquinas each developed Christian understanding of society, though different, was no less comprehensive.

[81] Calvin, *Institutes*, IV. xii. 23; IV. xix. 34.

[82] Calvin, II. viii. 44.

[83] "Intramundane asceticism" comes from Troeltsch, *Social Teaching*, vol. 2, 607. "Protestant work ethic" comes from Max Weber, *The Protestant Ethic and the Spirit of Capitalism*, trans. Talcott Parsons (London: Allen and Unwin, 1930); originally *Die protestantische Ethik und der Geist des Kapitalismus* (1905).

[84] Calvin, *Institutes*, IV. xx. 2.

[85] Calvin, IV. xx. 8.

Calvin believed the purpose of government is set by God, not by nature or the will of those governed, and denied any reason for general rebellion.[86] Magistrates, he said, are "vicars of God" who "cannot be resisted without God being resisted at the same time."[87] But he also opened the possibility of resisting and even replacing wicked rulers by distinguishing respect owed to a governing office from the person occupying that office.[88] It is "the first duty" of subjects, he said, to honor the office rulers hold no matter how wicked they become.[89] But while opposing rebellion arising from a population at large, Calvin went on to say lower magistrates, the *magistrats inférieurs*, should "withstand, in accordance with their duty, the fierce licentiousness of kings."[90]

Lastly, Calvin held that rulers need, on occasion, to use deadly force.[91] He accepted the just war ethic followed by Augustine and said rulers who "keep their hands clean of blood" while allowing wicked men to "range about with slaughter and massacre" are "guilty of the greatest impiety."[92] He claimed "the reason for waging war which existed of old still persists today" and "Christ . . . has changed nothing in this respect."[93] But Calvin also cautioned rulers when using deadly force "to guard particularly against giving vent to their passions even in the slightest degree."[94]

Calvin sometimes is criticized for paradoxes inherent to biblical ethics but, as discussed in Chapter 2, paradoxes are neither wrong nor contradictory. Paradoxes in Calvin's teaching include his view that moral will is free of external constraints while enslaved to its own fallen state, his approval of amassing wealth while insisting it cannot be pursued for its own sake, and his stress on social improvement without reaching social perfection. While these paradoxes are biblical and legitimate, Calvin's ethics is vulnerable to criticism in three ways.

The first problem in Calvin's ethical teaching is that trying to build a sanctified society in fallen circumstances led him to expect social transformation to a degree only possible if

---

[86] Calvin, IV. xx. 2; IV. xx. 9.
[87] Calvin, IV. xx. 6; IV. xx. 23.
[88] Calvin, IV. xx. 22.
[89] Calvin, IV. xx. 22; IV. xx. 25.
[90] Calvin, IV. xx. 31.
[91] Calvin, IV. xx. 11.
[92] Calvin, IV. xx. 10–12.
[93] Calvin, IV. xx. 12.
[94] Calvin, IV. xx. 12.

Christians possess all power and the Church is sovereign over defining and enforcing the ethic by which all is governed.[95] Calvin separated church and state in organizational terms but made the state functionally subordinate to the ethical teaching of the church.[96] So, although he distinguished the institutions organizationally, he did not leave the state free to refuse the ethical instruction of the church. Piety, he said, is "the first concern" of rulers since "it is fitting that they should labor to protect and assert the honor of him whose representatives they are."[97]

The second problem is that making the state functionally subordinate to the ethical teaching of the church led Calvin to deny religious liberty. He did not give the church temporal powers, but he expected pious rulers of their own free will to coerce acceptance of and compliance with the one true faith.[98] Thus, Calvin bluntly states, "I now commit to civil government the duty of rightly establishing religion" and "I approve of a civil administration that aims to prevent the true religion . . . from being . . . defiled with impunity."[99]

These first two problems led to a third, which is that Calvin sided with the papacy, against Luther, in legitimizing wars of religion fought on crusade terms. He not only accepted the ethic of just war but also embraced using a crusade ethic of war. Human governors, he believed, are ordained of God, not only to see "that men breathe, eat, drink, and are kept warm," but also to prevent "idolatry, sacrilege against God's name, (and) blasphemies against his truth."[100] This led Calvin to think war could be an instrument of religion, and when it is, he then believed the more God's honor is at stake the less restrained war should be.[101]

---

[95] Calvin pressed this to such an extent he once insisted residents of Geneva had to sign articles of faith to be citizens of the city. See Roland H. Bainton, *The Age of Reformation* (New York: Reinhold, 1956), 50.

[96] Troeltsch, *Social Teaching*, vol. 2, 627.

[97] Calvin, *Institutes*, IV. xx. 9.

[98] Calvin, IV. xx. 9.

[99] Calvin, IV. xx. 3.

[100] Calvin, IV. xx. 3.

[101] This is not addressed in Calvin's *Institutes*, but he stresses in several other places that war should not be restrained where the honor of God is at stake. See John Calvin, *Calvini opera*, vol. viii (8), in *Corpus reformatorum*, vol. xxxvi (36), ed. Guilielmus Baum, Eduardus Cunitz, and Eduardus Reuss (Brunsvigae, DE: Schwetschke et Filium, 1870), 476; John Calvin, *Calvini opera*, vol. xxiv (24), in *Corpus reformatorum*, vol. lii (52), ed. Guilielmus Baum, Eduardus Cunitz, and Eduardus Reuss (Brunsvigae, DE: Schwetschke et Filium, 1882), 360; and John Calvin, *Calvini opera*, vol. xliv (44),

All three problems in Calvin's ethical teaching arise from a perfectionist element in what he thought human government could and should try to achieve in the present world outside the Church where Christians live in mixed society with others. Seeing no right to be wrong and no reason to limit power in pursuing ethical truth as he saw it blinded Calvin to the risk of trusting men in power with using it to coerce faith and action, not just in the Church but in society and not just domestically but internationally.

Ethics of the Anabaptist Movement (1523–1600)

The Anabaptist movement began as a collection of dissenters who rejected Luther and Calvin as well as the Catholic Church. "Anabaptist" was a term applied to any person or group claiming to restart the church rather than reforming the existing institution. The name thus refers to a range of nonconformists from Melchior Hoffman (1495–1543), Thomas Müntzer (1488–1525), Jan Matthys (1500–1534), and John of Leiden (1509–1536), who thought launching the New Jerusalem justified violence, to Menno Simons (1496–1561), Felix Manz (1498–1527), Conrad Grebel (1498–1526), and Jakob Hutter (1500–1536), who repudiated violence at all costs. This sixteenth-century movement generated a perfectionist version of Christian ethics associated with the Swiss Brethren, Hutterites, Mennonites, and Amish and embraced today by the Sojourners community, "social justice Christians," and the "emergent church."

Because the movement began with revolutionaries mixed with pacifists,[102] no single Anabaptist group represents the whole. The ethical teaching of early Anabaptists was not monolithic, and so to be true, we must focus more on what they shared than on how they differed. Abraham Kuyper observed that Anabaptists in general believed "the circle of baptized believers was in duty bound to take all civil life under its guardianship and remodel it."[103] That

---

in *Corpus reformatorum*, vol. lxxii (72), ed. Guilielmus Baum, Eduardus Cunitz, and Eduardus Reuss (Brunsvigae, DE: Schwetschke et Filium, 1890), 346.

[102] J. Denny Weaver observes that historians have divided over how to interpret Anabaptist beginnings, with some claiming they were original revolutionaries who became pacifists after Münster, and with others claiming they were original pacifists who never were revolutionaries. Most now realize Anabaptism began with original revolutionaries mixed with original pacifists, and neither sort can be excluded. Weaver, "Anabaptism," in *Evangelical Dictionary of Theology*, ed. Walter A. Elwell, 2nd ed. (Grand Rapids: Baker, 2001), 54.

[103] Abraham Kuyper, *Lectures on Calvinism* (Grand Rapids: Eerdmans, 1931), 31.

is true but not all there is. Anabaptists also all believed how one lives life (practical ethics) is more important than how one systematizes doctrine, all thought ethics had more to do with obeying commands than understanding principles, and all aimed to realize Christ's millennial kingdom on earth—not just individually but socially and not just someday but now.

Anabaptists also all agreed God is the only ethical authority and, together with Lutherans and Calvinists, they, too, rejected Catholic reliance on natural law philosophy. But they did not agree on the best source of ethical revelation. All used Scripture but in different ways. Some elevated the Old Testament over the New (which led to polygamy, theocracy, and crusade); some rejected the Old Testament moral law, replacing it with the Sermon on the Mount (which led to nonresistance, refusing oaths, and withdrawing from politics); and some subordinated Scripture to what they claimed was continuing revelation through the inner witness of the Spirit (which led to abolishing private property, titles, and accumulating wealth).

Anabaptists rejected the Lutheran church-world ethical dualism along with the Catholic clergy-laity ethical dualism. But instead of embracing Calvin's view of an unchanging universal ethic, they took the monastic ethic of personal perfection, socialized it, and applied it to everyone. When this proved impossible to achieve without violence, they retreated from immediate universalization and adopted a form of Luther's dualism without including his idea of Christians living by two ethical systems at once—one for inside and the other for outside the church.[104] Thus, in effect, Anabaptists held that all Christians (not just priests, monks, and nuns) must live by Luther's inside ethic wherever they are and must strive (where they can in the world outside their communities) to replace Luther's outside ethic with his inside ethic.

Eventually, Anabaptists came to share a common set of values with eight features: discipleship, holy community, brotherly love, simplicity, strict discipline, detachment, nonviolence, and endurance. *Discipleship* meant imitating Christ in radical terms. *Holy community* meant viewing ethics in social and not merely individual terms. *Brotherly love* meant not allowing any

---

[104] This shift took place at a meeting following the Münster Rebellion (1534–1535) held in Bocholt, Germany, in August 1535. At this meeting, leaders from various Anabaptist groups worked to unify their convictions, and the violent Anabaptists accepted a compromise, maintaining that the time for fighting non-Anabaptists had not yet arrived and they would use no more force until it did. Anabaptist groups at this meeting included survivors of Münster, Batenburgers (who agreed with the Münsterites), David Joris (a compromised figure), and followers of Menno Simons (who repudiated the Münster violence).

Christian to go naked, homeless, or hungry. *Simplicity* meant renouncing materialism, being generous, and avoiding extravagance. *Strict discipline* meant shunning sinful Christians and excommunicating the unrepentant. *Detachment* meant refusing to swear oaths or to participate in civil life outside their own holy communities.[105] *Nonviolence* meant no military service, not defending themselves, and opposing capital punishment. And *endurance* meant suffering adversity without complaint.

Despite laudable qualities, like imitating Christ and stressing generosity, Anabaptist ethics also has serious problems. One is that Anabaptist ethics confuses the believer-unbeliever distinction with the Catholic clergy-laity distinction, leaving no place for Christians to go into the world to engage, evangelize, and be a healthy moral influence on nonbelievers. A second is Anabaptist ethics denies that God's creational ethic—the one affirmed at Sinai—still applies after the cross and is relevant for Christians living today. A third is, in contrast to Calvin's unchanging universal ethic and Luther's division of ethics by circumstance, Anabaptist ethics discontinues God's moral rule and claims a new and completely different ethic is now replacing the one God used before Jesus came. A fourth is Anabaptist ethics substitutes human efforts to realize social perfection in the present world for Christ's millennial rule in the world to come. And a final problem is many, if not all, Anabaptists tend to express the Catholic works-righteousness view of salvation more than the Protestant view of salvation *sola fide* (by faith alone).[106]

Anabaptists were harshly persecuted in the sixteenth century, and thousands were killed by Catholics and Protestants alike, which leads to wondering why it happened. The reason heard most often is that opponents failed to comprehend their differences and blamed them all for stirring up the German Peasants' War (1524–1525) and Münster Rebellion (1534–1535). While partly true, that is not the main reason. The greater motive was that Anabaptist convictions provoked fear in those responsible for maintaining order and justice in the larger world. When Anabaptists refused to swear oaths of loyalty, refused to defend their cities, refused to participate in civil life, and instead criticized economic prosperity and proclaimed a

---

[105] Not all Anabaptists required radical civil withdrawal. Pilgram Marpeck, a South German Anabaptist, developed a mediating position. But since European governments in the sixteenth century all enforced religious unity under a human ruler, most did eventually.

[106] Walter Klaassen, "Anabaptist Ethics," in *Westminster Dictionary of Christian Ethics*, ed. James F. Childress and John Macquarrie (Philadelphia: Westminster, 1986), 21.

new kingdom was replacing all present governments, their ethics seemed dangerous no matter how they otherwise stressed peace and love. The persecution of early Anabaptists was terribly wrong. But because of it, they became strong proponents of religious liberty, and through their influence, Christian ethics now includes a consensus that civil power must never be used to coerce matters of faith.

Ethics of the Jesuit Movement (1500–1700)

The Catholic response to the Protestant challenge that erupted in the sixteenth century was the Counter-Reformation (1545–1648), a renewal movement led by Ignatius of Loyola (1491–1556) who founded the Society of Jesus (*Societas Jesu*), otherwise known as the Jesuits. This was a new sort of religious order consisting of clerics who did not lead services (like priests) and did not withdraw into monasteries (like monks) but who instead lived in the world where they tried to be a good moral and spiritual influence. The Jesuits reacted to Protestantism out of loyalty to the papacy and were strongly influenced by mystical experiences claimed by their founders.[107]

Ignatius trained followers through his one major work, *Spiritual Exercises*, which was a series of prayers and meditations meant to shape their interior lives. Those who became Jesuits swore absolute loyalty to the Pope, took vows of poverty and chastity, and devoted their lives to evangelization, education, and charity work. Over time, they spread the Catholic faith around the world, popularized a method of prayer and meditation, and founded hundreds of schools. But their approach to Christian ethics relied more on Aristotle than on Scripture, and they considered good behavior essential to salvation rather than basing it on faith alone.

The Jesuits produced many moral theologians, including Francisco de Suárez (1548–1617), who became the greatest scholastic thinker after Aquinas (1225–1274). Suárez rejected the absolute power of kings and claimed the right to make human laws resides in the whole body of mankind.[108] He believed the legitimacy of human government comes from a social contract to which people consent but only if they remain subject to the Catholic Church. Suárez followed the just war tradition, saying, "War itself is not intrinsically evil," and "if

---

[107] Thomas O. Kay, "Monasticism," in *New Dictionary of Christian Ethics & Pastoral Theology*, ed. David J. Atkinson et al. (Downers Grove, IL: InterVarsity, 1995), 600.

[108] Francisco de Suárez, *A Treatise on Laws and God the Lawgiver* 3.2.

waged defensively, it may even be a moral necessity."[109] But he also accepted wars of crusade, claiming, "Even when war is aggressive, it is not evil in itself, but may be right and necessary."[110]

Jesuit ethics was strongly criticized for embracing a form of Catholic casuistry based on probabilism, a notion that started with Aquinas but was further developed and applied by Suárez. Probabilism was a form of ethical subjectivism that held any action can be justified for which reasonable arguments are given, even if better arguments support the opposite case. This provoked vigorous debate with those holding a biblically based, non-Aristotelian, non-scholastic approach to Christian ethics, including the French thinker Blaise Pascal (1623–1662), who thought Jesuit ethics threatened adherence to moral norms and engendered laxity.[111]

Ethics of Puritanism (1564–1700)

The Puritans were Protestants living in the sixteenth and seventeenth centuries who worked to reform personal and social ethics in England and America.[112] They continued the Bible based, Augustinian, non-Aristotelian stream of Christian ethics, and Mark Noll credits them with making "as serious an attempt as has ever been made in the English speaking world to establish their lives on the basis of biblical instruction."[113] They thought the monastics were right to renounce the world but were wrong to withdraw from it, and, with Calvin, the Puritans held to a timeless, unified ethic and believed it was man's duty to make everyone everywhere conform to God's sovereign rule.

---

[109] Francisco de Suárez, "Is War Intrinsically Evil?" in *A Treatise on the Three Theological Virtues: Faith, Hope, and Charity*, Disputation XIII.

[110] de Suárez.

[111] Blaise Pascal, *Provincial Letters*, 1656–1657.

[112] Those who stayed to reform the Church of England from within were "non-separating Puritans," and those who left it "separating Puritans" or "Separatists." But the term "Puritan" included both groups. The Pilgrims who traveled to America in 1620 on the *Mayflower* were a group of separating Puritans, while the settlers who arrived later in 1629 with John Winthrop (1588–1649) were non-separating Puritans.

[113] Mark A. Noll, "Puritanism," in *Evangelical Dictionary of Theology*, 2nd ed., ed. Walter A. Elwell (Grand Rapids: Baker, 2001), 973.

Godliness, sobriety, and self-examination were distinguishing features of Puritan personal ethics. Godliness meant becoming "God-ruled" in every action, thought, and desire. Sobriety meant not frittering life away on superficialities. Self-examination meant daily resisting the world, the flesh, and the devil. They drank alcohol but opposed drunkenness, valued the arts but opposed licentious themes, and because music is able not only to honor God but also to corrupt, they banned musical instruments in worship services and sang psalms in church acapella.

They stressed gender roles, family worship, and honoring sex and marriage. Husbands should lead, provide, and protect, and wives should nurture their families under male authority. Fathers were to lead family devotions every day, and *Of Domesticall Duties* (1622) by William Gouge (1575–1653) gave detailed instructions for doing so. They affirmed the goodness of sex and did not venerate virginity. They opposed sexual immorality but not sex itself and made sex in marriage a duty to the extent that one Puritan settler was excommunicated for not having sex with his wife.[114]

The Puritans stressed the virtues of industry, diligence, and thrift while condemning materialism. Every day had to be lived in view of eternity. Hard work kept sin at bay and idleness was the Devil's workshop. They rejected feudalism and pursued economic independence. They no longer considered poverty a virtue and thought it was most often the consequence of personal irresponsibility and laziness. But they were not hardhearted and encouraged philanthropy, while condemning the pursuit of wealth for its own sake or for squandering on lavish personal comforts.

Along with pursuing godliness in personal, family, and economic life, the Puritans developed a special interest in political ethics and led a religiously inspired revolution that executed King Charles I (1600–1649) and replaced the British monarchy with a short lived commonwealth under Oliver Cromwell (1599–1659). Never have Protestants tried harder to govern on Christian terms, and, although Puritan influence diminished in England after 1659, it remained strong in North America where it shaped the constitution and early governing of the United States.

---

[114] Thomas Foster, "Deficient Husbands: Manhood, Sexual Incapacity, and Male Marital Sexuality in Seventeenth-Century New England," *William and Mary Quarterly* 56/4 (October 1999): 726–27.

The Puritans aimed to make society a "City on a Hill,"[115] but they did not think social perfection could be achieved by inaugurating the millennial rule of Christ on earth as the Anabaptists imagined. They only hoped to improve conditions in a sin-cursed world pending Christ's return. They believed church and state were separate institutions both ordained by God, and since both are under God, the Puritans thought the functions of these separate institutions could and should be arranged to coordinate with each supporting the other. This led the Puritans to affirm a functional, but not an ethical, separation of church and state. Government, they believed, should assist and never interfere with the ministry of the church, and this included punishing violations of God's moral law.

Puritan ethics had strengths that served to improve personal and social life, such as minimizing crime, strengthening family relationships, and spurring economic development. But it had weaknesses as well. Puritan ethics tended to reduce everything to prescriptions leaving little room for wisdom or discretion, and this caused the movement to produce a Protestant version of Catholic casuistry. The Puritans mixed Old Testament ceremonial stipulations regarding the Sabbath (never meant to endure or apply to everyone) with God's universal and everlasting moral law and so condemned actions like writing letters and cooking meals as being sinful depending on when they were done. While claiming religious freedom for themselves, they did not extend it to others and once in power limited freedom of conscience to their own members. For these reasons, Ernst Troeltsch claims the Puritans introduced ethical legalism to a degree previously unknown among Protestants.[116]

Ethics of Quakerism (1650–1800)

The Quakers were a small group of reformers who arose in England during the seventeenth century and came to influence the world well beyond their few numbers. They were viciously persecuted by Catholics and Puritans alike who thought Quakers were anarchists because they denied all creeds, rejected worship practices like baptism and communion, never recognized clergy, erased social distinctions, challenged established authorities both civil and ecclesial,

---

[115] Proclaimed at the founding of the Massachusetts Bay Colony in John Winthrop's 1630 sermon aboard the ship *Arbella*.

[116] Troeltsch, *Social Teaching*, vol. 2, 680.

and elevated what they called "Inner Light" over the Bible, orthodox theology, and historic doctrines of the church. Their founder, George Fox (1624–1691), had little education but claimed to have had a vision in which God ordered him to declare a new ethic launching a "Lamb's War" (without weapons of this world) in which Christ would conquer the world— not just individually but socially, not just religiously but politically, and not just in the future but right away.[117]

Some incorrectly classify the Quakers as Puritans,[118] but they were different groups with completely different ethical views. The Puritans stressed original sin while the Quakers denied it. The Puritans prioritized the Bible while the Quakers marginalized it. The Puritans were social realists while the Quakers were social idealists. The Puritans justified war while the Quakers were pacifists. Lastly, Quaker ethics had three distinguishing characteristics never associated with Puritans: a spirit of mysticism that resisted tradition, doctrine, and objective ethical standards; a spirit of leveling that resisted religious, social, and political distinctions; and a spirit of brotherhood that resisted the use of force.

Mysticism led Quakers to reduce ethical truth to perceptions of "Inner Light" disconnected from Scripture and having no accountability to higher authority. The greatest Quaker intellectual, Robert Barclay (1648–1690), claimed the Bible is "not the principle ground of all truth" and is only "a secondary rule" subordinate to the inner light everyone has regardless of faith.[119] Leveling led Quakers to reject gender roles in church, but not in the family, commerce, or politics; to reject honorific titles and customs, such as bowing or tipping their hats, but not to the extent of ceasing to cooperate with magistrates and kings; and to reject class distinctions, but not to the extent of equalizing income. Brotherhood led Quakers to reject war but not to the extent of criticizing the conscience of soldiers or refusing to participate in wars in noncombatant positions. Quakers opposed the world but not entirely, meaning they pursued ideals while cooperating with contradictions undermining them. They rejected war and coercion but accepted civil government and supported military service. They rejected slavery but not private property, and they rejected clergy while accepting the role of elders. The

---

[117] H. Larry Ingle, *First Among Friends: George Fox and the Creation of Quakerism* (Oxford: Oxford University, 1994).

[118] Beach, Niebuhr, and White all misclassify Quakers as Puritans (Beach and Niebuhr, *Christian Ethics*, 307, 309; White, *Christian Ethics*, 249, 253).

[119] Robert Barclay, *Apology for the True Christian Divinity*, III. v.

Quakers thus withdrew from the world in partial ways while also remaining partly engaged with the world hoping to change it.

Quaker ethics grew to influence Western thought in some positive ways, the greatest being that it influenced the American founders to declare "all men are created equal" and "are endowed by their Creator with certain unalienable rights."[120] But Quaker ethics had glaring deficiencies as well. Its radical intuitionism led to anarchic antinomianism because Quakers had no way to distinguish "Inner Light" from their own desires, and the collapse of Quaker government in Pennsylvania proved a state could not operate on Quaker ethics in a fallen world and survive. The Quakers compromised their own ideals, not by accepting dualism, but by applying them selectively. They were unorthodox Christians who denied the necessity of the cross, redefined the gospel, and pursued self-perfection without objective accountability. In the end, they were ethical intuitionists who tried changing the outside world by focusing within themselves and tried transforming themselves and the world without transforming human nature.

Ethics of Anglican Rationalism (1570–1780)

The Age of Reason that started in the sixteenth century and lasted into the eighteenth arose mainly because upper-class Anglicans feared the Puritans and Quakers were undermining the historic union joining the Church of England to the British crown. These upper class Anglicans scorned what they called "enthusiasm," preferring rather to rely on dispassionate reason in place of ancient texts claiming to come from God. Richard Hooker (1554–1600), the movement's first proponent, in *Laws of Ecclesiastical Polity* (1594), formulated what became known as the Anglican *via media* (middle way) by siding, on the one hand, with Protestants in rejecting papal authority and, on the other, with Catholics in rejecting reliance on the Bible alone. But Hooker did this by elevating reason over the Bible together with the pope. John Locke (1632–1704), a second voice in this movement, claimed Christianity can

---

[120] Quotations from *The Declaration of Independence* (Philadelphia: Second Continental Congress, passed July 4, 1776). For how Quakers influenced Thomas Jefferson and the Founding Fathers with these ideas, see William Comfort, Francis Hass, Gregg Neel, and Stanley Yarnell, eds., *Remember William Penn* (Harrisburg, PA: William Penn Tercentenary Committee, Pennsylvania Historical Commission, 1944).

be "according to reason" or "above reason" but can never be "contrary to reason,"[121] and he wrote *The Reasonableness of Christianity* (1695) to prove Christianity is justified based on reason apart from revelation. The strongest proponent was Joseph Butler (1692–1752), who, in *Fifteen Sermons* (1726) and *On the Nature of Virtue* (1736), reconceived Christian ethics as based on reason alone and nothing else.[122]

These rationalists took the scholastic synthesis that, in the Middle Ages, mixed philosophy with theology and not only introduced back into Protestantism notions the Reformers rejected but also went beyond the scholastics to deny the Bible had any necessary role in Christian ethics. They viewed the ethical problem challenging human life in Greek rather than biblical terms, meaning they viewed it as ignorance rather than slavery to sin. Whereas the Reformers distrusted human nature corrupted by sin, the rationalists trusted human nature the way it is, saw no conflict between self-love and benevolence, and made self-love the "chief security of our right behaviour toward society."[123] They made Christian ethics autonomous and claimed, "man is . . . by his very nature a law to himself,"[124] even though this required faith in human reason that was every bit as dogmatic as faith in God and his Word.

By reconceiving Christian ethics in autonomous, self-conceived (philosophical) terms, Anglican rationalism reduced Christian ethics to the mundane, self-referential, humanly imaginable, naturally achievable, and historically immediate, while erasing everything transcendent, transformational, paradoxical, impossible, and not yet. It reimagined the relation of Christianity to ethics as one of illustration more than illumination, of acceptability more than accountability, and of confirmation more than transformation. Perhaps, with the exception

---

[121] John Locke, *An Essay Concerning Human Understanding* (1689), book vi, chapter 17, number 23.

[122] Butler so disputed biblical authority in Christian ethics he once complained, "pretending to extraordinary revelations and gifts of the Holy Ghost is a horrid thing, a very horrid thing." Cited by C. F. Allison in *New Dictionary of Christian Ethics & Pastoral Theology*, ed. David J. Atkinson, David F. Field, Arthur Holmes, Oliver O'Donovan (Downers Grove, IL: InterVarsity, 1995), 209. Also cited in *Oxford Essential Quotations*, ed. Susan Ratcliffe (Oxford: Oxford University Press, 2017).

[123] Joseph Butler, "Sermon I: Upon the Social Nature of Man" (preached 1726), in *Fifteen Sermons Preached at the Rolls Chapel* (Cambridge: Hilliard and Brown, 1827); republished in Joseph Butler, *Sermons* (New York: Robert Carter & Brothers, 1858).

[124] Joseph Butler, "Preface," *Fifteen Sermons Preached at the Rolls Chapel* (Cambridge: Hilliard and Brown, 1827); republished in Joseph Butler, *Sermons* (New York: Robert Carter & Brothers, 1858).

of Locke,[125] what most characterized the movement was how it reconceived Christian ethics as "ending with God," when heretofore it had always "started with God." By taking the Bible, God, transcendence, and transformation out of Christian ethics, Anglican rationalism took the "Christianity" out of Christian ethics and so anticipated the emergence of Protestant liberalism in the late nineteenth and early twentieth centuries.[126]

Ethics of Pietism (1650–1875)

Pietism arose as a movement protesting spiritual coldness and moral laxity in state-run Protestant churches in Germany at the end of the seventeenth century. But over the next centuries, it came to affect Protestants all over the world.[127] Early leaders of the movement were Philipp Jakob Spener (1635–1705), who sought to revitalize the faith by organizing small groups (*collegia pietatis*) within existing churches; August Hermann Francke (1663–1727), who founded many schools and social service institutions; and Nicholas Ludwig von Zinzendorf (1700–1760), who organized a group of refugees into a community that sent missionaries around the world and grew to become the Moravian church.[128]

Pietists were people of the heart who rejected cold intellectualism focused on doctrinal purity and sought to revive the affectional side of faith and ethics by cultivating devotion to Christ and passion for saving souls and practical benevolence. Pietist ethics had four primary traits. It stressed personal experience, preferred inner transformation over external effects, relied on the Bible directly over doctrine, and had a bent toward perfectionism. The

---

[125] Locke's *First Treatise of Government* (1689) relies on faith in the authority of biblical revelation, while his *The Reasonableness of Christianity* (1695) relies on faith in autonomous human reason apart from revelation.

[126] Beach and Niebuhr go as far as to ask, "If the theological element be an ingredient necessary for Christian ethics," then "in what sense" could Joseph Butler's "ethical theory be called Christian?" (Beach and Niebuhr, *Christian Ethics*, 333).

[127] The definition of "Pietism" varies depending on contextual focus. Widely, it denotes kindred spiritual revivals that spread throughout the world. Narrowly, it refers only to the second Reformation among Protestants in Germany. I am here using it in the wider sense.

[128] The main works expressing, developing, or promulgating the ethics of Pietism include Johann Arndt, *True Christianity* (1606); Philipp Jakob Spener, *Pia Desideria* (1675); August Hermann Francke, *On Christian Perfection* (1690); and William Law, *Serious Call to a Devout and Holy Life* (1729).

movement stressed intimacy with God but differed from mysticism in subjecting religious experience to biblical validation. Pietists, like the mystics, took an ascetic approach to personal ethics, but they never forgot the Bible also requires evangelizing the lost and loving needy neighbors. Pietist ethics thus featured a tension that rejected "the world" and "worldliness" as a realm of evil, while at the same time calling Christians to confront evil in the world through evangelism, education, and benevolence. Pietist insistence on uniting personal holiness with serving the needy reflected the ethics of monasticism. But rather than separating super holy Christians from ordinary Christians, they separated truly serious Christians from worldliness while urging all to serve and evangelize others.

The preference Pietists had for inner transformation over external effects influenced how they approached social and political ethics. Like Jesus, they focused on changing hearts and ignored social and political structures. For this reason, the movement never challenged existing systems, and Pietist ethics never went beyond personal life to address social, economic, or political power structures. Placing stress on living only for God while minimizing doctrine left Pietists vulnerable to notions of reaching personal perfection before Christ's second coming. They believed personal perfection meant holding nothing back from God and took Christlikeness to be the ethical ideal, but members of the movement never agreed on the degree to which, and on what terms, Christians could reach Christlike perfection under present conditions. Critics have accused Pietists of emotionalism, subjectivism, and espousing a fatalism that limits reform to changing individuals and nothing more. But the movement was never escapist and managed to inject Protestant ethics with a spirit of devotion, stress on personal transformation, and insistence on uniting evangelism with benevolent service that has continued ever since.

CHAPTER 6

HISTORY, FIGURES
& MOVEMENTS
JOHN WESLEY TO EMERGING TRENDS

This chapter continues introducing readers to historical Christian ethics as an academic subcategory within the larger field of Christian ethics. The previous chapter started with the ethics of the early Church and continued through the ethics of Pietism. This chapter starts with the ethics of John Wesley and continues to emerging trends.

Ethics of John Wesley (1703–1791)

John Wesley (1703–1791), an Anglican cleric and theologian from Epworth, England, about 150 miles north of London, and the founder of what became Methodism, was a leading figure among eighteenth-century British Pietists. He is worth separate focus in the history of Christian ethics, not just because his followers separated from Anglicanism, but because he formulated a new approach to Christian ethical understanding that deviated greatly from that of Augustine, the Reformers, and the Puritans. Over against predestination limiting those elected for salvation, Wesley held that all can be saved and those not saved are limited only by their own free will. Over against eternal security, he held that good works are motivated in part by fear of losing salvation. And, over against partial sanctification prior to Christ's return, he taught Christians must achieve ethical perfection before going to heaven. Wesley combined Pietist passions for holiness, heart conversion, and small group accountability with how monasticism used rigorous self-discipline to pursue sanctification, how the Reformers trusted Scripture alone, and how Puritans rejected worldliness while engaging the world. He stressed personal holiness while calling for social action and taught that conversion involves two stages of ethical development. In the first stage, believers are credited with the perfect righteousness of Christ, and in the second stage, the Spirit helps them grow to perfection.[1]

Wesley's personal ethics centered on his notion of "entire sanctification," by which he meant that, after conversion, and before death, every believer must become "so far perfect, as not to commit sin."[2] But Wesley reduced the meaning of "sin" only to doing wrong on purpose,[3] and he reasoned Christians must reach perfection in this life because, while the righteousness of Christ "imputed" by faith "entitles" believers to heaven, we do not "qualify" for heaven until the Spirit finishes "imparting" the total righteousness of living without sin.[4] This doctrine is not widely accepted because most Protestants have followed Augustine and the Reformers in believing that, until Christ removes the power and presence of sin, and not only the penalty of sin, moral perfection is an impossible ideal for which we strive but can never reach.

Wesley did not think salvation is limited to preparing ourselves for heaven without loving others here on earth and said, "The Gospel of Christ knows of no religion, but social" and "no holiness, but social holiness."[5] This led Wesley to fight for better prison conditions, offer loans to keep people out of debtors' prison, oppose the sale of hard liquor, found a school for poor children, establish a home for widows, dispense free medical services, and condemn

---

[1] John Wesley, *The Lord Our Righteousness*, 1765.

[2] John Wesley, *A Plain Account of Christian Perfection*, 1777.

[3] Shelton, "Perfection, Perfectionism," 906 (see chap. 5, n. 12).

[4] Wesley, *The Lord Our Righteousness*, 1765; John Wesley, *The New Birth*, 1788. Also see Robert G. Tuttle, Jr., "Wesley, John," in *Evangelical Dictionary of Theology*, 2nd ed., ed. Walter A. Elwell (Grand Rapids: Baker, 2001), 1267; Charles W. Brockwell, "John Wesley's Doctrine of Justification," *Wesleyan Theological Journal* 18/2 (1983): 18–32.

[5] John Wesley, *Preface to Hymns and Sacred Poems* (1739), in *The Works of John Wesley* (Grand Rapids: Zondervan, 1958), 14:321.

slavery. He viewed economic ethics as stewarding assets owned ultimately by God and urged believers to gain all you can, save all you can, and give all you can.[6] The first required industry, diligence, and productivity. The second guarded against waste, hoarding, and luxury, and the third aimed to please God by maximizing generosity and minimizing self-interest. Methodists have since eased what Wesley's third principle requires. Wesley actually intended something like Basil the Great (330–379), who thought Christians should keep nothing for themselves beyond basic subsistence, but Methodists today soften this to allow accumulating personal wealth.

Wesley's personal and social ethics were expansive, but his political and military ethics were not. Wesley told ministers not to address politics unless to support the government,[7] and while assuming good rulers should govern on Christian terms, he never dealt with resisting bad ones. He favored monarchy over democracy and thought American independence was unjustified because "no governments under heaven are so despotic as the republican" and "no subjects are governed in so arbitrary a manner as those of a common-wealth."[8] Wesley was no pacifist but opposed war so strongly he never discussed what was justified. He thought war "a horrid reproach . . . to all reason and humanity,"[9] which has led some to wonder if he allowed war at all. Methodists are thus divided over military service, with some resisting and others not. Wesley never specified what to do and seems to have left it to personal conscience.

Ethics of Jonathan Edwards (1703–1758)

Jonathan Edwards (1703–1758) was the leading Calvinist of the eighteenth century. But unlike Calvin, who relied on nothing but Scripture, Edwards took a syncretic approach, mixing philosophy with theology to conceive Christian ethics in terms going beyond biblical revelation. Edwards did not take the Catholic approach of relying on Aristotelian natural law and instead took up philosophical notions more popular in his day. From John Locke (1632–1704), Edwards adopted the notion that ideas come from sensations; from the Cambridge

---

[6] John Wesley, *On the Use of Money*, 1744.
[7] John Wesley, *What Are the Rules of a Helper?*, 1744.
[8] John Wesley, *A Calm Address to Our American Colonies*, 1775.
[9] John Wesley, *The Doctrine of Original Sin*, 1756.

Platonists, he adopted the notion that material things spatially exist in the mind of God; from Thomas Hobbes (1588–1679) and John Locke (1632–1704), he adopted thinking liberty is doing what we want instead of what we should; and from the third Earl of Shaftesbury (1671–1713) and Francis Hutcheson (1694–1746), he adopted the notion of virtue permitting no self-love whatsoever.[10]

Unlike Aquinas and the Anglican Rationalists, Edwards located virtue in the emotional self rather than in the intellectual self. He insisted virtue aims at "Being in general" and values benevolence only for its own sake. Edwards, therefore, argued Christian ethics has no place for self-love and concluded natural affections, like parental love and pity, are just splendid vices and not virtuous at all.[11] He broke with the Reformers, Calvin, and even Wesley by distinguishing God from the Word of God, and this led Edwards to locate ethical authority not in the Bible itself, but in God beyond the Bible. Edwards also claimed God gives Christians a sixth sense by which we have ethical knowledge straight from God separate from the Bible.[12] He believed this enables Christians to apprehend what he called "the beauty of the Godhead," "the divinity of Divinity," and "the infinite Fountain of good" in and of itself directly and thus to have ultimately accurate personal knowledge of "true moral good" apart from Scripture.[13] This meant Edwards believed we can acquire ethical knowledge from inner feelings outside of and beyond what the Bible says, even though he never thought such knowledge ever contradicts anything the Bible says.

Edwards believed the ethical change that occurs in personal regeneration cannot remain internal because love aims toward something called "Being in general." When regeneration occurs this aim produces disinterested benevolence toward others, not just for eternity but in this present life as well. But the applied elements of his ethical thought were undeveloped and not always consistent. Edwards made establishing the kingdom of God a major theme in Christian ethics, but he limited what the kingdom of God requires to individual salvation and character development and never discussed how it applies to work, labor relations, political life, civil citizenship, war and peace, or dealing with imperfect rulers. He encouraged acts of

---

[10] Armand A. Maurer, "Edwards, Jonathan," in *The Encyclopedia of Philosophy*, vol. 2, ed. Paul Edwards, (New York: Macmillan, 1967), 461.

[11] Jonathan Edwards, *The Nature of True Virtue*, 1765.

[12] Maurer, "Edwards, Jonathan," 461.

[13] Jonathan Edwards, *A Treatise Concerning Religious Affections*, 1746.

individual charity toward needy neighbors but never addressed improving social, economic, or political circumstances.[14] And, even though Edwards held that God created all men equal, he also owned slaves and did not seem to have noticed the inconsistency.[15] He mixed theology with philosophical ideas that were fashionable at the time but few have followed since, and his ethical teaching has not influenced Christians much beyond his own time.[16]

Edwards is criticized for idealizing disinterested benevolence because it conflicts with how the Bible requires loving neighbors as ourselves (Lev 19:18; Matt 19:19; Mark 12:31; Luke 10:27; Rom 13:9; Gal 5:14; Jas 2:8), seeking rewards for ourselves (Matt 5:12; Matt 10:42; Mark 9:41; Luke 6:23; 1 Cor 3:8; Phil 3:14; 2 John 1:8), and laying up treasures for ourselves (Matt 6:20), all of which presume there is a proper form of self-love. Edwards countered the cold rationalism of British Rationalism by reaffirming the emphasis Augustine placed on moral affections. But the openness Edwards had to feelings as a source of ethical knowledge apart from Scripture left later Christians vulnerable to mistaking their own desires and appetites for the Word of God.

Ethics of the Social Gospel Movement (1890–1920)

The nineteenth century saw the emergence of a movement to reconstitute Christian ethics by interpreting the kingdom of God based on ideas from Charles Darwin (1809–1883) and Karl Marx (1818–1883) rather than from what the Bible says.[17] Figures like Washington Gladden (1836–1918), Francis Peabody (1847–1936), Walter Rauschenbusch (1861–1918), and George Herron (1862–1925) urged Christians to focus on saving institutions rather than souls because they promised that would turn bad men into good.[18] This development, called

---

[14] Jonathan Edwards, *The Duty of Charity to the Poor*, 1732.

[15] Frank Viola, "The Shocking Beliefs of Jonathan Edwards," ch. 7 in Frank Vida, *ReGrace: What the Shocking Beliefs of the Greatest Christians Can Teach Us Today* (Grand Rapids: Baker, 2019), citing Kenneth P. Minkema, "Jonathan Edwards's Defense of Slavery," *Massachusetts Historical Review* 4 (2002): 23–60.

[16] Mark A. Noll, "Edwards, Jonathan," in *Evangelical Dictionary of Theology*, 2nd ed., ed. Walter A. Elwell, (Grand Rapids: Baker, 2001), 368.

[17] Walter Rauschenbusch gave a speech in 1905, later published in *The Kingdom* 1 (December 1907), in which he urged churches to follow Karl Marx.

[18] Walter Rauschenbusch, *Christianizing the Social Order* (New York: Macmillan, 1912), 125.

the social gospel movement, aimed to reshape social structures while redefining sin, minimizing the roles of personal responsibility and individual accountability, demoting biblical authority, and dismissing the many social ministries founded by Evangelicals in the nineteenth century as misguided, ineffective, or insufficient.[19]

The social gospel reduced the kingdom of God to humanly conceived social ideals it claimed people can achieve on their own without regeneration by the Holy Spirit and having to wait for the second coming of Christ.[20] It denied human depravity and claimed people will stop sinning if private property and authority roles are replaced with voluntary systems based on natural human affection and sentiment. The atoning work of Christ was rejected in favor of politics to such an extent that Rauschenbusch declared, "sin is not a private transaction between sinners and God" and reconceived salvation as "redeeming the historical life of humanity" through human initiative.[21]

The social gospel not only limited Christian ethics to social ethics but also changed what social ethics requires by eliminating transcendence, exaggerating human potential, misconceiving the nature of sin, minimizing the power of sin, and leaving sinners condemned to judgment and alienated from the mercy of God. In the name of the gospel, it preached an entirely different gospel than was preached by Jesus and the apostles (2 Cor 11:4; Gal 1:8–9).[22] In the name of affirming the Bible, it replaced biblical authority with human authority. In the name of pursuing the kingdom of God, it replaced the rule of God with political

---

[19] Some have suggested the social gospel arose because Evangelicals were ignoring social needs, but this is not historically accurate. Nineteenth-century Evangelicals founded a vast number of surprisingly effective social ministries that in retrospect dealt with social problems of the day far more effectively than the flurry of entitlement programs, inspired by the social gospel, that have since replaced them. See Marvin Olasky, *The Tragedy of American Compassion* (Washington, DC: Regnery, 1992); Frank Watson, *The Charity Organization Movement in the United States* (New York: Macmillan, 1922); Walter Trattner, *From Poor Law to Welfare State: A History of Social Welfare in America* (New York: Free Press, 1974).

[20] Walter Rauschenbusch, *Theology for the Social Gospel* (New York: Macmillan, 1918), chapter 13.

[21] Rauschenbusch, chapters 6 and 10.

[22] Wogaman is wrong to say, "Rauschenbusch was able to ground the movement solidly in mainstream Christian tradition" (Wogaman, *Christian Ethics*, 197 [see chap. 5, n. 2]). Just using the term *gospel* is not the true gospel if not faithful to the Word of God, just naming "Jesus" does not name the true Jesus if not faithful to the Word of God, and using words and terms in the Bible in new ways is not the Word of God if not faithful to what they meant when issued by God.

activism and social organizing. In the name of theology, it substituted philosophy. In the name of discipleship, it declared Jesus failed and that we must finish his mission. And in the name of Christianity, it declared Christianity began the wrong way and needs to set a new course.

The problem with the social gospel was not insisting Christian ethics has a social component but supposing Jesus failed and we can do better.[23] It changed the aim of Christianity from something we await from God to something we achieve for ourselves. It imagined a sinless world can be generated without transforming sinners and that Christ's millennial rule can be realized without Christ also because we no longer need await his return or no longer think he is coming back in a literal sense. Like the Münsterites of the sixteenth century, the social gospel movement tried erasing the already-and-not-yet tension in Christian ethics and differed from them only by relying on legislation rather than insurrection. In the end, the social gospel produced large-scale defections from historically faithful Christianity and divided Christian ethics into liberal and conservative streams that have continued ever since.

Ethics of Contemporary Catholicism (1891–present)[24]

Roman Catholic ethics today still relies on how scholastics in the Middle Ages mixed theology with Aristotelian natural law philosophy. But this has not prevented Catholics from exploring other possibilities—some of which the Vatican has embraced (John Courtney Murray, 1904–1967; Karl Rahner, 1904–1984; Bernard Häring, 1912–1998) and some it has rejected (Hans Küng, 1928–2021; Charles Curran, b. 1934). Starting with *Rerum novarum* in 1891, the Vatican has grappled with the most contentious issues troubling life in the modern world, and the Second Vatican Council (1962–1965) tried to focus Catholic thought less on philosophy and more on Scripture. While Catholic ethics no longer relies on the scholastic approach as

---

[23] Huebner says, "Rauschenbusch seems to suggest that Jesus may not be our best model" because after all Jesus "was himself not successful in realizing the kingdom of God." Huebner, *Introduction to Christian Ethics*, 327 (see chap. 5, n. 2).

[24] Here, I am using the term *ethics* in the broad sense of including all moral thought whether theological, philosophical, or mixed. That is how most use the term today and is how it is used throughout this text. But readers should know many Catholic writers, even today, still use the term *ethics* as it was used in the Middle Ages, meaning they use it only for human philosophy and so distinguish *ethics* from moral theology.

heavily as before, strong accents still remain, and, although the Vatican has, at times, criticized Marxism, it has also adopted notions borrowed from Marxist philosophy.[25]

Distinctives marking Catholic ethics today include greater emphasis on relating to God personally; defending the existence and application of universal norms; more openness to the way contextual differences affect ethical assessment; accepting religious liberty as a universal right; and stressing Scripture over tradition, faith over reason, grace over nature, and Christ over the Church. Rahner,[26] and later Pope John Paul II (1920–2005),[27] have led contemporary Catholics to reaffirm the ethical significance of relating to God in personal terms. Pope Paul VI (1897–1978) and Pope John Paul II both defended the reality and relevance of universal norms, based on which they declared abortion, artificial contraception, slavery, and sex trafficking inherently evil activities impossible to ever justify.[28] Rahner, Häring, and Josef Fuchs (1912–2005) helped Catholics understand some moral assessments vary with culture, intention, or perception.[29] John Courtney Murray (the Catholic theologian) persuaded the Vatican to stop saying human governments must obey the church and punish heretics and instead to support religious liberty as a universal right.[30] Rahner, Häring, and Pope John Paul

---

[25] Charles E. Curran, "Official Roman Catholic Social Teaching," in *Westminster Dictionary of Christian Ethics*, ed. James F. Childress and John Macquarrie (Philadelphia: Westminster, 1986), 433.

[26] James R. Bretzke, SJ, "Roman Catholic Moral Theology," in *Dictionary of Scripture and Ethics*, ed. Joel B. Green (Grand Rapids: Baker, 2011), 691; and Charles E. Curran, "Modern Roman Catholic Moral Theology," in *Westminster Dictionary of Christian Ethics*, ed. James F. Childress and John Macquarrie (Philadelphia: Westminster, 1986), 390.

[27] In the encyclical *Sollicitudo rei socialis* (*The Social Concern*) issued December 30, 1987.

[28] In the encyclicals *Humanae vitae* (*Of Human Life*) issued July 25, 1968, *Veritatis splendor* (*The Splendor of Truth*) issued August 6, 1993, and *Evangelium vitae* (*The Gospel of Life*) issued March 25, 1995.

[29] Bretzke, "Catholic Moral Theology," 692; and Long, *A Survey of Christian Ethics*, 94 (see chap. 1, n. 49).

[30] John Courtney Murray, "The Problem of Religious Freedom," *Theological Studies* 25 (December 1964): 503–75; John Courtney Murray, "Religious Freedom," in *The Documents of Vatican II*, ed. by Walter M. Abbot and Joseph Gallagher (New York: America, 1966), 673–96; John Courtney Murray, "Religious Liberty and Development of Doctrine," *The Catholic World* 204 (February 1967): 277–83; John Courtney Murray, *Religious Liberty: Catholic Struggles with Pluralism* (Louisville: Westminster/John Knox, 1993); Long, *Survey of Christian Ethics*, 251; Wogaman, *Christian Ethics*, 237.

II encouraged Catholics to give Scripture, faith, grace, and Jesus greater roles in how they conceive Christian ethics.[31]

Despite these good points, contemporary Catholic ethics has weaknesses as well. Like some Protestants, Catholics, too, have struggled with tension between affirming human fallenness and finitude on the one hand and desiring to solve social problems on the other, as well as affirming the kingdom of God on earth on the one hand and awaiting Christ's return before reaching the fullness of his earthly kingdom on the other.[32] Division among Catholics has strained relationships with the Vatican over whether to affirm a uniquely Christian ethical order, whether to affirm universal norms, and whether Catholics can dissent from what the Vatican teaches and remain in good standing.[33] Lastly, ethical positions taken by the Vatican have not always been consistent, and encyclicals issued by one pope have been countermanded by encyclicals issued by a later pope. For example, the notion of "subsidiarity" (that social needs must be handled at the lowest level of competent authority) was used in *Quadragesimo anno* (1931) to oppose enlarging government and then in *Mater et magistra* (1961) and *Pacem in terris* (1963) was reinterpreted to require expanding government. Some encyclicals have promoted private property and opposed redistribution, and others have opposed private property and called for redistribution.[34] Some have praised free enterprise, and others have praised socialism.[35] Whereas *Pacem in terris* (1963) espoused pacifism rather than just war, *Gaudium et spes* (1965) espoused just war rather than pacifism.

---

[31] In the encyclicals *Sollicitudo rei socialis* (*The Social Concern*) issued December 30, 1987, *Veritatis splendor* (*The Splendor of Truth*) issued August 6, 1993, and *Evangelium vitae* (*The Gospel of Life*) issued March 25, 1995.

[32] Curran, "Modern Roman Catholic Moral Theology," 390.

[33] Curran, 392.

[34] *Divini redemptoris* (1937) condemned communism and affirmed private property as a universal moral right. But *Quadragesimo anno* (1931) and *Populorum progressio* (1967) both criticized private property and expected government to redistribute wealth by force if necessary.

[35] *Octogesima adveniens* (1971) and *Laborem exercens* (1981) both affirmed free enterprise. But *Mater et magistra* (1961) and *Populorum progressio* (1967) both criticized free enterprise and called for using civil power to force worldwide wealth redistribution.

Ethics of Neo-Orthodoxy (1918–1980)

Word War I (1914–1918) marked the end of the social gospel as a major influence in Christian ethics and sparked the rise of a new approach reacting against naïve faith in human perfectibility. This new approach, called neo-orthodoxy,[36] returned to affirming historically orthodox views about sin, salvation, the kingdom of God, and the mission of the Church, and took a more conservative, though not entirely orthodox, view of Scripture. While the movement reaffirmed Augustinian and Reformational doctrines regarding human nature and the world, it adopted a subjective approach to the Word of God. It returned to affirming the value of Scripture but not enough to restore the ultimate authority of Scripture in Christian ethics.

Neo-orthodoxy refused to elevate reason, philosophy, and science over the Word of God and denied that the kingdom of God can be reduced to humanly achieved visions of perfection. But it was undermined by influences stemming from dialecticism, existentialism, and higher critical methods of biblical interpretation. Neo-orthodox theologians distinguished God from the Bible, and in the name of affirming God's transcendence over humanity, paved the way for elevating personal feelings and experience over what the Bible says. With Augustine, they affirmed the centrality of Divine love in Christian ethics. But they distinguished the biblical text from encountering God himself, and this led successors to consider existential situationism. They respected the Bible, but not enough to view it as having objective authority, and because they thought ultimate moral authority comes from experiencing God moment by moment in personal terms rather than from the Bible itself, they ended up denying the reality and relevance of rules and principles in Christian ethics.

Karl Barth (1886–1968)

The first major neo-orthodox theologian was Karl Barth (1886–1968), who was driven to rethink Christian ethics by World War I and emerged as Hitler's greatest intellectual opponent during World War II. Barth believed Christian ethics must never mix with philosophy and is as opposed

---

[36] As applied to this movement, the term "orthodoxy" refers to historic Christian faith and practice and not to the state-church faction ruled from Constantinople that in AD 1095 divided from the state-church faction ruled from Rome.

to human reason as it is to human sin.[37] Right living, he believed, is a privilege, and obeying God expresses freedom and love. He claimed Christian love determines what is good and right, but this love does not come from self and is interpreted and performed only in, for, and through Jesus Christ. Barth held that ethics comes from nothing other than the commanding God who transcends culture, the Church, and even rationality. And he even claimed God does not need to follow the Bible because he viewed the Bible as no more than human words about God having no divine authority in themselves. Instead, like Jonathan Edwards, Barth argued God's ethical authority is best found directly from the inwardly experienced Jesus, the Divine-Man now "present to us . . . and one with us as our Lord."[38] But for Barth, unlike Edwards, what believers know from Jesus within themselves is more authoritative and can even counter or set aside what the Bible says. Barth held this because he thought what believers apprehend from Jesus within themselves is directly of God, whereas the Bible only contains words of men about God, making it less directly of God and not as reliable. Of course, Evangelicals disagree.

Barth saw how striving for justice stirs conflicts with vested interests in a sinful world, and, with that, maintained that we cannot create the kingdom of God in the present world filled with sinners. Instead, we must live by faith in light of God's promises. The church must not usurp the state, even if rulers become "idolatrous" and the state becomes "demonic."[39] He thought we can do nothing to speed Christ's coming kingdom and can only anticipate its arrival. So, while Barth emphasized God's real transcendence and the reality of human depravity, he denied the Bible is the Word of God itself and had little hope of improving social conditions in the present world filled with sin and sinners.[40]

Dietrich Bonhoeffer (1906–1945)

Dietrich Bonhoeffer (1906–1945) was trained by Barth and wrote profoundly on Christian ethics in the few years he had before being martyred by the Nazis. Bonhoeffer attacked what

---

[37] Karl Barth, *Ethics*, 22, 44 (see chap. 1, n. 26). White, *Christian Ethics*, 339 (see chap. 1, n. 69).

[38] Barth, *Ethics*, 322–23.

[39] Karl Barth, *Church and State*, 1939. Originally *Justification and Justice*.

[40] For this reason, Reinhold Niebuhr once criticized Barth's "transcendental irresponsibility." John Macquarrie, *Twentieth Century Religious Thought* (London: SCM, 1963), 324.

he called "cheap grace" and insisted Christian discipleship is costly.[41] He distinguished the ultimate from the penultimate in Christian ethics in order to clarify how ethics in the present world relates to or compares with ethics in the world to come. It is a difference that, while acknowledging God's unchanging character, also acknowledges that what God requires in social and political relationships works out differently among sinners in sinful circumstances than among sinless people in sinless circumstances.

For now, social and political perfections are out of reach. Even though we should try to make things better, we should not think we can generate social or political perfections under present circumstances. In the present sinful world, we see "the hungry man needs bread and the homeless man needs a roof; the dispossessed need justice and the lonely need fellowship; the undisciplined need order and the slave needs freedom."[42] Bonhoeffer held that we must address such needs, but we should do so only because it pleases God and expresses God's love for people in need and not because we imagine it is possible to erase hunger, homelessness, loneliness, injustice, disorder, and oppression altogether.

Some criticize Bonhoeffer for saying Christianity must be "worldly" and "religionless." But by "worldly," he did not mean we should lower standards and rather meant, since God is in the world, we should stop acting as if he is not here with us. And, by becoming "religion-less," Bonhoeffer did not mean we should stop believing God is real and worshiping him, but only that we should not reduce Christianity to rituals and ought to practice it as living in a real relationship with Christ himself. But Bonhoeffer should be criticized for denying the existence of fixed moral rules, for teaching the Bible reveals no ethical principles that are "universally valid and timeless," and for supposing what God requires is given to individuals in ways that apply to themselves alone and no one else.[43] Because of this Ed Long says that "with Bonhoeffer we are moving toward a situational ethic."[44]

---

[41] Dietrich Bonhoeffer, *The Cost of Discipleship* (New York: Macmillan, 1963), 45–60.
[42] Bonhoeffer, *Ethics* (New York: Simon & Schuster, 1995), 136.
[43] Bonhoeffer, 220, 273.
[44] Long, *A Survey of Christian Ethics*, 155.

Reinhold Niebuhr (1892–1971)

Reinhold Niebuhr (1892–1971) started as a social gospel idealist but lost faith in human perfectibility after World War II. He never lost interest in social concerns but, after returning to an orthodox view of human nature, he developed a realist approach to Christian ethics. Rejecting illusions of perfection, he interpreted social ethics in terms that stopped assuming men can establish the social dimension of God's kingdom on earth through power politics. For Niebuhr, pursuing social perfections in anthropocentric naturalistic terms always betrays pursuers into corruptions of their own making.[45] Like the Pied Piper of Hamelin,[46] the attraction of impossible perfection is counterproductive, as it leads to destroying the best possible and leaves pursuers worse off than before.

As far as ethics is concerned, Niebuhr believed we live in a world governed by tension between the ideal and the real.[47] Ideals are impossible, and the best we can achieve is never ideal. We should keep trying to improve things. But love, Niebuhr explained, is an "impossible possibility," which means it is an ideal able to motivate and illuminates what we do even though we can never reach perfection. The best we can do is make better approximations of a justice in social relationships that never entirely satisfies what perfect love requires.

By returning to an orthodox view of human nature and the world, Niebuhr exposed critical weaknesses in what the social gospel envisioned, but Niebuhr had weaknesses of his own. The tension he stressed between the ideal and real was similar to the ultimate-penultimate tension in Bonhoeffer's thought. But, unlike Bonhoeffer, Niebuhr did not believe in Christ's literal return.[48] Therefore, unlike Bonhoeffer's ultimate, Niebuhr's ethic of presently impossible social perfection remains impossible forever, and unlike Bonhoeffer's penultimate, Niebuhr's ethic of

---

[45] Niebuhr, *An Interpretation of Christian Ethics*, 12 (see chap. 1, n. 6).

[46] The Pied Piper of Hamelin is an old German fairy tale related by the Grimm brothers. Jacob Grimm and Wilhelm Grimm, *Grimm's Fairy Tales* (Scotts Valley, CA: CreateSpace, 2018).

[47] Grimm and Grimm, 5.

[48] Niebuhr held that Jesus' teaching of a literal second coming was an "error . . . due to an almost inevitable illusion of thought which deals with the problem of the relation of time and eternity." For Niebuhr, New Testament teaching of a literal *Parousia*, a teaching he admits came from Jesus and "was followed both by St. Paul and the early church," must be reinterpreted to exclude literal fulfillment because "it is important to take Biblical symbols seriously but not literally." Reinhold Niebuhr, *The Nature and Destiny of Man*, vol. 2, *Human Destiny* (New York: Scribner's, 1943), 50.

presently possible imperfection never ceases to be imperfect. In other words, for Niebuhr, the kingdom of God not only is beyond reach for now but never fully arrives and never will.

Paul Ramsey (1913–1988)

Paul Ramsey (1913–1988) was a student of Reinhold Niebuhr's brother, H. Richard Niebuhr, and continued the realist tradition in Christian ethics that came through Augustine and was modified by Barth, Bonhoeffer, and Niebuhr. Like Barth and Bonhoeffer, Ramsey took a Christocentric view of Christian ethics and analyzed how Christian love and the image of God, as revealed in Christ, applied to the Vietnam War, nuclear weapons, civil disobedience, divorce, race relations, and questions arising in medical ethics.

The main theme in Ramsey's ethical thought was that humanly natural, self-interested conceptions of right and wrong must be refashioned by the selfless love expressed in the teaching of Jesus and demonstrated most clearly by what he did on the cross. Ramsey did not think social structures in a fallen world are able to operate on such love, but, like Reinhold Niebuhr, he thought such love shows the direction we must go to improve them, however imperfectly. The church, he believed, can offer ethical insight on civil matters. But he also held that the Church has no right to engage or even resist political power in its role as the Church. Ramsey valued justice. But when it came to improving social conditions and making them more just, he preferred taking a nonresistant approach to pursuing civil rights through power politics.[49] Ramsey used just war principles to argue nuclear war may be justified, criticized planning to bomb Soviet cities because that aims to kill civilians on purpose, and was one of the earliest Christian ethicists to tackle questions in the area of medical ethics.[50]

Ramsey was perhaps the most biblical proponent of neo-orthodoxy, but his work in Christian ethics can be criticized in two ways. First, Ramsey rather oddly held that, although Jesus is "the Christian ideal for human character," he "may not have been the happiest man or even the wisest man."[51] The problem is that doubting the wisdom of Jesus clashes with

---

[49] Paul Ramsey, *Christian Ethics and the Sit-In* (New York: Association, 1961).

[50] Joseph Fletcher's *Morals in Medicine* (Princeton, NJ: Princeton, 1954) predated Ramsey's *The Patient as Person: Explorations in Medical Ethics* (New Haven, CT: Yale, 1970) and *Fabricated Man: The Ethics of Genetic Control* (New Haven, CT: Yale, 1970) by sixteen years.

[51] Ramsey, *Basic Christian Ethics*, 193 (see chap. 1, n. 69).

submitting to his ethical authority. A second problem is inconsistency in how Ramsey regards the authority of Scripture. For, although Ramsey criticized establishing Christian ethics on any ground other than the Bible, he also recommended that we should learn what we can from philosophers and not follow the Reformers too closely.[52]

Ethics of Modern Liberalism (1920–1990)

The social gospel ended as a movement with World War I, but the ethics of modern liberalism carried forward some of the same ideas that led to forming two related factions—one Protestant and the other Catholic. The Protestant faction proposed "situation" ethics and was led by figures like Anders Nygren (1890–1978) and Joseph Fletcher (1905–1991), and the Catholic faction proposed "liberation" ethics and was led by figures like Gustavo Gutiérrez (b. 1928) and James H. Cone (1938–2018). Both raised a single humanly conceived ideal to the place of ultimacy and relativized everything to it. Both factions thus approached Christian ethics circumstantially as an essentially human enterprise, even though each started with a different ultimate ideal. The situation ethics of Nygren and Fletcher prioritized sentimental feelings, and the liberation ethics of Gutiérrez, Cone, and others prioritized liberation from different social inequities.

In the situation ethics of Nygren and Fletcher, only one thing is morally good in and of itself, and that is "love," which they viewed as individually perceived sentimental affection. Because of this, they concluded objectively fixed rules, norms, principles, or standards do not matter. Furthermore, they held that every situation is so unique that, when making ethical decisions, there is no prior precedent and comparing one situation to another is impossible. So, Nygren declared, "where love is, no other precepts are requisite,"[53] and Fletcher announced, "Jesus had no rules or system of values" and "even the Ten Commandments may be thrown aside if they conflict with love."[54]

In the liberation ethics of Gutiérrez and Cone, theologians claim to speak for what they define as an oppressed socially (not spiritually) defined population whose mistreatment

---

[52] Ramsey, xiii, xxi, 340.
[53] Anders Nygren, *Agape and Eros* (London: SPCK, 1941), 454.
[54] Fletcher, *Situation Ethics*, 33 (see chap. 4, n. 17).

is used to redefine Christian ethics for everyone. Marxist class analysis is used to divide individuals into competing social classifications—with one opposing another—and this division is used to organize support for a political movement demanding a reordering of social relationships, not between individuals but groups of people defined by group identities rather than personal character and responsibility. Gutiérrez reconceives Christian ethics based on economic poverty in third world countries—especially South America—and Cone reconceived Christian ethics based on the sociopolitical mistreatment of Blacks in North American culture.[55]

No version of modern liberal ethics starts with the Bible or aligns with how Christian ethics started and was passed on through history but rather starts with a present personal or sociopolitical experience based on which sin, salvation, and the aim of Christianity are redefined. Modern liberal versions of Christian ethics still refer to Christ, the Bible, and even early Christianity. But these are reconceived to require different standards and goals based on experiences that vary from place to place, time to time, or person to person and that propose solving problems through social organizing and power politics. Even though situational and liberational ethicists often claim to represent Christ, the Bible, or early Christianity, and even though they speak of the kingdom of God on earth, modern liberals all end up taking genuine Christianity out of Christian ethics altogether. Nygren and Fletcher substituted personal sentiment for the love of God, Gutiérrez reduced salvation to power politics, and Cone substituted Black Power for reconciling sinners to God.

It therefore came as no surprise when Pope Pius XII in 1952 condemned situation ethics for opposing the will of God by justifying sin and promoting sinful behavior. Nor was anyone surprised when Joseph Fletcher, in 1967, one year after publishing *Situation Ethics*,

---

[55] For Gutiérrez, see Gustavo Gutiérrez and Gerhard Ludwig Müller, *On the Side of the Poor: A Theology of Liberation* (Maryknoll, NY: Orbis, 2015); Gustavo Gutiérrez, "Reflections from a Latin American Perspective," in *Irruption of the Third World: Challenge to Theology,* ed. Virginia Fabella and Sergio Torres, (Maryknoll, NY: Orbis, 1983), 227–37; and C. Douglas McConnell, "Gutiérrez, Gustavo," in *Evangelical Dictionary of Theology*, 2nd ed., ed. Walter A. Elwell, (Grand Rapids: Baker, 2001), 531. For Cone, see James Cone, *A Black Theology of Liberation* (Maryknoll, NY: Orbis, 1970); James Cone, *The Cross and the Lynching Tree* (Maryknoll, NY: Orbis, 2011); and David Clyde Jones, "Cone, James H.," in *Evangelical Dictionary of Theology*, 2nd ed., ed. Walter A. Elwell, (Grand Rapids: Baker, 2001), 284.

renounced Christianity and claimed he really was an atheist who accepted no doctrine but his own.[56]

Ethics of Neo-Pacifism (1960–present)

Neo-pacifism refers to a new movement that approaches Christian ethics much like modern liberals because it, too, aligns everything to a single social ideal. Modern liberals reduce ethics to nothing but individually experienced "sentiment" or to nothing but "liberation" from differences between one social identity and another, and neo-pacifists reduce ethics to nothing but "nonviolence." But I am treating this movement separately because, while those in this movement elevate humanly conceived ideals over the Bible like modern liberals, some contemporary pacifists are Evangelicals who honor the ethical authority of Scripture.[57] Today's Evangelical proponents of pacifism are not neo-pacifists but present-day proponents of an earlier pacifism associated with *The Schleitheim Confession* (1527) and the likes of Menno Simons (1496–1561) in the sixteenth century. To avoid associating contemporary Evangelical pacifists with modern liberals, however indirectly, I am treating the neo-pacifist movement in Christian ethics separately.

The main figures responsible for neo-pacifism as a movement in Christian ethics are John Howard Yoder (1927–1997), James William McClendon, Jr. (1924–2000), and Stanley Hauerwas (b. 1940). John Howard Yoder was a Mennonite who studied under Karl Barth and then defended pacifism against the social realism of neo-orthodoxy. Yoder broke with aspects of his own Anabaptist tradition as well. For, unlike other Anabaptists, he was not content to leave the present world to itself while waiting for a new world to come but rather insisted Christians must spread pacifist thinking in the world even now. Yoder held that we are now living in two coexisting eons of history, each operating on a different ethic—one subjecting sinners to the kingdom of God the Son and another introducing life in the kingdom of God the Father.[58] But, while Yoder claimed to be radically Christ-centered and biblical, he was nei-

---

[56] "Joseph Francis Fletcher," Your Dictionary, http://biography.yourdictionary.com/joseph-francis-fletcher.

[57] Present-day Evangelical pacifists include M. Daniel Carroll, William R. McGrath, Dale W. Brown, and Ronald J. Sider.

[58] Yoder, *The Christian Witness to the State*, 10 (see chap. 4, n. 1).

ther because he reinterpreted Jesus, the Bible, and Christianity in view of prior commitment to nonviolence over everything else. Yoder rose to prominence but then lost credibility after confessing to charges of sexual misconduct and losing credentials as a minister and teacher in the Mennonite church.[59]

James William McClendon Jr. (1924–2000) started as a Southern Baptist minister. But he was dismissed from the faculty of Golden Gate Baptist Theological Seminary for misconduct, after which he left the Southern Baptist Convention, changed his theology, and spent the rest of his life trying to reconceive theology and Christian ethics.[60] McClendon built on Yoder by supposing the way Christian ethics relates to God should be reversed. So, rather than starting with God, he thought we should start with humanity, and rather than conforming humanity to the Word of God, he sought to conform the Word of God to humanity.[61]

Stanley Hauerwas (b. 1940) is a United Methodist minister who is now the greatest shaper of postmodern pacifism in contemporary Christian ethics. Hauerwas rejects the social gospel and liberation theology, along with neo-orthodoxy, but he also denies objective moral order, biblical inerrancy, transcendence, and that Christian ethics existed in the early Church. Along with Luther, Barth, Bonhoeffer, and Yoder, Hauerwas, too, insists Christian ethics is theology, not philosophy.[62] But he goes on also to claim Christian ethics is evolutionary and relative, not fixed and universal, because it is nothing more than "a community's wisdom about how certain actions are prohibited or enjoined for the development of a particular kind of people."[63]

Hauerwas believes two coexisting ethical systems are clashing one against the other—one based on a "gospel" of nonviolence and the other on natural law—and Christians are people in the business of replacing natural law thinking with pacifism.[64] Hauerwas claims pacifism is a "gospel" ethic but then says "one is mistaken to ask if . . . stories of God in Scripture . . .

---

[59] Huebner, *Introduction to Christian Ethics*, 575–76.

[60] Huebner, 593.

[61] The first volume in McClendon's three volume series, *Systematic Theology* (Nashville: Abingdon, 1986) is titled *Ethics* because he reverses the traditional order of theological treatment by starting with ethical life and ending with God, rather than starting with God and ending with ethical life.

[62] Hauerwas, *The Peaceable Kingdom*, xv (see chap. 1, n. 64).

[63] Hauerwas, xiii, 17, 33, 54, 63.

[64] Stanley Hauerwas, "September 11, 2001: A Pacifist Response," *South Atlantic Quarterly* 101 (Spring 2002), https://www.today.duke.edu/showcase/mmedia/features/911site/hauerwas.html.

are true."[65] So, rather than trust the Bible, he, too, places prerational faith in pacifism itself and then redefines Christ, Christianity, and Christian ethics based on that. Hauerwas believes Christianity is committing ourselves to living without war rather than trusting Christ for salvation,[66] which leads him to reconceive Christian theology and ethics based on aligning life to a different authority, different Christ, and different gospel altogether.[67]

Ethics of Contemporary Paganized Christianity (1970–present)

Paganized Christianity now constitutes the far end of the liberal stream in Christian ethics (used here in the academic as opposed to biblical sense) that began when the social gospel movement divided the field into liberal and conservative factions. Here, I am using "Christian" in the academic sense that includes what scholars claim to be doing however far it strays from biblical fidelity. Paganized "Christian" ethics is far from anything Christian in the biblical sense.

The social gospel movement in Christian ethics ended with World War I, but variations in the field have arisen since, following that same trajectory. All have reconceived Christian ethics in ways that minimize personal sin, eliminate transcendence, reduce the kingdom of God to a preferred social ideal, and turn salvation into social reform through political activism. Some have aligned ethics to personal sentiment and others to different humanly conceived social ideals. But the most recent version is one supposing to align Christian ethics with paganism. Proponents of this version on the liberal side of Christian ethics argue pagan ethics—especially in regard to sex—is not alien but is really a better form of Christian ethics. These not only say there is nothing wrong with what the Bible calls "sin," but also say that "sinning" is how people save themselves.

James B. Nelson (1930–2015) taught Christian ethics at a United Church of Christ (UCC) seminary for thirty-two years and was one of the first to justify unbiblical forms of sexual expression among professing Christians. His life mission was reuniting sexuality with

---

[65] Hauerwas, *Peaceable Kingdom*, 25.

[66] Hauerwas redefines Christians as "people who believe that God will have them exist through history without the necessity of war." *Against the Nations: War and Survival in a Liberal Society* (Minneapolis: Winston, 1985), 196.

[67] Huebner notes how some think Hauerwas teaches a "wholly different Christianity" (Huebner, *Introduction to Christian Ethics*, 615).

spirituality by teaching Christians to trust the flesh over the Bible.[68] So, rather than sinners being reconciled to God through repentance and faith in Jesus Christ, he taught that all can unite with God through sexual passion.[69] Nelson did not use the term but knew he was "paganizing" Christian ethics because, in reuniting sexuality with spirituality, he did not think the answer lay in returning to what the Bible says but rather in adopting pre-Christian pagan ideas about sex and religion.[70] So, whereas the Bible warns that indulging the flesh leads to spiritual death (Rom 8:13), Nelson believed doing so assures salvation.[71]

Rosemary Radford Ruether (b. 1936) is a feminist theologian who has spent most of her life urging ministerial students to paganize Christian ethics.[72] She explains that, as a student at Claremont Graduate School, "I was influenced by two brilliant classicists, Robert Palmer and Philip Merlan at Claremont. Both of these men preferred the culture and philosophy of Greco-Roman antiquity to Christianity. Their perspective transformed my stance toward Christianity. I learned . . . . presuppositions about the superiority of Yahwism to Ba'alism, Christianity to paganism were no longer possible."[73] Ruether replaces the biblical view of God with goddess worship and replaces faith in biblical revelation with faith in sexual sensations.[74] She denies souls are helpless to save themselves,[75] thinks believing the Bible causes people to sin,[76] and claims "sexual pleasure between lovers . . . or giving birth to a baby" is what unites us to God.[77]

---

[68] James B. Nelson, "Reuniting Sexuality and Spirituality," *Christian Century* (February 25, 1987): 187–90.

[69] James B. Nelson, *Body Theology* (Louisville: Westminster/John Knox, 1992), 23.

[70] Nelson, 15–28, and Nelson, "Reuniting Sexuality and Spirituality," 187–90.

[71] James B. Nelson, *Embodiment: An Approach to Sexuality and Christian Theology* (Minneapolis: Augsburg, 1978), 79.

[72] Rosemary Radford Ruether, "Feminist Theology and Spirituality," in *Christian Feminism: Visions of a New Humanity*, ed. Judith Weidman (San Francisco: Harper & Row, 1984), 16.

[73] Rosemary Radford Ruether, "Asking the Existential Questions: How My Mind Has Changed," *Christian Century* (April 2, 1980): 375.

[74] Rosemary Radford Ruether, *Woman-Church: Theology and Practice of Feminist Liturgical Communities* (San Francisco: HarperSanFrancisco, 1992), 189.

[75] Rosemary Radford Ruether, *Women and Redemption: A Theological History* (Minneapolis: Fortress, 1998), 275.

[76] Rosemary Radford Ruether, *Sexism and God-Talk: Toward a Feminist Theology* (Boston: Beacon, 1983), 68–69.

[77] Rosemary Radford Ruether, *Introducing Redemption in Christian Feminism* (Cleveland, OH: Pilgrim, 1998), 103.

Virginia Ramey Mollenkott (b. 1932) grew up Plymouth Brethren and attended Bob Jones University, but she has since spent most of her career trying to conform Christian theology and ethics to paganism.[78] Mollenkott recommends that Christians join witches' covens to learn how to connect sensuality with spirituality,[79] replaces biblical ethics with the sort followed by pagan shamans,[80] uses demons for ethical guidance,[81] not only reimagines deity in pagan terms but also claims to be "God herself,"[82] and claims fleshly desires can be indulged however you want with no fear of judgement.[83] But, if Mollenkott trusts the flesh over the Word of God and thinks witches and shamen have better theology and ethics than biblical Christians, why does she not renounce Christianity completely, and why especially does she still claim to be an "Evangelical" Christian? The answer, in her own words, is because she wants to "subvert" what Evangelical Christians think and teach about Christian ethics.[84]

Ethics of Contemporary Evangelicalism (1950–present)[85]

Contemporary Evangelicals are those who now continue the Bible-based, Augustinian, non-Aristotelian stream of Christian ethics that the social gospel abandoned in the early twentieth century and liberals have continued to oppose. The ethics of contemporary Evangelicals is

---

[78] Mollenkott thinks Christian ethics should be "fused" with pagan ethics. Virginia Ramey Mollenkott, "Re-Imagining Church as Worshipping Community," *1993 Re-Imagining Conference* (Apple Valley, MN: Audiotapes, Resource Express, Album One, Tape 11–1B).

[79] Virginia Ramey Mollenkott, "An Evangelical Feminist Confronts the Goddess," *Christian Century* (October 20, 1982): 1044–1046 and *Sensuous Spirituality: Out of Fundamentalism* (New York: Crossroad, 1992), 97.

[80] Mollenkott, *Sensuous Spirituality*, 74.

[81] Mollenkott, 19.

[82] Mollenkott, 17.

[83] Mollenkott, 16, 27.

[84] Virginia Ramey Mollenkott, "A Call to Subversion," *The Other Side* (July–August 1999): 14–19.

[85] I use *Evangelical* here in the sense it is defined and used by John D. Woodbridge, Mark A. Noll, and Nathan O. Hatch in *The Gospel in America* (Grand Rapids: Zondervan, 1979) to mean "heirs of the Protestant Reformation" who are "identified by the *gospel*" and confession of "Christ as the one who delivers from the consequences of sin and who brings new life" (p. 14). And the modifier *contemporary* is warranted because Evangelicalism as a movement in Christian history started in the eighteenth century. See Mark A. Noll, *The Rise of Evangelicalism: The Age of Edwards, Whitefield, and the Wesleys* (Downers Grove, IL: Intervarsity, 2003).

rooted in the version of Augustinian moral theology recovered in the Protestant Reformation. It is passed on more through Calvin than Luther but inherits their common reliance on Scripture over treating human reason, experience, or sentiment as authorities in their own right. But, while rooted in Augustine and the Reformers, contemporary Evangelical ethics is influenced as well by post-Reformational Protestant developments that include Puritan concern for holy community and responsible government, Pietist concern for transforming the heart and personal devotion, and Wesleyan concern for economics and serving those suffering hardship.

Evangelical ethicists all affirm *Sola Scriptura*. But while Evangelicals all used to think this required continuing to hold the antipathy Calvin and Luther shared toward mixing Christian ethics with philosophical theories relying on human reason, experience, or sentiment apart from Scripture, a division has arisen among Evangelicals over whether this antipathy is truly necessary. Some Evangelicals now embrace the way Catholics traditionally mix philosophy with theology and think this may not, in every case, conflict with Protestant commitment to *Sola Scriptura*. At the same time, other Evangelicals still believe using philosophy even to frame Christian ethical understanding undercuts the transcendence of Scripture. At root, this division concerns whether Evangelicals should think Christian ethics rests on special revelation from God and nothing else, or rests, to some degree, on what human reason conceives unrelated to whether people believe in God or recognize his authority. This text assumes Evangelical ethics should stay in line with the spring from which it arose.

On applied ethical issues, contemporary Evangelicals are united on affirming the sanctity of human life, of marriage, and binary sexuality, and together oppose adultery, pornography, homosexual desires and behavior, slavery, sex trafficking, gambling, and alcohol and drug dependency. But Evangelicals hold different positions on whether Christians may initiate divorce for adultery or desertion; whether the biblical truth norm permits deception; whether God requires or resists gender roles in the church and home; whether corporeal punishment for children is required, permitted, or no longer allowed; whether to prohibit, discourage, allow, or ignore masturbation; whether civil justice should include death penalties; whether forgiven sins of divorce, homosexual behavior, child abuse, or murder disqualify ministerial ordination for life; and whether to encourage or oppose voting for flawed but comparatively better political candidates, however despicable.

Leading proponents articulating contemporary Evangelical ethics include Cornelius Van Til (1895–1987), C. S. Lewis (1898–1963), John Murray (1898–1975), Helmut Thielicke (1908–1986), Francis A. Schaeffer (1912–1984), Jacques Ellul (1912–1994), Carl F. H. Henry (1913–2003), John M. Frame (b. 1939), Oliver O'Donovan (b. 1945), Gilbert C. Meilaender (b. 1946), and Wayne A. Grudem (b. 1948).[86] We will now survey what each of these has contributed to contemporary Evangelical ethical understanding.

Cornelius Van Til (1895–1987)

Cornelius Van Til (1895–1987) was a Presbyterian theologian, Christian ethicist,[87] and apologist some have credited as having been the greatest Calvinist mind since Calvin himself.[88] Van Til graduated from Calvin College, briefly attended Calvin Theological Seminary, and then transferred to Princeton, graduating with a PhD in 1927. He started teaching at Princeton but soon left to help found Westminster Theological Seminary, where he taught for forty-three years.

Van Til criticized the theology and ethics of Barth, claiming these were fatally compromised by Kantian philosophy, and he disputed how Lewis spoke of non-Christians having a natural knowledge of ethical truth, arguing they only know something formally similar and "it is wrong to say that the unbeliever has . . . correct notions as to content."[89] This was

---

[86] These are the main proponents, but there are others too numerous to discuss individually in this chapter. Others who have taken, or are taking, part in articulating contemporary Evangelical ethics include Harold O. J. Brown (1933–2007), Norman L. Geisler (1932–2019), Joe E. Trull (b. 1935), William Edgar (b. 1944), Paul D. Feinberg (1938-2004), John S. Feinberg (b. 1946), Dennis P. Hollinger (b. 1948), Scott B. Rae (b. 1954), myself (b. 1950), and of course many others. I do not include Edward John Carnell (1919–1967) or Arthur F. Holmes (1924–2011) as major proponents because, while Evangelical, neither went much beyond philosophical theories based on human speculation.

[87] Van Til's contributions as an Evangelical ethicist are found in *New Modernism: An Appraisal of the Theology of Barth and Brunner* (Philadelphia: P&R, 1946), *Common Grace* (Philadelphia: P&R, 1947), *Defense of the Faith* (Phillipsburg, NJ: P&R, 1955), *Christianity and Barthianism* (Phillipsburg, NJ: P&R, 1962), and *Christian Theistic Ethics* (1955) (see chap. 1, n. 36). His thought, including his ethical teaching, is described and analyzed by John M. Frame in *Van Til: The Theologian* (Cleveland, OH: Pilgrim, 1976) and in *Cornelius Van Til: An Analysis of His Thought* (Phillipsburg, NJ: P&R, 1995).

[88] Frame, *Cornelius Van Til: An Analysis of His Thought*, 44.

[89] Cornelius Van Til, *The Defense of the Faith*, revised 1963 edition (Phillipsburg, NJ: P&R, 1963), 59, and *A Christian Theory of Knowledge* (Phillipsburg, NJ: P&R, 1969), 296. Also see Van Til,

because Van Til did not think Christian ethics should be considered in ways that accept beliefs antithetical to truth. True Christian ethics, he taught, begins with truth about God, creation, and Scripture, and starting with false views of God, or autonomous reason, never arrives at anything really true.[90] Thus, Van Til criticized mixing theology with philosophy, argued there is no neutral ground between them, and insisted that ethical thinking, like ethical living, is subject to God's sovereignty. He believed that how one pursues ethical knowledge must bow to God's authority and so concluded those who never submit never attain it.

We may admire how Van Til honored God's sovereignty over ethical thought, but his approach has weaknesses as well. He was right to insist non-Christians inevitably suppress natural revelation. But he contradicted himself by saying unbelievers have no true knowledge at all and then saying they are judged for suppressing truth they have all along.[91] Van Til offered penetrating insight on the falsity of non-Biblical ethics, but his rhetoric sometimes went beyond what Scripture actually says.

C. S. Lewis (1898–1963)

C. S. Lewis (1898–1963) was an Anglican writer and literary scholar whom many consider to have been the greatest Evangelical proponent of Christian ethics of the twentieth century.[92]

Christianity and Barthianism, 263–264, and Van Til, *New Modernism*, vii–viii.

[90] Walter A. Elwell, "Van Til, Cornelius," in *Evangelical Dictionary of Theology*, 2nd ed., ed. Walter A. Elwell, (Grand Rapids: Baker, 2001), 1,237.

[91] Frame, *Cornelius Van Til: An Analysis of His Thought*, 189, 398.

[92] Lewis's contributions as an Evangelical ethicist are found in *The Problem of Pain* (see chap. 2, n. 51), *Mere Christianity* (see chap. 2, n. 4), "Right and Wrong as a Clue to the Meaning of the Universe," in *The Case for Christianity* (New York: MacMillan, 1943), *The Abolition of Man* (Oxford: Oxford, 1944), *The Weight of Glory and Other Addresses* (New York: MacMillan, 1949), *Christian Reflections* (Grand Rapids: Eerdmans, 1967), *God in the Dock: Essays on Theology and Ethics,* ed. Walter Hooper (Grand Rapids: Eerdmans, 1970), and *Virtue and Vice: A Dictionary of the Good Life*, edited by Patricia S. Klein (New York: HarperSanFrancisco, 2005). His thought including his ethical teaching is described and analyzed by Clyde S. Kilby in *The Christian World of C. S. Lewis* (Grand Rapids: Eerdmans, 1964); by Gilbert C. Meilaender in *The Taste for the Other: The Social and Ethical Thought of C. S. Lewis* (Grand Rapids: Eerdmans, 1978); by Scott R. Burson and Jerry L. Wallis in *C. S. Lewis & Francis Schaeffer: Lessons for a New Century from the Most Influential Apologists of Our Time* (Downers Grove, IL: InterVarsity, 1998); and by David Baggett, Gary R. Habermas, and Jerry L. Walls, eds., in *C. S. Lewis as Philosopher: Truth, Goodness and Beauty* (Downers Grove, IL: InterVarsity, 2008).

Lifestyle differences distinguished him from Evangelicals in the United States, but he was theologically Evangelical and claimed to be "a dogmatic Christian untinged with Modernist reservations and committed to supernaturalism in its full rigour."[93] Lewis has been called an apologist, but he did far more to explain and apply Christian ethics in theological terms than he did using philosophy to support and defend Christianity in secular terms nonbelievers find acceptable.[94]

Lewis denied that Christianity offers a new ethic because it concerns an ordering that stands exactly where it has always stood.[95] He described worthy living as becoming "clean mirrors filled with the image of a face that is not ours."[96] He saw that Christian ethics involves tension between enjoying gifts of creation and ultimately taking delight in nothing other than God.[97] And he held that Christian ethics is the only objectively true ethics there is, so if any other view is true, then Christianity and Christian ethics are false.[98]

Lewis noticed that "human beings, all over the earth, have this curious idea that they ought to behave a certain way, and cannot really get rid of it."[99] But he rejected natural law philosophy and only affirmed what the Bible says in Romans 1. Lewis warned readers not to think he was using the "Stoical or medieval . . . doctrine of Natural Law" because he meant to deny that men can, on their own, devise any objectively true ethical system and only to observe that "whenever ethical discussion begins we find already before us an ethical code whose validity has to be assumed before we can even critique it."[100] Indeed, Lewis went so far as to say, "the most dangerous thing you can do is to take any one impulse of your own nature and set it up as the thing you ought to follow at all costs" because there is not one "which will not make us into devils if we set it up as an absolute guide."[101]

---

[93] C. S. Lewis, *On Ethics*, in *Christian Reflections* (Grand Rapids: Eerdmans, 1967), 44.

[94] This is well defended by Meilaender in *The Taste for the Other*.

[95] Lewis, *On Ethics*, 46, 55.

[96] C. S. Lewis, *Readings for Meditation and Reflection*, ed. Walter Hooper (New York: HarperCollins, 1992), 39.

[97] Lewis, *God in the Dock*, 148. Meilaender also discusses this in *Taste for the Other*, 20–44.

[98] Lewis, *God in the Dock*, 108–9.

[99] Lewis, *Mere Christianity*, 21.

[100] Lewis, *On Ethics*, 55.

[101] Lewis, *Mere Christianity*, 23–24.

John Murray (Protestant; 1898–1975)

John Murray (1898–1975), the Protestant, not to be confused with John Courtney Murray (1904–1967), the Catholic, who lived and wrote over the same years, was a Presbyterian theologian and Christian ethicist who came to the United States from Scotland, taught briefly at Princeton, and then left with Van Til to found Westminster Theological Seminary, where he taught until retiring and moving back to Scotland in 1967.[102] John Murray had a reputation for exegetical expertise, and his *Principles of Conduct* was used as a primary text for ethics courses at Evangelical seminaries for decades.

Murray believed biblical ethics is the only true ethics, held that ethics is always essentially religious rather than philosophical, and said nothing regulates conduct "apart from the fear of God and the promotion of that fear among men."[103] Murray differed from natural law philosophy in two ways, first, by holding that "only those who experience union with Christ . . . are able to embrace his principles of conduct" and, second, by insisting, apart from what the Bible says about the holiness of God, any ethical knowledge one has inevitably disintegrates.[104]

Murray understood that all men have a moral conscience linked to bearing the image of God and that Christian love fulfills moral obligations. But he also taught that the origin of ethical truth is not human reason, human hearts, or human sentiment, but is, and only is, the will of God.[105] Murray also insisted biblical worship and biblical ethics must not be divorced, but he held to this only because he thought biblical ethics complements biblical worship and not because he thought them the same.[106] Now, many (myself included) think they are identical because the Bible indicates what vehicles (rituals) of worship should carry are lives submitted to and serving God's ethical judgment and authority (Amos 5:21–24).

---

[102] Murray's contributions as an Evangelical ethicist are found in *Divorce* (Philadelphia: P&R, 1953), *Redemption Accomplished and Applied* (Grand Rapids: Eerdmans, 1955), *Principles of Conduct* (see chap. 3, n. 1). and *The Imputation of Adam's Sin* (Grand Rapids: Eerdmans, 1959).

[103] Murray, *Principles of Conduct*, 47.

[104] Murray, 202.

[105] Murray, 19–26.

[106] Murray, 162–63.

Helmut Thielicke (1908–1986)

Helmut Thielicke (1908–1986) was a Lutheran theologian and Christian ethicist who, with Barth and Bonhoeffer, was a member of the Confessing Church in Germany that resisted Hitler's Nazi regime.[107] After the war, Thielicke went on to author one of the largest works in Christian ethics ever written. His *Theologische Ethik* (1958) first appeared in German in four volumes. Portions were then published separately by different publishers as they were translated into English. A complete (though abridged) English version of Thielicke's text titled *Theological Ethics* was ultimately published by Eerdmans in 1979 and was composed of three volumes, titled *Foundations*, *Politics*, and *Sex*.

While Thielicke did not explicitly affirm inerrancy, he was an Evangelical Christian, not only because he claimed to be but also because he accepted the Bible as fully reliable and once declared, "In everything I have said I have wished to be an advocate of the Holy Scriptures" because "what I am interested in is respect for the Word of God and not its depreciation or relativization."[108] He thought nature, history, experience, and philosophy are all never more than indirect and always speculative sources of understanding, whereas the Bible declares the Word of God with absolute directness and authority.

Thielicke sided with Van Til and Barth who, despite their other differences, both rejected autonomous attempts to reach ultimate truth from the bottom up. Thielicke taught that Christian ethics is incompatible with thinking "man no longer needs to receive the Word which binds and looses him, because man now speaks that word himself."[109] He understood Christian ethics may seem interchangeable with other systems as to behavior standards but realized these always diverge as to source of authority, view of reality, and motivation.[110] There can be, he said,

---

[107] Thielicke's contributions as an Evangelical ethicist are found in his four-volume German work *Theologische Ethik* (Tübingen, DE: Mohr, 1958–1959), *The Ethics of Sex* (New York: Harper & Row, 1964), *The Evangelical Faith* (Grand Rapids: Eerdmans, 1974–1977), and his three-volume English work *Theological Ethics* (see chap. 1, n. 69). His ethical teaching is described and analyzed by Richard A. Higginson in *The Contributions of Helmut Thielicke to Theological Ethics* (Manchester: University of Manchester, 1982).

[108] Helmut Thielicke, *Between Heaven and Earth* (New York: Harper & Row, 1965), 13, 16.

[109] Thielicke, 13.

[110] Thielicke, 20–27, 51.

"no such thing as autonomy of the various spheres of life" and so maintained there is no reality to other systems rivaling the only ethics there is, which is and only can be Christian ethics.[111]

Francis A. Schaeffer (1912–1984)

Francis Schaeffer (1912–1984) was a Presbyterian pastor, theologian, and Christian ethicist, whose work was interdenominational and whose thought influenced Evangelicals world-wide.[112] Schaeffer was not a highly trained scholar but had a passion for bringing God's truth to bear on real life at every level that invigorated Christian thought and action more than any other Evangelical of his day, including the evangelist Billy Graham.

Schaeffer challenged Evangelicals to engage ethical issues in the culture but also warned against accommodating ethics to culture.[113] Separating God from reason, he explained, denies any basis for reason or ethics at all and leaves modernity with a tragic sense of "cosmic

---

[111] Thielicke, 36, 38.

[112] Schaeffer's contributions as an Evangelical ethicist are found in *Escape from Reason* (London: Inter-Varsity Fellowship, 1968), *The God Who Is There* (London: Inter-Varsity Fellowship, 1968), *Death in the City* (London: Inter-Varsity Fellowship, 1969), *The Mark of the Christian* (Downers Grove, IL: InterVarsity, 1970), *The Church at the End of the 20th Century* (Downers Grove, IL: InterVarsity, 1970), *Pollution and the Death of Man: The Christian View of Ecology* (Wheaton, IL: Tyndale, 1970), *True Spirituality* (Wheaton, IL: Tyndale, 1971), *The Church Before the Watching World: A Practical Ecclesiology* (Downers Grove, IL: InterVarsity, 1971), *He Is There and He Is Not Silent* (see chap. 2, n. 36), *Back to Freedom and Dignity* (Downers Grove, IL: InterVarsity, 1972), *The New Super-Spirituality* (Downers Grove, IL: InterVarsity, 1972), *Two Contents, Two Realities* (Downers Grove, IL: InterVarsity, 1974), *How Should We Then Live?* (Westchester, IL: Crossway, 1976), Francis Schaeffer and C. Everett Koop, *Whatever Happened to the Human Race?* (Old Tappan, NJ: Revel, 1979), *A Christian Manifesto* (Westchester, IL: Crossway, 1981), and *The Great Evangelical Disaster* (see chap. 3, n. 25). His thought, including his ethical teaching, is described and analyzed by Colin Duriez in *Francis Schaeffer: An Authentic Life* (Wheaton, IL: Crossway, 2008), by Lane T. Dennis, ed., in *Francis A. Schaeffer: Portraits of the Man and His Work* (Wheaton, IL: Crossway, 1986), and by Ronald W. Ruegsegger, ed., in *Reflections on Francis Schaeffer* (Grand Rapids: Zondervan, 1986).

[113] Francis A. Schaeffer, *A Christian Manifesto*, in *The Complete Works of Francis A. Schaeffer*, vol. 5 (Wheaton, IL: Crossway, 1982), 320–21, 369–71, 451–97. Francis A. Schaeffer, *The Great Evangelical Disaster*, in *The Complete Works of Francis A. Schaeffer*, vol. 4 (Wheaton, IL: Crossway, 1982), 320–21, 369–71, 401–5.

alienation."[114] Schaeffer held that severing ethics from the Bible "makes ethics equal to no ethics" and, "if the truth of the Christian faith is in fact *truth*, then it stands in antithesis to the ideas and the immorality of our age."[115] Since philosophical ethics operates apart from the Bible, he claimed it really offers "no categories of truth, and no categories of right and wrong," and leads to thinking "in the area of all values, ethics, meaning and love there is nothing but silence."[116] He believed meaningless subjectivity is now all that remains in the modern world and the only way to recover objectively grounded meaning and morals is to reaffirm the only real source of ethical truth, which is the triune God revealed most clearly in the Bible.

Schaeffer got Evangelicals to begin opposing legalized abortion, warned against practices devaluing human life, anticipated sexual paganism, inspired what became the Christian Right in American politics, and although he was Presbyterian, stimulated the resurgence restoring biblical fidelity in the Southern Baptist Convention.[117] Francis Schaeffer passed away in 1984, but his writings still invigorate Evangelicals engaging the most pressing ethical issues of our day.

Jacques Ellul (1912–1994)

Jacques Ellul (1912–1994) was a sociologist, historian, and Christian ethicist who was a lifelong lay member of the Reformed Church of France, a Protestant denomination with Calvinist origins, even though Ellul was himself more influenced by Luther than Calvin. Ellul

---

[114] Schaeffer, *Manifesto*, 423–30; Francis A. Schaeffer, *The Church at the End of the Twentieth Century*, in *The Complete Works of Francis A. Schaeffer*, vol. 4 (Wheaton, IL: Crossway, 1982), 12–14; Francis A. Schaeffer, *He Is There and He Is Not Silent*, in *The Complete Works of Francis A. Schaeffer*, vol. 1 (Wheaton, IL: Crossway, 1982), 295.

[115] Francis A. Schaeffer, *Whatever Happened to the Human Race?*, 290 (see chap. 1, n. 81); Schaeffer, *Evangelical Disaster*, 320.

[116] Francis A. Schaeffer, *The Church before the Watching World*, in *The Complete Works of Francis A. Schaeffer*, vol. 4 (Wheaton, IL: Crossway, 1982), 130.

[117] This comes from a personal conversation with Paige Patterson who, with Paul Pressler, played the pivotal role in leading the Southern Baptist Resurgence.

was born, raised, and spent most of his life in Bordeaux, France.[118] As a university student, he was first attracted by Marxism but then converted wholeheartedly to faith in Christ. Ellul participated in the French Resistance during World War II and was dismissed from the faculty at Strasbourg for opposing the Vichy government. Then from 1944 until retiring in 1980, he served as Professor of the History and Sociology of Institutions at the University of Bordeaux.

Ellul was not neo-orthodox, but he liked how Barth defended the traditional Augustinian and Protestant view that revelation transcends human reasoning. Like Barth, but also like Luther, Calvin, Van Til, Murray, and Thielicke, Ellul too held that "philosophical presuppositions" must be ever examined "in the light of revelation" and never allowed to substitute man-centered substitutions for divinely revealed truth.[119] And for this reason, Ellul maintained a view of Christian ethics that resisted how liberation theologians mix Christianity with Marxism and how Catholics rely on natural law philosophy.

Ellul argued that freedom in Christ requires Christians to refuse assimilating to forms and forces of sinful society. We are in the world but can never be of the world. As a historian, Ellul admitted how back in the Middle Ages natural law philosophy seemed to offer common ground on which Christians and non-Christians could agree on moral issues. But that lasted only as long as no one disputed the existence of God establishing moral order, and we now live in a world in which non-Christians no longer believe natural law philosophy includes thinking God is needed. Ellul held that natural law philosophy now no longer provides even the appearance of common ground because what natural law now means to non-Christians reduces to a sort of ethical naturalism completely contrary to Christian ethics.[120]

---

[118] Ellul's contributions as an Evangelical ethicist are found in *The Theological Foundation of Law* (Paris: Delachaux et Niestlé, 1946), *The Presence of the Kingdom* (London, SCM, 1951), *The Technological Society* (New York: Vintage, 1964), *The Political Illusion* (New York: Vintage, 1965), *Violence: Reflections from a Christian Perspective* (New York: Seabury, 1969), *The Meaning of the City* (Grand Rapids: Eerdmans, 1970), *The Ethics of Freedom*, 3 vols. (1973–1984) (see chap. 1, n. 69), *The Subversion of Christianity* (Grand Rapids: Eerdmans, 1984), and *What I Believe* (Paris: B. Grasset, 1987). His ethical teaching is described and analyzed by David W. Gill in *The Word of God in the Ethics of Jacques Ellul* (Metuchen, NJ: Scarecrow, 1984).

[119] Ellul, *The Ethics of Freedom*, 8.

[120] Jacques Ellul, *The Theological Foundations of Law* (New York: Doubleday, 1947, 1960).

Carl F. H. Henry (1913–2003)[121]

Carl F. H. Henry (1913–2003) was a Baptist journalist, theologian, and Christian ethicist who reminded the world life is fleeting but the Word of God is forever and while Jesus saves souls, he also cares about loving neighbors.[122] With nonbelievers, Henry argued biblical ethics is both credible and true, and with believers, he argued it requires engaging social issues as well as evangelizing. Generally, Henry criticized secularists for abandoning God, liberal Christians for abandoning transcendence, and fundamentalists for ignoring social problems.

Although very important, Henry's most essential contribution to Christian ethics was not urging Evangelicals to address racism, materialism, and poverty, but rather was resisting pressure to mix Christian ethics with philosophy and to rely as much on autonomous reason as on revelation. Henry saw value to engaging philosophy but never used it to explain Christian ethics, always called philosophy "speculative" to make clear it has no authority compared to the Word of God, and warned that "every proposal to arrive at the content of Christian ethics by a synthesis of speculative morality and revealed morality minimizes the extent to which secular ethics is forged from the standpoint of revolt."[123] Henry differed from others in the

---

[121] Carl Ferdinand Howard Henry was born to Karl F. Heinrich and Johanna Väthröder, German immigrants to the United States, who changed their family name to Henry because of anti-German sentiment during World War I.

[122] Henry's contributions as an Evangelical ethicist are found in *The Uneasy Conscience of Fundamentalism* (Grand Rapids: Eerdmans, 1947), *Christian Personal Ethics* (see chap. 1, n. 2), *Aspects of Christian Social Ethics* (Grand Rapids: Eerdmans, 1964), *Frontiers in Modern Theology* (Chicago: Moody, 1966), *Evangelicals at the Brink of Crisis: Significance of the World Congress on Evangelism* (Waco, TX: Word, 1967), *A Plea for Evangelical Demonstration* (Grand Rapids: Baker, 1971), *Evangelicals in Search of Identity* (Waco, TX: Word, 1976), his six-volume *God, Revelation and Authority* (Waco, TX: Word, 1976–1983), *Christian Mindset in a Secular Society: Promoting Evangelical Renewal & National Righteousness* (Portland, OR: Multnomah,1984), *Twilight of a Great Civilization* (Westchester, IL: Crossway, 1988), and *Toward a Recovery of Christian Belief* (Wheaton, IL: Crossway, 1990). His thought, including his ethical teaching, is described and analyzed by Bob E. Patterson in *Carl F. H. Henry* (Waco, TX: Word, 1983), by G. Wright Doyle in *Carl Henry: Theologian for All Seasons* (Eugene, OR: Pickwick, 2010), and by Matthew J. Hall and Owen Strachen, eds., in *Essential Evangelicalism: The Enduring Influence of Carl F. H. Henry* (Wheaton, IL: Crossway, 2015).

[123] Henry, *Christian Personal Ethics*, 148.

field by insisting not even the *imago Dei* can unite non-Christian with Christian ethics and claiming sin corrupts so profoundly that "revelational instruction derived exclusively from Scripture" is needed to get it right.[124]

If Schaeffer did more than anyone of his day to fire Evangelical zeal for ethical witness, Henry, at the same time, did more than anyone to justify faith in the ethical authority of Scripture. In the generation following World War II, Thielicke and Ellul shaped Evangelical ethics in Europe, Henry shaped Evangelical ethics in the United States, and Schaeffer mobilized Evangelicals from around the world for ethical witness on a global scale.

John M. Frame (b. 1939)

John M. Frame (b. 1939) is a Presbyterian theologian, philosopher, and Christian ethicist noted for applying the Bible to contemporary issues and developing a triperspectival method of ethical analysis.[125] Frame was influenced by, but also critical of, Van Til and has taught theology and philosophy at Presbyterian seminaries all his professional life.[126]

Frame believes Christian ethics is the only real ethics and dismisses all non-Christian thought as "flawed, not only in its conclusions, but also in its initial understanding."[127] He

---

[124] Roy W. Butler, "Henry, Carl F. H.," in *Baker's Dictionary of Christian Ethics*, ed. Carl F. H. Henry (Grand Rapids: Baker, 1973), 288; also see Henry, *Christian Personal Ethics*, 146.

[125] Frame's primary contributions as an Evangelical ethicist are found in "Reformed Ethics," in Carl F. H. Henry, ed., *Baker's Dictionary of Christian Ethics* (Grand Rapids: Baker, 1973), 571–72; *Inerrancy: An Unbiblical Concept?* (Philadelphia: Westminster, 1978); *Medical Ethics: Principles, Persons, and Problems* (Phillipsburg, NJ: P&R, 1988); *Perspectives on the Word of God: An Introduction to Christian Ethics* (see chap. 2, n. 2); *Apologetics to the Glory of God: An Introduction* (Phillipsburg, NJ: P&R, 1994); *Worship in Spirit and Truth* (Phillipsburg, NJ: P&R, 1996); and *Doctrine of the Christian Life* (see chap. 1, n. 69). His ethical teaching is described and analyzed by Harold Netland in "Apologetics, Worldviews, and the Problem of Neutral Criteria," *Trinity Journal* 12/1 (1991): 39–58, by Cornelius P. Venema in "The Doctrine of God: A Theology of Lordship," *Mid-America Journal of Theology* 14 (2003): 153–66, and by John J. Hughes in *Speaking the Truth in Love: The Theology of John M. Frame* (Phillipsburg, NJ: P&R, 2009).

[126] Frame started work on a doctoral dissertation in philosophical theology at Yale University, but he left without finishing and never completed the degree requirements. For Frame on Van Til, see Frame, *Cornelius Van Til: An Analysis of His Thought*.

[127] Frame, *Doctrine of the Christian Life*, 10.

says his own "ultimate allegiance . . . is to the Christ of Scripture" and "not to scholarly canons of respectability," and he criticizes others for mixing philosophy with theology.[128] But Frame uses philosophical categories and systems himself in formulating a method of analysis involving three perspectives he thinks unite "deontological," "teleological," and "existential" philosophical systems if linked to elements of divine lordship. Thus, Frame connects God's authority with deontological philosophy, God's control with teleological philosophy, and God's presence with existential philosophy.[129] He treats the Ten Commandments at length. But he uses categories for analyzing them that all come from philosophy, not the Bible, and in doing so breaks with the stream of Christian ethics that through history has refused to mix philosophy with theology because the Word of God transcends and never submits to human speculation.

Evangelicals generally appreciate how Frame discerns complexity in moral revelation, regards Christian ethics as exclusive, and affirms biblical authority. But Evangelicals do not all agree with how he uses philosophy to impose order on revelation already ordered according to the holiness, love, and glory of God. Connecting philosophical systems with divine attributes does not prevent association with non-biblical ideas in the autonomous, humanly conceived sources from which they come, and that leaves Frame's triperspectival method at best confusing and at worst perverting.

Oliver O'Donovan (b. 1945)

Oliver O'Donovan (b. 1945) is an Anglican priest, theologian, and university professor who may be the greatest mind in the field of Christian ethics today.[130] O'Donovan is known for examining the structure of Christian ethics, developing political theology, surveying the history of Christian ethics, and defending the sanctity of human life, biblical sexuality, and the

---

[128] Frame, *Cornelius Van Til: An Analysis of His Thought*, 18, 46.

[129] Frame, *Doctrine of the Christian Life*, 49–51, 132, 240, 317.

[130] I refer here to the last years of the twentieth and early years of the twenty-first centuries.

ethic of just war.[131] He is respected by liberals and conservatives alike, even though his work is unapologetically Evangelical.[132]

O'Donovan insists "the foundations of Christian ethics must be evangelical," by which he means "Christian ethics must arise from the gospel of Jesus Christ" else "it could not be *Christian* ethics," meaning there would be nothing uniquely and distinctively *Christian* about what Christianity believes or teaches on the subject.[133] O'Donovan, therefore, insists that "the exploration of Christian moral concepts must always, in the first place, be the work of theology" rather than of philosophy.[134] Though O'Donovan accepts the value of reason, he also insists Christian ethics should never be reduced only to what human reason and experience allow as if divine revelation is not required.

O'Donovan does not only claim that Christian ethics is theological rather than philosophical, is Christ-centered rather than man-centered, and is gospel-centered rather than nature-centered. He goes on to insist that Christian ethics centers especially on God's raising Jesus from the dead,[135] and that is because Scripture says, "The new life upon which the very possibility of ethics depends" entails "a new birth into a living hope *through the resurrection* of Jesus Christ from the dead" (1 Pet 1:3, emphasis mine). From this, O'Donovan argues that, by "the achievement of salvation in the death and resurrection of Christ," Christian ethics not

---

[131] O'Donovan's primary contributions as an Evangelical ethicist are found in *Principles in the Public Realm: The Dilemma of Christian Moral Witness* (Oxford: Clarendon, 1984), *Resurrection and Moral Order, The Desire of Nations: Rediscovering the Roots of Political Theology* (Cambridge: Cambridge, 1996), *From Irenaeus to Grotius: A Sourcebook in Christian Political Thought* (see chap. 5, n. 2), *Common Objects of Love* (see chap. 2, n. 84), *The Just War Revisited* (New York: Cambridge, 2003), *Bonds of Imperfection: Christian Politics, Past and Present* (Grand Rapids: Eerdmans, 2004), and *Ethics as Theology: An Introduction*, 2 vols. (Grand Rapids: Eerdmans, 2013–2014). His ethical teaching is described and analyzed by Paul G. Doerksen in *Beyond Suspicion: Post-Christendom Protestant Political Theology in John Howard Yoder and Oliver O'Donovan* (Carlisle, UK: Paternoster, 2009), by R. T. France and Alister E. McGrath in *Evangelical Anglicans: Their Role and Influence in the World Today* (London: SPCK, 1993), and by David H. McIlroy in *Trinitarian Theology of Law: In Conversation with Jürgen Moltmann, Oliver O'Donovan and Thomas Aquinas* (Carlisle, UK: Paternoster, 2009).

[132] For example, Hauerwas, a postmodern liberal, considers O'Donovan's work in political theology "the most accomplished contribution to Anglican ethics since World War II" (Hauerwas, "September 11, 2001: A Pacifist Response")

[133] O'Donovan, *Resurrection and Moral Order*, 11. Note my earlier reference to this in chap. 1, n. 69.

[134] O'Donovan, 8.

[135] O'Donovan, 13.

only looks back to reaffirm "the order of creation" but also "forward to what is anticipated there, the kingdom of God."[136] In this way, O'Donovan shows how fundamental theology, and not philosophy, is what ultimately explains why Christian ethics is unchanging yet transforming, objectively real yet subjectively relevant, universal yet personal, and realistic about human sin and finitude yet headed for ultimate perfection.

Gilbert C. Meilaender (b. 1946)

Gilbert C. Meilaender (b. 1946) is a Lutheran theologian, professor, and Christian ethicist who thinks deeply about the sanctity of human life and served on the President's Council on Bioethics (2002–2009). But Meilaender is not just a bioethicist and has also addressed many other areas of ethics, including work, friendship, sex and marriage, the nature of Christian ethics, the limits of politics, and the ethical thought of Lewis.[137]

Like most who have shaped contemporary Evangelical ethics, Meilaender, too, sees ethics as essentially theological, not philosophical, and warns that, because Christian ethics "must begin from faith," it must not be reduced to nothing uniquely Christian.[138] But that makes it hard to relate Christian moral values to others in the world. So, while he says that "Christian moral knowledge is built upon no foundation other than the biblical narrative of God's dealing

---

[136] O'Donovan, 26.

[137] Meilaender's primary contributions as an Evangelical ethicist are found in *The Taste for the Other, Friendship: A Study in Theological Ethics* (Notre Dame, IN: University of Notre Dame, 1981), *The Theory and Practice of Virtue* (Notre Dame, IN: University of Notre Dame,1984), *The Limits of Love* (see chap. 4, n. 81), *Morality in Plague Time: AIDS in Theological Perspective* (St. Louis: Concordia, 1989), *Faith and Faithfulness* (see chap. 4, n. 80), *Body, Soul, and Bioethics* (Notre Dame, IN: University of Notre Dame, 1995), *Bioethics: A Primer for Christians* (Grand Rapids: Eerdmans, 1996), *Working: Its Meaning and Its Limits* (Notre Dame, IN: University of Notre Dame, 2000), *Forming Life, Forming Youth: Lutheran Perspectives on Contemporary Ethical Issues* (Valparaiso, IN: Valparaiso University, 2000), *Things That Count: Essays Moral and Theological* (Wilmington, DE: ISO, 2000), *Love Taking Shape: Sermons on the Christian Life* (Grand Rapids: Eerdmans, 2002), *The Freedom of a Christian: Grace, Vocation, and the Meaning of Our Humanity* (Grand Rapids: Brazos, 2006), and *Neither Beast Nor God: The Dignity of the Human Person* (New York: New Atlantis, 2009). His ethical teaching is analyzed by Mark W. Foreman in "Living through the Tension: Religion and Public Policy in the Thought of Gilbert Meilaender," (PhD diss, University of Virginia, 2008).

[138] Meilaender, *Faith and Faithfulness*, 126.

with his world,"[139] Meilaender also thinks it is "best to describe Christian ethics as a two tiered ethic—in part general and able to be defended on grounds not particularly Christian; in part singular, making sense only within the shared life of the faithful community."[140] Thus, he affirms the uniquely Christian nature of Christian ethics but also claims it is good for everyone.

Meilaender strongly opposes dividing the human race into persons and nonpersons and suggests using the term *human dignity* for capacities characteristic of our species but that vary from person to person, and using the term *personal dignity* for what is shared equally by all and never changes.[141] Evangelicals all agree with distinguishing variable from invariable aspects of dignity, but some do not agree with Meilaender's formulation and think it makes more sense to use *human dignity* for what everyone shares equally and to use *personal dignity* for what varies from person to person depending on character, ability, maturation, degeneration, genetics, or material circumstances.

Wayne A. Grudem (b. 1948)

Wayne A. Grudem (b. 1948) is a Baptist theologian and seminary professor best known for defending biblical gender roles.[142] He cofounded the Council for Biblical Manhood and Womanhood (CBMW) in 1987 with John Piper and Wayne House, served as president of

---

[139] Gilbert Meilaender, "The Singularity of Christian Ethics," *Journal of Religious Ethics* 17/2 (Fall, 1989): 107.

[140] Meilaender, *Faith and Faithfulness*, 20.

[141] Meilaender, *Neither Beast Nor God*, 8.

[142] Grudem's primary contributions as an Evangelical ethicist are found in John Piper and Wayne A. Grudem, *Recovering Biblical Manhood and Womanhood: A Response to Evangelical Feminism* (Wheaton, IL: Crossway, 1991), *Business for the Glory of God: The Bible's Teaching on the Moral Goodness of Business* (Wheaton, IL: Crossway, 2003), *Evangelical Feminism and Biblical Truth: An Analysis of More than 100 Disputed Questions* (Colorado Springs: Mulnomah, 2004), *Countering the Claims of Evangelical Feminism: Biblical Responses to the Key Questions* (Sisters, OR: Mulnomah, 2006), *Evangelical Feminism? A New Path to Liberalism?* (Wheaton, IL: Crossway, 2006), *Politics according to the Bible* (Grand Rapids: Zondervan, 2010); Charles Colson, Wayne Grudem, and Peter Lillback, *Biblical Perspectives on Business Ethics: How the Christian Worldview Has Shaped Our Economic Foundations* (Basking Ridge, NJ: Center for Christian Business Ethics, 2012), *How Christians Should Relate to Government* (Grand Rapids: Zondervan, 2012), *The Poverty of Nations: A Sustainable Solution* (Wheaton, IL: Crossway, 2013), and *Christian Ethics* (see chap. 1, n. 67).

the Evangelical Theological Society from 1999 to 2000, and has taught at Evangelical schools his whole career.[143]

Grudem's expertise is in biblical Greek and New Testament studies, but his interests range into systematic theology and Christian ethics. He is known for relying on the ethical authority of Scripture alone, meaning he does not use philosophy to structure or interpret what the Bible says. Thus, Grudem carries forward traditional Protestant rejection of syncretism in Christian ethics. His contributions to Christian ethical understanding mainly deal with applying biblical truth to issues where they are challenged or rejected in the culture. Grudem's work applying biblical ethics is extensive, but what makes him a major figure in contemporary Evangelical ethics is a 1,296-page volume published in 2018, titled *Christian Ethics: An Introduction to Biblical Moral Reasoning*.

Grudem is respected for applying biblical standards to contemporary issues, but his introduction to Christian ethics as a field of study does not distinguish biblical ethics as an academic subclassification in the larger field with relying on Scripture for ethical authority. Consequently, Grudem's text focuses on biblical analysis so narrowly, he introduces, the field without covering the history of Christian ethics, systems of moral theology, or philosophical theories treated from a biblical worldview and without alerting readers to how contemporary developments in the field are perverting Christian ethics by substituting experiences, affections, pleasures, and humanly conceived ideals for the Word of God.

Grudem's text introducing Christian ethics interacts with how scholars interpret Bible passages but hardly mentions moral theologians, interacts with fellow Evangelicals but hardly mentions non-Evangelicals working in the field, and discusses the meaning of Scripture passages without explaining how biblical revelation relates to philosophical theories. This is problematic for an introductory textbook because it is one thing to rely on Scripture and another to treat part of a field of study as the whole, and it is one thing to affirm truth and another to so narrow categories of scholarship that a field of academic study includes nothing with which one disagrees. Grudem offers superb work in biblical and applied ethics, but

---

[143] Grudem taught at Bethel College from 1977 to 1981, taught at Trinity Evangelical Divinity School from 1981 to 2001, and started teaching at Phoenix Seminary in 2001, where he still teaches as I write in 2019.

his text introducing Christian ethics as a field of study needs to be supplemented, by the sort of coverage this text provides.[144]

Emerging Trends

The study of Christian ethics is not static and has developed throughout history ever since the close of the New Testament. There are two reasons that the study of Christian understanding and practice develops over time. Jesus mentioned the first in saying there will be no end to what is found and brought out of the treasure stored in God's written revelation (Matt 13:52). The second is that, while God's truth never changes (Ps 119:89), ways the Devil and the world attack it change all the time (Matt 16:23), and although this causes perversions, it also causes faithful Christians to seek biblical answers and thus to articulate and defend unchanging truths of God in new ways. Trends emerging in Christian ethics as this book is written in the early twenty-first century reflect how Evangelical scholars are pulled in different directions by influences in the culture that include deconstructionism, anti-foundationalism, sensualism, egoism, emotivism, postmodernism, and neo-paganism.

Evangelical scholars are continuing to articulate and defend biblically grounded revelation essential to Christian faith and practice, but fractures are appearing among Evangelicals working in Christian ethics. Many, like O'Donovan in *Resurrection and Moral Order* (1986), Grudem in *Christian Ethics: An Introduction to Biblical Moral Reasoning* (2018), Mark Liederbach and Evan Lenow in *Ethics as Worship: Moral Discipleship to the Glory of God* (2021), and myself in this text, still do not rely on human philosophy, but some, like Geisler in *Christian Ethics: Options and Issues* (1989), Hollinger in *Choosing the Good: Christian Ethics in a Complex World* (2002), Rae in *Moral Choices: An Introduction to Ethics* (1995), and Frame in *The Doctrine of the Christian Life* (2008), mix humanly devised philosophical theories with what the Word of God reveals. While most Evangelicals still distinguish natural law theology from natural law philosophy, some, like Stephen Grabill

---

[144] Readers need to know I trained under Grudem at Trinity Evangelical Divinity School and owe even more to his mentoring, encouragement, and personal example since that time. The disagreement expressed in these pages is reluctant and premised on sharing his dedication to biblical fidelity and commitment to teaching truth without compromise.

in *Rediscovering the Natural Law in Reformed Theological Ethics* (2006) and Craig Boyd in *A Shared Morality: A Narrative Defense of Natural Law Ethics* (2007), think Evangelicals should now align with how Catholic moral theology has long adopted a syncretic approach mixing theology with philosophy.

Besides this, others who are Evangelical because they affirm biblical inerrancy and essential doctrines are now joining a trend started by liberals, like Hauerwas in *A Community of Character* (1981) and Hans Frei in *Theology and Narrative* (1993), who reconceive Christian ethics using a less-fixed "narrative" rather than "systematic" approach. Those doing so include Grenz in *The Moral Quest: Foundations of Christian Ethics* (1997) and Brian McLaren in *Everything Must Change* (2009) and *A New Kind of Christianity* (2011). And some who once were thought to be Evangelical have since forsaken biblical fidelity and Evangelical identity. These scholars must be classified as post-Evangelical and include Smedes in *Choices: Making Right Decisions in a Complex World* (1986), Stassen in *Authentic Transformation: A New Vision of Christ and Culture* (1995), Jim Wallis in *On God's Side* (2013) and *The (Un)Common Good: How the Gospel Brings Hope to a World Divided* (2013), and Gushee in *The Sacredness of Human Life* (2013) and *Changing Our Mind* (2014).

On the other side of the field to Evangelicals, the movement to paganize Christian ethics continues in the work of scholars such as Rita Nakashima Brock in *Journeys by Heart: A Christology of Erotic Power* (1988) and Eugene F. Rogers, Jr., in *Sexuality and the Christian Body: Their Way into the Triune God* (1999). And the popularity of postmodern philosophy is generating a whole new classification that combines how neo-pagans reaffirm spirituality with how post-liberals reduce ethics to nothing more than personal perspectives. In this vein, Patrick Nullens and Ronald Michener in *The Matrix of Christian Ethics: Integrating Philosophy and Moral Theology in a Postmodern Context* (2010) are proposing to reinterpret biblical revelation to align with postmodern philosophy rather than relying on biblical revelation to criticize how postmodern philosophy deconstructs divine authority and corrupts understanding the Bible.

Conclusion

The history of Christian ethics consists of responding to many trends arising out of variations in Christian understanding affecting teaching and behavior. Differences have arisen between

Cappadocians and Alexandrians, between legalists and libertarians, between Catholics and Protestants, between Calvinists and Lutherans, between Presbyterians and Baptists, between ethical unionists and ethical dualists, between royalists and independents, between triumphalists and separatists, between hierarchialists and congregationalists, between transformationalists and quietists, between universalists and communitarians, between proponents of continuity and of discontinuity, between social idealists and social realists, and between those hoping in political power and those fearing it. But the history of Christian ethics has reached a stage at which the greatest differences now are caused by how the field has divided into utterly opposed streams generally labelled "liberal" or "conservative." The difference separating one stream from the other reduces to answering two questions: "Should teachers and practitioners of Christian ethics accept God's Word as the final, ultimate, and only ethical authority?" and "Should those who study and articulate Christian ethics treat the Bible as the Word of God itself or merely as a record of what men have thought about it?"

Everything else in Christian ethical doctrine, practice, and tradition depends on how we answer these questions because nothing other than the Word of God establishes ethical truth that is objective, universal, and unchanging. In other words, nothing but the Word of God is above and beyond human manipulation. Nothing else relating to human life also transcends it such that we either must submit to higher authority on terms we do not control or must try to redefine it in ways we control ourselves. This is the difference now dividing Christian ethics into ever more radically contrary streams of thought.

All the deconstructionism, anti-foundationalism, sensualism, egoism, emotivism, postmodernism, and neo-paganism now erupting in work done in Christian ethics as a field of study lies downstream from the divide that occurred when the social gospel movement detached the study of Christian ethics from biblical orthodoxy. And, even now, the only thing keeping Evangelicals from going the same way is the doctrine of *Sola Scriptura*—not reason, not reaffirming natural law philosophy, not learning from Catholic moral theology, and not making up new pious definitions for commonly known philosophical categories. The only thing keeping Evangelicals from joining the rest is biblically revealed truth, studied and interpreted according to biblically revealed categories, and nothing else. The neo-orthodox movement that reaffirmed the Word of God in Scripture and recentered Christian ethical understanding on Christ and the gospel resisted sliding into ethical depravity for a time, but it collapsed because the movement was not anchored firmly enough in Scripture alone. Barth was on to something when he insisted moral theology stands by the Word of God alone. But he failed to follow through himself and, in his own work, allowed Kantian epistemology, mixed with Pietistic inwardness, to sever faith in the biblical text being, and not just containing, the Word of God.

The problem Barth faced, and that Christian ethics must always face, is that mixing biblical revelation with human philosophy—any human philosophy at all—inevitably destroys fidelity to *Sola Scriptura*. Philosophical syncretism first weakens faith in Scripture by assuming it is not adequate on its own, which so destroys faith in Scripture it leads to usurping Scripture and then to abandoning Scripture altogether. Any humanly devised philosophical system or terminology has the same affect—if not right away, then ultimately. The Word of God is ethically sufficient. It is fully adequate all by itself and never bows to anything else. Only the Word of God is worth trusting as the Word of God, and since Jesus ascended back up to heaven, the biblical text is the only reliable Word of God we have. It is true that Christ lives in our hearts, and it is true that the Holy Spirit informs conscience convicting the world of sin and assuring Christians of fellowship with God. But we cannot distinguish the inner Christ from ourselves, and we cannot distinguish the Holy Spirit from fleshly appetites, other than by evaluating our feelings and sentiments according to the biblical text. There is not, and never will be, any discrepancy between the Word of God within and the Word of God written. So, if any difference arises between what we sense or feel and what the Bible says, we can and must rely on *Sola Scriptura* and nothing else.

Looking ahead, it is not hard to see what the near future holds. If trends continue, what now divides Christian ethics will grow to divide the whole world into those faithful to the ethical authority of the Bible and those rejecting it to accommodate an ethic of sensuality. But we should not be surprised. Jesus warned that, before he returns, false teachers of Christian ethics will divide the institutional church so badly the love of many for God will grow cold and members will hate and betray one another (Matt 24:10–13),[145] and Paul added that, in the last days, conflict between an ethic of sensuality and fidelity to the Bible will divide the

---

[145] In these verses, what Jesus says will occur especially concerns the false teaching of "Christian ethics." It does not refer to misrepresenting theological doctrines in a general way because Jesus says what drives these events will be "lawlessness" (Matt 24:12). Lawlessness in Scripture refers to ignoring, revising, or abandoning God's moral law, and the study and practice of God's moral law is of course Christian ethics.

whole world (2 Tim 3:1–6). We need only remain faithful. Jesus wins the conflict, and we must only endure (Matt 10:22; 24:13; Mark 13:13).

This concludes our introduction to historical Christian ethics, and the next chapter will introduce readers to how Christian ethics relates to, interacts with, is different from, and criticizes philosophical ethics.

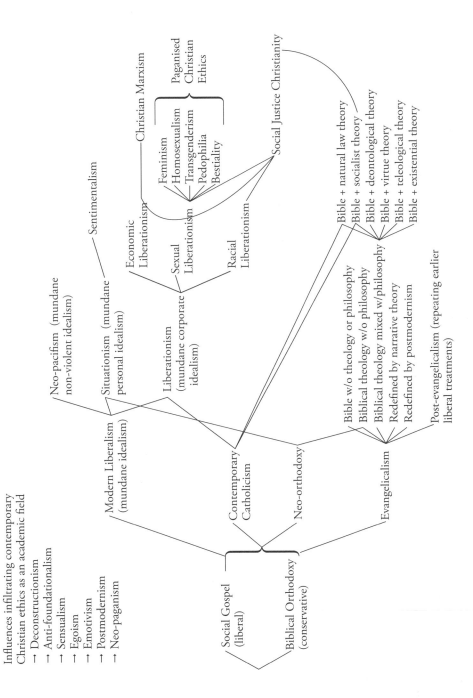

Developments in Christian Ethics Since the Social Gospel Split with Biblical Orthodoxy

CHAPTER 7

PHILOSOPHY, SPECULATION & THEORY

T his chapter introduces readers to philosophical Christian ethics as an academic subcategory within the larger field of Christian ethics.[1] This portion of the field examines,

---

[1] The most important literature in philosophical Christian ethics includes John Locke, *The Reasonableness of Christianity* (1695); Joseph Butler, *Fifteen Sermons upon Human Nature* (1726); Moreland and Craig, *Philosophical Foundations*, esp. 391–460 (see chap. 1, n. 38); Edward J. Carnell, *A Philosophy of the Christian Religion* (Grand Rapids: Eerdmans, 1952); Long, *A Survey of Christian Ethics* (see chap. 1, n. 49); George F. Thomas, *Christian Ethics and Moral Philosophy* (New York: Scribner's, 1955); K. Ward, *Ethics and Christianity* (London: Allen and Unwin, 1970); John Finnis, *Natural Law and Natural Rights* (Oxford: Clarendon, 1980); Finnis, *Fundamentals of Ethics* (see chap. 1, n. 35); Norman L. Geisler, *Ethics: Alternatives and Issues* (Grand Rapids: Zondervan, 1971); Arthur F. Holmes, *Ethics: Approaching Moral Decisions* (Downers Grove, IL: InterVarsity, 1984); Geisler, *Christian Ethics* (see chap. 1, n. 55); Norman L. Geisler, *Contemporary Issues and Options* (Grand Rapids: Baker, 2010); Eric Osborn, *The Beginning of Christian Philosophy* (Cambridge: Cambridge, 1981); Cook, *The Moral Maze* (see chap. 2, n. 2); John Warwick Montgomery, *Human Rights and Human Dignity* (Grand Rapids: Zondervan, 1986); Frame, *Perspectives on the Word of God* (see chap. 2, n. 2); Rae, *Moral Choices*, (see chap. 1, n. 9); Basil Mitchell, *Morality: Religious and Secular* (Oxford: Clarendon, 1980); Alasdair MacIntyre, *After Virtue*, (see chap. 4, n. 1); Alasdair MacIntyre, *Whose Justice? Which Rationality?* (Notre Dame, IN: University of Notre Dame, 1988); Lovin, *Christian Ethics: An Essential Guide* (see chap. 1, n. 47); R. Scott Smith, *Virtue Ethics and Moral Knowledge*

interacts with, and criticizes various theories about the meaning, nature, and source of ethical knowledge, ethical authority, and ethical accountability, doing it from a Christian point of view. Some doing work in this area also take concepts, terms, classifications, or definitions from these theories and use them along with what the Bible says. But Evangelicals hold different views on how much, if at all, that can be done without compromising.

How Philosophical Ethics Differs from Christian Ethics

Philosophical ethics and Christian ethics are not the same thing. Philosophical ethics and Christian ethics cover the same ground, ask the same questions, and use reason in much the same way as theological ethics, leading some to suppose there is not much difference, but that is not the case. They really are very different things and must not be confused. To understand what makes them different, we must start with seeing what is not different, and on that point, it is especially important to realize that Christian ethicists and philosophers both use reason—one no less than the other. Christian ethicists (both Bible scholars and theologians) who love God "with all your mind" (Matt 22:37; Mark 12:30; Luke 10:27) use reason just as vigorously and consistently as any philosopher. Philosophical and Christian ethics do not differ as to subject, questions, or reason, but rather are distinguished from each other as to starting point, perspective, finitude, authority, and comprehensiveness.

Whereas Christian ethics starts with revelation, philosophical ethics starts with human experience.[2] Whereas Christian ethics is theocentric (God-centered), philosophical ethics is

---

(Aldershot, UK: Ashgate, 2003); Stuart C. Hackett, *The Rediscovery of the Highest Good* (Eugene, OR: Wipf & Stock, 2009); R. Scott Smith, *Naturalism and Our Knowledge of Reality: Testing Religious Truth-Claims* (Farnham, UK: Ashgate, 2012); R. Scott Smith, *In Search of Moral Knowledge: Overcoming the Fact-Value Dichotomy* (Downers Grove, IL: InterVarsity, 2014); Anderson, *Christian Ethics in Plain Language* (see chap. 1, n. 52); Craig Vincent Mitchell, *Charts of Christian Ethics* (Grand Rapids: Zondervan, 2006); Calvin P. Van Reken, *Principia Meta-Ethica* (Eugene, OR: Pickwick, 2015); and Craig Boyd and Don Thorsen, *Christian Ethics and Moral Philosophy: An Introduction to Issues and Approaches* (Grand Rapids: Baker, 2018).

[2] I agree with Pannenberg, who says what sets theological ethics apart from philosophy is not the degree to which one or the other does or does not use reason, but rather is the opposed ways each conceives "its ethical foundation." Pannenberg, *Ethics*, 57 (see chap. 4, n. 1). What I refer to here as "starting point" means the same thing. This means I do not agree with Van Til's claim that "for Christians the difference between theological and philosophical ethics can be no more than one

anthropocentric (man-centered).[3] Whereas Christian ethics trusts transcendence, philosophical ethics only trusts the space-time-material world. Whereas Christian ethics bears divine authority (is dogmatic) and only speculates on aspects not directly addressed in what God says, philosophical ethics never goes beyond speculating, never truly obligates, and never actually holds anyone to account. And whereas Christian ethics tries to be comprehensive, philosophical ethics tries to reduce ethics to a single ideal, rule, goal, or virtue.

This last difference is especially interesting and worth considering more. How can ethical understanding presume truth about all there is (even things no one has yet encountered) and still hang together with all the parts fitting each other properly? Human philosophers claim to perceive universal truths but inevitably base the coherence needed for any valuing theory to work by taking a preferred ideal, rule, goal, or virtue and making it a *Grundnorm* (most basic principle) from which everything else derives meaning, validity, and authority.[4] Because philosophers start with human experience and human rationality, they never select anything beyond human limits. So, whatever philosophers select inevitably conflicts with reality as a whole. Nothing they select explains the whole for the same reason no one can explain how plants grow without considering the sun. Parts of the growing process can be studied just looking at plants themselves, digging in the soil around them, and examining their roots. But nothing on earth explains what energizes the process, and supposing the entire growing process can be explained just by studying plants and soil inevitably produces reductionistic explanations.

In contrast to this, Christian ethicists seek coherence in ways that include more. Starting with revelation from God, as theologians, they are driven to include everything under God's

---

of emphasis." Van Til, *Christian Theistic Ethics*, 5 (see chap. 1, n. 36). By using "emphasis" for the distinction, Van Til supposes the difference between what God reveals and men conceive is nothing more than a matter of stress or focus. That is, Van Til supposes there is no difference other than variations explained by which part of the same reality is in view. That, I think, is both wrong and dangerous. What distinguishes revealed ethics from what men conceive is foundational, not focal, and is a matter of supremacy, not stress.

[3] Emil Brunner held the main difference between philosophical and Christian ethics is what each presumes about the source of ultimate authority, with one looking to man and the other to God. Brunner, *The Divine Imperative*, 86 (see chap. 2, n. 39).

[4] The legal philosopher Hans Kelsen coined the term *Grundnorm* to indicate a most basic order, rule, or principle underlying, establishing, and so giving cohesion and legitimacy to a system of laws by which people live. See Hans Kelsen, *Pure Theory of Law* (Berkeley, CA: University of California, 1967).

authority—even things beyond what they, as finite human beings, experience or can fully grasp. They know the ruler of all things though they have not, as limited human beings, experienced all things under his authority. Philosophers find that the more they assume a theoretical system covers, the harder it gets to explain how one thing orders everything else, and they also find that it gets easier to explain how one thing orders the rest the less they assume a theoretical system covers. But, because Christian ethicists are theologians starting with revelation, they start already knowing what holds everything together (Col 1:17) and have no problem including all reality even though the whole includes things no one has yet experienced, discovered, or considered.

Unlike philosophical ethics, Christian ethics is so very inclusive the entirety cannot be reduced to a single *Grundnorm*. But this enormous inclusivity does not leave Christian ethics incoherent, jumbled, or disordered because there is something else generating the coherence needed for ordering the whole. Reality is not ordered by a basic ideal, rule, goal, or virtue but by a person. Christians know what orders all reality is not something but someone. It is not a what but a who. It is not something abstract, theoretical, inanimate, or impersonal but God himself.[5] John referred to this comprehensive ordering when declaring Jesus is the *Logos* (John 1:1), a term that, to Greek philosophers, especially the Stoics following Heraclitus (c. 535– c. 475 BC), signified the power holding the universe together, the operation by which reality runs as a whole, and so the principle explaining how everything in the universe is given unity, coherence, and meaning.[6]

Philosophers trying to explain the coherence of ethics inevitably leave out things Christian ethicists know to include, as they realize explaining the coherence of ethics will not succeed

---

[5] True Christian ethics, whether biblical or theological, has no single basic rule or ideal from which all others arise. But there is an ultimate motive, which is loving God (Matt 22:37; Luke 10:27); there is an ultimate source of authority, which is the will of God (Rom 12:2; Col 1:9–10); there is an ultimate source of accountability, which is the judgment of God (Rom 14:12; Heb 9:27); there is an ultimate goal, which is the glory of God (1 Cor 10:31; Col 3:17); there is an ultimate obligation, which is serving or worshiping God (Deut 6:13; Col 3:23); there is an ultimate measure, which is the holiness of God (Lev 20:26; 1 Pet 1:16); and there is an ultimate dread, which is the fear of God (Deut 10:12; Matt 10:28).

[6] Daniel W. Graham, "Heraclitus," in *Cambridge Dictionary of Philosophy*, ed. Robert Audi, 3rd ed. (New York: Cambridge, 2015), 453–54. Francis E. Peters, *Greek Philosophical Terms: A Historical Lexicon* (New York: New York University, 1967), 110–12.

apart from starting with the moral ruler of the universe. Philosophers sometimes argue toward arriving at what they know the Bible says about the character and purposes of God.[7] But even when doing that, philosophers treat God himself and relating to him properly as conclusions and not what is central or essential to how they conceive the meaning and nature of ethics.

Philosophical Christian Ethics vs. Christians Doing Philosophical Ethics

To qualify as "Christian" ethics, and not just ethics understood the same way by Christians and non-Christians alike, philosophical Christian ethics never contradicts anything the Bible teaches and never sacrifices Christian worldview assumptions. These boundary conditions are, or at least should be, respected even when considering knowledge we suppose everyone has, or at least should have, based on common experience, common ability, and common reasoning apart from anything the Bible says. Some do this more faithfully than others, and some even claim to be doing philosophical Christian ethics when employing ideas or methods contrary to the Bible or the God of the Bible. If so, we should ask if what they do really is "Christian" at all. Just because someone doing philosophical ethics claims to be "Christian" does not mean anything that person does is philosophical Christian ethics. Whether it is or not depends on if what God reveals is considered in relation to philosophy. To be philosophical Christian ethics, the work a person does must be more than just what anyone claiming to be "Christian" says based only on philosophy unrelated to Christianity.

Why Do Philosophical Christian Ethics?

If, in order to be philosophy (and not theology), philosophical ethics never starts with God, never accepts revelation, never trusts anything beyond human experience in the present world, never reaches certainty, always places faith in autonomous human reason while dismissing faith in revelation, and always reduces ethics to something less than it really is, why then should Christians consider philosophical ethics? Are the differences separating Christian ethics from philosophical ethics so great they have nothing to do with one another? Does the

---

[7] Examples of this are John Locke, *The Reasonableness of Christianity* (1695), and Joseph Butler, *Fifteen Sermons upon Human Nature* (1726).

very notion of philosophical Christian ethics turn out to be self-contradictory, incoherent, or even dangerous?

Readers should not think we are taking it that far. While trusting the reasoning of fallen humanity in place of revelation is wrong and while God considers it foolish to follow "the world's wisdom" debated by philosophers (1 Cor 1:20), this does not mean Christians must never have anything to do with philosophical ethics, never have anything to do with examining how others think, or never do anything with things in philosophical ethics that are compatible with what God says. Rather, it means we must see philosophy for what it is and not trust human authority to explain, frame, define, limit, interpret, and so distort or corrupt ethical truth revealed by God. Reasoning that only considers ethical truth revealed by the Word of God is theology, not philosophy. But Christians also need to understand and engage human-centered philosophical theories about ethics and are foolish if we do not try at least to understand how others think before debating how we differ.

It is important, however, that we not confuse engaging man-centered philosophical ethics on Christ-centered terms with using philosophical ethics to explain, frame, define, limit, interpret, and so distort or corrupt ethical truth revealed by God. Biblical truth is what Schaeffer called "true truth,"[8] and only true truth from God, centered on God, and interpreted in relation to God is reliable for ordering how we think of ethical reality—never the other way around. Ethical truth based on what God reveals can and should be used to shape what we think of philosophical ethics, but philosophical ethics must not be used to shape what we think of what God reveals. Studying philosophical ethics is part of philosophical Christian ethics, but we must not allow it to undermine faith in God and what he says. Philosophical Christian ethics may go beyond criticizing and sometimes use ideas in philosophical ethics that are compatible with revelation. But we must never reduce revelation to philosophy and must never substitute one for the other.

Philosophy & Revelation

Revelation is truth known from God, and philosophy is human speculating without necessarily believing anything God says or even that he exists. Theological Christian ethics evaluates

---

[8] Schaeffer, *Escape from Reason*, 21 (see chap. 6, n. 112).

what we know from revelation, and philosophical Christian ethics studies theories based on what men know, or imagine they know, without revelation. But reason can, as easily, be used to analyze revealed truths as theories that do not suppose ethics comes from God. Reason does not stand alone as a source of truth in its own right but is only an instrument we use to analyze what comes from whatever source of truth we presuppose.

Christian ethics starting with revelation is able to assess, accept, and use truths in philosophical ethics that align with Christianity. But philosophical ethics is never able to accept anything not explainable on human terms without God. In other words, Christian ethics has standing to assess philosophical ethics based on human experience without revelation, but philosophical ethics based on human experience without revelation always lacks standing to assess Christian ethics—not because it starts with something higher and better, but because it does not. For this reason, Christian philosophical ethics presupposes a Christian worldview while examining theories that do not.

I have said already that studying different philosophies of ethics and using elements compatible with Christianity has a place in Christian ethics, but doing so has limits that cannot be violated without elevating man over God. Studying philosophical ethics can be used to understand how men without the Bible think about moral reality and are inhibited from understanding it adequately, and philosophical ideas accepted by non-Christians may sometimes be used to gain a hearing that leads them to faith. Should that happen, how those so converted think of ethics must shift rather significantly. At least, what they think about the meaning and nature of ethical reality and source of ethical authority must change from what it was before coming to faith.

While agreeing to a place in Christian ethics for using elements in philosophical ethics found compatible with revelation, we must be careful when doing so to avoid using philosophy to explain, define, or classify the Christian understanding of ethical reality itself. Doing that turns the meaning, nature, and truth of divine revelation upside down. Raising philosophy over revelation elevates theory over dogma, treats philosophy as having greater authority than theology, and places man over God, which is idolatrous. Presuming philosophical ethics has thought supremacy conforms God to man rather than man to God, explains the superior by the inferior rather than the inferior by the superior, elevates earth over heaven rather than heaven over earth, reduces infinity to limitations of finitude rather than conceiving finitude in the larger scope of infinity, and gauges transcendence by the mundane rather than the mundane by transcendence. The difference concerns something most important, which is whether we live in God's moral reality or claim to be morally autonomous—not only as to accountability but also as to how we think, which means not only as to how we behave but also as to how we classify, define, and explain the meaning and nature of ethics itself.

Using philosophy to open the minds and hearts of non-Christians to God's moral revelation is one thing, but using it to explain God's moral revelation is something else. The first glorifies God (1 Cor 10:31), while the second does not. The first uses philosophy in service of revelation, while the second limits revelation to philosophy. The first uses revelation to interpret philosophy, while the second uses philosophy to interpret revelation. The first prioritizes revelation over philosophy, while the second prioritizes philosophy over revelation. The first treats the mind of God as sovereign over human minds, while the second treats human minds as sovereign over the mind of God. Van Til was wrong to take this distinction so far as to make God's sovereignty contrary to common grace, but he was right about insisting God is sovereign over how we think of ethics as well as over what it contains.[9] Barth was wrong to sever the Word of God from Scripture and reduce it to sentiment, but he was right to insist that theology transcends philosophy and "philosophy cannot . . . go beyond the Word of God . . . if it is not to become (a false) theology."[10]

Christian ethics is not Christian without Christ, and the right ordering of reality is never independent of God revealed in Christ. Christian ethics is real ethics, and real ethics is Christian ethics. Philosophical Christian ethics can evaluate, criticize, and sometimes use truths found in philosophical ethics, but Christian ethical thought never submits to, never is limited to, and never is reducible to any philosophy. Rather, it is that Christian ethical thought, including work in the portion known as philosophical Christian ethics, always relativizes, always redefines, and always reconceives philosophical speculating by the ethical reality

---

[9] For God's sovereignty eclipsing common grace, see Van Til, *A Christian Theory of Knowledge,* 296 (see chap. 6, n. 89). Frame says that "although Van Til affirms the ambiguity of the unbeliever's position under common grace, he nevertheless often writes as though the unbeliever knows and affirms no truth at all and thus is not at all affected by common grace." Frame, *Cornelius Van Til: An Analysis of His Thought,* 189 (see chap. 6, n. 87). For God's sovereignty over human thought, see Van Til, *Christian Theistic Ethics,* 32, and John M. Frame, "Van Til and the Ligonier Apologetic," *Westminster Theological Journal* 42:2 (Fall 1985): 282.

[10] Barth, *Ethics,* 22, 36, 40–44 (see chap. 1, n. 26); White, *Christian Ethics,* 340 (see chap. 1, n. 69). Quotation is from Barth, *Ethics,* 44.

revealed in the Bible as centering on, coming from, and fulfilled in the person, mission, and work of Jesus Christ.[11] As Van Til asserts, "The God of Scripture is the ultimate category of interpretation for man in every aspect of his being," and as Barth once famously declared, "On the field of ethical deliberation," theological (i.e., Christian) ethics "advances the claim that it is the one that with its investigation has the last word which absorbs all others."[12]

Philosophical Christian ethics studies how philosophy relates to revelation and so how philosophical ethics relates to theological and biblical ethics. Done properly, philosophical Christian ethics shows how the biblical and theological absorb the philosophical—not the other way around. Revelation is foundational to a properly formed Christian worldview, and a properly formed Christian worldview based on revelation is foundational to assessing philosophy—to assessing all humanly devised systems of thought—not the other way around.[13] That is why this text introducing Christian ethics as a whole starts with biblical ethics, moves to theological and historical ethics, and only then considers philosophical ethics. Other introductions to the field often start with philosophy and only then consider the rest. But that suggests human thought is able to absorb revelation without distortion, which never can be done and must be resisted. When the Apostle John declared Jesus is the *Logos* (John 1:1), he was absorbing philosophy into revelation—not the reverse.

Categories of Ethical Action

We will now consider two rational tools used for analyzing ethical issues. We are treating them in this chapter on philosophical Christian ethics, but they are neutral as to worldview and pertain as much to theological as to philosophical reasoning. The first deals with categories of ethical action and the second deals with assessing ethical responsibility. The first considers

---

[11] This view differs with my doctoral mentor Ed Long, who says, "It is impossible to understand Christian ethics without some appreciation of philosophical ways of dealing with moral issues," and also believes that "in order to understand Christian ethics as a field of discourse, it is important to have at least a bird's-eye view of ethical discourse as found in moral philosophy" (Long, *A Survey of Christian Ethics*, 3).

[12] Van Til, *Christian Theistic Ethics*, 20. Barth, *Ethics*, 19–20.

[13] The title for *Philosophical Foundations for a Christian Worldview*, by Moreland and Craig, reverses this relation and must be questioned. What the book contains prioritizes revelation over human thought in the way it accesses philosophical ideas. So, the title seems contrary to what the authors say.

"actions" (things done) and the second considers "actors" (those doing things). The first will be treated in this section and the second will be treated in the next.

All human actions are subject to ethical evaluation, a fact that follows from living under a Creator who rules all. But just because all actions are subject to ethical evaluation does not mean all are right or wrong in the same way. Some actions are completely right or completely wrong all the time, but others can be unwise but not always wrong, can be fine whether you do them or not, or can be optional and yet worth praising if you do them. So, to clarify differences, it is possible to identify four classifications: ethically indifferent actions, ethically discretionary actions, ethically obligatory actions, and ethically supererogatory actions.[14]

Ethically indifferent actions are those that can be done, or not, with impunity either way.[15] These are actions that make no moral difference since they incur no moral praise or blame under any circumstance. They are not morally discretionary (either wise or foolish), not morally obligatory (either mandated or prohibited), and not morally supererogatory (heroic).

---

[14] The Scottish philosopher Thomas Reid (1710–1796) classified actions into "good, bad, and indifferent." Thomas Reid, *Essays on the Active Powers of Man* (1788), chap iv, para ix. I take Reid's classifications to align with "mandates," "prohibitions," and "indifferent actions," which means Reid did not address "discretionary" or "supererogatory" actions. John and Paul Feinberg also identify three categories: the permissible, the obligatory (subdivided into mandates and prohibitions), and the supererogatory. Feinberg and Feinberg, *Brave New World*, 19 (see chap. 1, n. 38); or John S. Feinberg and Paul D. Feinberg, *Ethics for a Brave New World*, 2nd ed., (Wheaton, IL: Crossway, 2010), 24. But their "permissible" classification aligns with what others call "indifferent actions," which means they do not deal with discretionary actions either. Lastly, Paul McNamara proposes eight classifications: the obligatory, the morally optimal, the minimum morality demands, the supererogatory, the morally optional, the morally indifferent, the morally significant, and the permissibly sub-optimal (Paul McNamara, "Making Room for Going beyond the Call," *Mind* 105 [July 1996]: 415). I find McNamara helpful, but he expands classifications more than necessary. His "optional" and "indifferent" classifications are indistinguishable, his "optimal" and "permissibly sub-optimal" classifications are subcategories of his "morally significant" classification in the same way "wise and foolish actions" are subcategories of what I call "discretionary" actions, and his "the minimum morality demands" and "obligatory" classifications are indistinguishable, as both refer to the same mandates and prohibitions. I thus arrive at four classifications: the indifferent, the discretionary (subdivided into wisdom and folly), the obligatory (subdivided into mandates and prohibitions), and the supererogatory.

[15] The term *indifferent* comes from Cicero's use of the Stoic term ἀδιάφορα (*adiaphora*), meaning things neither morally good nor bad, which translated into Latin is *indifferens*. Marcus Tullius Cicero, *On the Ends of Good and Evil*, 45 BC, iii. 16. For the term in Stoic philosophy, see Eduard Zeller, *Stoics, Epicureans and Sceptics* (London: Longmans, Green and Co., 1870), 218.

In ethical terms, they are merely "okay" and nothing more. Examples of ethically indifferent actions include getting regular exercise, having a favorite music style, choosing what to wear in the morning, and eating with chopsticks rather than with a knife and fork. Actions of this kind can be healthy or unhealthy, stylish or gauche, polite or rude, fitting or unfitting, but doing them or not makes no ethical difference. It must be noted, however, that actions in this category can shift out of it when taken to extremes, such as when eating unhealthy food becomes deadly, clothing styles become immodest, or music becomes rebellious. That actions are ethically indifferent does not mean they are outside ethical assessing but only means they are of a kind that makes no ethical difference either way.

Ethically discretionary actions are those that are wise or foolish.[16] Being wise is not just praiseworthy but required, and being foolish is not just blameworthy but forbidden. But what is wise or foolish takes discretion, which is a form of ethical assessing that applies standing principles to changing circumstances. In other words, discretion uses relative moral judgment to assess risk levels, likely outcomes, cost benefits, or perceptions affecting a course of action. Ethically discretionary actions are not morally indifferent (those not making any moral difference) because being wise or foolish makes a moral difference, but they are not obligatory (mandated or prohibited) either. Seeking wisdom and shunning folly is obligatory. But whether acting one way or another is wise or foolish depends on circumstances, and for that reason, such actions are not obligatory on their own. Ethically discretionary actions also are not morally supererogatory (heroic) because while wisdom is praiseworthy and folly is blameworthy, being one and not the other is not optional but required.

Examples of ethically discretionary actions include drinking alcohol, watching R-rated movies, talking with drug dealers, and taking young children to live in the jungle surrounded by dangerous animals and diseases far from emergency medical help.[17] Doing things like this

---

[16] Richard Whately recognizes "discretion" as a category of ethical action in his *Introductory Lessons on Morals*. Richard Whately, *Introductory Lessons on Morals, and Christian Evidences* (Cambridge: John Bartlett, 1857), 34. Beyond that, my classifications of discretionary, wise, and foolish actions align with what McNamara terms "the morally significant, the morally optimal, and the permissibly sub-optimal" (McNamara, "Going beyond the Call," 415). This differs with the Feinbergs because their "permissible" classification only includes indifferent actions and does not include discretionary actions.

[17] This is what my parents did with their young children, which included me, a younger sister, and later a younger brother. My two youngest siblings were born after we left living in the jungle. Our

may seem foolish but can be wise depending on the stakes. Drinking alcohol can be medicinal, watching an R-rated movie can be a way of teaching valor, talking with drug dealers might stop something worse, and taking a family to live in danger far from emergency medical help might be the only way to evangelize people unreached by the gospel.

Ethically obligatory actions are those that mandate or prohibit doing, or not doing, things regardless of circumstance.[18] Ethical obligation is a power by which people are bound to do, or not do, certain things classified as duties that take the form of commands, rules, standards, or customs set by an authority superior to and with jurisdiction over those bound by them. Philosophers have different ideas about where the obligating authority in ethical duty comes from and have suggested it might come from universal reason, human nature, cultural tradition, social pressure, peer pressure, personal choosing, coercion, or a combination of these. But theologians know that obligation in ethical duty only comes from God as promulgated by the Word of God. Ethically obligatory acts are not morally indifferent (those not making any moral difference), not morally discretionary (either wise or foolish), and not supererogatory (heroic).

Ethical obligations come in two forms, one positive and the other negative. Positive ethical obligations are mandates that cannot be avoided without censure (moral blame), but just doing what is mandated earns no praise, as Jesus explains in Luke 17:9–10. Examples of ethical mandates include feeding babies, keeping promises, paying taxes honestly, honoring parents, and driving the speed limit. Negative ethical obligations are prohibitions that can never be done without censure (moral blame), but just avoiding what is forbidden is not praiseworthy either. Examples of ethical prohibitions include not molesting children, not

---

parents, Ernie and Mertie Heimbach, were first-contact pioneer missionaries who brought the gospel to the Hmong of Northern Thailand. The jungles where the Hmong lived were far from the nearest medical facility and filled with tigers and venomous snakes, as well as diseases such as malaria, yellow fever, dengue fever, cholera, typhus, and tuberculosis.

[18] Recent work on ethically obligatory actions include Mark A. Brown and José Carmo, *Deontic Logic, Agency and Normative Systems* (Berlin: Springer-Verlag, 1996); Roderick M. Chisholm, "The Ethics of Requirement," *American Philosophical Quarterly* 1 (1963): 147–53; John F. Crosby, "Person and Obligation," American Catholic Philosophical Quarterly 79/1 (2005): 91–119; and Stephen Darwall, "Moral Obligation: Form and Substance," *Proceedings of the Aristotelian Society* 110/1 (2010): 31–46.

murdering parents, not lying on job applications, not cheating on tests, not rebelling against civil authority, and not taking God's name in vain.

Ethically supererogatory actions are those going beyond the call of duty.[19] These are acts of heroism that matter greatly but cannot be required.[20] They are not morally indifferent (those not making any moral difference), not morally discretionary (either wise or foolish), and not morally obligatory (either mandated or prohibited). Like indifferent actions, they are optional, and no one is blamed for not doing them. Also, unlike obligations but like discretionary actions, supererogatory acts are praiseworthy. But praising actions that go beyond what duty requires differs from praising wisdom in four ways. First, acting wisely is obligatory, and going beyond duty is not. Second, what acting wisely requires changes from situation to situation, and going beyond duty is measured in reference to obligations that never change and stay the same for everyone everywhere. Third, acting wisely is discretionary, and going beyond duty is sacrificial and not discretionary at all. Fourth, acting wisely earns praise only if achieved, whereas going beyond duty is praised just for being attempted even if the attempt fails. Examples of ethically supererogatory actions include laying down your life to save others, bearing punishment deserved by others, paying expenses owed by others, risking death to care for people dying of dangerous diseases, and giving away all you have to feed the poor.

---

[19] Recent work on understanding ethically supererogatory actions includes Marcia Brown, "Kantian Ethics and Supererogation," *The Journal of Philosophy* 84/5 (1987): 237–62; David Heyd, *Supererogation: Its Status in Ethical Theory* (Cambridge: Cambridge, 1982); McNamara, "Going beyond the Call," 415–50; Gregory Mellema, *Beyond the Call of Duty: Supererogation, Obligation, and Offense* (Albany, NY: SUNY, 1991); Michael Stocker, "Supererogation and Duties," in Nicholas Rescher, ed., *Studies in Moral Philosophy* (Liverpool, UK: Basil Blackwell, 1968), 53–63; Gregory Trianosky, "Supererogation, Wrongdoing, and Vice," *Journal of Philosophy* 83 (1968): 26–40; and Michael J. Zimmerman, "Supererogation and Doing the Best One Can," *American Philosophical Quarterly* 30/4 (1993): 373–80.

[20] McNamara cautions, "There is no ordinary use of this term (*supererogation*) to guide us, and its use among philosophers is hardly uniform." My use aligns with McNamara in "Going beyond the Call," 416; the Feinbergs in *Brave New World*, 19 (1993) and 24 (2010); and Moreland and Craig in *Philosophical Foundations*, 443.

Factors for Assessing Ethical Credit, Blame, and Responsibility

Focus in the last section was on classifying actions, but focus in this section shifts to what makes agents, the doers of action, worthy of moral praise or blame. This tool, like the first, is neutral as to worldview and, though we are dealing with it here, pertains as much to theological as to philosophical reasoning. All actions for which people are responsible presuppose they are done freely, are done for good reasons, and are good things to do.[21] But, since these are distinct from one another, they also may conflict in moral terms. Acts may be done freely for bad reasons, may be well intended but bad things to do, or may be good but coerced or done by mistake. So, even if actions are good to do, it still makes sense to ask if those doing them deserve praising, and, even if actions are bad to do, it still makes sense to ask if those doing them deserve blaming. From this, we can see three factors are required to assess when a person deserves moral praise or blame, and these are that he must have acted by free moral will, have acted with a morally worthy motive, and have done something morally right to do. All three must be present to earn praise. Without the first, a person is neither praised nor blamed regardless of the other two, and, without the second or third, a person is blamed even if the others are met.

Morally Free Will

The first factor affecting when a person deserves praising or blaming is that he must have acted by "morally free will."[22] People are fairly judged only for actions emerging from their own wants and interests without others limiting or preventing them from doing what they would do left to themselves. No one earns moral credit except for what is done freely, and no one is blamed for doing what he cannot help or cannot do no matter what he wishes. A person doing good things against his or her will is not praised, a person forced to do bad things

---

[21] Henry Calderwood mentions three factors for assessing ethical credit but then oddly overlooks freedom of moral action while supposing a person's motive and purpose are separate things. Henry Calderwood, *Handbook of Moral Philosophy*, 3rd ed. (London: Macmillan, 1974), 19.

[22] For discussion of various kinds of free will, see David Basinger and Randall Basinger, eds., *Predestination and Free Will* (Downers Grove, IL: InterVarsity, 1986); Nicholas Rescher, *Free Will: A Philosophical Reappraisal*, 2nd ed. (London: Transaction, 2015); Joseph Keim Campbell, *Free Will* (Malden, MA: Polity, 2011).

against his or her will is not blamed, and the degree to which a person is morally responsible increases or decreases in relation to the degree to which he is free to do what he wants.

More precisely, the philosopher Nicholas Rescher explains that moral freedom hinges on "the agent's autonomy in relation to the operative motivations for his act, with that act as unfree to the extent that those motivations are not his own but externally imposed upon him."[23] Rescher also observes that moral freedom is a negative, rather than positive freedom, because it refers only to acting without external interference and does not entitle persons to being able to change outside things.[24] In other words, free moral will does not include getting others to give you what you want, getting others to do for you what you want, and being able to do anything you cannot do on your own. It only includes doing what you want left to yourself as you are. My free moral will is not compromised unless someone tries to stop me from doing what I can and would do without anyone hindering me.

So, if bank robbers fleeing with stolen money jump in my car and order me at the point of a gun to drive them away, I am not responsible for helping them escape because, in that case, I am forced to act against my will and not with it. And, if someone is coerced on threat of losing his job to donate resources to a good cause, he earns no praise because the act, even though good, is not done freely. But, if someone drowns because I cannot swim, I am not responsible for killing him just because I might have saved him had I been a swimmer.

This can lead Christians to wonder how what the Bible says about us being slaves to sin (John 8:34; Rom 6:20) relates to how fair God is in holding us responsible for sinning. Does the free moral will presupposed when holding people responsible mean God unfairly condemns us for doing what we cannot help and unfairly judges us by standards we cannot achieve? If not, is it because God's transcendence exempts him from needing to be fair? Or is there a different answer? To address this, we must admit God is transcendent, which means he is more than we are and relates to things differently than we do. But while God transcends us, he is also consistent, is not arbitrary, and expects human justice to reflect divine justice. In other words, fairness in how God holds us responsible must, in some way, be connected to fairness in how we hold others responsible. Human fairness may not be the same as divine fairness in all respects, but it cannot be entirely different. This does not mean divine justice must

---

[23] Rescher, *Free Will*, 39.
[24] Rescher, 45.

measure up to human justice, but God's justice cannot be unrelated to human justice. The challenge is for us to find what in divine justice is the same, even if more, than human justice. More precisely, it is to find what in presupposing free moral will is the same for God as for us.

The answer lies in distinguishing "inner" from "outer" freedom. It lies in distinguishing freedom in relation to what lies outside us from freedom in relation to what lies inside us. The notion of free will presumed in moral responsibility only concerns outside freedom and says nothing about inside freedom, and this is as true for divine as for human justice. God judges us fairly as free agents in the outside sense of nothing external stopping us from choosing what we want. But we are at the same time not free to want other than we want. And this distinction is the same for God as for us. Human fairness only requires outside, not inside, freedom; and divine fairness also is fully warranted by the outside freedom we have to act as we want, even though we are not free in the inside sense to want or do things against fallen human nature.[25]

Two further observations are in order here. First, this combination of being morally free outside but not inside is the same for God as for us. God is entirely unconstrained in the outside sense. No one tells God what to do, and no one hinders God from doing anything he wants. Yet, God is also not free in the inside sense to want or do anything against his nature. In this way, our being externally free while not free to act contrary to our nature is no different from how God is externally free while not internally free to act against his nature. Second, it is amazing that, even though it is perfectly fair for God to hold us responsible as externally free agents, He nevertheless cares so much about our inner slavery to sin that he took on himself the punishment we deserve. Indeed, his loving mercy is so astonishing, the only ones who must bear punishment for their own sinning in the end are those who freely choose to bear it only because they do not want God's mercy more than clinging to their sins (John 3:19).

---

[25] Evangelical theologians vary on the degree to which men can, or cannot, act against fallen human nature. But all agree no one is able to always oppose fallen human nature so as to never act sinful. In this way, even those who think we can sometimes resist temptation do not think we can always do so. Some Bible scholars see the dilemma described in Romans 7:14–24 as referring to how Christians struggle between wanting to please God and feeling the pull of fallen human nature, whereas others think it describes how unbelievers are ruled by fallen human nature and never act righteously. But everyone agrees, "All have sinned and fall short of the glory of God" (Rom 3:23). For contrasting views Evangelicals hold on free will, see Basinger and Basinger, *Predestination and Free Will.*

Morally Worthy Motive

The second factor needed to ascertain when one deserves moral praise or blame is having a morally worthy motive. Just acting freely is not enough. What one does must also be for good reasons. One's intentions really do matter, and we are always responsible for what we intend one way or the other. A good motive is required to earn moral praise, and just having a bad one deserves blaming. Doing good things for bad reasons, or even just for pragmatic reasons, earns no moral praise. No one is praised for doing good things in order to deceive and lead others astray. But doing good things just to make money, or just to get elected, or even just to make friends and nothing else, is not worth moral praise either, even if these motives are not necessarily wrong. Motives are not worth praising in a moral sense just because they make good business, political, or personal sense.

Jesus affirmed this when explaining how doing good merely to impress others earns no credit with God (Matt 6:1–6) and again when he blamed Pharisees for appearing righteous while "inside you are full of hypocrisy and lawlessness" (Matt 23:27–28). The Apostle Paul affirmed the same when declaring "everything that is not from faith is sin" (Rom 14:23), by which he meant doing good things for any ultimate reason other than for God not only earns no ultimate praise, but is ultimately sinful. In fact, Paul went so far as to insist no behavior, even martyrdom, earns the doer any credit without the right motive: "If I give away all my possessions to feed the poor, and if I surrender my body to be burned, but do not have love, it profits me nothing" (1 Cor 13:3, NASB).[26]

Here we must point out that there is a big difference between what the philosopher Immanuel Kant (1724–1804) said and what the Bible says on this topic. Kant held that only acting from duty—with no self-interest—ever deserves moral credit, and so he claimed having any interest in personal advantage can be prudent but disqualifies earning moral praise.[27]

---

[26] I am here following the longest held majority translation tradition of this passage, which does not agree with the Christian Standard Bible (CSB) that renders it "give over my body in order to boast." The difference between "burned" and "boast" is uncertainty over a single letter. I prefer the majority tradition because remaining able to boast after sacrificing one's body makes little sense, whereas burning martyrs at the stake was well known to the letter's first recipients.

[27] Immanuel Kant, *Groundwork for the Metaphysics of Morals*, 1785, ak. 4:397. Also: Immanuel Kant, *Groundwork for the Metaphysics of Morals*, ed. and trans. Allen W. Wood (New Haven, CT: Yale, 2002), 13.

In that case, Kant said, "the action, however it may conform to duty and however amiable it is, nevertheless has no true moral worth," which means those so motivated earn no moral praise either.[28] The problem with this is how Kant's position contradicts what Jesus taught in the Sermon on the Mount (Matt 5:12), in the parable of the talents (Matt 25:14–30), and in discussing his second coming (Matt 16:27). Jesus indicated repeatedly in these passages that seeking personally advantageous rewards from God, both now and in heaven, is a morally worthy motive for ethical action. The Apostle Paul taught the same, maintaining that rewards promised by God ought to incentivize good behavior (1 Cor 3:12–15) and earning "an imperishable crown" ought to motivate how we live, just like prizes motivate athletes to win races (1 Cor 9:25–27).

Unlike Kant, Jesus taught that morally worthy motivation is a matter of priority rather than exclusivity. He explained that, while seeking God's promised blessings should not be our primary ethical motivation, it may and should be a morally worthy secondary motive (Matt 6:33). According to Jesus, we must seek first the kingdom of God and his righteousness. But, after that, we may and should, in a secondary sense, also seek the good things by which God rewards living on his terms, things that may even include what we need to eat, drink, and wear (Matt 6:31). This means Kant was wrong, and, rather than say as he did that only acting from duty alone deserves praising, we should instead say, as Jesus and Paul did, that persons deserve moral praise when acting for good reasons. These reasons may and should include seeking those things by which God incentivizes (rewards) good behavior—things both spiritual and material and that make an advantageous personal difference both now and in the age to come.[29]

Morally Right Action

The third factor needed for assessing when persons deserve praise or blame is doing something morally right. Just acting freely and with good intentions is not enough. What one does must be morally right as well. It must be a good thing to do. Acting freely with a good motive does

---

[28] Kant, *Metaphysik der Sitten*, ak. 4:398; and Kant, *Metaphysics of Morals*, 14.

[29] This means John and Paul Feinberg too are wrong where they say, "We follow Immanuel Kant's understanding on this matter." Feinberg and Feinberg, *Brave New World*, 22 (1993), 27 (2010).

not justify doing wrong. No one doing bad things with good intentions deserves praise, and no one is blameless for doing bad things on purpose whether with good intentions or not.

Paul, in writing to early Christians in Romans, strongly denied that having a good motive ever absolves responsibility for doing wrong: "But if by my lie God's truth abounds to his glory, why am I also still being judged as a sinner? And why not say, just as some people slanderously claim we say, 'Let us do what is evil so that good may come'? Their condemnation is deserved!" (Rom 3:7–8) and, "What should we say then? Should we continue to sin so that grace may multiply? Absolutely not!" (Rom 6:1–2).

In fact, Paul goes so far as to say just thinking like this shows one is not really saved—has not "died to sin" (Rom 6:2) and remains under "condemnation" (Rom 3:8). In other words, Paul claims no honest Christian thinks this way and anyone who does cannot be a true believer. He challenges anyone tempted toward thinking this and claiming to be Christian to consider theological reality, asking, "Are you not aware that all of us who were baptized into Christ Jesus were baptized into his death?" Because if so, Paul explains, you should realize salvation through Christ presupposes dying to sin so that "just as Christ was raised from the dead . . . , so we too may walk in newness of life" (Rom 6:3–4).[30] Thus, not only can no one use good intentions to escape blame for doing wrong, not only can no one earn moral praise without acting morally, and not only can no one deny responsibility for choosing to do anything he knows is wrong, but Paul also says just wanting to use good motives to excuse sinning can never be reconciled with salvation.

Classifications in Philosophical Ethics

We turn now to consider philosophical ethics in the sense of ethical speculation without relying on the Bible or starting with Christian-worldview assumptions like transcendence, spiritual reality, fallen human nature, divine judgment, or redemption through Christ, and the existence of God, the Word of God, and the problem of sin. Philosophical ethics starts with human thought and never goes beyond human ability, experience, or imagination. We

---

[30] Paul explains the logic used here again where he says, "If One died for all, then all died. And He died for all so that those who live should no longer live for themselves, but for the One who died for them and was raised" (1 Cor 5:14–15).

just looked at two rational tools—categories of ethical action and factors for assessing ethical credit, blame, and responsibility—both of which pertain as much to theological as to philosophical thought because they are neutral as to worldview. In contrast to this, what we turn to now is not worldview neutral and often conflicts with what Christians believe. Yet, engaging philosophical ethics, even where it conflicts with divine truth, is part of Christian ethics in the same way that dealing with foreign leaders is part of what ambassadors do while serving their own countries even though foreign leaders sometimes oppose them.

In what follows, we will consider how philosophers classify (1) levels of ethical analysis, (2) ways of conceiving normative ethical systems, and (3) methods of attaining ethical knowledge.

Classifying Levels of Ethical Analysis

Philosophers recognize five levels of ethical analysis: metaethics, normative ethics, aretaic ethics, applied ethics, and descriptive ethics. Of these, two are believed to be non-normative in the sense of just dealing with facts—metaethics and descriptive ethics. The others are considered normative because they involve value judgments—normative ethics, aretaic ethics, and applied ethics. All do not agree on how many levels there are, but these five cover the whole range of philosophical discussion and make the best sense.[31]

Metaethics

A. J. Ayer, in 1949, started using the term *metaethics* for discussing the meaning and nature of ethics.[32] He thought then that metaethics was separate from doing ethics, but philosophers

---

[31] Douma, Moreland, and Craig distinguish normative from applied ethics but overlook aretaic ethics (Douma, *Responsible Conduct*, 7 [see chap. 1, n. 16]); Moreland and Craig, *Philosophical Foundations*, 404). Rae includes aretaic ethics but combines applied ethics with normative ethics (Rae, *Moral Choices*, 2nd and 3rd eds., 15, but note Rae drops "aretaic ethics" as a separate category in the fourth edition of his book). Anderson distinguishes normative from applied ethics but overlooks descriptive as well as aretaic ethics (Anderson, *Christian Ethics in Plain Language*, 5).

[32] This date comes from William S. Sahakian, *Philosophy* (Lincoln, NB: Cliff's Notes, 1968), 18, which refers to something prior to his using of the term in A. J. Ayer, *Philosophical Essays* (London: Macmillan, 1954), 246. Unlike *metaethics*, the term *metaphysics* has been around much longer, and Ayer obviously devised *metaethics* to indicate the ethical component of *metaphysics*.

now accept it as a level of analysis in the field. In Greek, μετά (*meta*) means along with, at the side of, leaning against, or after (and so perhaps also behind or beyond) and, linked with another word, refers to something presupposed by what that word is about. *Meta* linked with *ethics* thus suggests considering what ethics presupposes, and the term *metaethics* now refers to the level of analysis that considers what ethics is, where it comes from, and why anyone should care. Other terms for the same thing are *analytical ethics, critical ethics, theoretical ethics,* and perhaps *formal ethics,* and doing metaethics includes dealing with the epistemological metaethics, ontological metaethics, and linguistic metaethics.

Philosophers doing metaethics are sometimes glaringly inconsistent because, after claiming it is normatively neutral, they go on then to say things with enormous normative implications. So, Kai Nielsen has to explain, "If in claiming metaethical contentions are all normatively neutral, one answers" that they do not "alter one's normative ethical beliefs or attitudes . . . then one is surely mistaken."[33] Douma too acknowledges "metaethics always plays a role in the background of normative ethics" and "is just as value-laden as normative ethics."[34] The problem is that, while it alleges neutrality, metaethics always affects normative analysis and what philosophers doing metaethics assert under the guise of neutrality often attacks what Christian ethics stands for. When Ayers claims ethical statements are just blind ejaculations, he is by that also denying transcendence and asserting nothing is right or wrong in the same way for everyone.[35]

The reason metaethical assertions cannot avoid normative implications is they inevitably presume a worldview, make ultimate claims, and say things affecting everyone in ways imagined as having everlasting importance. When metaethics substitutes human words for the Word of God, it demands surrendering revelation to speculation, which is why Barth saw metaethics as idolatrous and believed it always falsifies true ethics.[36] But did Barth go too far?

---

[33] Kai Nielsen, "Ethics, Problems of," *The Encyclopedia of Philosophy*, vol. 3 (New York: Macmillan, 1967), 119.

[34] Douma, *Responsible Conduct*, 10.

[35] A. J. Ayer, *Language, Truth and Logic* (London: Gollancz, 1936) 107.

[36] Barth, *Ethics*, 17. Because this occurred before Ayer minted the term, Barth did not use the term *metaethics* directly. Instead, Barth referred to making metaphysical claims about ethics, which is the same thing.

And must metaethics always oppose Christian ethics? Answering depends on how metaethics relates to theology and on the nature of philosophy.

Ramsey once said, "Christian theological ethics is metaethics."[37] But he did not mean theologians take marching orders from philosophers and was just saying he thought metaethics and Christian theological ethics deal with the same thing. The conflict at root in this discussion comes from realizing there is only one ultimate reality and only one ultimate source of moral meaning and authority. Metaethics and theology might be compatible if they deal with the same thing, and Christian theology limits and controls metaethics. But if, as philosophers usually insist, they are not doing the same thing and metaethics claims supremacy over theology, or if they are thought to be doing the same thing because metaethics subsumes theology, then metaethics is a false theology that usurps Christian theology and always attacks Christian ethics. And, if philosophy starts with Christian worldview assumptions, then metaethics could possibly align with and supplement Christian ethics. But if, as philosophers usually insist, philosophy never starts with Christian-worldview assumptions, then metaethics always opposes Christian ethics by supposing men can define ultimate reality for themselves and can have a source of ultimate meaning and authority other than the Word of God.

Normative Ethics

Normative ethics is the level of ethical analysis that devises theoretical structures to explain how we should live, and these theoretical structures do not give just one or two norms for handling one or two issues but rather formulate systems by which to judge right from wrong all the time. Normative ethics refers to when philosophers try to explain what ethical thought requires overall, and, according to Nielsen, what they formulate reduces to answering three questions: "What is right and wrong?" "What is blameworthy and praiseworthy?" And "What is desirable or worthwhile?"[38]

Unlike metaethics, normative ethics does not analyze ethical language or logic but does overlap it by assuming a source of authority when formulating normative systems. Unlike

---

[37] O'Donovan, who studied under Ramsey, reports Ramsey held that "Christian theological ethics is metaethics, and the Christian community in all ages is a standing metaethical community of discourse" (O'Donovan, *Resurrection and Moral Order*, 8). I cannot find this elsewhere and so rely on O'Donovan for documentation.

[38] Nielsen, "Ethics, Problems of," 121.

applied ethics, normative ethics does not address issues but only seeks an overall way for distinguishing right from wrong. Unlike aretaic ethics, normative ethics focuses on actions over character, although virtuism (virtue ethics as a normative system) devises a system of right conduct based on what good character requires. And unlike descriptive ethics, normative ethics does not just describe what people think and do but claims rather to declare what really is right and wrong and to promote right over wrong.

For this last reason, normative ethics is sometimes called "prescriptive ethics" or "ethical prescriptivism." But these other terms can mean different things that must not be confused. Both can just be other names for normative ethics, but they can also refer to a kind of meta-ethical epistemology or to a kind of non-cognitive metaethical linguistic philosophy. So, to avoid confusion, the terms *prescriptive ethics* or *ethical prescriptivism* should not be used without clarifying which meaning is intended.

To formulate systems, normative theories all assume a source of ultimate authority and develop a way of framing ethical thought based on that. As James Fieser says, "The key assumption in normative ethics is that there is only one ultimate criterion of moral conduct, whether it is a single rule or a set of principles."[39] Consequently, normative ethical theories can be arranged according to the kind of source from which they think ethical authority derives, and doing that produces three general divisions—end-sourced systems, intrinsically-sourced systems, and self-sourced systems. These general divisions then each include particular systems, such as Marxism, utilitarianism, virtuism, normative rationalism, normative naturalism, divine command theory, or self-actualization ethics.[40]

---

[39] James Fieser, "Ethics," *The Internet Encyclopedia of Philosophy* (2006), http://www.iep.utm.edu/e/ethics.htm.

[40] All do not agree with subdividing normative ethics as I have. Geisler, Moreland, and Craig identify only two subdivisions (Geisler, *Christian Ethics*, 24; Moreland and Craig, *Philosophical Foundations*, 444); and, although Fieser identifies three subdivisions (Fieser, "Ethics"), his three are not identical to mine. The main reason for differing is that I treat egoism, developmentalism, and emotivism as self-sourced normative systems as well as metaethical linguistic philosophies. These must be treated as normative systems because they are driving how many now behave and are causing much controversy in contemporary culture.

Aretaic Ethics

The modifier *aretaic* comes from ἀρετή (*aretē*) that, in Greek, means virtue, uprightness, or moral excellence. Aretaic ethics, then, is the level of ethical analysis that considers what it means to be a good or bad person—usually without addressing whether specific actions are right or wrong. It refers to when philosophers try to distinguish good character from bad; to cultivate good character traits such as prudence, temperance, justice, and fortitude; and to avoid bad character traits, such as vanity, prodigality, vulgarity, and cowardice. Because aretaic ethics deals with states of character and not actions, it sometimes is called the "ethic of being."[41]

Aretaic ethics can be the same as virtue ethics, but that only is when virtue ethics is taken as a level of analysis and not a normative system. Some treat aretaic ethics as interchangeable with virtue ethics, but unless carefully qualified, that is not always the case. The problem is virtue ethics can mean two things and aretaic ethics only means one thing. Virtue ethics can mean a level of analysis or a normative system, and as a level of analysis, virtue ethics is the same as aretaic ethics. But, as a normative system, virtue ethics is something quite different. It is best, therefore, to use another term, like "virtuism," when referring to virtue ethics as a normative system, and when using it to mean the same as aretaic ethics then to explain that it is in that case only a level of analysis. Those who say "virtues without rules are blind" are criticizing virtue ethics as a normative system, not virtue ethics as a level of analysis. When virtue ethics is equivalent to aretaic ethics, it is not blind because, being only one level of analysis and not a comprehensive system, it does not exclude rules at all.

Applied Ethics

Applied ethics, sometimes called specialized ethics,[42] is the level of ethical analysis that addresses practical issues. As such, it covers a range of general specializations like sexual ethics, environmental ethics, racial ethics, political ethics, medical ethics, penal ethics, business ethics, and professional ethics, as well as the ethics of wealth and poverty, the ethics of life and death, and the ethics of war and peace. These general specializations, in turn, each include a number

---

[41] Grenz and Smith claim the term "ethic of being" is equivalent to "virtue ethics." Grenz and Smith, *Pocket Dictionary of Ethics*, 34, 125 (see chap. 1, n. 38).

[42] Douma, *Responsible Conduct*, 8.

of more narrowly defined specializations, such as dealing with the ethics of abortion, euthanasia, birth control, homosexuality, same-sex marriage, nuclear arms proliferation, surrogate mothering, genetic engineering, human cloning, human trafficking, racial profiling, illegal immigration, and climate change.

These general and particular specializations in applied ethics all fall into one of two very broad categories, either social ethics or personal ethics. Social ethics covers issues having to do with interacting with others, and personal ethics covers issues having to do with responsibility for yourself. Thus, social ethics deals with matters like justice (criminal and social), racism, poverty, marriage, parenting, work (labor), crime, and war, and personal ethics deals with matters like pornography, smoking, drinking alcohol, diet, gambling, illegal drug use, R-rated entertainment, and risk-taking.

Applied ethics is distinct from metaethics, normative ethics, aretaic ethics, and descriptive ethics but does not stand alone and depends largely on the metaethical and normative conceptions one adopts. However, this dependency is often assumed and not readily apparent. It is critical, therefore, when doing applied ethics, to identify worldview and source-of-authority assumptions underlying judgments and driving conclusions. These assumptions may be theological or philosophical, and, depending on which they are, judgments and conclusions in applied ethics can be dogmatic or speculative, fixed or changing, categorical or hypothetical, universal or unique.

Descriptive Ethics

Descriptive ethics is the same as moral sociology and is the level of ethical analysis that reports on how people think, act, or justify what they do. Descriptive ethics is a form of empirical research that only describes what attitudes, beliefs, values, or priorities people have without judging them. It concerns ethics only in the sociological sense of describing thought and behavior without saying whether it is right or wrong, good or bad. Descriptive ethics thus stands apart from *metaethics* (which considers the nature and meaning of ethics), *normative ethics* (which considers what distinguishes right and wrong), aretaic ethics (which considers what distinguishes good and bad), and applied ethics (which considers particular issues).

Descriptive ethics may study how one group thinks or behaves or may compare how different groups think or behave. When it compares different groups, it is the same as comparative ethics, but studying just one group, while descriptive, is not comparative. Research in descriptive ethics investigates perceived ideals and norms and records what things people in one group or another praise or blame and reward or punish as moral or immoral, in either social, legal, or political terms. Some dispute whether descriptive ethics really is doing ethics at all, but most accept it as a level of analysis in the field.[43] Saying, "Most Christians think same-sex marriage is wrong but some now are changing their minds" is a non-comparative descriptive ethical statement, and saying, "In Texas people think capital punishment is a good thing but in Massachusetts they do not," is a comparative descriptive ethical statement.

Classifying Ways of Conceiving Normative Ethical Systems

Normative ethics tries to explain how we should live and make ethical decisions. Unlike *meta-ethics,* it does not say what moral properties are, and unlike applied ethics, it does not say what to do in particular situations. Rather, normative ethics tries to explain what makes things right or wrong, good or bad. Systems in normative philosophical ethics all come with assumptions and, while these differ, they all start with an ultimate criterion—a single rule, principle, ideal, or feeling—and then insist all moral judgments follow from that one thing.

Philosophers often disagree on the meaning of terms and categories, and this occurs when discussing normative systems. They do not agree on the meaning of terms like *teleology* and *deontology* and do not even agree on how many classifications of normative thought there are because some claim there are two, others three, and others four.[44] We will order them here by the kind of source from which they think ethical authority derives, and doing this

---

[43] Moreland and Craig, *Philosophical Foundations*, 396

[44] Geisler, Moreland, and Craig list two classifications by which all normative systems must either be teleological or deontological. Geisler, *Christian Ethics*, 24; Moreland and Craig, *Philosophical Foundations*, 444. Rae starts with two different classifications by which all normative systems must either be action-oriented or virtue-based and goes on then to say the first classification has subcategories that are deontological, teleological, and relativist (Rae, *Moral Choices*, 3rd ed., 17 [see chap. 3, n. 6]). Fieser uses three classifications, which he lists as virtue theories, duty theories, and consequentialist theories (Fieser, "Ethics"). Hollinger identifies three classifications, which he lists as consequentialist ethics, principle ethics, and character or virtue ethics (Hollinger, *The Meaning of Sex*, 24 [see chap. 1, n. 35]). And Boylan uses four classifications, which he lists as intuitionism, virtue ethics, utilitarianism, and deontology (Boylan, *Basic Ethics*, 14–15 [see chap. 1, n. 31]).

produces three classifications: end-sourced systems, intrinsically-sourced systems, and self-sourced systems.[45]

End-Sourced Normative Ethical Systems

Normative systems in the end-sourced category are sometimes classified as forms of teleology, a term comprised of two Greek words: τέλος (*telos*), meaning "end" in the sense of purpose or goal, and λογίζομαι (*logizomai*), meaning "consider" or "ponder." Teleology first referred to Aristotle's virtue ethics, according to which each thing has its own intrinsic purpose and a thing's intrinsic purpose is different from all the rest. But the term has, in recent times, come to be used for thinking actions are right or wrong based on things "at the end," thus obscuring what distinguishes end-sourced theories from Aristotle's intrinsically-sourced theory.[46] So, to enhance clarity, I am using *end-sourced systems*, rather than *teleology*, for theories deriving ethical authority from things "at the end" and will treat Aristotle's theory later.

There are two kinds of end-sourced ethical theory. One kind is idealism and the other consequentialism. Systems in the idealism category are perfectionist, and those in the consequentialism category are productionist. Both treat ethics as objective (real outside yourself), fixed (unchanging), and universal (the same for everyone), and neither kind relies on anything intrinsic. Systems in the idealism category include Marxist ethics, situation ethics, Latin American liberation ethics, black liberation ethics, feminist ethics, homosexual ethics, and neo-pacifist ethics. Systems in the consequentialism category include act and rule utilitarianism, act and rule hedonism, asceticism, and altruism.

It is common for philosophers to think ethical systems pursuing ideals or practical effects conflict with systems stressing duties. But Christians should not agree because the Bible treats

---

[45] These are humanly conceived philosophical approaches, all of which contrast with presupposing *God-sourced* ethical authority.

[46] Ogletree says, "What I am calling consequentialist thought is often labeled *teleological*. I have avoided this term, however, because it is ambiguously used to refer to both consequentialist and perfectionist thought, obscuring the distinction between them." Thomas W. Ogletree, *The Use of the Bible in Christian Ethics: A Constructive Essay* (Philadelphia: Fortress, 1983), 42, n. 9. David C. Jones says similarity between the ideas of teleology and utility has led to "modern confusion of teleological ethics with consequentialism" (Jones, *Biblical Christian Ethics*, 20 [see chap. 2, n. 4]). And Jones says, "While some scholars have made the error of conflating teleology with utility, this is a false association, for the concepts are not identical" (Jones, *An Introduction to Biblical Ethics*, 8 [see chap. 2, n. 1]).

all three as important and not necessarily opposed. The difference for Christians is that ideals, practical effects, and duties do not operate independently, and each has a place in God's moral ordering. The advantage of end-sourced systems is that they stress how we are responsible for the impact of actions we control. But there are problems with reducing ethics to nothing else. Such theories assume we can predict what follows everything we do when no one is omniscient and long-term effects are especially hard to foresee. They justify social atrocities like ethnic cleansing, Hitler's "final solution," killing innocent people to advance science, abusing the environment, enslaving "less advanced" populations, and denying minority rights. They confuse doing right with having good intentions, and they reduce ethics to either pursuing impossibilities or desiring nonmoral values.

Intrinsically-Sourced Normative Ethical Systems

In contrast to end-sourced normative theories, others argue that some things are intrinsically right or good no matter what happens. Intrinsically-sourced systems assume what makes acts obligatory or character traits worthy is found in the way things are, and there are two main kinds: deontology and virtuism.[47] Deontological systems are duty-driven and virtuistical systems are essence-driven. All intrinsically-sourced systems contrast with end-sourced systems, but so do self-sourced systems, which will be covered next.

Deontology or duty-driven ethical systems

Deontology is an intrinsically sourced normative approach that focuses on behavior, claims some acts are right or wrong in and of themselves, and says these must be done or avoided no matter what happens. Deontology is not a single system but a set of systems that includes ethical rationalism as a normative system, ethical naturalism as a normative system, non-theological natural law as a normative system, and divine command theory as a normative system.[48]

---

[47] *Virtuism* is a term used here to distinguish virtue ethics treated as a normative system (virtuism) with virtue ethics treated as a level of analysis (aretaic ethics).

[48] "Divine command theory" can mean different things. It can refer to (1) a kind of deontological normative ethical system or (2) a kind of metaethical epistemology, both of which are philosophical, not theological. Some also use it to mean (3) accepting what the Bible says God commands, which is theological, not philosophical. As a philosophical system, divine command theory is a form of deontology that, while discussing divine commands, does not start with Christian worldview assumptions or

The term *deontology* comes from the Greek words δέον (*deon*), meaning "bond," "obligation," or "duty," and λογίζομαι (*logizomai*), meaning "consider" or "ponder." But what *deontology* means philosophically is disputed, and, philosophers agree on only two things—first, that deontology rejects consequentialism and second, that it prioritizes acting correctly over being a good person. Besides these two points, there is no agreement on what makes acts right or wrong, why right behavior has priority over good character, and whether moral norms exist outside human minds or only seem to. In fact, philosophers do not even agree on what deontology covers. Some think it refers to any normative theory other than consequentialism,[49] and others think it contrasts not just with consequentialism but with virtuism, idealism, and voluntarism as well.[50]

The advantages of deontology are that it holds people accountable to common standards and leaves room for doing more than required, but there are problems with it as well. The approach is associated with thinking moral absolutes are objective, meaning they exist outside human minds and whether people follow them or not.[51] But those saying this then also say the

---

biblical revelation, but instead speculates on things Christians believe (God's sovereignty, obeying his commands) using human reason based on human experience and nothing else. So divine command theory, as a deontological system, though it says things about God in relation to ethics, appears here as a philosophical system rather than as a system of theological ethics surveyed in chapter 4. In this book, the notion of divine command theory just meaning what the Bible says was addressed as biblical ethics in chapter 3. I do not agree with classifying biblical ethics as deontological, because I fear that subordinates biblical revelation to philosophy, divine authority to human authority, and dogma to speculation. As the Word of God transcends all words of men, so biblical ethics transcends philosophical classification. Studying and applying God's moral reality as revealed in the Bible is not reducible to a form of deontological philosophy because it is theological and not philosophical at all. Deontology and biblical ethics both affirm duties but in different ways. While deontological obligation is intrinsically sourced, biblical obligation is God-sourced. While deontology addresses duties in a way that includes nothing else, biblical ethics affirms a lot more than duties. And, while deontology has no place for love and admits nothing greater than doing duty for its own sake, pleasing God out of love goes beyond duties, not by replacing them, but by making it unnecessary to require what one loves and prohibit what one hates. In other words, biblical ethics is not deontological, in the same way, and for the same reason, good marriages cannot be reduced to what civil law demands on threat of execution.

[49] Robert G. Olson, "Deontological Ethics," in *The Encyclopedia of Philosophy*, vol. 2 (New York: Macmillan, 1967), 343.

[50] Long, *A Survey of Christian Ethics*, 6.

[51] For example, see Frame, *Doctrine of the Christian Life*, 102.

best example of deontology is the ethical philosophy of Immanuel Kant (1724–1804)—even though Kant claimed no one knows if norms really exist beyond just seeming real to people of good will.[52] A second problem is how deontology justifies disastrous consequences, like never suffocating a crying baby even to save hundreds hiding from terrorists bent on killing everyone they find. A third problem arises when deontologists explain obligation by appealing to notions so abstract nothing comes of them. This happens because philosophers cannot start with God without becoming theologians, and because of that, deontologists have no personal basis for justifying ultimate obligation and then, because of that, have trouble explaining how ethical authority obligates persons. Lastly, deontology never considers how attitudes affect assessing actions, and it is nonsense to think people doing the same thing for different reasons—one for love and one for hate—deserve equal praise or blame.

Virtuism or essence driven ethical systems

Because *virtue ethics* can refer either to a level of ethical analysis or to a class of normative ethics, it is best to use *aretaic ethics* when referring to virtue ethics as a level of analysis and *virtuism* when referring to virtue ethics as a class of normative ethics. Another problem arises when virtue ethics, as a class of normative ethics, is described as teleological and associated with end-sourced systems because, as mentioned earlier, *teleology* also means different things and is not always the same as end-sourced ethical thinking. So, to enhance clarity, I am using *virtuism* for this second intrinsically-sourced approach and will avoid calling it "teleological."[53] Systems of this kind do consider purposes, but they take an essence-driven rather than result-driven approach.[54] The difference is systems in the virtuism category are not end-sourced at all, and systems in the end-sourced category never start with anything intrinsic or essential.

---

[52] Immanuel Kant, *Critique of Pure Reason* (1781) A491/B519; Kant, *Groundwork for the Metaphysics of Morals*, Ak 4:451.

[53] Pojman says, "There is a teleological aspect in virtue ethics, but it differs from the kind usually found in utilitarianism, which asks what sort of action will maximize happiness or utility." Pojman, *Ethics*, 156 (see chap. 1, n. 38).

[54] Pojman says that, in systems of this kind, "virtues . . . have intrinsic value" (*Ethics*, 165); and Moreland and Craig say the same thing (Moreland and Craig, *Philosophical Foundations*, 458).

Virtuism, like deontology, is not a single system but a set of systems that includes self-denying eudaemonist virtue ethics, self-elevating virtue ethics,[55] true self-interest virtue ethics, self-creational virtue ethics, agent-based virtue ethics, exemplarist virtue ethics, and target-centered virtue ethics.[56] Like deontology, virtuism takes an intrinsically sourced approach, but unlike deontological systems, virtuistical systems reverse the relationship between character and behavior. Moral character is addressed in other approaches, but systems in the virtuism category prioritize goodness and being over rightness and doing either by deriving right behavior from good character or by defining right behavior by good character. This leads to thinking ethics is more a state of being than of following rules, and some even think virtues may be sufficient in themselves to make behavioral norms unnecessary.

The advantage of normative systems in the virtuism category is that they highlight the importance of moral character, can judge between people doing the same thing for different reasons, and are able to explain acts of heroism. But systems of this kind are criticized for self-centeredness, favoring self-interest over the common good, having nothing to guide behavior

---

[55] This refers to Aristotle's "virtue ethics," which some treat as teleological in the sense of being "end-sourced." But that is inaccurate. When Aristotle addresses "ends" (τέλοι) he refers to something he thinks is intrinsic. He did not think ethical obligation comes from something "at the end" and not present before, but rather thought it comes from something there from the start and present all along. One might also question whether Aristotle's virtue theory should be listed here at all. That is because Aristotle uses "ethics" (ἠθικὰ) so narrowly as to exclude his Πολιτικά (*Politics*), which goes to show his virtue theory is not a full ethics system in the sense meant today. I understand and share that concern but choose nevertheless to include Aristotle's theory simply because so many treat it as a full ethics system and leaving it out requires answering more questions than acquiescing to what most expect.

[56] For "self-denying eudaemonist virtue ethics," see Plato, Προταγόρας (*Protagoras*), Πολιτεία (*Republic*), Περὶ Ἀρετῆς (*On Virtue*); Timothy Chappell, *Values and Virtues* (Oxford: Oxford, 2006); Iris Murdoch, *The Sovereignty of Good* (London: Routledge, 1971). For "self-elevating eudaemonist virtue ethics," see Aristotle, Ἠθικὰ Νικομάχεια (*Nicomachean Ethics*), Ἠθικὰ Εὐδήμεια (*Eudemian Ethics*); Philippa Foot, *Virtues and Vices* (Oxford: Blackwell, 1978); Rosalind Hursthouse, *On Virtue Ethics* (Oxford: Oxford, 1999); Thomas Hurka, *Virtue, Vice, and Value* (Oxford: Oxford, 2001). For "true self-interest virtue ethics," see David Hume, *An Enquiry Concerning the Principles of Morals* (1751); Christine Swanton, *The Virtue Ethics of Hume and Nietzsche* (Oxford: Wiley Blackwell, 2015). For "self-creational virtue ethics," see Friedrich Nietzsche, *On the Genealogy of Morality* (1887); and Swanton, *The Virtue Ethics of Hume and Nietzsche*. For "agent-based virtue ethics," see Michael Slote, *Morals from Motives* (Oxford: Oxford, 2001). For "exemplarist virtue ethics," see Linda Zagzebski, "Exemplarist Virtue Theory," *Metaphilosophy*, 41(1/2): 41–57. For "target-centered virtue ethics," see Christine Swanton, *The Virtue Ethics: A Pluralistic View* (New York: Oxford, 2003).

when needed, lacking an objective basis for distinguishing good and bad, not being able to handle clashing virtues (as when kindness conflicts with justice), demeaning the value of sacrificial love, and having a naïvely optimistic view of human nature.

Self-Sourced Normative Ethical Systems or Ethical Relativism

A third classification in normative ethical philosophy include systems that conceive ethical authority not as end-sourced or intrinsically-sourced, but as self-sourced. These systems are not concerned with what is right or good but rather with what is most desired. Denying the reality or relevance of fixed principles and shared purposes, these systems instead stress personal feelings, being true to yourself, and not caring what others think. Rules do not matter, the common good does not matter, and even human nature does not matter. What is right for one may be wrong for another, what is good in one situation may be bad in another, and nothing applies to everyone the same except denying that anything applies to everyone the same.

This kind of ethical thinking arises because people who deny God exists and reject the relevance of any authority beyond themselves start thinking ethics is something they make up, and that leads to theories treating ethics as a matter of egoism (self-preference),[57] feeling fulfilled (self-actualization), or emotivism (non-rational self-expression).[58] All self-sourced systems are volitional, relativistic, subjective, and contrary to the Word of God, which means they all treat ethics as if it only applies to people choosing it, changes according to whim, is unrelated to anything beyond whoever makes it up, and reverses biblical good and evil. Theories of this kind are widely accepted today, but they also threaten social stability, are self-defeating, and usurp divine revelation.

This third approach in normative ethics comes in three forms: self-preference normative ethics, self-actualization normative ethics, and self-expression normative ethics.[59] The first,

---

[57] "Egoism" in philosophical ethics has two variants, one normative and the other metaethical. "Normative egoism" is a self-sourced system composed of asserting self over others. "Metaethical egoism" is a non-cognitive linguistic theory that reduces ethical speech to nothing more than self-assertion.

[58] "Emotivism" in philosophical ethics has two variants, one normative and the other metaethical. "Normative emotivism" is a self-sourced system composed of expressing sentiments others must affirm. "Metaethical emotivism" is a non-cognitive linguistic theory that reduces ethical speech to nothing more than expressions of mindless sentiment.

[59] For "self-preference ethics," see Ayn Rand, *The Virtue of Selfishness* (New York: Signet, 1964); Robert Ringer, *Looking Out for Number One* (New York: Skyhorse, 2013); and David Seabury, *The*

also known as "normative egoism," is the ethic of putting self first even if it hurts others. This ethic harms society by eroding social cohesion and is self-defeating because it never works when others know about it. The second, also known as "therapeutic ethics" or "normative developmentalism," uses novel ideas about feeling fulfilled to claim changeable things cannot change. This ethic discredits self-discipline and defeats itself by crushing real satisfaction. The third, also known as "normative emotivism," reduces moral judgment to expressing sentiment. Expressing sentiment is considered good, suppressing sentiment is considered bad, and getting others to affirm sentiment is thought so important one cannot be a moral agent otherwise. This ethic cannot distinguish moral good from manipulating others for selfish reasons and defeats itself by allowing no room for common goals.

Relating Christian ethics to normative philosophical categories

Is Christian ethics teleological (in the end-sourced sense)? It is partly similar, but even that part is not exactly the same thing. We must seek the glory of God in all we say and do (1 Cor 10:31), but just intending to glorify God does not justify breaking God's rules (Rom 6:1). And, even though seeking the glory of God seems similar to teleological philosophy, it is not exactly the same because Christian ethics is God-sourced, not end-sourced. Is Christian ethics deontological? It is partly similar, but again even that part is not exactly the same thing. There is an objective moral order holding us morally accountable no matter what we intend, feel, or choose, but if we only obey God outwardly, we are no better than "a noisy gong or a clanging cymbal" (1 Cor 13:1). Even though obeying divine commands seems similar to deontological philosophy, it is not exactly the same because Christian rules and principles are God-sourced, not intrinsically-sourced. Is Christian ethics virtuistical? It is partly similar, but even that part is not exactly the same thing either. We must love God with all of our heart, soul, strength, and mind (Luke 10:27), but loving God requires obeying all he commands (2 John 1:6). And even though loving God with all of our heart, soul, strength, and mind seems similar to

---

Art of Selfishness (New York: Julian Messner, 1964). For "self-actualization ethics," see John Dewey, "Self-Realization as the Moral Ideal," *Philosophical Review* 2/6 (November 1893): 652–64; Abraham Maslow, *Motivation and Personality* (New York: Harper, 1954); and Carl Rogers, *On Becoming a Person* (Boston: Houghton Mifflin, 1961). For "self-expression ethics," see Ayer, *Language, Truth and Logic*; C. L. Stephens, *Ethics and Language* (New Haven, CT: Yale, 1944); and Charles Taylor, *Philosophical Arguments* (Cambridge: Harvard, 1995).

virtuistical philosophy, it is not exactly the same because Christian virtues are God-sourced and neither intrinsically-sourced nor self-sourced.

When it comes to philosophical classifications, Christian ethics differs not by rejecting them completely but by starting from a different source of authority and claiming more is involved. In other words, Christian ethics is theological, not philosophical, and cannot be otherwise. It always must say that ethics depends more on what God says than on anything man says. It always must insist that understanding the meaning and nature of ethics depends more on revelation than on philosophy, more on faith than on speculating, and more on a transcendent point of view than on a worldly point of view. In the end, Christian ethics differs from philosophical ethics mainly because it presumes an authority and point of view transcending human speculation, which in turn reduces the best philosophy offers to nothing more than part truths best understood only within parameters of a larger, more complex reality ordered not by human reason, human observation, or human experience, but by the Word of God.

It is not wrong to say Christian ethics has teleological, deontological, or virtuistical similarities. But Christian ethics does not submit to philosophical classifications because it comes from a higher source, from God himself, and claims standing over philosophical ethics—not the other way around. Although Christian ethics can accept thinking some philosophical insights make relative sense, Christian ethics resists submitting to how any philosophy structures, classifies, or defines normative reality as a whole and rejects identification as a form of any humanly derived way of interpreting everything else.

Christian ethics has goals, aims, and purposes but cannot be reduced to a version of teleological ethics. It has rules, principles, and duties but cannot be reduced to a version of deontological ethics. It addresses character, motives, and dispositions but cannot be reduced to a version of virtuistical ethics. It is important that we understand Christian ethics is not something we devise to evaluate what God does but rather is something God devises to evaluate what we do. It is not something by which we define, understand, and classify God's moral reality, but rather is something by which God's moral reality defines, understands, and classifies us.

Classifying Methods of Attaining Ethical Knowledge

When classifying methods used for attaining ethical knowledge, also known as ethical epistemologies, we are not concerned with what makes things true, obligatory, or wise but with how things are learned or discovered to be true, obligatory, or wise. These are not the same and should not be confused.[60] For example, reason can be regarded as if it is what makes things right or wrong or just treated as a way of learning what is right or wrong based on something else, and, while thinking an impersonal reason is what makes things right or wrong is not compatible with Christianity, using reason to grasp what God requires is not just compatible but is, in fact, essential to loving God with our minds as well as other ways (Luke 10:27).

We are here once more dealing with something both theological and philosophical. Theologians deal with moral learning as seriously as philosophers, and the main difference is philosophers usually take one approach and reject others as opposing theories, while theologians usually take multiple approaches, treating them as complimentary. There are six ways of gaining ethical knowledge—six different ethical epistemologies—and these are ethical authoritarianism, ethical rationalism (as a way of attaining knowledge), ethical empiricism, ethical intuitionism, ethical relationism, and ethical existentialism. Using two or more of these together is called "mixed ethical epistemologies" or "ethical perspectivalism."

Ethical authoritarianism, also known as "imperativalism" or "prescriptivism,"[61] is thinking moral learning comes from taking orders and contrasts with thinking it comes by reason, experience, science, intuition, relationships, or choosing. Moral learning in the Bible is not limited to taking orders but includes it where it says, "Man does not live on bread alone but on every word that comes from the mouth of the LORD" (Deut 8:3), and Ockham's divine command theory is an example of someone using this ethical epistemology.

Ethical rationalism (as a way of attaining knowledge) means thinking moral learning comes from using reason, and philosophers taking this approach assume human reasoning does not require faith and usually either deny human nature is fallen or think sinners can reliably discern right and wrong with no help from God. This epistemology contrasts with

---

[60] Since Long's *A Survey of Christian Ethics*, Christian ethicists have tended to follow his classifying of ethical systems as reason-based, prescription-based, and relation-based. But this is problematic because Long's classifications do not distinguish normative systems from ethical epistemologies. I am here rectifying that insufficiency.

[61] The term *prescriptionism* is used in three ways: (1) as another way of referring to "normative ethics," (2) as referring to a non-cognitive metaethical theory that considers ethical statements to be nothing more than someone telling others what he wants, and (3) as referring to an epistemology. These three different meanings must not be confused, and failing to distinguish them will lead readers astray.

thinking moral learning comes by orders, science, intuition, relationships, or choosing. Moral learning in the Bible is not limited to human reasoning but includes it where we are told, "set your minds on things above, not on earthly things" (Col 3:2), and the natural law theory of Aquinas is an example of someone using this epistemology in Christian ethics.

Ethical empiricism is thinking moral learning comes from studying scientific facts, and the approach has two forms: epistemological experientialism and epistemological naturalism. The first says moral learning comes by trial and error through experiences, the second says it comes by observing things in nature, and the approach contrasts with thinking it comes by orders, reason, intuition, relationships, or choosing. Moral learning in the Bible is not limited to this method but includes learning from experiences (Ps 34:8) and from nature (Rom 1:20). Locke demonstrates using epistemological experientialism in *Concerning Human Understanding*, and Butler demonstrates using epistemological naturalism in *The Analogy of Religion*.

Ethical intuitionism is thinking moral learning comes from following an inner sense, or intuition, that operates like the physical senses except it apprehends moral laws believed to exist whether people accept them or not. This approach, too, has two forms: conscience theory and inspirationism. The first says moral learning comes by listening to an inner voice that warns against violating moral boundaries, and the second says it comes from listening to a supernatural being (like the Holy Spirit) indwelling us. Both contrast with thinking it comes by orders, reason, experience, science, relationships, or choosing, and, although moral learning in the Bible is not limited to intuition, it includes listening to conscience (1 John 3:21) and to the Holy Spirit (John 15:26). Joseph Ratzinger's *On Conscience* demonstrates using conscience theory in Christian ethics, and Bonhoeffer's *Ethics* demonstrates using inspirationism.

Ethical relationism is thinking moral learning comes through relating to others based on assuming the idea that being in a relationship precedes knowing what it requires. This epistemology also has two forms: epistemological exemplarism and epistemological situationism. The first says moral learning comes by following good examples, and the second says it comes by adapting to relational circumstances. Both forms contrast with thinking it comes by orders, reason, experience, science, intuition, or choosing, and, although moral learning in the Bible is not limited to relationships, it includes following good examples (John 13:15; 1 Cor 11:1) and adapting to relational circumstances (1 Cor 8:13; Phil 4:11). Thomas à Kempis demonstrates using epistemological exemplarism in Christian ethics in *The Imitation of Christ*, and

Joseph Fletcher demonstrates using epistemological situationism in *Situation Ethics* (though he does not do so in a biblical manner).

Ethical existentialism can either refer to a normative theory or to an epistemology. As a normative theory, it means thinking individuals create ethics for themselves by means of choosing,[62] but as an epistemology, it means thinking moral learning grows from accepting responsibility. Philosophers using this approach often equate ethical learning with making things up, but theologians avoid this by connecting moral choosing with trusting and obeying God. This epistemology contrasts with thinking moral learning comes by orders, reason, experience, science, intuition, or relationships, and, while moral learning in the Bible is not limited to choosing, it includes deciding what authority we make ultimate in our lives (Josh 24:15) and choosing to trust God without doubting (Jas 1:6). *Fear and Trembling* by Kierkegaard is an example of someone using this epistemology.[63]

Mixed ethical epistemologies, or ethical perspectivalism, is thinking moral learning comes in different ways that all aid ethical understanding. Philosophers sometimes say this means having to say ethics is never true in the same way for all, but theologians do not agree. Christian ethics does include a worldview element, but that does not make it merely relative (just for Christians) or subjective (just what people feel). Christian ethics admits to having a point of view but also says it is the ultimate point of view preempting all others. It claims to have standing by which all is judged and to apprehend an ethical reality to which all epistemologies must align. The perspective orienting Christian ethics transcends and relativizes all others because it is the one true all-encompassing perspective, revealed by God, according to which anything else is partial, relative, or insufficient. Henry's *Christian Personal Ethics* and Frame's *Perspectives on the Word of God* demonstrate using mixed ethical epistemologies in Christian ethics.[64]

---

[62] As a normative ethical theory, existentialism is a version of normative egoism, which is the same as self-sourced self-preference ethics.

[63] I did not mention Kierkegaard when surveying the history of Christian ethics because he starts with self in place of revelation and so conceives ethics in ways not necessarily Christian. Kierkegaard was a Christian man who approached philosophical ethics using existential epistemology.

[64] Frame's perspectives are more than epistemologies, but they include ways of acquiring moral knowledge.

Resolving Ethical Conflicts

The last topic addressed in this chapter concerns whether, why, and how to resolve ethical conflicts. Here we are again dealing with something both theological and philosophical, and how each views resolving ethical conflicts is affected by different worldview assumptions that produce very different answers to questions on the nature and number of ethical norms. Do ethical norms exist? Are they things people make up and do not matter objectively, or are they things that exist objectively and matter to everyone? If any exist objectively, how many are there? Do they interact and, if so, are they adaptable or fixed? If they are objective, universal, and fixed, can they have exceptions? Or must they never have exceptions no matter what? Different conceptions of ethical reality lead to different views on resolving ethical conflicts,[65] and philosophers and theologians have formulated eight possible positions.[66]

Antinomianism says objectively fixed norms do not exist and conflicts are impossible. Generalism says objectively fixed norms do not exist, flexible principles do exist, and conflicts need not arise because they bend. Situationism says one objectively fixed norm exists and conflicts do not arise because it is the only one. Regular nonconflicting absolutism says many objectively fixed norms exist but conflicts never arise because they are arranged never to conflict. Conflicting absolutism says many objectively fixed norms exist, and these sometimes conflict. If so, we must break lower ones to obey higher ones but doing this is wrong even though it is right. Graded absolutism (also called hierarchicalism) says many objectively fixed norms exist and sometimes conflict. If so, we must break lower ones to obey higher ones, and there is nothing wrong with doing this. Humble absolutism starts the same as regular non-conflicting absolutism but adds that we can be in situations we cannot figure out even though we should, and, if so, we must break lower norms to obey higher ones and seek forgiveness for not figuring out what we should. Finally, nonconflicting complex normism starts like regular nonconflicting absolutism and humble absolutism but adds that objectively fixed norms are

---

[65] This is converse to the claim by Jones that "different methods of resolution reveal widely divergent concepts of morality" (Jones, *Biblical Christian Ethics*, 126).

[66] The first six of these follow designations popularized by Geisler in *Ethics: Alternatives and Issues* and revised later in *Christian Ethics*. In these works, Geisler changes labels used for these six designations. This chapter uses terms from both sources based on what I think best conveys the meaning of each. The last two are new designations added by my colleague, Mark D. Liederbach, and myself.

not simple rules but have complexities that explain how what they require can be different when dealing with sinners as compared to God.

The first three positions clash with Evangelical Christianity because they start with philosophical assumptions incompatible with the Word of God. Antinomianism is incompatible because it denies there is any objective basis for ethics. Generalism is incompatible because it denies anything transcendent anchors ethical objectivity. Situationism is incompatible because, while it affirms a fixed norm, it denies multiple norms, like the Ten Commandments, and limits what the one norm requires to how sinners assess situations unaccountable to anyone else. When it comes to resolving ethical conflicts, Evangelicals are divided among five further options, all of which affirm God's authority and hold that his norms apply to all (are universal), never change (are fixed), and obligate whether we like them or not (are objective). Three of these—regular nonconflicting absolutism, conflicting absolutism, and graded absolutism (hierarchicalism)—are positions traditionally held by Evangelicals and two are new positions proposed for Evangelicals dissatisfied with the other options. These new positions are humble absolutism, which my colleague, Liederbach, proposes,[67] and nonconflicting complex normism, which I propose.

The strengths of regular nonconflicting absolutism, sometimes called unqualified absolutism, are affirming that God controls all things even in a fallen world and stressing how he promises "the way out" of every temptation (1 Cor 10:13). But proponents struggle with passages that, on plain reading, clash with what they expect and then evade problems that so narrow what norms mean as to leave little of what they ordinarily cover. Augustine so narrowed the meaning of truth as to claim even though Jacob thought he was lying to steal Esau's birthright, he was not because lying occurs only when there is no way of reversing what it means in a figurative sense.[68] John Calvin so narrowed the meaning of truth he concluded merchants selling counterfeit goods are not lying and neither is fabricating cover stories to deceive.[69] And Grudem alleges that truth does not cover nonverbal communicating even though he knows

[67] For Liederbach's position, see Mark D. Liederbach and Evan Lenow, *Ethics as Worship: The Pursuit of Moral Discipleship* (Phillipsburg, NJ: Presbyterian and Reformed, 2021), 261–75.

[68] Augustine, *Against Lying*, AD 420, sec. 24.

[69] John Calvin, *All the Works of John Calvin that Remain*, ed. by J. W. Baum, A. E. Cunitz, and E. Reuss, 59 vols. (Braunschweig: Schwetschke, 1863–1900), vol. 30, 161–62.

this is less than we usually think.[70] Then, like all positions traditionally dividing Evangelicals, regular nonconflicting absolutism, too, treats divine norms like one dimensional rules that fit human expectations and apply to relating to sinners the same as relating to God.

The strengths of conflicting absolutism, sometimes called tragic morality, the tragic moral choice view, or the impossible moral conflict view,[71] are recognizing that ethical conflicts are not imaginary and not narrowing the meaning of biblical norms to explain them away. But it clashes with saying Jesus was "tempted in every way as we are, yet without sin" (Heb 4:15), does not treat forgiven sinners returning to old sins like "a washed sow" returning "to wallowing in the mud" (2 Pet 2:22), and denies God provides "a way out" of all temptations (1 Cor 10:13). Like other positions traditionally dividing Evangelicals, conflicting absolutism treats divine norms like one-dimensional rules that fit human expectations and apply to relating to sinners the same as relating to God. It is nicknamed the "Dirty Hands" view because it says sinning can be ethical and unethical at the same time, which led Augustine to ask, "What can be more absurd" than to suppose "some sins are just?"[72]

The graded absolutism position, sometimes called hierarchicalism,[73] or views similar to it, was widely held in the early Church and is the position most commonly held by Evangelicals today.[74] The strengths of the position are recognizing that ethical norms do not have equal value, accepting that ethical conflicts are not imaginary, not limiting biblical norms to avoid problems with what they expect, and thinking ethical conflicts can be resolved without sinning. But it treats biblical ethics as not quite suitable for sinful conditions, makes God seem unable to fully anticipate what sinners will do, appears to say the unbreakable is breakable, and leaves sinners to decide on their own what to do if a right course is not obvious. And like other positions traditionally dividing Evangelicals, graded absolutism (or hierarchicalism)

---

[70] Grudem, *Christian Ethics*, 310–314 (see chap. 1, n. 67).

[71] Jones, *Biblical Christian Ethics*, 130–132; Frame, *Doctrine of the Christian Life*, 230–34; Grudem *Christian Ethics*, 188–201.

[72] Augustine, *Against Lying*, AD 420, sec. 31.

[73] Geisler first referred to this position as "hierarchicalism" (*Ethics: Alternatives and Issues*, 114–36) and later changed the title for this position to "graded absolutism" (*Christian Ethics*, 113–32).

[74] Grotius indicates that even Augustine acknowledged "nearly all" early Church theologians prior to himself held a position something like what we are calling "graded absolutism" (Hugo Grotius, *The Rights of War and Peace*, 1625, bk. 3, ch. 1, sec. 9.2).

treats biblical norms like simple rules that fit human expectations and apply to interacting with sinners the same as interacting with God.

No one thinks any of the positions traditionally dividing Evangelicals are entirely satisfactory, and Liederbach and I have considered whether God's Word offers something else. This reexamination has led Liederbach to formulate humble absolutism and me to formulate nonconflicting complex normism. Both try to be faithful to everything the Bible says, which includes affirming the multiplicity, objectivity, universality, and fixed nature of divine norms. Both also take ethical conflicts very seriously, hold God is entirely consistent, and acknowledge we are finite, fallen creatures. But there are differences.

Liederbach developed humble absolutism because other views seem to overlook how seriously conversion and growing sanctification affect our minds, and the strengths of this position are admitting we face conflicts we cannot figure out, affirming God controls things in a sinful world, recognizing human limitations, accepting responsibility for all we do, and not saying God judges people for things they cannot avoid. But the position is vulnerable to asking if it really is any different from regular nonconflicting absolutism on the one hand or conflicting absolutism on the other, and to the degree it is the same as one or the other, it must deal with how these are criticized as well. The position also does not seem entirely coherent. It says we face conflicts we cannot resolve without sinning yet insists we can escape them. It says Jesus faced everything we do without sinning yet claims we cannot handle them as Jesus did. It says Jesus never sinned because conflicts are not real yet says sinning is sometimes all we can do because conflicts are real to us. The problem is conflicts cannot be real and unreal at the same time, sinning cannot be avoidable and all we can do at the same time, and Jesus cannot have been tempted in all the ways we are, and not, at the same time. And, along with the other positions already dividing Evangelicals, humble absolutism also treats divine norms like one-dimensional rules that fit human expectations and apply to relating to sinners the same as relating to God.

I developed nonconflicting complex normism because all other options dividing Evangelicals, including humble absolutism, use the term *absolute* ambiguously (for things that are universal and fixed and for things with no exceptions) and treat divine norms as simple rules fitting what we expect. So I refer to "norms" instead of "absolutes" and accept the complex nature of divine norms when interpreting what they require. Divine norms are always universal and fixed, but while some have no exceptions (like never worshiping other gods or committing adultery), others do (like allowing a desperate person to eat bread only for priests, allowing farm animals to be rescued when work is prohibited, and requiring believers to stay unequally married to unbelievers even though unequal marriages to unbelievers are prohibited). In the Bible, exceptions to norms are fixed parts of how those never-changing norms are defined, which is not the same as needing to break fixed norms or altering them to fit situations.

The Bible reveals that all divine norms are complex in four ways. All have dimensions—a vertical dimension relating to God and a horizontal dimension relating to others like ourselves. All have internal aspects regulating character as well as external aspects regulating behavior (like not stealing and not wanting to). All have degrees, starting with a fixed core with no exceptions (like never committing murder), but also extending beyond that core to express the same obligation in ways that vary with intention and perception (like how not belittling others expresses the same obligation involved in not murdering them). And, while all divine norms are understandable, none are completely knowable because all apply transcendence to mundaneness, infinity to finitude, perfection to imperfection, purity to impurity, completeness to incompleteness, and sinlessness to sinfulness. Because of this, limiting how we understand divine norms to what we expect is a sure way of getting them wrong, and the only sure way of getting them right is accepting what the Word of God says whether we think it makes sense or not. We have to remember God says, "My thoughts are not your thoughts. Nor are your ways My ways . . . . For as the heavens are higher than the earth, so are My ways higher than your ways and My thoughts than your thoughts" (Isa 55:8–9). This passage refers to God's ethical norms as much as to other revelations, for while the passage may include more, it cannot exclude them.

Regular nonconflicting absolutism says Scripture tells us what we need to resolve all ethical conflicts but limits what norms require to less than commonly thought. Conflicting absolutism says Scripture does not tell us how to resolve all ethical conflicts, and where it is silent, doing wrong is right. Graded absolutism (or hierarchicalism) says Scripture tells us there is nothing wrong with resolving ethical conflicts by breaking lower norms to obey higher ones. Humble absolutism says Scripture tells perfect people how to resolve ethical conflicts but does not give imperfect people enough to resolve conflicts they cannot solve without sinning. But nonconflicting complex normism says divine norms must be interpreted in ways that are theocentric, not anthropocentric, and complex, not simplistic, and divine norms apply transcendence to mundaneness rather than thinking they must fit what we expect. Doing so enables imperfect people to resolve all ethical conflicts without limiting what divine norms cover, without sinning, and without having to break one norm to obey another.

Conclusion

In closing this chapter, it is important to note that, in relation to Christian ethics, philosophical ethics is at best partial and at worst idolatrous. Revelation transcends philosophy and can be used to explain and evaluate philosophical ideas. But philosophy never transcends revelation, and standing to explain or evaluate revealed truth as though human thinkers have standing over God and can reduce what God says to humanly devised categories. So, while aspects of philosophical ethics may sometimes correlate with true ethical truth revealed by the Word of God and where this happens may be used along with the Word of God, philosophical ethics should not be used to explain or evaluate the meaning and use of true ethical truth according to the Word of God. Doing that is not Christian ethics in the best and real sense but instead substitutes something competing against it, and mixing the two always perverts and never enhances Christian ethics in the best and real sense. For what men values never lasts (Isa 51:7–8; 1 John 2:17), "but the word of our God remains forever" (Isa 40:8; 1 Peter 1:25).

The next chapter will start introducing applied Christian ethics as a subcategory of the larger field and will discuss what applying the biblical truth norm requires.

CHAPTER 8

TRUTH, LYING & FAITHFUL COMMUNICATING

This is the first of five chapters that together introduce readers to applied Christian ethics as an academic subcategory within the larger field of Christian ethics.[1] Applied

---

[1] The most important literature in applied Christian ethics, or what also is called Christian social ethics, includes Troeltsch, *Social Teaching* (see chap. 5, n. 2); Rauschenbusch, *Christianizing the Social Order* (see chap. 6, n. 18); Reinhold Niebuhr, *Moral Man and Immoral Society* (New York: Scribner's, 1932); William Temple, *Christianity and Social Order* (London: SCM, 1937); T. S. Eliot, *The Idea of a Christian Society* (New York: Harcourt Brace, 1949); Thomas E. Jessop, *Social Ethics: Christian and Natural* (London: Epworth, 1952); Henry, *Aspects of Christian Social Ethics* (see chap. 6, n. 122); Joseph Fletcher, "Situations for Ethical Decision," in *Moral Responsibility: Situation Ethics at Work* (Philadelphia: Westminster, 1967); Norman L. Geisler, "Ethical Issues," in *Ethics: Alternatives and Issues* (Grand Rapids: Zondervan, 1971); Forell, ed., *Christian Social Teachings* (see chap. 5, n. 2); Cotham, *Christian Social Ethics* (see chap. 2, n. 84); Mott, *Biblical Ethics and Social Change* (see chap. 3, n. 1); Ronald Nash, *Social Justice and the Christian Church* (Milford, MI: Mott, 1983); Davis, *Evangelical Ethics*, chs. 2–12 (see chap. 1, n. 55); Norman L. Geisler, "Ethical Issues," in *Christian Ethics: Options and Issues* (Grand Rapids: Baker, 1989); Roger G. Betsworth, *Social Ethics: An Examination of American Moral Traditions* (Louisville: Westminster/John Knox, 1990); Joe E. Trull, "Issues in Christian Ethics," in *Walking in the Way: An Introduction to Christian Ethics* (Nashville: B&H, 1997); Dennis P. Hollinger, "Applying Christian Ethics in Culture and Society," in *Choosing the Good: Christian Ethics in a Complex World* (Grand Rapids: 2002); Anderson, *Christian Ethics in Plain Language*, chs. 6–22 (see chap. 1,

philosophical ethics is a category of philosophical ethics, and applied Christian ethics is a category of Christian ethics. Readers will remember that in the last chapter we discussed how Christian ethics engages but does not mix with philosophical ethics. So, in considering applied Christian ethics, it is important to understand that it is distinguished from the philosophical counterpart in the same ways and for the same reasons the field of Christian ethics is distinguished from the field of philosophical ethics.

We mentioned before, in Chapter 2, how this academic specialization sometimes is referred to as "specialized Christian ethics," "practical Christian ethics," or even "Christian social ethics" (this term refers to a subcategory of applied ethics but is sometimes confused with the larger category). But I prefer using the term *applied Christian ethics* over other terms because the other terms can be misleading in ways the term *applied Christian ethics* is not. Applying Christian values to everyday issues is always "social" in the sense of affecting relations with God and is usually "social" in the sense of affecting other people in some way as well. But issues of this sort are not always "social" in the social dynamics sense because some applied issues mostly concern self-discipline in ways that affect personal well-being, as when deciding whether or not to smoke or drink alcohol. So, to keep these distinct, it is best to distinguish personal issues from social issues by using the term *applied* when referring to both in the same academic subcategory in the field of Christian ethics. Even though it makes sense to label this subcategory "practical Christian ethics" because it concerns putting Christian values into "practice," the term *practical* can mistakenly suggest utilitarian thought, and, therefore, using the term *applied Christian ethics* avoids this problem as well.

Applying Christian values in real life requires self-discipline as well as interacting with others, which means putting Christian values into practice is rarely easy or convenient. And, even though applying Christian values distinguishes this part of the field from other parts, applied Christian ethics does not stand alone but rather depends on the rest. It addresses issues like abortion, euthanasia, capital punishment, birth control, homosexuality, racial

---

n. 52); Stott, *Issues* (see chap. 4, n. 8); Frame, *Doctrine of the Christian Life*, chs. 28–44 (see chap. 1, n, 69); Rae, *Moral Choices*, chs. 5–12 (see chap. 1, n. 9); Matthew L. Weaver, ed., *Applied Christian Ethics* (Lanham, MD: Lexington, 2014); Scott B. Rae, *Introducing Christian Ethics: A Short Guide* (Grand Rapids: Zondervan, 2016), chs. 5–12; Bruce Riley Ashford, *Letters to an American Christian* (Nashville: B&H, 2018); Boyd and Thorsen, *Christian Ethics and Moral Philosophy* (see chap. 7, n. 1); and Grudem, *Christian Ethics*, chs. 11–42 (see chap. 1, n. 67).

prejudice, wealth, poverty, and going to war, but it does not address them other than by drawing on other parts of the field. In other words, dealing with applied issues in Christian ethics depends on biblical, theological, historical, and philosophical Christian ethics. Thus, work in applied Christian ethics always takes an academically integrated, rather than isolated, approach.

While subsequent chapters introducing applied Christian ethics will each cover a range of applied issues, this chapter covers only one, that of communicating truly or without sin.[2] We are treating this one issue in greater depth, first, because of its significance in Scripture (God

---

[2] The most important literature on truth and lying in applied Christian ethics includes Augustine, *On Lying*, AD 395; Augustine, *Against Lying*, AD 420; Augustine, *On Faith, Hope, and Love*, AD 421; Thomas Aquinas, "Of Lying," in *Summa theologica*, AD 1265–1274, vol. 12, 85–98; Hugo Grotius, *The Rights of War and Peace*, 1625, bk. 3, ch. 1, secs. 6–20; John Henry Newman, *A Defense of His Life* (London: Longman, 1864); Charles Hodge, "The Ninth Commandment," in *Systematic Theology*, 3 vols. (Grand Rapids: Eerdmans, 1952, reprint from 1872), 3:437–463; Dietrich Bonhoeffer, "What Is Meant by 'Telling the Truth'?," in *Ethics* (New York: Simon & Schuster, 1995, reprint from 1949), 358–67; John Murray, "The Sanctity of Truth," in *Principles of Conduct: Aspects of Biblical Ethics* (Grand Rapids: Eerdmans, 1957), 123–48; Helmut Thielicke, "Compromise and the Limits of Truthfulness," in *Theological Ethics* (Grand Rapids: Eerdmans, 1979, reprint from 1958–1959), 1:520–566; Helmut Thielicke, "The Borderline Situation of Extreme Conflict," in *Theological Ethics*, vol. 1, *Foundations*, ed. W. H. Lazareth (Grand Rapids: Eerdmans, 1979, reprint from 1958–1959), 1:609–647; Fredrick Buechner, *Telling the Truth* (New York: HarperCollins, 1977); Sissela Bok, *Lying* (New York: Random House, 1978); Sissela Bok, *Secrets: On the Ethics of Concealment and Revelation* (New York: Random House, 1983); Boniface Ramsey, "Two Traditions on Lying and Deception in the Ancient Church," *Thomist* 49/4 (October 1985): 504–33; Peter A. Hicks, *Evangelicals and Truth* (Leicester, UK: Apollos, 1998); Diane M. Komp, *Anatomy of a Lie: The Truth about Lies and Why Good People Tell Them* (Grand Rapids: Zondervan, 1998); Joseph M. Stowell, *The Weight of Your Words: Measuring the Impact of What You Say* (Chicago: Moody, 1998); Allen Verhey, "Is Lying Always Wrong?" *Christianity Today* 43/6 (May 24, 1999): 68; Paul J. Griffiths, *Lying: An Augustinian Theology of Duplicity* (Grand Rapids: Brazos, 2004); Raymond A. Blacketer, "No Escape by Deception: Calvin's Exegesis of Lies and Liars in the Old Testament," *Reformation & Renaissance Review* 10/3 (2008): 267–89; Wayne Grudem, "Why It Is Never Right to Lie," in *Speaking the Truth in Love*, ed. John J. Hughes (Phillipsburg, NJ: P&R, 2009); Scott M. Sullivan, "In Defense of the *Falsiloquium*," *Classical Thomist* (July 19, 2012): 1–13, https://scottmsullivan.com/in-defense-of-the-falsiloquium/; Vern S. Poythress, "Why Lying Is Always Wrong," *Westminster Theological Journal* 75 (2013): 83–86; Christopher O. Tollefsen, *Lying and Christian Ethics* (New York: Cambridge, 2014); Matthew Newkirk, *Just Deceivers* (Eugene, OR: Pickwick, 2015); and Grudem, "Lying and Telling the Truth," in *Christian Ethics: An Introduction to Biblical Moral Reasoning* (Wheaton, IL: Crossway, 2018).

is "the God of truth," Ps 31:5, Isa 65:16; Jesus is "the truth," John 14:6; and the Holy Spirit is "the Spirit of truth," John 15:26, 16:13), second, because of how it affects the rest of Christian ethics, and, third, because there is such confusion and division among Christians on this one issue, we really should try sorting it out.

What is communicating truly? What does it demand of us? What is meant by lying? Is it the same as communicating untruly? Is it permissible or perhaps even necessary ever to lie? Does God prohibit lying even to the point of betraying innocent people to death? Or does God prohibit betraying innocent people to death even to the point of lying? Or is it always possible to reconcile never lying and never betraying innocent people? Helmut Thielicke says,

> The experiences encountered in rendering illegal assistance to the Jews during the National Socialist persecutions afford classic and terrifying examples of the conflict between life and truth. Such assistance sometimes took the form of striking names from the proscribed list, or of adding them to groups which were not earmarked for liquidation. A high price was exacted by the Gestapo for these steps. Men adopted such dubious means with a sense of anguish about having thus to plunge into direct association with evil without any knowledge of how it might all turn out. But it seemed more important to extend a brotherly hand to the persecuted than to avoid at all costs any personal contamination by association with criminals.[3]

Three examples from this time period, often mentioned when discussing the ethics of truth, come from different ways members of the ten Boom family in Nazi-occupied Holland during World War II struggled to be faithful Christians under terrible circumstances. The ten Booms had Jewish friends and worked hard to help them and others escape arrest and deportation to German death camps. When their operation was discovered, the enemy regime moved to close it, and as that happened, members of the family took different approaches to communicating truly even though each was trying to please and obey God at all costs.

Corrie ten Boom's married sister, Nollie van Woerden, betrayed her Jewish friend, Annaliese, to Nazi officers rather than saying anything contrary to what she knew, even though she realized doing so meant sending her friend off to die. Pointing to Annalise the Nazi officers asked, "Is this a Jew?" and Nollie answered, "Yes." When others criticized her rigid

---

[3] Thielicke, *Theological Ethics*, 588 (see chap. 1, n. 69).

honesty, Nollie denied responsibility, arguing God did not need her to lie to save Annalise. Amazingly, Annalise was later saved in a rare prison break that occurred before she could be shipped to a death camp.[4]

Corrie's niece, Nollie's daughter Cocky, faced something similar but handled it differently. Rather than speaking candidly, she deceived enemy soldiers looking for her brothers by telling them something partly true in a manner she knew would be taken the wrong way. Her brothers were hiding in a cellar under the kitchen floor that was entered through a trapdoor under the kitchen table. When the soldiers arrived, the trapdoor was covered by a rug, over which stood the kitchen table covered by a tablecloth. When asked, "Where are your brothers?" Cocky replied, "They're under the table." The soldiers flung back the tablecloth, guns ready, only to see nothing immediately under the table. And then, when Cocky burst out laughing, they thought she was mocking them and stormed out. They wrongly thought she referred only to the room they were in, which is exactly what she intended hoping they would judge her words falsely.[5]

Finally, Corrie ten Boom herself viewed truth in a way that allowed her to say and do things that were contrary to what she knew but fulfilled a mission assigned by God. She often planned, said, and did things she knew were not factually accurate in order to save Jewish lives. She obtained and distributed false identity cards and false ration cards. And when the Gestapo asked, "Where are you hiding the Jews?" Corrie answered, "I don't know what you're talking about" or "There aren't any Jews here," even though she knew exactly what they were talking about and was hiding Jews in a special "hiding place" in her house.[6]

How should we think the ethics of truth applies in situations like this? What does God expect us to say or do when they occur? Which member of the ten Boom family set the best example? Which course of action should we say pleases God the most? Should we give factually accurate answers to evil people at the cost of betraying innocent friends, thinking God will protect them without lying if he chooses the way Nollie did? Should we trick bad people into reaching false conclusions by using part truths in place of whole truths or by using words differently than understood by those addressed, the way Cocky did? Or should we prioritize

---

[4] Corrie ten Boom, *The Hiding Place* (Grand Rapids: Baker, 1971), 126–27.

[5] ten Boom, 106–7.

[6] ten Boom, 142, 144.

fidelity to good people relying on us for protection over giving accurate answers to bad people trying to harm them the way Corrie did?

As Jones observes, "Debate over this type of conflict situation has a long history in both philosophical and theological ethics."[7] Augustine once said long ago that "whether we should ever tell a lie if it be for someone's welfare is a question that has vexed even the most learned."[8] And, while God demands truthfulness (Exod 20:16; Zech 8:16; Eph 4:25), he also accepts something less than total candor in extenuating circumstances (1 Sam 16:1–5; 2 Kgs 6:14–20), uses lies for his own purposes (1 Kgs 22:19–23; 2 Thess 2:11), and commends the faith of people who demonstrated it by deceiving enemies of God (Josh 2:4–6; Heb 11:31; Jas 2:25). We turn now to how Christians have divided on this issue through history.

Two Traditions on Truth & Lying in Christian Ethics

Philosophers have argued over the meaning of truth and lying from earliest memory, and Plato justified lying for a good cause, while Aristotle denied it is ever justified.[9] But aside from philosophers arguing in human terms, Christian interpreters of Scripture also have a long history of dividing over the issue, with one tradition arguing that truth allows justified deception and the other arguing that it never does. Terms are used differently, and being truthful can mean fidelity to God, keeping faith with neighbors, keeping words consistent with thoughts, being consistent with facts, speaking in ways consistent with what others think you mean, or just communicating ethically, whatever that means. Lying can also mean not being faithful to God, not keeping faith with neighbors, not keeping words consistent with thoughts, being inconsistent with facts, speaking in ways different from what others think you mean, or just communicating unethically, whatever that means.

Division over the ethics of communicating truly has had as much to do with defining terms as with obeying and pleasing God throughout the history of Christianity. For example, if lying means communicating untruly, then lying (so defined) is never ethical by definition.

---

[7] Jones, *Biblical Christian Ethics*, 144 (see chap. 2, n. 4).

[8] Augustine, *Against Lying*, AD 420, 33.

[9] Plato, Πολιτεία (*Republic*), c. 380 BC, bk. 3, 389b–c; quoted by Jerome, *Apology against Rufinus*, c. AD 402, 1.18. Aristotle, Ἠθικὰ Νικομάχεια (*Nicomachean Ethics*), c. 340 BC, 4.7.

But if lying means using words contrary to facts, or contrary to what others expect, and being truthful means fidelity to what God requires, then if God requires hiding facts from people doing bad things, then lying (so defined) can be the same as being truthful (so defined). Differences like this have led to opposing traditions—the "lying is communicating contrary to neighbors" tradition and the "lying is communicating contrary to thoughts" tradition. Prominent Christians, like Augustine, Calvin, and, most recently, Grudem, have condemned the Hebrew midwives in Egypt (Exod 1:15–21) and Rahab in Jericho (Josh 2:1–7) for deceiving bad people to save lives, even though God rewarded them and made Rahab an example of the sort of faith he requires (Heb 11:31). But other equally prominent Christians, like nearly everyone in the early Church, Luther, and, most recently, Frame, have praised not only their intentions but what they did as well.

No Christian before Augustine condemned lying as thoroughly as he did, not because they ignored the issue but rather because they defined lying differently. Every Christian leader on record dealing with the ethics of truth before Augustine held that there are causes for which communicating falsely on purpose is not sinful and sometimes even necessary.[10] These included Clement of Alexandria, Origen, Hilary of Poitier, Ambrose, Gregory of Nyssa, Paulinus of Nola, Jerome, Chrysostom, Sulpicius of Severus, Abbot Alonius, and probably Tertullian and Lactantius as well.[11] In fact, Hugo Grotius (1583–1645) in the seventeenth century reported that Augustine, although he disagreed, nevertheless recognized he was opposing what had been the dominant teaching of the Christian world for three centuries before he rejected it.[12]

Clement of Alexandria (150–215) held that a Christian should never "speak falsehood though he should die by tortures," but then he also argued that a Christian "may deceive or tell an untruth . . . for the benefit of his neighbors" and believed that was acting "piously," "justly,"

---

[10] Boniface Ramsey, "*Mendacio, De/Contra mendacium*," in *Augustine through the Ages: An Encyclopedia*, ed. Allan D. Fitzgerald (Grand Rapids: Eerdmans, 1999), 556; Sullivan, "In Defense of the *Falsiloquium*," 9.

[11] Hugo Grotius lists Tertullian and Lactantius (an advisor to Emperor Constantine who Jerome admired as a Christian Cicero) as holding this view as well. But no one else mentions it, and I cannot confirm it from surviving sources. See Grotius, *The Rights of War and Peace*, 1625, bk. 3, ch. 1, sec. 9.2.

[12] Grotius, 1625, bk. 3, ch. 1, sec. 9.2. Grotius may have been referring to a source that no longer survives.

and "according to duty."[13] Origen (184–253) held that communicating contrary to thoughts can be necessary to obtain "some great good" and argued that deceiving bad people for good reasons cannot be wrong because God does that himself.[14] And Hilary of Poitier (310–368) believed "a lie is sometimes necessary and falsity is at times useful, as when one lies about a person hiding from a murderer," and claimed lying is wrong "only when another person is adversely affected."[15]

Ambrose (334–397), Bishop of Milan and mentor of Augustine, did not leave direct evidence that he justified communicating contrary to thoughts, but he did leave indirect evidence of doing so. Murder of all kinds, including self-murder (suicide), is considered sinful. But Ambrose argued that women who kill themselves to avoid rape not only do nothing wrong, but are moral heroes. Logically, if doing something extreme (suicide) is justified, then doing something less extreme (communicating contrary to thoughts) for the same reason has to be justified. So, because Ambrose commended suicide to avoid rape as ethical, it means he commended the ethics of lying in the sense of communicating contrary to thoughts to avoid rape as well.[16] Gregory of Nyssa (335–394), a bishop in Cappadocia (now Turkey), claimed deceiving bad people for good reasons only follows God's example because "it was by means of a certain amount of deceit" that God carried out his scheme to save us.[17] And the early Christian poet Paulinus of Nola in Italy (354–431) told a story of Christ reappearing to help a Christian escape persecutors by lying, after which Paulinus says "the Lord mocked at the baying hounds who were beguiled."[18]

Jerome (c. 347–420), the most revered Bible scholar in the early Church, agreed with Origen that communicating contrary to thoughts is justified to obtain "some great good."[19] Jerome held that "there are different ways of speaking" and "to teach a disciple is one thing;

---

[13] Clement of Alexandria, Στρώματα or *Stromata* (*Miscellanies*), c. AD 200, 7.8.51; 7.9.53–54.

[14] Origen, Στρώματα or *Stromata* (*Miscellanies*), c. AD 220, bk. 6. Original lost but quoted by Jerome in *Apology against Rufinus*, c. AD 402, 1.18; Origen, *Homilies on Jeremiah*, c. AD 240, hom. 20, ch. 20, vv. 7–12.

[15] Hilary of Poitier, *Homilies on the Psalms*, c. AD 361, 14.2–3.

[16] Ambrose, *Concerning Virgins*, AD 377, 3.7.32–37. Others who interpret Ambrose this way include Ramsey, "Two Traditions," 512, and Sullivan, "In Defense of the *Falsiloquium*," 9.

[17] Gregory of Nyssa, Η Μεγάλη Κατήχηση (*The Great Catechism*), c. AD 385, 26.

[18] Paulinus of Nola, *Poems*, c. AD 390, 16.72–74.

[19] Jerome, *Apology against Rufinus*, c. AD 393, 1.18.

to vanquish an opponent, another." So, if teaching, Christians must communicate what they have in mind with "frankness and openness" and, if disputing with someone serving the devil, Christians "are compelled to say not what they think but what is needful."[20] But when Augustine criticized this, Jerome asked that he "not bring the reproach of teaching the practice of lying upon me who am a follower of Christ."[21] Nevertheless, he never ceased distinguishing communicating contrary to thoughts for good reasons (which he justified) from lying in the sense of communicating sinfully (which he did not). So Jerome's insistence never to have taught "the practice of lying" clearly indicates he defined "lying" differently than Augustine.

Chrysostom (c. 347–407), Archbishop of Constantinople, distinguished "good deceit" from bad and wondered if "one ought not even to call a deceit at all," the sort mentioned in Jeremiah 20:7.[22] But, since the Bible uses the term, Chrysostom held that deception must be "good or bad according to the intention of those who practice it" and concluded that Scripture teaches it can even be "necessary to deceive and to do the greatest benefits by means of this device."[23] The Christian historian Sulpicius Severus (363–425) praised the behavior of someone who tricked St. Martin (a Roman soldier turned hermit) into accepting consecration as Bishop of Tours in Gaul (now France) by lying.[24] And the Desert Father Abbot Alonius (c. 405) defended pious lies (communicating contrary to thoughts) because "if one never lies many terrible things happen," such as delivering "over to execution" people who flee to you for protection.[25]

Augustine (354–430), Bishop of Hippo (now Annaba, Algeria), started a second tradition among Christians on the ethics of communicating truly that for centuries eclipsed the first. Augustine wrote two treatises—*De mendacio* (*On Lying*), written in AD 395, and *Contra mendacium* (*Against Lying*), written in AD 420—in which he discussed eight kinds of lying in the sense of communicating contrary to thoughts and condemned all of them, including those told to protect innocent lives, to avoid rape, and even to fulfill other duties. His eight kinds of sinful communicating were (1) communicating contrary to thoughts so as to corrupt

---

[20] Jerome, *Letter 48 to Pammachius*, AD 393 or 394.

[21] Jerome, *Letter 112 to Augustine*, AD 404.

[22] John Chrysostom, Ὁμιλίες για τοῦ Κολοσσεῖς (*Homilies on Colossians*), c. AD 396, *Homily XV*.

[23] John Chrysostom, Ἀπό την Ἱερατεία (*On the Priesthood*), c. AD 380, 1.8.

[24] Sulpicius Severus, *Life of St. Martin*, c. AD 415, ch. 9.

[25] Abbot Alonius, *Sayings of the Fathers: Those of Abbot Alonius*, c. AD 405, 4.

theological doctrine; (2) communicating contrary to thoughts so as to harm someone without benefiting anyone; (3) communicating contrary to thoughts so as to profit self at the expense of others; (4) communicating contrary to thoughts for the pleasure of doing it and nothing else; (5) communicating contrary to thoughts so as to enhance rhetorical style; (6) communicating contrary to thoughts so as to profit self without harming anyone; (7) communicating contrary to thoughts so as to benefit others spiritually, like giving them time to repent; and (8) communicating contrary to thoughts so as to save good people from bodily torture, defilement, or execution by bad people.[26]

Augustine developed his position using four steps. First, he defined truth as keeping words consistent with thoughts and defined lying as the opposite. He said,

> A man lies, who has one thing in his mind and utters another in words, or by signs of whatever kind . . . . Whence it comes to pass, that he may say a false thing and yet not lie, if he thinks it to be so as he says although it be not so; and, that he may say a true thing, and yet lie, if he thinks it to be false and utters it for true, although in reality it be so as he utters it. For from the sense of his own mind, not from the verity or falsity of the things themselves, is he to be judged to lie or not lie.[27]

Second, Augustine used these self-focused, conceptually defined terms to interpret biblical commands, thus giving them divine authority. Third, he discussed levels of sinfulness and argued that although lying in the sense of communicating contrary to thoughts is never justified, some lies are less wrong than others. Fourth, Augustine argued that the Bible never justifies communicating contrary to thoughts even though it seems to in places, and he did this using three strategies: by claiming a sinful behavior is mentioned without saying so, by claiming something contrary to what a speaker was thinking can be true in a figurative sense, or by claiming that communicating contrary to thoughts can be distinguished from a speaker's good intentions. Thus, Augustine claimed that Tamar's deception of Judah (Gen 38:1–30) was wrong even though the Bible never condemns it, claimed Jacob did not lie when stealing Esau's birthright (Gen 27:1–40) even though he thought he was, and claimed that when the

---

[26] Augustine, *On Lying*, AD 395, 25.
[27] Augustine, 3.

Bible makes Rahab an example of faith (Heb 11:31), it only commends her good intentions and not the way she expressed them.[28]

Christian teaching on the ethics of truth has divided over the "lying is communicating contrary to neighbors" tradition of the early Church and the "lying is communicating contrary to thoughts" tradition of Augustine ever since. Soon after Augustine, several challenged the biblical basis for his position. John Cassian of Rome (360–435) criticized Augustine for limiting God's blessing of Rahab to her intentions, arguing that it is more faithful to the text to say she was "approved by God . . . so as not only to incur no guilt of sin from it, but even to attain the greatest goodness."[29] Others like Dorotheos of Gaza (c. 505–c. 565) and John Climacus (579–649) did so as well.[30] But through the Middle Ages (476–1492) the church favored the Augustinian position, and Aquinas (1225–1274) added philosophical arguments to back Augustine's way of interpreting what the Bible says.

Aquinas discussed three kinds of true communicating—"moral truth," wherein speech and life conform to the mind; "ontological truth," wherein something conforms to its assigned purpose; and "logical truth," wherein something communicated makes rational sense—and he discussed three kinds of sinful communicating—"pernicious lies," being those done for bad reasons; "benevolent lies," being those done for good reasons; and "jocose lies," being those done for humorous reasons.[31] Aquinas claimed the first sort are "mortal sins" (those damning the soul), the second sort are "venial sins" (those not damning the soul), and the third sort are not sinful and perhaps should not be called lies at all. But, while he did not think benevolent lies are all that bad, Aquinas denied that they are allowed based on two philosophical arguments. Functionally, he argued, even benevolent lies must be wrong because the purpose of speech is expressing what we have in mind, and it must be wrong to speak contrary to that purpose. Socially, he argued, such lies also are wrong because we are social animals and cannot survive without accurate communication.[32]

---

[28] Augustine, *Against Lying*, AD 420, 30, 24, 34
[29] John Cassian, *Conferences of the Desert Fathers*, c. AD 420, part 2, conf. 17, ch. 17.
[30] Dorotheos of Gaza, Τοῦ Ὁσίου Πατρός Ἡμῶν Δωροθέου Διδασκαλίαι (*Discourses of Our Holy Father Dorotheos*), c. AD 542, 9. John Climacus, Κλῖμαξ (*Ladder of Paradise*), c. AD 615, 12.
[31] Aquinas, *Summa theologica*, AD 1265–1274, 2a–2ae, q. 110, art. 2.
[32] Aquinas, q. 110, art. 3 and q. 114, art. 2.

In leading the Protestant Reformation, Luther (1483-1546) also broke with Augustine, Aquinas, and Catholicism to reaffirm the "lying is communicating contrary to neighbors" position. Like the early Church, Luther took a God-focused, neighbor-love, relational rather than self-focused, conceptual, philosophical approach. He asked, "What harm would it do, if a man told a good strong lie for the sake of the good and for the Christian church?" and answered, claiming, "a lie out of necessity, a useful lie, a helpful lie . . . would not be against God. He would accept them."[33] Luther also did not think the Bible treats the midwives who lied to save lives as doing anything wrong and rather treats what they did as heroic and worth emulating.[34] And Luther's fellow reformer Martin Bucer (1491–1551) once advised a friend to employ a "holy lie" of the sort Rahab used because the Bible is full of them.[35]

After Luther and Bucer, Calvin (1509–1564) was the first Protestant to return to the "lying is communicating contrary to thoughts" position of Augustine and the medieval church. Like Augustine, Calvin, too, started with self-focused, conceptual definitions of truth and lying and interpreted the Bible based on them, rather than starting with the Bible and questioning human understanding of what these terms mean. Calvin condemned "all feigning whether in word or deed," including communication contrary to thoughts told to save lives, protect sexual integrity, or preserve national security.[36] Commenting on Rahab's deception, Calvin said,

> As to the falsehood, we must admit that though it was done for a good purpose, it was
> not free from fault. For . . . while our purpose is to assist our brethren . . . it can never
> be lawful to lie, because that cannot be right which is contrary to the nature of God.[37]

But then to say the Bible never condones lying in the sense of communicating contrary to thoughts, Calvin so narrowed the meaning of lying as to claim it does not include misleading

---

[33] Martin Luther, from notes kept by his secretary recording something Luther said at the Eisenach Conference, July 15, 1540, in Max Lenz, ed., *Correspondence: Of Count Philipp the Magnanimous of Hesse with Bucer* (Leipzig: Verlag von S. Hirzel, 1880), 1:373.

[34] Martin Luther, *Martin Luther's Works: The Complete Critical Edition*, 93 vols. (Weimar: H. Bohlau, 1883–1990), 16:15.

[35] Martin Bucer, "Letter to the Landgrave, July 18, 1540," in Lenz, *Correspondence*, 1:193.

[36] Calvin, *Ioannis Calvini*, 25:19.

[37] John Calvin, *Commentaries on the Book of Joshua* (1564), 47.

half-truths, making false impressions, selling counterfeit goods, and cover stories fabricated to lead others toward reaching false conclusions.[38] As a result, Grotius later accused Calvin and Catholics following Aquinas of employing "interpretations so repugnant to all practice that one may question whether it is not more satisfactory to admit . . . the use of false-hoods . . . than so indiscriminately to exempt such interpretations from the definition of falsehood."[39]

A century after Calvin, Grotius (1583–1645) returned to the more ancient "lying is communicating contrary to neighbors" tradition and expanded on it, arguing that communicating truly is not a matter of words aligning with thoughts but a matter of moral rights that vary with the character of those addressed. Grotius claimed that some people have no right to truth, and in such cases, false statements are not lies in the sense of violating obligation to be true. Rather, he argued, what makes a statement untrue is "violation of the existing and permanent rights of the person to whom a discourse, or particular signs, are directed."[40] As such, he believed communicating contrary to thoughts is not sinful when the person addressed is an infant; is insane; is not deceived even if others are; is wanting to be deceived; is subject to the speaker, as when Solomon said he would cut a baby in half (1 Kgs 3:16–28); is trying to kill or rape an innocent person; or is an enemy trying to destroy you, as when Elisha deceived enemy soldiers (2 Kgs 6:8–23).[41]

In 1864, Catholic Cardinal John Henry Newman (1801–1890) broke with the "lying is communicating contrary to thoughts" tradition followed by Catholics for centuries and sided with the position of the early Church, Luther, and Grotius. Newman especially criticized how Catholic scholars, and especially Jesuits, justified equivocation—mental reservations by which a speaker secretly uses meanings contrary to customary speech—while alleging to oppose lying in all cases. He argued equivocation is just lying by another name and said, "I can fancy myself thinking it was allowable in extreme cases for me to lie, but never to equivocate."[42] He also argued that, just as all killing and taking are not sinful even though the sixth commandment

---

[38] Calvin, *Ioannis Calvini*, 30:161; also see Blacketer, "No Escape by Deception," 278–79.

[39] Grotius, *The Rights of War and Peace*, 1625, bk. 3, ch. 1, sec. 17.3.

[40] Grotius, sec. 11.

[41] Grotius, secs. 12–20.

[42] Newman, *Apologia pro vita sua*, 360.

prohibits murder and the eighth prohibits stealing, so, too, all deceiving is not sinful even though the ninth commandment prohibits false witness.[43]

Like Newman, the Protestant theologian Charles Hodge (1797–1878), too, held that, as the sixth commandment does not prohibit all killing and requires that we study other Scripture to find when it is allowed, so the ninth commandment requires looking elsewhere to determine if or when false speaking beyond what the Decalogue prohibits is allowed.[44] Hodge concluded "a man is not bound to speak the truth," and "those to whom the declaration or signification is made have no right to expect him to do so" when accurate speaking violates obligations like protecting innocent lives or national secrets.[45] But others disagreed, and another Reformed theologian, Murray (1898–1975), opposed Hodge to reaffirm the "lying is communicating contrary to thoughts" position, claiming, "neither Scripture itself nor the theological inferences derived from Scripture provide us with any warrant for the vindication of Rahab's untruth" or "the propriety of untruthfulness under any exigency."[46]

Thielicke (1908–1986), Jones (1937–2017), and Frame (b. 1939), all Protestants, have further defended the "lying is communicating contrary to neighbors" position. Following World War II, Thielicke criticized the "lying is communicating contrary to thoughts" position for denying "the most profound of all the plights of conscience" and debasing those who deceived Nazis to save innocent Jews as if their decisions were based on nothing more than "unredeemed chimeras and complexes."[47] Jones believed the Bible gives murderers no right to accurate information and argued "to insist on verbal truthfulness in such circumstances is manifestly against the purposes for which God has given us speech."[48] Frame questions how those taking the "lying is communicating contrary to thoughts" position interpret Scripture because the Bible shows "a lie is not simply an untrue statement" but "is a word or act that intentionally deceives a neighbor in order to hurt him." Frame believes the Bible teaches "we have no obligation to tell the truth to people who, for example, seek innocent life" and thinks

[43] Newman, 358.

[44] See Frame, *Doctrine of the Christian Life*, 837, interpreting Charles Hodge, *Systematic Theology*, 3 vols. (New York: Scribner's Sons, 1872), 3:437–442.

[45] Hodge, 441.

[46] Murray, "The Sanctity of Truth," 139, 146.

[47] Thielicke, "The Borderline Situation," 610.

[48] Jones, *Biblical Christian Ethics*, 150.

those who, during World War II, betrayed innocent Jews to Nazi murderers rather than lie to protect them "misunderstood their ethical obligation."[49]

Most recently, Grudem (b. 1948), who trained under Frame, has broken with his teacher to once more defend the "lying is communicating contrary to thoughts" tradition associated with Augustine, Aquinas, medieval Catholicism, Calvin, and Murray. Like them, Grudem completely prohibits lying in the sense of communicating contrary to thoughts and interprets the Bible based on self-focused conceptual definitions rather than starting with the Bible and questioning human understanding of what terms mean. With Augustine, Aquinas, medieval Catholicism, Calvin, and Murray, Grudem also refuses to ever condone communicating contrary to thoughts even to save innocent lives. But he struggles to explain how this applies in real life, first saying we must never communicate contrary to what we think even with evildoers and then saying evildoers have no right to truth.[50] Finally, to explain places the Bible approves deception without giving up his position, Grudem, like others before, insists truthfulness does not apply to deceiving others by using false actions, false gestures or expressions, half-truths in place of the whole truth, and meanings you know others do not understand or expect.[51]

Analyzing the Divide in Christian Ethical Teaching

Generally, the "lying is communicating contrary to neighbors" tradition holds that communicating contrary to what we think is not always wrong because what makes communicating sinful is betraying a relational trust, and that is not always the same as aligning words with thoughts. In this tradition, communication that betrays relational trust owed to God and others is untrue (is lying), and communicating in ways that are faithful to God and others is

---

[49] Frame, *Doctrine of the Christian Life*, 839–40.

[50] Grudem, *Christian Ethics*, 328 (see chap. 1, n. 67).

[51] Grudem, 311–13, 328, 335–36. Whether he means to or not, when he praises the niece of Corrie ten Boom for using equivocation to deceive soldiers looking for her brothers and says he would neither tell Nazis where Jews were hiding nor "lie to them either" (Grudem, 327–28), Grudem is in danger of doing the sort of thing for which Catholic Cardinal John Henry Newman and Reformed Protestant theologian Charles Hodge so criticized the casuistry of medieval Jesuits (Newman, "Lying and Equivocation," in *Apologia*, 348–63; Hodge, "Mental Reservations," in *Systematic Theology*, 3:445–48).

true (not lying)—even if it does not always align words with thoughts. This leads to thinking there can be worthy reasons for communicating contrary to thoughts, such as when innocent life, sexual purity, or national security are endangered. So, if lying means speaking sinfully, then communicating contrary to thoughts is not always lying; and, if lying means communicating contrary to thoughts, then lying is not always sinful. This tradition holds that the Ten Commandments address sinful communicating the same way they address sinful killing and sinful taking, and just as killing and taking are not always sinful, so communicating contrary to thoughts is not always sinful either.

Similarly, the "lying is communicating contrary to thoughts" tradition generally holds that communicating contrary to what we think is always wrong because what makes communicating sinful is discord between what one communicates and what one has in mind, and that is not the same as how it affects relational trust. This tradition maintains that saying things not aligned with what you think is never allowed—even if it betrays good people and helps bad people do wicked things. This leads to thinking it is never right to communicate using words contrary to what you know and, thus, usually is never right to deceive other people on purpose.[52] Communicating in ways leading others to believe things you know are untrue usually is considered sin no matter what is at stake, no matter who is addressed, and no matter how badly it affects anyone. This tradition also holds that the Ten Commandments do not address sinful communicating in the same way they address sinful killing and sinful taking. So, even though proponents accept how the sixth commandment does not prohibit all killing and the eighth does not prohibit all taking, they nevertheless insist the ninth commandment prohibits all communicating contrary to thoughts, unlike how the sixth and eighth commandments address what they prohibit.

Divisions at Deeper Levels of Analysis

We should not think because Christian tradition is divided between two ways of interpreting obligation to communicate truly that the sanctity of truth is just a matter of choosing one or the other. Augustine himself admitted the issue "is, indeed, very full of dark corners, and has

---

[52] I say "usually" because some following this tradition justify using equivocation to deceive people so long as words are used in ways that are true "in a sense."

many cavern-like windings, whereby it often eludes the eagerness of the seeker; so that at one moment what was found seems to slip out of one's hands, and anon comes to light again, and then is once more lost to sight."[53] Not only are there variations within each tradition, but also deep layers of analysis offer multiple options affected by how they are interpreted.

First, we can ask if the character of God requires defining truthfulness in a preferred way or not. After defining "truthfulness" as someone affirming what he knows or believes, Murray connects it with obligation to conform to "God's truthfulness."[54] But does obligation to conform to God's character require Murray's preferred definition of "truthfulness"? Frame agrees we must conform to God's character but disputes Murray's prior definition since fiction is not unethical just because it is fictional.[55]

Second, there is no ethic of communicating truly without defining terms, and defining terms badly can shift the meaning of right and wrong to the point of calling "evil good and good evil" (Isa 5:20). Much rides on the meaning and nature of truth, but Christians have struggled with it for centuries. Everyone agrees God speaks "the truth" (Isa 45:19, ESV), Jesus is "the truth" (John 14:6), the Holy Spirit is "the Spirit of truth" (John 15:26; 16:13), and truth "leads to godliness" (Titus 1:1). But there is no commonly held Christian view of what communicating truly and untruly mean. Scientific truth is a question of aligning claims with scientific facts. But with what sort of thing should we say ethical truth aligns? Is it something conceptual, something relational, or something personal?

Third, it is naïve to think communicating truly is simple in the sense of involving only one factor. Many factors affect communicating truly, and passing information one to another always involves multiple levels of understanding and integrity. This makes any ethic of communicating truly complex, and in practice, one cannot really divorce one factor from the rest. Communicating in an ethically true manner always involves knowing, expressing (whether by words, writing, gestures, motions, or grunts), acting, relating, intending, and implying. None of these occurs separately, and each affects communicating in an ethically true manner to the degree it affects communicating in the first place.

---

[53] Augustine, *On Lying*, 1.
[54] Murray, "Sanctity of Truth," 127, 133.
[55] Frame, *Doctrine of the Christian Life*, 834.

Fourth, communicating truly has internal and external aspects and is not just one or the other. Acting truly is external, and intending to be true is internal. Expressing is external but comes from thoughts which are internal. Communicating starts with one person knowing something and ends with other people knowing something, which is internal at both ends but external so far as each is outside the other. Knowing is internal but involves information about external realities, and communicating ethically concerns the way internal knowing relates to external realities and gets from one mind into others. Saying something true is external, or at least involves something internal getting externalized, whereas being true is something internal with external effects. Ethical communicating involves both aspects and always does.

External actions fulfill internal desires, but how do they relate ethically? If a desire does not produce a bad action, is it bad on its own? Or must something externally bad happen to make it bad? Ethicists disagree, and some think there is nothing wrong with wanting to deceive so long as words align with external reality in clever ways others do not grasp, while others think just wanting to deceive is wrong regardless of how cleverly words line up with external reality.

Fifth, other categories of obligation in God's moral law have unconditional cores allowing no exceptions and conditional perimeters that apply the same category of obligation in ways that vary, and we can ask if the obligation to be truthful is like that. Jesus explained that beyond prohibiting murder, the sixth commandment also restricts insulting people, even though assessing that varies with culture, place, and time (Matt 5:21–22). It makes sense, therefore, to wonder if the sanctity of truth established in the ninth commandment is similarly constructed. Augustine, Calvin, and Grudem have denied there is any such distinction to be found in the obligation to be truthful, while others like Luther, Hodge, and Frame have argued there is.

Sixth, attempts to reduce truthfulness to a single thing appear to be ruled out by ethicists discussing multiple sorts of truth and lying. Augustine and Aquinas both started with defining truth in a single way and then discussed multiple sorts of truth and multiple sorts of lying. Augustine claimed there are eight kinds of lying, and Aquinas claimed there are three kinds of truth, all of which raises questions about whether truth and lying go back to the one way they were defined in the first place. Christians since Augustine and Aquinas have suggested truth and lying can be classified as formal, functional, material, relational, personal, and situational. Formal truth and lying regard whether communication fits reality. Functional truth and untruth regard whether it is used properly. Material truth and lying regard whether it fits material information. Relational truth and lying regard how it affects relationships and responsibilities. Personal truth and lying regard how it fits things inside yourself. And situational truth and lying regard how it fits circumstances. As a result, Thielicke thought something formally true may at times be functionally false and something formally untrue may at times be functionally true.[56] Similarly, Bonhoeffer thought formal lies are sometimes "more in accord with reality" than speaking words that are formally true.[57]

Seventh, we can ask if terms used in conceiving ethical truth are defined in self-centered, other-centered, or God-centered ways. It is one thing to interpret and apply what the Bible says about walking in truth after thinking we already know what "truth" means and something else to think we do not know what "truth" means before attending to what the Bible says. Any notion of truth or untruth that is not God-centered is man-centered, either in a self-centered or some other humanly experienced man-centered way. This difference is critically important because starting with any man-centered definition leads to misreading what the Bible says in ways that fit preconceived notions rather than letting the Bible reveal how we ought to think.

Ways Both Sides Fall Short

The traditions dividing Christian interpretation of communicating truly both get some things right because both respect Scripture, but neither is entirely right because both reach conclusions clouded by dubious preconceptions. One says truthfulness is about keeping good relationships, which is important but secondary and, thus, not entirely correct. The other says truth is about aligning words and thoughts, which, too, is important but secondary and, thus, not entirely correct. Both traditions treat secondary matters as if they are primary, when the Bible treats truthfulness as primarily concerned with being true to God in all we intend, say, and do (Rom 3:4).

So, rather than choose sides, we should identify strengths and weaknesses and take from each what can be used to formulate a more robust position transcending both. Addressing the "lying is communicating contrary to neighbors" tradition we need to ask,

---

[56] Thielicke, *Theological Ethics*, 552.
[57] Bonhoeffer, *Ethics*, 362.

1. Is it the same as personal relativism and, if not, how does it differ?

2. In what sense is it morally objective, fixed, and universal?

3. Is it completely consistent with the nature of God?

4. Does it contradict itself by saying wrong is right and right is wrong?

5. Does it compromise godliness with fallen human nature and the Devil?

6. Does it justify sinning?[58]

7. Does it interpret the Bible correctly, and is it faithful to all the Bible says?

8. Does it disconnect communicating truly from being true?

9. Does it elevate rights to life, property, or liberty over the right to true speech?

Addressing the "lying is communicating contrary to thoughts" tradition, we need to ask,

1. Does it reduce communicating truly to absurdities, like never claiming to be "fine" when not and allowing people to kill others in self-defense but never deceiving them?

2. Does it interpret what God says by what men say?

3. Does it define what truth means before considering what God says about it?

4. Does it require being more faithful to bad people than to good people?

5. Does it treat "truth" like an idol independent and above God himself?

6. Does it deny the doctrine of eternal security the way Augustine did?[59]

7. Does it read things into the Bible to explain away passages that do not fit expectations?

8. Does it exclude being true from the ethics of truth?

9. Does it elevate the right to true speech over rights to life, property, or liberty?

Division between the traditions comes down to different ways each assesses the wrong in communicating untruly. If truthfulness means preserving relational trust, the wrong in

---

[58] Augustine held that "he who says that some lies are just, must be judged to say no other than that some sins are just, and therefore some things are just which are unjust" (Augustine, *Against Lying*, 31).

[59] Augustine did not think Christians should lie to keep innocent people from being killed because he thought those doing so lose their own eternal life. He argued that "since . . . by lying eternal life is lost, never for any man's temporal life must a lie be told." Augustine's position against communicating contrary to thoughts even to save life came from denying eternal security because he held that for one to save another from death by speaking contrary to thoughts is to "slay his own soul in order that another may grow old in the flesh" (Augustine, *On Lying*, 9).

communicating untruly is betraying a trust relationship as measured by others trusting us and nothing else. If truthfulness means aligning words with thoughts, the wrong in communicating untruly is discord between them and nothing else. And, if truthfulness means fulfilling a mission assigned by God, the wrong in communicating untruly is hindering a divine mission or purpose however words align with thoughts and however it affects those trusting us for their own reasons.

The main difference between the Augustinian "lying is communicating contrary to thoughts" tradition compared to the early Church "lying is communicating contrary to neighbors" tradition has to do with how truth and lying are defined. What Christians held before Augustine was not precise, but they generally aligned communicating truly with neighbor love, making it relational, and during the age of persecution (AD 35–313), they justified communicating contrary to thoughts in order to save innocent people. But the weakness of this approach is that neighbor love can be interpreted in subjective-sentimental terms. Augustine meant to purge the church from ethical relativity and usually did that by relying on what the Bible says. But, when it came to interpreting the sanctity of truth, Augustine started with definitions of truth and lying not found in the Bible itself. Thus, neither of the traditions dividing Christian ethics defines communicating truly in genuinely God-centered terms, and that problem must be addressed.

What Scripture Says about Truth, Lying, & Faithful Communicating

The history of Christianity is divided on the ethics of truth, but God's ethical reality is not. This means we cannot treat the opposing traditions like items on a cafeteria line from which to select what we like. The coherence of God demands a coherent answer, and that leaves three options. Perhaps the "lying is communicating contrary to neighbors" tradition is correct and the other wrong. Perhaps the "lying is communicating contrary to thoughts" tradition is correct and the other wrong. Or perhaps what the Word of God reveals transcends both traditions. Christians have, until now, sided with one tradition or the other, but I think it is time we consider whether Scripture offers a third option transcending both—one that defines truth, truthfulness, deception, and lying in ways that are neither neighbor-focused nor self-focused but God-focused. It is time to stop thinking we already know what terms mean from dictionaries and philosophers and to, instead, admit we cannot really understand them before

God tells us. Now we will survey what the Bible says on the subject and after that will consider how the pieces fit together.

The Bible Stresses Truth and Condemns Violating Truth

To understand what the Word of God reveals concerning the ethics of communicating truly, we must start with how it identifies truth with God and violating truth with rejecting him. God declares, "I the LORD speak the truth," and then says, "I declare what is right" (Isa 45:19, ESV; compare with John 17:17). God not only communicates accurately but also is the source and measure of truth. Everything true is of God, and nothing else is true. Moses announces that the "name" of God, meaning his essential character, is "righteous and true" (Deut 32:3–4). This does not mean God measures up to truth as if truth is something higher and greater existing independently but rather means God being "Truth Itself" is consistent with himself. When Scripture says God is "the God of truth" (Ps 31:5; Isa 65:16), it means he is not just true or truthful but is that to which all truth aligns and is that according to which all things are held to account. Therefore, everything God says is true (2 Sam 22:31; Ps 119:160), everything he reveals proves true (Prov 30:5, ESV), everything God does is true (Ps 25:10), nothing contrary to God is true (Prov 30:5), God never is untrue (Num 23:19; Titus 1:2), and God "remains faithful forever" (Ps 146:6) because God's character never changes (Num 23:19; Heb 6:18; 13:8; Jas 1:17). And God requires we be true (Ps 51:6) and "speak truth to one another" (Zech 8:16; see also Eph 4:25) because he means for us to be like him (Lev 19:2; 20:7; 1 Pet 1:16). Living in truth "leads to godliness" (Titus 1:1) and assures God's blessing and protection (Ps 91:4). The mystery of the Trinity is involved because, not only is truth identified with God the Father (Ps 31:5), but also with God the Son (John 14:6) and with God the Holy Spirit (John 14:17; 15:26, 16:13; 1 John 5:6).

This makes communicating truly a sacred obligation and, as Murray explains, violating truth contradicts "that which God is."[60] Not only does the ninth commandment prohibit "false testimony against your neighbor" (Exod 20:16), but there are numerous passages in the Bible censoring communication contrary to God (Lev 19:11; Job 27:4; Ps 5:6; 31:18; 58:3; 63:11; 101:7; 119:104; 119:163; 120:2; Prov 12:22; 13:5; 14:5; 17:7; 26:28; 30:8; Isa

---

[60] Murray, "The Sanctity of Truth," 125.

59:4; Jer 9:5; Eph 4:25; Col 3:9; 1 Tim 1:10; Jas 3:14; Rev 21:8). God hates "a lying tongue" (Prov 6:17), "no lie comes from the truth" (1 John 2:21), Christians must never do anything "against the truth, but only for the truth" (2 Cor 13:8), and the Church is meant to be "the pillar and foundation of the truth" on earth (1 Tim 3:15).

But There Are Passages in the Bible Condoning Deception

Although the Bible stresses the sanctity of truth and condemns violations, a number of passages treat communicating contrary to known facts and deceiving others on purpose with no hint of disapproval, and several passages go so far as to commend and reward doing so. These include:

- The Hebrew midwives deceived Pharaoh to save babies (Exod 1:15–21).
- Rahab deceived a king to save spies (Josh 2:1–7; 6:17, 25; Heb 11:31; Jas 2:25).
- God ordered Israel to ambush the men of Ai (Josh 8:3–8).
- Jael deceived the Canaanite general Sisera (Judg 4:18–21; 5:24–27).
- God fabricated a cover story for deceiving King Saul (1 Sam 16:1–5).
- Michal deceived her father Saul to protect David (1 Sam 19:12–17).
- David told Jonathan to cover his absence by deceiving his father Saul (1 Sam 20:6).
- Jonathan deceived his father Saul to cover David's absence (1 Sam 20:28–29).
- David deceived Ahimelech the priest about his mission (1 Sam 21:2).
- David deceived the people of Gath by feigning madness (1 Sam 21:13).
- David deceived King Achish about the places he was raiding (1 Sam 27:10).
- David deceived King Achish about where his true loyalty lay (1 Sam 29:8–9).
- God ordered David to ambush the Philistines at Rephaim (2 Sam 5:22–25).
- David ordered Hushai to deceive Absalom with bad advice (2 Sam 15:34).
- Hushai deceived Absalom by giving intentionally bad advice (2 Sam 17:5–13).
- God decreed Absalom be ruined by Hushai's deceitful advice (2 Sam 17:14).
- A woman deceived Absalom's men to save David's men (2 Sam 17:19–20).
- God sent a "lying spirit" to deceive King Ahab (1 Kgs 22:19–23; 2 Chr 18:20–22).
- The prophet Elisha deceived Syrian troops sent to arrest him (2 Kgs 6:14–20).
- Jeremiah deceived people to keep God's message to King Zedekiah secret (Jer 38:24–27).

- God said he will himself deceive false prophets (Ezek 14:9).
- God will send strong delusion causing bad people to believe what is false (2 Thess 2:11).

These passages all deal with deceiving bad people and treat doing so either as if nothing is wrong or as if it is a good thing. In some cases, ethical approval is implied because deceivers are treated as heroes, and in others, approval is expressed directly and clearly because God actually blesses deceivers for deceiving. In one case, the deceiver (Rahab) is commended as demonstrating the sort of faith God desires even though she proved it speaking contrary to known facts, and in five cases, God causes bad people to be deceived to their ruin, either by commanding good people (like Joshua, Samuel, and David) to deceive them or ordering spirits to the same purpose. God does this sometimes to punish the wicked, enable a righteous person to fulfill an assigned mission, and save innocent people needing protection.

Those denying that Scripture anywhere approves communicating contrary to facts argue none of these passages says what it seems to, and they do this using strategies, such as:

- Claiming that what the ninth commandment prohibits applies in the same unconditional way to circumstances beyond what the text actually says;
- Denying that obligation to communicate truly applies to nonverbal communicating;
- Claiming that communicating truly allows deceiving by methods not understood by those addressed (equivocation);
- Denying that the biblical truth ethic includes being true;
- Claiming that sinning with good intentions is praiseworthy, contrary to Romans 3:7–8;
- Claiming that circumstances and distinctions not mentioned in the Bible can be used to explain passages that do not fit expectations;
- Defining terms in ways not coming from the Bible and that are self-centered rather than God-centered.

The passages most often debated in relation to interpreting the sanctity of truth, and that those following Augustine find hardest to explain, are where God protects and rewards the Hebrew midwives in Egypt (Exod 1:15–21), where God protects, rewards, and treats Rahab in Jericho as a role model (Josh 2:1–7; 6:17, 25; Heb 11:31; Jas 2:25), and where God fabricates a cover story for deceiving King Saul (1 Sam 16:1–5). These all treat deceiving bad people to fulfill missions assigned by God in a positive manner, and so either offer unique insights or unique challenges to interpreting what the Word of God reveals about the sanctity of truth.

Even though God blessed the Hebrew midwives (Exod 1:20), and even though James says God-pleasing faith is inseparable from faithful action (Jas 2:22), Augustine could not believe God approved their deception of Pharaoh and rather argued that God only approved their intentions.[61] But distinguishing intentions from what was communicated is unconvincing, first, because it is not mentioned in the text and, second, because it conflicts with the New Testament, saying good intentions for bad behavior are themselves unworthy (Rom 3:7–8). Others favoring Augustine have suggested what the midwives said may have been factual because Hebrew women may really have given birth more rapidly than Egyptians. But that is problematic as well because the text indicates that Pharaoh was tricked on purpose into believing something untrue, and even if what the midwives said was factual "in a sense," it was not the true and real reason they disobeyed Pharaoh. Thus, even by this second argument, what the midwives said was at best "true" only by equivocation, and nearly everyone considers that less than truthful.

Even more is at stake with how Scripture treats Rahab because no one doubts she communicated contrary to what she knew using words to convey false information to save spies hiding in her house. In Rahab's case, there was no equivocation and no way of claiming what she said was true in some factual sense. Rahab knowingly communicated something she knew was not so and did it very much on purpose, so interpreters must decide whether God condoned what she said as ethical and true or considered it lying and sinful. Augustine held that, although Rahab can be commended for placing herself in peril to save others and for preferring the God of Israel over the gods of her own people, nevertheless, "in that she lied" she is not "meant to be imitated."[62] But, in separating the ethics of Rahab's communication from the worthiness of her intentions, Augustine not only once more used a distinction not found in the text and contrary to the inseparability of faith and action (Jas 2:22) but then assessed what she said contrary to what the Bible says itself.

Scripture twice records that Rahab spoke as she did because she feared God (Josh 2:9; Josh 2:11), elsewhere establishes fearing God as a principle assuring ethical purity (Ps 19:9; 25:12;

---

[61] Augustine, *Against Lying*, 32.
[62] Augustine, 34.

Prov 3:7; 14:2; 16:6; 8:13), and once even declares it is the very thing guaranteeing truthful communication: "To fear the LORD is to hate . . . perverse speech" (Prov 8:13). Thus, mentioning that Rahab spoke as she did because she feared God is the Bible's way of saying she communicated truly the way God defines it. Her communication was true according to the "God of truth" (Ps 31:5; Isa 65:16), even though she lied the way men often define it.

Beyond this, the Bible reveals in multiple ways that God truly was pleased, not just with what Rahab intended, but with what she said. We know this, first, because the whole event is given as a good—not a bad—example of proving the sort of faith God desires (Heb 11:31). We know this, second, because what Rahab said turning the men of Jericho from her door is referred to as the "work" of faith (more than a feeling or intention) according to which God credited her "as righteous" (Jas 2:25) in exactly the same way offering Isaac was the "work" of faith (more than a feeling or intention) according to which God credited Abraham "as righteousness" (Jas 2:23). We know this, third, because her house was built "into the wall of the city" (Josh 2:15), and God miraculously kept it standing when the walls of Jericho fell (Josh 6:20–23). And we know this, fourth, because God honored Rahab by placing her in the Messianic line (Matt 1:5).

Scripture commends the faith expressed through what Rahab communicated so clearly and so often it is very hard to avoid seeing that she pleased God by doing and saying exactly as reported and not despite it. So, if how she communicated does not fit expectations, rather than explain away all the evidence, we should, instead, change what we expect to better fit what the Bible clearly says. Since the text treats Rahab as an ethical hero, we should not suppose she violated the sanctity of truth and should instead agree that she communicated truly—not in reference to the people of Jericho, not in reference to herself, and not even in reference to the spies, but in reference to God. She demonstrated what pleasing God requires in that circumstance.

A third passage affecting interpretation of the biblical truth ethic records God fabricating a cover story to deceive Saul so Samuel can anoint a successor king (1 Sam 16:1–5). This could be the most important of the passages on how "the God of truth" (Isa 65:16) who never lies (Num 23:19) views and defines communicating truly. Samuel had already told Saul God was rejecting him as king and was giving the kingdom to another (1 Sam 15:23–28), but Saul had the impudence to think he could stop this. So, when God ordered Samuel to carry out his plan, Samuel wanted to know, "How can I go? Saul will hear about it and kill me!" (1 Sam

16:2). Instead of intervening miraculously, God fabricates a cover story for deceiving Saul. God orders Samuel to "take a young cow with you and say, 'I have come to sacrifice to the LORD'" (1 Sam 16:2).

Some argue that the principle of aligning words with thoughts is not violated because cover stories only pretend something partly true is the whole truth,[63] just withhold pertinent information,[64] or merely conceal a real purpose without saying anything incorrect.[65] But, as Newkirk observes, the problem with this is "Samuel did not just conceal the true purpose of his visit" but communicated false information.[66] When people at an accident ask for a "doctor," it is one thing to say "I can't help" without explaining and something else to say "I'm a 'doctor'" because you have a degree in theology. The setting makes all the difference, and at an accident scene, calling yourself a "doctor" means claiming you are medically trained. The first way of responding just withholds information, whereas even though what the second claims is factual "in a sense," it is spoken in a context you know those addressed will take falsely.

The problem with following the Augustinian interpretation of this passage is the cover story God fabricated is like the second way of responding, not the first. Samuel's real purpose for visiting Bethlehem was anointing a new king, and the cover story claimed it was something else. It deceived Saul into thinking something false and so was "lying" in the sense of communicating something other than Samuel (and God) had in mind, other than Samuel (and God) knew Saul wanted to know, and other than Samuel (and God) knew Saul's emissaries would be asking.

We already know God never lies in the sense of communicating contrary to himself. But this account shows God sometimes expects us to communicate in ways causing others to think and believe things we know are not the case, and this is justified when communicating with people seeking to hinder us from fulfilling a divine mission the way Saul was seeking to hinder Samuel. This is consistent with God never lying as he defines it, but it exposes problems with defining it other ways. God never lies in the sense of communicating contrary to his own character, plans, or purposes, but he does sometimes communicate with bad people in ways

---

[63] Jones, *Biblical Christian Ethics*, 146.

[64] Kaiser, *Toward Old Testament Ethics*, 225–26 (see chap. 3, n. 1).

[65] Murray, *Principles of Conduct*. 139–40; Grudem, *Christian Ethics*, 311, 325, 335.

[66] Newkirk, *Just Deceivers*, 59.

contrary to what he knows. If we fear this makes God "a liar," the problem is not with God but with defining terms in ways other than God does himself. The difference is crucial, and we should not mix them up.

God Is Not Always Straightforward

Some passages mention God sending a "lying spirit" or "strong delusion," causing bad people to believe something false (1 Kgs 22:19–23; 2 Chr 18:20–22; 2 Thess 2:11), and theologians debate whether this means God uses the sinfulness of bad people against them or means God deceives bad people himself. However these passages are interpreted, two other passages clearly indicate that God adjusts how he communicates according to the character of those addressed and sometimes even communicates contrary to what he knows in order to foil or destroy bad people.

Psalm 18:25–26 says, "With the faithful you prove yourself faithful, with the blameless you prove yourself blameless, with the pure you prove yourself pure, but with the crooked you prove yourself (something)."[67] But what? Translators struggle with that last word. The Christian Standard Bible and the New International Version use "shrewd," the English Standard Version uses "torturous," the New American Standard Bible uses "astute," the King James Version uses "unsavory," and the New Revised Standard Version uses "perverse." Should we think God is perverse or simply astute or shrewd? If this passage means only to say God is astute or shrewd, why would he be astute or shrewd only with bad people and not good people? Should we think God is tortuous rather than straight, or is unsavory rather than reputable? The wide range of translations shows there is no English word that easily captures what this text reveals.

The Hebrew term is תִּתְפַּתָּל (titpatāl), which derives from פָּתַל (pātal), meaning "twist" in a form, meaning to show oneself twisted, cunning, tortuous, crafty, sly, wily, or even perverse or deceitful. It can mean astute or shrewd but only in the negative sense of devious and not in the positive sense of being keen minded. We should not think God ever is, or ever pretends to be, sinful, and, since it is about ways God communicates, the passage must be saying people

---

[67] This prayer of David appears twice in Scripture, once in Psalm 18 and once in 2 Samuel 22. The word in question differs slightly between these two places, but scholars agree Psalm 18 provides the earlier more reliable record of what David initially penned.

who justify sinning find God communicating with them in ways that seem hard and perhaps even seem "wrong" as they see it. But there is a difference between just seeming false to a bad person and communicating in terms that really are false, and settling which Scripture intends depends on the tense used for the Hebrew verb expressed in English as "prove yourself."

The core idea is that to those who want truth, God communicates clearly, and to those who do not, he communicates in ways hard to grasp, not necessarily because it is too profound for human minds but rather just because some people are not worthy of it. The character of God never changes (Num 23:19; Jas 1:17; Heb 13:8). Truth as God defines it stands forever (Ps 146:5–6). Nothing God says is untrue (Ps 25:10). But this says God adjusts his manner of communicating according to our willingness to receive what he communicates. It reveals that God not only conceals truth from unworthy people but also, to some extent, distorts what they perceive. To clarify this further, we need to consider something God reveals in Ezekiel.

In Ezekiel 14:7–9 God says, if someone "separates himself from me, setting up idols in his heart and putting his sinful stumbling block in front of him," then "I, the LORD, will answer him myself" first by acting hostile toward him. Then, if that person gets a prophet to tell him what he wants to hear, not only will that prophet be deceived but when it happens, "it was I, the LORD, who deceived that prophet." What we must note is that God says he will himself communicate contrary to what is the case. Since Augustine defines this to be "lying," the passage clearly reveals that God does not define "lying" as Augustine did, which in turn means we should not use the Augustinian definition for interpreting what the Bible says about it.

These passages together (Ps 18:25–26; Ezek 14:7–9) clearly reveal that God not only acts against bad people directly and in person but at times also deceives them directly and in person. And God does this not only by withholding information, not only by letting bad people deceive themselves, and not only by using emissaries but sometimes even by communicating contrary to what he knows in order to foil and destroy them. It is again important to reiterate that God never lies in the sense of saying, doing, or implying anything contrary to his own character, plans, and purposes (Num 23:19). But we also need to understand that God does, sometimes directly and intentionally, deceive bad people. And, "because as he is, so are we in this world" (1 John 4:17), and since God commands us to be holy as he is holy (Lev 19:2; 1 Pet 1:16), this means we should do so as well in similar circumstances.

God's Ways Are Past Comprehending Fully

When interpreting what the Bible says about communicating truly, it is important to affirm God's transcendence as in, "How unsearchable are his judgments and untraceable his ways!" (Rom 11:33b). Here, Paul uses two terms for how God's handling of ethical matters transcends human comprehending. One is ἀνεξεραύητα (*anexerauēta*), meaning "beyond the ability of human minds to explain," and the other is ἀνεξιχνίαστοι (*anexichniastoi*), meaning "beyond the ability of human minds to fully grasp." Both terms indicate that God defines and applies ethical matters in ways beyond human ability to comprehend fully. God reveals all we need to know, but there always comes a point at which we must accept his "judgments" (his assessing of right and wrong) and his "ways" (his handling of ethical norms) even though we do not understand them completely.

When it comes to communicating truly, this means we must always, at some a point, just accept what the Bible says, even if it does not fit the way we define things or think makes the best sense. So, if someone explains communicating truly in a fashion that, to us, makes perfect sense, it is good evidence that their explanation either is wrong or in some way distorts how God defines and applies truth, truthfulness, deception, and lying. This is another reason to suspect the Augustinian interpretation. It is suspect not only because it is self-referential (is defined by aligning "my" words with "my" thoughts), denies God's commendation of the Hebrew midwives and Rahab, makes God "a liar" for telling Samuel to communicate false information, and rejects what the Bible says about God communicating contrary to what he knows, sometimes directly and in person, but also because it is does not trust God beyond human comprehending. The early Church interpretation, too, is suspect to the extent that it allows separating neighbor love from loving God himself or prioritizes loyalty to anyone over loyalty to God.

When Romans 11:36 says, "From him and through him and to him are all things," it means all genuinely accurate ethical understanding is God-centered. It means all ethical truth is defined by God, measured in reference to God, revealed by God, and accountable to God. If we ask, Where does God get his knowledge of truth? The answer is he gets it from himself as measured by his holiness and defined by his heart as is seen where Scripture says, "According to your own heart, you have brought about all this greatness" (2 Sam 7:21, ESV), and, "According to your own heart, you have done all this greatness" (1 Chr 17:19, ESV). To say God communicates truly (Ps 33:4) or is the "God of truth" (Ps 31:5; Isa 65:16) means God reveals his heart and is fully consistent. He does not get it from men defining it in human terms in their own way. He does not get his knowledge of truth from philosophers, no matter how wise, and he certainly does not get it from human dictionaries, no matter how commonly accepted or logical. And, because the true meaning and nature of truth is from God, measured by God, and defined by God rather than men on their own terms, a full understanding of truth will always be more than we grasp or define on our own.

God, in Isaiah, explains the reality and importance of his ethical transcendence in relation to human understanding, saying, "My thoughts are not your thoughts, and your ways are not my ways . . . . For as heaven is higher than earth, so my ways are higher than your ways, and my thoughts than your thoughts" (Isa 55:8–9). If God's thoughts are not our thoughts because they are as vastly different in a superior way as "heaven is higher than earth," then when God condescends to communicate in ways we comprehend, it is always in terms not exactly as he thinks. The Augustinian interpretation calls this "lying" when, of course, God never lies (Num 23:19). So we should be saying, rather, that God is always consistent with himself, and that alone establishes God's view of ethical truth.

When Scripture says, "God is not a man, that he might lie" (Num 23:19), it first means truth as God defines it is not affected by human conventions, and no matter how many agree, it is not accurate if God does not define it that way. Second, this verse also says no way humans define truth without God is entirely correct. Thus, anyone who defines truth on his own without God, in terms he thinks it makes the best sense, is lying as God defines it. This does not make sense to everyone, and no one grasps it fully. But that is only because the truth ethic revealed in Scripture comes from a person whose ways are past human ability to comprehend fully (Rom 11:33).

Communicating Truly Is Inseparable from Being True

Some, following Augustine, interpret the truth ethic revealed in Scripture as only concerned with communicating and not also including obligation to be true.[68] Those doing this, in most

---

[68] Augustine, *On Lying*, 3, 5; Augustine, *On Faith, Hope, and Love*, 6, 18; Calvin, *Institutes of the Christian Religion*, 1536, 2.8.47–48; Murray, *Principles of Conduct*, 133; Grudem, *Christian Ethics*, 311–12.

cases, also claim that the obligation to communicate truthfully only applies to speaking and writing and does not cover gestures, behavior, relationships, character, or ways we accept, handle, and carry out responsibilities. They realize these are important but do not think they are part of the same ethic as communicating truthfully. I strongly disagree because it imposes a distinction not found in Scripture, and the Bible so clearly treats communicating truly and being true as a single ethic.

God not only communicates truly but is "Truth Itself." He is the essence, measure, origin, and definer of truth. He is the one without which nothing is true. So, as we communicate more truly, we also become more and more true as God is true, and as we become more true as God is true, we also communicate more and more truly. This interconnection is expressed where John says, "If we say, 'We have fellowship with him,' and yet we walk in darkness, we are lying and are not practicing the truth" (1 John 1:6), adding later that "when he appears, we will be like him" and "everyone who has this hope in him purifies himself just as he is pure" (1 John 3:2–3). In other words, John says the truth ethic is something practiced and not just something verbalized. It is something we become and not just something we convey.

Jesus says truth is something we are "of," which means the truth ethic covers more than communicating alone: "Everyone who is of the truth listens to my voice" (John 18:37b). He also connected communicating truly with being true when correcting what some religious leaders wrongly thought, telling them, "What comes out of the mouth comes from the heart, and this defiles a person. For from the heart come evil thoughts, murders, adulteries, sexual immoralities, thefts, false testimonies, slander. These are the things that defile a person; but eating with unwashed hands does not defile a person" (Matt 15:18–20). Jesus was addressing the nature of Old Testament dietary laws but also was saying, while words and actions are important, a person's inner character (heart) is inseparable from communicating truly. In fact, he was saying that, while both are important, being true really matters more than what a person happens to say or do considered independently.

In the Bible, being true is the same as being faithful—primarily to God and secondarily to others—and what I am saying is the Bible treats fidelity as essential to communicating truly. This makes being true (or faithful) and communicating truly (or faithfully) one thing, not two things.[69] They are sides of the same coin, aspects of a single ethic, one requires the

---

[69] Kaiser, *Toward Old Testament Ethics*, 222.

other, and one without the other is both meaningless and impossible. This interconnection is affirmed in a vision of Christ's second coming later given the apostle John: "Then I saw heaven opened, and there was a white horse. Its rider is called Faithful and True" (Rev 19:11). When Jesus returns, the most obvious thing to observe will be that he is faithful and true. Not just faithful and along with that also true as separate things but faithful and true expressing a single reality, not just about his identity but about the ethic of truth revealed in and through Jesus Christ as well. All creation will see that Jesus not only communicates truly but is true. He communicates truly because his being is "Truth Itself." Emphasizing both means that when Jesus appears at the close of history, we will see that his truthfulness and being true are one and the same and, while that interconnection will be obvious the moment he returns, it is present already in the ethic of truth revealed in and through the Word of God.

Accurate Communication Can Be Ethically False

One way the truth ethic in Scripture contrasts with both the "lying is communicating contrary to neighbors" tradition and the "lying is communicating contrary to thoughts" tradition is that in two places, communicating accurately is considered untrue in the sense of being sinful. The first is where Doeg the Edomite betrays David (1 Sam 22:9–10), and the second is where Judas Iscariot betrays Jesus (Matt 26:21–25, 45–49; Mark 14:18–21, 43–45; Luke 22:3–6, 21–23, 47–48; John 17:12; 18:2–3). In both places, a person who spoke in line with what he was thinking and communicated facts accurately is nevertheless treated as having lied in the sense of speaking in a blameworthy manner. Doeg the Edomite and Judas Iscariot are both judged as communicating untruly, and yet neither of the traditional ways Christians have interpreted communicating truly can explain why.

The Augustinian "lying is communicating contrary to thoughts" tradition must conclude that Doeg said nothing violating its definition of truth, and the early Church "lying is communicating contrary to neighbors" tradition cannot explain why Doeg, being from Edom, should not have felt more neighborly toward Saul than David. The Bible also treats the betrayal of Jesus by Judas as horribly wrong (John 17:12). Yet, the Augustinian tradition again must conclude that Judas did not sin in what he said, first, because what he told the chief priests was consistent with what he was thinking and, second, because he never said anything inaccurate when greeting Jesus with a kiss. And the early Church tradition, once more, cannot explain why, in strictly human terms, Judas should not have been more loyal to leaders of his people than to an outcast criticizing them. It is just not possible to say Doeg the Edomite and Judas Iscariot communicated untruly in the sense of speaking in a morally blameworthy manner unless communicating truly is measured by something greater than their own thoughts or neighborly feelings.

Bonhoeffer deals with this by saying, "There is a truth which is of Satan. Its essence is that under the semblance of truth it denies everything that is real. It lives upon hatred . . . of the world which is created and loved by God . . . . God's truth judges created things out of love, and Satan's truth judges them out of envy and hatred."[70] And Thielicke considers it where he says,

> He who himself lives in untruth covertly changes even the objective truths which he happens to speak into untruths. What is formally true, true in form, can be falsified by what it is that actually dwells in this form. Pornographic literature, for example, may contain objectively correct statements concerning erotic and sexual processes. Yet in pornography the parcels of truth are integrated into a perverse system of values and thus become unequivocal lies.[71]

James, in the New Testament, shows that, in biblical terms, communicating truly depends more on a speaker's state of heart than on aligning words with what he thinks or can rationalize as neighborly: "If you have bitter envy and selfish ambition in your heart, don't boast and deny the truth . . . . For where there is envy and selfish ambition, there is disorder and every evil practice" (Jas 3:14–16). This says a bad heart makes anything communicated ethically false even if it is factually accurate, aligns with what you think, or is possible to consider neighborly in some way. Yet, this sort of false communicating is considered true according to the "lying is communicating contrary to thoughts" position and can even be considered true according to the "lying is communicating contrary to neighbors" position if rationalized in human terms. Doeg the Edomite and Judas Iscariot can be said to have violated the ethic of truth revealed in Scripture if, and only if, lying is defined as "communicating contrary to God." No other position is sufficient to explain why the Bible treats their communicating as untrue.

---

[70] Bonhoeffer, *Ethics*, 361.
[71] Thielicke, *Theological Ethics*, 552.

What the Ninth Commandment Does and Does Not Say

God both ordered and revealed the essential nature of ethical communication in the ninth commandment delivered to Israel at Mount Sinai. This commandment declares, "Do not give false testimony against your neighbor" (Exod 20:16; see Deut 5:20). It prohibits something specifically referred to as "false witness," does so unconditionally, and aims to protect people classified as רֵעֲךָ (rēʿakā), translated "your neighbor." Because God issued this command audibly (Exod 20:1), we must assume words used not only are accurate but express what God intended in the best possible way. That is, we must assume God knew what he was saying and had reasons for expressing himself exactly this way and not some other way.

The vocabulary of the ninth commandment refers to communicating in a binding format, such as testifying in a court of law, entering an irrevocable covenant, or swearing to something with life-or-death implications. No one questions the value of communicating truly at such times, but the narrowness of the commandment means what it directly addresses is less than most expect. Because the commandment defines the essential nature of communicating truly, because it comes audibly from the mouth of God, and because God never says anything by mistake and always has good reasons for saying what he says exactly the way he says it, we must take the narrowness of the ninth commandment seriously and not think we could do a better job saying what God meant than he did himself. Understanding this command requires asking the following questions: (1) "What exactly did God command?" (2) "Why did God put it so narrowly?" And (3) "How does the sanctity of truth revealed in this command apply in broader circumstances?"

The word עֵד (ʿēd) translated "witness" is a technical term referring to someone or something validating a claim or promise secured by God through an oath, invoking a curse (usually that God strike the oath maker dead) should the words sworn or the one swearing prove untrue.[72] Proverbs says a partner in crime "dare not testify" (be a witness) when "he is put under oath" (Prov 29:24, NIV[1984]). What fills this role usually is a person, as in the ninth commandment, but can be a symbolic object (Josh 24:27).[73] In any event, the authority guaranteeing what is

---

[72] Rooker, *The Ten Commandments*, 153 (see chap. 3, n. 80); Raymond Westbrook, ed., *A History of Ancient Near Eastern Law*, 2 vols. (Boston: Brill, 2003), 1:34.

[73] Carl Schultz, "ʿēd. Witness," in R. Laird Harris, Gleason L. Archer, Jr., and Bruce K. Waltke, eds., *Theological Wordbook of the Old Testament* (Chicago: Moody, 1980), 649.

sworn is God himself, as in "God (is) a witness (עֵד, 'ēd) between you and me" (Gen 31:50). The word שֶׁקֶר (shāqer), translated "false," also connotes communication established on oath but negatively, as in "covenant-breaking" when parties fail to live by sworn promises or treaties.[74]

Neither term says anything about what people swearing oaths think and only concerns whether they are faithful primarily to God (Gen 21:23) and secondarily to others, who in the ninth commandment are classified as "your neighbor." Who then is a "neighbor" in the ethical sense employed in the ninth commandment? Since the term specifies a particular relational category, it cannot refer to just anyone, but the term is also rather broad. In the Old Testament, a "neighbor" was a member of one's community (Lev 19:18), and Jesus later enlarged application to anyone in need whom we encounter and are able to help. In the parable of the Good Samaritan (Luke 10:29–37), Jesus showed that proximity and ability incur neighbor-helping obligation even beyond ties like family, friendship, community, race, and religion.

Thus, the ninth commandment clearly, directly, and unconditionally prohibits swearing falsely in the name of God, in formal circumstances, to the detriment of a needy person we can help. But this narrowness also means the ninth commandment does not, in the same clear, direct, unconditional way, address, or necessarily even prohibit, communicating inaccurately or in misleading ways in other circumstances. Nor does it, in the same clear, direct, unconditional way, address, or necessarily require, always being candid with everyone all the time. It does not directly address what communicating truly requires when not swearing to it in the name of God. It does not address what communicating truly requires outside formal circumstances, like testifying in courts of law or entering covenants. It does not directly address how communicating truly relates to aligning words with thoughts. And, while it addresses neighbors, it does not explain how to handle competing neighbor loyalties or how obligation to communicate truly relates to factual accuracy. So, why not?

Despite the narrowness of the ninth commandment, everyone agrees it does more than establish courtroom proceedings and undergirds obligation to communicate truly in an

---

[74] Hermann J. Austel, "שָׁקַר (shāqar) deal falsely, be false," in R. Laird Harris, Gleason L. Archer, Jr., and Bruce K. Waltke, eds., *Theological Wordbook of the Old Testament* (Chicago: Moody, 1980), 955; William L. Moran, "Review: *Psalm 89* by G. W. Ahlström," *Biblica* (1961) 42:239; Max Wagner, "Beitrage zur Aramaismenfrage im alttestament," *Supplements to Vetus Testamentum* (1967) 16:364–365; D. Winton Thomas, "Review: *Les inscriptions araméennes de sfiré* by André Dupont-Sommer," *Journal of Semitic Studies* (1960) 5:282.

overall sense as well.[75] But how does it apply beyond the words God used in the first place? Some argue the narrowness of the ninth commandment should be interpreted as prohibiting a particularly hateful example of lying in a manner ruling out any inaccurate communicating to the same unconditional terms even though that is not exactly what the text says.[76] The problem with this interpretation is presuming God did not say exactly what he meant and supposing we can do it better, when we should rather assume God knew what he was doing and said exactly what he meant in the best possible way. This better starting assumption leads to thinking that how God phrased the ninth commandment reveals the unconditional core at the center of the sanctity of truth stated the way God defines it. The Ten Commandments are more than simple rules, and each gives the unconditional core at the center of ten categories of obligation in God's ordering of ethical reality. The ninth commandment defines the sanctity of truth and, like the other commandments defining other categories of ethical obligation, the ninth commandment shows that the sanctity of truth has an unconditional core allowing no exceptions, but outside that core, applies obligation to communicate truly in conditional terms to broader circumstances beyond "false testimony against your neighbor."[77]

Trusting God to have phrased the ninth commandment in the best possible way leads to realizing unconditional obligation to communicate truly could not have been stated more broadly without adding exceptions, and this clarifies when obligation to communicate truly is absolutely "unconditional" and when it is "conditional," depending on something. If so, on what does obligation to communicate truly depend when it is conditional? According to Scripture, it depends on fearing God, as in "To fear the LORD is to hate . . . perverse speech" (Prov 8:13). The ultimate condition governing ethical communication in all cases is fearing God and, even beyond the unconditional core establishing the sanctity of truth as revealed

---

[75] Calvin, *Institutes* 2.8.47 (see chap. 4, n. 1); Hodge, *Systematic Theology*, 3:437; Murray, *Principles of Conduct*, 132; J. Douma, *The Ten Commandments,* 313 (see chap. 3, n. 80); Jones, *Biblical Christian Ethics*, 149; Rooker, *Ten Commandments*, 160; Frame, *Doctrine of the Christian Life*, 831, 834; Grudem, *Christian Ethics*, 309–310.

[76] Calvin, *Institutes*, 2.8.47; Grudem, *Christian Ethics*, 318.

[77] This agrees with where Grudem follows theological consensus in saying the ninth commandment "is not intended to prohibit *only* this specific kind of false speech" (Grudem, *Christian Ethics*, 309) but disagrees with how Grudem follows Calvin in supposing broad application of the ninth commandment continues to be unconditional beyond what it narrowly stipulates (Grudem, *Christian Ethics*, 318; Calvin, *Institutes*, 2.8.47).

by God's narrow phrasing of the ninth commandment, we always communicate truly, not in reference to our own thoughts or in reference to neighbors in and of themselves but only in reference to God himself.

The "Lying Is Communicating Contrary to God" Position

The two positions that have divided traditional Christian treatment of the truth ethic are both essentially anthropocentric—one measuring truth by consistency with neighbors and the other by consistency with thoughts. Yet, the Bible treats ethical truth as essentially theocentric, as in "I am the LORD . . . who declares what is right" (Isa 45:19b), and this theocentricity includes the meaning, nature, and relevance of truth. This has led to formulating what can be referred to as the "lying is communicating contrary to God" position. On this, we should agree with Bonhoeffer, who says, "One does not owe truthful speech to this or that individual man, but solely to God," and if the measure we use "is not . . . the God who entered into the world in Jesus Christ," then we are using "some metaethical idol." Accordingly, "If one is to speak truthfully, one's gaze and one's thought must be directed towards the way in which the real exists in God and through God and for God."[78]

What truth means and requires is not something we accurately grasp apart from God. Truth is not something by which we measure God but is something by which God measures us, and so we should not approach interpreting Scripture using the way men or dictionaries define truth but rather should approach it assuming we do not already know what truth means and need God's instruction. We must not think communicating truly requires more consistency with anyone or anything than with God himself, and we best learn what he requires by attending to the way he instructs and responds to people he assigns missions, such as saving babies (Exod 1:15–21), saving spies (Josh 2:1–7), anointing a new king (1 Sam 16:1–5), or causing bad people to make self-destructive decisions (1 Kgs 22:19–23; 2 Chr 18:20–22).

In the Bible, obligation to communicate truly and be true has two dimensions: one vertical in relation to God and one horizontal in relation to others. Communicating truly and being true involves both God and others and, while obligation to communicate truly and be true is always "unconditional" in relation to God, it is never more than "conditional" in

---

[78] Bonhoeffer, *Ethics*, 359–60.

relation to others, always depending on how it affects fidelity to God. The Bible refers to this condition as "the fear of God," and a diagram of the dimensions structuring the truth ethic in biblical terms is as follows:

Dimensions of the Truth Norm

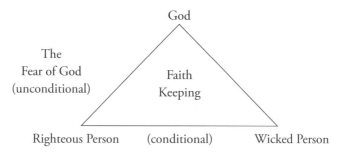

Scripture tells us that "to fear the LORD is to hate . . . perverse speech" (Prov 8:13) and then also tells us the Hebrew midwives and Rahab communicated as they did because they "feared" God (Exod 1:17; 1:21; Josh 2:9; 2:11). Because of this and because Scripture regards the act by which Rahab protected the spies as a good example of faith pleasing God (Heb 11:31), we should stop treating these accounts as "hard" and should instead accept them as places where God explains how the way he defines communicating truly and being true differs from what we expect. God uses these accounts to show how communicating must be unconditionally true and faithful to himself and needs be no more than conditionally true and faithful to anyone or anything else. We must come to accept that the midwives and Rahab did not violate but rather demonstrated communicating truly the way God defines it.

The sanctity of truth is ultimately personal and relational, not abstract and impersonal. "Ultimate Truth" is a person (John 14:6), not a concept, principle, or rule standing off by itself over, against, or behind God. All truly true truth comes from, relates to, and serves God (Rom 11:36), and obligation to communicate truly and be true reduces to fidelity to God himself and nothing else. Communicating truly primarily concerns fidelity to he who is "Truth Itself," and how it relates to neighbors, thoughts, or facts is never more than secondary. Keeping faith with neighbors, our own thoughts, and facts make relatively good sense but are not absolutes in their own right. What they mean is subordinate to God, and we know how they apply from what the Word of God says—whether or not it agrees with what we think makes the most sense. He "declares what is right" (Isa 45:19b), and fearing him is the key to avoiding "perverse speech" (Prov 8:13).

Jesus declares he is himself "the way, *the truth*, and the life" (John 14:6, my emphasis) and John describes him as "full of grace and *truth*" (John 1:14, my emphasis). Jesus is not simply someone who, compared to some abstract principle or human definition of truth, is found to measure up. Rather, as God himself, Jesus is the source, measure, and end of all that is truly true. He is not just a version of, or an example of, or an instance of truth conceived in terms other than himself, but rather is "Truth Itself." Pilate asked, "What is truth?" (John 18:38) after Jesus claimed, "Everyone who is of the truth listens to my voice" (John 18:37b). Pilate's question showed he understood Jesus was saying something momentous. Jesus was addressing more than something spiritual, private, and merely personal and was saying truth, all truth, all communicating truly and being true, all accuracy and meaning, all genuinely reliable existence, behavior, understanding, and passing information one to another—whether ethical, theological, or scientific—is of and through himself in such a way that conceiving it any other way is false, perverted, and ultimately deceptive.

Jesus is that without which nothing is true, and the Bible identifies anything less with Satan, calling him not just a liar, or just a father of lies, but "*the* father of lies" (John 8:44, my emphasis). Satan is the ultimate source of all sinful communication, and what makes communicating sinful (ethically wrong) is not just a question of loyalty to neighbors in and of themselves, nor is it a question of inconsistency between what a person says and thinks. Rather it is a question of pleasing the Devil and elevating something over God, and Jesus in particular, the way Satan does. Ethics is, at heart, a matter of worship, and there are just two options. We can worship God or some guise of the Devil, and it is either one or the other with no middle ground: "Whoever wants to be the friend of the world becomes the enemy of God" (Jas 4:4b). Our communicating can be in step with God or with the Devil, and conceiving truth other ways skews or ignores the essential ethical question at the heart of all truly true truth: "True by what measure?" or "True to whom?" You cannot be true to the Devil and to Christ at the same time, and you cannot communicate truly with both, in reference to both, or with the emissaries of both at the same time. Fidelity to ultimate truth requires infidelity to ultimate falsehood. As revealed in Scripture, communicating truly comes from Christ (1 Pet 3:15–16) and communicating untruly comes from hell (Jas 3:6).

Affirming the "lying is communicating contrary to God" position does not mean we need to discard the traditional positions altogether. Only the "lying is communicating contrary to God" position is sufficient to capture all the truth ethic revealed in Scripture means and requires, but there is room to think the other positions add value, so long as they support and do not conflict with the primary position. That is, we can treat the traditional principles as having subordinate roles pointing toward what the ultimate principle most often requires. Niebuhr suggested equality and liberty serve as "regulating" principles pointing toward what Christian love most often requires in social interactions,[79] and we can similarly employ protecting neighbors and keeping words consistent with what we have in mind as "regulative" principles pointing toward what the truth ethic revealed in Scripture most often requires in relation to God.

As regulative principles, the two traditional ways of interpreting the truth ethic aim toward Christ just as all Old Testament regulations aim toward him (Rom 10:4). They serve but do not restrict what pleasing Christ requires because sometimes what pleasing Christ requires transcends what the regulative principles suggest when interpreted apart from Christ. Christ controls the degree to which the regulative principles apply, not the other way around. Pleasing Christ is the only absolute governing ethical truth, and the regulative principles are forever subordinate and relative to what pleasing him requires. They point toward what communicating truly and being true usually, but do not always, require. And, where the Word of God says something different, we trust the Word of God. We follow the "primary" principle, not the regulative principles.

In closing, it is worth noting this "lying is communicating contrary to God" position affirms something Allen Verhey observes by saying, "God is Truth, but truth is not a second god."[80] This is the same as saying, while God defines truth, truth does not define God. There is a connection, but it is not reciprocal. It is not reversible. What we know of truth says something of God but does not define him. It does not limit him and at best only reflects him.

---

[79] Reinhold Niebuhr, *Pious and Secular America* (New York: Scribner's, 1958), 66; Niebuhr, *The Nature and Destiny of Man*, 2.254 (see chap. 6, n. 48) ; Reinhold Niebuhr, "Christian Faith and Natural Law," *Theology* (February 1940): 89; and Niebuhr, *Love and Justice*, ed. D. B. Robertson (Gloucester, MA: Peter Smith, 1976), 50.

[80] Verhey, "Is Lying Always Wrong?", 68.

And, to know truth truly we must focus on God rather than on what we imagine based on something else. What truth means depends on God, not the other way around, and is rather like how a piece of art testifies to the ability of an artist, but an artist does not testify to the ability of a piece of art.

Conclusion

From what we have learned, how should we evaluate the different approaches to truth and lying taken by members of the ten Boom family? Nollie was so candid she betrayed a Jewish friend to Nazi officers rather than saying anything factually false. Cocky was not as forthcoming and instead offered a part truth as if it was the whole truth so as to deceive enemy soldiers looking for her brothers. And Corrie flatly denied hiding Jews to protect Jews she was hiding. Which of them communicated most truly? Which of them best understood the truth ethic revealed in Scripture? Which of them was most true and faithful to Christ? All did the best they could. But that does not mean anything goes because communicating truly is something fixed regardless of intentions. While crediting all of them with desiring to glorify God and meaning to do the right thing, this is how I think we should evaluate their different approaches.

Nollie meant well but did the wrong thing. She communicated truly, as most define it, but not the way God does. Yet, God made up for her well-meant error by saving her friend by others who disobeyed civil laws to break her out of prison. Cocky equivocated, which is using words with hidden meanings in order to deceive. Some Christians think her equivocating was justifiable because what she said was true "in a sense." But most ethicists consider this wrong, or at least undesirable, because it deceives others knowingly and on purpose and because it uses words in ways that are not true as others comprehend them. I think what Cocky did was devious and tricky but not wrong in that circumstance because it parallels God telling Samuel to deceive bad people with a cover story (1 Sam 16:1–5). Yet, I also think she could more easily have denied knowing where her brothers were, and it is hard to make her an example because most people are not as clever at hiding the meaning of words on the fly the way she did. I also would caution that it is dangerous to employ because equivocation is sinful if used in any situation other than one in which God requires it. Thus, in the end, Corrie was the one I think set the best example of communicating truly the way God defines it. She spoke contrary to known facts not just to save people but to fulfill a divine mission. And she did so not because she especially liked the people she saved in and of themselves, nor because she claimed to make up new rules, but only because she sought to please Christ. She communicated truly and was true as God defines it even though it is not what most think. She did what the Hebrew midwives and Rahab did (Exod 1:15–21; Josh 2:1–7), who were commended as moral heroes.

This study of the truth ethic revealed in and by the Word of God demonstrates how God's ordering of ethical reality is at once highly complex and united by deep simplicity centered on God himself. It demonstrates, as well, the paradoxical nature of revealed ethics. For the biblically revealed ethic of truth—of communicating truly and being true—while consistent, absolute, universal, and unvarying, nevertheless runs contrary to human expectations. It is not self-contradictory but bears marks of coming from a mind transcending our own. It is not what most think because it is more complex than most expect, deeper than most expect, and measured by a standard higher than most expect. It is, nevertheless, easy enough for anyone trusting God to grasp, and its edges are plain enough to convict the worst sinners as knowing better and having no excuse. It is also sufficient to guide what we say and do in all situations arising in a fallen fallible world from communicating in everyday affairs to communicating under persecution.

The next four chapters will continue introducing applied Christian ethics. But, rather than concentrating on a single issue, the next four chapters will introduce applied issues grouped by similarities. The next chapter will cover applied issues mainly to do with personal duties and discipline, the chapter after that will cover sexual issues that are both social and personal, and the last chapters will cover applied issues to do with social dynamics—one focusing on issues to do with governing and one focusing on issues involving social dynamics other than governing.

CHAPTER 9

ISSUES IN PERSONAL LIFE

ABORTION; BIRTH CONTROL; ASSISTED REPRODUCTION; EUTHANASIA; BIOMEDICAL ETHICS; GAMBLING; ALCOHOL, TOBACCO & DRUG ABUSE

This is the second of five chapters introducing readers to applied Christian ethics as an academic subcategory of the larger field of Christian ethics. Applied Christian ethics deals with a range of practical issues raised by questions concerning the way what Christians know from moral revelation, established doctrine, and teaching through history informs engaging ethical challenges that emerge in everyday life. Whereas the last chapter dealt with a single applied issue at length, the remaining chapters are organized to address groups of associated issues and thus cover each in less depth together. Books can and have been written on each issue, so readers need to realize we are now introducing groupings of issues together and, thus, will cover specific issues more briefly than in the previous chapter. There are more applied issues than can be mentioned here, so the listing in this book is not exhaustive. And, for those that are, readers should not expect to find in these chapters everything needed to engage them successfully. What we have will serve that purpose. But to be best prepared, readers should supplement what these chapters offer with more reading and research. In other words, these chapters provide a start to understanding the issues covered but are not meant to finalize readiness for effective ethical witness.

The present chapter covers issues associated with "personal" as opposed to "social" ethics. There is a sense in which all ethical issues are personal since they always involve people, and subjecting objects and animals to ethical analysis makes no sense. Where "personal ethics" is distinguished from "social ethics," the term refers to issues affecting individuals as opposed to those involving the way people act in groups or interact with groups. This chapter introduces issues in personal ethics in the sense of dealing with moral matters that concern individual goods more than the common good and that affect individual responsibility, discipline, and character more directly than general welfare, social stability, and civil justice.[1]

Abortion

The number of induced abortions performed in the United States has risen to astounding levels, and the ethics of abortion is one of the most controversial issues of our day. The number of American lives lost in all wars is about 1,196,500.[2] But the number of American lives lost to abortion between 1973, when it was legalized beyond saving a mother's life, and 2018 is more than 60 million. So, more than fifty times as many American lives have been lost to unnecessary abortions than to wars, and this astounding disproportion has arisen all in the space of forty-six years (or a single lifetime). The holocaust in Nazi Germany claimed about six million innocent Jewish lives, but the number of innocent lives lost to abortion in the United States is ten times greater. The transatlantic slave trade cost about 12 million African lives. But between 1973 and 2017, more than 19 million African

---

[1] It is true that individual behaviors can affect social interactions and individual goods affect the common good if compounded. But the distinction made here is clear despite this practical overlap.

[2] Data comes from Megan Crigger and Laura Santhanam, "How many Americans have died in U.S. wars?," *PBS News Hour*, May 24, 2015, updated May 27, 2019, www.pbs.org/newshour/nation /many-americans-died-u-s-wars.

Americans were killed in the womb,[3] which means the number of African American lives lost to abortion is now 50 percent more than were lost in the slave trade. This is a major ethical issue that matters, not only to families, not only to friends and neighbors, and not only to the nation, but to God.

Abortion refers to stopping something that has started, and, applied to pregnancy, it refers to ending lives that have started and are not just planned or anticipated. The term is broad since it covers all the ways lives can end before birth, and the ethics of abortion is much affected by what causes them to occur. We need first to distinguish "spontaneous" from "induced" abortions. Spontaneous abortions are those that occur naturally with no outside intervention, and these include missed implants and miscarriages. Missed implants are when life is conceived but fails to implant in the uterus and passes out of the mother's body. Miscarriages are when a baby starts growing in the womb and then dies of natural causes or is rejected by the mother's body too early to survive. The number of spontaneous abortions is hard to determine, but one study indicates about 70 to 75 percent of all conceptions either fail to implant or miscarry.[4] When this happens, it is tragic but not immoral. Someone dies, and it is appropriate to grieve and hold funeral services. But there is nothing immoral about spontaneous abortions because no one does anything wrong.

Ethical criticism of abortion all concerns those that are "induced," which means someone chooses and then does something to kill a baby.[5] The numbers mentioned at the start of this section are only for induced abortions and do not include spontaneous abortions. Induced abortions are classified in three ways: "therapeutic," "eugenic," and "elective." These all are controversial, but differences between them can affect ethical analysis.

Therapeutic abortions are those performed to save the life or health of a mother. Some pregnancies threaten a mother's life. A conceived life sometimes attaches inside the fallopian tube before getting to the uterus and, unless it is aborted, the baby and mother both will die. Some mothers have hearts so weak that carrying a baby to term will kill them. And, if a

---

[3] Data comes from "Black Abortions by the Numbers," Right to Life of Michigan, https://rtl.org /outreach/.

[4] Allen J. Wilcox, et al., "Incidence of Early Loss of Pregnancy," *New England Journal of Medicine*, 319/4 (July 28, 1988): 189–94.

[5] Those justifying induced abortions sometimes deny it kills babies. But life in the womb is a baby from conception, so induced abortions do indeed kill babies.

pregnant mother develops cancer, treating her cancer will kill the baby and carrying the baby to term means not saving the mother by treating her cancer soon enough.

These are life-for-life situations in which saving a mother requires killing her baby and doing nothing means either losing two lives instead of one (in the case of ectopic pregnancy or a mother's weak heart) or choosing to let a mother die when she could be saved (in the case of maternal cancer). These situations involve tragic moral choices. Saving two lives is not possible. At best, one can be saved, and the only question is whom to save at the expense of the other. It is not wrong to abort life to save life, and no one is obligated to sacrifice his or her life for others. If a mother chooses to give her life for her baby, it is supererogatory and worth praising, but she cannot be blamed for choosing to live at the expense of her child.

But therapeutic abortions include more than those needed to save mothers from dying. They also include those induced just for health reasons, and the ethics involved is very different. These abortions take place where a mother's life is not at risk. Carrying a baby to term will not kill her, and the only concern is that it might affect her physical, emotional, psychological, or relational health.[6] Scripture does not allow this sort of abortion because, even though maternal health is important, it is not more important than the sanctity of human life.

Eugenic abortions are those performed to avoid having a handicapped child. Perhaps a child is deformed, has Down's syndrome, or has sickle cell anemia. Or perhaps no one knows, and those involved just fear something could be wrong. These are pregnancies that will continue to term unless stopped. So, to avoid having a handicapped child or to reduce chances of having one, doctors will advise parents to abort the child they have on the way and try again. Handicapped children are not easy to raise, and the prospect of one is hard to take. But this does not justify killing them. There is more to it, but one problem with aborting for eugenic reasons is it treats children like merchandise ordered from Amazon rather than gifts of God, which conflicts with the sanctity of human life.

Elective abortions are a third sort of induced abortion. These are abortions performed even though a mother's life or health are not at risk and there is nothing wrong with the baby. These simply are "pro-choice" abortions, and any reason will do. Perhaps a mother does not

---

[6] In *Doe v. Bolton*, 410 U.S. 179 (1973), the US Supreme Court ruled that for purposes of law, abortion for a mother's "health" includes factors that are "physical, emotional, psychological, (or) familial."

feel ready to start a family, does not think she can afford another child, wants a boy instead of a girl, or just does not want pregnancy to interfere with something else, so she chooses to abort the child in her womb. The term "pro-choice" is a euphemism shifting attention from what really is at stake to something else. No one disagrees with moral freedom to choose when to conceive children or not, and the only real disagreement is about when that freedom is over because a choice is made. Evangelicals are "pro-choice" up until conception and only criticize extending freedom to choose beyond that. In the Bible, terminating human life on purpose is justified only when people forfeit moral title to their lives by committing capital offenses or killing or threatening to kill others without justification or authority.

Understanding the ethics of abortion requires interpreting what the Word of God says about the sanctity of human life, and the most important passage on what it means is Genesis 1:27, where we are told, "God created man in his own image; he created him in the image of God; he created them male and female." This says the ethical value of human life does not come from humanity but God. It is a matter of reflecting or expressing something beyond ourselves, which makes it something we cannot generate or loose, do not share with animals, do not control, do not own, and all bear the same regardless of gender, age, intelligence, health, wealth, or social status. It is not distributed more to some than others, and so what is wrong with violating the sanctity of human life is also the same for all unrelated to different qualities of life. Nevertheless, the ethical value of human life is neither self-justifying nor ultimate. It is high but is not the highest thing there is because God is higher, and the ethical value of human life is "derived," meaning it comes from a source greater than itself.

In Genesis 9:5–6, we are told what maintaining the sanctity of human life requires, which is that anyone who kills another without warrant must be treated as forfeiting title to his or her own life. God thinks the sanctity of human life cannot be maintained without requiring murderers to pay a price equal to the wrong they do, and nothing short of losing their own lives is equal to the lives wrongly taken from their victims. Exodus 20:13 and Deuteronomy 5:17 show that God mandates honoring the sanctity of human life and prohibits violations. The obligation incurred is not optional because God commands it. The command in these passages was issued to Israel but specifies something universal and timeless. The obligation involved began at creation and only was reaffirmed at Sinai. Exodus 21:22–25 and Psalm 139 give insight on how to assess the sanctity of life at the margins of life by clarifying who is covered and to what degree.[7] These passages reinforce how the ethical value of human life is the same for everyone regardless of status or state. Qualities of life change over time, but the ethical value of human life stays constant whether we are just conceived or fully grown, sick or healthy, conscious or unconscious, wealthy or poor, male or female, skilled or unskilled. The sanctity of human life has no scale for decreasing obligation to respect the weak and least able among us.

Ezekiel 13:19 guards against misinterpreting the sanctity of human life because we are told it is just as wrong to "spare those who should not live" as to "put those to death who should not die." The sanctity of human life is not interpreted properly unless we understand it requires executing those forfeiting their right to life just as much as it requires guarding the lives of those who do not. Finally, in Matthew 5:21–22, Jesus teaches that the sanctity of human life even prohibits maligning others. Words do not harm physically but can diminish respect for life. Murder violates the sanctity of human life, and so does putting others down, perhaps not as badly, but it matters. Thus, Jesus shows that the sanctity of human life prohibits anything not in line with valuing life as a gift of God, even if only in speaking.

Applying what Scripture says about the sanctity of life makes sense to Christians, but what about others? The value of human life matters to God whether people realize it or not, and the sacredness of life affects the ethics of abortion whether people are Christian or not. So, if the sanctity of human life is universal and not just for Christians, is there a way to apply it without violating the separation of church and state? Is there a way to translate the ethic in secular terms that will not get dismissed as narrowly theological and thus irrelevant to public policy? This most often is done by affirming a common sense of human dignity obligating everyone to respect the personhood of everyone else.

All agree that we should guard the lives of innocent persons and that murdering persons is terribly wrong. So it seems reasonable to put the sanctity of life in secular terms by arguing abortions are wrong because murdering innocent people violates human dignity. But, while this is true, using it to argue the pro-life position hardly ever works in secular terms because

---

[7] For a detailed discussion on interpreting the Exodus passage, see H. Wayne House, "Miscarriage or Premature Birth: Additional Thoughts on Exodus 21:22–25," *Westminster Theological Journal* 41/1 (1978):108–23. And for more on both passages, see Frame, *Doctrine of the Christian Life,* 718–22 (see chap. 1, n. 69).

the opposing sides do not agree on what "personhood" means. Most often what brings debating abortion in secular terms to a standstill is not disagreement over murder but disagreement over whether abortions kill persons or not. If they do, then abortions are wrong because murder is wrong. But, if not, then nothing is wrong with inducing them and the only problem is trying to stop them.

Those arguing the pro-life position take an "essential view" of personhood, meaning they believe it is something essential to human existence. An essential feature is one without which a thing cannot exist. Thus, it is not marginal or optional, does not develop, and never grows or diminishes. It is possible for acorns to exist without becoming oak trees, but acorns cannot exist without being material because there are no immaterial acorns. Similarly, the essential view of personhood says every human life is a person because human life is not possible without being one. As such, all human lives are persons from conception, and killing them is the same as killing adults.

Those arguing the pro-choice position take a "developmental view" of personhood, meaning they believe it is something that grows and may diminish depending on the degree to which human lives manifest nonessential functional criteria, such as consciousness, ability to distinguish self from non-self, rationality, mobility, ability to sense pain and pleasure, or ability to communicate.[8] As such, even though many humanly conceived lives evolve into persons (achieve personhood), some never do, some fail to evolve fully, and some lose personhood after reaching it as criteria making them persons atrophy. This treats human lives becoming persons like acorns becoming oak trees. No acorn is an oak tree until it grows up. Some eventually grow into fully developed oak trees. But some acorns never grow at all, and others become plants that never grow past the seedling stage. Similarly, the developmental view of personhood claims that human lives do not start as persons and only evolve into persons as they grow up. By such thinking, human lives are not always persons, exist without being persons for a time after conception, and may not even start evolving into persons until after

---

[8] Although proponents of this view think various functional criteria must be met to be a person, there is no standard list for what these criteria should be. Some propose appointing a committee of experts for getting this done. But then we would want to know what kind of expertise we should think qualifies anyone to render such decisions. And we would want to know, as well, who can be trusted with power as vast as deciding the ethical value of everyone else in the world.

they are born. Based on this, it is argued that abortions do not kill persons and there can be nothing wrong with inducing them.

What makes defending the sanctity of human life using personhood arguments in secular terms difficult is that it is terribly hard to change how a secular person views personhood in order to change how he thinks about abortion. Most cling to developmental thinking just because they know it justifies the outcome they strongly prefer, and because of that, using personhood arguments in public policy situations usually ends with no one changing his or her mind. But there is a more effective way to advance the sanctity of human life in secular terms, and that is by approaching it as God does in the Bible without mentioning personhood at all.

Ironically, defending the pro-life position on abortion this way is both more biblical and more persuasive in secular terms. Although it is true that we are persons from conception, there is a better chance of changing how secular people see the ethics of abortion if we instead focus on general obligation to protect innocent human life. First we will look at what makes this approach more biblical and then we will explain what makes it a more effective way to advance the pro-life position in secular arenas outside the Christian community.

The concept of personhood arose during the Trinitarian debates of the fourth and fifth centuries, when theologians needed a way to indicate what makes God three without denying monotheism.[9] To reference this new concept, theologians took the Greek word πρόσωπον (prosōpon), meaning face, countenance, or outward manifestation, and extended it to indicate a living entity relating to God.[10] Since this conception arose well after God already had revealed in his Word all we need to know about the sanctity of human life, it means God conveyed the

---

[9] "Person," Wikipedia the Free Encyclopedia, last modified October 26, 2021, https://en.wikipedia .org/wiki/Person; Owen Barfield, *History in English Words*, 2nd ed. (Great Barrington, MA: Lindisfarne, 2002), 59–60; Jean D. Zizioulas, *Being as Communion* (Crestwood, NY: St Vladimir's, 1985), 27. For further reading, see Cornelia J. de Vogel, "The Concept of Personality in Greek and Christian Thought," in *Studies in Philosophy and the History of Philosophy*, vol. 2, ed. John K. Ryan (Washington, DC: Catholic University of America, 1963): 20–60; and M. William Ury, "The Concept of Person," in *Trinitarian Personhood: Investigating the Implications of a Relational Definition"* (Eugene, OR: Wipf & Stock, 2002), 79–101.

[10] The concept was translated into Latin as *persōna*, which before that just meant a mask or role in a play, and that Latin translation then became the English word "person." The point is, our notion of personhood was unknown before it arose out of the Trinitarian debates, and imprecision before that can be seen where Paul struggles to express a similar idea in 2 Corinthians 4:6—even using πρόσωπον (prosōpon)—centuries before the conception we know now arose.

ethic some other way and must have considered it more effective. That other way was to focus on general obligation to protect innocent human life without mentioning personhood at all.

In Scripture, the ethical wrong or guilt of violating the sanctity of human life is put in terms of "shedding innocent blood." God says, "Do not kill the innocent and the just, because I will not justify the guilty" (Exod 23:7). Cities of refuge are established so "innocent blood will not be shed" (Deut 19:10). Murderers must be executed to purge the land from "the guilt of shedding innocent blood" (Deut 19:13). There is a curse on "anyone who takes a bribe to shed innocent blood" (Deut 27:25, ESV).[11] David asks Saul, "Why would you sin against innocent blood by killing David for no reason?" (1 Sam 19:5). A wicked man "kills the innocent" (Ps 10:8). God hates "hands that shed innocent blood" (Prov 6:17) and judges those who rush "to shed innocent blood" (Isa 59:7). Residents of Jerusalem are condemned for filling the city "with the blood of the innocent" (Jer 19:4). And God warns King Zedekiah of Judah not to "shed innocent blood" (Jer 22:3). The thing here to see is how the Bible conveys the sanctity-of-human-life ethic in terms of general obligation to protect all human life apart from guilt or innocence. It starts with honoring the value of life in everyone alive, and the only exception is where one forfeits the title one has to the gift of life.

But, while focusing on general obligation to protect innocent human life is more biblical than focusing on obligation to maintain the meaning of personhood, it is also a more effective strategy for advancing the pro-life position on abortion in secular terms. And that is because it is very hard for anyone running for office to openly oppose the idea that human government should protect innocent human lives. Without quoting Bible verses or discussing faith convictions, it is possible simply to affirm that the most important principle distinguishing civilized from uncivilized societies is whether they believe those responsible for governing others must protect innocent human life. Societies affirming this become civilized no matter how

---

[11] The ASV and NIV translate the wrong done in this verse as killing "an innocent person" (ASV) rather than shedding "innocent blood." But translating the verse this way reads into it a conception not understood at that time. The Hebrew is נֶפֶשׁ (*nepeš*), which indicates a living human, or soul, or inner being. It does not include animals but includes any human life regardless of condition. So the word is in a way close to what the essentialist view of personhood indicates today. Besides anachronism, there is another problem with using *person* for translating this verse, which is that competing views of personhood leave the English meaning ambiguous in ways not in the text. Thus, it is best I think to avoid "person" for translating this verse.

primitive they are to begin with, and societies that cease to affirm this start losing civilized status no matter how advanced they are to begin with.

Shifting strategy for promoting the pro-life position in public policy away from personhood arguments and toward general obligation to protect innocent human life has power to redirect the abortion debate in favor of life over death. Whereas using personhood arguments in secular terms ends with stalemates that never change minds, using general obligation to protect innocent human life is able to change minds and votes. No one can deny that what humans conceive is alive (not dead), is human (like conceives like), is actual (not just potential), is distinct (not the mother or father), is unique (not a copy), and is innocent (not guilty of anything). These are scientific facts not open to dispute. By definition, obligation to protect innocent human life begins when human life begins. And, because it is a matter of existence, not development, the obligation applies to all human lives regardless of condition, leaving no room to permit induced abortions for any reason other than saving a mother's life. Candidates running for office will feel pressured to agree, and candidates denying obligation to protect innocent human life are not likely to be elected. Debating abortion ethics this way is more effective outside the Christian community because it has power to refocus moral opinion that personhood arguments do not.

Recommended further reading on the issue of abortion includes Francis J. Beckwith, *Politically Correct Death: Answering the Arguments for Abortion Rights* (Grand Rapids: Baker, 1993); Megan Best, *Fearfully and Wonderfully Made* (Kingsford, AU: Matthias, 2012); Richard L. Ganz and C. Everett Koop, eds., *Thou Shalt Not Kill: The Christian Case against Abortion* (New Rochelle, NY: Arlington House, 1978); Robert P. George and Christopher Tollefsen, *Embryo: A Defense of Human Life* (New York: Doubleday, 2008); and Scott Klusendorf, *The Case for Life: Equipping Christians to Engage the Culture* (Wheaton, IL: Crossway, 2009).

Birth Control

Birth control is managing the number and spacing of children and refers to methods used either to prevent or terminate pregnancy. This means the ethics of birth control is tied closely to the sanctity of life, sex, and marriage. For Christians, the issue only concerns sex in marriage. People in extramarital affairs wish to control pregnancy as well, and immoral types of birth control are wrong no matter who uses them. But that is not in view here because methods properly married couples may use are not moral for others to use. When assessing the ethics of birth control, the main questions are, "May properly married couples try to control getting pregnant?" and then, "If so, what methods may they use?"

Within Christianity, most opposition to birth control comes from the Catholic Church, but some Protestants oppose it as well.[12] Catholic opposition comes from valuing how nature links sex to having children and deciding it is evil to disconnect them.[13] But such thinking comes from natural law philosophy rather than from the Bible and distorts Christian ethics by elevating speculation over revelation, deriving obligation from observation (the naturalistic fallacy), and universalizing something impossible to universalize (thinking it must be wrong to interfere with any natural process). As Frame observes, "It also is natural for hair to grow indefinitely . . . . But that doesn't prove hair should never be cut."[14]

Among Protestants, the Quiver Full movement also opposes birth control but for biblical reasons.[15] Proponents argue that controlling or limiting conception conflicts with treating children as blessings of God (Deut 7:13–14; Ps 113:9; 127:3), ignores God's command to procreate (Gen 1:28; 9:1, 7), and lacks faith in God's power to control fertility (Gen 20:17–18; 21:1–2; 29:31; 30:17, 22; Exod 23:26; Deut 7:14; 1 Sam 1:5; Ps 113:9; 127:3; Isa 8:18; Rom 4:19–20). Relying on Scripture is better than relying on philosophy. But just using Scripture

---

[12] For a good treatment on how Catholic tradition opposes birth control, see Davis, *Evangelical Ethics*, 44–49 (see chap. 1, n. 55). For a good treatment on how some Protestants oppose birth control, see Grudem, *Christian Ethics*, 754–58 (see chap. 1, n. 67).

[13] For centuries, the Roman Catholic Church held to the claim made by Clement of Alexandria (150–215) that sex in marriage is not allowed "other than to procreate children" because separating sex from procreation "does injury to nature" (*Pedagogus* 2.10.95.3). But starting with *Casti connubii* in 1930, the Vatican has allowed sex in marriage to avoid procreation using the rhythm method because this is judged to be "natural." This, however, shifted what "natural" means from "according to a thing's inherent purpose" to nothing more than "not artificial" or "not fabricated." The meaning is not the same, and the natural law ethics involved is not the same.

[14] Frame, *Doctrine of the Christian Life,* 783.

[15] These are Evangelical Protestants who "eschew even behavioral forms of birth control and seek large numbers of biological offspring to build the kingdom of God." Darlene Fozard Weaver, "Birth Control," *Dictionary of Scripture and Ethics*, ed. Joel B. Green (Grand Rapids: Baker, 2011), 102. Proponents include Mary Pride, *The Way Home* (Westchester, IL: Crossway, 1985); Samuel Owen, *Letting God Plan Your Family* (Wheaton, IL: Crossway, 1990); Sam Torode and Bethany Torode, *Open Embrace: A Protestant Couple Rethinks Contraception* (Grand Rapids: Eerdmans, 2002).

is not the same as interpreting it correctly, and on this issue, I dispute how the Quiver Full movement interprets Scripture along with Catholic reliance on natural law philosophy.

Christians opposing birth control, whether Catholic or Protestant, tend to think sex in marriage has only one purpose, when Scripture says it has many purposes that include procreation (Gen 1:28; 9:1, 7), companionship (Gen 2:18), relational union (Gen 2:24; Mal 2:15; Matt 19:4–6), enjoyment (Song 1:2; Eccl 9:9), godly offspring (Mal 2:15), and guarding against temptation (1 Cor 7:5; 1 Thess 4:3–5). Children are indeed blessings of God (Gen 1:28; Ps 127:5). But this truth does not satisfy everything sex in marriage is for and does not stand alone, and the Bible nowhere says it must be in view every time couples get intimate. Setting one purpose off by itself when the Bible mentions several hinders proper understanding of what the Bible teaches about how sex, marriage, and having children interconnect.

Managing reproduction to please God requires understanding how different divine mandates go together. There is a procreation mandate to be fruitful and multiply (Gen 1:28). But other important mandates include a dominion mandate requiring us to learn about and control natural processes (Gen 1:26), a stewardship mandate requiring us to manage well everything God entrusts to our care (Gen 1:28; 2:15), and a missional mandate requiring us to evangelize the world (Matt 28:19–20). God has arranged these different mandates to harmonize, with no single mandate predominating or preempting the rest. So the procreation mandate cannot obligate couples to have as many children as possible because taking it that way conflicts with God's equally important commands to control natural processes and be good stewards of what he places in our care. Severing the procreation mandate from the others even interferes with evangelizing the world because it is harder to send large families on missionary endeavors than smaller ones.

It is important, also, to understand that the procreation mandate applies to us corporately, not individually. God did not tell Adam and Eve to "fill the earth" (Gen 1:28) all by themselves but rather expected their descendants to multiply and spread out over future generations. The procreation mandate is for the human race as a whole and never obligated couples to seek children every time they have sex. So, because married couples may have sex for other biblical purposes besides having children, and because the procreation mandate applies corporately not individually, there is nothing wrong with married couples using contraceptives to manage the number and spacing of children while continuing intimate relations. God even calls some to avoid marriage, sex, and children altogether (Matt 19:12; 1 Cor 7:26–35, 38, 40), which shows that general duty to reproduce does not apply to everyone the same all the time. And, if divine calling exempts some from general duty to procreate altogether, it stands to reason that divine calling grants exceptions to the same general duty when it comes to sex in marriage as well.

Just because couples are allowed to manage human reproduction does not mean they may avoid pregnancy for any reason they like. Some motives are worthy, and others are not. It is wrong to use contraceptives for selfish reasons like pursuing a lavish lifestyle, keeping a youthful figure, or maximizing free time. But there is nothing wrong with postponing children to finish education, spacing children to enhance marital relations, or limiting the number of children to better parent those one has already. Couples trying to avoid pregnancy must accept any child God gives them. Pregnancies may be unplanned by human parents, but no child is unplanned by God.

Furthermore, just because couples are allowed to manage reproduction, and have good reasons for it, does not mean they may use any method whatever. Some methods are permissible, and others are not. Birth control methods are classified as "abortifacients," "continents" (methods practicing continence), and "contraceptives." Abortifacients prevent conceived life from implanting and include intrauterine devices (IUDs), mifepristone or RU-486 (the abortion pill marketed as Mifeprex), levonorgestral or LNG (the morning after pill marketed as Plan B), and ulipristal acetate (the morning after pill marketed as Ella). Continents keep sperm out of a woman's body when she is fertile and include *coitus interruptus* (withdrawing before ejaculation), the rhythm method (timing past menstrual cycles), the basal temperature method (monitoring changes in body temperature), the sympto-thermal method (monitoring changes in vaginal mucus as well as body temperature), and permanent methods like vasectomy (for men). Contraceptives prevent sperm already in a woman's body from reaching an egg, and these include temporary methods like condoms, sponges, spermicides, diaphragms, cervical caps, and hormonal controls preventing ovulation, as well as permanent methods like tubal ligation (for women).

When assessing methods of birth control, the main thing distinguishing permissible from impermissible methods—aside from limiting sex to marriage (Heb 13:4), proper motivation (Phil 2:3), responsible practice (1 Cor 7:3), and loving communication (Col 3:14)—is how they relate to the sanctity of human life. Methods that work by blocking conception are permitted, and methods that work by killing after conception are not because they "put those to death who should not die" (Ezek 13:19).

The biggest question dividing Evangelicals on the ethics of birth control concerns whether or not it is permissible to use methods putting life at risk if they fail to work contraceptively. All contraceptive methods risk failing. Whereas some just risk unplanned pregnancy, others like "the pill" risk aborting life if they fail to prevent conception. Birth control pills have three effects. The first suppresses ovulation, which is contraceptive. The second thickens the mucous plug at the mouth of the womb, which hinders sperm from entering the womb and is contraceptive at well. The third hardens the lining of the womb, making it less receptive (though not entirely hostile) to implantation if the contraceptive effects do not work and life is conceived unexpectedly. The risk involved is very low and occurs only if the mucous barrier fails, ovulation suppression fails, sperm get into the right fallopian tube at the moment an unexpected egg presents, and fertilization takes place. But, unlike the first and second effects, this third much less likely effect is abortifacient. So, does risking this unlikely tertiary effect mean we have to classify the pill as abortifacient rather than contraceptive and make it immoral ever to use?

To be fair, the threat using the pill poses to innocent human life never materializes unless the two far more likely contraceptive effects both fail to work and life is conceived despite them. But the risk involved, however unlikely and unintentional, is nevertheless real and known just as we know there is a real though very unlikely unintended risk of killing another person every time we drive a car. In fact, the risk to life involved is about the same in both cases.[16] The risk is very unlikely but not zero. It is not intended but is known about, and it is

---

[16] To put things in perspective, every life faces an unavoidable risk of abortion from failing to implant. The ambient risk to life from failing to implant is near 70 percent (Gavin E. Jarvis, "Early Embryo Mortality in Natural Human Reproduction," US Library of Medicine, National Institutes of Health, June 7, 2017), which compares to a 0.3 percent risk to women (less than one out of 100) of getting pregnant over a one year period if the pill is used properly. If a couple has sex once a week, their risk of unintended pregnancy while using the pill is 0.00625 percent each time they have sex. And, if used with a spermicide or condom, the added risk to life caused by using the pill is about the same as odds of killing someone accidentally while driving a car, which is about 0.000107 percent (Matt Schmitz, "Are the Odds Ever in Your Favor? Car Crashes Verses Other Fatalities," *Cars.com News*, October 16, 2015, https://www.cars.com/articles/are-the-odds-ever-in-your-favor-car-crashes-versus -other-fatalities-1420682154567). The question is whether adding 0.000107 percent to the 70 percent

indirect because killing another person is not the reason for doing what is done. The ethical question is whether far more likely benefits make minimal, unintended, indirect risks to life worth taking, and we must be consistent. So, if the sanctity of life ethic allows driving cars, it must allow using the pill.

Life is full of minimal risks accepted in view of likely benefits, and most Evangelicals think there is nothing wrong with using the pill for its primary, far more likely contraceptive benefit because risking life is not the same as taking it, unintended effects are not the same as intended effects, indirect tertiary consequences are not the same as primary results, and very unlikely possibilities are not the same as likely outcomes. Whatever is decided, Christians ought to respect conscience differences (Eph 4:2–3; Col 3:12–14), and if some sense obligation to avoid using the pill, others should respect that (Rom 14:13–23). But the grace of respecting conscience differences works both ways, and those sensing obligation to avoid the pill should not criticize those using the pill with a free conscience and should, as well, make sure they are handling all low risks to life the same way.[17]

Recommended further reading on the issue of birth control includes: Daniel Doriani, "Birth Dearth or Bring on the Babies? Biblical Perspectives on Family-Planning," *Journal of Biblical Counseling* 12/1 (Fall 1993): 24–35; Linda K. Bevington, et al., eds, *The Pill: Addressing the Scientific and Ethical Questions of the Abortifacient Issue* (Deerfield, IL: Center for Bioethics and Human Dignity, 2003); Randy Alcorn, *Does the Birth Control Pill Cause Abortions?*, 8th ed. (Sandy, OR: Eternal Perspectives, 2007); William R. Cutrer and Sandra L. Glahn, *The Contraception Guidebook: Options, Risks, and Answers for Christian Couples* (Grand Rapids: Zondervan, 2005); Mary Eberstadt, *Adam and Eve after the Pill: Paradoxes of the Sexual Revolution* (San Francisco: Ignatius, 2012); and R. Albert Mohler, Jr., "Can Christians Use Birth Control?," *Journal for Biblical Manhood and Womanhood* 18.1 (2013): 7–9.

---

ambient risk every life already faces of failing to implant makes a measurable ethical difference. The ambient 70 percent risk of failing to implant all life faces after conception is a low estimate that could be higher. As such, the increased risk to life caused by using the pill is lost in the +/- uncertainty ranges surrounding the unavoidable natural risk of failing to implant all conceptions face anyway.

[17] On what consistency requires, see L. Bovens, "The rhythm method and embryonic death," *Journal of Medical Ethics* 32(6), (June 2006): 355–56, posted by the National Institutes for Health, https://www.ncbi.nlm.nih.gov/pmc/articles/PMC2563373/.

Assisted Reproduction

"Assisted reproduction" refers to methods and procedures developed to alleviate infertility. Adoption used to be the only way infertile couples could have children, and assisted reproduction now promises them opportunities to have biological children of their own. Birth control makes copulating possible without having babies, and assisted reproduction makes having babies possible without copulating.

The possibilities opened by assisted reproduction challenge us to think deeply about how biblical norms apply in new situations, and degenerating ethical attitudes altering the vocabulary of conception makes this especially important. Leon Kass writes,

> Consider the views of life and the world reflected in the following different expressions to describe the process of generating new life. Ancient Israel, impressed with the phenomenon of transmission of life from father to son, used a word we translate as "begetting" or "siring." The Greeks, impressed with the springing forth of new life in the cyclical processes of generation and decay, called it *genesis*, from a root meaning "to come into being." . . . . The premodern Christian English-speaking world, impressed with the world as given by a Creator, used the term "pro-creation." We, impressed with the machine and the gross national product (our own work of creation), employ a metaphor of the factory, "re-production."[18]

We can use "reproduction" to address methods and procedures but should keep using "procreation" to indicate the meaning and nature of what they achieve.

Many specialized terms are used when applying ethical thought in this area. "Ova" are single cell eggs released by a woman's ovaries and are what females contribute to conception. "Sperm" are the cells males contribute to conception. "Gametes" are the same as sperm and eggs. "Fallopian tubes" carry eggs from a woman's ovaries into her womb and are where conception naturally occurs. "Conception" takes place when a sperm and egg unite forming a new life. "Fertilization" is the same as conception. A "womb" is the organ in which babies grow. A "uterus" is the same as a womb. "Gestation" is growing a baby in the womb or uterus. A "zygote" is the earliest stage of life that starts with conception and is the same as a fertilized

---

[18] Leon R. Kass, *Toward a More Natural Science* (New York: Free Press, 1985), 48.

egg. A "blastocyst" is the next stage of life and occurs when a zygote becomes a ball of identical cells while passing down a fallopian tube into the womb or uterus. An "embryo" is the stage of life after that and starts when a blastocyst divides into two sorts of cells, some becoming placenta and some becoming the baby. Normally, the embryo stage starts when a newly conceived life implants in the womb or uterus, but it can start in laboratory conditions as well.

Assisted reproduction is a rapidly advancing specialization in medical science that offers new ways to have children. Each new way requires ethical analysis, and this requires addressing situations not directly mentioned in Scripture. Moral revelation in Scripture is not exhaustive but, nevertheless, provides a sufficient basis for answering any ethical question that can ever arise. New situations do not mean we get to make up new ethical rules. Nothing is, or ever will be, outside the rule of God, and, because Scripture is sufficient for all faith and practice, we must look for principles in Scripture by which to answer questions that could not be asked before advances in science made them possible. The principles in Scripture most pertinent to the ethics of assisted reproduction concern obligation to respect the sanctity of life, marriage, procreating, getting pregnant, and parenting.

The oldest and most widely practiced methods of assisting reproduction are two forms of intrauterine insemination (IUI), formerly called artificial insemination (AI): one using sperm from a woman's husband and one using sperm from a donor. IUI involves inserting sperm into the uterus artificially and is often combined with using high powered drugs that force the ovaries to release multiple eggs all at once rather than at the normal rate of one a month. IUI and fertility drugs both raise chances of conceiving. But using them together risks starting more pregnancies than desired and sometimes starts more than a woman can survive. When this happens, lives conceived are allowed to grow to the embryo stage and then those deemed surplus are removed and either killed, frozen, or used for experiments.

Intrauterine insemination by husband (IUIH) uses sperm from a woman's husband and used to be known as artificial insemination by husband (AIH). Intrauterine insemination by donor (IUID) uses sperm from an anonymous donor and used to be known as artificial insemination by donor (AID). Both methods collect sperm by masturbation that an embryologist not married to the woman getting pregnant uses to impregnate her artificially. These insemination methods make it easier for sperm to reach eggs in the normal location, and using them with fertility drugs makes sure eggs are there when sperm arrive. But beyond that conceiving and implanting take place normally.

In vitro fertilization (IVF) is a third method of assisting reproduction that involves mixing sperm with eggs in a lab. It is "in vitro" (in glass) because fertilization takes place in a glass petri dish and contrasts with fertilizing "in vivo" (in a living thing), which is how it occurs in natural intercourse, IUIH, and IUID. IVF requires obtaining eggs from an egg source (either the wife or a donor) and sperm from a sperm source (either the husband or a donor) and uniting the gametes in a lab. Resulting zygotes are allowed to become embryos that are ranked by health, sex, or other desired characteristics, and then based on that ranking, decisions are made as to how many and which to save or discard. Lastly, IVF requires an embryologist to insert the favored embryos into a woman's uterus (either the wife or a surrogate), where they have a chance to implant and develop.

IVF, too, boosts chances of succeeding by fertilizing more eggs than needed. But, unlike the insemination methods, IVF goes beyond just allowing and actually inserts more embryos than needed into a woman's uterus. This means IVF always produces multiple embryos and IUI does only if combined with using fertility drugs. Finally, in IVF, those who procreate (unite sperm with eggs) and impregnate (achieve pregnancy) are embryologists who neither supply the gametes nor are married to the women getting pregnant.

Gamete intrafallopian transfer (GIFT) and zygote intrafallopian transfer (ZIFT) are two more ways of assisting reproduction. GIFT injects a mixture of eggs and sperm into the fallopian tubes where it is hoped conception and implantation will follow in the normal fashion. Thus, GIFT enhances chances of pregnancy more naturally than IVF. But, since multiple eggs are injected with sperm, GIFT also typically produces more embryos than needed, which leaves couples needing to decide what to do with them. ZIFT is similar to GIFT, except zygotes produced by IVF in the lab are transferred into the fallopian tubes rather than just a mixture of eggs and sperm. These become blastocysts while descending into the uterus and then become embryos when they implant. ZIFT differs from normal IVF because what is conceived in the lab is transferred at an earlier stage and placed higher in the reproductive system. But ZIFT has all the same ethical problems as regular IVF. GIFT does not use embryologists to procreate as in IVF and ZIFT, but GIFT and ZIFT both use embryologists to impregnate women outside marriage.

Besides methods that make conceiving easier, assisted reproduction now offers four methods of surrogacy. Surrogacy refers to a woman gestating (carrying) a baby in her womb for other people. Surrogacy arrangements are legally complicated, but the ethics involved is not.

Surrogacy started in order to give women too weak to survive pregnancy, or with wombs too damaged to carry babies, a chance to have biological children without getting pregnant. But demand has expanded to service people desiring biological children without getting pregnant for other reasons, like staying in shape for athletic events, LGBTQ+ men wanting a child related to one of them, or just skipping the inconvenience. Surrogacy can be either partial or full and either commercial or altruistic, and this produces four different methods: "partial commercial surrogacy," "partial altruistic surrogacy," "full commercial surrogacy," and "full altruistic surrogacy."

Partial surrogacy, also known as genetic surrogacy, is when a woman is inseminated with sperm from the husband of a couple wanting a child. This woman then conceives, carries his baby, and, after giving birth, turns the baby over to that man and his wife. This is partial surrogacy because, while sperm come from the man arranging with another woman to have a child, the woman agreeing to it is the biological mother, and in most states, she has a legal right to change her mind and keep the baby no matter what was arranged. Full surrogacy, also known as gestational surrogacy, is when a woman agrees to carry a child for other people and has no genetic relation to it. Embryos are created by IVF using gametes from the couple arranging the surrogacy. One of the resulting embryos is then transferred into the surrogate's womb, and she carries it in place of the biological mother. In most states, a full surrogate has no rights to the baby and must turn it over no matter how she feels. Partial surrogacy was more common, but now is hardly practiced because the law makes obtaining babies this way so uncertain.

Commercial surrogacy is when a surrogate carries a baby in her womb to make money, and altruistic surrogacy is when a family member or close friend carries it just for love. Both forms pay for living and medical expenses. But an altruistic surrogate gets nothing more, and a commercial surrogate profits from it. Commercial surrogacy can cost more than $100,000. First, the surrogate makes about $30,000. Her living and medical expenses add to that, a broker charges for arranging connections, lawyers charge legal fees, and fertility clinics charge for screening, IVF, and implantation. Despite how much it costs, full commercial surrogacy is now by far the most common form of surrogacy, with full altruistic surrogacy following a distant second, and both forms of partial surrogacies are rather infrequent.

The biggest problems with surrogacy are treating women like human incubators and violating the uniqueness of marriage. All methods of surrogacy depersonalize something God made personal, make shallow something God made profound, and add others to something

God made exclusive. Commercial surrogacy also cheapens something God made priceless. Altruistic surrogacy avoids treating babies like commodities but still treats them like instruments for indulging desires rather than persons valued in their own right. All the surrogacy methods use embryologists to perform procreating and impregnating actions outside marriage.

Intracytoplasmic sperm injection (ICSI) is a tenth method now available to assist reproduction. ICSI goes beyond making it easier for sperm to find eggs and actually injects sperm into eggs. Like IVF, it unites gametes in the lab. But in IVF, sperm fertilize eggs on their own; whereas, in ICSI, an embryologist picks up a single sperm with a fine glass needle and injects it directly into a single egg. This usually fertilizes an egg producing a zygote, but it also fails to screen out sperm that are weak or unhealthy. Because conception takes place in the lab, ICSI requires transferring the resulting zygote into a fallopian tube or transferring the resulting embryo into a womb. Another problem with ICSI is that, while inserting a sperm more deeply into an egg makes fertilization more likely, it also raises the risk of damaging the egg and either destroying it or producing an abnormal child. Destroying an egg is not the same as destroying a person. But alleviating childlessness does not justify producing damaged children, and the sanctity of life does not allow do-overs. Then ICSI, too, uses embryologists to procreate and impregnate outside the uniqueness of marriage. It could be said that ICSI places procreating in the hands of third-party embryologists more directly and completely than any other method.

The most recent, and also least ethically objectionable, method of assisting reproduction is embryo or zygote adoption. This possibility does not promise biologically related children but does allow infertile women to give birth to children carried in their wombs. As commonly practiced, all reproductive methods involving IVF, and even the IUI methods when combined with high-powered fertility drugs, produce more zygotes or embryos than desired or can be safely carried. Something must be done with these, so they are either killed right away, donated to researchers who kill them in experiments, or frozen and stored at the clinics producing them.

Freezing means these innocent humans could die in storage or in the thawing process, but some can survive if transferred into wombs and given a chance to flourish. The procedure used is the same as for full surrogacy, but the action is heroic because it rescues "those stumbling toward slaughter" (Prov 24:11) and treats life as sacred rather than a commodity (Prov 6:26). Transferring lives into the wombs of rescuers means embryologists impregnate them outside marriage as occurs in IVF, GIFT, ZIFT, surrogacy, and ICSI, but the action's heroic nature justifies it just as saving babies in Egypt justified deceiving Pharaoh (Exod 1:19–21). The action is allowed to save innocent lives that would otherwise perish.

We should empathize with the longing of childless couples, but no one should think methods and procedures like in vitro fertilization (IVF), egg harvesting, sperm donating, embryo transfer, surrogacy, screening desirable characteristics, sperm injection, selective reduction, or freezing embryos are not tempting us to view childbearing in ways less than sacred. The Bible gives no reason to avoid benefits solving malfunctions of reproduction any more than benefits solving malfunctions of our digestive, circulatory, or urinary systems. But we must do so without lessening the sanctity of life, marriage, procreating, getting pregnant, and parenting.

Many of the procedures used with methods assisting reproduction conflict with the sanctity of life beginning at conception, and many also take procreating and impregnating actions outside the uniqueness of marriage. And there is more. We also must resist the way methods assisting reproduction tempt us to change how we view what the Bible calls "father[ing]" (Gen 4:18, 20; 5:3, 4, 6, 9) children and considers equal to God "form[ing] you from the womb" (Isa 44:2) and God "knit[ting]" life together in a "mother's womb" (Ps 139:13). It is what the KJV refers to as *begetting* in order to capture something grand enough to include the incarnation of Christ (John 3:16) as well as common everyday biological reproduction. According to Scripture, children come to us from God as gifts of God (Ps 127:3) and we are blessed to have them (Gen 17:16). But, however much children might be desired, we must not think God owes us children. No one deserves children. No one is entitled to them. Having children is good, but we must worship the giver, not the gift. While considering what methods assisting reproduction promise, we must neither idolize children nor depersonalize, commodify, or commercialize them. We must not forget adoption builds families without new methods assisting reproduction, and God views building families by adoption as heroic and akin to how we get to be members of his family (Eph 1:5).

Recommended further reading on artificial reproduction includes: Oliver O'Donovan, *Begotten or Made?* (Oxford: Oxford, 1984); Donald DeMarco, *Biotechnology and the Assault on Parenthood* (San Francisco: Ignatius, 1991); John Robert, *Children of Choice* (Princeton, NJ: Princeton, 1994); Scott Rae, *Brave New Families* (Grand Rapids: Baker, 1996); Brent Waters, *Reproductive Technology* (Cleveland, OH: Pilgrim, 2001); Liza Mundy, *Everything Conceivable* (New York: Knopf, 2007); Megan Best, *Fearfully and Wonderfully Made* (Downers Grove, IL: InterVarsity, 2012); Scott Rae, *Outside the Womb* (Chicago: Moody, 2011); and Matthew

Arbo, *Walking through Infertility: Biblical, Theological, and Moral Counsel for Those Who Are Struggling* (Wheaton, IL: Crossway, 2018).

Euthanasia

Abortion, birth control, and assisted reproduction all address how the sanctity of human life applies when life begins, and euthanasia addresses how it applies at the end. There is life after death, God promises eternal life, and we expect to rise from the dead. Unless Jesus returns before we die, death is something all must experience (Ps 89:48; 1 Cor 15:22; Heb 9:27), and euthanasia deals with how we approach it. How should we behave when dying is imminent, and what if someone is dying in terrible pain?

Euthanasia is a compound term comprised of two Greek words: εὖ (*eu*, good) and θάνατος (*thanatos*, death). In Greek, euthanasia literally means "good death," and both elements are essential to understanding what it means. First, the term involves a notion of good, and second, it involves applying that notion to dying. That is very general, and the issue needs defining more exactly. The problem of defining euthanasia more exactly is clouded by disagreement. Evangelicals who agree on the sanctity of human life sometimes clash on the ethics of euthanasia, but that mostly comes from explaining what euthanasia means in different ways. A narrow definition makes it easy to condemn completely and a broad definition makes it harder. We should use a broad definition because, even though a narrow definition simplifies analysis, it fails to resolve hard situations many families must address. So, while some Evangelicals define euthanasia narrowly,[19] we, here, understand euthanasia to cover a range of practices involving if or when it would be moral to influence by action or nonaction either the timing or methodology of death, or both, in order to achieve some notion of good.

Subclassifications of euthanasia come from recognizing three distinctions, which are whether what is done or not is voluntary or involuntary, active or passive, or direct or indirect. The first recognizes there is an ethical difference between killing someone who does not

---

[19] This is a broad definition that contrasts with limiting euthanasia to physicians helping patients commit suicide (Rae, *Introducing Christian Ethics*, 112 [see chap. 8, n. 1]), limiting it to mercy killing (Frame, *Doctrine of the Christian Life*, 737), or limiting it to actions and excluding decisions to forego measures that simply delay death (Grudem, *Christian Ethics*, 587).

want to die and killing someone who does. Life belongs to God, and we cannot give others permission to kill us. But killing an innocent person who does not want to die is worse than killing someone who does. The second recognizes there is an ethical difference between killing someone and letting someone die, and the third recognizes there is an ethical difference between killing yourself and having someone else do it. "Direct" means death comes at the hand of the person dying, and "indirect" means it comes at the hand of someone else. Together, these distinctions produce eight subclassifications: (1) voluntary-active-direct euthanasia, (2) involuntary-active-direct euthanasia, (3) voluntary-passive-direct euthanasia, (4) involuntary-passive-direct euthanasia, (5) voluntary-active-indirect euthanasia, (6) involuntary-active-indirect euthanasia, (7) voluntary-passive-indirect euthanasia, and (8) involuntary-passive-indirect euthanasia.

Euthanasia broadly defined covers many situations, some of which have special names. "Death with dignity" refers to when patients forego life-prolonging treatments in order to spend their last days surrounded by friends and family at home rather than drugged up in hospitals surrounded by people they hardly know. It is euthanasia because decisions are made aiming for a notion of good that affects the timing and methodology of death, and this sort falls in the voluntary-passive-direct subclassification. Death with dignity is permitted because, as Meilaender observes, Christians are not vitalists.[20] We view life as sacred, but we also neither treat life as self-justifying nor as the greatest good there is. With Christ, we think some things worth dying for (John 15:13) and do not believe we need always to extend life no matter what (Luke 23:46). Death with dignity is able to affirm the sanctity of life even while recognizing the priority of goods like faith, family, and freedom that justify not delaying death longer than necessary.

Special names for other situations having to do with euthanasia are "mercy killing" (putting someone in pain out of his or her misery), "death selection" (choosing to meet death on your own terms), "suicide" (self-murder to escape personal problems), "physician-assisted suicide" (suicide by physician rather than self), and "ethnic cleansing" or "genocide" (killing members of social groups to achieve corporate goals unrelated to personal responsibility, conduct, or character). These, too, are forms of euthanasia, but, unlike death with dignity, these

---

[20] Gilbert Meilaender, "Living Life's End," *First Things* (May 2005): 17.

other forms clash with the sanctity of human life, biblical neighbor love, and a Christ-centered view of ethical reality.

The main dangers associated with arguments used to justify euthanasia are denying the sanctity of human life, misjudging the value of suffering, and misapprehending the relation we have to life. According to Scripture, the sanctity of human life comes from realizing it belongs to God, who prohibits killing anyone apart from guilt. We must respect and protect the lives of everyone alive except where God says a person does something forfeiting his or her title to life (Gen 9:6; Ezek 13:19). The difference is innocence. God hates "hands that shed innocent blood" (Prov 6:17), and that means we may never kill anyone for reasons other than guilt no matter what good we intend. This precludes active euthanasia and killing passively by neglect but does not rule out accepting the dying process when keeping someone alive only slows it down.

This leads to a question over which most Protestants disagree with most Catholics, and that is whether withdrawing artificial life support (artificial breathing, artificial blood circulation, and artificial nutrition and hydration) is "killing" or "letting die." Is it murder or just a way of accepting mortality? Catholic theologians, influenced by natural law philosophy, argue that withdrawing artificial life support amounts to murder because breathing, circulating blood, eating, and drinking are natural necessities without which no one lives. But Protestants generally think sustaining life artificially with no hope of recovery, though it can be heroic, is not obligatory. With no hope of recovery, withdrawing artificial life support amounts to accepting the natural dying process. By this understanding, withdrawing artificial life support simply allows dying patients to die and does not kill them. Because of this difference, most Protestants treat taking dying patients off artificial life support as a form of passive euthanasia,[21] and most Catholics treat it as a form of active euthanasia.

Besides active euthanasia violating the sanctity of human life, other problems with arguments used to justify euthanasia (arguments like appealing to quality of life, to personal autonomy, or to notions of mercy or compassion) are they tend to misjudge the value of suffering and to misapprehend the relation we have to life. They misjudge the value of suffering

---

[21] For more, I recommend Erik M. Clary, "Embracing PVS 2.0 (The 'Permanent? Vegetative? State'): Medical Research Beckons Ethicists Considering the Issue of ANH Withdrawal to Adopt a More Challenging Situational Narrative," *Ethics & Medicine* 33/1 (Spring 2017): 43–53.

by assuming it has no value or higher purpose and must therefore be worthless, irredeemable, and something to avoid at all costs. But that is not biblical because God uses suffering to produce positive results (Rom 5:3–5; 1 Pet 1:6–7) that far outweigh anything lost (2 Cor 4:17). Arguments used to justify euthanasia also tend to misapprehend life in two ways: first, by treating life like property and, second, by treating life like something with which we can do whatever we please rather than as something belonging to God we get to use.

Most people do not think of euthanasia until a loved one is hospitalized with a serious disease or injury or is in failing health due to old age. When that happens, hard decisions must sometimes be made, and knowing what is or is not allowed is especially challenging when a loved one is dying in terrible pain. Few are prepared to make life and death decisions affecting loved ones, so here are some guidelines:

1. Do what can be done to relieve pain without killing the patient or hastening death.
2. Do not force a patient to undergo procedures that (a) no longer provide any foreseeable benefit or (b) either cannot, or can no longer, assure healing or recovery.
3. Do not do anything in view of dying until losing hope of recovery.
4. Do not help a patient take his or her own life (commit suicide) no matter how strongly that person insists.
5. Painkillers that do not hasten natural death (do not cause death to occur more rapidly than if a patient is left without artificial life support) are morally acceptable.
6. Painkillers that do hasten death (do cause death to occur more rapidly than if a patient is left without artificial life support) are not morally acceptable.
7. Finally, if a patient's life is being sustained artificially, and there is no hope of recovery, then withdrawing artificial life support is allowed because it simply amounts to accepting the natural death process. This is permissible because (a) mortality is God's decision, and (b) there is no duty to slow the approach of natural death artificially after passing all hope of recovery. But, while this is allowed, it is not required, and deciding to withdraw artificial life support is up to the patient or to the family member authorized to make life-and-death decisions on the patient's behalf.

To conclude, we should oppose active euthanasia in all forms and should oppose passive euthanasia so long as hope of recovering remains. Jesus establishes this latter principle in the parable of the Good Samaritan (Luke 10:25–37) by criticizing the priest and Levite for not helping a dying traveler who could be saved, and James does as well (Jas 4:17). But this suggests we may also accept passive euthanasia after losing hope of recovery. Hastening death beyond the pace it approaches without interference is not permitted, not even after losing hope of recovering and not even to alleviate great suffering. That is because we may never destroy innocent human life (Exod 20:13; 23:7). But, if someone is dying with no hope of recovery, slowing death artificially is not obligatory, even if heroic, and withdrawing artificial life support is allowed. The Bible does not require dying patients to fight death as long as possible, no matter what, and faith requires trusting God who both wills our mortality and promises resurrection. We should agree here with Frame, who says,

> It is not wrong for a Christian to refuse medical treatment, out of recognition that the treatment could be burdensome to his family and fellow believers. I suspect that the apostle Paul, had he lived in our time, would not have wanted to be kept indefinitely on artificial life support, when the expense of that could have been used for ministry. His desire to go on living was only for the sake of ministry (Phil. 1:20–26); otherwise, he preferred to leave this world and be with Christ.[22]

Recommended further reading on the issue of euthanasia includes Zakyah Basri, *Euthanasia: Mercy or Murder?* (Bloomington, IN: AuthorHouse, 2012); Kathryn Butler, *Between Life and Death: A Gospel-Centered Guide to End-of-Life Medical Care* (Wheaton, IL: Crossway, 2019); Nigel M. de S. Cameron, *The New Medicine: Life and Death after Hippocrates* (Wheaton, IL: Crossway, 1991); Neil M. Gorsuch, *The Future of Assisted Suicide and Euthanasia* (Princeton, NJ: Princeton, 2006); Derek Humphrey, *Final Exit*, 3rd ed. (New York: Dell, 2002); John F. Kilner, *Life on the Line: Ethics, Aging, Ending Patients' Lives, and Allocating Vital Resources* (Grand Rapids: Eerdmans, 1992); David Jeffrey, *Against Physician Assisted Suicide* (New York: Radcliffe, 2009); Wesley J. Smith, *Culture of Death* (San Francisco: Encounter, 2000); Joni Eareckson Tada, *When Is It Right to Die? A Comforting and Surprising Look at Death and Dying*, updated ed. (Grand Rapids: Zondervan, 2018).

---

[22] Frame, *Doctrine of the Christian Life*, 739.

Biomedical Ethics

Biomedical ethics is a compound term that combines *bioethics* with *medical ethics*. Medical ethics deals with healthcare delivery and examines things like the character, conduct, and responsibilities of medical professionals, patient rights, physician-patient relations, and healthcare decision-making. Bioethics deals with the biosciences and any sort of biotechnology and examines questions related to molecular biology, cellular biology, human biology, developmental biology, microbiology, immunology, embryology, geriatrics, genetics, genomics, physiology, biochemistry, biophysics, pharmacology, toxicology, bioinformatics, biotechnology, and bioengineering. These fields overlap but are not the same because medical ethics focuses on patients and physicians while bioethics focuses on scientists, lab personnel, and research subjects. This means biomedical ethics includes dealing with assisted reproduction, but as we covered that already, it will not be treated here.

Brent Waters identifies three phases in the evolution of contemporary medical ethics. First, there was the "patient-as-fellow-person" phase, then the "patient-as-autonomous-person" phase, and now the "patient-as-consumer" phase.[23] The first patient-as-fellow-person phase was led by Christian theologians like Paul Ramsey, whose books *Fabricated Man* (Yale, 1970), *The Patient as Person* (Yale, 1974), and *The Ethics of Fetal Research* (Yale, 1975) defined the field before secularists moved in. In that first phase, healthcare was treated more like persons of equal worth dealing with problems together than like experts solving problems for nonexperts. But the first phase collapsed for lack of agreement on what constitutes a person, since some thought anyone alive is a person and others thought diminished capacities made patients less than a person.

The second patient-as-autonomous-person phase began with philosophical books like *Principles of Biomedical Ethics* (Oxford, 1979) by Tom Beauchamp and James Childress. The personhood problem was not resolved but most agreed patients should make life and death decisions for themselves. And if patients are not competent, then surrogates must make ultimate decisions for them. This led to four principles generally viewed as guiding all medical decisions: non-malfeasance (never harm patients on purpose), beneficence (do things only to

---

[23] Brent Waters, "Disembodied Bioethics: The Incarnation, Embodiment, and Late Modern Medicine" (paper presented at the seventieth annual meeting of the Evangelical Theological Society, Denver, CO, November 14, 2018).

benefit patients), justice (never benefit one patient at the expense of others), and autonomy (never treat patients without informed consent). This last principle held that patients or their surrogates had the last say on life-or-death decisions and prevented physicians from playing God, but it allowed patients or surrogates to play God for themselves because the patient-as-autonomous-person stage had no place for transcendence.

Medical ethics is transitioning now (in the early 21st century) to a third patient-as-consumer phase. Rather than treating patients as persons equal to physicians or even as autonomous decision makers, healthcare professionals are shifting to treating patients as consumers to be satisfied. The second stage replaced theologians with philosophers, and the third stage is replacing philosophers and theologians with market managers. The second stage shifted ethical focus from patient healing to patient autonomy, and the third is shifting ethical focus from patient healing and autonomy to patient satisfaction. The earlier stages treated physicians as being there to solve problems, but this third stage treats them like salesmen there to meet desires. So, if patients want to boost a function, resist aging, or die painlessly, that is what they should get.

Although bioethics focuses on research, not healthcare, and on scientists, not physicians, shifts in medical ethics are affecting bioethics as well. The human race has struggled with problems of mortality since the fall. We are immortal souls in mortal bodies. As Paul observes, "We have this treasure in clay jars" (2 Cor 4:7) and look forward to a time when mortality will be "swallowed up by life" (2 Cor 5:4). But in recent years, the biosciences and biotechnologies have made spectacular advances toward overcoming problems of mortality, promising not only to cure genetic diseases, replace failing organs, and slow degenerative disorders but even to control and perhaps enhance the constitution of every living thing.

Those making these advances do it for three reasons: therapy, prevention, and enhancement. Initially, the only aim was to solve medical problems—to cure diseases, restore lost functions, and correct abnormalities. But a second aim arose, which was not only to solve medical problems but also to prevent them. The first sought to restore good health and the second to preserve it, and this second aim led to producing immunizations, inoculations, preventive healthcare measures, nutrition supplements, and germicides. Now a third aim is rising that seeks to enhance organisms beyond their natural best by boosting functionalities past anything in nature. This third aim seeks more than healing or health and attempts rather to produce things that are "super"-natural or "trans"-natural by transforming things into something different than before. This requires Christian ethicists to assess many matters never addressed before, and I will summarize the main ones.

"Recombinant DNA technologies," "gene editing," "gene splicing," and "gene therapies" all refer to introducing genes into existing cells to treat or prevent diseases or to enhance abilities. Procedures used for this are classified as "somatic" or "germline." Somatic procedures affect a single patient and no one else, and germline procedures affect not just a single patient but all future descendants of that patient. These procedures can be used to heal and restore by replacing defective genes with healthy ones, but they also tempt those knowing how they work to go beyond curing diseases by either making designer children or making germline changes affecting future generations in the name of improving or redefining humanity.[24]

"Organic cloning" refers to generating organisms genetically identical to an original. Cloning occurs naturally in some plants and insects, and scientists have reproduced sheep and cows asexually using laboratory techniques. Now scientists, ethicists, politicians, and lawyers are debating whether researchers should be allowed to clone humans artificially. Genetic duplications of an organism can be generated in the lab two different ways: first, by "artificial embryo twinning" and, second, by "somatic cell nuclear transfer." Artificial embryo twinning mimics the process that produces identical twins naturally. A life generated sexually by uniting a sperm and egg is divided at the zygote stage in a Petri dish. This produces identical twins who then are transferred to a womb and allowed to gestate. Whether it happens naturally or not, twinning divides an undeveloped zygote that starts with sexual reproduction and does not duplicate a fully developed organism.

By contrast, somatic cell nuclear transfer does duplicate a fully developed organism and does it without sex. Somatic cells are cells with two complete sets of chromosomes (DNA), meaning they can be any cell in a fully developed organism other than a sperm or egg, and a nucleus is the compartment in a cell that holds its chromosomes (DNA). In somatic cell nuclear transfer, embryologists take a somatic cell removed from an organism being cloned and extract its nucleus. Then, they take an egg from a female of that species, remove the single strand nucleus out of that

---

[24] David Cyranoski and Sarah Rearden, "Chinese Scientists Genetically Modify Human Embryos," *Nature* (April 22, 2015), www.nature.com/news/chinese-scientists-genetically-modify-human -embryos-1.17378; Rae, *Introducing Christian Ethics*, 104–5; Brent Waters, *From Human to Posthuman* (Burlington, VT: Ashgate, 2006).

egg, and replace it with the dual set nucleus taken from the somatic cell. The former egg cell with its new somatic (dual set) nucleus then starts behaving like a fertilized egg, is allowed to develop into an embryo in the lab, and finally is implanted into a surrogate mother to gestate. This produces an organism genetically identical to the one providing the somatic nucleus transferred into the enucleated egg and does it in a way different from twinning and completely without sex.

There is nothing wrong with cloning plants and animals to improve nutrition and food supplies. But cloning humans by somatic cell nuclear transfer runs into major ethical problems, not only because the process makes and destroys many innocent lives before one survives, but also because it makes marriage irrelevant to reproducing, makes procreating unnecessary to human survival, separates "life-making" from "love-making," and redefines parenthood.[25]

Stem cell research aims to control the genetic switches that tell cells what to become, and stem cell therapy uses controlling these switches to restore lost parts or functions. Fully developed cells are "unipotent," meaning all genetic switches are off except one, and for that reason, they can be just that one thing and nothing else. But stem cells are cells with more than one genetic switch left on, which means they can become different things if given the right signals. Furthermore, stem cells can be at different stages along the path of assignment, with some being "totipotent," some being "pluripotent," and some being "multipotent." Totipotent stem cells can become anything, including a whole new person, because no switches are off, and the ultimate totipotent stem cell is a fertilized egg. Pluripotent stem cells have some switches turned off but not many, and these can become anything in one of three very general categories depending on which switches are on or off. They can become anything in either the brain-related category, the bone-related category, or the organ-related category, but they cannot become a whole new person. Multipotent stem cells are even more specialized but are still more versatile than unipotent cells. More switches are turned off than in pluripotent cells, but they still can become more than one thing.

Power to control stem cells promises amazing things like growing new flesh and blood body parts to replace or regenerate parts lost to disease, accidents, or degeneration, and the main ethical questions relating to this research area concern how researchers get the cells on which they

---

[25] Daniel R. Heimbach, "Cloning Humans: Dangerous, Unjustifiable, and Genuinely Immoral," *Valparaiso University Law Review* 32/2 (Spring 1998): 633–59.

work. "Zygotic stem cells" are totipotent stem cells obtained by killing zygotes, "embryonic stem cells" are pluripotent stem cells obtained by killing embryos, and "adult stem cells" (also called "somatic stem cells") are mostly multipotent stem cells obtained from sources like bone marrow, umbilical cord blood, skin, or teeth that do not require harming anyone. Now that researchers have learned how to reprogram cells and can turn any somatic (adult) cell back into pluripotent or totipotent stem cells, it no longer is necessary to kill anyone to get them.[26]

"Nanotechnology" is manipulating atoms or molecules to produce materials and devices with special properties, and "nanomedicine" is using nanotechnologies to benefit human health. Recent advances in nanotechnology and nanomedicine are revolutionizing the biosciences and contemporary healthcare. Nanomedicines improve the lives of patients with kidney disease, fungal infections, elevated cholesterol, multiple sclerosis, chronic pain, asthma, and emphysema. Nano materials, such as carbon nano tubes, nano crystals, nano wire, and nano shells, are being used to treat cancer. And progress is being made on developing nanotechnologies to treat degenerative neurological disorders like Parkinson's and Alzheimer's.

Neuroenhancers are pills, liquids, or devices that enhance cognitive, social, emotional, or motor functionalities. Some boost memory beyond normal, some boost concentration beyond normal, and some boost sex beyond normal. Modafinil is a drug that decreases fatigue, increases vigilance, reduces daytime sleepiness, and improves mood, and Viagra is a pill that enhances sexual arousal in men. Some neuroenhancers are used to overcome ailments like narcolepsy, sleep apnea, and attention deficit disorder. But neuroenhancers prescribed for therapeutic reasons can be easily abused, and marketers are now promising to boost functions and abilities in healthy people beyond natural limits.

The newest biotechnologies include "artificial intelligence" (AI), "cyborgs," "chimeras," and "hybrids." AI refers to machines that mimic human learning and problem solving, and automated image analysis is an example of using AI in health care. Cyborgs are beings with a mix of organic and biomechatronic parts, and a man with a bionic eye, computerized hearing, and prosthetics is a cyborg. Chimeras are beings with parts from different parent organisms

---

[26] Alexander Meissner, et al., "Direct Reprogramming of Genetically Unmodified Fibroblasts into Pluripotent Stem Cells," *Nature Biotechnology* 25 (2007): 1177–81. And, of course, cloning by somatic cell nuclear transfer involves turning a somatic (adult) non-stem cell nucleus into a totipotent stem cell nucleus.

that may or may not be of the same species. A patient with an eye from an organ donor is one sort, and growing a human ear on the body of a mouse is the other sort. Hybrids are beings with genes from different species in the chromosomes of the nuclei in every cell in their bodies. Mules are horse-donkey hybrids, and newly developed fruit hybrids include cherry-plums (cherry + plum), plumcots (plum + apricot), and tangelos (tangerine + pumelo). These trends promise to restore or replace lost functionalities but also blur what distinguishes normal from abnormal, natural from unnatural, and one species from another. And some developments are now aiming to produce beings that are better than human.[27]

Biotechnology is a multifaceted, fast developing field, and we cannot analyze all new ethical challenges here. But we can mention some general concerns. We should neither be naïve nor alarmist. We must not let the dazzle of amazing promises blind us to ethical dangers, nor should we criticize new things just because they are new. As Christians, we cannot forget that, until transformed at the resurrection, human nature is fallen and mortal, and, while it is good to hope for immortality on God's terms, we must not seek eternal life without our Creator. Beyond that, we must reject all procedures that violate the sanctity of human life, the sanctity of marriage, and the sanctity of paternity, and we must not seek powers that dehumanize humanity by blurring it with animals or trying to surpass it.

Recommended further reading on the issue of biomedical ethics includes: Daniel R. Heimbach, "Cloning Humans: Dangerous, Unjustifiable, and Genuinely Immoral," *Valparaiso University Law Review* 32/2 (Spring 1998): 633–659; John F. Kilner, Nigel M. de S. Cameron, and David L. Schiedermayer, *Bioethics and the Future of Medicine* (Grand Rapids: Eerdmans, 1995); Gilbert Meilaender, *Bioethics: A Primer for Christians*, 3rd ed. (Grand Rapids: Eerdmans, 2013); C. Ben Mitchell and D. Joy Riley, *Christian Bioethics* (Nashville: B&H, 2014); James C. Peterson, *Genetic Turning Points* (Grand Rapids: Eerdmans, 2001); David VanDrunen, *Bioethics and the Christian Life* (Wheaton, IL: Crossway, 2009); Brent Waters, *From Human to Posthuman* (Burlington, VT: Ashgate, 2006); and Brent Waters, *This Mortal Flesh: Incarnation and Bioethics* (Grand Rapids: Baker, 2009).

---

[27] Waters, "Disembodied Bioethics"; John Wyatt, "The New Biology," in John Stott, *Issues Facing Christians Today*, 4th ed. (Grand Rapids: Zondervan, 2006), 428.

Gambling

Gambling is transferring ownership of something of value based on chance, using a contrived risk to settle winners who gain at the expense of losers, all without anyone doing anything to earn or forfeit the value exchanged and without producing anything constructive. All gambling favors one or a few at the expense of others and does it for the questionable thrill of getting for nothing something others lose. Life is full of risks, and no one can avoid making decisions on matters that are uncertain. But every decision affected by uncertainty is not gambling any more than all cars come from Detroit or all art is worth collecting. Distinctions separate one risk from another, and, based on these, some qualify as gambling and some do not.

Profitmaking in industry, commerce, or sales is not gambling because it does not rely exclusively on chance and, even though profitmaking always deals with uncertainty, attempts are made to minimize what is uncertain and to maximize constructive results. Profitmaking also does not transfer owning anything others have based on chance. Investing is not gambling because investors study market conditions and buy or sell based on skilled interpretation, and investing cannot succeed unless the enterprises invested in produce constructive results. Farmers also do not gamble when planting crops even though harvests are always affected by powers beyond their control. For, while farmers take risks, they also try hard to minimize uncertainties and produce constructive results.

Insurance is not gambling because it spreads the burden of possible losing rather than exploiting it. Buyers of insurance and insurance companies both try to minimize the risk of losing assets, while gambling does the opposite. Using chance to settle equal claims that cannot be shared is not gambling. Tossing a coin to decide which team starts on offense decides something based on chance. But this is not gambling because no value is exchanged and the side winning a coin toss gets nothing at the other side's expense. Games, like Monopoly, that use chance only to entertain are not gambling because, even though players win and lose, game results are affected as much by skill as by chance and nothing of value is exchanged. Giving and accepting gifts is not gambling because, even though receivers get something without working for it and givers transfer something of value, the exchange is other-centered rather than self-centered, is done out of love rather than acquisitiveness, elicits satisfaction in givers rather than regret, and elicits gratitude in receivers rather than delight at others losing what they gain.

Some think gambling is stealing, but these are not the same. Gamblers who cheat by rigging results do steal from other players, but those who gamble fairly do not. Yet, even when gamblers do not steal from other players, they can steal from God by squandering wealth he owns (Deut 10:14; Ps 50:12) and is trusting them to use for his glory (1 Cor 10:31). Even honest gambling risks squandering something God owns and does with it something God never does because he controls "power to gain wealth" (Deut 8:18) and leaves nothing to chance (Isa 46:10). It is as if a friend trusted you with something he owns and you squandered it instead of using it wisely and returning it with interest (Matt 25:27).

Finally, faith in God is not gambling even though they look the same to unbelievers. From a man-centered naturalistic perspective, there is no difference between relying on God and relying on chance because what distinguishes them is transcendent. Both rely on something people do not see or control. But faith relies on the one true God who really does control everything, and gambling relies on chance, which controls nothing. Faith depends on the known and knowable character and power of God, and gambling depends on something unknown and unknowable with no character or power at all. Faith trusts someone certain and reliable, and gambling trusts something completely uncertain and unreliable.

Because of these differences, practices in the Bible that relied on God were not gambling even though they look like gambling to unbelievers. Joshua cast lots to distribute territory after entering the Promised Land (Josh 18:10), and David cast lots to assign priestly duties to the descendants of Aaron (1 Chr 24:3–19). They did this at God's direction (Exod 28:30; Num 27:21; 1 Chr 24:19) as a way of finding what he wanted them to do, for "the lot is cast into the lap but its every decision is from the LORD" (Prov 16:33). Casting lots was last used in the New Testament when the apostles asked God to reveal who should take the place of Judas (Acts 1:21–26), and after that, it was replaced by guidance of the Holy Spirit (Acts 13:2; 15:28).

Faith in God to control things humans cannot was also built into the justice system of ancient Israel (Num 5:11–31). If a husband thought his wife was unfaithful but had no proof, he was instructed to take her to a priest who would ask God to reveal if she was guilty or not. The priest was to mix dirt from the tabernacle floor into a bowl of holy water, put it in the woman's hands, place her under oath, and have her swear innocence to God. He then was to write curses on a scroll, wash the ink of those curses into the dirty water, and have her drink the dirty water mixed with ink from the curses. If the woman was guilty, God caused her belly to swell and her womb to shrivel (Num 5:27). But, if she was innocent, God protected her health and ability to have children (Num 5:28). These practices were not gambling because they came from God and were not devised by man, relied on faith not on chance, and did not transfer owning any value apart from love or labor.

Christians are divided on the ethics of gambling. Catholics, Anglicans, Lutherans, and Presbyterians generally have permitted gambling in moderation; Baptists, Methodists, and Brethren generally have opposed all gambling; and this denominational variation underlies division among Evangelicals as well. The main argument for the "gambling in moderation" position is to say gambling is not prohibited in the Bible and then to add we must not go beyond what the Bible says. All Christians agree it is wrong to gamble covetously or in ways that compromise worship, discourage gainful work, or interfere with marriage, family, or community responsibilities. But, as long as people do not cross these boundaries, the "gambling in moderation" position says we must honor Christian liberty, must not bind the consciences of other people, and must not claim each and every act of gambling is contrary to the Word of God.

As opposed to this, the "all gambling is wrong" position argues either that the Bible prohibits all gambling by implication or that the Bible not only prohibits gambling implicitly but explicitly as well. The first version of the "all gambling is wrong" position agrees with saying the Bible never prohibits gambling directly but then argues that the Bible prohibits all gambling indirectly. The second version disagrees with saying the Bible never prohibits gambling directly and instead argues the Bible not only prohibits gambling implicitly but explicitly as well. This second version of the "all gambling is wrong" position is the one I think is most true to what God reveals in Scripture. Even though it is common to say the Bible never prohibits gambling directly and at most prohibits gambling indirectly, I think the Bible not only prohibits all gambling indirectly but directly as well.

Evangelicals do not agree on this, and I respect the integrity of those who think otherwise. I recognize, too, that arguing this position must guard against falling into legalism. There is no virtue in adding to Christian ethics more than God requires, and doing that (however well intended) is strongly condemned throughout the Bible (Deut 4:2; 12:32; Prov 30:6; Rev 22:18–19). But there is danger in both directions. We must neither command where Scripture is silent nor give liberty where Scripture commands. We must not say God requires more than he does (Rev 22:18; Luke 11:46), but we also must guard against taking away anything God really does require (Deut 4:2; 12:32; Prov 30:6; Rev 22:19).

Here, then, is why I think we have to say the Bible not only prohibits all gambling indirectly by implication but also prohibits it directly and explicitly. First, the Bible prohibits all gambling indirectly because it either violates or tends to violate biblical obligations:

1. To love others sacrificially the way Jesus loves us (John 15:12).
2. To treat others as we wish to be treated ourselves (Matt 7:12; Luke 6:31).
3. Not to make ourselves rich at the expense of the poor (Prov 22:16).
4. Not to try serving God and money at the same time (Matt 6:24).
5. Not to worship (trust in) anything besides God (Exod 20:3; 1 Tim 6:17).
6. Not to covet possessions (Exod 20:17) or to love money (1 Tim 6:10).
7. Not to keep bad company (Ps 1:1; 1 Cor 15:33).

Second, the Bible prohibits all gambling indirectly because it either violates or tends to violate biblical principles, such as:

1. Loving neighbors as ourselves (Lev 19:18; Matt 19:19; Gal 5:14; Jas 2:8).
2. God supplying all we need (Phil 4:19).
3. God blessing industry (Ps 128:2; Prov 10:22; 12:11).
4. Life not consisting in the abundance of possessions (Luke 12:15).
5. Being satisfied with what we have (Heb 13:5).
6. Being good stewards of what God provides (Matt 25:27; 1 Cor 4:2; 1 Pet 4:10).
7. Not being enslaved to appetites of the flesh (Gal 5:13).

Third, the Bible prohibits all gambling indirectly because it clashes with biblical wisdom, which

1. Honors God for providing the wealth we have (Prov 3:9).
2. Honors productive work (Prov 22:29; Eccl 2:24).
3. Does not exploit the poor (Prov 22:16, NIV$_{1984}$).
4. Does not trouble family relations (Prov 15:27).
5. Does not trouble social relations (Prov 28:25).

6. Does not invite loose spending (Prov 13:11, ESV, NLT).

7. Is not a companion of fools (Prov 13:20).

Fourth, I believe the Bible also prohibits all gambling directly and explicitly because

1. It says those who gamble (place faith in chance) "abandon the LORD" (Isa 65:11).

2. It says God does not accept winnings that cost nothing (2 Sam 24:24).

3. It says we must not benefit ourselves at the expense of others (1 Cor 10:24).

Even though many say the Bible does not prohibit gambling per se, and I do not want to go beyond what Scripture requires, I must conclude gambling in the sense of transferring anything of value based on nothing but chance is not only not sanctioned in Scripture and is not only prohibited in Scripture indirectly but is prohibited in Scripture directly. The biggest reason I have for taking this position is that Isaiah 65:11 says placing faith in chance directly contradicts faith in God. We must not dismiss the "Fortune" and "Destiny" mentioned in this verse as merely referring to ancient pagan deities and practices no one worships or employs anymore. God, there, is objecting not merely to ancient pagan deities and practices but also to anyone placing faith in chance rather than in himself. By declaring sinful the very thing that defines gambling, God, in this verse, prohibits all gambling directly. Even when unintended, gambling always puts chance into a place God has, and never shares, in relation to providing wealth and welfare (Deut 8:18; Prov 10:22; Matt 6:33; Rom 11:36). It is not stated as clearly, or as often, as other biblical prohibitions, but I think there is enough evidence to say the Bible prohibits gambling explicitly and not only by implication.

Recommended further reading on the issue of gambling includes: Larry Braidfoot, *Gambling: A Deadly Game* (Nashville: Broadman, 1985); Kenneth Kantzer, "Gambling: Everyone's a Loser," *Christianity Today* (November 25, 1983): 12–13; William Mackenzie, *The Ethics of Gambling* (Philadelphia: Altemus, 1896); Robert Mortimer, *Gambling* (London: Century, 1933); Rex Rogers, *Gambling: Don't Bet on It* (Grand Rapids: Kregel, 2005); John Stapleford, *Bulls, Bears, and Golden Calves: Applying Christian Ethics to Economics* (Downers Grove, IL: InterVarsity, 2002); Randy Starr, *Gambling: What the Bible Says* (Dallastown, PA: Starr, 2015); and Alan Wolf, and Erik Owens, eds., *Gambling: Mapping the American Moral Landscape* (Waco, TX: Baylor, 2009).

Alcohol, Tobacco & Drug Abuse

Recreational Alcohol Consumption

People drink alcohol because it affects the central nervous system in ways that begin favorably because it brightens how people feel, eases tensions, and relaxes social barriers. But the effects of alcohol soon turn negative because continued drinking impairs speech, hampers motor control, distorts judgment, makes people aggressive, and causes them to black out. Drinking to excess is drunkenness, drunkenness is highly addictive, and the addiction of alcoholism destroys mental and physical health, ruins relationships, hampers economic and social functions, fosters crime, and, if not stopped, leads to premature death either from deadly accidents or bad health. More than 88,000 people die from alcohol-related causes in the United States every year, and the cost of alcohol abuse every year in the United States—measured in terms of crime, lost productivity, and healthcare—surpasses $249 billion.[28]

The Bible condemns drunkenness but never bans consuming alcohol, and as a result, Evangelicals are divided over whether it is best to abstain or to drink in moderation while stressing Christian freedom and personal responsibility. When assessing what the Bible says about drinking alcohol, we cannot overlook how often the Bible portrays responsible drinking in a positive light. Giving wine to God symbolizes fellowship with him (Exod 29:40; Lev 23:13), vats overflowing with wine indicate God's blessing (Prov 3:9–10), lacking wine is a curse (Deut 28:30), drinking wine "with a cheerful heart" (Eccl 9:7) is an appropriate way to celebrate good standing with God, free wine for anyone who thirsts indicates the good life God gives believers (Isa 55:1), Jesus revealed his glory by changing water into wine (John 2:11), and Jesus also used not wasting good wine by storing it the right way to illustrate handling the gospel properly (Mark 2:22). Beyond this, the Bible recommends drinking wine for medicinal purposes (1 Tim 5:23), allows using the mind numbing effects of strong drink to help people in pain or hopeless situations forget their misery (Prov 31:6–7), and even credits the mood-altering effects of social drinking as a gift from God (Ps 104:15).

---

[28] "Fact Sheets—Alcohol Use and Your Health," Centers for Disease Control and Prevention, accessed January 3, 2018, https://www.cdc.gov/alcohol/fact-sheets/alcohol-use.htm; "Trends & Statistics," National Institute on Drug Abuse, http://drugabuse.gov/related-topics/trends-statistics.

At the same time, the Bible very strongly condemns drunkenness and addiction (Prov 23:20–21; Isa 5:11; 1 Cor 5:11; 6:12; Eph 5:18). Drunkenness is a deed of darkness (Rom 13:12–13) and an act of sinful human nature (Gal 5:19–21) that not only is sinful in itself but represents spiritual-moral collapse at the end of the world (Rev 14:8; 17:2). Christians must not associate with drunkards (1 Cor 5:11), and people who persist in drunkenness will not inherit the kingdom of God (1 Cor 6:10; Gal 5:21). The Bible very clearly warns that inebriation is perilous, "Wine is a mocker, beer is a brawler," and whoever they lead astray "is not wise" (Prov 20:1). It muddles the brain (Isa 28:7), deadens proper judgment (Prov 31:4–5), causes many troubles (Prov 23:29–35), is humiliating (Gen 9:21; 19:30–38), takes away understanding (Hos 4:11), and destroys spiritual perception (Isa 5:11–12). And the Bible cautions that morally permissible behavior is not always wise or helpful (1 Cor 10:23) and applies this to say we should not insist on freedom to eat or drink things that cause others to stumble (Rom 14:13, 20–22; 1 Cor 8:9, 13).

Finally, although the Bible does not prohibit all drinking of alcoholic beverages, it does require certain people to abstain at certain times for certain reasons. Under the Mosaic covenant, leaders and people set apart by vows or special callings were required to abstain from drinking alcoholic beverages. Kings had to abstain lest they pervert justice (Prov 31:4–5), priests had to abstain when on duty (Lev 10:8–11), people fulfilling Nazirite vows had to abstain for a set time (Num 6:2–4, 20), Sampson and John the Baptist were called by God to abstain for life (Judg 13:7; Luke 1:15), the Rechabites abstained to keep themselves pure (Jer 35:1–19), and Daniel and his friends did as well (Dan 1:8–16). This shows that the Bible regards abstaining from alcohol as an ideal even though in most cases whether and how that ideal is pursued is left to the discretion of individuals or those charged with leading others. It could even be that Old Testament approval of the mood-altering effects of controlled social drinking (Ps 104:14–15; Eccl 10:19) is superseded in the New Testament with being filled by the Holy Spirit (Eph 5:18).

There is room to hold different biblically informed convictions about abstaining or drinking in moderation. We can say neither that the Bible prohibits drinking alcohol nor that abstaining has no biblical basis. Rather, we need to understand that biblical ethics treats the issue as a matter of wisdom and not of obligation. We must pursue wisdom (Prov 4:6–7; Eph 5:15) and shun foolishness (Eph 5:17; 2 Tim 2:23). But these things require exercising moral discretion because what separates what is wise from what is foolish often varies with situation and circumstance. Given the devastating physical, mental, relational, and financial effects of drunkenness, alcoholism, and alcohol-related accidents, it is my judgment that in contemporary culture, recreational, nonmedicinal consumption of alcohol is never really necessary or wise, and because of that, it is better now to abstain than to insist on freedom to indulge.

Those disagreeing with this position because they suppose it requires more than the Bible itself must not condemn or act superior toward those agreeing with it, and those agreeing with this position must not condemn or act superior toward those who think they are free to consume alcohol in self-disciplined moderation. Evangelical Christians can disagree about this and remain in fellowship, and the two sides can together follow biblical teaching by fighting drunkenness, alcohol abuse, and alcoholism.

Smoking Tobacco

The practice of smoking tobacco began in North America, was brought to England by Sir Walter Raleigh in the late sixteenth century, was first marketed for alleged medicinal value, and then was strongly opposed by King James I of England (1566–1625), who also authorized the King James Version of the Bible. King James not only denied that smoking had medicinal value but called it "a custom loathsome to the eye, hateful to the nose, harmful to the brain, and dangerous to the lungs,"[29] and even tried unsuccessfully to stop the practice and keep it from spreading.

The nicotine in tobacco is an addictive substance like alcohol. It can seem innocuous because it does not change behavior or cause accidents, but this difference is deceptive because, unlike drinking alcohol, there is no safe level of smoking. All smoking endangers human health, primarily of smokers but of people exposed to secondhand smoke as well. Health problems caused by smoking include lung cancer, coronary heart disease, stroke, chronic bronchitis, and emphysema. Smoking also raises the risk of getting rheumatoid arthritis, tuberculosis, and certain eye diseases; and it can lead to problems with the immune system as well.

Smoking is the leading cause of preventable death in the world, even surpassing the number of deaths caused by alcohol. More than 7 million people worldwide die from smoking every year, on average, smokers die ten years sooner than nonsmokers, and the annual

---

[29] King James I of England, *A Counterblaste to Tobacco* (1640).

economic cost of smoking in the United States exceeds $300 billion.[30] Recently, vaping has been marketed as a healthier alternative to smoking tobacco, but doctors have started battling an outbreak of life-threatening illnesses related to vaping. Because of this, the Centers for Disease Control and Prevention has advised not vaping until more is known, and researchers fear the practice may prove more deadly than traditional tobacco products.[31]

Smoking tobacco or nicotine products was unknown in Bible times, so is not addressed in Scripture as such. But biblical principles, warnings, and wisdom pertaining to alcohol generally apply to smoking as well. Given what we now know about the harmful effects of smoking, we can say it is foolhardy and very unwise. But that alone does not make smoking sinful any more than doing other dangerous things—like swimming in shark–infested waters or riding a motorcycle in traffic—is inherently sinful. Jesus once explained, "It's not what goes into the mouth that defiles a person but what comes out of the mouth (from the heart)—this is what defiles a person" (Matt 15:11), and Paul adds, "The kingdom of God is not eating and drinking (or smoking), but righteousness, peace and joy in the Holy Spirit" (Rom 14:17).

When assessing the ethics of doing something dangerous where no duty is involved and it only concerns pleasures of the body, Christians need to consider three biblical principles. First, we cannot treat our bodies carelessly because they belong to God (1 Cor 6:19–20). Second, we must only do with our bodies what glorifies God (1 Cor 10:31). Third, we must weigh long-term effects and avoid things leading to death even if they seem initially pleasant (Prov 14:12). Based on these, I conclude that, even though smoking is not inherently sinful, it is a "way of death" foolish to follow in view of all we know today, and it, therefore, is wise to avoid the practice. But I also believe this is a matter of personal responsibility and that civil government should not step in to prevent voluntary smoking by making the practice illegal and punishing violators by law.

---

[30] "Smoking & Tobacco Use: Fast Facts," Centers for Disease Control and Prevention, updated February 6, 2019, http://cdc.gov/tobacco/data_statistics/fact_sheets/fast_facts/index.htm; National Institute on Drug Abuse, "Trends & Statistics."

[31] Sheila Kaplan and Matt Richtel, "The Mysterious Vaping Illness That's Becoming an Epidemic," *The New York Times*, August 31, 2019; "Outbreak of Lung Illness Associated with Using E-cigarette Products: Investigative Notice," Centers for Disease Control and Prevention, posted September 11, 2019, http://cdc.gov/tobacco/basic_information/e-cigarettes/severe-lung-disease.html.

Drug Abuse

Assessing the ethics of drug abuse does not address using drugs medicinally in prescribed ways but only concerns using mind- or body-altering chemicals for recreational, self-pleasing, or other nonmedically prescribed reasons. A drug is any chemical other than foodstuffs that is ingested, injected, or administered for a desired effect on a biological system, and drug addiction is becoming psychologically or physically dependent on using a chemical to the point of losing ability to restrict or discontinue using it voluntarily.

Using mind- or body-altering chemicals nonmedicinally is dangerous and can be very addictive. Between 1999 and 2017, there were more than 700,000 drug overdose deaths in the United States, an average of 130 Americans die every day from overdosing on drugs, and the annual economic cost of drug abuse in the United States surpasses $271 billion.[32] The dangers of using mind- or body-altering chemicals without medical supervision vary by type, but all are deadly.

Warnings in the Bible against drunkenness apply to drug abuse as well, and biblical principles that relate to the subject without mentioning it directly include:

1. Needing to be sober-minded as the end times approach (1 Pet 4:7).
2. Cultivating self-control as a Christian virtue and fruit of the Spirit (Gal 5:23; 2 Pet 1:6).
3. Treating our bodies as temples of God (1 Cor 6:19).
4. Caring for our bodies because they do not belong to us but to God (1 Cor 6:19–20).
5. Being a good moral influence in a bad world (Matt 5:13–16).
6. Not being enslaved to anything other than God (1 Cor 6:12).
7. Realizing addiction to any natural pleasure is foolish (Prov 21:17).

It may be that beyond this the Bible also prohibits abusing mind- or body-altering drugs directly when it condemns occultic practices. The word for such practices in the New Testament is φαρμακεία (*pharmakeia*), from which we get "pharmacy" and "pharmaceutical." The word in Greek can refer to drugs, sorcery, witchcraft, or magic arts because in the ancient

---

[32] "Understanding the Epidemic," Centers for Disease Control and Prevention, accessed September 12, 2019, http://cdc.gov/drugoverdose/epidemic/index.html; National Institute on Drug Abuse, "Trends & Statistics."

world, using mind- or body-altering drugs and occult practices were so intertwined that where the Bible condemns one (Gal 5:20; Rev 9:21; 18:23; 21:8; 22:15), it likely condemns the other as well. People differ on whether this connection remains relevant today. But I think it is dangerous even now to assume abusing drugs is spiritually unrelated and rather believe we still should fear that it not only endangers physical and mental life and health but also leaves abusers vulnerable to "cosmic powers" and "spiritual forces in the heavens" (Eph 6:12).

We have treated alcohol, tobacco, and drug abuse together because they are ethically similar. All three concern personal ethics, each raises questions about whether Scripture prohibits them or not, handling each requires moral discretion making it as much a matter of wisdom as of duty, and, in each case, assessing responsible action requires dealing with perceptions and how it affects other people as much as maintaining purity in the eyes of God. The Bible shows all appetites of the body can be abused and managing them requires the virtue of self-control.

Recommended further reading on issues of alcohol, tobacco, and drug abuse includes Ollie Batchelor, *Use and Misuse: A Christian Perspective on Drugs* (Leicester, UK: InterVarsity, 1999); Tom Breeden and Mark L. Ward Jr., *Can I Smoke Pot? Marijuana in Light of Scripture* (Adelphi, MD: Cruciform, 2016); Andre Bustanoby, *The Wrath of Grapes: Drinking and the Church Divided* (Grand Rapids: Baker, 1987); Christopher C. H. Cook, *Alcohol: Addiction and Christian Ethics* (New York: Cambridge, 2006); Kenneth L. Gentry, *The Christian and Alcoholic Beverages: A Biblical Perspective* (Grand Rapids: Baker, 1986); June Hunt, *Alcohol and Drug Abuse* (Peabody, MA: Hendrickson, 2013); David Kessler, *A Question of Intent: A Great American Battle with a Deadly Industry* (New York: PublicAffairs, 2001); and Robert A. Morey, *The Bible and Drug Abuse* (Grand Rapids: Baker, 1973).

Conclusion

This chapter has been the second of five chapters introducing applied Christian ethics as a subcategory of the larger field of Christian ethics, and in it, readers were introduced to applied issues that are mainly personal in nature. Life is intertwined, and issues of this kind sometimes affect other people. But they are treated as "personal" because they do not involve social dynamics as much as personal welfare, personal responsibility, and personal discipline. The present chapter addressed abortion, birth control, assisted reproduction, euthanasia, biomedical ethics, gambling, and alcohol, tobacco, and drug abuse. Some may question treating abortion, euthanasia, and biomedical ethics in the personal ethics category, but, while they certainly affect other people, I covered them here because they concern personal duties, not group interactions.

The next chapter will take up sexual issues, which are never just personal or just social but always are both at the same time. That means the next chapter will introduce readers to issues at the interface between personal ethics and social ethics. It will cover issues with features similar to both and not reduceable entirely to either one side or the other.

CHAPTER 10

ISSUES IN SEXUAL LIFE

SEXUAL MORALITY; MARRIAGE & SAME-SEX MARRIAGE; DIVORCE & REMARRIAGE; HOMOSEXUALITY; TRANSGENDERISM; PORNOGRAPHY; PROSTITUTION

This is the third of five chapters introducing applied Christian ethics as an academic sub-category within the larger field of Christian ethics. The last chapter introduced applied issues in the personal as opposed to social classification, meaning it dealt with issues focusing more on individuals than groups and more on matters affecting people themselves than relating to others. Applied issues in the social as opposed to personal classification will be covered in two chapters after this one. But the issues in this chapter are not easily classified as either entirely personal or entirely social because they are both. They have to do with how individuals behave but in ways more connected with others than issues covered in the previous chapter. And, even though they connect with others more than issues in the last chapter, they also focus less on group connections than issues covered in the next chapters.

Because issues in this chapter all concern sex, we could suppose "sexual life" might be classified as a third category under applied ethics, but that overlooks how sexual issues always are personal and social at the same time. So, rather than classify issues in sexual life as a third category *separate from personal and social* ethics, this chapter treats them as transitional, meaning we think they always are as personal as they are social, even though we know they never are so personal as to be socially irrelevant and never are so social as to be personally irrelevant. The reason sexual issues cannot be reduced to just one of the two classifications into which issues in applied ethics commonly divide is because, even though sexual intimacy is so personal it should be kept private, the relationships, responsibilities, and results produced by sexual intimacy affect social life in ways that matter to everyone in very public ways.

Sexual Morality

Sexual morality deals with the meaning, nature, and purposes of sex, which means it provides a framework for dealing with questions about the ethics of behaviors, relationships, desires, functions, roles, identities, or commitments relating to sex. Not only does sexual morality address something very important, we also happen to be living in times when no area of applied ethics is more controversial. These days, the United States, Western culture, and perhaps the entire world is being rocked by notions about sexual morality that deny moral revelation and challenge not only what the Bible says about marriage, ordination, and gender roles but also essential matters of faith such as sin, salvation, the gospel, and the identity of God. This section covers how the Bible frames sexual morality in contrast to other ways people now think about it, and issues dealing with more specific questions relating to sex will be addressed after this.

Biblical Sexual Morality

Sex between the first man and woman was among the many things declared "very good" by God at creation (Gen 1:31). Besides affirming the goodness of sex, Scripture goes on to say the human sexual relation is enormously significant because it touches on bearing the image of God, the thing making us not only different but better than everything else in the space-time-material universe. The human sexual relation touches on bearing the image of God because it is the next and only other thing mentioned along with first revealing that enormously significant ethical truth (Gen 1:27).

Sex is both a gift and a very important responsibility. God's gift of sexual intimacy is given only for men and women to use relating to each other as husbands and wives in opposite-sex marriages. But the values regulating how people use this gift matter to everyone—to those who are single as well as those who are married, to families as well as neighbors and friends, to societies and civilizations as well as churches, businesses, and nations, and it matters most of all to God (Heb 13:4). Thus, everyone shares responsibility for handling sex the right way.

God designed sex to be something we enjoy. It is something God wants us to find satisfying, honorable, and attractive, but only as we live by his standards and not just any way we please. Sex is not moral just because we enjoy it. Passions of the flesh can stimulate pleasurable sensations, and that alone is morally deceptive (Gal 6:7–8). When it comes to judging when sex is right or wrong, the flesh is not trustworthy (Gal 5:16–17) because human nature is fallen. Sex is moral only when aligned to God's standards. This seems foolish to people who think good sex aligns with indulging the flesh, but the irony is that pleasing God works better than pleasing ourselves. Sex that is aligned to please God rather than ourselves turns out to be a lot more enjoyable than we imagine going our own way.

Christians agree sex is natural, enjoyable, and fulfilling, and we agree it affects hearts, minds, and souls as well as bodies. But Christians do not agree with reducing sex to entertainment, using the flesh as a moral compass, assuming passion cannot be controlled, or dismissing sexual norms as just matters of taste. Instead, Christians consider sex to be so important it matters to God, and we think it is so precious, sex needs protecting in exclusive, lifelong relationships run on unconditional will-based love that endures regardless of health, wealth, or feelings.

According to the Bible, sex has two functions: a generative function (Gen 1:28) and a unitive function (Gen 2:24). While these functions help regulate moral sex, they are not what make sex morally right or wrong. They are not the compass for moral sex for two reasons: first, because the moral aim for everything is God's glory (1 Cor 10:31), and that includes sex (1 Cor 6:18–20), and second, because what establishes biblical morality in all areas is God's holiness (Lev 11:44–45; 19:2; 20:7; 1 Pet 1:15–16), and that includes sex as well (1 Thess 4:3–4). According to Scripture, moral sex is a matter of keeping sex holy, and sexual immorality is wrong because it is unholy. What holiness means in relation to sex is not something we get to define ourselves. It does not come from philosophers, the dictionary, or anything we feel.

Rather, the holiness on which sexual morality in the Bible relies is specific to the one true God. It is the character of God in Scripture, and that alone requires believing what the Bible says.

What then does holiness in relation to sex look like? According to Lewis, "The old Christian rule is, 'Either marriage, with complete faithfulness to your partner, or else total abstinence.'" Then, Lewis adds,

> This is so difficult and contrary to our instincts, that obviously either Christianity is wrong or our sexual instinct, as it now is, has gone wrong. One or the other. Of course, being a Christian, I think it is the instinct which has gone wrong.[1]

Lewis summarizes biblical sexual morality in very general terms by stressing the single most important boundary condition. But biblical sexual morality has more than one boundary, and examining Scripture carefully reveals that God has a three-part structure to what sexual holiness requires. First, there are principles that establish the essential nature of moral sex as determined by the one who knows it best—the Creator himself. Then, there are prohibitions that help protect and preserve moral sex. Finally, there are promises that incentivize practicing sex God's way.

The Bible reveals seven principles that establish the essential nature of moral sex and together explain what practicing sexual holiness looks like. These are positive because they show us what God is for (not against) when it comes to sex, and they are essential because all of them are required for any sexual behavior, relation, or desire to be moral. If one of these is absent, a sexual behavior, relation, or desire is wrong even if other principles are present. These seven principles of essential moral value are that sex must always be (1) personal or relational, (2) exclusive or unique, (3) intimate or profound, (4) fruitful or productive, (5) selfless or sacrificial, (6) complex or multidimensional, and (7) complementary in the sense that holy sex unites corresponding sexual differences.[2]

Most people know the Bible prohibits many sexual behaviors, and for that reason, some accuse the God of Scripture, and thus Christians, of hating sex. While the Bible does prohibit many sexual behaviors, it is not because God hates sex, but the opposite. The real reason is

---

[1] C. S. Lewis, *Mere Christianity*, 90 (see chap. 2, n. 4).

[2] For a discussion of where and how these principles are revealed in Scripture, please see chapter 7 in my book, *True Sexual Morality* (see chap. 1, n. 41).

that God values sex so highly that prohibitions are issued to help make sure we do not lose what he wants us to have. In other words, God thinks having the best sex is so good for us that barriers are needed to keep people from missing the best sex possible before realizing what they are doing. The prohibitions relating to sex in the Bible are not arbitrary or cruel because each protects one or more of the positive values essential to having the best sex—not only in a moral sense but relationally and experientially as well.

Scripture issues sixteen sex-related prohibitions:

- No sex outside of marriage.
- No sexual worship (spiritualized prostitution).
- No sexual commerce (economic prostitution).
- No homosexual sex.
- No sex with animals (bestiality).
- No sex or marriage with close relatives (incest).
- No pedophilia.
- No sexual violence.
- No lustful sexual desires (inner adultery).
- No intentional gender confusion.
- No sex during a woman's period.
- Strong opposition to divorce.
- Strong opposition to spiritually mixed marriage.
- Strong opposition to sexual immodesty.
- Opposition to polygamy.
- Opposition to fellowship with sexually immoral Christians.

The Bible does not put these prohibitions in a fixed order. But some ranking is involved because Jesus rebuked religious teachers of his day for neglecting "the more important matters of the law" (Matt 23:23). So, even though there is no official ranking of sex-related prohibitions in Scripture, the listing above does approximate the relative standing each sex-related prohibition has compared to the rest.

Finally, in addition to principles of essential value and prohibitions protecting them, the three-part structure ordering sexual holiness in the Bible includes promises that bless pursuing sex God's way. Biblical sexual morality not only starts positively but also ends positively. These promises incentivize moral sex by making it desirable in morally worthy ways. God made us creatures of desire, and, when it comes to keeping sex moral, the main problem we have is not with having strong desires but with not desiring what we should as we should. So the key to keeping sex holy is not the ability to suppress desires but the ability to channel them properly, and that comes with learning to aim them the right way. God cares about this so much that he helps us by promising four results worth desiring that incentivize obeying his rules. These four incentives are that God promises to bless keeping sex holy with abiding joy, genuine satisfaction, exemplary honor, and pure allure.

Abiding Joy

The first blessing God promises for keeping sex holy is joy. When God brought Eve to Adam, he responded with joy (Gen 2:23), and God later even orders husbands to seek the joy promised for practicing moral sex with their wives (Prov 5:18–19). Obeying God produces joy, and disobeying ruins it (Prov 10:28). Everyone longs for joy. But sinners substitute pleasure for joy only to be disappointed because it never delivers what they most long for. Substituting pleasure for joy disappoints because they are not the same and pleasure is not nearly as good. Pleasure is fleeting, while joy abides. Pleasure fades, while joy gets better and better. Pleasure has limits that end with pain or death, while joy is limitless and never causes pain. And, while suffering cancels pleasure, joy endures suffering and rises above it (Heb 12:2).

Genuine Satisfaction

The second blessing for keeping sex holy is a powerful sense of well-being that starts in the soul and touches all levels of human existence—physical, emotional, psychological, and spiritual. Besides joy, God orders husbands also to pursue the satisfaction promised those who practice sex his way (Prov 5:19). Real satisfaction cannot be reached without obeying God first because God only "fulfills the desires of those who fear Him" (Ps 145:19). Sex never satisfies when people disobey God (Ps 16:2; 90:14) because seeking it outside God's will destroys the real thing. Truly satisfying sex blesses obedience and is out of reach to people who elevate sex over God.

Exemplary Honor

The third blessing God promises for keeping sex holy is a sense of honor that comes with earning deserved respect, ultimately from God but in most cases from family members and neighbors as well. Honor connects worthiness with reputation and, while this can seem unimportant in superficial relationships, it matters a lot in profound ones. Sex is profound because God designed sex to link us with others in ways that matter a lot, and sex practiced the right way generates honor and respect. In general, God says, "Those who honor me I will honor, but those who despise me shall be disgraced" (1 Sam 2:30). Therefore, moral sex earns honor (1 Thess 4:4; Heb 13:4), and immoral sex earns dishonor (Prov 6:32–33).

Pure Allure

The fourth blessing God promises for keeping sex holy is pure allure. This is power to attract the attention, love, and dedication of someone worth having as an intimate partner in an exclusive lifelong relationship. This power works two ways because it repels unworthy prospects while also inspiring the right sort to think you are worth pursuing, worth staying pure for, worth denying all others in the world for, and worth making commitments for that last for life. In other words, it is power to attract an authentic soulmate while repelling pretenders who put on a good show but only want to ravish you and leave. Pure allure does this by the power of modesty. Modesty does not say "no to sex" but rather says "yes to sex only with the right person at the right time" and "no to everyone else." Modesty says, "yes to sex only with someone worthy, only with someone who denies everyone else, and only with someone who commits to marriage and lifelong fidelity." When Rebekah met Isaac, "she took her veil and covered herself" (Gen 24:65), and this inspired him to marry and love her (Gen 24:67). And Solomon indicates that modesty produces sexual allure even after couples get married (Song 6:5).

Four counterfeit views now compete against the influence of biblical sexual morality in Western culture, and these are "romantic sexual morality," "playboy sexual morality," "therapeutic sexual morality," and "pagan sexual morality." These views are counterfeit, not only because they do not come from God, but also because they deceive by offering something good and delivering something bad instead. Like lures for catching fish, they use something relatively good to hide something bad that tricks the unwary into giving up something precious.

Romantic Sexual Morality

This view, also known as the "affectional" or "sentimental" view, bases sexual morality on romantic feelings. The role of romantic affection in sexual relationships is elevated to the place of God and made a moral compass. Sexual behaviors, relationships, desires, and commitments are justified based on affectionate feelings alone. Sex is thought moral if people "love" each other in a spontaneous sentimental way, and when their feelings change, sex becomes wrong and relationships depending on them evaporate. Since sentimental feelings are spontaneous, no one can be responsible for how they come and go. As a result, what justifies sex does not remain constant, and faithless partners are not blamed for leaving, for having sex with others, or for breaking marriage vows. It all depends on feelings no one can help. By this view, sexual fidelity is immoral after the feelings thought to justify sex go away, and the only thing romantic sexual morality considers truly wrong is for jilted partners to object by hanging on and not letting faithless partners go.

Christians can say romantic sexual morality is right to think love has a connection with sex, sex should be saved for someone we love, and something is wrong with unloving sex or sex unrelated to love. But romantic sexual morality conflicts with Scripture by reducing sexual relationships and anything depending on them—such as marriages, families, or the fabric of society—to fatalism. It mistakes sentimental feeling for the sort of love that is "strong as death" (Song 8:6) and keeps promises, fulfills responsibilities, and remains faithful no matter how feelings of sentimental affection rise or fall. For Christians, romantic feelings make morally good sex special but are not what make sexual behaviors, relationships, desires, or commitments moral in the first place.

Playboy Sexual Morality

This view, also known as the "natural impulse" or "biological" view, bases sexual morality on pursuing pleasure connected with sex. Sexual pleasure is sought for its own sake, and nothing is ruled out except behaving in ways that hinder pleasure because they are not consensual or threaten someone's health or well-being. Advocates claim desiring sexual pleasure is biologically natural and denying it is unnatural, and then they make this a moral compass for sex. Pursuing anything that stimulates pleasure is considered moral, and disciplining or denying opportunities for pleasure is considered immoral. Consequently, marriage, sexual fidelity, and even insisting on affection are treated as relatively unimportant. What makes sex moral is pleasure and not holiness or even love. Sex partners aim for the glow of successful performance and nothing else matters. Partners need not care for one another and may not even know each other's names. Personal relationships are not expected and tend to be avoided because they complicate opportunities to pursue pleasure with whoever comes along.

Christians can agree with thinking pleasure connected with sex is a good thing. God is not anti-pleasure and designed sex to be something we like and enjoy. Christians do not disagree with the playboy view over affirming sexual pleasure but over using it as a moral compass. Playboy sexual morality contradicts Scripture by deifying sexual pleasure, ignoring the fallen state of human nature, trusting "desires that wage war against the soul" (1 Pet 2:11), reducing sex to something self-centered and impersonal, treating partners as objects rather than persons, and trivializing marriage and family life.

Therapeutic Sexual Morality

This counterfeit justifies sex based on theories about how it affects human psychology. Sex is considered morally right or wrong based on how it relates to things like mental health, psychological stability, or personal growth. Proponents say people actualize themselves through sex and must fulfill sexual desires to become whole persons. Such thinking came from ideas that arose in various psychological theories, and these came then to be seen as what makes sex moral or not. Therapeutic sexual morality says no sexual behavior is right or wrong in the same way for everyone because that comes from satisfying desires that vary from person to person. This view says people are obligated (psychologically and, thus, morally) to pursue sex in whatever ways they find fulfilling, and the only thing it condemns is failing to support what people do to satisfy whatever sexual desires they have.

When it comes to therapeutic sexual morality, Christians agree with thinking sex has a psychological component, satisfies a need for personal interconnection, and affects meaningful human existence. But Christians do not agree with using ideas from theories of psychology as a compass for moral sex. Therapeutic sexual morality conflicts with Scripture because it replaces God with psychological self-satisfaction, and that leads Christians also to disagree with how therapeutic sexual morality relies on a developmental view of personhood, treats sex in a self-centered and non-relational way, denies that sexual morality has any objective basis, and thinks nothing is wrong with fallen human nature.

Pagan Sexual Morality

Ironically this counterfeit is both the most recent view of sexual morality to arise in contemporary culture and the most ancient in human history. Pagan sexual morality recognizes how sex is spiritual, considers sex a good way to harness spiritual power, and then makes using sex to harness spiritual power a compass for what makes sex moral or not. Pagans think spirituality assures morality and then, because all sex is spiritual, they conclude all sex must be moral and the more intense the better. They understand a spiritual world permeates the material world and think that, while spiritual power affects material things, material things can also be used to access and control spiritual power. Pagans think spiritual power running the cosmos can be drawn into our bodies and controlled by intense material experiences—the most powerful being those that are sexual.

Pagan sexual morality is both the nearest and most diametrically opposed counterfeit to biblical sexual morality. It is nearest because it sees how sex is spiritual and treats this as the most important truth about sex. The difference is pagans think any spirituality is necessarily good and holy and Christians do not. The Bible teaches the Devil and sin are spiritual and yet are unholy, evil, and bad. And because Christians know some spiritual things are good and others bad, we cannot go along with how sexual pagans reduce spirituality to sexuality, think people save themselves through sex, and believe sex turns people into gods and goddesses who control the cosmos. So, even though pagans and Christians both agree sex is spiritual, pagan sexual morality also is diametrically opposed to biblical sexual morality. It treats the Devil as a hero and God as a villain, reverses sin and salvation by saying spiritual life requires sinning and avoiding sin destroys it, and denies the deity of Christ because he never sinned or had sex.

Recommended further reading on the issue of sexual morality includes Daniel Akin, *God on Sex* (Nashville: B&H, 2003); Denny Burk, *What Is the Meaning of Sex?* (Wheaton, IL: Crossway, 2013); William Cutrer and Sandra Glahn, *Sexual Intimacy in Marriage* (Grand Rapids: Kregel, 1998); Daniel R. Heimbach, *True Sexual Morality: Recovering Biblical Standards for a Culture in Crisis* (Wheaton, IL: Crossway, 2004); Dennis P. Hollinger, *The Meaning of Sex* (Grand Rapids: Baker, 2009); Peter Jones, *The God of Sex: How Spirituality Defines Your Sexuality* (Colorado Springs, CO: Victor, 2006); Paul Ramsey, *One Flesh: A Christian View of Sex Within, Outside and Before Marriage* (Bramcote, UK: Grove, 1975); Helmut Thielicke, *The Ethics of Sex* (New York: Harper and Row, 1964); Carl R. Truman, *Strange New World:*

How Thinkers and Activists Redefined Identity and Sparked the Sexual Revolution (Wheaton, IL: Crossway, forthcoming 2022); and Philip Turner, *Sex, Money & Power* (Cambridge, MA: Cowley, 1985).

Marriage & Same-Sex Marriage

The meaning and practice of marriage has become one of the most hotly contested issues of our age. Gone are the days when Americans commonly affirmed "mom, baseball, and apple pie," where "mom" stood for honoring traditional roles in marriage. What was thought essential to American identity and social survival now is attacked, not just by a few but many, not just by maverick lawyers but the Supreme Court of the United States, and not just in secular settings but in religious settings as well. Ethical conflict over marriage is driven by two premises—first alleging the legitimacy of homosexual behavior and second alleging there is no socially relevant difference between same-sex and opposite-sex relationships. The second will be addressed here, and the first will be addressed when dealing with homosexuality later in this chapter.

According to Scripture, marriage is a covenant institution that involves a uniting performed by God (Matt 19:6), joining a man and a woman in an exclusive, lifelong, conjugal relationship of love, provision, and support superseding previous family loyalties, transforming all social commitments, and constituting the proper medium for having and raising children. This is true for every marriage, whether those getting married agree or not, and it even applies where human authorities redefine marriage. Redefining marriage by human agencies (kings, governments, or courts) never changes the real thing, so in theological and ethical terms, redefined "marriages" are not actual marriages at all.

Marriage was established at creation when God made the first woman as a corresponding helper (עֵזֶר כְּנֶגְדּוֹ, *ʿezer kʾnegdō*) for the first man and united them in a way that affirmed they had equal value without erasing the significance of sexual differences and their assigned roles in marriage (Gen 1:27). The Bible does not say everyone must get married, but it does connect marriage with the kind of relationship we are made to have with God (Eph 5:32). In God's plan, getting married has three elements: leaving, cleaving, and becoming one flesh (Gen 2:24; Matt 19:5). "Leaving" denotes establishing a new social unit distinct from what came before. "Cleaving" denotes an ongoing life transition. And "becoming one flesh" denotes forming an intimate relational connection at all levels—sentimental, physical, psychological, and spiritual.

The new social unit generated by marriage is procreatively structured, monogamous, complementary, and lifelong. The male-female distinction is fundamental to how God structured marriage at creation (Gen 2:18–24) and aligns it with God's procreational mandate (Gen 1:28). This procreational structure is not optional but rather is essential for all real marriages, whether particular married couples go on to have children or not, and that is because man-woman married couples provide the proper setting for having and raising children (Gen 1:28; 4:1–2). The procreational structure of real marriage obviously clashes with the new prototype set forth in our day that denies marriage has any connection with procreating at all.

Besides being procreatively structured, marriage is intended to be monogamous, meaning it is designed to unite one man and one woman. God first created one man, Adam (Gen. 2:7), and then made one woman, Eve (Gen 2:22), each in separate acts. Then he brought the one man and one woman together in a marriage that was monogamous. God did not make multiple wives for Adam or multiple husbands for Eve. The formula was just one of each, and Jesus, in the New Testament, reaffirmed that God from the beginning intended marriage to be monogamous and never altered that design (Matt 19:4–6).

It is true that some Old Testament saints had multiple wives and that God never tells men with many wives to go back to having one by divorcing the rest. But that does not mean God ever made polygamy morally discretionary. Although Scripture never bans polygamy in general terms, it does command leaders to avoid it. Kings must not "acquire many wives" (Deut 17:17), and church leaders may not have more than one wife at a time (1 Tim 3:2, 12; Titus 1:6). Scripture also makes clear that polygamy always disrupts family harmony (Gen 16:4–5; 30:1–2; 1 Sam 1:6–7; 1 Kgs 11:3). So, even though Scripture only tells leaders not to have multiple wives, it treats monogamy as best for everyone, and even though polygamy is not treated like adultery, it always disqualifies people from serving as role models for marriage.

Besides being procreatively structured and monogamous, husbands and wives also have complementary roles in marriage, meaning they have functions that differ in ways that go together without one being better than the other. Men and women have equal worth because both are made in the image of God (Gen 1:27). But they have different roles in marriage that apply regardless of circumstances or culture. The equality of husbands and wives does not mean they have interchangeable responsibilities. As Jones observes, "To be equal is not to be identical, and justice requires taking relevant differences into account."[3] In a marriage, the husband is assigned to lead in a manner that is selfless, sacrificial, and loving (Eph 5:23, 25–28), and this means he must do all he can, consistent with following Christ, to ensure marriage to his wife succeeds by securing her well-being on all levels—spiritual, material, and emotional. The wife is assigned to cooperate with her husband in marriage (Eph 5:22–24), and this means she must do her best, consistent with following Christ, to ensure marriage to her husband succeeds by supporting his leadership.

Finally, besides being procreatively structured, monogamous, and complementary, marriage is also meant to last for life. Marriages on earth do not last forever (Matt 22:30) because they end at death (1 Cor 7:39). But they should not end before that, and Jesus reaffirmed that God wants marriages to be lifelong (Matt 19:6). So, even though couples do not stay married after one of them dies (Rom 7:2–3; 1 Cor 7:39), God does not want people abandoning marriages before that (Mal 2:14–16). We will discuss divorce and remarriage in the next section and are here only noting that divorce is inherently tragic. It always results from sin and falls short of what marriage should be.

Prior to the twenty-first century, no society ever treated marriage as relating to same-sex relationships.[4] In 2001, Western countries started legalizing same-sex marriages, and the Supreme Court legalized them in the United States when it handed down the *Obergefell* decision in 2015. Since then, LGBTQ+ advocacy groups have portrayed opponents as bigots with no good reason for disagreeing, and those holding a traditional view of marriage have claimed that a right to disagree needs protecting as a matter of religious liberty.

Before *Obergefell*, the main argument for legalizing same-sex marriage was that it simply was a matter of treating everyone equally and would change nothing for anyone except same-sex couples wanting to marry each other. But opponents responded that there was no unequal treatment in existing marriage laws relating to same-sex attracted individuals without redefining legal marriage and predicted that, if marriage was legally redefined to remove what distinguishes opposite-sex from same-sex relationships, people disagreeing would be persecuted.

---

[3] Jones, *Biblical Christian Ethics*, 166 (see chap. 2, n. 4).

[4] See Edward Westermark, *The History of Human Marriage* (New York: Allerton, 1922). Also, in his dissent to the *Obergefell* decision, Chief Justice Roberts reports that lawyers who petitioned in favor of same-sex marriage conceded they were "not aware of any society that permitted same-sex marriage before 2001." *Obergefell v. Hodges*, 576 U.S. 644 (2015), Roberts, C. J. dissenting. I.A (4).

Today that shift has occurred, and Christians are facing two challenges, one regarding what marriage means in society and the other regarding civil rights.

The first challenge Christians face relating to marriage following *Obergefell* is that what marriage means in society at large now conflicts with what it means according to God and human history. In constitutional terms, what marriage means has been redefined to align with what homosexuals wanted in order to use government to force others to accept their behavior. In US law, marriage now is nothing more than a way of getting others to affirm private feelings that contribute nothing of public significance (like having and raising children to be good citizens). It has become just a way of affirming sexual desires and no longer indicates a procreationally structured institution essential to social survival. The court, in *Obergefell*, first redefined marriage and then, and only then, was able to claim there is "no difference between same- and opposite-sex couples" in regard to it.[5] So we now live in a culture that defines legal "marriage" differently than real marriage.

The second ethical challenge Christians face following *Obergefell* is that debate over the new right same-sex sexual partners have to "marry" now focuses on religious liberty. The question has become whether or not to allow religious exemptions for institutions and people who do not agree with affirming the new right. This arises because what government affirms is not neutral, and persecution arises when the power of civil law is used to enforce legal rights that conflict with strongly held ethical standards grounded in religious convictions. Legalizing same-sex marriage means what was normal is normal no longer, what was universal now is optional, and the newly conceived marriage right for same-sex sexual partners must be conceded throughout society whether people like it or not. As a result, ever since same-sex marriage was declared a constitutional right, schools, businesses, and the armed forces have been working to get everyone to accept same-sex sexual desires and behavior as normal and good and to marginalize, and even penalize, anyone who resists.

Christians now want government to affirm that a constitutional right to disagree based on religious convictions has priority over the new marriage right for same-sex sexual partners

---

[5] Daniel R. Heimbach, "The Insidious Logic of the Court's Marriage Decision," Ethics and Religious Liberty Commission, July 10, 2015, https://erlc.com/resource-library/articles/the-insidious -logic-of-the-courts-marriage-decision.

and that not only should churches, synagogues, and mosques be exempted but also individuals who have religiously based objections to treating same-sex marriages as real marriages. But LGBTQ+ advocates disagree and are arguing religious liberty must give way to the marriage right for same-sex sexual partners the way some were forced to accept racial equality for African Americans despite holding strong convictions against it.[6]

Recommended further reading on the issue of marriage includes Christopher Ash, *Marriage* (Vancouver, B. C.; Regent, 2003); Henry Brandt and Kerry L. Skinner, *Marriage God's Way* (Nashville: B&H, 1999); Maggie Gallagher, *The Abolition of Marriage: How We Destroy Lasting Love* (Washington: Regnery, 1996); Robert P. George and Jean Bethke Elshtain, *The Meaning of Marriage* (Dallas: Spence, 2006); Sherif Girgis, Ryan T. Anderson, and Robert P. George, *What Is Marriage?* (New York: Encounter, 2012); Daniel R. Heimbach, *Why Not Same-Sex Marriage: A Manual for Defending Marriage against Radical Deconstruction* (Sisters, OR: Trusted Books, 2014); Gordon Hugenberger, *Marriage as a Covenant* (Grand Rapids: Baker, 1998); Timothy Keller, *The Meaning of Marriage* (New York: Dutton, 2011); Andreas J. Köstenberger and David W. Jones, *God, Marriage, and Family*, (Wheaton, IL: Crossway, 2010); Glen T. Stanton, *Why Marriage Matters* (Colorado Springs: Pinon, 1979); and Gary Thomas, *Sacred Marriage* (Grand Rapids: Zondervan, 2000).

Divorce & Remarriage

The Bible regards marriage as very important. It is something sacred, a covenant institution established by God and accountable to him. So, of course, God strongly opposes terminating marriages before physical death separates one partner from the other.

---

[6] This was argued at length by Chai Feldblum, who served in the former Obama Administration. See Chai R. Feldblum, "Moral Conflict and Liberty: Gay Rights and Religion," *Brooklyn Law Review* 72:1 (2006): 61–123. And Beto O'Rourke, an unsuccessful Democratic candidate for president, made this a campaign promise in 2019 (Caleb Parke, "Beto threatens tax-exempt status of churches if they don't support gay marriage," *Fox News,* October 11, 2019, https://www.foxnews.com/politics/beto-church-of-tax-exempt-status-gay-marriage).

That God strongly opposes divorce is clear in both the Old and New Testaments. The prophet Malachi announces,

> The LORD is acting as the witness between you and the wife of your youth, because you have broken faith with her, though she is your partner, the wife of your marriage covenant. Has not the LORD made them one? In flesh and spirit they are his . . . . So guard yourself in your spirit, and do not break faith with the wife of your youth. "I hate divorce," says the LORD God of Israel, "and I hate a man's covering himself with violence as well as with his garment," says the LORD Almighty. So guard yourself in your spirit, and do not break faith. (Mal 2:14-16, NIV$_{1984}$)[7]

In the New Testament, Jesus says the same when declaring, "What God has joined together, let no one separate" (Matt 19:6; Mark 10:9). And Paul affirms it again where he says,

> To the married I give this command—not I, but the Lord—a wife is not to leave her husband. But if she does leave, she must remain unmarried or be reconciled to her husband—and a husband is not to divorce his wife. (1 Cor 7:10-11)

---

[7] I use the 1984 translation of the New International Version (NIV$_{1984}$), which agreed with universal translating tradition of these verses followed by Christians for nineteen centuries and for even more centuries of textual interpretation by Jewish scholars. But a break with this long tradition of interpreting and translating took place among English translators in the early twentieth century, starting with the English Standard Version (ESV) and then spreading to other translations, including the NIV. This break changes the meaning of the text by shifting the subject (in v. 16) from God to a man divorcing his wife, translating the noun *divorce* as a verb, and making *hate* a feeling in the heart of unfaithful men rather than how God views divorce. These changes transform the single most powerful statement in Scripture against divorce into a warning merely to avoid bad feelings when divorcing. Revising translation this way is grammatically impossible because a noun (*divorce*) cannot be translated as a verb (*who divorces*). The main reason given for breaking with long-established tradition is that the subject who acts in v. 16 is put in third person (he hates) rather than in first person (I hate). This subject was long understood, by Jews and Christians alike, to be God referring to himself, and not men divorcing their wives. Recent English translators have forgotten that the reason God refers to himself in third person rather than first person is an ancient Hebrew rhetorical device used in prophetic speech to underscore something God declares from a very lofty and official position. It is a device something like using the royal "we" in English when rulers refer to themselves in their ruling capacity. See Andrew S. Malone, "God the Illeist: Third-Person Self-References and Trinitarian Hints in the Old Testament," *Journal of the Evangelical Theological Society*, 52/3 (September 2009): 499–518.

These passages show how strongly God opposes divorce. In fact, he hates divorce and says it makes a marriage covenant (pictured as a cloak, Ruth 3:9; Ezek 16:8) look like a garment splattered with blood worn by a murderer who has killed a victim (Mal 2:16, NIV$_{1984}$).

In biblical terms, marriage is not something we do to ourselves, even with God's blessing. Rather, we are joined in marriage by God (Mal 2:15; Matt 19:6), and for that reason, it is presumptuous to think we can undo marriages ourselves. Divorcing assumes we can unmake something God makes. It assumes we can do away with something for which we answer ultimately to God and not just to each other, our families, our neighbors, or even to the Church. The Bible says, "In flesh and spirit they are his" (Mal 2:15, NIV$_{1984}$). No one actually undoes anything God does, so marrying another person after wrongful divorce simply adds sinning by adultery to sinning by illegitimate divorce. It compounds one sin with another.

Mark reports that Jesus taught, "Whoever divorces his wife and marries another commits adultery against her" and, "if she divorces her husband and marries another, she commits adultery" (Mark 10:11–12). So, whether a husband or a wife initiates wrongful divorce, Jesus taught, if either marries another person, he or she commits adultery because the first marriage continues in the eyes of God. Where divorce is not justified, not even innocent parties have any right to remarry, and Matthew and Luke explain that a third party who marries a wrongly divorced person commits adultery as well (Matt 5:32; Luke 16:18).

But even though God opposes divorce very strongly, he does not oppose it absolutely in the sense of allowing no exceptions. God who joins couples in marriage also permits divorce under limited conditions. We see this in several places: first, in the law of Moses, where God allows divorce based on "something indecent" (עֶרְוַת דָּבָר, *'erwaṯ dāḇār*, Deut 24:1); second, where Jesus says something translated "sexual immorality" (λόγου πορνείας, *logou porneias* in Matt 5:32 and πορνεία, *porneia* in Matt 19:9) justifies divorce; third, where Jesus says putting God first may cost losing a wife (Luke 14:26; 18:29); and fourth, where Paul says a Christian may accept divorce initiated by a nonbelieving spouse (1 Cor 7:15).

Thus, God permits divorce in some cases, but there is much debate over how best to interpret grounds he allows. No one says divorce is ideal and, even where it is allowed, divorce remains an exception to the good of staying married. When Jesus discussed grounds for permissible divorce (Matt 19:3–12), he qualified it by saying "it was not like that from the beginning" (Matt 19:8). So, while God permits divorce under limited conditions, it is a concession to how persistent sin—referred to as "the hardness of your hearts"—affects family relationships, and, when addressing divorce, Jesus focused on keeping marriages together and not on escaping problem marriages.

Evangelicals agree God usually opposes divorce even though he gives grounds for some kind of exception. But Evangelicals divide over how best to interpret the grounds God allows and over whether remarriage is allowed after acting on those grounds. This division usually reduces to whether Christians can initiate divorce without sinning after starting sex in marriage, and what happens after that. Put another way, the big question is whether divorce is allowed after consummating marriage, and the follow-up question is, if so, whether remarriage is allowed after getting divorced on permissible grounds.

In writing the church at Corinth, Paul explained that Christians do not sin if they accept divorce initiated by unbelievers (1 Cor 7:15). Even so, Paul gives Christians no grounds for initiating divorce themselves without sinning. If an unbelieving spouse agrees to remain married, a Christian must stay married to that unbeliever and not get divorced. But, if an unbelieving spouse initiates divorce (for any reason), the Christian spouse may then accept divorce without sinning. The unbeliever may incur guilt, but the believer does not. Any guilt assigned is not shared, and the Christian is responsible only to avoid contentiousness (1 Cor 7:15).

Division among Evangelicals over permitting divorce is not over whether a Christian may accept and go through with divorce initiated by an unbelieving spouse, but, rather, is over whether a Christian may ever initiate divorce himself or herself and, if so, on what grounds. There are two main views. A majority view among Evangelicals, sometimes called the Erasmian view,[8] holds that adultery, and perhaps other unfaithful actions as well, gives Christians grounds to initiate divorce without sinning; and a minority view, also held by some Evangelicals, contends that Christians may never initiate divorce without sinning, even if a spouse commits adultery.

The majority view assumes that the grounds God allowed for divorce through Moses, and the grounds Jesus mentioned when explaining what that was (Matt 5:32; 19:9), must both apply to marriages after couples exchange vows and become sexually active. In other

---

[8] This is because Desiderius Erasmus of Rotterdam (1466–1536) was the first in the history of Christianity to argue this view. No one interpreted biblical teaching on divorce this way before the late fifteenth century.

words, those holding the majority view think whatever grounds the Bible permits must apply to terminating consummated marriages, and they assume the grounds allowed must include adultery and perhaps other sex-related sins as well. Furthermore, they think, because Jesus dealt with grounds in the Mosaic law allowing husbands to initiate divorce without sinning, it must be that Christians also are allowed to initiate divorce without sinning.

Everyone holding this majority view agrees physical adultery gives Christians grounds to initiate divorce. But all do not agree on whether other grounds, like abandonment or abuse, are included beyond that. Some argue grounds permitting divorce must include more because Moses and Jesus used terms that often cover more than physical adultery alone,[9] and others resist this because of how including more conflicts with a high view of marriage.

Against this majority view, other Evangelicals argue that, while God allows Christians to accept divorce initiated by an unbelieving spouse (for any reason), he never allows Christians to initiate divorce, even for adultery.[10] Those holding this minority view criticize the majority view for some or all of the following reasons.

First, they criticize the majority view for treating marriage like a contract when Scripture reveals marriage to be a covenant (Mal 2:14; Prov 2:17). In a covenant, duty to be faithful remains intact however faithless the other partner may be (Ezek 16:59–60; Hos 3:1), and claiming that obligation to stay married ceases if a partner commits adultery treats marriage like a contract in which obligation to be faithful ceases when other parties do not keep their end of the bargain.

Second, they criticize the majority view for missing how the Mosaic grounds for divorce, as inaugurated, only applied to a stage in Semitic marriage called betrothal that has no parallel to the way marriage is practiced in Western culture. The Mosaic grounds applied to a period during which couples were considered legally and morally married (not just engaged) even

---

[9] For example, William F. Luck, *Divorce and Remarriage: Recovering the Biblical View* (San Francisco: Harper & Row, 1987).

[10] Some non-Evangelicals accept this reading of the Bible more easily that many Evangelicals. For example, Ramsey says "divorce on account of adultery is as far removed from the teaching of Jesus as divorce would be for any of the other reasons prevalently considered . . . . Different degrees of seriousness . . . give no ground for begging the question in Christian ethics in favor of divorce under one circumstance only, since divorce for any reason is absolutely different from no divorce at all." Paul Ramsey, *Basic Christian Ethics* (Louisville: Westminster/John Knox, 1993, orig. 1950), 72.

before making vows to God and becoming sexually active,[11] and terminating their relationship during this pre-vow, pre-sex stage was considered divorce of the sort Joseph planned in Matthew 1:18–19. The mild grounds Moses allowed in Deuteronomy 24:1 (עֶרְוַת דָּבָר, *'erwaṯ dābār*, something indecent) fits a high view of marriage only if applied to the pre-vow, pre-sex betrothal stage of Semitic marriage and not later, which explains how Moses could allow divorce for "something indecent" and yet at the same time say nothing can justify divorce if a woman was a virgin when she commenced sex with her husband (Deut 22:13–19).

Third, they criticize the majority view for interpreting the Mosaic grounds for divorce in a way that conflicts with other parts of Mosaic law. Moses required death for adultery (Deut 22:22). So, if the law was self-consistent, whatever grounds Moses allowed could not have permitted divorce for adultery short of capital punishment whether during betrothal or after.

Fourth, they criticize the majority view for thinking Jesus changed how the grounds Moses provided applies when the Bible says he did not (Matt 5:18). If the grounds Moses allowed did not include adultery and did not apply after making vows to God and becoming sexually active, and if Jesus did not change any of that, he could not have added adultery as grounds nor could he have applied it after marriages are consummated.

Fifth, they criticize the majority view for failing to explain how the disciples could have been shocked by what they heard Jesus say (Matt 19:10). Limiting grounds for divorce to adultery was not shocking to Jews with a high view of marriage, and if Jesus allowed divorce for mild reasons, his disciples would have thought him permissive. They knew Jesus held a high view of marriage and opposed leniency, so the only thing the disciples could have thought impossibly unrealistic was if Jesus did not allow divorce even for adultery.

Sixth, they argue that the majority view fails to explain how Mark, Luke, and Paul could have summarized Jesus' teaching on divorce without mentioning grounds making it permissible (Mark 10:2–12; Luke 16:18; 1 Cor 7:10–11). If Jesus allowed terminating consummated marriages for any reason, then leaving that out makes no sense. But, if what Jesus allowed did

---

[11] On the betrothal stage of Semitic marriage, see John Piper, "Divorce and Remarriage: A Position Paper," Desiring God, July 21, 1986, https://www.desiringgod.org/articles/divorce-and-remarriage-a -position-paper; G. F. Moore, *Judaism in the First Centuries of the Christian Era*, vol. 2 (New York: Schocken, 1971); Joachim Jeremias, *Jerusalem at the Time of Jesus* (Philadelphia: Fortress, 1969); and Abel Isaksson, *Marriage and Ministry in the New Testament*, trans. Neil Tomkinson (Lund, Sweden: Gleerup, 1965).

not apply to their readers, leaving it out makes complete sense. Mark, Luke, and Paul were writing to Gentile (non-Semitic) readers who did not practice a pre-vow, pre-sex betrothal stage in marriage, so the grounds Jesus allowed did not relate to them and mentioning it could have led them astray.

Seventh, they criticize the majority view for being unable to explain why Jesus used a broad term (πορνεία, *porneia*, sexual immorality) rather than a precise one (μοιχεία, *moicheia*, adultery) when referring to grounds for divorce. If Jesus meant adultery, why did he not say so? Or at least why did Matthew not use the Greek for adultery (μοιχεία, *moicheia*) when translating what Jesus said?

Finally, they criticize those holding the majority view who say Jesus allowed terminating consummated marriages for acts of adultery but not for simply wanting to commit adultery because distinguishing these components treats the seventh commandment in a way Jesus rejected (Matt 5:28). And they criticize other proponents of the majority view who say because Moses allowed divorce for "something indecent," Jesus must have allowed divorce even for desiring adultery, because doing that denies that Jesus held a high view of marriage (Matt 19:6).

Besides dividing over grounds for initiating divorce without sin, Evangelicals also divide over whether people who get divorced on permissible grounds can remarry. Evangelicals agree that marrying another person is wrong if getting divorced was not justified in the first place. But what about marrying another person after justified divorce? Some deny remarriage is allowed even after permissible divorce because Jesus held that victims of unjustified divorce (those not incurring guilt) commit adultery if they remarry (Matt 5:32; Luke 16:18). These also argue that this view was taught in the early Church; that a covenant joined by God cannot be undone; that Malachi says a divorced wife still "is your partner, the wife of your marriage covenant" (Mal 2:14, NIV₁₉₈₄); and that Paul says believers who divorce one another "must remain unmarried or be reconciled" (1 Cor 7:11).

But other Evangelicals hold that remarriage after permissible divorce is allowed because, where God permits divorce, it is logical to assume he includes freedom to remarry. They also argue that, while no one is able to undo a covenant God establishes, God can do it himself; that Paul says believers allowed to accept divorce initiated by unbelievers are "not bound" (1 Cor 7:15), which means they are free to remarry; and that Paul also says a person "released" (permissibly divorced) from a marriage does not sin if he or she remarries—"if you do get married, you have not sinned" (1 Cor 7:27–28).

Recommended further reading on the issue of divorce and remarriage includes Jay E. Adams, *Marriage, Divorce, and Remarriage in the Bible* (Grand Rapids: Zondervan, 1980); Andrew Cornes, *Divorce & Remarriage: Biblical Principles* (Grand Rapids: Eerdmans, 1993); Guy Duty, *Divorce and Remarriage* (Minneapolis, MN: Bethany, 1967); Stanley A. Ellisen, *Divorce and Remarriage in the Church* (Grand Rapids: Zondervan, 1977); William A. Heth and Gordon J. Wenham, *Jesus and Divorce* (Nashville: Thomas Nelson, 1984); Wayne H. House, ed., *Divorce and Remarriage: Four Christian Views* (Downers Grove, IL: InterVarsity, 1990); David Instone-Brewer, *Divorce and Remarriage in the Bible* (Grand Rapids: Eerdmans, 2002); John J. McArthur, Jr., *On Divorce* (Chicago: Moody, 1985); John Murray, *Divorce* (Philadelphia: P&R, 1961); and Gordon J. Wenham et al., *Remarriage after Divorce in Today's Church* (Grand Rapids: Zondervan, 2006).

Homosexuality

Few issues in applied ethics are as controversial as homosexuality. This makes moral witness difficult, but we cannot ignore the issue because God addresses it in Scripture, and it affects people around us. The term *homosexuality* can mean different things and may indicate feeling aroused by members of the same sex, having romantic aspirations toward someone of the same sex, having once had sex with a same-sex partner, having sex with same-sex partners all the time, identifying with the LGBTQ+ community, or identifying with the term for any reason at all. But it never means all these at once. Scientists now say there is no empirical basis for it, and what people communicate by it is clouded by how it is perceived socially, morally, and politically. Evangelicals once assumed *homosexuality* and *heterosexuality* had accepted definitions. But that is no longer the case. So, I, here, will refer to *homosexuality* without assuming agreement on what it means.

Some claim the Bible says little about same-sex sexual desires or behavior and treats the subject marginally, but that is not correct. Same-sex sexual desires and behavior are both condemned in interlocking passages throughout the Bible, and accepting, practicing, and promoting same-sex sexual desires and behavior is regarded as paradigmatic of rejecting divine authority (Rom 1:22–23; Rev 21:27; 22:15). The Bible first condemns the practice implicitly by telling us God, at creation, envisioned sex in a way that was incompatible with same-sex sexual desires and behavior. God made sex to occur within man-woman marriages. When "a man leaves his father and mother and bonds with his wife . . . they become one flesh" (Gen 2:24). This sets the pattern for sex as much as for marriage and defines the proper use of sex as excluding same-sex relationships and desires.

Same-sex sexual desires and behavior also clash with the main thing God made sex to satisfy. Before God made sex, the Bible does not say Adam lacked companionship (he had many animal friends), rational communication (he talked with God every day), or even ability to reproduce (though he needed that as well). Rather, it says God made sex to satisfy Adam's need for "a helper corresponding to him" (עֵזֶר כְּנֶגְדּוֹ, *ʿēzer kᵉnegdō*, Gen 2:18, 20). Adam needed a corresponding other. He did not lack a same-sex partner but one made differently in a fashion meant to unite with him. Presenting it this way shows uniting corresponding difference to be essential to the nature of human sexuality, and, finally, same-sex sexual desires and behavior also clash with the generational mandate (Gen 1:28) and role we have in preserving human continuity (Gen 2:24).

Along with condemning same-sex sexual desires, and behavior by implication, when reporting on how God made sex at creation, the Bible also condemns it explicitly in many places. Same-sex sexual behavior is directly forbidden in moral law: "You are not to sleep with a man as with a woman; it is detestable" (Lev 18:22; 20:13). Before that, when God destroyed Sodom and Gomorrah, we are told he acted as "Judge of the whole earth" (Gen 18:25), meaning he enforced standards that apply to everyone and acted in "fierce anger" (Deut 29:23), meaning he truly hated what they did. While the people of Sodom did many wicked things, parading (Isa 3:9) deviant sex (Jude 7) and same-sex sexual desires and behavior in particular was treated by God as the last straw demanding immediate intervention. We know this because Ezekiel lists characteristic sins of Sodom from least to greatest ending with "detestable acts" (תּוֹעֵבָה, *tōwʿēbâh*, Ezek 16:50), a term signaling reference to where same-sex sexual behavior is prohibited in moral law (Lev 18:22; 20:13).

Besides forbidding same-sex sexual behavior, the Bible also forbids desiring it. Doing anything God forbids is sin, but wanting to is as well. Jesus said it is wrong not only to have adulterous sex but also to desire it (Matt 5:27–28). But we must be careful at this point. Experiencing temptation is not the same as entertaining it. It is not sin to be tempted (Heb 4:15) but is sin to accept or enjoy feeling tempted (Jas 1:15). The sin line is crossed when temptation is not resisted (Jas 4:7). Unresisted temptations are lusts that "wage war against the soul" (1 Pet 2:11), and this applies to desiring same-sex sexual intimacy no less than to other temptations.

When forbidding same-sex sexual desires and behavior, the Bible adds that no one can excuse it either. Violators deserve punishment, and, if that occurs, God says it is "their own fault" (Lev 20:13). Because God made us, this especially means no one can blame same-sex sexual desires or behavior on how God made them. But, along with prohibiting same-sex sexual behavior and desiring it, the Bible also promises that anyone violating God's standard can be forgiven and homosexual identity can be forsaken. A person who repents for sinning this way is "washed," "sanctified," and "justified" (1 Cor 6:11). And, when that happens, that person not only stops practicing same-sex sexual activities but also ceases to be so identified.

The only place the Bible mentions people who practice same-sex sexual behavior using terms equivalent to "homosexual" is where Paul says some in the Corinthian church had been μαλακοὶ (malakoi, men and boys who submit to be used homosexually) and ἀρσενοκοῖται (arsenokoitai, men who have sex with men). The Holy Spirit inspires Paul to say, "Some of you used to be like this" (1 Cor 6:11) using a verb tense indicating something no longer the case. Paul says these are Christians who had been but no longer are homosexual. In other words, they became former homosexuals. In this way, the Bible says there are no same-sex identified Christians, only some who used to identify with the practice before converting. This does not mean Christians may never struggle with same-sex attraction. It only means Christians do not identify with it because we identify with Christ (Matt 10:25; Rom 8:29; Gal 2:20; Col 3:10) and no longer with temptations to forsake him (Rom 8:12; Gal 5:24; Col 3:9).

If the Bible challenges feelings or behavior, we must change them to conform to what the Bible says, but some are trying to revise biblical interpretation in order to affirm same-sex desires and behavior. One might think these would reject the Bible as erroneous. But they do not because they are trying to change what Bible-believers believe. This effort is ironic because people who deny inerrancy are trying to revise how people who affirm inerrancy understand what the Bible says.

In order to deny that destroying Sodom and Gomorrah (Gen 19:1–29) shows God condemning same-sex sexual desires and behavior, revisionists used to argue that those cities were destroyed for attempted rape, not for sex between consenting same-sex attracted partners, and now they usually argue Sodom and Gomorrah were destroyed for inhospitality and not anything to do with sex. But neither argument makes sense. The first fails because the text nowhere suggests what the men at Lot's door wanted would have been fine if his visitors consented, and limiting God's judgment to what happened at Lot's door makes him a monster for demolishing "the entire plain, all the inhabitants of the cities, and whatever grew on the ground" (Gen 19:25). The second argument fails because it cannot explain why Lot suggested sex with his daughters in place of what the men at his door came for, makes God a villain for killing those trying to apply reasonable hospitality practices (the men at Lot's door) and saving those causing problems (Lot and his family), and conflicts with Jude saying Sodom and Gomorrah were punished for sexual deviancy (Jude 7).

To deny that the passages in moral law prohibit all same-sex sexual desires and behavior (Lev 18:22; 20:13), revisionists claim they only prohibit using same-sex sexual intimacy in cult prostitution and do not apply to loving sex between same-sex sexual partners. But this, too, makes no sense because, although Leviticus does include passages dealing with worship procedures, the passages forbidding same-sex sexual behavior list moral rules, not worship procedures. Revisionists take one prohibition out of context and ignore the rest. Incest, adultery, and bestiality are prohibited on the same list with same-sex sexual behavior, and no one suggests these only deal with worship procedures and are not moral rules. If incest, adultery, and bestiality are morally prohibited, then same-sex sexual behavior is as well.

Finally, in order to dismiss the relevance of Romans 1:18–32, revisionists claim it only condemns same-sex sexual activity between non same-sex attracted partners and does not apply to same-sex sexual activity between partners who are born same-sex attracted. This fails because it relies on a thesis few scientists support, denies inspiration by supposing the text cannot apply to future findings an ancient writer did not know about, denies inerrancy by supposing what the text means can be wrong unless changed to affirm what scientists say, and defies logic by assuming the passage addresses a non-problem by condemning sex practiced in a way no one wants.

These days, denying the legitimacy of same-sex sexual behavior based on Scripture strikes many as unfair. We hear constantly that same-sex sexual behavior is normal, it is impossible to change, and all sexual orientations deserve equal treatment. Two notions underlie these claims: first, that satisfying sexual desires is essential to happiness and health and, second, that same-sex sexual orientation is innate. Both undermine Christian ethics but must be understood to address today's culture and those influenced by such thinking. The first conflicts with Jesus teaching an ethic of self-denial (Matt 16:24; Mark 8:34; Luke 9:23), and the second rejects the Word of God in favor of dubious science.

Assuming obligation to satisfy sexual desires is the same as saying we should trust the flesh in place of God, and that is something the Bible warns against: "We are not obligated to the flesh to live according to the flesh, because if you live according to the flesh, you are going to die" (Rom 8:12–13). Indeed, according to the Bible, no appetite of the flesh can be trusted (Gal 5:16–17) and, unless disciplined, will destroy us (Rom 8:6; Gal 6:8). Here, I agree with Stephen Holmes, who says, "Our sexual desires are not in pressing need of being fulfilled; they are in pressing need of being mastered and reordered so that we may grow into Christlikeness."[12]

This does not single out people attracted to same-sex sexual activity. No one is free to pursue appetites of the flesh however he wants, and, in this regard, people desiring same-sex sexual activity are no different than anyone else. We all must reform the sexual appetite to align with what God requires, and no sexual appetite starts where it should. There is no sexual appetite that does not need reforming. Sexual desires always need redirecting to meet standards transcending how we feel.

The other notion underlying today's sense of unfairness is thinking sexual orientation is predetermined. But, besides conflicting with Scripture, this also relies on a scientific claim for which there is little basis, and most evidence points the other way.[13] Critics point out, and some self-identifying as "queer theorists" point out as well, that homosexuality and heterosexuality have always been social constructs that replace thinking sex joins people made for each other with thinking sex simply satisfies feelings that vary from person to person.[14] This shift in perceiving sexuality is dubious because most scientists now say no one is born same-sex attracted. For example, Mayer and McHugh, in their exhaustive review of scientific studies

---

[12] Stephen Holmes, "Listening to the Past and Reflecting on the Present," in *Two Views on Homosexuality, the Bible, and the Church*, ed. Preston Sprinkle (Grand Rapids: Zondervan, 2016), 184.

[13] Lawrence S. Mayer and Paul R. McHugh, "Sexuality and Gender," *The New Atlantis* 50 (Fall 2016): 14.

[14] Hanne Blank, *Straight: The Surprisingly Short History of Heterosexuality* (Boston: Beacon, 2012); Gore Vidal, "Sex Is Politics," *Playboy* (January 1979); Jonathan Ned Katz, *The Invention of Heterosexuality* (Chicago: University of Chicago, 2007); Brandon Ambrosino, "I Wasn't Born This Way: I Chose to Be Gay," *The New Republic* (January 28, 2014); Michael W. Hannon, "Against Heterosexuality," *First Things* 241 (March 2014): 27–34.

on this subject, report that "there is virtually no evidence that anyone, gay or straight, is 'born that way' if that means their sexual orientation was genetically determined."[15]

Instead of acting like a fixed trait, it turns out homosexual identity usually disappears spontaneously over time. Satinover reports that, since the mid-nineties, "there has existed solid epidemiologic evidence, now extensively confirmed and reconfirmed, that *the most common natural course for a young person who develops a 'homosexual identity' is for it to spontaneously disappear unless that process is discouraged or interfered with by extraneous factors*."[16] And, agreeing with this, Mayer and McHugh say, "There is now considerable scientific evidence that sexual desires, attractions, behaviors, and even identities can, and sometimes do, change over time."[17] This does not mean same-sex attractions are easily overcome. It only means change is possible, and now scientists agree with what the Bible has said all along (1 Cor 6:11).

Having noted what science does and does not say, it is important to acknowledge two qualifications. First, while there is no reason to think anyone is born same-sex attracted, there are environmental factors—like prenatal hormones and child sexual abuse—that can raise chances of having disordered sexual feelings. These do not make people unavoidably same-sex attracted because most affected by them do not respond that way. They just correlate with a slightly higher than usual susceptibility. Second, many studies have documented a connection linking same-sex sexual behavior with risking poor health, mental problems, partner violence, and suicidality at rates much higher than average. Some blame this on stress caused by stigmatization. But, while stigmatization accounts for some disparity, it does not account for most of it.

To summarize, same-sex sexual desires and behavior are condemned consistently throughout the Bible, and revisionist reinterpretations are not persuasive. God declares it abominable, it violates creation, no one can say God made them same-sex attracted, and there are no exceptions. For Christians, our identity is in Christ, not in ways we are tempted. We have "put off the old self with its practices and have put on the new self" (Col 3:9–10), and "those who belong to Christ Jesus have crucified the flesh with its passions and desires" (Gal 5:24). It is

---

[15] Mayer and McHugh, "Sexuality and Gender," 14, 31.

[16] Jeffrey B. Satinover, "The Trojan Couch," *NARTH Conference Reports* (2005), 24; Jeffrey B. Satinover, "How the Mental Health Associations Misrepresent Science," in Daniel Heimbach, *Why Not Same-Sex Marriage* (Sisters, OR: Trusted Books, 2014), 447.

[17] Mayer and McHugh, "Sexuality and Gender," 50.

not sin to be tempted but is sin not to crucify it. It is not sin to need help resisting but is sin to view any temptation as essential. And that is why the Bible says, "Consider yourselves dead to sin and alive to God in Christ Jesus" (Rom 6:11). At the same time, the Christian community must treat people experiencing same-sex attraction with love, compassion, and patience. We offer good news of forgiveness and change, but we do it without treating sexual orientation as something fixed or essential, without affirming same-sex sexual desires, and without compromising the Word of God.

Recommended further reading on the issue of homosexuality includes Alan Branch, *Born This Way?* (Wooster, OH: Weaver, 2016); Denny Burk, "Is Homosexual Orientation Sinful?" *Journal of the Evangelical Theological Society* 58/1 (March 2015), 95–115; Denny Burk and Heath Lambert, *Transforming Homosexuality* (Phillipsburg, NJ: P&R, 2015); James DeYoung, *Homosexuality* (Grand Rapids: Kregel, 2000); Donald Fortson and Rollin Grams, *Unchanging Witness: The Consistent Christian Teaching on Homosexuality* (Nashville: B&H, 2016); Robert Gagnon, *The Bible and Homosexual Practice* (Nashville, TN: Abingdon, 2001); Michael W. Hannon, "Against Heterosexuality," *First Things* 241 (March 2014): 27–34; Stanton Jones and Mark Yarhouse, *Homosexuality* (Downers Grove, IL: InterVarsity, 2000); Lawrence S. Mayer and Paul R. McHugh, "Sexuality and Gender," *The New Atlantis* 50 (Fall 2016): 1–143; Jeffrey Satinover, *Homosexuality and the Politics of Truth* (Grand Rapids: Baker, 1996); Jeffrey Satinover, "The Trojan Couch," *NARTH Conference Reports* (2005); Thomas Schmidt, *Straight and Narrow?* (Downers Grove, IL: InterVarsity, 1995); and John Stott, *Homosexual Partnerships? Why Same-Sex Relationships Are Not a Christian Option* (Downers Grove, IL: InterVarsity, 1984).

Transgenderism

"Transgenderism" is claiming a gender identity not matching one's biological sex. Transgenderism adds the notion of gender identity to the notion of sexual orientation. Sexual orientation distinguishes sexual attraction from what reproduction requires, and gender identity distinguishes gender perceiving from sexual anatomy. Advocates for homosexuality want to normalize same-sex attraction without reconceiving gender and anatomy, but transgenders detach gender from anatomy and may or may not think sexual orientation goes with it. Thus, one trans woman may claim to be straight although anatomically male and desiring sex with men, and another may claim to be lesbian although anatomically male and desiring sex with women.

The term *transgender* is used in different ways for different reasons, so it helps to recognize three subclassifications. The "trans-of-migration" refers to switching from one binary gender category to the other, the "trans-of-between" refers to defining oneself on a spectrum between the binary genders without embracing either entirely, and the "trans-of-beyond" refers to positioning oneself by denying binary gender categories altogether. Some pursue transgendered identity only in psychological terms, others do it socially as well by changing their names, pronouns, dress, and behavior, and still others go on to modify their bodies surgically.

Until recently, *sex* and *gender* were more or less synonymous, and older books still use them that way. But transgenderism is changing that, and in circles distinguishing them, *sex* indicates "biological sex," which is considered external and objective, and *gender* indicates "gender identity," which is considered internal and subjective. Gender identity has two elements—*gender perception* is feeling a certain way and *gender expression* is conveying that feeling.

Other related terms are *cisgender*, *gender dysphoria*, and *gender deconstruction*. Transgenders refer to non-transgenders as "cisgenders" using the Latin prefix "cis-," meaning "same as," to indicate persons identifying with a gender aligned with biological sex, and that is because it reflects how *transgender* uses the Latin prefix "trans-," meaning "across from," to indicate persons identifying with a gender not aligned with biological sex. Feeling transgendered may be welcomed or not, and if not, the American Psychiatric Association (APA) considers it a disorder called "gender dysphoria." But, according to the APA, what is wrong depends on what a person considers unwelcome. If a person does not welcome feeling transgendered, then the problem is considered psychological. But, if a person does not welcome having a body not matching how he feels, the problem is considered anatomical, and the APA prescribes sex-reassignment surgery and cross-sex hormone therapy. Finally, *gender deconstruction* refers to reconceiving classifications either by adding possibilities along a bipolar spectrum (the trans-of-between) or by denying what some call gender "stereotypes" altogether (the trans-of-beyond).

Transgenders are not hermaphrodites. In humans, hermaphroditism is a rare malformation that occurs at conception leaving a child with an extra X chromosome that leads to having both male and female sex organs. The difference is hermaphrodites are biologically ambiguous and transgenders are not. Transgenders do not have ambiguous bodies and yet claim they have feelings of a gender not aligned with their bodies. Hermaphrodites do not constitute a third sex, genetic malformation does not put human sexuality on a spectrum between male and female, and the possibility is no reason for treating gender as something fluid, optional, or reversible.

Some think that because the human authors did not know about transgenderism and the Bible does not address it by name, it must be silent on the issue. But that is incorrect.[18] Because the Bible is the Word of God, it is ethically sufficient, meaning it contains everything needed for faith and practice for all time, for the future as well as the past, and so includes everything needed to address the ethics of transgenderism. Indeed, the Bible reveals ten ethical truths that clearly establish how God wants us to approach the issue.

First, the Bible says God created humans "male and female" (Gen 1:27; 5:2), which tells us manhood and womanhood are not arbitrary perceptions but essential properties. What determines maleness and femaleness is not fluid but fixed and is rooted in fact, not feeling. Second, the Bible links gender identity, our maleness and femaleness, to the biological binary needed to fulfill the mission God assigned the human race to reproduce and "fill the earth" (Gen 1:28). Third, the Bible teaches that human nature is fallen. It is compromised by sin that corrupts our desires and circumstances (Gen 3:1–24; Rom 8:20). But, while this affects all we do, it does not allow us to revise God's creational design by separating gender from anatomy.

Fourth, Christ, in the New Testament, reaffirmed that God still connects gender with biological sex by asking, "Haven't you read . . . that he who created them in the beginning made them male and female?" (Matt 19:4). Fifth, the Holy Spirit through Paul requires us to express gender in sexually aligned ways (1 Cor 11:7–15). Sixth, the Bible demands that we keep "spirit, soul, and body" blameless for the sake of Christ (1 Thess 5:23). This obligates us to connect elements constituting ourselves in the manner Christ requires, and, since that includes aligning gender with sex, transgenderism is wrong to suppose we can treat them otherwise.

Seventh, in Deuteronomy 22:5, God forbids crossdressing to disregard the value of distinguishing one gender from the other. This is not ceremonial law because it does not concern worship rituals, and it is not civil law because it is not administrative. It is part of God's unchanging moral law because crossdressing is declared "detestable" (תּוֹעֵבָה, *tōw'ēbâh*),

---

[18] Here, I disagree with Scott Rae, who says transgenderism "is another area in which the Bible is silent." *Introducing Christian Ethics,* 155 (see commentary in chap. 8, n. 1).

which links it to moral law in Leviticus (Lev 18:22; 20:13). Since differences in the way men and women dress vary with culture, time, and circumstance, the enduring wrong prohibited is dressing to signify moral rebellion. It does not rule out sharing a jacket on a cold night but, rather, precludes dressing to convey disrespect for the moral value of aligning gender with anatomy.

Eighth, the Bible condemns altering our bodies to express lies. In the Old Testament, men who crush or remove sex organs could not enter "the LORD's assembly" (Deut 23:1), and Paul, in the New Testament, condemns "those who mutilate the flesh" (Phil 3:2). While the first addresses trying to alter sexual identity and the second addresses unnecessary circumcision, both convey a principle that also applies to sex reassignment surgery and cross-sex hormone therapy. Altering the body to express a lie is foolish and immoral. Ninth, the Bible refers to inner perceiving as the "heart" and warns against trusting it for moral guidance. According to the Bible, what is used to justify transgenderism is morally deceitful (Jer 17:9), inclined toward evil (Gen 6:5), good at hatching evil plans, and irrational when challenged by reality (Eccl 9:3). Tenth and finally, the Bible reveals that the key to overcoming false inner perceiving like feeling transgendered is "put[ting] to death what belongs to your earthly nature: sexual immorality, impurity, lust, evil desire, and greed" (Col 3:5). Thus, affirming that our "old self" is crucified with Christ is the key to rendering sin unable to rule in our bodies (Rom 6:6; also Gal 5:24).

Of course, those affirming transgenderism see it differently. Advocates now claim the idea of sex determining gender is outdated and want ethics, psychology, medicine, and law all to take a fluid approach affirming it. But they cannot agree on what justifies such a radical shift. Some say there must be a biological basis for doing so, while others say transgenderism is justified by feelings alone. Some say it is volitional and others deny it, some say babies are born genderless and others say they are born hardwired in some undiscovered way disconnected from sex, and they all say cultural influences play a huge role in how a person perceives gender. But scientists have yet to find anything objective supporting these claims, transgenderism cannot be a choice and impossible to resist at the same time, and it makes no sense to suppose gender identity is both shaped by culture and hardwired.

While researchers have found nothing to justify treating cross-gender identification as natural or normal, they have proven it is very unhealthy. Compared to the general population, transgenders "are at substantially increased risk of suicidal ideation, suicide attempts, and completed suicide," and they experience substance abuse, anxiety, and depression at rates impossible to blame on social stress.[19] Some suggest these problems should be solved by sex reassignment surgery and hormone therapy, but Paul McHugh, perhaps the foremost scientific and medical expert on the subject, disagrees emphatically. According to McHugh, changing a person's sex "is biologically impossible" and "people who undergo sex reassignment surgery do not change from men to women or vice versa." Thus, he concludes, "encouraging surgical intervention is in reality to collaborate with and promote a mental disorder."[20]

Treating feelings as if they justify detaching gender from sex is impossible to reconcile with biblical ethics. Yet, while Christians cannot affirm transgenderism and must expose lies corrupting ethical analysis, we should empathize with people struggling with cross-gendered feelings and need to realize we can offer them more help than people collaborating with how they feel because they fail to understand fallen human nature. God defines us, "and not we ourselves" (Ps 100:3, KJV). We are creatures made by God who cannot redefine ourselves, and we are sinners whose deepest problems require a Savior, not surgery.

Accepting God's alignment of gender with sex is much like trusting him with other aspects of embodied identity like race, fertility, and intellect. But more could be at stake because, while marriage and reproducing will not continue in heaven (Matt 22:30; Mark 12:25; Luke 20:35), gender aligned with anatomy lasts forever. We will have resurrected bodies that remain gendered even as the body of Jesus remained recognizably male after rising from the dead (1 Cor 15:21; 1 Tim 2:5; Rev 1:13), and that means gender aligned with anatomy must be more important to God than fulfilling our temporary duty to reproduce. So it appears transgenderism may challenge the way God orders ethical reality even more seriously than homosexuality in that it scrambles something eternal and not just temporal.[21]

Recommended further reading on the issue of transgenderism includes Ryan Anderson, *When Harry Became Sally: Responding to the Transgender Movement* (New York: Encounter, 2017); James Beilby and Paul Eddy, eds., *Understanding Transgender Identities: Four Views* (Grand Rapids: Baker, 2019); J. Alan Branch, *Affirming God's Image: Addressing the Transgender*

---

[19] Mayer and McHugh, "Sexuality and Gender," 59, 70.

[20] Paul McHugh, "Transgender Surgery Isn't the Solution," *Wall Street Journal* (June 12, 2014).

[21] Daniel R. Heimbach, "The Unchangeable Difference: Eternally Fixed Sexual Identity for an Age of Plastic Sexuality," *Biblical Foundations for Manhood and Womanhood*, ed. Wayne Grudem (Wheaton, IL: Crossway, 2002), 275–89.

Question with Science and Scripture (Bellingham, WA: Lexham, 2018); Craig Kline and David Schrock, "What Is Gender Reassignment Surgery?," *Journal of Biblical Manhood and Womanhood* 20/1 (2015): 35–47; Paul McHugh, "Surgical Sex," *First Things* (November 2004): 34–38; Paul McHugh, "Transgender Surgery Isn't the Solution," *Wall Street Journal* (June 12, 2014); Lawrence Meyer and Paul McHugh, "Sexuality and Gender: Findings from Biological, Psychological, and Social Sciences," *New Atlantis* (Fall 2016): 10–143; Andrew Walker, *God and the Transgender Debate* (Epsom, UK: Good Book, 2017); and Mark Yarhouse, *Understanding Gender Dysphoria* (Downers Grove, IL: InterVarsity, 2015).

Pornography

Even though the problem of sexual lust was mentioned when considering sexual morality generally, the enormous influence of pornography in today's culture warrants giving it attention in a separate section. The word *pornography* comes from combining two Greek words—πόρνη (*pornē*), meaning "whore" or "something lewd," and γραφή (*graphē*), meaning "writing" or "drawing"—and the term in English refers to material designed to arouse erotic passion. Pornography does not just convey information about sex. Medical texts do that and are not pornographic. The difference is pornography has a prurient or seductive quality, and medical texts do not. Pornography has two classifications: "hardcore pornography" and "softcore pornography." Hardcore pornography focuses on genitals and acts of sexual intercourse, while softcore pornography does not go that far.

Pornography has been a growing problem in the United States for at least a century. It moved from the shadows into the mainstream when *Playboy Magazine* was launched in 1953 and has become more and more open, accessible, explicit, and tolerant of aberrant behaviors since that time. Advances in communication technology have caused the smut industry to explode. Annual revenue generated by pornography now exceeds $97 billion worldwide and exceeds $13 billion in the United States alone. The number of pornographic webpages has grown to over 260 million, and sex is the most searched-for topic on the internet.[22]

---

[22] "Porn Industry Archives," Enough Is Enough: Making the Internet Safer for Children and Families, accessed April 15, 2020, https://enough.org/stats_porn_industry_archives.

Some say the Bible does not address pornography,[23] but again, that is not true. The term does not appear, but the Bible addresses what makes pornography alluring and sinful at great length. Pornography is communication, and "lust of the flesh" (1 John 2:16) is what pornography arouses in people using it. Understanding pornography as an ethical issue starts with recognizing how it is meant to arouse unholy sexual thoughts and desires, and this alone makes it inherently immoral. But there is more in the Bible relating to pornography than just declaring it wrong, for the Bible also details how it interrelates with other important matters, like having good character, establishing good marriages, raising good children, maintaining good social relations, and being in good standing with God.

Ethical rejection of pornography in the Bible is capsulized where Jesus explains that just looking at a woman the wrong way violates the moral boundary limiting sex to man-woman marriage (Matt 5:28). Jesus taught that God prohibits both inner and outer adultery, and he showed that sinful thoughts about sex violate not just one but two of the Ten Commandments. It breaks the seventh, prohibiting adultery, and also the tenth, prohibiting wrong desires. And, when he did this, Jesus also showed that the ethical order served by these commands is eternal. It remains as relevant in the New Testament as in the Old Testament.

Jesus made sure we would know using pornography is inherently immoral. But beyond that, the Bible adds at least ten more truths relating to the ethics of pornography. First, it tells us God knows everything we think and desire (Jer 17:10; Heb 4:13) and someday will use this knowledge to judge "what people have kept secret" (Rom 2:15–16). Second, it says God cares about keeping sexual thoughts and desires pure. Job makes a covenant with his eyes "not to look lustfully at a young woman" (Job 31:1, NIV[1984]) because God sees what he is doing (Job 31:4). Solomon warns against looking at women using their bodies to arouse sinful desires (Prov 6:25). And Peter equates "eyes full of adultery" with "wickedness" (2 Pet 2:14–15).

Third, it warns that sinful desires lead to sinful actions, and the more one cultivates sinful desires the harder it is to keep from expressing them outwardly. "The corruption that is in the world" arises "because of evil desire" (2 Pet 1:4), and what sinning produces begins when one "is drawn away and enticed by his own evil desire" (Jas 1:14). Fourth, it says giving yourself to

---

[23] For example, Erin Dufault-Hunter says, "The Scriptures remain relatively silent on this topic." Erin Dufault-Hunter, "Pornography," in *Dictionary of Scripture and Ethics*, ed. Joel B. Green (Grand Rapids: Baker, 2011), 607.

pornography enslaves and ultimately destroys you. Pornography is a false prophet promising freedom to indulge "fleshly desires and debauchery" while making users "slaves of corruption" (2 Pet 2:18–19). No one gets away without getting hurt (Prov 6:29), and the one who tries "lacks sense" and "destroys himself" (Prov 6:32). Fifth, it says using pornography defiles a person's mind, conscience, and even his or her soul. Jesus says immoral sexual thoughts are the sort of thing that "defile a person" (Matt 15:19–20), Paul says they corrupt both "mind and conscience" (Titus 1:15), and Peter says they "wage war against the soul" (1 Pet 2:11).

Sixth, it says pornography hurts people we should love. God says to "love your neighbor as yourself" (Lev 19:18; Matt 22:39; Mark 12:31), but pornography causes users to "transgress against and take advantage of a brother or sister" (1 Thess 4:6). The world equates lust with love, but that is a moral and relational lie. Using images of a person to feed an appetite unrelated to knowing a person is not loving but transgressing against that person. Seventh, it says pornography turns the heart away from God and incites his wrath. Loving pornography shows a person does not know God (1 Thess 4:5), does not love God (1 John 2:15), and is making himself an enemy of God (Jas 4:4). Thus, it makes God angry (Eph 2:3) and moves him to reserve special punishment for "those who follow the polluting desires of the flesh" (2 Pet 2:10).

Eighth, it reveals that those who use pornography can turn from it and be forgiven (1 Cor 6:11). Ninth, it warns that refusing to give up pornography keeps a person from being saved and going to heaven (Rev 21:8).[24] Christians can struggle with pornography, but embracing pornography and refusing to struggle against it means one is not a Christian. Tenth, it reveals that overcoming the allure of pornography requires loving God more than self (Rom 6:13; 13:14; Gal 5:16), putting the flesh to death (Rom 8:13; Gal 5:24; Col 3:5), and disciplining everything you think, desire, and look at (Rom 12:1–2; 2 Cor 10:5; 1 Thess 4:4–5; 2 Tim 2:22).

When dealing with pornography in secular settings, the question is whether it harms anyone, and those defending pornography will claim there is no evidence it does. But this is not true and must be refuted.

---

[24] John is told that the "sexually immoral" will be assigned to "the lake that burns with fire" (Rev 21:8). The word translated "sexually immoral" is πόρνοις (*pornois*), the same Greek word from which English word *pornography* is mainly derived. In the original language, the term refers to those who cling to any kind of sexual sin. So, although this reference covers more than consumers and purveyors of pornography, it certainly includes them.

First, we need to argue that pornography is bad for those using it because it harms them spiritually, mentally, physically, and socially. Christians know that the worst damage done by pornography is spiritual because it alienates one from God, works against God, and makes God angry. But, if people around us do not care about that, we can point to other damages, such as how pornography harms those using it by impairing their social attitudes and perceptions. Viewing pornography increases tolerance for sex that is deviant, violent, or even criminal by conditioning them to perceive others as commodities rather than persons,[25] and researchers have found that even brief exposure to violent pornography leads to antisocial attitudes.[26]

Besides harming users spiritually and mentally, pornography also harms them physically and socially. Using pornography leads to compulsive sexual behavior that increases chances of getting sexually transmitted diseases and leads to addiction that interferes with normal living.[27] The addictive power of pornography comes from a hormone that keeps users coming back for more, and a survey of pornography addicts found all were impaired in important aspects of their lives as a result of their addiction.[28]

Pornography is bad not only for those using it but also for others close to them. Men given to pornography are less committed to their wives, women married to them feel betrayed, and this often leads to infidelity and divorce. Children in such circumstances are more likely to be abused, child pornography victimizes children, and commercializing sexual images of women demeans their humanity by treating them as objects to ogle rather than people to honor, cherish, and respect. Finally, pornography weakens the fabric of society. According to the FBI, pornography consumption is the most common factor shared by sexually violent

---

[25] Patrick F. Fagan, "The Effects of Pornography on Individuals, Marriage, Family and Community," *Research Synthesis* (Washington, DC: Family Research Council, December 2009), accessible at: https://www.frc.org/issuebrief/the-effects-of-pornography-on-individuals-marriage-family-and-community.

[26] Edward Donnerstein, "Pornography and Violence against Women," *Annals of the New York Academy of Science* 347/1 (June 1980): 277–88.

[27] Kristian Daneback, Michael Ross, and Sven-Axel Månsson, "Characteristics and Behaviors of Sexual Compulsives Who Use the Internet," *Sexual Addiction & Compulsivity* 13/1 (August 2006): 53–67.

[28] Fagan, "Effects of Pornography"; Victor Cline, *Pornography's Effects on Adults and Children* (New York: Morality in Media, 1990); Donald Black, Laura Kehrberg, Denise Flumerfelt, and Steven Schlosser, "Characteristics of 36 Subjects Reporting Compulsive Sexual Behavior," *American Journal of Psychiatry* 154/2 (February 1997): 243–49.

serial murderers,[29] police officers report that pornography influences criminal activity, and the Mafia has long played a major role in the porn industry.[30]

Pornography is entirely contrary to biblical sexual morality. While promising good sex, it destroys truly good sex by reducing it to a passing, impersonal, non-relational, self-centered, and shallow physical experience that interferes with developing and maintaining a sexual relationship that is lasting, meaningful, profound, multidimensional, complementary, and approved by the Creator who made sex to work that way. Sadly, pornography pollutes the mind (Rom 8:6), burns the soul (1 Pet 2:11), offends God (Rom 1:24), and, beyond that, threatens good health, good relations, and good society. Pornography's bad effects cannot be solved without dealing with the moral problem underlying them, and there is no doing that without avoiding pornography altogether. Therefore, as the Bible says, "Let us cleanse ourselves from every impurity of the flesh and spirit, bringing holiness to completion in the fear of God" (2 Cor 7:1).

Recommended further reading on the issue of pornography includes Stephen Arterburn and Fred Stoeker, *Every Man's Battle* (Colorado Springs: WaterBrook, 2000); Barna Group, *The Porn Phenomenon: The Impact of Pornography in the Digital Age* (Ventura, CA: Barna, 2016); Victor B. Cline, *Pornography's Effects on Adults and Children* (New York: Morality in Media, 1990); Charles Colson, and Tom Minnery, *Pornography: A Human Tragedy* (Wheaton, IL: Tyndale, 1986); Neil Malamuth, and Edward Donnerstein, eds., *Pornography and Sexual Aggression* (New York: Academic, 1984); Michael McManus, ed., *Final Report of the Attorney General's Commission on Pornography* (Nashville: Rutledge, 1986); Raymond C. Ortland, Jr., *The Death of Porn* (Wheaton, IL: Crossway, 2021); Samuel L. Perry, *Addicted to Lust: Pornography in the Lives of Conservative Protestants* (New York: Oxford, 2019); William M. Struthers, *Wired for Intimacy: How Pornography Hijacks the Male Brain* (Downers Grove, IL: InterVarsity, 2009); and John White, *Eros Defiled: The Christian and Sexual Sin* (Downers Grove, IL: InterVarsity, 1977).

---

[29] "The Men Who Murdered," *FBI Law Enforcement Bulletin* 54/8 (August 1985): 4.

[30] *Attorney General's Commission on Pornography: Final Report,* July 1986 (Washington, DC: US Department of Justice); and Robert M. Press, "FBI's Big Pornography Crackdown Reveals Organized Crime Influence," *The Christian Science Monitor* (February 19, 1980).

Prostitution

Prostitution is the last issue covered in this chapter introducing applied issues to do with sex. As with the previous issue, we also touched briefly on prostitution earlier when considering sexual morality in general, and as before, this, too, deserves singling out. However, in this case, it is not because of anything new but because the issue is so old. Despite that, prostitution as an applied issue in Christian ethics is sadly all but ignored in most texts, and that is strange because the issue not only is very old but also is treated at length throughout the Bible.

Prostitution is engaging in sex outside marriage for compensation, which means it treats marriage as irrelevant, minimizes emotional investment, selects partners rather indiscriminately, interacts non-relationally, keeps expectations transient, and considers pregnancy a problem to avoid and not a blessing to welcome. Today prostitutes are sometimes called "sex workers," which is a euphemism coined in 1978 by prostitutes' rights activist Carol Leigh to avoid negative moral connotations. But using the euphemism requires discretion. For, while using it can lower some barriers, it also clashes with biblical references and hinders ethical honesty.

Types of prostitution are classified by sort, method, or coupling. Classifying by sort distinguishes "cultic" prostitution (practiced for spiritual reasons) from "commercial" prostitution (practiced for economic reasons). Classifying by method distinguishes "temple" prostitutes (who meet clients inside places of worship) from "street" prostitutes (who meet customers out in public places), "brothel" prostitutes (who meet clients inside places established for that purpose), and "escort" prostitutes (who arrange meetings by phone or computer and meet clients in rented rooms). And classifying by coupling distinguishes "courtesans" (women taking male clients), "gigolos" (men taking female clients), "hustlers" (men taking same-sex clients), and "lesbian" prostitutes (women taking same-sex clients).

Different things motivate people to become prostitutes, and the most common is seeking material gain. But people can be motivated by social or spiritual gain as well. Seeking social gain motivates entering prostitution in cultures where hospitality includes providing sex, and seeking spiritual gain motivates prostitution in areas practicing sex worship. Statistics on the size and scope of prostitution are hard to determine because prostitutes mostly operate outside the law, give no receipts, do not report earnings, and do not like answering questions. Estimates are that about 42 million prostitutes throughout the world are producing over $180 billion annually, and that, of these, nearly 2 million operate in the United States, generating about $14 billion annually.

Most societies throughout history have allowed prostitution to some degree, and those banning prostitution have not always enforced laws against it. In the ancient world, it was practiced widely in connection with pagan worship, and Jews and Christians broke with paganism by condemning it. The Church has always opposed prostitution but not always strongly. Augustine (354–430) and Aquinas (1225–1274) thought prostitution was evil but had to be tolerated to keep sexual violence and sodomy from running rampant.[31] As a result, the medieval church tolerated prostitution. The Protestant Reformers then opposed it completely, and this difference has divided Protestant from Catholic ethics ever since.

Prostitutes operated in the American colonies, and, during the American Revolution, so many followed the Continental Army they caused army leaders to worry about losing soldiers to venereal diseases. In the early nineteenth century, over 200 brothels flourished in lower Manhattan, in the mid-nineteenth century, gold rush profits brought prostitutes to mining towns in the Wild West, and during the Civil War so many prostitutes lived with soldiers protecting our nation's capital under the command of General Hooker that *hooker* became a slang term for prostitute.

Legal opposition to prostitution did not start in the United States until World War I and then more to keep soldiers healthy than for moral reasons. It was widely legal before that but by 1915 had become illegal nearly everywhere in the United States. It stayed legal in Alaska until 1953, and it now is legal only in some rural parts of Nevada. But attitudes are changing once more. Groups advocating prostitution began forming in the 1970s and now include COYOTE (Call Off Your Old Tired Ethics), FLOP (Friends and Lovers of Prostitutes), and HIRE (Hooking Is Real Enjoyment), and, although prostitution is illegal in California by state law, the cities of Berkeley and San Francisco no longer enforce state laws prohibiting prostitution.

The Bible uses different terms for "prostitute," and understanding them is key to interpreting how God treats the issue. Terms used for "prostitute" in the Old Testament are קְדֵשָׁה (*qᵉḏēšāh*), indicating a female cult prostitute who takes opposite-sex clients; קָדֵשׁ (*qāḏēš*),

---

[31] Augustine, *On Order*, 2.4; Aquinas, *Summa theologica*, II.II, q. 10, xi.

indicating a male cult prostitute who takes same-sex clients; זוֹנָה (zōnâh), indicating a female commercial prostitute who takes opposite-sex clients; and כֶּלֶב (keleb), meaning "dog" used for a male commercial prostitute who takes same-sex clients. Terms used for "prostitute" in the New Testament are πόρνη (pornê), indicating a female prostitute either cultic or commercial; πόρνος (pornos), indicating a male prostitute also either cultic or commercial; and κύνες (kunes), which is the New Testament equivalent of כֶּלֶב (keleb) in the Old Testament, meaning "dog" and used for a male commercial prostitute who takes same-sex clients.

These terms together show that the Bible addresses two kinds of prostitution—cultic and commercial—and, while God opposes both, he deals with them differently. Some say the Bible does not forbid prostitution or patronizing prostitutes,[32] but neither claim is correct. The Old Testament clearly prohibits both kinds of prostitution (Deut 23:17; Lev 19:29) and opposes patronizing them (Hos 4:14), and the New Testament condemns patronizing any prostitute in terms allowing no exception (1 Cor 6:15–17). But that is not all the Bible says on the subject.

Besides prohibiting cult prostitution, the Bible also says it provokes God to "jealous anger" (1 Kgs 14:22–24), God expects good rulers to eradicate it (1 Kgs 15:12; 22:46; 2 Kgs 23:7), becoming a cult prostitute proves having "a godless heart" (Job 36:13–14), patrons forfeit their right to life (Num 25:1–5), and it stands for ultimate spiritual rebellion because it rejects true worship of the true God and not just individually, but leads others to as well (Rev 17:1–2).

Besides prohibiting commercial prostitution, the Old Testament says violators deserve execution, but how violators get executed depends on how they relate to spiritual leaders. If a daughter of a priest becomes a commercial prostitute, she is burned to death (Lev 21:9), but others guilty of the same are stoned (Deut 22:20–21). There is debate over whether executing commercial prostitutes is limited to the civil law of ancient Israel or is part of enduring moral law. However we answer that question, we need to see that executing prostitutes in the Old Testament underscores how strongly God disapproves of what they do.

Other stipulations in the Old Testament are that God will not accept earnings of a commercial prostitute regardless of gender (Deut 23:18); a high priest cannot marry one, but

---

[32] Robin Parry, "Prostitution," in *Dictionary of Scripture and Ethics*, ed. Joel B. Green (Grand Rapids: Baker, 2011), 640; Wilda W. Morris, "Prostitution," in *Holman Bible Dictionary* (Nashville: Holman Bible, 1991), 1144.

others can (Lev 21:7); treating someone as a commercial prostitute is shameful (Gen 34:31); being forced into commercial prostitution is a curse (Amos 7:17); and shaming by commercial prostitutes is doubly dishonoring (1 Kgs 22:38). Scripture also warns that commercial prostitutes depersonalize clients (Prov 6:26; Joel 3:3; Nah 3:4), use seduction to entrap them (Prov 7:10; 23:27–28), and develop hardened moral attitudes (Jer 3:3; Ezek 16:30; Hos 2:2). As for patronizing commercial prostitutes, the Bible says it lacks sense (Prov 7:7), squanders assets on "strangers" (Prov 5:10), proves bad character (Prov 23:28), ruins wealth (Prov 29:3), and can cost your life (Prov 7:23). And, even though cult prostitution offends God more severely, the Bible also uses consorting with commercial prostitutes to symbolize spiritual infidelity (Num 15:39; Jer 5:7; Ezek 16:30; 23:44; Hos 9:1).

While the Bible condemns prostitution, it also treats prostitutes and their clients with understanding and extends hope to those willing to repent. Tamar is judged more righteous than Judah despite acting as a prostitute (Gen 38:26), and Judah is forgiven for patronizing her (Gen 49:8; Matt 1:3). Rahab is spared, honored for her faith, and accepted into the family of God, despite having been a commercial prostitute (Josh 6:17; Matt 1:5; Heb 11:31; Jas 2:25). God tells Hosea to marry and faithfully love a commercial prostitute to demonstrate how God loves Israel despite Israel's unfaithfulness (Hos 3:1). And Jesus forgave repentant prostitutes (Matt 21:31; Luke 7:48), treated them with understanding (Luke 7:39–46), and taught that God forgives and restores repentant sinners using a parable about a father who forgives and restores a repentant son who squanders all he has on commercial prostitutes (Luke 15:30).

Other things revealed in Scripture regarding prostitution are that, while God expects human rulers to eradicate cult prostitution (1 Kgs 15:12; 22:46), he does not expect good rulers necessarily to rid the present world of all commercial prostitutes (1 Kgs 3:16–28). Being conceived and raised by a prostitute does not mean God has no purpose for your life (Judg 11:1). God understands prostitutes and their clients, but never takes it lightly. For, while God forgives those who repent, he also warns that no one refusing to repent will be in heaven (Rev 22:15).

Having surveyed what the Bible says on prostitution, a few concluding observations are in order. First, God regards cultic prostitution as worse than commercial prostitution. Both sorts are prohibited, and both are used to symbolize spiritual infidelity. But cultic prostitution makes God angrier, calls for eradication, not suppression, is sanctioned immediately rather than handled patiently, and is considered more evil and corrupting than commercial prostitution. Second, being self-righteous is worse than being a prostitute because Jesus once told self-righteous critics, "Prostitutes are entering the kingdom of God before you" (Matt 21:31). Third, sex outside marriage given freely is worse than charging for it because God condemns Israel as "unlike (worse than) a prostitute because you scorned payment" (Ezek 16:31). Fourth, paying for sex with a prostitute is worse than getting paid for it because God condemned Israel as worse than a commercial prostitute because "you paid a fee instead of one being paid to you" (Ezek 16:34).

Finally, patronizing commercial prostitutes is worse than being one because God told Israel, "I will not punish your daughters when they turn to (commercial) prostitution . . . because the men themselves consort with (commercial) harlots" (Hos 4:14, NIV$_{1984}$). The distinction God makes here is opposite what human societies do, which is look down on women who earn a living as prostitutes while excusing men who patronize them. Some condemn this as a double standard based on thinking no distinction should be made.[33] But, although what human societies do should be condemned, the problem God has is not with judging the parties differently but with assessing differences between them the wrong way around. When judging men and women regarding prostitution, God does not use a sexist double standard but uses different standards justified by divinely assigned gender roles. God treats men and women the same when it comes to violating marriage (Lev 20:10) but not when it comes to expecting men to act as moral-spiritual leaders, and that is why God thinks men patronizing prostitutes do something worse than women accepting payment to have sex with them.

Recommended further reading on the issue of prostitution includes William Acton, *Prostitution Considered in Its Moral, Social, and Sanitary Aspects* (London: Churchill, 1862); Arthur L. Mackey, Jr., *The Scarlet Thread of Redemption: Moving Forward from Prostitution to Proclamation* (Roosevelt, NY: Mackey Productions, 2015); Caroline Norma and Melinda T. Reist, eds., *Prostitution Narratives: Stories of Survival in the Sex Trade* (North Melbourne, AU: Spinifex, 2016); Sharon S. Oselin, *Leaving Prostitution: Getting Out and Staying Out of Sex Work* (New York: New York University, 2014); Michael Rutter, *Upstairs Girls: Prostitution in the American West* (Helena, MT: Farcountry, 2005); Teela Sanders, Maggie O'Neill, and Jane Pitcher, *Prostitution: Sex Work, Policy and Politics* (London: SAGE, 2009); William W. Sanger,

---

[33] James B. Nelson, "Prostitution," in *The Westminster Dictionary of Christian Ethics*, ed. James F. Childress and John Macquarrie (Philadelphia: Westminster, 1986), 513; Morris, "Prostitution," 1144.

The History of Prostitution: Its Extent, Causes, and Effects throughout the World (Jacksonville, FL: Heritage, 2014).

Conclusion

This chapter has introduced how Christian thought applies to ethical issues to do with sex, sexuality, sexual identity, and interacting as sexual creatures bearing the image of God. We considered the meaning, nature, and purposes of sex as given in the Word of God, and, with that, surveyed norms God says apply to sexual behavior. After that, we addressed a range of particular issues having to do with sex selected because of their importance or contemporary relevance, and we did this keeping focus on what it takes to be what God made us and live up to what he intends.

This has been the third of five chapters that together introduce readers to applied Christian ethics as an academic subcategory within the larger field of Christian ethics, and, in it, we treated issues to do with sex as transitional between applied issues that are primarily personal in nature and those that are primarily social in nature. We did that because issues in sexual ethics are as personal as they are social, meaning they always are social even though personal and always are personal even though social. Now, in the last two chapters, readers will be introduced to applied ethical issues that always are more social than personal in nature.

CHAPTER 11

ISSUES IN SOCIAL LIFE

GOVERNMENT & POLITICS; RELIGIOUS LIBERTY; WEALTH & POVERTY; CAPITAL PUNISHMENT; WAR & PEACE; TERRORISM

This is the fourth of five chapters introducing applied Christian ethics as a subcategory in the larger field of Christian ethics, and it is the first of two chapters introducing applied issues that are mainly social as opposed to personal. That means we now will focus on how Christian faith and belief apply to issues more to do with relating to other people than to individual life. The previous chapter addressed issues spanning both applied classifications because they are as personal as they are social, and we now will address issues that are mainly social.

Dealing with such issues usually is referred to as Christian social ethics, but some now use the term *public theology*. Using this new term requires care as it is not well established and can be misunderstood.[1] Public theology is the same as Christian social ethics only if it applies

---

[1] For example, some might take qualifying "theology" by "public" as agreeing with a non-biblical public-private distinction in how God's authority applies, and some could even see it as acquiescing to civil disqualification of theologically based participation in public affairs. No Christian affirming

Christian theological thought and not some other ultimate perspective, and social ethics is the same as Christian public theology only if it applies moral revelation from the Word of God and not just moral philosophy, which never transcends human-centered speculating.

God made us relational creatures (Gen 1:27–28), so, in a sense, all ethical issues are social. But, while personal issues involve some relating like interacting with God (Ps 139:7) or buying drinks at a bar, they are not what social ethics usually considers. As commonly used, *social ethics* deals with external (or perhaps civil or public) responses to material needs in a collective referred to as society. Thus, *social ethics*, as the term is commonly used, refers to something less than everything the Bible considers relevant and often attracts thinking contrary to pleasing God (Rom 8:7–8). It is important, therefore, that Christians understand God's Word well enough to distinguish biblical truth from what is culturally popular.

Government & Politics

Government is a structure of authority by which people living together are directed, and, while it can be used of directing religious, family, or even personal life, it is used here of directing civil life. Government is one of three institutions God arranges for humans to rule humans in a fallen world (Dan 2:21; 4:17; John 19:11; Rom 13:1), the others being family and church. *Politics* is a related term that refers to activities by which individuals or groups strive to achieve, retain, or direct governing power, usually in the area of civil life.

As an issue in applied Christian ethics, government is complex because it spans the interrelation of religion, law, and morality, each of which entails a different sort of life-controlling authority. *Religion* concerns convictions and commitments regarding a source of ultimate meaning and purpose and so involves different worldviews (about human nature, reality, and ultimate authority) and dimensions (individual and corporate). *Law* concerns structures, standards, and processes for allocating rights and duties, and for holding people accountable and, as such, involves different classifications (cultic, moral, and civil) and kinds (rules, standards,

---

"public theology" means this, but the term can render public influence with secularists susceptible to unwarranted rejection. Of course, prefacing "social ethics" with "Christian" can do the same. But whereas secularists might possibly accept "Christian" as describing a constituency in mixed society, they will not agree to "theology" informing civil matters.

and principles). *Morality* concerns ascertaining and applying ultimate right and wrong and, as such, involves different aspects (external, internal, and directional), elements (guidelines, mandates, and ideals), components (conduct, character, and goals), expressions (beliefs, traditions, and customs), and levels (private, public, and universal).

These together constitute a network of authority structures that affect us all the time but in different ways. Only one divine authority (only one worldview concerning God) is true, and others are false. But human government does not control what people think and should not try to referee what they believe. This network of authority structures affects different areas of human life, such as personal life, family life, social life, and political life. Their structures can be distinguished conceptually, but in real life, they interconnect and cannot be separated. Religious convictions determine moral convictions, and moral convictions determine respect for law. The fact is civil governing runs on laws that do not endure unless sustained by moral convictions, and moral convictions do not arise apart from faith convictions determined by religion. The institutions of church and state can be separated. But religion, law, and morality have intersecting functions that together serve the common good. Without religion, there is no morality in politics, and without morality in politics, there is no justice in governing.

When applying Christian thought to government, the things Christians want to know are how the power of Christ relates to human power, whether and to what degree the responsibilities of church and state overlap, and how tensions between them get resolved. More answers are offered than can be treated here, and since most reflect specific situations, we will focus on revelation and not survey all of them. Despite differences between the theocracy of ancient Israel and how God deals with other nations, the Bible provides a single consistent approach to governing in the present world. The Bible does not provide a single way of organizing society, or of structuring political life, so as to best govern sinful people in the fallen world. But it does provide a coherent way of thinking about it that applies to everyone the same way through history. The theocracy of Israel envisioned how God will govern a perfect world but was not meant to serve as a model for sinners ruling sinners. The best passages for that are not those about living in the Promised Land but those about living in mixed society with nonbelievers as revealed to Daniel and Nebuchadnezzar in the Old Testament and revealed through Jesus, Paul, and Revelation in the New Testament.

In the Old Testament, when Israel lost independence for rejecting the rule of God and was placed under pagan rule in Babylon, God remained sovereign and promised to restore them. But he also used it to explain the way human governing relates to him no matter how pagan. For this reason, the book of Daniel provides more on God relating to sinners governing sinners than any other book in the Bible and does so in universal terms not affected by shifting politics.

This, then, is what God tells Daniel and Nebuchadnezzar about how he relates to governing imperfect people in imperfect circumstances:

- God does not expect compliance with policies interfering with godliness (Dan 1:8).
- Godly people should respect those governing while avoiding compromise (Dan 1:8; 6:21).
- God controls all wisdom and power affecting government (Dan 2:20).
- God controls the rise and fall of political history (Dan 2:21).
- God controls wisdom and knowledge needed by political advisors (Dan 2:21).
- God gives wisdom and power to political advisors who seek it from him (Dan 2:23).
- God knows what will happen and has a plan for political history (Dan 2:28).
- God controls whatever sovereignty, power, strength, and glory rulers have (Dan 2:37).
- God controls what rulers are able to rule (Dan 2:38).
- When pushed, godly people obey God rather than human rulers (Dan 3:18, 28; 6:10).
- The sovereignty of God over human governing is everlasting (Dan 4:3, 34; 6:26).
- The sovereignty of God over human governing is universal (Dan 4:25, 32; 5:21).
- The sovereignty of God over human governing cannot be destroyed (Dan 6:26).
- God bestows ruling power on anyone he wants (Dan 4:25, 32; 5:21).
- God wants rulers to accept being accountable to him for how they rule (Dan 4:26).
- No human governing limits God's supremacy over it (Dan 4:35).
- The sovereignty of God over human governing is eternally true and just (Dan 4:37).
- God never loses control and can always humble rulers who resist him (Dan 4:37).
- God sets himself against rulers who set themselves against God (Dan 5:23).
- The life breath of every human ruler depends on God (Dan 5:23).
- God controls the course in life taken by every human ruler (Dan 5:23).

- All should fear "the living God," including all human rulers and governments (Dan 6:26).
- God is able to rescue anyone out of the hands of wicked rulers (Dan 6:27).

The essential points in Daniel are that all human governing is accountable to God, whether or not those in power know it or agree. However governing power is acquired in human terms, God controls who gets it, wants those getting it to use it wisely, and considers it wicked for rulers to act as if they take his place. This means there is an irony to human governing, which is that no human sovereignty is sovereign in relation to God. All power on earth comes from God, all rulers are accountable to God for how they rule, and this accountability is direct, meaning God deals with them himself without using another person or agency.

The New Testament approaches human governing the same way Daniel does but adds more on living under bad rulers. All rulers are accountable to God, whether they rule well or not. But what happens when rulers turn against God, use power for evil, and rebel against God knowingly and on purpose? Should we cooperate with or try to stop them? And beyond that, how much should we tolerate from imperfect rulers who do a few things right and many other things wrong?

Human governing was not a major topic in what Jesus taught during his time on earth, but he did affirm its necessity and validated government even in the hands of unbelieving rulers (John 19:11). Beyond this, he also expected rulers to defend national security (Luke 14:31), establish monetary systems, levy taxes, and enforce compliance (Matt 17:24–27; 22:17–21; Mark 12:14–17; Luke 20:22–25). While considering government valid and essential, Jesus also criticized abusing power (Matt 16:6; Mark 8:15; Luke 12:1), did not yield to threats (Luke 13:32), told followers to expect opposition (Matt 10:17–18; John 15:20), and warned them not to trust unbelievers in authority (Matt 16:6; Mark 8:15; Luke 12:1). Jesus wanted those he taught to influence the world for good (Matt 5:13–16), but not by revolting (John 6:15), and told them to accept those using power unfairly (Matt 5:41). He distinguished "things that are Caesar's" from "things that are God's" (Matt 22:21; Mark 12:17; Luke 20:25) but without limiting God's sovereignty. Jesus was not separating human governing from God and only meant that cooperating with nonbelievers governing positions is not disloyalty to God even if those in power do not know or accept him.

The passages most studied by Christians looking for what the Bible teaches about government are Romans 13:1–7 and 1 Timothy 2:1–2. But, while these passages are important, they do not stand alone and essentially reaffirm what is already revealed through Daniel and Jesus. Paul, in Romans and 1 Timothy, highlights what Christians need to know when governed by non-Christians, but he does not address what to do if Christians rise to power or suffer terrible persecution. Rather than give a political theory or blueprint for governing, Paul only explains very generally how God relates to governing and wants Christians to cooperate with whatever governing situation he allows.

In writing early Christians in Rome, Paul stresses seven points about relating to human government. First, it is instituted by God however it comes to power. Second, God wants rulers to punish behavior that is bad and to reward (or at least recognize) behavior that is good. Third, God authorizes rulers to exercise power over life and death in order to get this done. Fourth, God wants Christians to be good citizens (to submit) and not bad citizens (to rebel) no matter who is in power. Fifth, God authorizes rulers to raise taxes to support what they do. Sixth, God wants Christians to go along with whatever governing he allows. Seventh, God wants Christians to respect and honor those governing however they handle it. And then, writing to Timothy, Paul adds that Christians should ask God to help rulers provide civil tranquility (1 Tim 2:1–2).

Finally, God, in Revelation, reveals how terribly bad human government can become even though he never loses control. Government can stop serving its proper purpose and become a beast empowered by the Devil that demands worship, blasphemes God, wages war on the saints, and conquers the world (Rev 13:1–8). Nevertheless, God remains sovereign, and this end time demonic state can only do what he permits (Rev 13:7). At the right time, God will destroy it (Rev 18:8) and rescue the saints (Dan 12:1; Matt 24:13, 22; Rev 18:4). He will do this himself and not use proxies (Rev 17:14), and, when Christians are persecuted by this demonic state, their fidelity through it will glorify God (Rev 2:10; 12:11).

The hardest questions Christians ask relating to government are: "Must Christians always respect and honor bad rulers?" "May Christians ever try to overthrow and replace bad government?" And "What should those governing attempt with the power they have?" One reason these questions are hard is because we want, on the one hand, to make things better, and bad people in power do very bad things. On the other hand, God institutes all governing authorities and wants us to cooperate with them. Another reason they are hard is because, outside the theocracy of ancient Israel, the Bible focuses on cooperating with those ruling us and does not address how we should use power if it falls in our hands.

Christians must "submit" to all governing (Rom 13:1; 1 Pet 2:13–14), but our duty to obey is not absolute, for "we must obey God rather than people" (Acts 5:29). God requires that we accept those governing us, but only as they serve his purposes. We must do as they say, but not if they countermand God. God does not require doing whatever government requires and, if it requires disobeying God, we must refuse. God establishes all governing authorities (Rom 13:1) but does not authorize misgoverning. He sometimes allows bad people to govern, but he does not authorize them to do or require bad things.

Christians also must "respect" and "honor" all governing authorities (Rom 13:7; also note 1 Pet 2:17). This means showing deference to the role government has in our lives and does not mean we should be blind to bad character or trust untrustworthy people. Jesus warned against trusting misguided people (Mark 8:15), praised being shrewd (Luke 16:8), and called Herod "that fox" (Luke 13:32), so what Paul and Peter require does not rule out circumspection, using good judgment, or even standing up to a governing official unworthy of the authority he has.

Christians are divided over whether God allows us to support revolutions to replace bad governments. Some, following Augustine, think Christians must endure whatever governing there is no matter how bad because Paul says God institutes "the authorities that exist" and resisting "is opposing God's command" (Rom 13:1–2).[2] Others, following Calvin, think Paul only prohibits private citizens and allows lower officials to protect those in their care by resisting or replacing higher officials who assault them.[3] And some, like Thomas Müntzer, who led the German Peasants' War (1524–1525), and John of Leiden, who helped lead the Münster

---

[2] Augustine says, "Christ's servants . . . are bidden, if need be, to endure the wickedness of an utterly corrupt state, and by that endurance to win for themselves a place of glory . . . in the Heavenly Commonwealth, whose law is the will of God" (*The City of God*, II.19).

[3] Calvin says, "Any magistrates . . . appointed to restrain the willfulness of kings" have a duty "to withstand . . . the fierce licentiousness of kings . . . who violently fall upon and assault the lowly common folk" (*Institutes of the Christian Religion*, IV.xx.31), and elsewhere says, "Earthly princes lay aside their power when they rise up against God, and are unworthy to be reckoned among the number of mankind" (*Commentaries on the Prophet Daniel* [1561], lecture xxx, on Daniel 6:22).

Rebellion (1534–1535), even have thought believers must use violence in the name of governing for God if imperfect rulers do not step aside willingly.

Christians dividing over the first two positions debate whether Calvin's distinctions (between officials and private individuals and between lower and higher officials) are in the text or read into it, but the third position is not properly Christian because it perverts what the Bible actually says. Still, we need to analyze this third position to avoid making the same mistake. The difference between biblically worthy politics and revolution in the name of ruling for God reduces to whether God wants us to impose sovereignty in his name right now and, in human terms, by using violence, or wants us to wait until Jesus returns and does it himself.

Nothing in the Bible indicates that God wants believers to replace bad government, much less take over the world, before God does it himself. In the Old Testament, after Israel loses independence, God does not tell his people to overthrow foreign rulers but rather to serve them (Jer 29:7), and in the New Testament Jesus tells believers to await his return (Matt 24:42; Luke 21:36) rather than immediately to rule for him politically, to endure mistreatment rather than to stop it (Matt 10:22; 24:13; Mark 13:13), and, if necessary, to be faithful unto death (Rev 2:10). The tragedies of the Münster Rebellion and the Peasants' War came from a nonbiblical view of political perfection and is why Baptists were feared in the American colonies.[4]

We know from Scripture that political perfection is possible in Paradise (Isa 2:4; Mic 4:3; Rev 21:4; 22:3). But that is yet to come (Dan 9:26) and is not presently possible in a world where Satan deceives and destroys (1 Pet 5:8; Rev 12:9; 20:7–8). Until Jesus rids the world of sin and sinners, Christian political ethics can only be realist, not perfectionist. We can imagine a perfect world, ruled perfectly by perfect rulers who assure perfect justice. But that is future and not possible for us to achieve now no matter how hard we try. For now, the best we can imagine exceeds human finitude and fallenness. Wanting political perfection so badly we deny real world limits makes things worse, not better. In fact, pursuing political perfection

---

[4] This also is why theologians who saw the horrors of Nazism were so keenly aware of how dangerous it is to pursue political perfection before the return of Christ. Thus, Bonhoeffer stressed preserving the "penultimate" for the sake of the "ultimate" (*Ethics*, 133 [see chap. 6, n. 42]); Niebuhr insisted on the "relevance of an impossible ideal" (*An Interpretation of Christian Ethics*, 83 [see chap. 2, n. 57]); Ellul spoke of "tension between the Already and the Not Yet" (*The Ethics of Freedom*, 11 [see chap. 1, n. 69]); and Thielicke of "walking between two worlds" (*Theological Ethics* [see chap. 1, n. 69], 147).

without waiting for Jesus spawns evil in two directions. It leads those governing to be tyrants (Zeph 1–3:3) and those governed to be anarchists (Deut 12:8; Judg 21:25) or revolutionaries (Ps 2:1), either because they believe no one needs governing (anarchy) or believe they can rule perfectly after taking over (revolution).

While God is sovereign over all human affairs, including human government and politics, he is not imposing his political rule on the world right now. And he does not authorize or expect the church to impose divine sovereignty on politics in his name either. This does not mean God does not care or will not do something about it, for Jesus will impose universal political rule when he returns. But, for now, the kingdom rule of God is a voluntary individual matter residing "within you" (Luke 17:20–21, NIV$_{1984}$), and is not a matter of using civil power to stop sinners from sinning or to force unloving people to love others against their will. For now this means we must not confuse the role of the state with the role of the church. We must not mix what God wants of civil rulers and politicians with spreading the kingdom of God in human hearts.

The third hard question is, "What should those in power do with it?" Should they only punish and praise (Rom 13:3)? Or should they also try making things better than they are? It is one thing to submit and another to be in charge. What difference should it make if a Christian rises to power, not by revolution but peacefully? What goals should be set and what difference should it make? Answering is affected by what we think of human nature. The less limited we think we are the more we suppose government can do, and the more limited we think we are the less we suppose government can do. How we view human nature also affects what we think causes the problems we face. Is the main cause having a sin nature or just not having the same stuff? Is it selfishness or just not having good education? Is it something in our hearts or something in the outside world? How these questions get answered affects whether we think government can eliminate problems or only restrain them.

Misperceiving human nature leads to misperceiving problems and affects whether we think government can solve them. Christians should not expect power in the hands of finite, fallen people to do what only God can. God changes people from the inside out, and human governing can do no more than try to change people from the outside in, even though it cannot determine or control what people think or desire. Government can affect external things but cannot change human nature. It can limit what selfish, hateful, greedy people do but cannot stop what makes them bad, and it can praise what loving, compassionate, responsible people do but cannot control what makes them good. Even people doing good things out of relatively good hearts are never perfectly good all the time. So, even the best human governing possible only makes relative improvements and never reaches perfections that require perfect people.

The Bible does not envision a single best way to organize governing systems in the present world. But neither does it say those in power should not try making things better, so long as they accept human finitude and fallenness and limit governing to external things. Because we can imagine more than is possible, governing is tempted to cross these boundaries, and doing that makes things worse, not better. Human governing can make things relatively better, but never perfect. Perfect society will come, but only in a world without sinners. It is worth longing for, but not ahead of schedule. For now, those governing must not confuse making things better with making things perfect, and those governed must not think any governing can make things perfect before Jesus returns.

Christians have divided through history on how much to be involved in politics, and it may be there is no fixed answer. Being salt and light (Matt 5:13–16) in a dark and rotten world includes being a good moral influence in all areas of life, including government and politics. But the manner and extent to which Christians ought to be involved in politics is not reducible to a mathematical formula and cannot be measured in materials ways. It is a tension or dialectic that comes out appearing the same as simply doing the best we can under whatever circumstances happen to apply. But, despite variations affecting the moral influence Christians have on politics, there are hazards to avoid when doing so, and these include (1) reducing the gospel to politics, (2) acting as if we can rid the world of sin and sinners before Jesus comes back, (3) doing nothing at all to resist wicked behavior, or (4) thinking human governing power can do what only God can do, which is turn bad people into good people by transforming them from the inside out.

Recommended further reading on the issue of government includes Lawrence Adams, *Going Public* (Grand Rapids: Baker, 2002); Harold Berman, *The Interaction of Law and Religion* (Nashville: Abingdon, 1974); Greg Forster, *The Contested Public Square* (Downers Grove, IL: IVP, 2008); Wayne Grudem, *Politics according to the Bible* (Grand Rapids: Zondervan, 2010); P. C. Kemeny, *Church, State, and Public Justice: Five Views* (Downers Grove, IL: IVP, 2007); Richard John Neuhaus, *The Naked Public Square* (Grand Rapids: Eerdmans, 1986); Francis Schaeffer, *A Christian Manifesto* (Westchester, IL: Crossway, 1981); James Skillen, *The Good of Politics* (Grand Rapids: Baker, 2014); and Gary Smith, ed., *God and Politics: Four Views* (Phillipsburg, NJ: P&R, 1989).

Religious Liberty

Religious liberty, as an applied issue in Christian ethics, lies at the intersection of religion, civil law, and morality. It involves all three elements, and none reduces to the other, which makes religious liberty both strategic and complex. The issue concerns the relation of civil governing to religious life when both have moral missions to fulfill. It deals with whether those governing should leave religious life alone or try to control it because what people worship matters so much to social justice and civil stability. What makes the issue challenging is that religious liberty requires government to stay out of something that makes a big difference to what it does.

Defining *religious liberty* needs updating from how it was conceived earlier. It once was conceived in terms of not having a state church and allowing Christians to disagree with each other without involving the state.[5] But that did not necessarily include treating other belief systems the same way, and *religious liberty* today must include more than limiting the way government treats Christians. These days the greatest opposition to religious liberty no longer comes from one Christian group using civil power to suppress other Christian groups but comes from Islamic groups bent on erasing all resistance and from secular ideologies bent on silencing all disagreement. *Religious liberty* can no longer be defined in uniquely Christian terms and now requires defining in a broader way that seeks for all religions and belief systems the same freedom from civil interference it seeks for Christianity.

Religious liberty now means immunity from civil coercion that forces institutions or individuals to act contrary to sincerely held belief system (i.e., religious) convictions or to accept or reject such convictions, together with being allowed, within limits (such as no human sacrifice, no revolution, and no denying others the same treatment), to act on such convictions and to spread them to others. While it is personal, ethical, and religious, the issue also is social, political, and public in nature, meaning it supposes society and its institutions must respect freedom of religion in a public and legally protected manner. It applies to institutions

---

[5] Barnette, *Introducing Christian Ethics*, 169 (see chap. 1, n. 60); Trull, *Walking in the Way*, 272, 277 (see chap. 1, n. 55).

(like churches, synagogues, and mosques) as well as individuals, has positive as well as negative aspects (like freedom to evangelize as well as immunity from coercion), and applies to functionally religious ideologies (like communism, progressive secularism, LGBTQ+ worldview ideology, and antireligious atheism) as well as traditional religions (like Christianity, Judaism, Islam, Buddhism, and Hinduism).

Other related terms include *persecution* and *tolerance*. *Persecution* refers to experiencing or inflicting injury or harassment because victims hold beliefs contrary to those in positions of power, and *tolerance* either means having an attitude of forbearance toward beliefs and behaviors you do not share or means treating with respect opinions and practices conflicting with your own. *Tolerance* implies disagreement, and that leads some to oppose using it. But, where truth matters, the term cannot be avoided even though we should defend others being free of civil coercion to believe and practice convictions God says are false and foolish.

Religious liberty only concerns how civil life relates to religious life in a world filled with sin and sinners. There is no religious liberty in relation to God, and there will be no religious liberty in the new earth where God will govern perfect people in perfect circumstances. When that happens, there will be no freedom to oppose the way God rules, but neither will we want to. Religious liberty also should not be confused with the freedom we have in Christ (Luke 4:18; John 8:36; Rom 8:2; Gal 5:1). That freedom refers to escaping punishment for offending God and has nothing to do with immunity from human powers. One is spiritual and the other civil. Thus, one can be spiritually free while civilly persecuted, and one can be civilly free while spiritually enslaved.

Religious liberty is neither ideal nor eternal. It refers to something in this life that will not apply when Jesus returns, and it seeks immunity in civil life for things God hates and will punish. For these reasons, the ethics of religious liberty takes a "realist" (not perfectionist) approach that separates the state from institutions serving belief systems (not just churches but ideological institutions as well). But this is qualified by understanding that ethics depends on belief systems that cannot be separated from politics without leaving politics morally blind and understanding also that religious liberty in real life must be balanced against government needing to protect peace and order. In other words, while honoring religious liberty, governments need also to protect society from abuses in the name of "religious liberty" that threaten other people.

If religious liberty is a good thing, why do people oppose it? Some oppose it because religious liberty requires tolerating things they consider wrong, or they think it threatens political authority, think error has no rights, think disagreement hinders achieving social goals, or think it masks prejudice and hate. These reasons all reduce to perfectionist thinking that fears disagreeing with preferred beliefs, associates politics with what people worship, supposes evil comes from disagreeing with what they worship, and so confuses the mission of government (defending justice and civil order) with the mission of religion (saving people from evil). Such thinking is mistaken but affects many people, including Christians. Until the Second Vatican Council, Catholics opposed religious liberty, thinking the Church, as God's representative on earth, must control all areas of life both civil and religious. Theodore Beza (1519–1605), John Calvin's successor in Geneva, considered religious liberty "a most diabolical dogma, because it means that everyone should be left to go to hell in his own way."[6]

Religious liberty has four classifications formed by two distinctions, one between two conceptions of civil freedom and the other between two levels of civil freedom. There are two mutually incompatible conceptions of civil liberty—"ordered liberty" and "autonomous liberty." The first is responsible, duty-bound, and tethered to a sense of moral authority beyond manipulating because it lies beyond self. It is freedom to be accountable to authority transcending civil government. The second is irresponsible, licentious, and not tethered to any authority past manipulating because it is entirely self-focused. It is freedom from accountability to anyone or anything, not just in respect to civil law, but in respect to any authority other than self. Furthermore, civil liberty as to religious life applies at two levels—"institutional liberty," which is corporate, and "individual liberty," which is personal.

Together, these produce four classifications of civil liberty in relation to religion or belief systems: (1) ordered liberty for institutions, (2) autonomous liberty for institutions, (3) ordered liberty for individuals, and (4) autonomous liberty for individuals. These classifications all hold that matters of faith and practice, whether traditionally religious (like Christianity, Judaism, Islam, Buddhism, and Hinduism) or functionally religious (like communism, progressive secularism, LGBTQ+ worldview ideology, and antireligious atheism), should be free of civil coercion. But they do not have the same value in terms of God and society because

---

[6] Theodore Beza, *On Heretics*, 1554.

autonomy in the name of religion, having no obligation to higher moral authority, foments chaos, whereas responsible freedom in the name of religion to follow moral obligation beyond self as well as government restrains chaos. In other words, moral autonomy destroys social order and moral discipline secures it.

The Bible does not tell us to expect fair treatment in the present world and rather warns that we must expect religious persecution. That means we should affirm religious liberty but know, as well, that it is hard to achieve and persecution is normal. Shadrach, Meshach, and Abednego were thrown into a burning furnace for refusing to worship an idol (Dan 3:1–30); Daniel was thrown into a den of lions for praying to God rather than a human ruler (Dan 6:1–28); heroes of faith in the Bible include some who died by stoning, being sawed in two, and by the sword rather than deny or disobey God (Heb 11:37); Jesus warned, "If they persecuted me, they will also persecute you" (John 15:20) and told us to "pray for those who persecute you" (Matt 5:44); there will be terrible religious persecution just before Jesus returns (Dan 12:1; Matt 24:21–22; Mark 13:19–20); and God will bless those who are faithful unto death (Rev 2:10). If Christians are in power, we must not persecute others for three reasons: first, because Jesus excluded "things that are God's" from the jurisdiction of human government (Matt 22:21); second, because Jesus opposed using force to get people to follow him (Luke 9:54–55); and third, because Jesus refused to politicize the kingdom of God in the present world (John 6:15).

Religious liberty in relation to civil power is relatively new in human history. Until the eighteenth century, rulers all thought they needed uniformity of religion to assure national morality and good order. Tragically, many Christians also mistakenly thought civil power could force people to believe and follow the right faith, and well-known Christian leaders like Augustine, Aquinas, and Calvin justified persecuting religious dissent. In Europe, Catholics and Protestants both wanted only their churches to operate in areas they controlled, and dissenters like Baptists, Mennonites, Quakers, Puritans, Methodists, and Huguenots were forced to flee to the "new world" of North and South America.

Such thinking led to the Thirty Years War fought in Central Europe between 1618 and 1648. This was a conflict between Protestants and Catholics that resulted in the deaths of over 8 million people, making it one of the bloodiest wars in history. Beyond this, Anglicans in England persecuted Catholics, Puritans, Baptists, Quakers, and Presbyterians; Presbyterians in Scotland persecuted Catholics, Anglicans, Baptists, and Quakers; and Lutherans in Switzerland

and Germany persecuted Anabaptists, Mennonites, and Brethren. Because of this, the Baptist leader Balthasar Hübmaier urged Christians everywhere to give up trying to coerce religious uniformity and to affirm religious liberty instead.

Support for religious liberty took root when Europeans moved to North America and founded the United States, and this happened for two reasons: first, because many settlers had fled religious persecution in Europe and second, because forming a new nation required uniting people from different religious backgrounds. Some regions of the new nation started with state churches (Congregationalism in New England, Catholicism in Maryland, and Anglicanism in New York, Virginia, the Carolinas, and Georgia) which later declined, and Pennsylvania and Rhode Island rejected a state church from the start. All the American colonies soon started tolerating religious differences, and they finally agreed to protect religious liberty throughout the new nation when the original states ratified the US Constitution and Bill of Rights.

Achieving religious liberty is highly praiseworthy. Yet, it cannot survive without ongoing popular support and perpetual defending by those in power, and these factors determine whether one generation passes it on to the next. Achieving religious liberty has always been rare, and, while some countries have followed the United States on this issue, religious liberty remains rare in the world. Support for it in the United States is waning as trends in the culture lead more and more to consider it harmful and perhaps dangerous.

Outside the United States, religious liberty is threatened by the rising influence of militant Islamic and Hindu movements, and in the United States, it is threatened by two triumphalist idealisms—secular progressivism and LGBTQ+ normalizing ideology—that are functionally religious because they frame ethical understanding for everything else including civil law, civil liberties, and constitutional interpretation. These ideological movements are triumphalist because they try to push freedom to believe and practice other belief systems (like Christianity) out of civil life—out of the common arenas of society—so that, should they succeed, only people sharing their one preferred belief system (functional religion) will be free to participate and those not going along will be persecuted.

This can be seen in little ways, like a sixty-three-year-old blind lady, in 2019, being threatened with jail for sharing her faith in a public park in Rhode Island. But sadly, the shift now weakening religious liberty in our culture is taking place in much bigger ways as well. In 2006, Chai Feldblum, an LGBTQ+ activist who clerked for Justice Blackmun on the Supreme

Court, wrote a law article showing how religious liberty stands in the way of forcing everyone to accept LGBTQ+ identity rights and arguing that, where they conflict, LGBTQ+ identity rights must preempt religious liberty in American law.[7] In 2016, the US Commission on Civil Rights declared that religious liberty must not be allowed to mask "discrimination, intolerance, racism, sexism, homophobia, Islamophobia," and "Christian supremacy," and said government officials must limit religious liberty when it protects what they deem "bigoted" or "phobic" by their own beliefs regardless of how historic or sincere religious convictions held by others might be.[8]

Richard John Neuhaus observes that the Supreme Court is now standing religious liberty in America "on its head" by reinterpreting the religion clauses in the Bill of Rights to mean the opposite of what the framers intended. Now, rather than protecting religious life from infringing by the state, they treat them as protecting public life from the influence of religion, and, rather than securing a protection right for religion, they treat them as securing a protection right against religion.[9] Lastly, the Supreme Court, since 2003, has handed down a string of LGBTQ+ normalizing decisions—*Lawrence v. Texas* (2003), *Obergefell v. Hodges* (2015), and *Bostock v. Clayton County* (2020)—that have embedded logic into constitutional law detrimental to religious liberty just the way Chai Feldblum anticipated.

Recommended further reading on the issue of religious liberty includes Roland H. Bainton, *The Travail of Religious Liberty* (New York: Harper, 1951); Daniel R. Heimbach, "Contrasting Views of Religious Liberty," *Journal of Law and Religion* 11/2 (1994–1995): 715–731; John Courtney Murray, *The Problem of Religious Freedom* (Westminster, MD: Newman, 1965); John Courtney Murray, *Religious Liberty* (Louisville: Westminster/John Knox, 1993); Thomas White et al., eds., *First Freedom*, 1st ed., (Nashville: B&H, 2007); Philip J. Wogaman, *Protestant Faith and Religious Liberty* (Nashville: Abingdon, 1967); and Perez Zagorin, *How the Idea of Religious Tolerance Came to the West* (Princeton, NJ: Princeton, 2003).

---

[7] Feldblum, "Moral Conflict and Liberty," 61–123 (see chap. 9, n. 6).

[8] "Peaceful Coexistence: Reconciling Nondiscrimination Principles with Civil Liberties" (Washington, DC: US Commission on Civil Rights, September 7, 2016).

[9] Richard John Neuhaus, "The Upside-down Freedom," *Christianity Today*, December 9, 1988, 24–26.

Wealth & Poverty

The Bible has much to say about wealth and poverty and refers to it more than to marriage, parenting, or the return of Christ. This does not make the subject more important but does show that God understands the trouble we have with it. Some extreme views are perpetrated about what the Bible teaches on the ethics of wealth and poverty. One view reduces all good to being wealthy and all bad to being poor, and another claims it is impossible to be good and wealthy at the same time. But neither is valid because godly people are found in Scripture at vastly different economic levels. Abraham, Job, and Daniel were rich; Amos, Ezekiel, and Jesus' father Joseph were middle income; and Jeremiah was poor. So the amount we have cannot alone settle how we stand with God.

The term *wealth* comes from *weal*, an Anglo-Saxon word indicating abundance. It is used in phrases like having a "wealth of knowledge" or "wealth of experience." But, while *wealth* is used other ways, it most often refers to material abundance. Used this way, *wealth* refers to having more, and usually a lot more, than needed just to get by and thus being able to afford luxuries, take time off, and employ others. The term *poverty* derives from *paupertas*, a Latin word for having less than adequate means. *Poverty*, thus, indicates a state in which people struggle to get by, and it can range from having little (paucity) to having nothing at all (destitution).

The Old Testament mainly uses five Hebrew words to identify where people stand materially, but these Hebrew words focus more on what people experience than how much they have. The עָשִׁיר (*āšîr*) are the well off. The עָנִי (*ānî*) are the oppressed. The דַּל (*dal*) are those teetering on disaster. The רוּשׁ (*rûš*) are the needy, those who for lack of necessities suffer hunger, thirst, or insecurity. And the אֶבְיוֹן (*'ebyôn*) are those who must beg to survive.

Similarly, the New Testament uses five Greek words to identify where people stand materially, but these Greek words focus less on what people experience and more on how much they have. The πλούσιος (*plousios*) are the upperclass who have plenty and have time to pursue interests beyond earning income. The τεχνίτης (*technitēs*) are upper middleclass craftsmen, artisans, builders, and small business owners. The εργάτης (*ergatēs*) are lower middleclass workers with no special skills and who get by on manual labor. The πένης (*penēs*) are the top of the low class. They are relatively poor but not destitute. And the πτωχός (*ptōchos*) are the lowest of the low. These are people so poor they cannot support themselves and will die unless others help them.

Wealth and poverty are addressed throughout Scripture, but Proverbs deals with it extensively and offers the following:

- It is better to be poor and righteous than to be wealthy and wicked (Prov 16:8; 19:1).
- It is better to be poor and humble than to be wealthy and proud (Prov 16:19).
- It is better to be poor and fear God than to be wealthy without God (Prov 15:16).
- It is better to eat simply with loved ones than to feast with those who hate you (Prov 15:17).
- It is better to eat plain food in peace than to feast surrounded by tension (Prov 17:1).
- Wealth is a buffer in hard times, but the poor have no buffer (Prov 10:15).
- Wealth attracts friends, and poverty alienates them (Prov 19:4).
- Everyone likes handouts, but even relatives avoid beggars (Prov 19:6–7).
- The generous are enriched, but no one likes people who are stingy (Prov 11:25–26).
- Oppressing the poor dishonors God, and helping the poor honors Him (Prov 14:31).
- God rewards people who help the poor (Prov 19:17).
- Laziness leads to poverty, and working hard builds wealth (Prov 10:4; 24:33–34).
- Negligence loses wealth and diligence builds it up (Prov 10:4).
- No discipline makes you poor, but learning from mistakes helps you avoid it (Prov 13:18).
- The diligent gain power, and the lazy squander what power they have (Prov 12:24).
- The wealthy have influence, and the poor do not (Prov 14:20).
- Some are made poor by injustice (Prov 13:23), and doing that offends God (Prov 14:31).

The Bible views wealth ambiguously, treating it as good or bad depending on how it is acquired, used, or valued. Wealth can be a gift of God or something he condemns, and it can move people to thank God or tempt them to forsake him. So, the sage in Proverbs asks God for "neither poverty nor wealth . . . . Otherwise I might have too much and deny you . . . or I might have nothing and steal profaning the name of my God" (Prov 30:8–9).

On the good side, God blessed Abraham with riches (Gen 13:2), made Job rich (Job 1:10), allowed Satan to take it (Job 1:12), and then made Job wealthier than before (Job 2:12);

and some New Testament Christians, like Joseph of Arimathea (Matt 27:57–60), Barnabas (Acts 4:6–7), and Lydia (Acts 16:14), were wealthy as well. The Bible never doubts it is possible to be godly and wealthy at the same time. But it distinguishes valuing wealth the right way from lusting for it, earning it the right way from stealing it, and using it the right way from using it badly. Acquisitiveness is condemned (1 Tim 6:10), but diligence, thrift, and saving are praised (Gen 41:35–36; Prov 6:6–8; 10:5, 15). Honest riches come from God (Deut 8:18; 1 Chr 29:12) and can be used to honor God (Prov 3:9), serve others (1 Tim 6:18–19), and support ministries (Acts 2:45; 24:17). So there is nothing inherently wrong with getting and being wealthy.

But, while wealth can be good, it is not the greatest good and has a bad side. Some wealthy people are righteous, but some, like King Ahab (1 Kgs 21:1–16) and Herod the Great (Matt 2:16), are terribly evil. Evil things associated with wealth in the Bible fall into four categories. Wealth is acquired badly if gained by violence (Mic 2:2; 6:12; Jas 5:6), oppression (Isa 10:1–2; Amos 2:6–8; 4:1), deception (Mic 6:11–12), or using ministry to enrich yourself (1 Tim 6:5). Wealth is used badly if flaunted (Isa 3:16–23; 5:8; 1 Tim 2:9; Jas 5:5), used for evil purposes (Ps 52:7; Isa 3:15; Mic 2:1–2; Jas 2:6–7), or spent with callous disregard for people in need (Eccl 5:13; Amos 4:1–4; Jas 5:1–5). Wealth is viewed badly if loved in place of God (Ps 62:10; Heb 13:5) or used to justify arrogance (1 Tim 6:17), ingratitude (Deut 8:12–14; Hos 2:8), or coveting (Exod 20:17; Deut 5:21; Mic 2:1–2). And wealth is trusted badly if trusted to do what only God does. Wealth cannot satisfy (Eccl 5:10), give life meaning (Luke 12:15), assure favor with God (Rev 3:17), or shield us from God's judgment (Prov 11:4, 28; Ezek 7:19; Zeph 1:18; Jas 5:1–5; Rev 18:15–16). It has no eternal value (Eccl 5:15–16; Prov 27:24; Matt 6:19–20; 1 Tim 6:7), dwindles quickly (Prov 23:4–5; Eccl 5:11), can be stolen (Eccl 6:2; Matt 6:19), cannot stop death (Ps 49:10–12, 16–17; Jas 1:11), and will be squandered after you die (Eccl 2:18–21).

Jesus warned that wealth can deceive people into misvaluing things (Matt 13:22; Mark 4:19), can compete with serving God (Matt 6:24), can hinder discipleship (Mark 10:23), and can choke spiritual growth (Matt 13:22; Mark 4:18–19; Luke 8:14). Thus, wealth often is linked to idolatry (Deut 8:12–19; 32:15–16; Isa 2:7–8; Ezek 7:20; Hos 2:5–9). But evils associated with wealth are all in us and not in riches themselves. The ethical problem is not with how much we have but with how we regard what we have (Prov 28:20). And we solve it not by changing how much we have, but by focusing on the value of knowing God over all we have (Jer 9:24; 1 Cor 1:31).

Having considered what the Bible says about wealth, we turn now to what it says about poverty. Taking them in this order is important because wealth precedes poverty in both time and theology. God, in time, made a rich world lacking nothing until sin entered the picture, and, in theology, one does not properly understand sin and judgment without first understanding the rich goodness of God and of all he plans and provides.

Ultimately the reason for poverty is fallen human nature. Poverty did not exist at Creation (Gen 1:31) and will not exist in the new heaven and earth (Rev 21:4). Even now, it exists only because of disobedience, separation from God, and the curse God imposed on material things affecting our survival (Gen 3:17–19). God knows and cares about the "poor" (דַּל, *dal*; Prov 19:17), but poverty is not inherently good, never was, and never will be. It is part of the present fallen world where it causes suffering (Prov 10:15), isolates people from family and friends (Prov 14:20; 19:4, 7), puts them at the mercy of others (Prov 18:23), and tempts some to reject or dishonor God (Prov 14:31; 17:5).

God controls who is wealthy and poor: "The LORD brings poverty and gives wealth; he humbles and he exalts. He raises the poor (דַּל, *dal*) from the dust and lifts the needy (אֶבְיוֹן, *ebyôn*) from the trash heap. He seats them with noblemen and gives them a throne of honor" (1 Sam 2:7–8). In the present world, God does not eliminate poverty because he allows freedom to sin. But, he controls the process by blessing and restraining, pities the "poor" (דַּל, *dal*) and "helpless" (אֶבְיוֹן, *ebyôn*; Ps 72:13), and will solve their problems someday (Isa 29:19). God promised there would be no "poor" (אֶבְיוֹן, *ebyôn*) in Israel if only they obeyed him (Deut 15:4-5). But, knowing they would not, God also said they would always have poor people (אֶבְיוֹן, *ebyôn*) among them (Deut 15:11), and Jesus said the same (πτωχός, *ptōchos*; Matt 26:11; Mark 14:7; John 12:8). Individuals can work their way out of poverty (Prov 10:4), but no society can solve the social problem because fallen humanity cannot change fallen human nature.

God strongly condemns oppressing the poor, weak, and vulnerable (Isa 1:23; 3:14–15; Jer 2:34; 22:13; Ezek 18:10–13; Amos 2:7; 4:1; 5:11; 8:4–7; Mic 2:1–2), wants those who can to help them (Exod 23:11; Lev 19:10; Deut 15:7–8, 11; Luke 12:33; 1 John 3:17), and blesses those who do (Deut 15:10; Ps 41:1–3; Prov 14:21). But God prohibits favoritism in courts of law (Lev 19:15) or in church (Jas 2:1–7) based on economic status. Justice requires treating all the same regardless of what they have, not giving all the same regardless of working. God considers us moral agents, not machines that operate the right way only under the right conditions.

If forced to choose one or the other, the moral value of righteousness far exceeds the economic value of material things: "The little that the righteous person has is better than the abundance of many wicked people" (Ps 37:16). In a perfect world, moral and economic value go hand in hand. But in a fallen world, they sometimes conflict, and where that happens, we must prefer righteousness with poverty over wealth with wickedness. This does not mean wealth and righteousness are always opposed, but we live in a world in which one does not assure the other (Ps 73:3, 13; Jer 12:1; Mal 3:14–15). In the present world, righteousness does not guarantee wealth, and wealth does not guarantee righteousness. Where these do not match up, we must trust God will, in his time, correct the equation (Ps 37:7–9). But, even now, moral and economic values are not necessarily opposed, for righteousness does not always mean being poor and poverty does not always mean being righteous.

While material poverty is not good and does not make anyone good, there is, in the Bible, a spiritual "poverty" that is worthy in the eyes of God. We must take care because there are two sorts of spiritual "poverty," one good and one bad. The church at Laodicea is criticized for being spiritually "poor" (πτωχός, *ptōchos*) in a bad way (Rev 3:17), and God blesses people who are spiritually "poor" (πτωχός, *ptōchos*) in a good way (Matt 5:3). Good spiritual "poverty" is reaching out to God the way David does in Ps 40:14, and God favors it because he wants us to approach him in totally dependent humility the way poor people plead for help (Isa 66:2).

It is true that, in a fallen world, wicked people hate the righteous and often oppress them (Matt 5:10), but those impoverished for righteousness are righteous before and not made righteous by it. Righteousness is the reason, not the result. Materially "poor" people (πτωχός, *ptōchos*) do tend to be more open to the gospel (Jas 2:5) than rich people who think they "need nothing" (Rev 3:17). But even so, material poverty does not earn credit with God all by itself.

Jesus said some extraordinary things about possessing things and assisting the poor. He told his disciples to "sell your possessions and give to the poor" (Luke 12:33), said no one can be a disciple without renouncing "all his possessions" (Luke 14:33), had "no place to lay his head" (Matt 8:20; Luke 9:58), wants us to follow his example (John 13:15), sent his disciples on a mission trip with "no staff, no traveling bag, no bread, no money" and no "extra shirt"

(Luke 9:3), and challenged a rich young ruler to "sell all you have and distribute it to the poor" (πτωχός, *ptōchos*; Luke 18:22). While taking these statements to heart, we must not misinterpret them.

Jesus did not say poverty saves anyone, did not make it the ideal way to live, and did not say Christians could not have possessions. Rather, he insisted on giving God priority over all we have, never letting money and possessions determine how we live, and using all we have to please and honor God. Jesus did not dispute having possessions and using them properly. He did not sell the family business when going into ministry (Mark 6:3), relied on people who supported him "from their possessions" (Luke 8:2–3), and commended an unjust steward for using "worldly wealth" shrewdly (Luke 16:9).

When Jesus told his disciples to "sell your possessions and give to the poor" (Luke 12:33), he did not want them to impoverish themselves but to share some of what they had with people needing help. When declaring no one can be a disciple without renouncing "all his possessions" (Luke 14:33), Jesus did not stop Christians from owning things but, rather, meant no one can be a Christian without surrendering everything to his lordship. In sending his disciples on a mission trip without supplies (Luke 9:3), Jesus was teaching a lesson about trusting God, not setting a precedent (Luke 22:35–36). And, in telling the rich young ruler to "sell all you have and distribute it to the poor" (πτωχός, *ptōchos*; Luke 18:22), he was challenging him as an individual, not issuing a universal command. What Jesus required of the rich young ruler cannot be universalized without conflicting with what Jesus did himself (he did not sell the family business that was supporting Mary in Nazareth) and the way he assumed his disciples would have means to help the poor "whenever you want" (Mark 14:7).

What the Bible says on the ethics of wealth and poverty can be summarized as follows:

1. God as Creator ultimately owns everything in the world (Ps 50:10–12).
2. We are responsible to God for stewarding the world's resources (Gen 1:26–28), and thanking him for what he gives honors God (Prov 3:9), as does using it to help others (Prov 19:17; Matt 25:31–46).
3. Those who can should support themselves and their families (1 Tim 5:8) and not depend on others (2 Thess 3:10–12).
4. Those who can should voluntarily (Mark 14:7) share some of what they earn or produce with those not able to support themselves (Eph 4:28).

5. Christians should first care for other believers (Deut 15:7; Mark 7:27; Rom 15:26; Gal 2:10; 6:10; 1 John 3:17) and then, as they can, should help others as well (Gal 6:10).

6. No one should exploit anyone needing help (Prov 14:31; Ezek 22:29; Amos 2:7).

7. A well-governed society rewards honest work (Prov 10:4), discourages folly and laziness (2 Thess 3:10), and helps the needy find ways to achieve economic independence by working (Deut 14:29; Lev 19:9–10).

Recommended further reading on the issue of wealth and poverty includes Randy C. Alcorn, *Money, Possessions, and Eternity* (Wheaton, IL: Tyndale, 2003); E. Calvin Beisner, *Prosperity and Poverty* (Wheaton, IL: Crossway, 1988); Craig L. Blomberg, *Neither Poverty nor Riches* (Grand Rapids: Eerdmans, 1999); Steve Corbett and Brian Fikkert, *When Helping Hurts: How to Alleviate Poverty without Hurting the Poor* (Chicago: Moody, 2009); George Gilder, *Wealth and Poverty* (San Francisco: ICS, 1993); R. Glenn and William R. Duggan, *The Aid Trap* (New York: Columbia Business School, 2009); David W. Jones and Russell S. Woodbridge, *Health, Wealth & Happiness* (Grand Rapids: Kregel, 2011); Robert D. Lupton, *Toxic Charity* (New York: HarperOne, 2011); Marvin N. Olasky, *The Tragedy of American Compassion* (Washington: Regnery, 1995); Jay W. Richards, *Money, Greed, and God* (New York: HarperOne, 2009); and John Schneider, *Godly Materialism: Rethinking Money & Possessions* (Downers Grove, IL: InterVarsity, 1994).

Capital Punishment

Capital punishment is execution by governing authority to penalize crime. In the Western world, the crime penalized only concerns murder—taking human life without justification—so in applied ethics, capital punishment deals with the duty governments have to maintain respect for human life. Ethical debate focuses on whether governments must do this by executing murderers or can do it in other ways. Capital punishment is the harshest form of civil punishment because it ends a person's earthly existence, and doing that cannot be reversed.

Capital punishment has been practiced all through history. But in our day, many nations have abolished it, and the United States is the last major Western nation still executing murderers. Other than the United States, India, Japan, and Singapore, nations still practicing capital punishment are mostly ruled by communism (other than Russia) or Sharia law. There was a movement in the United States to declare it unconstitutional, and executions were halted while the Supreme Court deliberated. But in 1972, the Court ruled it constitutional, and since then, some states practice capital punishment and others do not.[10] Opinion polls show that about 75 percent of Americans support executing murderers, and more states do than not. But the rate of executions is low, and in states practicing capital punishment, less than 24 percent of those sentenced to die are actually executed. This means murderers sentenced to die in the United States are three times more likely to avoid it on appeal than to have it carried out.

Advocates think executing murderers is what justice demands, and opponents think murderers do not deserve to die and executing them devalues human life. Christians disagree about what the Bible teaches; some say it requires capital punishment at least for murder, and others say it was authorized in the Old Testament but not anymore. Disagreeing on this issue either separates Christians affirming biblical inerrancy from those denying it, or it separates those who believe moral law in the Old Testament still applies from those who believe Jesus started a different approach to morality that replaces moral law in the Old Testament. In 2018, Catholics were shocked when the Vatican announced that, even though it long taught that the Bible authorizes capital punishment, Catholics should now believe capital punishment violates biblical ethics.[11] Comparatively, Evangelicals mostly favor capital punishment and still believe the Bible requires it at least for premeditated murder.

The ethics of capital punishment starts with understanding the sanctity of human life, and the most important passage in the Bible explaining it is, "God created man in his own image; he created him in the image of God; he created them male and female" (Gen 1:27). The sanctity of human life is the ethical value assigned it by God, which makes it derived and not original to us. It reflects something beyond us and is not something we make up, choose, control, or define ourselves. The sanctity of human life is given by God, which means others cannot take it from us. Every human life has the same sanctity regardless of gender, age, intelligence, health, wealth, or social status, and violating the sanctity of life held by others is wrong the same way no matter who it is. While the ethical value of human life is high, it is not the

---

[10] As of September 2020, capital punishment is allowed in twenty-eight of the fifty states, as well as under federal law and military law. It is not allowed in twenty-two states, and that number has been growing.

[11] New revision of number 2267 of the Catechism of the Catholic Church on the death penalty (Holy See Press Office, August 2, 2018).

highest there is, is not self-defining, and is not what decides right and wrong for everything else. Only God is ultimate, self-defining, and decides right and wrong, and some things are worth dying for (Dan 3:17–18). Yet, even though the right we have to life cannot be taken, it can be forfeited by taking it from others without God's approval (Exod 21:14; Lev 24:17; Num 35:33; Deut 19:21; Ezek 13:19).

When God renewed the creation ordinance with Noah after the flood, he ordered the human race to maintain respecting the sanctity of human life by executing murderers: "Whoever sheds human blood, by humans his blood will be shed, for God made humans in his image" (Gen 9:6). This says the sanctity of human life is maintained by the life-for-life principle. Taking someone's life without God's approval forfeits title to your own. The price paid must equal the wrong done, and nothing short of taking a murderer's life is equal to wrongly taking another person's life. In the eyes of he who defines the sanctity of life, a victim's life is worth no less than a murderer's life. It is worth exactly the same because it is not "worthless" to God.

Genesis 9:6 applies "retributive justice" to punishing murder cases. Punishing murder must equal the wrong of murder. Obligation to punish murderers retributively is universal and timeless, not only because it comes from God, but also because it guards the value of bearing God's image, which is universal and timeless. The Bible applies retributive justice to other crimes besides murder (Exod 21:23–25), but Genesis 9:5–6 makes it essential to maintaining respect for the sanctity of human life. Equally shared reflection of God's image demands taking the life of someone who takes God's gift of life from another person without God's approval. God does not allow taking more than a murderer's life—he does not allow killing a family to avenge one person—but he never accepts less either.

Opponents sometimes argue Genesis 9:6 only predicts what murderers should expect and does not prescribe capital punishment per se. But it can only be prescriptive, and not merely predictive, for several reasons: (1) God "requires" (Gen 9:5) capital punishment for murder; (2) it is grounded in his creation of humanity; (3) it upholds respect for the image of God in us which is universal and timeless; (4) it links retributive justice to human life; and (5) God later issues more laws doing exactly what he requires in Genesis 9:6.

Opponents sometimes claim that capital punishment violates the sixth commandment by quoting the King James Version to say, "Thou shalt not kill" (Exod 20:13, KJV). But this translation misleads because, although the sixth commandment forbids violating the sanctity of human life, it does not forbid capital punishment. What it forbids is (רָצַח, *rāṣaḥ*), which only refers to taking human life when not warranted by guilt. It forbids murder but not executing murderers, a fact demonstrated in the immediate context where God says, "If a person schemes and willfully acts against his neighbor to murder him, you must take him from my altar to be put to death" (Exod 21:14). So murderers break the sixth commandment, but executing them does not.

There are many death penalties in the laws God gave Moses at Sinai, and opponents of capital punishment sometimes claim it is inconsistent to execute murderers if we do not also practice the other death penalties. But this does not hold because distinguishing the other death penalties from executing murderers comes from God, not moral inconsistency. The other death penalties issued in Mosaic law only applied to ancient Israel and never were given to the rest of the world. They never were regarded as universal or timeless, but capital punishment for murder predates Sinai. It goes back to Noah and applies to the entire human race. The other death penalties are consistent with God's unchanging character (Ps 102:27; Mal 3:6; Heb 13:8; Jas 1:17) and are not undeserved. But God does not require all nations to use them the way he requires using capital punishment in the case of murder.

The most important New Testament text on capital punishment is where Paul says governing authorities carry "the sword" (μάχαιρα, *machaira*) to bring God's "wrath on the one who does wrong" (Rom 13:4). Opponents say Paul's reference to "the sword" only symbolizes governing authority and does not legitimize capital punishment, but this substitutes a different meaning than first intended. "The sword" in Romans 13:4 must legitimize capital punishment for several reasons. First, the Romans had specific symbols for different sorts of governing authority, and "the sword" stood for authority to take human life, and not just governing in general, because they used the fasces (a bundle of sticks bound together with an axe) to symbolize governing in general. Second, Paul had to know his Roman readers would take "the sword" to include capital punishment. Third, Mosaic law demands executing murderers, and an expert in Mosaic law like Paul would not take a different view. And fourth, Paul endorsed capital punishment when he told Festus, the Roman procurator of Judea, "If . . . I did anything wrong and am deserving of death, I am not trying to escape death" (Acts 25:11).

Two other New Testament texts sometimes used to oppose capital punishment come from the life and teaching of Jesus. In the Sermon on the Mount, Jesus says that, rather than demand justice, Christians should turn the other cheek (Matt 5:38–39) and love their enemies (Matt 5:44). And, when scribes and Pharisees asked Jesus to rule on a woman caught in adultery, knowing Mosaic law required putting her to death (Deut 22:22–24), Jesus dismissed her saying, "neither do I condemn you" (John 8:11). Opponents of capital punishment say Jesus, in these passages, did away with it and so should we, but advocates disagree, saying Jesus could not have replaced God's moral law in the Old Testament because it reveals the character of God (Lev 11:44–45; 19:2; 20:7; 1 Pet 1:16), which never changes (Num 23:19; Ps 102:27; Mal 3:6; Heb 13:8; Jas 1:17).

In the Sermon on the Mount, Jesus did not do away with Old Testament moral law but rather explained how personal and social (or governing) ethics relate to justice in different ways. Government is not just unless it is retributive. But persons acting on their own and who are not responsible for others must not be retributive because God assigns that to government. When Jesus dismissed the woman caught in adultery (John 8:11), he did not cancel her death penalty but simply followed Mosaic requirements, which did not allow executions unless two or more witnesses were there (Deut 17:6; 19:15). When Jesus dismissed her, no witnesses remained. As God, he knew she was guilty and told her to stop sinning. But, as a man, he had not witnessed what she did. Jesus did not abolish, but rather affirmed, capital punishment.

Some opposing capital punishment take what they call the "seamless garment" view, which claims that a consistent human life ethic must reject capital punishment along with abortion, euthanasia, assisted suicide, and war.[12] But this denies how God views capital punishment in relation to the sanctity of human life. The way God views the relation is given where he criticizes prophets (moral teachers) who "lie to my people" when "you put those to death who should not die and spare those who should not live" (Ezek 13:19). Here, God says, "sparing those who should live" violates the sanctity of human life as badly as killing those "who should not die." God sees no contradiction between the sanctity of human life and capital punishment, and the "seamless garment" view is wrong to think so. Murderers and nonmurderers do not have the same right to life, and the "seamless garment" view, not capital punishment, is what conflicts with the way God views the sanctity of human life.

Finally, the passage that most clearly shows that God requires human authorities to execute murderers is where he declares, "You are not to accept a ransom for the life of someone

---

[12] The term *seamless garment* was coined in 1971 by Roman Catholic pacifist Eileen Egan and then popularized by Cardinal Joseph Bernardin, Archbishop of Chicago, starting in 1983.

who is guilty of murder; he must be put to death . . . . Do not defile the land where you live, for bloodshed defiles the land, and there can be no atonement for the land because of the blood that is shed on it, except by the blood of the person who shed it" (Num 35:31, 33). In this passage, God requires that all rulers, and not just ancient Israel, use capital punishment to preserve valuing human life. Murder—the taking of human life without justification— corrupts society, and the integrity of society is not restored without executing murderers. Anything less is insufficient, and punishing murderers insufficiently lowers general respect for the sanctity of human life in societies failing to execute them.

Opponents of capital punishment sometimes argue that since no human authority is per- fect, we must ban it to make sure no innocent people are executed. Advocates agree authorities should try to avoid mistakes, but then say they also should keep executing murderers while taking precautions not to kill the wrong people. The problem is that, in a sinful world, justice with no risk of imperfection is impossible. We can only have imperfect justice or none at all. So hard though it seems, we must accept God using imperfect rulers exercising capital punish- ment to preserve the sanctity of human life among imperfect people in an imperfect world.

Recommended further reading on the issue of capital punishment includes Ronald Gleason, *The Death Penalty on Trial* (Ventura, CA: Nordskog, 2008); Wayne House and John Howard Yoder, eds., *The Death Penalty Debate: Two Opposing Views of Capital Punishment* (Waco, TX: Word, 1991); C. S. Lewis, "The Humanitarian Theory of Punishment," in *Readings in Ethical Theory*, Wilfred Sellars and John Hospers, eds. (New York: Meredith, 1970), 646–50; James Megivern, *The Death Penalty: An Historical and Theological Survey* (Mahwah, NJ: Paulist, 1997); Gilbert Meilaender, "Capital and Other Punishments," *First Things* (November 2001): 8–10; Oliver O'Donovan, *Measure for Measure: Justice in Punishment and the Sentence of Death* (Nottingham, UK: Grove, 1977); Erik Owens, John Carlson, and Eric Elshtain, eds., *Religion and the Death Penalty* (Grand Rapids: Eerdmans, 2004); and Ernest Van den Haag and John Conrad, *The Death Penalty: A Debate* (New York: Plenum, 1983).

War & Peace

As an issue in applied Christian ethics, war and peace deals with how governing protects justice and national security. It concerns God wanting good rulers to resist bad rulers in the present world, and that makes it one of the most consequential issues we face. War maims and destroys people made in God's image, and yet, because we live in a sinful world, tranquility comes at the price of wrongs that cannot be stopped without war. Men long for peace but find it elusive. Peace, rather than becoming more likely with advances in human knowledge and ability, instead has become less likely, and the likelihood of war, rather than decreasing, instead has increased. Among sinners in a sinful world, war is perennial, peace is fleeting, and now we have weapons so powerful it is possible to annihilate everyone on earth at the push of a button.

War is when nations or groups use deadly force to contest power, and the term can be used nonmaterially as well as materially. Nevertheless, in this section, we are using *war* only for nations using deadly force to contest material power in material ways. *Peace* is harder to define because it can mean different things that do not go together. Generally, it indicates what exists between times of war, but beyond that, *peace* can mean four things. Since the English word *peace* is not precise, we will use words from Hebrew, Greek, Latin, and Arabic—*shālôm*, *eirēnē*, *pax*, and *al-Islam*—to avoid mixing them up. These words from other languages all mean "peace" but in different ways that enable us to comprehend how *peace* means different things.

Peace in the Hebrew *shālôm* sense is realized prosperity and can be seen where David says, "May peace be in you. Because of the house of the LORD our God, I will pursue your prosperity" (Ps 122:8–9). This first meaning conceives *peace* in terms that are positive and substantive. It is experiencing the blessing of God (Ps 128:5–6), which is more than just not fighting or a chance to thrive. It is actually thriving because of what God gives us.

Peace in the Greek *eirēnē* sense focuses on order and coherence. The word comes from a root meaning things are lined up and is the term from which we get the English word *irenic*, meaning "harmonious" and "orderly." This second meaning conceives *peace* in terms that are positive and formal. It is more than just not fighting but does not include prospering unless people take advantage of the opportunity it provides.

Peace in the Latin *pax* sense means nothing more than nonviolence and is related to quietness, not because it is the same thing, but only because people are quiet when they stop fighting. This third meaning conceives *peace* in terms that are negative and formal, meaning it is defined as not something and offers a chance at something else.

Peace in the Arabic *al-Islam* sense means acquiescing to authority. It is submitting to someone who defeats you. It is getting along with a conqueror. This fourth meaning conceives *peace* in terms that are negative and substantive, meaning it involves relinquishing independence to a power demanding absolute control.

Over time, Christians have articulated three ways of viewing the ethics of war and peace, all of which reject evil and value peace. But they conceive evil and peace in different ways that lead to formulating different ethics relating to war. These are "pacifism," "crusade," and "just war," and they exhaust the logical possibilities for formulating ethics of war and peace. Glen Stassen suggests another way,[13] but it is impossible without misconceiving the standard paradigms. I mentioned how there are four conceptions of peace, then said they lead to formulating different ethics, and now am saying there are three, and only three, of them. The reason for three ways of formulating the ethics of war and peace, and not four, is because *shālôm* and *al-Islam* are two sides of a single more complex notion of *peace* we can discern in Scripture.[14]

Pacifism starts with peace in the *pax* sense of nonviolence and sees evil in terms of violence. Accordingly, pacifists think war is never justified because evil is never justified. Pacifist Christians always criticize, oppose, and stay out of any war that comes along, but they disagree on whether war on earth can be stopped before Jesus comes back. "Optimistic pacifism" believes it can, and "pessimistic pacifism" does not think so. They disagree on whether participating in war is wrong only for Christians ("community pacifism") or is wrong for everyone ("universal pacifism"). In the first case, they pray that non-Christians on a preferred side will win, and in the second case, they cannot pray for any side to win no matter what is at stake. And they disagree on whether they are allowed to only turn the other cheek ("nonresistant pacifism") or can use nonviolent tactics to hinder or stop others from going to war ("resistant pacifism").

Arguments for Christian pacifism are that Jesus (1) blessed peacemakers (Matt 5:9), (2) told us to turn the other cheek (Matt 5:39), (3) taught us to love our enemies (Matt 5:44; Luke 6:27), (4) rebuked Peter for using a sword (Matt 26:52), and (5) went to the cross without defending himself, and that Paul told us (6) to "live at peace with everyone" (Rom 12:18), and (7) to "conquer evil with good" (Rom 12:21). Those who criticize Christian pacifism dispute how it assumes Jesus started a different ethic in the New Testament than God used in the Old Testament, assumes what the Sermon on the Mount teaches applies to

---

[13] Glen H. Stassen, ed., *Just Peacemaking: The New Paradigm for the Ethics of Peace and War* (Cleveland, OH: Pilgrim, 2008).

[14] This can be seen in how Scripture portrays "peace" with God. Positively, God blesses all who love and serve him, and, negatively, he demands unconditional surrender, never negotiates, and destroys all opposition.

government, and assumes Jesus meant civil nonviolence in every place he referred to peace. Critics reject the first because Jesus is "the same yesterday, today, and forever" (Heb 13:8) and, as "the angel of the LORD," fought battles and led wars in the Old Testament (Exod 23:20–23; Num 22:23; 2 Kgs 19:32–35; 1 Chr 21:16; Isa 37:33–37). They reject the second because the Sermon on the Mount was given to guide individual behavior and not to change how governments operate (Lev 27:29; Num 35:31; Ezek 13:19; Rom 13:4). And they reject the third because when Jesus spoke of peace, he was usually referring to reconciling sinners to God (John 14:27), and in the one place he clearly addressed civil nonviolence, Jesus denied launching a pacifist ethic, saying, "I have not come to bring peace but a sword" (Matt 10:34).

Crusade starts with peace in the *shālôm + al-Islam* sense of submitting to God (or ultimate authority) and sees evil in terms of opposing God (or ultimate authority). Crusade, therefore, treats war as a good way to eliminate evil and achieve peace in the sense of creating a world in which no one opposes totalitarian rule by one ultimate authority. It is easy to think that, if war is ever justified, the alternative to pacifism might be crusade because it uses war to rid the world of imperfection. Characteristically, crusades are led by religious figures like a prophet, pope, or imam, or by ideologues like Hitler who function that way. Crusade does not limit deadly force, ignores the odds, accepts no compromise, sees no difference between combatants and non-combatants, demonizes opponents, executes prisoners, never surrenders, and never ends because the perfection motivating war is never fully achieved.

God authorized crusade war when punishing the Midianites for corrupting Israel (Num 31:1–54), giving Israel the Promised Land (Deut 20:16–18; Josh 6:17, 24; 8:26–27; 9:24; 10:28–40; 11:8, 11, 14), and enforcing true worship in Israel (Deut 13:12–17). But the Bible never makes it a human option. In the Bible, divinely authorized crusade occurs only when God initiates it (Num 31:1–2), leads it (Exod 14:14; Deut 1:30; 3:22; 20:4; Josh 5:13–15; 10:42; 2 Chr 20:29), and does it in a way participants can verify (Josh 3:7–13; Rev 19:11–16). When Pope Urban II launched crusade war in the Middle Ages, he violated biblical restrictions and stained the reputation of Christ. Until Jesus returns, the kingdom of God advances in voluntary spiritual terms (Luke 17:20–21) and not in physical coercive terms (John 18:36; 2 Cor 10:4). Until then, the alternative to pacifism is not crusade but an ethic referred to as "just war."

While differing from one another, pacifism and crusade are both perfectionist, meaning they conceive war and peace in ideal terms, but just war takes a realist approach, meaning it recognizes there are limits to what sinners can do in fallen circumstances. It accepts that sinners cannot create a world with no war no matter how hard we try and accepts that, until Jesus comes back, the best we can do is restrain war without getting rid of it. Just war regrets war and tries to minimize it but at the same time understands good rulers must sometimes go to war to keep wickedness from running rampant.

Just war starts with peace in the *eirēnē* sense of existing order and sees evil in terms of disrupting what existed before tensions arose. Peace in the just war ethic is not an ideal that never exists in real life but rather is something imperfect that previously existed. Because of this, the evil just war tries to overcome is unjustified action one nation takes against another that upsets previous cooperation between them. In other words, war is warranted to rectify violations of previous cooperation. In the same way, the justice defended in just war is not ideal justice but the realistic justice of undoing unjustified actions in order to restore what existed before it happened.

The ethic of just war is a long-practiced tradition sometimes said to have started with Augustine,[15] but that is incorrect. The just war ethic actually comes from two far older sources—one biblical and the other classical. On the classical side, it comes from practices ancient Greeks followed when fighting other Greeks and were commonly accepted well before Plato (428–348 BC).[16] On the biblical side, it comes from rules God, even earlier, required Israel to follow when fighting outside the Promised Land (Deut 20:10–15, 19–20) and principles God applied when criticizing the war actions of Gentile nations surrounding Israel (Amos 1:3–2:3). The just war ethic coming from these hitherto separate sources was discovered by theologians like Ambrose (340–397), Augustine (354–430), and Aquinas (1225–1274) to be essentially the same. These Christian theologians carried it forward, as did philosophers like Francisco de Vitoria (1486–1546) and Hugo Grotius (1583–1645), making just war a tradition shared by Christians and non-Christians alike. Pacifism and crusade have had Christian proponents. But just war has always been the majority ethic on war and peace held by Christians and has always been the majority ethic on war and peace guiding Western civilization.

Since just war opposes unnecessary war but also thinks it is, at times, necessary, the ethic is framed by two questions: (1) "When is going to war justified?" and (2) "How should justified

---

[15] Anderson, *Christian Ethics in Plain Language*, 210 (see chap. 1, n. 52); Rae, *Moral Choices*, 299 (see chap. 1, n. 9).

[16] Bainton, "The Classical Origins of the Just War," 33–43 (see chap. 5, n. 29); Stott, *Issues*, 106 (see chap. 4, n. 10).

war be conducted?" Answering these questions has produced two lists of guiding principles. Those answering the first are classified as *jus ad bellum* (principles before war), those answering the second are classified as *jus in bello* (principles in war), and some are split because they answer both questions and versions appear in both classifications.[17] In the listings below, Bible references supporting each principle are provided with its title.

Jus ad Bellum Principles

1. *Just cause* (1 Kgs 10:9; Ps 82:3–4; Prov 2:7–8; 29:4; Isa 56:1; Heb 11:33–34; Rev 19:11). There must be an act of injustice that going to war will correct. It is not right to go to war unless needed to right a wrong action one nation takes against another.

2. *Competent authority* (Ps 144:1; Rom 13:1). Deciding when to go or refrain from war is on the shoulders of those in authority responsible for upholding justice and assuring civil order and national security. Those without governing authority cannot take a nation to war.

3. *Comparative justice* (1 Sam 2:3; Dan 5:26–28; 1 Cor 11:17). If justice is divided, what is at stake on your side must be more than what is at stake on the other. It is not right to go to war knowing it will cause more harm than good.

4. *Right intention* (Ps 34:14; 120:6–7; Zech 8:16; Rom 14:19; Heb 12:14; 1 Pet 3:11). The situation desired by going to war must be peace in the sense of returning to relationships in place before they were disrupted. It is not right to go to war for glory or to punish, humiliate, or conquer.

---

[17] Eric Patterson proposes adding *jus post bellum* as a third category of just war principles. But this is neither historical nor widely accepted. Indeed, it is conceptually impossible because post-war principles are ideals and not real-world restraints on using force. It cannot be done without changing the essence of just war thinking so much as to erase what distinguishes it from crusade and pacifism. "Just war" is ethical realism and "crusade" and "pacifism" are forms of ethical idealism. While crusade and pacifism aim to achieve things not existing before, just war aims only to restrain what threatens existing conditions or to restore what they were. Trying to mix in with just war things to achieve is like mixing oil and water. They simply do not mix. See Eric Patterson, "Finishing Well," in *Just War Thinking* (Lanham, MD: Lexington, 2007), Eric Patterson, *Ethics Beyond War's End* (Washington, DC: Georgetown, 2012); Eric Patterson, *Ending Wars Well: Order, Justice, and Conciliation in Post-Conflict* (New Haven, CT: Yale, 2012).

5. *Last resort* (Prov 3:31–32; 15:1; Rom 12:18). All realistic nonviolent alternatives must be exhausted before going to war. It is not right to go to war if what needs correcting can be corrected another way.

6. *Probability of success/ad bellum* (Luke 14:31–32; 2 Cor 8:12). There must be a realistic chance of victory. It is not right to go to war knowing there is no chance of winning.

7. *Proportionality of projected results/ad bellum* (Luke 9:62; 14:28–30). The good expected by winning must be more than the expected cost of winning. It is not right to go to war knowing it will cost more than it will be worth.

8. *Right spirit/ad bellum* (Ps 68:30; 120:6–7; Eccl 7:9). Going to war must be decided with regret. War is tragic even if necessary, and it is wrong to go to war with zeal, glee, or hate.

Jus in Bello Principles

1. *Proportionality in the use of force* (Deut 20:10–11, 19; Amos 1:11). The amount of deadly force used in war must not exceed what is needed to achieve military goals. It is never right to do more harm than good.

2. *Discrimination* (Gen 18:23, 25; Deut 20:13–14, 19–20; Amos 1:6, 9, 13). Those using deadly force must distinguish combatants from noncombatants and military targets from nonmilitary targets and must never destroy noncombatants or nonmilitary targets on purpose. It is never right to purposely harm or kill noncombatants or to purposely damage or destroy nonmilitary targets.

3. *Avoidance of evil means* (Ps 34:14; Amos 1:3, 6, 9, 13; 2:1; Rom 12:17). Some actions are inherently evil and must not be used even if it affects winning or losing. Inherently evil means include raping, pillaging, sexually abusing, desecrating holy places, dishonoring the dead, executing prisoners, executing civilians, selling captives into slavery, salting fields, cutting down fruit trees, ruining a nation's economy, or breaking families apart to dispirit the populace. It is never right to win by acting wickedly.

4. *Good faith* (Ps 5:6; Prov 12:22; Isa 33:7–8; Hos 10:4; Amos 1:9; Dan 11:23). Enemy soldiers are fellow human beings and not animals or devils. Promises made must be kept so treaties can be negotiated and nations reconciled after war ceases.

5. *Probability of success/in bello* (Luke 14:31–32; 2 Cor 8:12). If, while fighting, all hope of victory fades, commanders must surrender and rulers give up. It is not right to keep fighting with no hope of winning. There is no glory in dying for a lost cause.

6. *Proportionality of projected results/in bello* (Luke 14:28–30). If, while fighting, the cost of winning escalates beyond what winning is worth, commanders must surrender and rulers give up. It is not right to keep spending, destroying property, and losing lives toward winning after what it costs to achieve goes beyond what justifies fighting. It is not right to keep fighting when winning is no longer worth what it costs to win.

7. *Right spirit/in bello* (Ps 68:30; Prov 10:23; Eccl 7:9; Amos 1:11; Matt 5:43–44). Soldiers must regret needing to harm and destroy others. They must neither enjoy fighting nor hate enemies. Enemy combatants are neighbors they must love even when fighting for justified reasons.

Most Evangelical scholars see two contrasting ethics of war in the Bible—a crusade ethic and a just war ethic—and do not think it teaches pacifism at all. The Bible shows how God sometimes authorizes crusade war but only when he launches and leads it, and the Bible also shows that God ordinarily wants rulers to follow just war principles when having to fight. What mainly distinguishes just war from pacifism is that pacifism seeks social perfection and just war takes the realistic approach Jesus told us to follow in the parable of the weeds (Matt 13:24–30). They differ also in that just war accepts and pacifism rejects seeing God as the only one able to rid the world of war (Ps 46:9; Isa 2.4; Mic 4:3) and needing to wait for Jesus to accomplish that when he returns (Rev 21:4; Isa 9:7). In seeking peace, we need to avoid two pitfalls: imagining a world with no war can be achieved before Jesus comes and does it and doing nothing because we know a world with no war will not be achieved before Jesus comes and does it. The first is the error of naïve sentimentalism. The second is the error of cynical realism.

One question that often comes up when Christians consider war and peace is, "Was Jesus a pacifist who taught pacifism?" Jesus is the Prince of Peace (Isa 9:6; Luke 1:79), but the peace he offers is reconciling sinners to God, not civil tranquility among sinners in a sinful world. In the Sermon on the Mount (Matt 5:3–48), Jesus did not address, much less change, how government uses military power (Rom 13:4). He went to the cross to save sinners (John 1:29), not to launch a new ethic replacing Old Testament moral revelation (Matt 5:18). He rebuked Peter for using a sword (Matt 26:52) to hinder the mission he had from the Father

(Matt 26:39, 42), not to keep Christians out of the army, and we know that because Jesus earlier that evening told his disciples to buy swords and use them after he departed (Luke 22:36). Jesus denied teaching pacifism (Matt 10:34) and said wars will continue until he comes back (Matt 24:6). He assumed kings must sometimes go to war (Luke 14:31–32). He did not practice nonviolence when cleansing the temple (John 2:15). He praised the character and faith of military officers without criticizing their profession (Matt 8:5–10). Before being born in Bethlehem, Jesus was "the angel of the LORD" who fought battles and led armies in the Old Testament (Josh 5:14; 2 Kgs 19:35; 1 Chr 21:16; Isa 37:36). He will again fight and lead armies at the end of history (Rev 19:11–15; 20:7–9). And, since he is the God who never changes (Heb 13:8) and authorized war in the Old Testament (Ps 144:1), Jesus could not have been a pacifist who taught pacifism.

Another question is, "Was the early Church pacifist?" Pacifist Christians say it was. Although some early Christians were pacifist, most were not, and pacifism has never been the majority ethic on war taught by the Church. Neither the Bible nor history supports the pacifist narrative, and we know this on strong evidence. Pacifism conflicts with how the Bible reports that the earliest Gentile converts were soldiers in the Roman army (Matt 8:5–10; Luke 3:14; Acts 10:1–8, 34–35; 16:29–34; Phil 1:12–13; 4:22) who never repented for their profession, never were urged to leave the army, and whose faith was confirmed by the Holy Spirit while remaining in military service (Acts 10:44–47). The pacifist narrative relies on Tertullian and Origen, two theologians who were disciplined by the early Church for heresy. It ignores how there is no record of the early Church penalizing members for serving in the military even though records exist for behaviors that were penalized. It conflicts with how early Christians in the army were martyred for not worshiping the emperor but never for refusing to fight. It conflicts with how the early Church buried Christian soldiers in the catacombs with epitaphs honoring their profession. It conflicts with how, only 100 years after the New Testament, Christians made up a large portion of the Thundering Legion commanded by Marcus Aurelius. And, it conflicts with how Tertullian, the earliest Christian to defend pacifism, reports that when he wrote, so many Christians were serving in the Roman army the empire would collapse if they all left, a situation that could not have arisen if the early Church was teaching it was sinful to join the army, was refusing membership to soldiers, or was excommunicating Christians who disobeyed.[18]

---

[18] Tertullian, *Apology*, AD 197, 37.

Recommended further reading on the issue of war and peace includes Roland H. Bainton, *Christian Attitudes toward War and Peace* (Nashville, TN: Abingdon, 1960); Robert G. Clouse, ed., *War: Four Christian Views* (Downers Grove, IL: InterVarsity, 1981); Daniel R. Heimbach, "Crusade War in the Old Testament and Today," *Journal for Baptist Theology and Ministry* 9/1 (Spring 2012): 40–56; Daniel R. Heimbach, "Did Jesus Teach an Ethic of Pacifism?," *CSB Apologetics Study Bible* (Nashville, TN: B&H, 2017), 1295; Daniel R. Heimbach, "The Problem of Universal Ethics for Christian Pacifists," *Journal of Faith and War* 1/1 (Fall 2009); James Turner Johnson, *Just War Tradition and the Restraint of War* (Princeton, NJ: Princeton, 1981); and Heath Thomas, Jeremy Evans, and Paul Copan, eds., *Holy War in the Bible* (Downers Grove, IL: InterVarsity, 2013).

Terrorism

The ethics of terrorism relates to the ethics of war and peace. But we are dealing with it separately, first, because terrorism goes beyond regular warfare; second, because even though nations have used terrorism, it now is most often used by other entities; and third, because terrorism dominates world news. This applied issue considers how Christians should think about terrorism and whether, and in what ways, governments should address violence that threatens justice and security but is driven by belief systems outside what they control.

Defining *terrorism* is controversial because it indicates something very bad, and there is no commonly accepted basis for deciding why that is. This lack of agreement keeps the world from arriving at a universal definition, so different entities are left using different definitions. But, ironically, even though no one agrees on how it should be defined, everyone, except terrorists themselves, treats terrorism as being something criminal, unjustified, and immoral. Since we cannot evaluate the ethics of terrorism without defining it, our definition will be that terrorism is a psychological tactic, sometimes used in wars of crusade, by which inherently evil methods are used to frighten opponents into submitting to domination by a conquering ideological or religious authority. Furthermore, this using of inherently evil methods to frighten opponents into submitting is carried out by nations or movements made up of people sharing a belief system justifying it.

Terrorists justify what they do in cosmic rather than civil or political terms, claim totalitarian rather than jurisdictional authority, and seek global rather than regional domination.

They do not operate institutionally and are not accountable because they act on beliefs with no chain of command. Terrorists fight a war that is ideological and physical at the same time, they operate on principles that work only in their favor and are not reciprocated, nothing limits the methods or amount of force they use, and they do not distinguish combatants from noncombatants and do not distinguish military targets from civilian targets.

Terrorism is not new. Ashurnasirpal II, king of Assyria from 883 to 859 BC, was notorious for terrorizing opponents. Some he skinned alive and displayed their skins to intimidate survivors; some he entombed alive or impaled on stakes. He mutilated captives by cutting off their hands and feet and letting them bleed to death. Others he blinded or cut off their noses, lips, and ears and displayed them in a heap. Once, he decapitated every man in a defeated city and made a tower of their heads to terrify their families. He ordered soldiers to rape children—both girls and boys—and then burned these abused children alive. He also disemboweled pregnant women, and once had everyone in a defeated city stripped naked and driven into the desert where he left them without food and water to die of exposure, starvation, and thirst.

Vlad the Impaler (1431–1476) is another figure in history notorious for terrorizing. Vlad was a prince who ruled Walachia, now part of Romania, who in the fifteenth century kept Ottoman invaders out of Europe. He poisoned wells, burned crops, and sent diseased people to infect enemy camps; and he disemboweled, beheaded, skinned, and boiled enemies alive. But this fifteenth century prince was especially famous for impaling captured enemy soldiers on stakes inserted up their rectums and out their mouths. And he finally used this tactic on a grand scale to terrorize the Ottomans into retreating by lining their route to battle with 20,000 previously captured Ottoman soldiers impaled on a forest of stakes.

While nations like Assyria and rulers like Ashurnasirpal II and Vlad the Impaler used terror tactics years ago, most terrorism now comes from movements without national boundaries or systems of accountability. And, although some comes from drug cartels and insurrections, most terrorism today is perpetrated by Islamic militants seeking world domination. We have, in recent years, seen an explosion of terrorism fomented by clerics bent on imposing their view of God's kingdom on everyone else on earth. A few Muslim leaders decry it while blaming Western freedoms they say aggravate Muslim sensitivities. But most Muslim leaders say nothing and lend tacit support to clerics who urge Muslims to terrorize non-Muslims by attacking anyone they think opposes Islam or even just symbolizing believing something different.

The most vivid act of Islamic terrorism in our day occurred on September 11, 2001, when nineteen Islamic militants hijacked four planes filled with passengers and used them to carry out suicide attacks on targets in the United States. Two crashed into the north and south towers of the World Trade Center in New York, a third crashed into the Pentagon, and a fourth intended for the White House crashed in Pennsylvania when passengers stormed the cockpit. This event caused 2,977 civilian deaths, wounded more than 25,000 others, and resulted in more than $10 billion in property damage, making it the single most deadly terrorist attack in history.

The world has been fighting Islamic terrorism ever since, not just in the United States but throughout the world. While precautions have been taken to thwart major incidents, smaller incidents have occurred, and continue to occur, on a regular basis, including one taking place on October 29, 2020, as this was written. In this incident, three people were killed in a knife attack on Christians gathered for worship in a church in France. A young man shouting "Allahu Akbar" (God is greatest) beheaded an older woman, cut a man's throat, and stabbed a young woman to death. These victims were guilty only of being in church and were selected symbolically to send a message meant to terrorize non-Muslims, and especially Christians, throughout the world.

It is easy to criticize terrorism in just war ethical terms. But it means nothing to terrorists because they reject just war and use crusade thinking to justify what they do. Unlike just war, crusade justifies killing motivated by religion, or an ideology that functions religiously, which means that to combat terrorism by Islamic militants we must understand how they perceive terrorism differently than we do. We must understand how religiously inspired crusade thinking differs from just war thinking, the main differences being as follows:

- Religiously inspired crusade perceives terrorism as an effective way to wage unconditional war against enemies of God, whereas just war perceives terrorism as something never allowed and justifies war only when needed to undo relative acts of injustice disturbing civil tranquility.
- Religiously inspired crusade perceives terrorism as serving God, whereas just war perceives war as serving the state and treats terrorism as something civil authorities can never justify.
- Religiously inspired crusade fights for the source of ultimate right and so thinks anything done against people opposing ultimate right is justified, including terrorism.

Just war limits what can be done to enemies by distinguishing combatants from non-combatants, avoiding evil means like terrorism, and restricting the use of force to the least needed to achieve limited (not global) material (not religious) objectives.

- Religiously inspired crusade will give enemies who surrender a chance to convert but, if not, will terrorize them to intimidate others and does not keep promises made to enemies, such as agreeing on terms to cease fighting. Just war spares enemies who surrender, treats prisoners humanely, and will cease fighting on negotiated terms.

- Religiously inspired crusade uses terrorism to impose religious ideals, whereas just war aims to restore a previous state of civil tranquility and views terrorism as hindering that purpose.

- Religiously inspired crusade seeks world conquest and uses terrorism to punish people getting in the way, whereas just war seeks only to reverse something violating previous tranquility and never uses war, much less terrorism, to punish anyone.

- Religiously inspired crusade opposes the value system of enemy societies and will terrorize people and things perceived as symbolizing values other than its own, whereas just war only opposes unwarranted actions and never uses terrorism to attack value systems for any reason.

- Religiously inspired crusade treats war as a calling for zealous saints to terrorize enemies of God, whereas just war treats war as a last resort, kills enemies with regret, and treats terrorism as something evil that must not be used for any reason.

- Religiously inspired crusade needs no declaration of war and, in this way, secures the element of surprise by which terrorism operates, whereas just war believes war must be declared by rulers of states and sees terrorism as violating this requirement.

- Religiously inspired crusade turns war into a permanent state (because totalitarian global ideals are never fully realized) and makes terrorism something good to use anywhere at any time, whereas just war makes war something that stops when limited objectives are reached and treats terrorism as something wrong no matter what stakes are involved.

Frame admits not being a Quran scholar, but he, nevertheless, claims the Quran "warrants peaceful coexistence of Muslims with non-Muslims" and, based on that, assumes Muslims supporting terrorism must represent a "brand of Islam" contrary to what most Muslims believe.[19] But that is not exactly true. This is not to say all Muslims are terrorists or favor terrorism, but we cannot be wise and fair unless we understand that Muslims are not able to reject terrorism and take the Quran literally at the same time and unless we understand, as well, that those favoring terrorism are just doing what it says. The Quran tells Muslims to get along with other Muslims but does not say the same about non-Muslims. Instead, the Quran views regions of the world not ruled by Muslims as regions where Muslims are at war with non-Muslims, and in these regions, the Quran commands them to "strike terror into the enemy of God and your enemy" (The Quran, 8:60, trans. N. A. Dawood) by crucifying them or striking off their heads, hands, or feet, in order to intimidate the whole non-Muslim world (The Quran, 5:33–34; 8:12–16; 47:3, trans. N. A. Dawood). Unlike the way Christians who take the Bible literally must reject terrorism, Muslims who take the Quran literally cannot. Muslims cannot renounce terrorism without saying the Quran does not mean what it says, and that is why Muslims so rarely criticize terrorism and usually keep quiet when terrorist attacks occur.

The Bible, too, speaks of "terror" in relation to God (1 Sam 11:7; 2 Chr 19:7; Ps 9:20; Isa 2:10, 19, 21), including when he sends Israel to war (2 Chr 14:14; 17:10). But the Bible addresses it differently than the Quran. God "terrifies" those resisting him (Exod 15:16; 23:27; 1 Sam 14:15; Job 27:20; Jer 32:21), but he does this himself without using inherently evil methods. The "terror" of God comes from comprehending his majesty (Job 13:11; 31:23; Isa 2:10, 19, 21), which is his infinite purity and power. It never comes from people using inherently evil methods to make enemies fear God for fear of their own humanly terrorizing behavior. God is not a terrorist, never allows anyone to employ evil for any reason, and, instead, condemns and punishes people who do (Ps 10:17–18; 14:4–5; Isa 17:14; 30:31–33; Jer 49:15–16; 50:33–36; Amos 1:3, 13). Indeed, while the Assyrians terrorized the ancient world, God declared, "Woe to him who builds a city with bloodshed and founds a town with injustice!" (Hab 2:12).

How then should Christians respond to terrorism, and what can governments do to combat religiously driven terrorism today? On the first question, we can take comfort in knowing

---

[19] Frame, *Doctrine of the Christian Life*, 664 (see chap. 1, n. 69).

that God cares about what we face (Jer 17:17), and we can affirm that those who fear God need fear nothing else (Ps 23:4; 27:1; Isa 8:12–13; Heb 13:6; 1 Pet 3:14). We have God's protection (Deut 31:6; 2 Sam 22:3; Ps 5:11–12; 37:39–40; 91:14–15; 121:7; Prov 18:10; 29:25; Isa 41:10; Nah 1:7), and that includes God's protection from terrorists using evil methods (Ps 64:1; Jer 30:5–7). Terrorists do not intimidate God (Isa 47:12), and he promises a future without them (Isa 54:14). Until then, Jesus says we must find ways to love and do good to enemies who hate, curse, and mistreat us (Luke 6:27–28), and that includes finding ways to love and do good to terrorists who hate Christians and use evil methods to attack who we are and what we believe.

The second question is harder to answer. Western nations have so far reacted only to effects of terrorism without addressing the underlying cause. They have made it harder to hijack airplanes or bomb military bases, shopping centers, and schools but have done little to combat how terrorists think and justify what they do. And terrorists see this as weakness and lacking will to resist. Another factor complicating the way Western nations respond is that they affirm religious liberty and keeping religion out of politics, and terrorists do not. Still, Western nations would do better if they took the following steps. First, they can try harder to understand how the crusade thinking of terrorists differs from just war thinking. Second, they can focus on how terrorists think religious ideology is more important than military power and should factor that into planning. Third, they can think harder about how the threat terrorism poses cannot be stopped without addressing how terrorists think and should factor that into planning as well. Fourth, they can find ways to foster accountability of a sort that matters to nations or movements enabling terrorist operations. For example, they can do more to organize international resistance, can pass binding resolutions, and can urge religious leaders to hold clerics accountable for promoting terrorism. Fifth, they must not compromise just war ethics by using terrorism to fight terrorists. And sixth, they can work on better ways to minimize physical threats by relying on superior technology, superior military assets, and superior education.

Recommended further reading on the issue of terrorism includes Jean Bethke Elshtain, *Just War against Terror* (New York: Basic, 2003); Mark Gabriel, *Islam and Terrorism* (Lake Mary, FL: FrontLine, 2002); Boaz Ganer, *Global Alert: The Rationality of Modern Islamist Terrorism* (New York: Columbia, 2015); Richard Hess and Elmer Martens, eds., *War in the Bible and Terrorism in the Twenty-First Century* (Winona Lake, IN: Eisenbrauns, 2008); Susanne Martin and Leonard Weinberg, *The Role of Terrorism in Twenty-First-Century Warfare* (Manchester, UK: Manchester

University, 2017); Nick Megoran, *The War on Terror: How Should Christians Respond?* (Downers Grove, IL: IVP, 2007); Stephen Nathanson, *Terrorism and the Ethics of War* (Cambridge, UK: Cambridge, 2010); Uwe Steinhoff, *On the Ethics of War and Terrorism* (Oxford, UK: Oxford, 2007; Isaac Taylor, *The Ethics of Counterterrorism* (London: Routledge, 2018).

Conclusion

This has been the fourth of five chapters introducing applied Christian ethics as a subcategory in the larger field of Christian ethics and is the first of two chapters introducing applied issues that are social as opposed to personal in nature. The present chapter addressed a range of applied issues all relating to government, its nature and role, duties and limits, and challenges good responsible governing must address. We first addressed government and politics in general and then addressed religious liberty, wealth and poverty, capital punishment, war and peace, and finally terrorism. The actual number of issues concerning government are innumerable, but this covers the most pertinent. Issues like this are highly contested, so there is a vast literature on each. This chapter has simply introduced them but has tried doing it in a way that is balanced and insightful as well as succinct. Issues like this are sometimes called "public policy" issues and that means they figure in political campaigns. But, while they have political implications, this chapter has treated them on a biblical and theological (rather than political) basis.

The next chapter will continue introducing social issues in applied Christian ethics. But it will move past issues having to do with governing and will take up issues involving interactions that may, in some ways, affect governing but that also involve dynamics beyond what human rulers control.

CHAPTER 12

MORE ISSUES IN SOCIAL LIFE

RACISM; SLAVERY; HUMAN TRAFFICKING; CREATION CARE; GLOBAL WARMING; USING TECHNOLOGY; ENGAGING CULTURE

This is the last of five chapters introducing applied Christian ethics as a subcategory in the larger field of Christian ethics and is the second of two chapters discussing various issues that are mainly social in nature as opposed to those that are mainly personal or a mixture of both. We were covering the various subcategories comprising the larger field of Christian ethics mostly in single chapters. All but historical Christian ethics were covered in one chapter, and we covered that in two. But we are taking five chapters to cover applied Christian ethics, not because it is more important, but simply because we now face so many applied issues that covering them even briefly just takes more time. We focused in the last chapter on social issues mainly having to do with governing, and we now will focus on social issues that, although they affect using civil power, are, nevertheless, bigger than just that element of social life. In other words, we now will consider social issues affected as much by human nature as by human governing and that involve faith and culture as much as civil law, public policy, and politics.

Racism

Racism has a long history of corrupting people, nations, cultures, and even churches. The issue is as relevant now as it ever was, and dealing with it is as contentious and polarizing now as it ever was. To understand racism, we must first understand *race*, a term once believed to indicate divisions in the human species determined by variations in skin color, hair type, and facial structure. This, coupled with Darwinian evolutionary theory, led to supposing that a hierarchy of races justified evil practices like segregation, slavery, and genocide. But, having learned that the human genome is 99.9 percent the same in all people,[1] scientists now say that conception has no basis in fact. Biological variations exist but do not warrant racial divisions. There is only one race—the human race—which includes everyone made in the image of God and descended from Adam and Eve.

Another related term is *ethnicity*, which concerns group identities based on nonessential traits that can be physical, cultural, or both. Nonessential physical traits include things like skin color, hair type, and facial features, and cultural traits include things like nationality, religion, language, dress, cuisine, and customs. If *race* indicates what all have in common, then *ethnicity* means something else. But, if *race* is linked to nonessential differences dividing us from one another, then it reduces to *ethnicity*. So, if *race* and *ethnicity* are not exactly the same, *race* must indicate something we are and *ethnicity* something we learn, *race* must refer to what unites us and *ethnicity* to what divides us. As such, *ethnicity* refers to nonessential differences and *race* to what is humanly essential and distinguishes us from other life forms like angels, animals, or plants.

Accordingly, *racism* refers to misconstruing race and ethnicity in ways alleging to justify evil attitudes and behavior toward other people. It refers to judging people based on misconstruing human identity. Like ethnicity, racism is learned, but whereas ethnicity does not claim to have a scientific basis, racism does, even though none exists. And, whereas ethnicity offers no basis for judging people, racism does, even though no such basis exists. Definitions of *racism* vary, with some focusing on individuals, leaving no room for collective responsibility, and some focusing on collectives, leaving no room for individual responsibility. But racism

---

[1] Human Genome Project Information Archive, 1990–2003, US Department of Energy, Office of Science, Office of Biological and Environmental Research, accessible at: https://web.ornl.gov/sci/techresources/Human_Genome/research/index.shtml (updated April 09, 2019).

involves both. It involves individual attitudes and behavior and also involves social structures favoring some over others based on misconstruing their humanity.

Although racism is expressed and defended in new ways, it is not new in human history. The ancient Greeks thought they were superior to everyone else on earth, not only culturally, but by nature. And, to support this prejudice, Aristotle claimed that there are two different human natures, one superior to the other, and from that, concluded it was "advantageous and just" for Greeks to act superior and treat others as beneath them.[2]

Racism fueled the ideology that caused the Nazis to launch World War II (1939–1945) and perpetrate the Holocaust (1941–1945). Hitler saw history in terms of different races competing for dominance and, in *Mein Kampf,* claimed Jews were hindering the rise of an Aryan "master race." The Nazis believed that a racial hierarchy determines human value, that those who first settled Europe were a "master race," and that science justified exterminating races hindering their preeminence. They conducted thousands of experiments trying to justify their racist theories. But they never found any evidence and only managed to murder innocent victims on a scale surpassing anything ever known before.

Racism not only arose long ago and in other countries, but it also has corrupted Americans. It was written into the Constitution when the drafters decided enslaved blacks were only worth three-fifths the value of whites. That variation did not address blacks who were free, but in the *Dred Scott* (1857) decision, the Supreme Court ruled even blacks who were free had no constitutional rights, and reaction to that racist decision was a factor leading to the Civil War (1861–1865).

After the Civil War, efforts to end racism led to passing the Thirteenth Amendment, abolishing slavery; the Fourteenth Amendment, guaranteeing equal protection; and the Fifteenth Amendment, guaranteeing the right to vote. But a white supremacist movement arose that, for a century, denied racial equality, and it would take the Civil Rights Act of 1965 to reassert what these amendments guaranteed. Racist laws and practices, referred to as "Jim Crow,"[3] arose to hinder treating blacks the same as others. People were segregated by skin color in

---

[2] Aristotle, Πολιτικὰ (*Politics*) 1.2.1251a32–34; 1.5.1255a38–39.

[3] Jim Crow was a song and dance character, played by a white entertainer in blackface, who portrayed stereotypes of black people in nineteenth-century theater productions. The name became shorthand for laws and practices demeaning black people between the Civil War and the civil rights movement.

every situation imaginable. There were white-only schools, white-only playing fields, white-only graveyards, white-only eating areas, white-only restrooms, white-only drinking fountains, white-only shopping, and white-only transportation. Military units and prisons were divided by skin color, and mixed marriage became a huge taboo.

But Jim Crow would not have been effective without the detestable practice of lynching. From 1882 to 1968, 4,743 lynchings occurred in the United States,[4] all conducted by white mobs. Most victims were black, and nonblack victims were lynched mainly for helping blacks. Perpetrators rarely got punished, whites in power turned a blind eye, and many white Christians failed to condemn it.

Christians have both fought against and perpetuated racism. White Christians led efforts that transformed race relations in the British empire, and Christians led the movement to abolish slavery in America.[5] But racism did not end with slavery, and since the end of slavery, Christian opposition *to racism* in America has been led by black Christians like Martin Luther King, Jr. (1929–1968), Ralph Abernathy (1926–1990), and Fred Shuttlesworth (1922–2011), with white Christians saying little or even hindering their efforts. Tony Evans observes that, in America,

> The church endorsed the myth (of black inferiority) when it was silent to the immorality of parishioners who bred slaves for profit and pleasure. The church endorsed the myth when it forced blacks to sit in the rear of churches—if they were allowed access at all. The church endorsed the myth when white denominations established schools for biblical learning that excluded African-Americans who desired training in God's Word.[6]

Some even invoked Christianity to justify racism. The Ku Klux Klan (KKK) mixed an alleged "Christianity" with racist nationalism to form an ideology excluding all but Protestant

---

[4] *Lynching, Whites & Negroes, 1882–1968* (Tuskegee, AL: Tuskegee University Archives, 2010).

[5] The most influential of these were Elijah Lovejoy (1802–1837), Lyman Beecher (1775–1863), Edward Beecher (1803–1895), Harriet Beecher Stowe (1811–1896), Charles Finney (1792–1875), Charles T. Torrey (1813–1846), Theodore Weld (1803–1895), and William Lloyd Garrison (1805–1879). Indeed, Alvin J. Schmidt observes that most who led the American abolitionist movement were Christian clergy. See *How Christianity Changed the World* (Grand Rapids: Zondervan, 2004), 279.

[6] Tony Evans, *Oneness Embraced* (Chicago: Moody, 2011), 100.

whites. Theodore G. Bilbo (1877–1947), a Klansman, twice elected governor of Mississippi (1916–1920; 1928–1932), and twice elected US senator from Mississippi (1935–1947), wrote a book attacking mixed marriages and integration, claiming, "Nothing could be more foreign to the ideals of the Christian religion than miscegenation and amalgamation."[7]

Catholics, Episcopalians, Methodists, Presbyterians, and Northern Baptists in America all compromised with racism to some degree. But Southern Baptists exceeded the rest because the Southern Baptist Convention (SBC) was founded in 1845 to show there was nothing wrong with white Christians enslaving blacks. As Albert Mohler says, the SBC "was founded by men who held to an ideology of racial superiority and who bathed that ideology in scandalous theological argument."[8] One hundred and fifty years later, the SBC officially apologized in a resolution that read, "We recognize that the racism which yet plagues our culture today is inextricably tied to the past; and . . . we apologize . . . repent . . . ask forgiveness . . . (and) . . . commit ourselves to eradicate racism in all its forms."[9] After that, Fred Luter, in 2012, became the first African American elected president of the SBC, and Rolland Slade, in 2020, became the first African American elected chairman of the SBC Executive Committee. Mixing racism with Christianity shames the name of Christ and hinders evangelism. But Christians can bear witness by repenting for, as well as avoiding, sin and by apologizing for, as well as condemning, wrongs.

The Bible rarely mentions skin color (Song 1:6; Jer 13:23; Acts 13:1), and where *race* appears in English translations, the term usually refers to humanity and has nothing to do with skin color. The Christian Standard Bible (CSB) uses *race* in a different sense when translating Acts 7:19. But even this does not support dividing humanity into different races. The word translated "race" in Acts 7:19 is γένος (*genos*) meaning "generation" and there refers to ancestors living at the same time and not to essential differences dividing humanity.

---

[7] Theodore G. Bilbo, *Take Your Choice: Separation or Mongrelization* (Poplarville, MI: Dream House, 1947), 88.

[8] R. Albert Mohler, Jr., "Conceived in Sin, Called by the Gospel: The Root Cause of the Stain of Racism in the Southern Baptist Convention," in *Removing the Stain of Racism from the Southern Baptist Convention*, eds. Jarvis J. Williams and Kevin M. Jones (Nashville: B&H, 2017), 3.

[9] "Resolution on Racial Reconciliation on the 150th Anniversary of the Southern Baptist Convention," The Southern Baptist Convention, June 1, 1995, https://www.sbc.net/resource-library/resolutions/resolution-on-racial-reconciliation-on-the-150th-anniversary-of-the-southern-baptist-convention/.

Opposition to racism in the Bible is not only linguistic but theological, and theological opposition is revealed in ten ways. First, all humans are created in the image of God for the purpose of glorifying God. There is no essential difference in the value of being human because all bear the image of God equally regardless of nonessential differences (Gen 1:27; Isa 64:8; Mal 2:10). And we are all made for the same and equal purpose of glorifying God (Isa 43:7). Second, all humans are descended from the same parents, not once but twice. Everyone is descended not only from Adam and Eve (Gen 1:28; 2:22–24; 3:20; Acts 17:26) but from Noah and his wife as well (Gen 9:1; 10:32). We do not come from evolutionary variations in pre-human life forms but are members of one family all descended from the same original parents.

Third, God loves all humans the same regardless of nonessential differences. God cares for everyone the same (Deut 32:8; Acts 17:26). He chose Israel for special treatment not because they were better (Deut 7:7) but to bless the world through them (Gen 12:3; 18:18; 26:4; 28:14; Acts 3:25; Gal 3:8). Fourth, God offers salvation to all humans equally (John 3:16; Acts 15:9; Rom 5:17–18; 1 Cor 12:13; Eph 2:13–16; Col 3:11; 1 Tim 2:4; 2 Pet 3:9; 1 John 2:2; Rev 14:6). Fifth, all humans redeemed by Christ are equal members of a new creation (Rom 8:16–17; 2 Cor 5:17; Gal 3:28; Col 3:10–11). Sixth, all humans redeemed by Christ will be equally valued in paradise (Rev 5:9–10; 7:9). Seventh, God wants his people to love others regardless of nonessential differences. In the Old Testament, God's people are told to "regard the alien who resides with you as the native-born among you. You are to love him as yourself" (Lev 19:34). In the New Testament, Jesus extended this to include "enemies" (Matt 5:43–44; Luke 6:27).

Eighth, God condemns and punishes racist attitudes and behavior. God condemns it because it profanes godliness (Mal 2:10), and he punishes it because that is what he did when Miriam and Aaron criticized a marriage for racist reasons (Num 12:1). What God punished in that case was racism because the reason given for Miriam and Aaron objecting was that the woman married was "Cushite," meaning she had dark skin (Jer 13:23). God did prohibit marriage to "foreign women" (Deut 7:3; 1 Kgs 11:1–2; Ezra 9:2, 10–12), but that was for spiritual and not racial reasons (Deut 7:4; 1 Kgs 11:2; Ezra 9:14).

Ninth, the early Church opposed racism. The apostles resolved conflict over feeding Hellenistic widows by adding Hellenistic leaders to oversee the feeding ministry (Acts 6:1–6), the first convert from a region outside the Roman Empire was black (Acts 8:26–39), and one of the elders who commissioned Paul and Barnabas is identified as "Simon who was called Niger" (Acts 13:1). *Niger* is Latin for "black man." So this elder is literally identified as "Simon the black man," and it is reasonable to suppose he was a black man from North Africa who moved to Antioch, heard the gospel, came to faith, and then rose to leadership in the first Gentile church. Tenth, every human transformed by Christ is called to Christlike humility that destroys pride giving rise to racism (Phil 2:3–8).

Two misinterpretations have been used to claim the Bible justifies racism—one is the "mark of Cain" rationale and the other is the "curse of Canaan" (or Ham) rationale. The mark of Cain rationale misinterprets Genesis 4:11–15. When God banished Cain for murdering Abel, Cain complained that "whoever finds me will kill me." So God said anyone murdering Cain would be punished and put a mark on Cain that would keep others away. Some have claimed this marking made Cain a black man, and, as a result, blackness marks people as being cursed by God. But this is completely bogus. The Hebrew word translated "mark" (אוֹת, *'ôṯ*) never refers to skin color, God did not say Cain's mark would pass on to future generations, and, since Cain's descendants all died in the flood, the mark of Cain could not refer to anyone today even if it was passed on to his descendants.

The curse of Canaan rationale misinterprets Genesis 9:18–27. Canaan was the youngest son of Noah's second son Ham, and the curse in this story (sometimes erroneously referred to as the curse of Ham) applied to Canaan and not to Ham. After the flood, Noah got inebriated and passed out in his tent, and someone discovering him made a joke of it. It is not clear who that was, but the text implicates Canaan since Noah treats him as responsible. Another clue is that the culprit is identified as being Noah's "youngest son" (Gen 9:24). Ham was not Noah's youngest son (Gen 5:32; 7:13; 10:1). But Canaan was Ham's youngest son (Gen 10:6), could have been Noah's youngest grandson when the incident occurred, and Hebrew often uses *son* (בֵּן, *bēn*) for offspring without generational precision.[10] Shem and Japheth respect their father's dignity by covering him, and, afterward, Noah blessed Shem and Japheth and cursed Canaan saying, "He will be the lowest of slaves to his brothers" (Gen 9:25). This text was used to

---

[10] I question how best to translate Genesis 9:22, which identifies who violated Noah's dignity. Making Ham the perpetrator leaves Noah cursing a grandson for something he did not do. But, if Noah acted fairly, then Ham was not responsible and Genesis 9:22 must be different than translated. I think the Hebrew might be translated to say, "And Canaan whose father was Ham saw the nakedness of his ancestor and told his relatives." If that is correct, it resolves Noah's seeming injustice.

defend enslaving and considering blacks inferior prior to the Civil War, but this interpreta-tion, too, is completely wrong. If anything, black people are descended from Ham's older sons Cush, Mizraim, and Put and not from his youngest son Canaan (Gen 10:15–19). Canaan's descendants settled Sidon (Phoenicia), Sodom and Gomorrah, and the Promised Land (land of Canaan). Sodom and Gomorrah were destroyed by God (Gen 19:24–25), Canaanites in the Promised Land were destroyed by Joshua (Deut 7:1–2), and the Bible says nothing con-necting Canaan's line with Africa. The curse of Canaan simply has nothing to do with Africa or blackness.

Having reviewed how the Bible treats racism, we need to consider, "What differences should we celebrate and not celebrate?" Racism is bad because it claims differences exist that do not or claims other differences matter in ways they do not. Some differences are real and good and should be celebrated and others are bad or unreal and should not be celebrated. So, what makes the difference? Other than distinguishing reality from nonreality, it is important to recognize some things are essential, unchanging, and shared equally, and other things, though real, are not essential, may or may not change, and are not shared equally.

Since no essential differences divide the human race, we should not celebrate pretending they do. Pretending something unreal is a lie and we should not celebrate lies. Such things not only include pretending there are different races but also pretending spiritual or moral truth is not objectively fixed and can vary with time, place, or culture. Differences of this kind are tragic, and pretending they are valid is not something to celebrate. While essential things never change and are the same for all, nonessential things can vary and be used to divide peo-ple. Differences of this kind can be mutable or immutable and can be benign or malignant.

Diverse nonessential immutable things (like skin color) are benign and should be cele-brated, and diverse nonessential mutable traits (like culture) can be benign or malignant since they are matters of choice and responsibility. Benign nonessential mutable differences include language, music, dress, and customs, and diversity of this sort is worth celebrating. But malignant nonessential mutable differences like racism, child sacrifice, and cannibalism are immoral, and we should not celebrate that sort of diversity. There is tension to celebrating human unity and diversity, and balancing them requires biblical wisdom. In any case, cele-brating diversity should not divide us, and celebrating unity should not demean differences God finds equally pleasing.

The Christian answer to racism is humble, self-sacrificing love (Phil 2:3–8) that starts with converting hearts and leads to systems treating everyone the same regardless of skin color. Governments can outlaw racist behavior but cannot change hearts or reconcile the oppressed with oppressors. We should abolish racist laws, and we should acknowledge and try to reverse racist effects that persist even after abolishing racist laws and policies. But that will not stop racism because it grows from roots only reached by the gospel. The gospel insists selfish pride must give way to enter God's kingdom (Matt 19:24; Mark 10:25; Luke 18:25), and that means racism clashes with getting saved. Christians may struggle with sin, including racism. But refusing to struggle means we are not saved in the first place.

Recommended further reading on the issue of racism includes Anthony B. Bradley, *Liberating Black Theology* (Wheaton, IL: Crossway, 2010); Michael Emerson and Christian Smith, *Divided by Faith* (Oxford: Oxford, 2000); Tony Evans, *Oneness Embraced* (Chicago: Moody, 2011); Spencer Perkins, and Chris Rice, *More than Equals* (Downers Grove, IL: InterVarsity, 1993); John Piper, *Bloodlines: Race, Cross, and the Christian* (Wheaton, IL: Crossway, 2011); Clarence Shuler, *Winning the Race to Unity* (Chicago: Moody, 2003); Stephan Thernstrom and Abigail Thernstrom, *America in Black and White* (New York: Simon & Schuster, 1997); Walter Strickland and Dayton Howard, eds., *For God So Loved the World* (Nashville: B&H, 2020); Raleigh Washington and Glen Kehrein, *Breaking Down Walls* (Chicago: Moody, 1993); and George Yancey, *Beyond Racial Gridlock* (Downers Grove, IL: InterVarsity, 2006); Jarvis J. Williams, *Redemptive Kingdom Diversity: A Biblical Theology of the People of God* (Grand Rapids: Baker, 2021); Mark A. Noll, *God and Race in American Politics: A Short History* (Princeton, NJ: Princeton, 2008).

Slavery

Slavery is often associated with racism but is not the same thing. Racism is a sinful attitude, and slavery is a sinful action. The two go hand in hand, but not always. Racism can lead to enslaving people, and enslaving people can lead to racism. But in either case, it does not happen every time. Racism can exist without enslaving people, and people can be enslaved with no connection to racism. Still, even though enslaving people is not always racist, it quite often is.

There are different kinds of slavery, and evaluating the issue depends on what people have in mind. A broad definition covers more than contemporary readers expect and makes it hard to condemn in all cases but, while defining it narrowly makes it easy to condemn, it excludes much of what God says about it. So, we will define *slavery* broadly as a state of bondage in which persons lacking customary freedom are controlled by others to the point of determining where and how they live, how they work, how they fare, and how they relate to others. Defined this broadly, *slavery* covers a range of bondage conditions that may be voluntary or involuntary, temporary or permanent, and humanitarian or inhumane. This broad definition goes beyond contemporary expectations but does so to cover all the Bible includes on the issue.

Four sorts of slavery are covered under this very broad definition. "Humanitarian slavery" is a state of voluntary, temporary, humanitarian bondage that the poor use to save themselves and make a new start. "Prisoner of war slavery" is a state of involuntary, permanent, non-humanitarian and sometimes inhumane bondage in which people defeated in battle are made to labor for those defeating them. "Progressive slavery" is a state of temporary and mostly humane bondage that can be voluntary or involuntary in which people without land or income advance their standing in life. "Chattel slavery" is a state of involuntary, permanent, inhumane bondage in which people are kidnapped and treated as things rather than human beings with inalienable worth, dignity, and rights. Two related terms are *abolition*, which is working to end slavery, and *abolitionism*, which is thinking slavery must end. Unless otherwise specified, these terms refer to the movement that ended slavery in the Western world, and, more particularly, they refer to insisting slavery must end immediately rather than gradually.

Slavery has existed in various forms all throughout history. The Assyrians and Babylonians obtained slaves by attacking peaceful people and taking captives. Israelites could sell themselves into slavery to escape destitution (Exod 21:2; Lev 25:39–43; Deut 15:12–18), could take prisoners of war as slaves (Deut 20:10–11), and could acquire foreign slaves in other ways (Lev 25:44–45). Slavery was part of the Greco-Roman economy when the New Testament was written.

The Arab Muslim slave trade began ten centuries before Europeans took it up. Muslims invading Europe first enslaved whites, but as Europe grew stronger, they turned to Africa and enslaving blacks. The number of Africans enslaved by Europeans totaled 12.5 million, of which 388,000, or just 3.1 percent, were sold in North America. But the number of mostly

Africans enslaved by Arab Muslims over fourteen centuries (from the seventh to the twentieth) was at least 18 million, and some believe that is low and the number could be over 180 million.[11] The European slave trade was horrendous but was eclipsed by the Arab Muslim slave trade, which began earlier, enslaved more, and continued more than a century after it ended in the West. Those enslaved by Arab Muslims exceeded those enslaved by Europeans by at least 44 percent. But the difference may have been 14.4 times as much or have exceeded the Europeans by 1,440 percent.

From the seventeenth to nineteenth centuries, Western nations did not enslave prisoners of war but rather kidnapped Africans and transported them under hideous conditions for sale in the Americas.[12] While Arab Muslims marketed enslaved Africans in the Eastern world, nations, including the Portuguese, Spanish, French, Dutch, Danish, English, and Americans, did the same thing for three centuries, marketing them in the Western world despite the influence of Christianity. Christians were not united, and some, to their shame, defended slavery, while others fought against it. The sermons of men like John Wesley (1703–1791) and Charles Finney (1792–1875), reforms of Christian statesmen like William Wilberforce (1759–1833), and agitations of Christian activists like Harriet Beecher Stowe (1811–1896) led to abolishing slavery first in Great Britain (1833), then in Europe (1811–1846), then in the United States (1865), and finally in South America (1888). By contrast, legal slavery continued in the Muslim world into the second half of the twentieth century, and, when slavery was abolished, the incentive came mainly from diplomatic pressures generated by Western Christians and not from moral changes in Islam.

Slavery is addressed extensively in the Bible but not as readers might expect. It condemns kidnapping people to enslave them but allows acquiring slaves in other ways. It tells slaves to accept freedom if masters offer it but to work willingly for those who do not. This may seem dissonant, but the ethics of it resolves on realizing the Bible addresses different sorts of slavery, all of which were very different from slavery in America.

The Mosaic law sanctioned two sorts of slavery—humanitarian slavery for poor Israelites who could not provide for themselves, and prisoner of war slavery for foreigners defeated

---

[11] Shaun Snapp, "Did Slavery Ever Stop in Arab Countries?," *Brightwork Research & Analysis,* September 1, 2019, https://www.brightworkresearch.com/did-slavery-ever-stop-in-arab-countries/.

[12] Of the 12.5 million Africans loaded onto Atlantic slave ships, only 11 million survived.

after attacking Israel unjustly. Under humanitarian slavery, Israelites were allowed to accept a "brother" who "becomes destitute and sells himself to you" (Lev 25:39). This sort of slavery functioned as a welfare program to ensure people falling on hard times were cared for and given a way to recover. It was not an entitlement program because it required beneficiaries to work and be responsible for what they got, and although it limited independence, it was voluntary and temporary, and restored the impoverished to self-supporting independence.

The second sort found in Mosaic law was prisoner of war slavery. Besides Israelites who temporarily sold themselves to survive poverty, Israelites could also purchase male and female slaves "from nations around you" (Lev 25:44) and "from aliens residing with you" (Lev 25:45). Unlike Israelites in humanitarian slavery, these foreigners could be "slaves for life" and left "to your sons . . . as property" (Lev 25:46). But, since God condemns enslaving peaceful people (Exod 21:16; Amos 1:6, 9), oppressing foreigners (Exod 22:21; 23:9), and violating the image of God (Gen 9:6; Jas 3:9), what God allowed assumes strict limits. Acquiring such slaves certainly included foreigners defeated after attacking Israel unjustly (Deut 20:11), and when that happened, those enslaved included everyone on the other side, not just men but women and children who had no one to care for them if left behind (Deut 20:14). This second sort may also have included foreigners who sold themselves to Israelites without first attacking them (Josh 9:24–27). In any case, Israel was not allowed to attack peaceful people to enslave them as the Assyrians and Babylonians did (2 Kgs 15:29; 24:16), and anyone involved in manstealing was executed not only if they stole Israelites (Deut 24:7) but anyone at all (Exod 21:16).

Non-Israelite slaves were treated differently than Israelites. They belonged to their masters (Lev 25:45–46), unlike Israelites, who belonged to God directly (Lev 25:42); could be sold, unlike Israelites, who could not be sold (Lev 25:42); were "slaves for life" (Lev 25:46), unlike Israelites, who were freed after six years (Exod 21:2; Deut 15:12) or on the Year of Jubilee (Lev 25:40), whichever came first; and could be treated "harshly," unlike Israelites, who could not (Lev 25:43, 46). But "harsh" treatment only refers to physical discipline and did not mean masters could abuse, injure, or kill foreign slaves. Israelites could not "oppress" foreigners (Exod 22:21; 23:9). And, no matter what sort of slave it was, if a master inflicted permanent injury, however minor, that slave was set free (Exod 21:26–27); if a master killed a slave, that master was executed the same as murdering anyone else (Exod 21:12, 20); and if a slave ran away, that slave could not be returned and had to be received as a free member of whatever community he fled to (Deut 23:15–16).

Most importantly, differences in how slaves in the two Mosaic categories were treated ceased if a foreign slave converted to faith in God. Conversion transformed non-Israelites into Israelites, as in the case of Rahab (Josh 6:25) and Ruth (Ruth 1:16), who became ancestors of David (Matt 1:5); in the case of some Gittites (Philistines from Gath), one of whom hosted the ark in his home for three months (2 Sam 6:10–11; 1 Chr 13:13–14); and in the case of a contingent who joined David's army (2 Sam 15:19–22; 18:1–2). This means conversion also transformed permanent involuntary prisoner of war slaves who were foreigners into temporary voluntary humanitarian slaves who were Israelites. Neither sort was dehumanizing, abusive, or had anything to do with race. Slaves in one category were better off than slaves in the other, but slaves in the lower category could shift to the higher and be freed if they wanted.

A third sort we are calling progressive slavery is found in the New Testament, and we refer to it as "progressive" because in this sort of slavery, slaves could advance their standing and eventually either purchase their freedom or stay employed as they were. Slaves in the first-century Greco-Roman world performed manual labor but also were doctors, administrators, investors, and intellectuals. They managed finances, administered businesses, ran cities, and commanded ships in the Roman navy. Some were highly educated to the extent that philosophers and educators often were slaves.

A Greco-Roman slave, or δοῦλος (*doulos*), could be paid, save up to purchase his freedom, and be entrusted with enormous responsibility. The Athenian silver mines were managed by a slave, many running what served as banks were slaves, and, in the parable of the talents (Matt 25:14–30), Jesus showed it was not surprising to entrust this sort of slave with millions of dollars.[13] New Testament slaves were more like employees with employer-provided benefits, privileges, and power than like captives forced to labor against their will for people abusing them. They passed freely among others, had more social status and money than day laborers (Matt 20:1–15), and those who sought independence usually attained it by the time they were thirty. They had more self-determination, social respect, and assets than either sort of slave in the Old Testament, and all three were nothing like slaves in America.

The New Testament condemns slave traders who kidnap people (1 Tim 1:10) and, while it tolerates the existing institution, it does not recommend it and redefines the master-slave

---

[13] In contemporary terms, the slave receiving ten talents was entrusted with $3 million, the slave receiving two talents with $1.2 million, and the slave receiving one talent with $600,000.

relationship in a way that ends it. Slaves are told to serve masters willingly (Eph 6:5; Col 3:22) not only if they are "good and gentle" but even if they are "cruel" (1 Pet 2:18), to not talk back or steal from them (Titus 2:9–10), to serve Christian masters "even better" (1 Tim 6:2), and to accept their enslaved status though they should accept freedom if offered (1 Cor 7:20–21). Masters must not threaten slaves (Eph 6:9), must treat them "justly and fairly" (Col 4:1), must realize God treats slave and free alike (1 Cor 12:13; Gal 3:28; Col 3:11) and does not prefer them over slaves (Eph 6:9), and must treat a Christian slave "as a dearly loved brother" (Phlm 16).

The New Testament does not directly attack slavery as an institution. But it condemns kidnapping and abusing slaves and not only requires they be treated well but as equals, which in effect, destroys what makes the institution evil and causes it to collapse. By requiring slavery to operate on love and equality, the New Testament gives bad people no reason to have slaves and good people reasons to free them. It assures the end of abusive involuntary bondage but not as most expect because it does so in a way that is voluntary rather than involuntary, relies on faith rather than force, employs the gospel rather than government, and ends up destroying the institution in terms that are peaceful rather than violent and cooperative rather than combative.

The institutions of humanitarian slavery and prisoner of war slavery sanctioned in the Old Testament and of progressive slavery tolerated in the New Testament all were entirely different from slavery in America. What was formerly practiced in American was chattel slavery, the worst form of bondage ever devised in human history. In biblical terms, chattel slavery was the sort practiced by the Assyrians and Babylonians and never by Israelites or even by first-century Greeks and Romans. Chattel slavery reduces people made in and bearing God's image to the level of things and treats them so badly the evilness of it cannot be overstated. In our history, free Africans not only were kidnapped but also were transported to America in horribly inhumane conditions; not only were transported inhumanely but also were sold as merchandise in open air markets where they were stripped bare and branded like cattle; not only were sold inhumanely but also were cruelly disciplined by masters who could beat, injure, rape, or even kill them with impunity; not only were disciplined inhumanely but also were treated cold-heartedly by masters who could sell them without notice, separating husbands from wives and children from parents, and could literally work them to death; and not only were treated inhumanely by masters but also were treated inhumanely by American law, which provided no protection and no path to freedom, and punished runaways and anyone helping them. All this was interpreted and justified by racist lies and prejudice.

The sorts of slavery found in the Bible should not be taken as approving chattel slavery, which is unloving, harmful, and fundamentally wrong because it demeans and dishonors people made in and bearing the image of God. American slaveholders wrongly alleged the Bible allowed it by conveniently failing to distinguish chattel slavery from the sorts found in Mosaic law and addressed in the New Testament. The Bible shows that all slavery can be abused and no form is ideal. It shows that some forms can be tolerated within strict limits, but also shows that chattel slavery is now, and always has been, totally unbiblical, immoral, and evil because it deeply offends those abused, deeply offends our shared humanity, and deeply offends God. Chattel slavery is wrong for all the reasons racism is wrong but is worse. Chattel slavery exceeds the evil of racism by treating people as if they do not bear God's image, or as if bearing God's image does not matter, and by not merely devaluing humanity but denying it altogether. Indeed, by biblical standards, everyone involved in American chattel slavery deserved execution (Exod 21:16).

Recommended further reading on the issue of slavery includes Hector Avalos, *Slavery, Abolitionism, and the Ethics of Biblical Scholarship* (Sheffield, UK: Sheffield Phoenix, 2013); James O. Buswell, *Slavery, Segregation, and Scripture* (Grand Rapids: Eerdmans, 1964); David B. Davis, *In the Image of God: Religion, Moral Values, and Our Heritage of Slavery* (New Haven, CT: Yale, 2001); David B. Davis, *Inhuman Bondage* (New York: Oxford, 2006); David B. Davis, *The Problem of Slavery in Western Culture* (New York: Oxford, 1966); Charles Elliott, *The Bible and Slavery* (Cincinnati: Poe & Hitchcock, 1863); Thomas Sowell, *Economic Facts and Fallacies*, 2nd ed. (New York: Basic, 2011); and Shelby Steele, *Shame: How America's Past Sins Have Polarized Our Country* (New York: Basic, 2015).

Human Trafficking

Slavery has not vanished in the twenty-first century but, rather, has assumed different forms now referred to as "human trafficking." It is tragic that slavery remains a problem after being officially abolished throughout the world, and it is alarming to discover that enslaving people now is more prevalent than ever before. Efforts to stop it are being made but are making little headway because the industry is driven by enormous profitability coupled with rising pools of vulnerable people caused by political unrest, economic disparities, relational dysfunctions, and drug abuse.

In 2004, human trafficking was the second largest criminal industry in the world and now may be the largest. In 2004, it was tied for second place along with illegal arms trafficking and was surpassed only by illegal drug trafficking. But it has since been the world's fastest growing criminal enterprise, which means it could already have become the world's largest criminal industry. In 2018, the Global Slavery Index reported that 45 million people were enslaved around the world, and that means more are enslaved today than ever before. Arriving at that total depends on who is counted and where data comes from. Nevertheless, it is likely that the number of people enslaved today is at least one third greater than the total number of people captured and sold by slave traders in the previous fourteen centuries.

Human trafficking is a multibillion dollar criminal business driven by demand for cheap sex, labor, and goods magnified by world unrest and the effects of globalization on travel, commerce, and communication. In just nine years, from 2005 to 2014, annual profits from human trafficking rose from $44 billion to $150 billion and now must be closer to $200 billion. Profits like this, coupled with the low risk of being caught and prosecuted, is leading criminal enterprises to prefer human trafficking over other riskier pursuits.

Human trafficking is an umbrella term for all the ways victims can be abused for the benefit of those abusing them, and specific forms include "sex trafficking," "labor trafficking," "child soldier trafficking," and "organ trafficking." Actions that qualify as human trafficking include recruiting, transporting, harboring, receiving, selling, buying, or using persons in ways that require threats, fraud, or physical force to control them. It is not the same as human smuggling because smuggled individuals give permission to be smuggled across borders and pay smugglers large sums for getting them across. In human trafficking, victims do not consent to being victimized. Another difference is that in smuggling everyone involved is guilty, but in human trafficking only traffickers are guilty, and victims are not.

"Sex trafficking" is when threats, fraud, or physical force is used to make someone engage in a commercial sex act, and forms of sex trafficking include sexual slavery, sexual exploitation, and bride kidnapping. Sexual slavery is claiming to "own" someone and so being entitled to make that person engage in sexual activities against his or her will. Sex tourism is traveling to another country to purchase sex from people with far less income, but the anti-trafficking community is now replacing the term *sex tourism* with the terms *extraterritorial sexual exploitation* or *extraterritorial commercial sexual exploitation* in order to focus on how the activity harms victims rather than focusing on the perpetrator's reason for traveling. Bride kidnapping is a form of sexual slavery in which women are abducted and raped by men claiming them as "wives" against their will. Alleging to "marry" abducted women against their will is a pretext for rape and sexual enslavement, and most nations consider it a sex crime.

As the Islamic State in Iraq and Syria (ISIS) lost income from oil, taxation, and extortion, the terrorist group turned to sex trafficking to finance operations. In 2014, ISIS attacked the Yazidi homeland in northern Iraq, killing thousands of Yazidi men and abducting 5,000 to 7,000 Yazidi women and girls. These abducted women and girls then were sold as sex slaves or "awarded" to ISIS fighters who claimed them as "wives" and raped them. Marketing them as sex slaves generated $30 million for ISIS in 2016 alone, and an estimated 3,000 Yazidi women and girls were still enslaved in 2019.

"Labor trafficking" is when threats, fraud, or physical force is used to make people work in conditions they cannot escape, change, or reject. It is often combined with "debt bondage," which is using fees charged for transportation, lodging, or food, or interest charged on small initial loans, to keep workers from regaining independence. "Domestic servitude trafficking" is labor trafficking in residential circumstances in which workers cannot escape their employment, are underpaid, if paid at all, are not given benefits (like time off) or protections (like a minimum wage) common to other workers, and are not able to move around freely.

Qatar, a small country on the shore of the Persian Gulf, has 300,000 official citizens but employs about 2.5 million foreign workers in enslaved conditions. These foreign workers, comprising 80 percent of Qatar's population, come mainly from Asian countries and are treated as slaves even though slavery is officially illegal there. They are paid so little they cannot afford to go home, often have their passports taken away, are charged fees they cannot repay, and then are fined for late or nonpayment of these "loans." The Qatar government does not allow them to leave without paying off all they allegedly "owe," and they have no legal rights under Qatari law, meaning they can be murdered, raped, or extorted by their employers with impunity. These workers remain in perpetual debt with no way out and are thus in effect "owned" by their Qatari masters.

"Child soldier trafficking" is when children are forced to serve, or deceived into serving, as slaves by armed forces, paramilitary organizations, or rebel groups. Child soldiers are made to fight alongside adults and may also be used as porters, cooks, guards, attendants, messengers, or spies usually for no pay at all, and girls tend to also be used as sex slaves by older soldiers. When ISIS took control of large areas in Iraq and Syria in 2014, they developed a program called "Cubs of the Caliphate." Children abducted from new territories were indoctrinated, given weapons training, and deployed as human shields and suicide bombers. For example, in 2016, ISIS fighters loaded a twelve-year-old child with explosives, sent him to infiltrate a Kurdish wedding party, and then blew him up, killing him along with fifty-three wedding guests.

"Organ trafficking" is when people are exploited to obtain organs, which are removed and sold on the black market. Victims rarely receive what induces them to sell an organ, some lose organs despite refusing to sell them, and some are kidnapped and killed for their organs. It is hard to say how many organs are trafficked this way, but in 2015 the World Health Organization (WHO) estimated 12 to 13 thousand organs were being trafficked annually and that it was generating yearly profits of $840 million to $1.7 billion. Eritreans constitute 95 percent of the refugee population living on the Sinai Peninsula, and recent reports indicate that traffickers are kidnapping Eritreans and removing corneas, kidneys, and livers, which generally kills the victim.

In 1949, the United Nations adopted the *Convention for the Suppression of the Traffick in Persons and Exploitation of the Prostitution of Others*, which encouraged member nations to pass laws prohibiting sexual exploitation, and, in 2000 the United Nations adopted the *Protocol to Prevent, Suppress and Punish Trafficking in Persons*, which broadened the definition of trafficking persons to include any of the ways people can be victimized. The United States passed the *Trafficking Victims Protection Act* in 2000, and then passed two related laws—the *William Wilberforce Trafficking Victims Protection Reauthorization Act* and the *Child Soldiers Prevention Act*—in 2008. But passing laws is one thing, and enforcing them is another. Criminalizing human trafficking is much easier than catching traffickers and putting them out of business. Enforcement could be better even in the United States and is lax to nonexistent in many other parts of the world. Beyond this, many nonprofits, both secular and religious, have sprung up to aid, rescue, and serve victims, but these efforts, though very commendable, are miniscule compared to the worldwide need.

All forms of human trafficking, whether sex trafficking, labor trafficking, child soldier trafficking, or organ trafficking, are versions of chattel slavery, which is wrong because it treats human beings contrary to their God-given dignity and, in biblical terms, clashes with what the ethic of neighbor love requires. Human trafficking is an enormous ethical challenge for human governments and Christian ministries alike. It is easy to renounce but not easy to eliminate. It is easy to vote against but not easy to stop. It is easy to pass laws against but not easy to catch and convict people breaking those laws. It is easy to get some nations to deny traffickers freedom to operate but not easy to get all nations to deny it all over the world. And, while Christians can love and assist a few victims, we cannot keep traffickers from finding more victims. What makes human trafficking so challenging to address is that the issue is not simply accidental or incidental but is primarily intentional and strategic. It also is not simply a local or individual problem but is primarily a systemic and institutional problem. Differences like these make the issue more intractable than most and show that overcoming it requires cooperation and ability on a scale finite humans cannot attain without supernatural intervention.

This does not mean we should do nothing or should not resist the problem as much as we can. It only means we must not be naïve and should not think one or two things will solve the problem. Government has a role to play, and Christian ministries do as well. Government cannot provide family, friends, and faith, and ministries cannot kick down doors and arrest traffickers. Neither can do what the other does, and neither can succeed without the other. Even so, the best we can do is restrain wicked behavior without supposing we can rid the world of what causes it in the first place (Rom 13:3–4). Laws and policies can restrain what bad people do but cannot make them good—only Christ does that. And ministries can love and assist victims in the name of Christ but cannot give them victory over their experiences— only Christ does that.

Recommended further reading on the issue of human trafficking includes: Kevin Bales and Ron Soodalter, *The Slave Next Door* (Oakland, CA: University of California, 2010); Nita Belles, *In Our Backyard: Human Trafficking in America* (Grand Rapids: Baker, 2015); Noel B. Busch-Armendariz et al., *Human Trafficking: Applying Research, Theory, and Case Studies* (Los Angeles: Sage, 2018); Marion Carson, *Human Trafficking, the Bible, and the Church* (Eugene, OR: Cascade, 2016); Marion Carson, *Setting the Captives Free: The Bible and Human Trafficking* (Eugene, OR: Cascade, 2015); Jeffrey Goltz et al., *Human Trafficking: A Systemwide Public Safety and Community Approach* (St. Paul, MN: West Academic, 2017); Raleigh Sadler, *Vulnerable: Rethinking Human Trafficking* (Nashville: B&H, 2019); Louise Shelley, *Human Trafficking: A Global Perspective* (Cambridge: Cambridge, 2010); and Wendy Stickle et al., *Human Trafficking: A Comprehensive Exploration of Modern-Day Slavery* (Los Angeles: Sage, 2019).

Creation Care

Issues involving creation care are getting more attention now than before, and this has exposed opposing convictions. Some think human development threatens the world, others think it makes the world a better place, and Christians wonder if we should pick sides or view it differently than others. Interacting with nature the right way has concerned people since before recorded history. But technologies have increased what humans can do, and science has made us more aware of how much we are altering the world. Creation care is important, not only because it is getting more attention but also because it matters to God and is connected to duties God assigned us at creation.

Before going further, we need to understand how some terms will be used in this section. *Environmental ethics* is the subfield in applied ethics dealing with human interaction with the natural world. *Creation care* is environmental ethics addressed from a Christian point of view, meaning it addresses the same questions based on what the Bible says. *Environmentalism* is ideology that explains obligation to care for things in nature without considering the role or reality of God. *Ecology* is the study of how organisms relate to each other and to things around them. An *ecosystem* is a community of organisms interacting with nonliving things around them. The *biosphere* is the sum of all ecosystems on earth, and *biodiversity* refers to how many different kinds of organisms exist either in a region or on the earth as a whole.

How people view interacting with nature depends on what they believe about human nature, human destiny, and the natural world itself, and just using the term *creation care* signals a starting point that differs from what many others assume when discussing environmental ethics. We will start by surveying different perspectives people assume when discussing environmental ethics, then will cover what constitutes a biblically revealed creation-care ethic, then will discuss different approaches Christian ethicists use when interpreting a creation-care ethic, and, lastly, will comment on how it all relates to current issues in environmental ethics.

People discussing environmental ethics assume one of four perspectives, which are either biocentrism, ecocentrism, anthropocentrism, or theocentrism. Biocentrism places biological life at the center of environmental ethics and assumes all living things have equal value. It ignores God, gives no special status to humans, assumes life forms exist for the sake of species survival, and only values nonliving things in terms of how they support living things. Ecocentrism is more inclusive in that it centers environmental ethics on the natural world as a whole, not just living things but everything else as well. It, too, gives humans no special status and ignores God in the biblical sense. But, while it denies creation, ecocentrism inclines toward worshipping nature, fears that developing the natural world diminishes deity, and treats spirituality as cruel because nature is cruel. Christians agree that nature matters to God but do not accept worshipping nature or normalizing cruelty. Anthropocentrism, too, ignores God but centers environmental ethics on valuing humans over everything else and denying other things have value or purpose other than what humans give them. So, if humans do not value something, it is treated as unimportant and worthless. This perspective criticizes the way humans interact with the environment only if it harms people and, if no one gets hurt, sees nothing wrong with however humans use nature.

Theocentrism contrasts with the previous perspectives by centering environmental ethics on a Creator who made the world instead of centering it on humans (anthropocentrism), nature as a whole (ecocentrism), or living things (biocentrism). But, while Christianity is theocentric, there are other versions besides the Christian version. Islam is theocentric but misperceives the rule of God, anthropology, redemption, and eschatology. Judaism is theocentric but misperceives Christ, redemption, and eschatology. Animists (like the Hmong people with whom I grew up in Thailand were before receiving the gospel) are theocentric but only know the Creator as a distant deity they lost touch with. Thus, theocentrism affects environmental ethics in a big way but does not alone provide a whole operating system for treating things in nature the right way or evaluating when something is wrong and needs to be corrected. It is just a perspective, and, while having the right perspective is critical in ethics, it does not include everything needed to handle decisions about right and wrong and what to do. So just because Muslims, Jews, and Animists affirm theocentrism does not mean they always will agree with Christians on environmental issues. They may agree on more things than biocentrists, ecocentrists, or anthropocentrists, but their thinking is not framed the same even though theirs, too, is theocentric.

Theocentrism refers to the perspective Christians should have on environmental ethics but is not the ethic itself. It is the starting point and not the whole thing. If interacting with nature is a parade, theocentrism is like getting off on the right foot and creation care is like marching the whole parade keeping in step while turning, stopping, and pivoting all at the right time in the right way. How then does the Word of God reveal an entire ethical system as to the significance, value, and purposes of things in the natural world and the role and responsibilities we have relating to them? Indeed, the creation-care ethic revealed in the Bible has at least twenty elements, and I can only mention each briefly here, even though each one has enormous implications and is worth discussing at length:

1. *God created everything in the natural world.* Because God made it all (Gen 1–2; Isa 40:28; 42:5; Jer 32:17; John 1:3; Col 1:16; Heb 1:2), dealing with nature matters to him. But as Creator, God also transcends what he made and is not himself part of nature (Exod 20:4; Rom 1:23).

2. *God owns everything in the natural world.* The earth and everything in it belongs to God (Job 41:11; Ps 24:1; 50:10–12). In a sense, the earth is given to us (Ps 115:16), but God has not given it away. We may use and develop what the earth contains, but what we do with it must always suit the real owner.

3. *God values and rejoices in everything in the natural world.* God made everything "good" (Gen 1:4, 10, 12, 18, 21, 25, 31; 1 Tim 4:4) and rejoices in all of it (Ps 104:31). Thus, everything in nature has value whether or not humans appreciate, use, or develop it (Matt 6:30).

4. *God sustains everything in the natural world.* God is what holds nature together (Col 1:17) and keeps it operating (Eph 4:6; Heb 1:3)—not just spiritually but materially, not just humans but the environment (Deut 28:11–12), not just animals (Ps 104:17–18; Matt 10:29; Luke 12:24), crops (Ps 104:14), trees (Lev 26:4; Ps 104:16), flowers (Luke 12:28), and germs (Deut 28:21; Ps 91:5–6) but natural resources (Ps 65:9–13; 104:10–13), not just water, air, and minerals, but even gravity, weather, and how the earth rotates and orbits the sun (Gen 8:22; Ps 104:5, 19–22; 121:6).

5. *God's reality and attributes are revealed in the natural world.* Nature proves God's reality because someone makes it work (Job 12:7–9), and it presupposes some of his non-visible attributes, including his power, divinity, righteousness, and faithfulness (Ps 50:6; 89:5; 97:6; 104:24; 111:2–3; Rom 1:20).

6. *God is glorified by everything in the natural world.* "The heavens declare the glory of God" (Ps 19:1) and "his glory fills the whole earth" (Isa 6:3). Everything in nature glorifies God (Ps 96:11–13; 97:1–6; 98:7–9; Rev 5:13), meaning it praises him (Ps 65:13; 93:3; 148:3–10; Isa 44:23). Thus, everything in nature has purpose whether needed by humans or not.

7. *There is a hierarchy of value in the natural world.* Humans are created in God's image (Gen 1:27) and have preeminence over other things (Ps 8:6–8). The environment has value, humans have more value, and God has the most value.

8. *Humans have delegated authority over the natural world.* God made humans to "rule" the rest of creation (Gen 1:26), but this does not mean we can do whatever we want. The authority we have is regal (because we are acting for earth's king), managerial (because we do not own the earth), benevolent (because we must treat the earth as God does), productive (because God wants the earth to flourish), delegated (because the role we have is not one that we have in our own right), cooperative (because there are laws of nature we can use but not change), and representative (because we only represent God when dealing with things in nature).

9. *Humans are responsible for the natural world.* Responsibility for things in nature began when God assigned Adam and Eve to "watch over" the Garden of Eden (Gen 2:15). The word translated is שָׁמַר (*šāmar*), which means nurture, protect, or exercise great care over. We not only have authority over the earth but are responsible for it.

10. *Humans are to fill the natural world.* God made us not only to rule and watch over the earth but also to "fill" it (Gen 1:28). We must propagate and occupy the planet. But, because the Bible says nothing about stopping, questions are raised as to whether population growth remains a God-given blessing or has become a problem we should stop.

11. *Humans are to develop the natural world.* Our calling to "subdue" the earth (Gen 1:28) means God wants us to bring out its latent potentialities. Developing the earth is intended not only to sustain human flourishing but also to glorify God (Ps 19:1). God did not place everything under our feet either to be ignored or to be trampled on (Ps 8:6; Heb 2:6–8).

12. *The natural world is able to provide all our material needs.* God made the earth good, beautiful, and bountiful (Ps 24:1–2; 33:1–9; 50:1–2; 65:5–13; 72:19), and the Bible never hints we might ever exhaust its resources (Phil 4:19). This does not mean we should waste them, but we also need not fear running out of necessary resources.

13. *Humans both transcend and are part of the natural world.* Humans are not only over nature but also in it. Nature relies on humans to flourish, and humans cannot flourish apart from nature. Those who harm nature harm themselves.

14. *The natural world is under a curse.* Nature was made "very good" (Gen 1:31) but was altered after the fall (Gen 3:17–18; Rom 8:20). So even nature untouched by humans is not pristine. It is good but not ideal, beautiful but also cruel, and filled with disasters, blight, predation, and diseases as well as resources. This allows us to deal with cruelty in nature without thinking God is cruel and, while we can mitigate natural dangers, we should not think they can be eliminated.

15. *God relates to the natural world apart from, as well as through, humans.* God has made two covenants with the earth and its creatures that go beyond human beings alone. He issued one at creation to assure the earth he would keep it going (Jer 33:20), and he issued a second after the flood to assure all creatures he would not destroy life on earth by water again (Gen 8:21–22; 9:9–17). And we must believe God will keep these covenants no matter what humans do.

16. *God wants humans to use things in nature without worshipping or abusing them.* We must not worship anything God made (Exod 20:4–5; Rom 1:22–23). God has given plants and animals to us for food (Gen 1:29; 9:2–3) but also wants us to treat the land with care (Exod 23:10–11), to avoid pollution (Deut 23:13), to conserve trees (Deut 20:19–20), to treat domestic animals kindly (Exod 23:5, 12; Deut 22:4; 25:4; Prov 12:10), and to respect wildlife (Deut 22:6).

17. *God's plan of redemption includes the natural world.* It was "subjected to futility" on account of the fall but is important enough to be included in what God saves (Rom 8:19–21). Humans are focal but will not be redeemed without the environment (Col 1:20).

18. *The natural world will be purged and renewed.* A day will come when the heavens will "pass away" and the elements "dissolved" (2 Pet 3:10). But, since the present world looks forward to inclusion in the future "freedom of God's children" (Rom 8:19–21), Peter does not mean the present world will be destroyed and replaced and, rather, means it will be purged and renewed.

19. *God will someday punish those who destroy the earth.* Revelation warns a time will come "to destroy those who destroy the earth" (Rev 11:18).

20. *God's relationship to the natural world centers on Christ.* Everything in the world was not only made by Christ but also for Christ (Rom 11:36). He started it (John 1:3; Col

1:16), rules it (Eph 1:20–22), holds it together (Col 1:17; Heb 1:3), and will transform it (Matt 19:28; Col 1:20). Which means those transformed by Christ should even now treat the earth in ways that reflect not only past creation by Christ but also future redemption through Christ.

All Christians assume a theocentric perspective on environmental ethics and affirm what the Bible says on creation care. But, when it comes to employing creation care as an ethical system, Christian ethicists have developed four different approaches by interpreting the human role in terms of either dominating, preserving, stewarding, or shepherding. The "dominion model" stresses how כָּבַשׁ (*kābaš*) and רָדָה (*rādâ*) in Genesis 1:28 are strong words that can mean "bring into bondage" and "tread upon" without much caring about what is subjugated other than forcing it to serve a master. But these terms need not always be interpreted harshly and must be taken benevolently when related to the rule of God. The dominion model is right to recognize the preeminence of humanity but is wrong to view nature as only existing to serve humanity.

The "preservation model" stresses duty to cultivate God-given resources while minimizing the impact humans have on nature. This model focuses on how, in Genesis 2:15, Adam is assigned to עָבַד (*ʿābad*) and שָׁמַר (*šāmar*), the first meaning to "cultivate," "work," "serve," or perhaps "worship," and the second meaning to "nurture," "protect," "exercise great care over," or perhaps "obey" in the sense of attending to instructions. The preservation model is right to recognize that nature has value beyond just serving humanity but is wrong to downplay human preeminence by elevating Genesis 2 over Genesis 1.

The "stewarding model" stresses avoiding waste and pollution because God wants us to use resources wisely and efficiently. The model focuses on being good managers or "stewards" of property entrusted to us but belonging to God. We can use and develop what God entrusts to us as long as we please him over just pleasing ourselves. The stewardship model is right to recognize how God owning everything affects how we interact with nature. But, while this is not wrong, the focus it places on managing obscures vision to go beyond mere managing to also work at enhancing the way nature glorifies God—not just by serving humanity but also by glorifying God directly.

The "shepherding model" builds on the stewarding model by stressing how the authority we have over the natural world is not only delegated but also representative and is not only managerial but also should imitate the way God leads us.[14] God is not a tyrant, a mere farmer, or just a good manager but rather leads like a shepherd (Ps 23:1; John 10:11–15) who exercises authority based on loving what he rules. The shepherding model adds bringing out the best in things not only to better ourselves but also to better how each thing in nature fulfills its own God-given purpose. Yes, humans are primary, and, yes, we can use nature to meet needs and better ourselves. But that is not all there is to it because everything God created has value and purpose regardless of how it serves us, and we should care about bringing the best out of things the way God does with us. The shepherding model stresses loving over controlling, enhancing over utilizing, and glorifying God over just not wasting or polluting things.

Because this section addresses what frames and constitutes a biblically revealed creation care ethic, we have little room to discuss the many issues now debated in environmental ethics. Such issues include whether population growth needs to be controlled, whether natural resources will run out if we do not restrict how much we use, whether chlorofluorocarbons (CFCs) threaten the ozone layer protecting the earth, whether deforestation threatens the earth's oxygen supply, whether we should stop development where it threatens biodiversity, whether and how to reduce waste disposal, how to reduce pollution and assure clean air, clean water, and clean energy, and whether we should try to stop or reverse climate change. These and other environmental issues need to be understood correctly, else we can easily make things worse in the name of trying to fix them. Just doing "something" is not better than doing "nothing" if what is done comes from misconceiving "problems" and "solutions."

When it comes to environmental ethics, understanding issues correctly depends not just on science but on how people understand human nature (including human finitude and fallibility), the nature and purpose of nature (creation), the reality, providence, and power of God, and the nature and direction of history (including natural history), which is why this section focuses on the latter. Science affecting environmental issues can be complex, but it is not hard to interpret from within a well-understood biblical view of creation care. This section has set forth framing sufficient to interpret whatever scientific claims arise, and the next section will

---

[14] This understanding of a "shepherding model" comes from Donald R. McDaniel, "Becoming Good Shepherds: A New Model for Creation Care" (PhD diss., Southeastern Baptist Theological Seminary, 2011).

take up the most controversial of the many issues debated in environmental ethics, that of climate change, otherwise known as "global warming."

Recommended further reading on the issue of creation care includes Richard Bauckham, *The Bible and Ecology* (Waco, TX: Baylor, 2010); E. Calvin Beisner, *Where Garden Meets Wilderness* (Grand Rapids: Eerdmans, 1997); Calvin B. DeWitt, *Caring for Creation* (Grand Rapids: Baker, 1998); Mark Liederbach and Seth Bible, *True North: Christ, the Gospel, and Creation Care* (Nashville: B&H, 2012); Bjørn Lomborg, *The Skeptical Environmentalist* (Cambridge: Cambridge, 2001); Douglas Moo and Jonathan Moo, *Creation Care* (Grand Rapids: Zondervan, 2018); Michael S. Northcott, *The Environment and Christian Ethics* (Cambridge: Cambridge, 1996); and Francis Schaeffer, *Pollution and the Death of Man* (Wheaton, IL: Crossway, 2011).

Global Warming

Whether or not humans are causing unprecedented heating of the earth that threatens global disaster is the most divisive issue in environmental ethics today. If it is true, then life on earth is at stake and stopping it is worth any cost. If it is not true, then a false alarm is being used to pressure people into doing things that are in themselves disastrous because they divert attention from real problems, destroy commerce, and make life harder for those least able to bear it.

"Global warming" is when the temperature of the earth goes up, and that raises questions as to why, if it is normal, and whether the earth will cool again. "Anthropogenic global warming" is global warming attributed to human activity, meaning it is something people think would not otherwise occur. "Climate" is averaging weather characteristics over various periods of time. "Climate change" is when averaged weather characteristics go up or down, are more or less severe, or occur more or less frequently. "Anthropogenic climate change" is climate change attributed to human activity, meaning it, too, is something people think would not otherwise occur. The "greenhouse effect" is the atmosphere reflecting heat radiating from the earth back toward the surface and so keeping it warmer than it would be otherwise. "Greenhouse gases" are gases in the atmosphere that together produce the greenhouse effect. Of these, water vapor is the most significant, being responsible for up to 95 percent of the greenhouse effect, and less significant greenhouse gases include carbon dioxide, responsible for about 4.5 percent, methane, responsible for about 0.25 percent, and other trace gases, responsible for a combination of about 0.25 percent. The *Intergovernmental Panel on Climate Change* (IPCC) is a body the United Nations set up in 1988 to inform the world about anthropogenic global warming and to propose ways to avert dangers it may cause.

Everyone knows the earth has been warming. But there is no agreement on whether it is problematic, and two views have evolved. One view says the earth is dangerously overheating and will become inhospitable unless we support a massive effort to stop it, and another view says the global warming we see today is within normal ranges and there is nothing to fear. We will survey these views, look at what the Bible says, and then make some comments.

The first view makes seven claims: (1) that there is no credible disagreement with a scientific consensus on global warming, (2) that the IPCC is the best source of trustworthy information on global warming and speaks for the consensus we must follow, (3) that global warming today is unprecedented, (4) that it is caused entirely or primarily by emissions coming from humans burning fossil fuels that are raising atmospheric CO_2 to levels upsetting the greenhouse effect, (5) that the earth's climate system is fragile and global warming is nearing a point of no return, (6) that unless it is stopped anthropogenic global warming will cause catastrophic events threatening life on earth, and (7) that stopping these events requires giving government more power and is worth any cost.

What this first view claims depends on believing the IPCC provides the best climate predictions possible, and what the IPCC says is that the current warming trend is unprecedented because it is higher and more rapid than has ever occurred before and that this unprecedented warming trend is driven by humans using fossil fuels because it started with the Industrial Revolution (1760–1840). Along with this, some IPCC-related scientists say the earth's climate system is so finely balanced that, if it warms just a few more degrees, it will reach tipping points after which irreversible feedback loops will make things rapidly worse until the earth becomes inhospitable. Tipping points include major ice sheets collapsing, major ocean currents shutting down, and oceans turning into acidic dead zones. The IPCC predicts storms and droughts will increase in frequency and intensity, crop productivity will drop precipitously, and diseases will surge. And some scientists related to the IPCC warn that, unless humans immediately stop using fossil fuels, these events will occur by the end of the twenty-first century.

The second view consists of seven parallel claims: (1) that climate science is not settled as to the rate and magnitude of warming caused by human actions and disagreement with the first view is highly credible, (2) that the IPCC is a political body with limited scientific credibility, (3) that global temperatures are cyclical and warming today is neither abnormal nor unprecedented, (4) that anthropogenic CO_2 in the atmosphere is not upsetting the greenhouse effect, (5) that the earth's climate system is not fragile and is not nearing a point of no return, (6) that greenhouse gas-induced global warming will not produce catastrophic results, and (7) that what advocates of the first view want us to do is unnecessary, foolish, and dangerous.

This second view starts by disputing the reality and relevance of an alleged scientific consensus and observes how just making the claim is itself unscientific. Some leading climate scientists have always disagreed with thinking global warming is problematic, and these have noted how appealing to a "consensus" to suppress dissent is incompatible with what real scientists actually do, which is compare evidence to hypotheses and analyze any anomalies they discover. "Consensus" does not matter to real scientists because they study how facts line up no matter how many accept one hypothesis or another.

This second view challenges the credibility of the IPCC because its forecasting of dire climate events is based on mathematical models that do not follow real world data. Climate models are fine if corrected by empirical evidence, but the IPCC was discovered to not be correcting climate models when real-world data did not match preferred results. This came to light when thousands of emails were discovered, first in 2009 and then in 2011, revealing people at the core of the IPCC were corrupting the peer review process, fabricating data, suppressing contrary evidence, and intimidating researchers who reached conclusions disagreeing with their views. This discovery, referred to as "Climategate," revealed that the IPCC was more political than scientific and caused it to lose much of its credibility.

The second view maintains that global temperatures are within normal ranges and not unprecedented, the earth is not in danger of overheating, the current warming trend either is not mainly caused by human activity or, if it is, then what is happening is a good thing, and no one can stop the earth's climate from changing. The earth's temperature changes all the time and, if we could stop it (which we cannot), doing so would be abnormal. In the earth's climate history, global temperatures have been both a lot warmer and a lot colder than now, so warming today is neither unprecedented nor abnormal. During the last ice age (2.6 million years ago), glaciers covered half the globe, sea levels were over 100 meters lower than today, and islands and continents now separated by seas were connected by land bridges. Since then, the earth has been in a warming cycle that is perfectly natural and, at least before 1960, had nothing to do with human activity because it started long before industrialization.

Humans burning fossil fuels do add CO_2 to the atmosphere but not significantly. It is hard to be precise, but the most reliable science suggests anthropogenic CO_2 comprises 0.117 percent of the gases causing the greenhouse effect. Thus, reducing it to zero would make no difference at all.

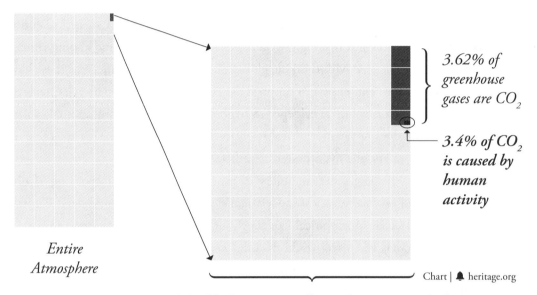

Entire Atmosphere

3.62% of greenhouse gases are CO_2

3.4% of CO_2 is caused by human activity

Chart | 🔔 heritage.org

This block represents all greenhouse gases, which comprise only 2% of the total atmosphere

Yet, even if humans burning fossil fuels has become a significant source of atmospheric CO_2, it would not be problematic because there is good evidence that more CO_2 in the atmosphere actually helps farmers grow more food.[15]

The second view thus rejects the first as resting on politicized science, ignoring climate history, and forecasting disaster based on normal variations in atmospheric CO_2 that actually benefit humanity. But, besides manipulating the peer review process and ignoring real-world evidence, the first view on global warming also clashes with the Word of God in seven ways. First, it conflicts with God designing a "very good" (Gen 1:31) earth because it assumes

---

[15] On this, see Robert Mendelsohn, *Climate Change and Agriculture* (Northampton, MA: Elgar, 2009).

the earth's climate system is so fragile humans can easily make it hostile to life on earth. Contrary to such thinking, the Bible treats the earth as the robust, resilient creation of a perfect Designer, and, while anything on earth can be abused, the climate system is made in a way that suppresses, and does not magnify, anything wrong humans do.

Second, it conflicts with God's covenant to maintain global stability. After the flood, God promised to keep global temperatures (cold and heat) aligned with human flourishing (Gen 8:22). Third, it exaggerates danger in nature to a degree surpassing the curse God imposed altering harmony between humanity and nature. The first view wrongly assumes nature can be rendered incompatible with human survival and not merely more difficult to cultivate. The curse made relying on nature harder to achieve but had more to do with growing food than with the atmosphere or climate. Although the curse disrupted relations with creation as a whole (Rom 8:20), it mainly had to do with disrupting productivity of "the ground" (Gen 3:17, 23; 5:29) and did not much affect seasons, temperature cycles, or day and night (Gen 8:22). It is safe, therefore, to assume that the curse did not place climate stability at odds with human flourishing.

Fourth, it clashes with how obeying God aligns with environmental responsibility. The first view assumes obeying God can become wrong and irresponsible if the earth changes so that continuing to obey threatens climate stability. Since the curse, God can and does alter the weather—but only to reward obedience or to punish disobedience and never the reverse (Lev 26:3–5, 14, 19–20; Deut 11:13–17; 28:1–2, 12, 23–24). The Bible never treats obeying God's command to subdue the earth (Gen 1:28) as ever becoming environmentally irresponsible. Fifth, it denies "God . . . richly provides us with all things to enjoy" (1 Tim 6:17). The Bible treats using natural resources like fossil fuels as inherently good and not something that ever becomes wrong or irresponsible, much less make the earth inhospitable to plants, animals, and humans.

Sixth, it views the earth's climate system in a manner that (1) conflicts with believing God controls things whatever sinners do and however the curse alters creation, (2) weakens faith in God as a good Creator, and (3) erodes gratitude to God for supplying all our needs (Ps 65:9–13; 147:14). Seventh, it clashes with God rebuking people who do not believe he controls the earth's climate system. The Bible strongly affirms God's sovereign control over climate and weather (Lev 26:18–20; Deut 28:12, 23–24; 2 Sam 21:1; 1 Kgs 17–18; Job 37:9–13;

Ps 107:23–38; 148:8; Amos 4:7–8; Matt 8:24–27), and he rebukes those who stop believing he controls "seasonal rains" and "guarantees to us . . . the harvest" (Jer 5:24). Taken together, these seven principles lead me to agree with Grudem, who suggests that "the underlying cause of fears of dangerous global warming might not be science but rejection of trust in God."[16]

Christians need to avoid opposing hazards when dealing with global warming. One is reacting based on fear, and the other is having no concern at all. Followers of Jesus Christ love and trust God unconditionally (Matt 22:37; Prov 3:5) and, because of that, fear nothing else (Isa 43:1; Mark 4:40). So fearing the human impact on nature cannot drive a Christian view of global warming. The view predicting global catastrophe not only rests on poor science but also tells us to live in fear rather than faith in God. We should be concerned about making the earth a better place and stopping environmental abuse, and that is why recycling and sustainable development make sense. But we should not fool ourselves into thinking that, by doing such things, we can somehow control the weather, the earth's temperature, or climate change.

Fearmongering corrupts politics, has no place in science or ethics, and violates the mind of Christ (Phil 2:5–8) that should characterize Christian witness in the world. It would be foolish not to recognize a crisis when one arises. But crying "wolf" sacrifices credibility, and crisis motivating used too often and out of proportion deadens how people respond. Even if real danger is involved, crisis motivating becomes counterproductive if it anticipates something so enormous it cannot be stopped, requires spending more than everyone together can afford, or requires a degree of cooperation everyone knows is beyond reaching.

There have been other times in history when pressure from a broadly held consensus made levelheaded thinking hard to maintain. Like Athanasius (296–373), who, in the fourth century, defended the eternal existence and sinless nature of Jesus Christ *contra mundum* (against the world), and like the astronomer Galileo Galilei (1564–1642),who, in the sixteenth century, opposed the consensus of his day that insisted the sun orbits the earth, what determines the ethics of global warming today is a matter of reality regardless of how many agree or not. Majority voting has a place in politics but has nothing to do with settling what is true in theology, science, or ethics.

---

[16] Grudem, *Christian Ethics*, 1142 (see chap. 1, n. 67).

Christian ethical thinking about global warming must focus on what really is true regardless of how many choose it, accept it, or prefer it. We must center on God, trust the Word of God, and then think for ourselves. We must not be stampeded by emotion, popular opinion, or fear, and we certainly must not, out of fear, start thinking fallen humans can be trusted with more governing power than is wise to place in anyone's hands (John 2:24–25). We must not "fear what they fear" (Isa 8:12) and should always suspect what sinners in a sinful world rally to (Matt 7:13; Rev 13:8). We should listen to "experts," but never blindly. We should never trust anyone for any reason over the Bible and should not even trust anyone over what we observe for ourselves—things such as natural systems being cyclical, the climate always changing, no one controlling the weather except God, CO_2 being a normal part of the air we breathe and good for crops, and the earth being in a warming cycle ever since glaciers covered half the planet, which means global warming today started long before humans began using fossil fuels.

In the Psalms, we are told, "God is our refuge and strength, a helper who is always found in times of trouble. Therefore we will not be afraid, though the earth trembles and the mountains topple into the depths of the seas, though its water roars and foams and the mountains quake with its turmoil" (Ps 46:1–3). Those who fear God do not fear global catastrophe. Why? Because God controls the natural world no matter what humans do, and this applies to the present fallen world, not a future sinless world, and applies even if catastrophic events occur. This does not license irresponsibility, but it does free us from feeling that survival depends on humans controlling more than is humanly possible.

Recommended further reading on the issue of global warming includes Christopher Essex and Ross McKitrick, *Taken by Storm: The Troubled Science, Policy and Politics of Global Warming* (Toronto, ON: Key Porter, 2007); Christopher Horner, *The Politically Incorrect Guide to Global Warming* (Washington: Regnery, 2007); Bjørn Lomborg, *Cool It* (New York: Knof, 2007); Patrick Michaels, ed., *Shattered Consensus: The True State of Global Warming* (Lanham, MD: Rowman & Littlefield, 2005); William Nordhaus, *A Question of Balance: Weighing the Options on Global Warming Policies* (New Haven, CT: Yale, 2008); Lawrence Solomon, *The Deniers: The World-Renowned Scientists Who Stood Up against Global Warming Hysteria* (Minneapolis, MN: Vigilante, 2008); Roy Spencer, *Global Warming Skepticism for Busy People* (Cornwall Alliance, 2018); and Roy Spencer, *The Great Global Warming Blunder* (New York: Encounter, 2010).

Using Technology

The French theologian and Christian ethicist Jacques Ellul said, "No social, human, or spiritual fact is so important as the fact of technology in the modern world. And yet no subject is so little understood."[17] He did not mean people do not realize life today swims in oceans of technology and did not mean people cannot use iPhones or computers. Rather, Ellul meant that, even though technology pervades our lives, few comprehend how much it affects their thinking, values, and relationships. We easily perceive technology's material effects—how it speeds communication, transportation, and manufacturing and how it increases health, data collection, and crops. But are we aware of how much technology affects ethics, not only when it comes to using it properly, but also when it comes to how it affects moral identity, moral formation, moral judgment, and moral accountability?

What the term *technology* means has changed over time. At first, it just referred to machines that enhance or extend human functions. Then, it was used to indicate any means of improving human efficiency, mechanical or not. But now, it covers even more and refers to any way humans interact with materials to enhance power, control, knowledge, movement, communication, comfort, or health. Thus, *technology* now includes anything from watches to the Internet, from drugs to nuclear weapons, and from artificial reproduction to artificial intelligence.

Other terms related to the subject include *technological*, *technological artifacts*, and *technological systems*. *Technological* is an adjective describing anything to do with developing, using, admiring, or simply cooperating with *technology*. But the adjective covers more than the noun because it can refer to a whole worldview or valuing system and not merely to technologies themselves. *Technological artifacts* are things like water heaters, fans, phones, missiles, TVs, and cars, meaning they are instruments used to enhance or extend human power, control, knowledge, movement, communication, comfort, or health. And *technological systems* are things like sewer lines, water lines, the electric grid, cell towers, and the Internet. They are things enabling *technological artifacts* to function but that usually attract little attention and might be disguised as trees, placed behind walls, or buried underground.

---

[17] Ellul, *The Technological Society*, 3 (see chap. 6, n. 118). In this quotation, I have taken the liberty of translating Ellul's reference to "la technique" as "technology" rather than "technique," because it is understood that what he meant corresponds more nearly to what English speakers mean by "technology."

What technology has achieved in our day has been dazzling. The space program took men to the moon and is exploring the solar system, computers have enhanced everything we do, genetics has increased crops, and iPhones and the Internet have launched an information age connecting the world. Advances have been so amazing and rapid that, for some, faith in technology has supplanted faith in God and possessing the latest device is treated like worship. But, looking past all this, we can see that, although technology increases power and knowledge, it does not increase the character or wisdom of those using it. Ethical judgment is needed because although using technology seems innocuous, it is enormously influential. It not only changes the way people communicate, shop, travel, work, play, and amuse themselves but also influences what people want, value, or even believe. It enhances ability to calculate, collect data, heal, fabricate, and disseminate information but also makes people vulnerable to new sorts of criminal activity (identity theft, mass shootings) and to deadlier accidents (airplane crashes, gas explosions).

The ethics of using technology has two components. We must assess how to use technology ethically and also must assess how using technology affects us ethically. The first starts with realizing every new ability acquired raises questions never asked before and requires controlling of a sort never needed before. For example, reproductive technologies are causing us to ask questions about what constitutes adultery. Does a third party technician performing the procreative act in a petri dish violate something unique to marriage even if the gametes come from a married couple and even if there is no genital contact? And examples of technologies calling for new controls include the accessibility of pornography to kids surfing the Internet, identity theft threatening financial security, driverless cars threatening new and different accidents, and drones programmed to kill as well as take photographs. Lewis observed, "Each new power won *by* man is a power *over* man as well" and "each advance leaves him weaker as well as stronger."[18] New technologies make life easier, faster, and more entertaining but also make errors more disastrous, accidents more deadly, and privacy harder to maintain.

Assessing how to use technology ethically is not enough because we also need to assess how using various technologies affects us ethically. Technology is not only a set of tools but also a set of life-shaping forces. The institutions of home, school, and church used to be the primary ways moral values got passed on from one generation to the next. But now the

---

[18] C. S. Lewis, *The Abolition of Man* (New York: Macmillan, 1947), 71 (emphasis his).

internet and electronic devices have become the main shapers of how most people think, feel, and make decisions about what is good, bad, or desirable—not just commercially but ethically. Using technology influences moral identity by drawing minds out of the real world into a virtual one in which they are ethically anonymous and detached, given a false sense of independence, allured by a sense of virtual transcendence, and have their sense of moral location shifted from shared values in a real-world community to a perceived sharing of values in an online community that is mostly imaginary.

Using technology also affects moral accountability, moral influence, and moral thinking. Ironically, it affects moral accountability in ways that are less and more at the same time. Accountability is less because anonymity on the Internet makes it less personal, less direct, and less likely. But accountability can also, in a way, be more because cyber cancel culture generates a sort of alternate accountability that is overwhelmingly intense, unforgiving, and sometimes deadly. New communication technologies extend moral influence globally, and this makes ethical witnessing quicker and more extensive. But terrorists can use it that way as well and, even when used for good, moral influence on the World Wide Web is less profound and life changing than personal witnessing and discipleship. While technology can disseminate moral truth, it can also corrupt how people think not just with moral lies but also in other more subtle ways, like making moral thought less analytical, more reactionary, and more emotional as well as reducing notions of "goodness" to efficiency and maximal output, leaving out righteousness, justice, holiness, and wisdom. Understanding this leads to asking, "Are we controlling technology or is technology controlling us?" "What is technology's proper place and how do we keep it there?" "Is it possible to use technology for good and in good ways while keeping it from being used for bad and in bad ways?" "How do we stay in control of how we use it and avoid bad effects?"

For Christians, the ethics of using technology grows out of understanding how it relates to the doctrines of creation, sin, and redemption. In terms of creation, technology is part of fulfilling God's mandate to "subdue" the earth (Gen 1:28). At creation, God put us in charge of developing, using, and managing the natural world. God did not intend that we simply enjoy things as they were without changing anything. Although we are not licensed to abuse things, God wants us to bring things under control, and doing that includes developing and using technologies that help us cure diseases, grow better crops, travel faster, and communicate more effectively. In terms of sin, technology is affected by the Fall that corrupted human nature

(Rom 5:17–19) and by the curse that made life difficult (Gen 3:17–19; 5:29). The Bible shows that technology can be used for bad (building the tower of Babel, Gen 11:1–9) as well as for good (building the ark, Gen 6:9–22), can compete with faith in God (Isa 31:1–3) as well as enhance it (1 Kgs 6:1–38), and can be used to kill and destroy (Isa 3:25; Joel 3:10) as well as to guard and protect (2 Chr 14:7; Isa 62:6). In terms of redemption, technology not only can be used to reduce present dangers (Deut 22:8) but also will be repurposed and shifted from destructive to constructive uses in Christ's millennial kingdom (Isa 2:4; Mic 4:3).

The Bible also teaches that just because something is permissible does not mean it is necessarily "beneficial" (1 Cor 6:12; 1 Cor 10:23), "builds up" (1 Cor 10:23), or cannot master you (1 Cor 6:12). So even if using a technology is permissible, we need to think about how it can be misused and, even if using it is not necessarily wrong, it could be that using a certain technology incurs risks that make using it unwise or dangerous—if not for all, then perhaps for children under a certain age, people without adequate training, or those lacking self-discipline.

The Bible treats technology as morally neutral in itself but also powerful in ways that can be used for good or bad or in ways that can have good or bad effects depending on the character, motives, and maturity of those using it. Technology is a tool, and human motives and ways of using technology can be good or bad even though the tool is itself benign. Technology itself is neither moral nor immoral. But technology can be developed for good or bad reasons, can be used for good or bad purposes, and can be used in good or bad ways. It can be developed and used in order to deceive, steal, reduce freedom, invade privacy, and promote false worship. Or it can be developed and used to glorify God, resist death and disease, create beauty, support families, minister to people in need, and spread the gospel. It can be used foolishly, carelessly, irresponsibly, and dangerously, or it can be used wisely, carefully, responsibly, and safely.

The difference is a matter of character, and limiting technology to good uses and preventing bad uses requires self-discipline in personal life and regulation in social life, both of which require understanding human nature in realistic biblical terms. Because human beings are fallen and finite, we must accept and act on the fact that no power in human hands can be trusted without setting boundaries that permit using it well but hinder using it badly. Failing to understand, accept, and act on this leaves individuals and groups vulnerable to technological manipulation and makes advances in technology threatening as well as promising. The key to this applied ethical issue lies in understanding and controlling ourselves and not in anything technological. The ethics of using technology is not itself technological. It is personal, relational, and spiritual because ethics cannot be reduced to a program, ethical problems are not solved by technology, and no technology will ever replace cultivating wisdom, character, and self-control.

Recommended further reading on the issue of using technology includes Albert Borgmann, *Technology and the Character of Contemporary Life* (Chicago: University of Chicago, 1984); Brian Brock, *Christian Ethics in a Technological Age* (Grand Rapids: Eerdmans, 2010); Andy Crouch, *The Tech-Wise Family: Everyday Steps for Putting Technology in Its Proper Place* (Grand Rapids: Baker, 2017); Jacques Ellul, *The Technological Society* (New York: Vintage, 1964); Jeff Orlowski, Davis Coombe, and Vickie Curtis, *The Social Dilemma* (Netflix, September 9, 2020); Sherry Turkle, *Reclaiming Conversation: The Power of Talk in a Digital Age* (New York: Penguin, 2015); and Carl R. Trueman, *The Rise and Triumph of the Modern Self* (Wheaton, IL: Crossway, 2020).

Engaging Culture

Engaging culture is the last applied issue covered in this book. There are similarities between it and the last issue, but they are not the same. Being technological can characterize culture, but technologies are not culture because artifacts are not culture. Culture is not a thing but a way of thinking, just as ethics is not a thing but a way of thinking. In fact, culture and ethics are connected because ethics is central to culture. Culture is more than ethics, but ethics is the hub from which valuing in a culture emanates. It is the part without which no culture exists. But, although artifacts are not culture itself, artifacts can and often do express or convey culture.

Culture refers to a system of beliefs, values, and behaviors characterizing a people group, and basic to it is a worldview that shapes how they interpret ethics, reality, and whatever gives them a shared sense of identity, meaning, purpose, and continuity. *Worldview* is the conceptional lens through which people interpret reality, understand the meaning and significance of all they do and experience, and make moral decisions. Without a worldview there is no ethics, and without ethics there is no culture. Every worldview produces ethics, and every ethic applied to living in society produces culture. Engaging culture, thus, refers to interacting with, participating in, or trying to influence the worldview and ethical system shaping the shared values, identity, behaviors, and thought patterns characterizing a people group.

Engaging culture requires understanding the nature of culture, and that involves at least five features. First, we must understand that culture is fabricated, meaning it is made up and does not occur naturally. This does not mean that the worldview and ethic culture builds on must be made up. There is a true worldview and true ethic, and people in a culture may not realize what they build on is made up. While the worldview and ethic in culture are not always made up, they often are (Rom 1:21). So dealing with the question is crucial when engaging culture. Second, we need to understand that culture is integrated, meaning it is not random. Something holds it together, and culture cannot be engaged effectively without finding the integrating principle. Third, we must realize culture is intergenerational, meaning it is passed on from one generation to another. Engaging culture affects future generations and not just people we are talking to. Fourth, we must understand that culture is comprehensive, meaning it is not partial. It affects everything in life. And, fifth, when engaging culture, we must understand that it is not morally neutral. Culture includes some matters of taste (such as cooking, crafts, styles, and whether men shave or not) that are morally neutral. But, more importantly, they also always include things that are not morally neutral such as a shared worldview and way of framing ethical thought.

Engaging culture effectively not only requires understanding the nature of culture but also understanding how engaging culture is different from similar issues. First, engaging culture is not the same as the interaction of church and state. Church and state are institutions, and culture is a way of thinking and valuing. These issues overlap because culture influences how institutions operate. But institutions do not define or control culture, and culture concerns more than institutions. Second, engaging culture is not the same as the interaction of politics and religion. Again, these issues are associated, but politics and religion are spheres of life and culture covers life as a whole. Like religion, culture assumes a worldview, and, like politics, culture involves community. But religion and politics have governing powers, and culture operates on social pressure. Third, engaging culture is not the same as the interaction of philosophy and theology. At least, it is not the same unless people treat philosophy as dogma. Then, what started as theory takes on worldview status and can become the valuing basis of culture. But, if that happens, philosophy becomes theology, and there is no distinction. The issues are not the same because philosophy and theology are different categories of thought, and engaging culture disputes a single category, which is the worldview and ethic characterizing a people group.

Fourth, engaging culture is not the same as debating what is secular or sacred because engaging culture disputes the distinction. There can be an alleged difference but no ultimate difference between secular and sacred because cultures are religious even when denying it. A culture can be highly Christian or highly non-Christian and can be highly religious in a traditional way (as in Catholic culture, Islamic culture, or Hindu culture) or highly secular in the sense of rejecting traditional religions. But, even when rejecting traditional religions, culture always assumes religion-like, value-framing authority over members of a people group. Culture always functions religiously in the worldview-ethics sense even when denying it.

God inaugurated culture when he ordered Adam and Eve to "be fruitful, multiply, fill the earth, and subdue it" (Gen 1:28). Theologians call this the "cultural mandate" because it includes creating community, social systems, and expressions of culture. God wants humans to create culture. But, when Adam and Eve disobeyed, their sin perverted human nature (Rom 5:17–19; Gal 5:19–21), and since then culture has been disordered because human nature is disordered. Since the fall, cultures can become better or worse, but the sort of culture sinners produce is never sinless and is often terribly wicked (Gen 6:5), even when impressive in other ways (Gen 4:17–22). Nevertheless, God values culture and wants to redeem it. Eating and drinking "for the glory of God" (1 Cor 10:31) are cultural patterns disciplined to please God, and culture will be part of the new heaven and new earth (Isa 65:21–23; Rev 21:10–14, 26), even though "everything in the world . . . . is passing away" (1 John 2:16–17).

H. Richard Niebuhr (1894–1962), in his classic book *Christ and Culture*, discusses five positions on Christianity and culture—Christ against culture, Christ of culture, Christ above culture, Christ and culture in paradox, and Christ the transformer of culture.[19] Niebuhr's five positions are often mentioned when discussing Christians relating to culture but are nearly as often misconstrued. They are not "strategies" for different circumstances, not "reactions" to different experiences, not "attitudes" expressing different feelings, and certainly are not "ideals." They are best interpreted as "views" on how Christian ethical thinking relates to the value-shaping power of culture in present world circumstances. "Christ," in Niebuhr's five views, is not the Church, or religion, or theology, and "culture," in his five views, is not the

---

[19] H. Richard Niebuhr, *Christ and Culture* (New York: Harper and Row, 1951). Readers should not confuse H. Richard Niebuhr with Reinhold Niebuhr, covered in chapter 6. They were brothers, with Reinhold being two years older than H. Richard. Both Niebuhrs were theologians who contributed to Christian ethical thought. But Reinhold was the more important figure being more widely read, more influential, and more sought after than H. Richard. *Christ and Culture* was H. Richard's only truly notable book, and Reinhold wrote many more.

state, or politics, or philosophy (even though these are affected). The views listed are ways of thinking Christian ethics ought to impact culture and, as such, have influenced how people holding them behave. They do not stand for what necessarily happens or would be ideal.

The main idea of the Christ against culture view is that there is one true ethic, Christians are the only ones who follow it, culture is hopelessly evil, and Christians must separate from culture and not try to improve it because it is a waste of time or doing so will corrupt us. Examples of people holding this view include Tertullian (c. 155–c. 220) in the early Church, Leo Tolstoy (1828–1910), and groups like the Mennonites, Quakers, and Amish. Criticisms of the view are that no one, not even proponents, is able to avoid culture completely, and it mistakenly assumes sin exists only in culture and not in Christians, clashes with Jesus sending us into the world (John 17:15–18), and leaves culture unchanged.

The main idea of the Christ of culture view is that there is a single reasonable ethic, and non-Christians understand it as well as or better than Christians, Christians should accommodate culture even at the cost of abandoning the Bible, and, if not, Christianity will become irrelevant. Examples of people holding this view include Gnostics in the early Church, Fredrich Schleiermacher (1768–1834), Albrecht Ritschl (1822–1889), Walter Rauschenbusch (1861–1918), and the social gospel movement. Criticisms of the view are that it distorts the biblical Jesus, denies biblical inerrancy, redefines sin, is naïve about human nature, follows the spirit of the world instead of the Spirit of God, and leaves culture unchanged.

The main idea of the Christ above culture view is that there is only one true ethic and Christians should take over and control culture in the name of God because only they know and follow the ethic on which God wants culture to operate. Examples of people holding this view include the Medieval Roman Catholic Church, Aquinas (1225–1274), Richard Baxter (1615–1691), and the Massachusetts Bay Colony (1628–1691). Criticisms of the view are that it preempts Christ in the name of ruling for Christ; does not accept how radically sin affects everyone, including Christians; substitutes coercion for conversion; confuses Christian community with living in mixed society; and is fragmentary because life in fallen circumstances never aligns with God perfectly no matter who governs or how much force is used.

The main idea of the Christ and culture in paradox view is that the world operates on two contrary ethics—one for the Christian community (operating on love without law) and one for non-Christian culture (operating on law without love)—that Christians live under both as they move in and out of the world for work and trade, and that the ethic of Christian community does not apply to culture and the ethic of culture does not apply to Christian community. Examples of people holding this view include Marcion in the early Church (85–160), Luther (1483–1546), the Lutheran church, Yoder (1927–1997), Martin Marty (b. 1928), and Hauerwas (b. 1940). Criticisms of the view are that it clashes with the self-consistency of God, denies the unity of moral law, requires Christians to live by contrary ethical systems, and leaves culture unchanged.

The main idea of the Christ the transformer of culture view is that there is only one true ethic and culture is fallen and compromised. But, while God does not want believers to impose his moral rule on nonbelievers, and while culture cannot be perfected before Jesus returns, it is possible even now to improve the ethics of culture as Christians participate and win converts. Examples of people holding this view include Augustine (354–430), Calvin (1509–1564), Wesley (1703–1791), and most Evangelicals today. It accepts the fallenness of culture while believing Christians can make a difference, recognizes the sovereignty of God without taking over ourselves, affirms the unity and universality of Christian ethics without substituting coercion for conversion, and does not confuse perfecting culture before Jesus comes back with the perfection God credits us based on faith in Christ. Niebuhr did not criticize this view because it most aligns with biblical Christianity.

If God cares about culture, why does he allow it to grow better or worse? The answer is the same as for why God allows individual people to grow better or worse. God wants us to have a heart for him (2 Chr 16:9), and heartedness is corporate (Jer 29:13–14) as well as individual. Culture is the collective heart of a people group. Improving culture does not save anyone because people are not saved collectively. Engaging culture is important because culture can lead to or away from Christ, and it functions that way because culture influences hearts as well as minds. Our collective lives will not matter at the "judgment seat of Christ" (2 Cor 5:10), but it is part of how God directs history (Job 12:23). Cultures rise and fall according to moral strength (Lev 18:24–28), and God lets it happen because he wants the collective hearts of people groups to seek (love) him just as he wants the hearts of individual people to seek (love) him. Furthermore, collective hearts cannot be coerced any more than individual hearts. Whether individual or collective, heart orientation is voluntary, and improving it is cultivated by moral influence more than mandated. Laws can align with or oppose the process. But laws only affect external behavior, and changing hearts, whether individual or collective, is a matter of redirecting desire.

Schaeffer (1912–1984) passed away in 1984 and was, at that time, the greatest prophetic voice of our day. His last book, *The Great Evangelical Disaster*, challenged Evangelicals not to accommodate culture on worldview and ethics. Schaeffer had earlier challenged Evangelicals to engage culture on both accounts, but his last challenge went the other way. Evangelicals heeded Schaeffer's earlier call, but some took it the wrong way. So Schaeffer challenged us not to confuse "engaging" culture with "accommodating" culture. Christian ethics should change culture and not the other way around. "Truth," he said, "*demands* confrontation; loving confrontation, but confrontation nevertheless. If our reflex action is always accommodation regardless of the centrality of the truth involved, there is something wrong."[20] Since then, Evangelicals have been active on many issues but not consistently and not without ever accommodating. Schaeffer's last challenge is as relevant as ever, and we must take it seriously for three reasons—because Jesus tells us to (Matt 10:16), it is our role in the world (Phil 2:15), and obligation to engage without accommodating culture will not cease until Jesus comes back (Matt 24:12–14).

Recommended further reading on the issue of engaging culture includes Augustine, *De civitate Dei* (*The City of God*); Emile Cailliet, *The Christian Approach to Culture* (Nashville: Abingdon, 1953); Greg Forster, *The Contested Public Square* (Downers Grove, IL: InterVarsity, 2008); Os Guinness, *The American Hour* (New York: Free Press, 1993); Carl F. H. Henry, *Twilight of a Great Civilization* (Westchester, IL: Crossway, 1988); James Davison Hunter, *Culture Wars* (New York: BasicBooks, 1991); Richard John Neuhaus, *The Naked Public Square* (Grand Rapids: Eerdmans, 1984); H. Richard Niebuhr, *Christ and Culture* (New York: Harper & Row, 1851); Oliver O'Donovan, *Common Objects of Love* (Grand Rapids: Eerdmans, 2002); Francis A. Schaeffer, *The Great Evangelical Disaster* (Wheaton, IL: Crossway, 1984); Henry R. Van Til, *The Calvinistic Concept of Culture* (Philadelphia: P&R, 1959).

Conclusion

This concludes the present chapter covering social issues having to do with the world or humanity as a whole. In this chapter, we considered racism, slavery, human trafficking, creation care, global warming, using technology, and engaging culture. These issues might seem diverse, but they all concern social issues larger than those just affecting families,

---

[20] Schaeffer, *The Great Evangelical Disaster*, 64 (see chap. 3, n. 25).

neighborhoods, or nations. There are more such issues we might have covered, issues like the ethics of international trade, international peacekeeping, or international food safety, and more such issues will emerge, like the ethics of militarizing space or mining other planets. We have treated global issues that are most relevant for now, and future books will address more as they become relevant or pressing.

This also concludes the section in this book introducing applied Christian ethics as an academic subfield within the larger field of Christian ethics. There is more to Christian ethics than applied issues because the field also includes biblical, theological, historical, and philosophical subfields. But applied Christian ethics is the largest subfield as measured by the attention scholars give it. Indeed, that is why we have given more chapters to it than the rest. Applied Christian ethics also is the *most practically useful* subfield because it is "where the rubber meets the road," meaning it deals with living life and not just thinking about it.

This last section started with a chapter dealing with a single very important issue—truth, lying, and faithful communicating—and then treated other applied issues by dividing the subfield into further subcategories—personal ethics, sexual ethics, social ethics having to do with governing, and social ethics having to do with the world.[21] This further subdividing of the subfield exhausts the possibilities, meaning there are no more subdivisions. More applied issues could be covered, and others will emerge. But there are no more subdivisions in applied Christian ethics because what structures God's ethical reality stays the same and nothing else exists. At least, there is no more to it now, and we will see if God has more in store in the "new heaven and . . . new earth" (Rev 21:1) when he makes "everything new" (Rev 21:5).

---

[21] Truth, lying, and faithful communicating is not a separate subdivision, but I am not sure where it best fits because it affects so much else. We could list it with personal ethics. But, of course, truth-telling matters to social as much as to personal life. And, if someone argues it must be a social issue, we might counter by noting it always involves personal integrity. Perhaps then we should acknowledge truth-telling straddles the personal-social divide the same as issues in sexual life. Truth-telling is not sexual. But it straddles the personal-social divide the same way. Thus, if pressed, I would list truth-telling along with issues in sexual life. Neither deserves treating as a different applied category on par with the personal-social divide. It simply is the case that neither truth-telling nor issues in sexual life are entirely personal or entirely social. Truth-telling and issues in sexual life both "straddle the fence."

REFLECTIONS

Schaeffer (1912–1984), in his last book, *The Great Evangelical Disaster*, challenged Evangelicals not to accommodate "the world spirit of our age."[1] He did this because it is the greatest possible threat to living the Christian life and, thus, to biblically faithful Christian ethics. Because it opposes "biblical truth and morality in the full spectrum of life," Schaeffer declared, "*to accommodate to the world spirit about us in our age is the most gross form of worldliness.*"[2] This is not extreme but exactly what the Bible says: "Do not love the world or the things in the world. If anyone loves the world, the love of the Father is not in him. For everything in the world—the lust of the flesh, the lust of the eyes, and the pride in one's possessions—is not from the Father, but is from the world" (1 John 2:15–16).

We are left in the world (John 17:15) to engage it as salt and light (Matt 5:13–16). This means interacting with sinners and sin (1 Cor 5:9–10), which puts us at risk of contamination and needing to be cleansed (John 13:10)—not for salvation but to keep channels open with God (1 John 1:9). But engaging sinners and sin in the present fallen world must not be confused with shifting the moral compass we live by. Ethical truth and reality is an "all or nothing" proposition: "If anyone loves the world, the love of the Father is not in him" (1 John 2:15). As a wheel cannot rotate around two hubs at once, so God's moral compass and what the world uses do not mix. They cannot be used at the same time. There is only one hub, and

---

[1] Schaeffer, *The Great Evangelical Disaster*, 37.
[2] Schaeffer, 37, 141, 142.

accommodating the spirit of this world any way at all is total infidelity to God. We must stand on one side or the other.

Deciding whether to please God or the world—whether to operate on biblically faithful Christian ethics or to operate on what the world uses—is a matter of heart orientation, something the Bible refers to as "love." This is not a sentiment but a desiring. What orients the ethics we use is a "want" that determines valuing everything else. Heart-orientating "love" aligns ethical thinking and behavior. It determines around which hub our ethical valuing rotates. And the problem we have is that, since the fall perverted human nature, our hearts are "more deceitful than anything else" (Jer 17:9). Left to themselves, our hearts aim at loving the wrong thing. The spirit of the world loves the flesh, and true ethics requires loving God rather than the flesh. The spirit of the world can be overcome only by cleansing our hearts "from every impurity of the flesh and spirit, bringing holiness to completion in the fear of God" (2 Cor 7:1).

The challenge is learning to want what God wants. We must cultivate hearts that love God over the world, heaven over earth, the Word of God over the flesh, and then value everything else in view of the ethics-orienting love we have for God. Jesus said, "Where your treasure is, there your heart will be also" (Matt 6:21), meaning what we ultimately want (treasure) reveals the ethic we live by. And what that is makes a huge difference because "the one who trusts in himself is a fool" (Prov 28:26) and "happy are those who . . . seek him [God] with all their heart" (Ps 119:2).

Christians have struggled throughout history to understand how the spirit of the world works against the Spirit of God, as both claim to define what distinguishes good from evil, ethical reality from ethical nonreality, and true moral thinking from false moral thinking. The contest started in Eden when the Devil tempted Eve to doubt God's goodness by asking, "Did God really say?" (Gen 3:1). Understanding what the contest involves and how to deal with it has occupied theologians for centuries and, other than the Bible, the greatest treatise on this contest has been Augustine's *The City of God*.

Augustine (354–430) interpreted the ethical flow of history in terms of two cities competing with each other. These cities are not the same as church and state because Augustine was not thinking of institutions but of the ethical clash between living for God and living for the world. He thought about how a God-centered ethic conflicts with a man-centered ethic and saw that what distinguishes them reduces to opposing "loves" in the heart-orientation sense.

He explained that these cities are "formed by two loves: the earthly by the love of self, even to the contempt of God; the heavenly by the love of God, even to the contempt of self."[3] They are opposing views of ethical reality, one framed by a this-worldly man-centered "love" and one framed by an other-worldly God-centered love.

But, while these "loves" both integrate life with others (they are cities), they are orientations that compete within every human heart. And, although Augustine knew philosophers propose different ethical systems, the difference he had in mind only concerned how loving God competes with any ethic framed by this-worldly "love." In his words, "There have arisen no more than two classes, as it were, of human society . . . . a city of men who choose to live carnally, and another of those who choose to live spiritually, each aiming at its own kind of peace."[4] Augustine realized that the loyalty contest between the spirit of the world and the Spirit of God not only affects integrating life with other people but also affects integrating life inside each of us. The two cities compete for dominance and loyalty within every heart, whether collective or individual.

Once, while serving as Deputy Assistant Secretary of the Navy for Manpower, I attended a banquet celebrating the birthday of the United States Navy and was seated next to the three-star admiral responsible for all recruiting, force structure, training, education, and discipline for both the US Navy and US Marine Corps. We started chatting politely, but the conversation got deeper on learning we had two things in common. We shared an interest in ethics and found we had served in the Tonkin Gulf during the Vietnam War at exactly the same time—I as a junior officer on one ship and he as commanding officer of another.

These connections led him to share how he learned something related to ethics in those days. Officers commanding Navy ships at sea hold something called "captain's mast," which combines the disciplinary role a father has in a family mixed with the role a judge has in criminal proceedings. This admiral told me how a captain's mast he conducted in the Tonkin Gulf during the Vietnam War opened his eyes to how the ethical landscape in American life was changing to the degree that military training needed revising. A young sailor was charged with stealing a "boombox" (a now obsolete form of entertainment technology) off another sailor's rack (bed) while the owner was taking a shower. When the owner

---

[3] Augustine, *The City of God*, XIV.28.
[4] Augustine, XIV.1.

found it missing, a search was conducted, and the missing boombox was discovered in this other sailor's locker.

At captain's mast the guilty sailor admitted everything, but the interesting thing was he had no idea what was wrong with what he had done. He had grown up in the inner city where it was assumed anything unattended is fair game and "stealing" only occurs when breaking in and taking something locked up. The admiral sharing this told me that captain's mast back in 1973 made him realize the Navy could no longer assume new recruits understand how to think ethically and convinced him Navy training had to start at a more basic level in order to build the good order and discipline military life requires. Addressing that became his career focus, and when we chatted, he was in charge of getting it done. That conversation took place in 1992, and since then, ethical breakdown in our culture has only gotten worse.

Another illustration of how ethical thinking in American culture has shifted occurred after I left government service and had been teaching at Southeastern Baptist Theological Seminary for more than twenty years. In 2017, I was asked to give a lecture at the Defense Intelligence Agency (DIA) as part of an ethical leadership series. I lectured on "The Greatest Military Leadership Challenge of Our Day: Cultivating the Warrior Ethic Sustaining Military Power," and it was well received and got broadcast globally. The audience was military and secular, and the main idea was that the sacrificial ethic on which military success depends cannot be cultivated unless military members resist trends in the culture and are loyal to a moral authority greater than their own appetites. National security ultimately depends on military members living for something worth dying for—something transcending personal survival—and, while religion secures that sort of ethic, contemporary culture does not.

Military commanders are limited by the separation of church and state and cannot tell soldiers and sailors what religion to affirm. But they also cannot cultivate a warrior ethic unless soldiers and sailors believe in something more than their appetites and personal survival. So the best commanders can do is work with chaplains to support whatever faith military members have in something greater than themselves. The challenge I presented was something George Washington understood and warned the nation to consider in the *Farewell Address* he delivered in 1796 after twenty years of distinguished public service:

Let us with caution indulge the supposition that morality can be maintained without religion. Whatever may be conceded to the influence of refined education on minds of peculiar structure, reason and experience both forbid us to expect that national morality can prevail in exclusion of religious principle.[5]

This message was taken to heart by the DIA in 2017. But the same message was deemed dangerously inappropriate two years later in 2019 when a colleague and I were asked to prepare seminars to help military leaders address why good order and discipline was breaking down in the United States Special Operations Command (USSOCOM). Writing this book was set aside for a month as I prepared, and the military leaders in charge were enthusiastic and kept expanding whom they wanted us to reach, not just in one region but across the nation. Then one week before starting, a military lawyer asked to review what I prepared and cancelled the whole thing. The message was exactly as presented at the DIA, and, in either case, I went no further than agreeing with George Washington. But the training I prepared for USSOCOM got cancelled because it clashed with a newly preferred ethical paradigm that now would cancel George Washington himself. The point is that the ethical climate in today's world is shifting and shifting rapidly. What was taken to heart in 2017 was deemed dangerously inappropriate in 2019. Our nation is becoming hostile toward the worldview and values on which it was founded. Christians can still influence non-Christians outside the Church, but it is getting harder.

This book is meant to resource courses introducing Christian ethics to ministerial students. But it is written in a way I hope appeals to more than scholars. It deals with scholarship but in a way that makes profound ideas easy to understand by any reader, including parents, teenagers, and interested laypeople. Academic references are made in footnotes, and further reading is suggested for those needing more. This book is unique because, although others introduce Christian ethics, this is the only one that introduces the entire field. Previous works have introduced biblical ethics, theological ethics, the history of Christian ethics, philosophical theories assessed from a Christian point of view, and applied ethics. But this is the first written introducing all of these together.

The first chapters dealt with the field overall—what Christian ethics means, what makes it important, what makes it different, how it has subcategories and has characteristic features. Later chapters introduced field subcategories—biblical ethics, theological ethics, historical

---

[5] George Washington, *Farewell Address*, September 19, 1796.

ethics, philosophical ethics, and applied ethics. Some previous introductions deal with the historical component and bypass the rest, and others deal with other components and bypass history. This book surveys the history of Christian ethics comprehensively but succinctly, leaving greater coverage to specialized publications. Yet, in doing that, this book brings the history of Christian ethics up-to-date and covers things others leave out. Protestants usually leave out Catholic doctrine, Catholics usually leave out Protestant doctrine, and this text gives readers a complete picture of how Christians have dealt with ethics through history. But even doing that succinctly required two chapters.

The last subcategory dealt with was applied Christian ethics, and five chapters were needed to introduce the full range of applied issues now challenging moral witness in the world. This could have been shortened but not without defeating the book's purpose, which is to train and resource Christians engaging the world in moral witness. New issues are emerging all the time (like transgenderism, human trafficking, and using technology), and it was important to address these along with perennial issues (like adultery, prostitution, and abortion). One perennial issue with a complex title—truth, lying, and faithful communicating—was given a chapter to itself. That was because true communicating affects so much else, and the Church has always been deeply divided on the issue—not between biblical Christians and those forsaking the Bible but between Bible-believing Christians on both sides. This book has tried not only to help readers understand that division but also to resolve it in a God-centered, biblical way.

This book is written with the future in mind. It is meant to resource ethical understanding, convictions, and faithfulness in days to come when standing against cultural pressures will be harder than today. The Church in America, and perhaps the world, is heading toward persecution that will focus on what ethic has priority and how it applies. Christians will be pressured to abandon biblically faithful Christian ethics and to redefine what they believe or adopt something else, and those taking neither option will be pressured to keep silent. We should not be surprised because Jesus said this would happen: "They will hand you over to be persecuted, and they will kill you. You will be hated by all nations because of my name. Then many will fall away, betray one another, and hate one another" (Matt 24:9–10).

Many cultural "Christians" will stop pretending and openly reject Christian ethics, and so few will remain. Jesus asked, "When the Son of Man comes, will he find faith on earth?" (Luke 18:8). This is worth examining. The "faith" referred to is not merely believing God exists and, rather, indicates people who are "saved." Jesus also was not referring simply to people going to heaven but to people who accept and practice God-pleasing Christian ethics. The question Jesus asked really was, "Will anyone still accept and practice God-pleasing Christian ethics when I come back?" He was not suggesting there might be no faithful Christians remaining at all when he returns because then no one would be left to rapture alive (Matt 24:40–41). Rather, Jesus was saying that when he returns, very few will be left who still take God seriously enough to accept and practice God-pleasing Christian ethics. Nearly all will have forsaken real ethics to go along with what the world considers ethical "progress." The problem with that, however, is that what sinners consider ethical "progress" is regression in the eyes of God (Isa 51:7–8).

Even though many will abandon faithful Christian ethics, those who do not will make a huge difference. Their fidelity under persecution will inspire many to reaffirm true ethical reality. Addressing what will happen during a worst-in-history persecution that will occur just before the end, Daniel says, "Those who have insight will shine like the bright expanse of the heavens, and those who lead many to righteousness, like the stars forever and ever" (Dan 12:3). Christian ethics will be the pivot point in a great awakening that will occur during persecution just before Jesus comes back. Stars never shine so bright as against a black sky, and Christians resisting moral compromise under persecution will "lead many to righteousness," righteousness being how the Bible refers to ethical purity. Peter adds, "The end of all things is near, therefore, be alert and sober-minded" (1 Pet 4:7), which means, in view of what lies ahead, get serious about resisting ethical compromise. This book is written to help with that.

Proverbs 4:18 says, "The path of the righteous is like the light of dawn, shining brighter and brighter until midday." This verse says being ethical as God views it involves a course in life that becomes ever more ethically worthy, ethically mature, ethically knowing, and ethically complete. Even now, we should expect to make progress toward an ethical perfection transcending our natural state because it seeks aligning with God's character and is empowered supernaturally. Living the Christian life progresses toward an ethical perfection we reflect but do not generate. It is something expressed in us but is not of us. Which is to say we become more clearly and truly perfect as we more clearly and truly manifest the character of him whose image we bear. The "midday" in Proverbs 4:18 (translated in the KJV as "the perfect day") indicates God's infinite perfection and, therefore, suggests that our growing ethical perfection will continue forever. Jesus touched on this as well when saying a time will come when "the righteous will shine like the sun in their Father's kingdom" (Matt 13:43). Someday we will "shine like the sun," but that shining will not be static.

The ethical perfection manifested through us in that day will be sinless but not infinite. Only God is infinitely perfect, and our perfection will be finite even after we are sinless. What these verses say is that people who reign with Christ in "their Father's kingdom" will keep growing in greater and greater conformity with God's ethical perfection forever. It is an increasing ethical perfection that Proverbs 4:18 refers to as "the light of dawn shining brighter and brighter." The process never ends because we can never cease approaching God's infinite perfection. We will reflect God's infinite perfection better and better as we approach it more and more nearly, and our increasing ethical perfection will not cease, not because sin remains, but because God's perfection is infinite and ours never is. In approaching the sun of God's infinite ethical perfection, we will never be the sun no matter how much our perfection increases despite continuing forever.

This book explains that path, but it is just a start, merely an introduction to something so grand it has no end and will never cease. If you are on the path, enjoy the journey. If you have not started, I hope this book motivates you to get started.

> *"Now may the God of peace, who brought up from the dead our Lord Jesus—the great Shepherd of the sheep—through the blood of the everlasting covenant, equip you with everything good to do his will, working in us what is pleasing in his sight, through Jesus Christ, to whom be glory forever and ever. Amen."*
> Hebrews 13:20–21

Soli Deo gloria

APPENDICES

APPENDIX A

CHRISTIAN ETHICS & BIBLICAL WORSHIP

This appendix supplements Chapter 3 by adding more to a full understanding of biblical ethics. Chapter 3 introduces readers to biblical ethics as an academic subcategory in the field of Christian ethics and stresses the foundational importance of biblical scholarship to the whole enterprise. But there is more we could have covered, and something we should consider in more detail is how the Bible treats ethics and worship as one and the same. Real Christian ethics as portrayed in the Bible and worship as portrayed in the Bible are not just connected but the same. Nothing about one is separate from or different than the other.

This is rarely addressed either in biblical scholarship or in Christian ethics.[1] But it should be. I did not say much on this before, but the connection was there. It was observable in how biblical ethics starts with God, centers on God, is accountable to God, and fulfills God's purposes, and it was observable, as well, when discussing how the first commandment frames ethics on having no "other gods besides me" (Exod 20:3). Readers should, therefore, already know biblical ethics is impossible without biblical worship and biblical worship is impossible

---

[1] A refreshing exception to this is *Ethics as Worship: Moral Discipleship to the Glory of God*, by my colleagues Liederbach and Lenow (see chap. 2, n. 1).

without biblical ethics. We now will examine how that is, starting with a general review of the topic, then showing how the biblical languages treat ethics and worship as one thing, then showing how biblical theology does as well, and then closing with comments on what this implies.

General Review of Ethics & Worship in the Bible

Things motivating people to worship God include his character, nature, and actions. God's holiness, lovingkindness, wisdom, truthfulness, and goodness motivate worship (Isa 6:3; Ps 115:1; 118:1–4; Rev 4:8), and affirming these amounts to affirming his ethical character. And, of God's character qualities, the one most inspiring worship affirming his character is God's holiness (Exod 15:11; 1 Chron 16:29; Ps 29:2; 96:9). God's glory, greatness, renown, eternality, invisibility, power, inapproachability, and fearsomeness motivate worship as well (Deut 32:3; 1 Chr 16:29; Ps 29:1–2; 68:34; 117:1–2; 1 Tim 1:17; 6:15–16), and affirming these amounts to lining up with God's authority. Finally, God's creation, revelation, protection, provision, and salvation also motivate worship (Ps 116:17; 118:1; Rev 4:11), and this last set of motivations amount to gratitude for what God does. Particular actions inspiring worship out of gratitude include supplying needs (Ps 31:19), answering prayers (Isa 64:4), preparing a future (1 Cor 2:9), the pleasure of his presence (Ps 16:11), satisfying (Ps 36:8), and both enlightening and giving life (Ps 36:9). And, of God's actions, the one most inspiring worship out of gratitude is saving us from sin and death (Rev 5:12).

Two observations can be made at this point. First, everything motivating biblical worship reduces to accepting the finality and goodness of God's ethical authority. All worship amounts to affirming God's worthiness to require ethical perfection as a matter of sharing his holiness (Heb 12:10). Second, while worship refers, at times, to "giving" God things (1 Chr 16:29; Ps 29:1–2; 96:8; Rev 5:12), this does not mean worship makes God greater than he is already. God never changes (Num 23:19; Ps 102:27; Mal 3:16; Heb 13:8; Jas 1:17), and giving him "power and riches and wisdom and strength and honor and glory and blessing" (Rev 5:12) only means worshipers recognize who God is, appreciate what God does, and submit to God's authority. Worship does not change God, but it certainly changes us. It changes our ethical standing and character by drawing us closer to him, and drawing closer to God aligns us better to him and makes us better reflections of him in the world.

Worship aligns the heart attitude or moral compass we live by, and true worship aligns all we think, say, do, and desire to the only true God (1 Cor 10:31; Col 3:17; 1 Pet 4:11). Worship aligning the heart attitude or moral compass we live by is what Jesus spoke of when telling the woman at the well, "True worshipers . . . worship the Father in Spirit and in truth" because "God is spirit, and those who worship him must worship in Spirit and in truth" (John 4:23–24). What Jesus meant is that authentic worship (worshiping "in truth") aligns the heart attitude or moral compass we live by on the only God who really exists (worshiping "in Spirit").

While the moral compass we live by is a heart attitude, what comes from it does not stay inside and is expressed in thoughts, words, actions, and desires that bear fruit for (and so reveal) what we worship. This goes wrong in two ways. We cannot worship "in Spirit and in truth" if the connection between inner and outer breaks down, and we cannot worship "in Spirit and in truth" if the moral compass we live by is set to anything other than the only true God. Worshiping other things is false and perverted (not worshiping "in Spirit and in truth"), and getting it right matters because it sets the moral compass we live by.

God said this when explaining that Satan fell from heaven because "your heart became proud" and it "corrupted your wisdom" (Ezek 28:17). Jesus said it when describing how "from the heart come evil thoughts, murders, adulteries, sexual immoralities, thefts, false testimonies, slander" and "these are the things that defile a person" (Matt 15:19–20). And Paul did, too, when saying, "The old self . . . is corrupted by deceitful desires" (Eph 4:22). These statements from different parts of Scripture all affirm how worship aligns the moral compass we live by. Ethical purity requires purity of worship, and false worship corrupts the ethical compass we live by. Ultimately what distinguishes an ethically good person from an ethically bad person is what he worships, and that is what Jesus referred to when saying, "Each tree is known by its own fruit. Figs aren't gathered from thornbushes, or grapes picked from a bramble bush. A good person produces good out of the good stored up in his heart. An evil person produces evil out of the evil stored up in his heart" (Luke 6:44–45).

Linguistic Analysis of Ethics & Worship

When translating what the Bible says on ethics and worship, translators must choose between English words, none of which fully express what the original Hebrew and Greek words say.

Both of the original biblical languages use terms that, when referring to God, do not separate living on God's terms from worshiping him. But English has no word that invariably means ethics and worship at the same time. So, whatever English word translators use seems to indicate a possible difference (between ethics and worship) not in the original text. This is not to say words in Hebrew and Greek do not get used different ways. It only is to say that words the Bible uses for worshiping God always mean living under and by his ethical authority, and words used for living under and by God's ethical authority always mean worshiping him. The biblical languages do not allow readers to think any difference exists between living in submission to God's ethical authority and worshiping God, and any impression English readers get that ethics and worship could be different does not come from the Bible itself but from having to use English words that do not fully convey what the original text says.

The word in Hebrew for "serving" in the sense of submitting to, accepting, and cooperating with authority, and thus working for, obeying, and living to please that authority, is עָבַד (*ābad*).[2] When used in relation to deity, עָבַד (*ābad*) means "venerate" or "serve unconditionally" and, thus, "worship." But in such cases, *worship* also means what *ethics* refers to in the sense of submitting to God's authority and living to please him. The logic is as follows:

- Ethics = living by and under God's authority
- Living by and under God's authority = serving God
- Serving God = עָבַד (*ābad*) used in reference to God
- עָבַד (*ābad*) used in reference to God = worship
- Therefore עָבַד (*ābad*) meaning worship = ethics

עָבַד (*ābad*) is always used for "worshiping" God and always, at the same time, also refers to submitting to his authority and living to please him. In such cases, עָבַד (*ābad*) refers to "living an ethically worthy life" defined on God's terms, obeying God's rules, fulfilling God's purposes, conforming to God's holiness, and seeking God's glory.

---

[2] Walter C. Kaiser, "עָבַד (*ābad*) **work**, **serve**" in *Theological Wordbook of the Old Testament*, vol. 2, ed. R. Laird Harris, Gleason L. Archer, and Bruce K. Waltke (Chicago: Moody, 1980), 639.

עָבַד (ʿāḇaḏ) is the word used in the Old Testament for how everyone must submit to, accept, cooperate with, and, thus, only obey and worship the one true God. God made this very clear when commanding Israel: "Fear the LORD your God, worship (עָבַד, ʿāḇaḏ) him" and "do not follow other gods" (Deut 6:13–14). And Jesus later quoted it as, "Worship the Lord your God, and serve only him" (Matt 4:10). Despite how clearly God made this obligation known, Israel and others violated the commandment regularly by submitting to, working for, obeying, and so worshiping false gods (Deut 7:16; 2 Kgs 10:18–19, 21–23). This angers God and corrupts those doing it (Exod 32:7).[3] People with corrupt hearts do not worship God, but worshiping false gods corrupts them further in the same way eating bad food makes you sick. No one should want to eat bad food. But, if someone does, it harms that person more than if he wanted to eat bad food but never did.

The noun form, עֶבֶד (ʿeḇeḏ), is used when addressing God in prayer (Exod 4:10; Ps 19:12, 14; 109:28) and means "your servant," "one who lives to please you," or "one who does your bidding." Using the noun in prayer amounts to telling God the one praying accepts his authority, lives to please him, and so worships him. The noun is used, as well, for people with duties in the tabernacle or temple and for people serving God in special roles like Abraham, Isaac, Jacob, Moses, Joshua, Caleb, David, and Hezekiah.[4] עֶבֶד (ʿeḇeḏ) is used in the Bible for slaves as well as for people who worship God,[5] and, although ethics and worship are the same when referring to God, they are not the same when referring to human masters—the main difference being that serving God is joyful and liberating (Exod 3:12; 4:23; 7:16; 10:26; 12:31; 15:20–21; Ps 22:31; 33:3; 43:4; 84:2; 98:4-6; 100:1–2) and serving a human slave master is not (Exod 1:13–14; 3:7). But the difference is not great. Slaves do not worship their masters, but they do not simply "work" for them either. In both cases, "serving" is rendered without pay and expresses submission to, acceptance of, and cooperation with an authority that controls everything a person does. Slavery and worship both require aligning words and actions to how an authority assesses what is worthy or not, is profitable or not, and is praiseworthy or

---

[3] While the CSB refers to worshiping the golden calf simply as having "acted corruptly," the ESV, KJV, NKJV, and NASB translations refer to it as having "corrupted themselves." I prefer the latter because it brings out how idol worship not only is a corrupt action but also has an ethical-spiritual corrupting influence on those doing it.

[4] Kaiser, "עָבַד (ʿāḇaḏ)" in *Theological Wordbook of the Old Testament*, 640.

[5] See my treatment of this in chapter 12.

not. Thus, slavery and worship are similar in that both require living by a sort of moral compass aligned to a power imposing it on us, judging us by it, and holding us accountable to it. So, even though human slavery is not fully equivalent to worshiping God, it is close and, for that reason, is easily abused by human masters who usurp God's role in the lives of people serving them.

One of the strongest texts in the Bible showing how עָבַד (*'ābad*) used in relation to God treats ethics and worship as one and the same is Genesis 2:15, a verse that tells of the mission God assigned Adam (and thus humanity). The Hebrew verbs conveying this are עָבַד (*'ābad*) and שָׁמַר (*šāmar*), the first meaning "to serve," "to work," or "to worship" and the second meaning "to watch over" or "to obey" in the sense of following orders or fulfilling a mission. English translations vary on what Genesis 2:15 refers to, but they all assume Adam's mission was limited to the garden of Eden and concerned farming, even though the previous chapter says God appointed Adam and Eve to rule the planet (Gen 1:28) and even though the verses following have to do with ethics (Gen 2:16–17).

The Christian Standard Bible (CSB) assumes Adam's mission was "to work it (the garden) and watch over it (the garden)." The English Standard Version (ESV) assumes it was "to work it (the garden) and to keep it (the garden)." The New International Version (NIV) assumes it was "to work it (the garden) and take care of it (the garden)." The New American Standard Bible (NASB) assumes it was "to cultivate it (the garden) and keep it (the garden)." And the King James Version (KJV) assumes it was "to dress it (the garden) and to keep it (the garden)." But there are insurmountable problems with reading the verse this way, and John Sailhamer makes a strong case for reading Genesis 2:15 instead to be saying (1) Adam's mission was "to worship and to obey," (2) the garden of Eden is the setting but not the object of Adam's mission, and (3) the object of Adam's mission is God himself.[6] Genesis 2:15 is the most important verse in the Bible on the overall mission God made Adam (and so humanity) to fulfill, and Sailhamer argues it is not simply to farm but to worship in the sense of living holy obedient lives (ethics).

Sailhamer's case for translating Adam's mission in Genesis 2:15 as "to worship and obey" is built on six arguments. Sailhamer's first argument is that the word used for "placing" Adam

---

[6] John Sailhamer, "Genesis" in *The Expositor's Bible Commentary*, vol. 2, *Genesis, Exodus, Leviticus, Numbers*, ed. Walter C. Kaiser and Bruce K. Waltke (Grand Rapids: Zondervan, 1990), 44–48.

in Genesis 2:15 is a different and more specialized word than is used for "placing" Adam in the garden seven verses earlier in Genesis 2:8. The word used earlier in verse 8 is the common term for "placing," but the word used in verse 15 is a word used elsewhere only in two ways: for "placing" in locations where God provides special rest or safety (Gen 19:16; Deut 3:20; 12:10; 25:19) and for setting things set aside to serve God (Exod 16:33–34; Lev 16:23; Num 17:4; Deut 26:4, 10). This vocabulary difference signals that the "placing" of Adam in Genesis 2:15 has more to do with putting him into God's service than with simply giving him a place to live and something to do. The writer uses it to let readers know Adam had a mission relating to God that started in the garden of Eden but applied anywhere he went.[7]

Sailhamer's second argument is that English translations of Genesis 2:15 all assume something grammatically impossible, and thus incorrect, when they make the garden of Eden the object of the verbs stating Adam's mission. The verbs each end with ה (*hê*), and a ה (*hê*) at the end of a Hebrew verb can either be a suffixed feminine pronoun meaning "her" or an infinitive ending used for making the verb a purpose statement. All English translations assume the ה (*hê*) endings to the verbs are pronouns referring to the garden of Eden. But, Sailhamer notes, that cannot be the case because "garden" in Hebrew (גַּן, *gan*) is masculine, and feminine pronouns cannot refer to masculine objects. The ה (*hê*) ending each of the verbs can only be infinitive endings, and nothing else is possible.[8]

Sailhamer's third argument is that the Jewish Hebrew language expert Umberto Moses David Cassuto (1883–1951) determined that the verbs in Genesis 2:15 had to have been infinitives in the original text and that the Masoretes were wrong to place a *mappiq*, or dot, in the final *hê's* and reading them as suffixed feminine pronouns (her) instead.[9] The Masoretes were Jewish scribes who, in the Middle Ages, added vowel points to the original Hebrew letters of the Old Testament text to show how they thought it should be read. The original text had no vowel markings and, before that, in places where the text could be read different ways, readers had to guess what was originally intended. What the Masoretes did worked well in most places but created problems if they read the wrong thing, and Cassuto determined that

---

[7] Sailhamer, 44–45.

[8] Sailhamer, 45.

[9] Sailhamer, 47–48, referring to Umberto Cassuto, *A Commentary on the Book of Genesis* (Jerusalem: Magnes, 1961), 122.

in Genesis 2:15 the Masoretic scribes had mistaken the final *hē's* as feminine pronouns when they should have read them as infinitives (verbal nouns).

Cassuto chaired the Biblical Studies Department at the Hebrew University of Jerusalem from 1938 to 1951 and was the leading authority on ancient Hebrew of his day and likely, too, was the strongest authority on it since the Masoretes themselves. Affirming the inerrancy of Scripture is limited to the original biblical text and does not require agreeing with how scribes in the Middle Ages thought it should be read. The letters of the original Hebrew text are inerrant, but the vowel points added by the Masoretes are not. Cassuto dedicated himself to reviewing what the Masoretes did and understood ancient Hebrew better than any non-Hebrew speaking scholar translating the text into English. So, while we should respect the Masoretes, Cassuto is more likely to have corrected them for reading the verbs in Genesis 2:15 as having suffixed feminine pronouns referring to the garden of Eden when the garden of Eden is masculine and there is nothing in the text to which feminine pronouns can refer.

Sailhamer's fourth argument is that taking the verbs in Genesis 2:15 as infinitives indicating that Adam's mission was "to worship and obey" also fits the narrative better. According to Sailhamer,

> The importance of these two infinitives can be seen in the fact that the narrative returns to precisely them in its summary conclusion of the state of mankind after the Fall. The man and woman were created 'for worship' (*lᵉ'obḏāh*, 2:15), but after the Fall they were thrown out of the garden 'to work the ground' (*la'ăḇōḏ 'eṯ-hā'ăḏāmāh*, 3:23). In the same way they were created 'for obedience' (*lᵉshomrāh*, 2:15), but after the Fall they were 'kept' (*lishmōr*, 3:24) from the tree of life.[10]

Sailhamer's fifth argument is that limiting Adam's assignment in Genesis 2:15 to "working" the garden of Eden leaves nothing in the narrative contrasting with how Adam is punished in Genesis 3:23. Sailhamer observes that "later in this same narrative (3:23) 'to work the ground' (*la'ăḇōḏ*) is said to be a result of the Fall, and the narrative suggests that the author had intended such a punishment to be seen as an ironic reversal of man's original purpose."[11] "Working the ground" is negative in Genesis 3:23, and English translations of Genesis 2:15

---

[10] Sailhamer, 48. The references in this quotation are to Genesis 2:15; 3:23; and 3:24.
[11] Sailhamer, 45.

all leave readers wondering how "working the ground" can be a blessing in one chapter and a punishment in the next.

Sailhamer's sixth argument is that translating Genesis 2:15 as "to worship and obey" also better fits the ethical focus marking the next two verses. After placing Adam in the setting described in Genesis 2:15, God commands him saying, "You are free to eat from any tree in the garden, but you must not eat from the tree of the knowledge of good and evil, for on the day you eat from it, you will certainly die" (Gen 2:16–17). These commands assume "that God alone knows what is good (tôḇ) for man and that God alone knows what is not good (raʿ) for him." Therefore "to enjoy the 'good' man must trust God and obey him" and, if man disobeys, it would be catastrophic because without God man cannot know what is truly good or bad.[12] Reading Adam's mission as "to worship and obey" fits the ethical focus marking the next verses and otherwise does not. Nothing obviously links farming with respecting God's ethical authority, but worshiping God in Genesis 2:15 is very obviously linked to respecting his ethical authority in Genesis 2:16–17.

The reason for examining Genesis 2:15 is that Sailhamer's arguments clearly show how עָבַד (ʿāḇaḏ) used in relation to God treats ethics and worship as one and the same. עָבַד (ʿāḇaḏ) in Genesis 2:15 is not a job but a mission and is not just a matter of giving Adam something to do but of setting his ethical compass. Taken together, the linguistic arguments just considered make a strong case for concluding that Genesis 2:15–17 is best rendered as

> The LORD God took the man and set him up in the garden of Eden to worship/live ethically and obey, doing it by commanding the man saying, "You may freely eat from any tree of the garden, but of the tree of the knowledge of good and evil you may not eat, for on the day you eat of it you will certainly die."

But, having agreed with Sailhamer's analysis, we need to consider how interpreting it like this affects the way some use translating עָבַד (ʿāḇaḏ) in Genesis 2:15 as "cultivate" to support the preservation model of creation care.[13] If עָבַד (ʿāḇaḏ) in Genesis 2:15 refers to worshiping God and accepting his ethical authority, can it still require preserving natural resources? One might think it disqualifies the preservation model, but that goes too far. Translating עָבַד

---

[12] Sailhamer, 45.

[13] Readers are referred to our discussion of this in Chapter 12.

(*'ābad*) in Genesis 2:15 to reveal how it connects worship with ethics does favor the steward-ship or shepherding models of creation care, but that does not mean we should waste natural resources. The final ה's (*hēs*) are not suffixed feminine pronouns referring to the garden of Eden (which is masculine), and translating עָבַד (*'ābad*) as "to worship" best portrays Adam's mission. But Genesis 2:15 still includes not wasting resources given by God because worship-ing God and living to please him are inseparable.

Viewing ethics and worship as the same is linguistically required in Greek as well as in Hebrew. But the connection in Greek is more complex, as Greek uses three different words for worship. Each Greek term has a slightly different emphasis, but each also treats ethics and worship as the same. The verb λατρεύω (*latreuō*) means "to worship" or "to serve" in the sense of obeying and fulfilling duties. Using this term emphasizes "being in submis-sion to or being someone serving" higher authority. It is doing what a higher authority demands, living in submission to that higher authority, or fulfilling duties assigned by that higher authority. It means doing as required. But λατρεύω (*latreuō*) focuses on external performance and so, used alone, may or may not include having the right heart attitude. It is used in Philippians to say Christians "worship (λατρεύοντες, *latreuontes*) by the Spirit of God" (Phil 3:3), and Paul adds "by the Spirit of God" to guarantee authenticity that could be questioned otherwise.

The verb προσκυνέω (*proskuneō*) means "to worship" or "to venerate" by falling down, bowing low, or prostrating before higher authority. Using this term emphasizes "expressing submission or acting as if serving" higher authority. It is posturing that alleges submission to higher authority but, as such, the worship expressed can be authentic or fake. The term is used where Jesus says, "An hour is coming . . . when the true worshipers (προσκθνηταὶ, *proskunētai*) will worship the Father in Spirit and in truth" (John 4:23). Here Jesus qualifies "worshipers" with "true" because outward posturing can be faked. The term also is used where Satan asks Jesus to "fall down and worship (προσκθνήσῃς, *proskunēsēs*) me" (Matt 4:9). Satan did not add "true," perhaps thinking it would make posing worship more tempting, but Jesus would not even fake worshiping Satan.

The verbs σεβάζομαι (*sebazomai*) and σέβομαι (*sebomai*) are variations of a word meaning "to worship" in the sense of "inwardly accepting" or "sincerely believing in" higher authority. Using these terms emphasizes the "heart attitude" or "inner acceptance" a person has toward higher authority. It is actually respecting, loving, and preferring that higher authority over others. These terms are used where Paul says people "worshiped (ἐσεβάθησαν, *esebathēsan*) . . . what has been created instead of the Creator" (Rom 1:25) and where Matthew quotes God saying, "They worship (σέβονταί, *sebontai*) me in vain" (Matt 15:9).

Theological Analysis of Ethics & Worship

Seeing how the Bible treats ethics and worship as the same depends on more than individual words and is revealed, as well, through what God commands, expects, and criticizes, and through what Satan really wants. Many passages in the Bible portray this connection, some of which include the following:

- "And now, Israel, what does the LORD your God ask of you except to fear the LORD your God by walking in all his ways (biblical ethics), to love him (ethics), and to worship (עָבַד, *ābad*, as in Gen 2:15) the LORD your God with all your heart and all your soul? Keep the LORD's commands and statutes (biblical ethics) I am giving you today, for your own good" (Deut 10:12–13).
- "You must follow the LORD your God and fear him (biblical ethics). You must keep his commands and listen to him (biblical ethics); you must worship (עָבַד, *ābad*, as in Gen 2:15) him and remain faithful to him (biblical ethics)" (Deut 13:4).
- "Therefore, fear the LORD (biblical ethics) and worship (עָבַד, *ābad*, as in Gen 2:15) him in sincerity and truth. Get rid of the gods your forefathers worshiped (עָבַד, *ābad*, as in Gen 2:15) beyond the Euphrates River and in Egypt, and worship (עָבַד, *ābad*, as in Gen 2:15) the LORD. But if it doesn't please you to worship (עָבַד, *ābad*, as in Gen 2:15) the LORD, choose for yourselves today: Which will you worship (עָבַד, *ābad*, as in Gen 2:15)—the gods your fathers worshiped (עָבַד, *ābad*, as in Gen 2:15) beyond the Euphrates River or the gods of the Amorites in whose land you are living? As for me and my family, we will worship (עָבַד, *ābad*, as in Gen 2:15) the LORD. . . . So the people said to Joshua, 'We will worship (עָבַד, *ābad*, as in Gen 2:15) the LORD our God and obey (biblical ethics) him'" (Josh 24:14–15, 24).

- "Above all, fear the LORD (biblical ethics) and worship (עָבַד, *ʿāḇaḏ*, as in Gen 2:15) him faithfully with all your heart. . . . However, if you continue to do what is evil (here ethical wrong is the opposite of worship which means worship is doing what is ethically right), both you and your king will be swept away" (1 Sam 12:24–25).

Each of these passages treats ethics in the sense of submitting to God's authority and living to please him the same as worshiping him. They show how ethics and worship are not just linked but are one and the same. Living life on God's terms is the same as worshiping God, and, being identical, the reverse is true as well. Not living on God's terms is not worshiping God, and that is made very clear in Amos where God says,

> Seek good and not evil (ethics) so that you may live . . . . Hate evil and love good (ethics); establish justice in the city gate (ethics) . . . . I hate, I despise your feasts (worship rituals)! I can't stand the stench of your solemn assemblies (worship services). Even if you offer me your burnt offerings and grain offerings (worship rituals), I will not accept them; I will have no regard for your fellowship offerings of fattened cattle (worship rituals). Take away from me the noise of your songs (worship music)! I will not listen to the music of your harps (worship music). But let justice (ethics) flow like water, and righteousness (ethics), like an unfailing stream" (Amos 5:14–15, 21–24).

Thus, ethics is worship itself and worship is ethics itself. Real ethics is real worship and real worship is real ethics. Diagramming it looks like this:

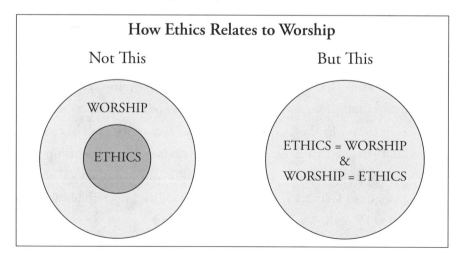

But worship and ethics being one and the same does not mean ethics measures up to experiences people associate with worshiping God. How we worship must measure up to real ethics and not the other way around. It must be that way because it is very easy to confuse worship vehicles with worship itself, and doing that easily leads to worshiping ourselves instead of God. Things done in a worship service like singing, praying, giving, and listening to sermons are vehicles that should convey worship to God. But vehicles of worship are not worship itself and should not be confused with what they carry any more than coffee cups should be confused with coffee or taxis should be confused with passengers. Vehicles can be empty and may carry the wrong thing. Coffee cups can carry mud, taxis can carry terrorists, and vehicles of worship can carry content that offends God.

What worship vehicles carry is ethics in the sense of submitting to God's authority and living to please him. Things done in a worship service like singing, praying, giving, and listening to sermons are ways of telling God we are living to please him. And, if that is not the case, what they carry is sinful living that causes God to say, "I can't stand the stench of your solemn assemblies . . . . I will have no regard for your fellowship offerings . . . . Take away from me the noise of your songs!" (Amos 5:21–23). The worship God wants is having hearts submitted to his authority and lives lived to please him, and, apart from these, what worship vehicles carry offends God no matter how well performed or how much they stir us up.

The principle of something is what defines it or makes it work, and the principle of worship is given in Romans 12:1. Translators struggle with how to translate the verse because, again, there is no English word meaning exactly what Paul says. Translators know Paul addresses worship, but what exactly does he mean? Translations into English vary widely. For example:

CSB: .... this is your true worship . . .

NIV$_{1984}$: .... this is your true and proper worship . . .

NLT: .... this is (~~your~~) truly the way to worship . . .

HCSB: ....this is your spiritual worship . . .

ASV: .... which is your spiritual service . . .

ESV: .... which is your spiritual worship . . .

NASB: .... which is your spiritual service of worship . . .

KJV/AKJV/Webster's ...... which is your reasonable service (~~worship~~) . . .

CEV: .... that's the most sensible way to serve God (~~worship~~) . . .

Darby/YLT: ……..…….   (which is) your intelligent service (~~worship~~) . . .

Aramaic Bible: …………..   which is (~~your~~) logical service (~~worship~~) . . .

The key to understanding what Paul says is realizing how the term λόγος (*logos*), when used to explain something, indicates a principle of operation.[14] Speakers of Greek at the time Paul wrote referred to the principle running the universe as "The Logos" in the manner John does when writing, "The Word (λόγος, *logos*) became flesh and dwelt among us" (John 1:14). John, in the opening of his gospel, told Greek readers the principle running the universe became flesh, and that is who Jesus was. This using of λόγος (*logos*) for the principle of something explains what Paul says about worship in Romans 12:1. Paul uses λόγικον (*logikon*)—the adjectival form of λόγος (*logos*)—the way John uses λόγος (*logos*). John uses λόγος (*logos*) to explain who Jesus was, and Paul uses λόγικον (*logikon*) to explain what worship is. So, when Paul says presenting "your bodies as a living sacrifice . . . holy and pleasing to God" is the λόγικον (*logikon*) of worship, he means sacrificial (unconditional) submission to God's authority (ethics) is the principle of worship, is what worship itself actually is.

If Paul's statement in Romans 12:1 is not convincing, there is no stronger proof for how the Bible treats ethics and worship as one and the same than is provided in the last way Satan tested Jesus after his baptism. The baptism of Jesus launched his public ministry, the aim of which was saving the world (John 1:29; 3:16; 4:42; 12:32), and the first step Jesus took after that was allowing Satan to test him. Satan tested Jesus three times in three ways. With each test, Satan tried to compromise Jesus, but Satan's last test (listed second in Luke, which does not give them chronologically) got to what he wanted most.[15] In it, "the devil . . . showed him all the kingdoms of the world and their splendor. And he said to him, 'I will give you all these

---

[14] "Logos," in *The Encyclopedia of Philosophy*, vol 5, ed. Paul Edwards (New York: Macmillan, 1967), 83.

[15] Matthew and Luke report the same three temptations of Christ (Matt 4:1–11; Luke 4:1–13) but order them differently. Matthew lists them chronologically, and Luke does not. We know this because Matthew uses Greek particles that indicate the temptations are presented chronologically (τότε, πάλιν), whereas Luke uses a general particle that indicates that the temptations may not be given chronologically (καὶ, καὶ). Another thing proving this is that Matthew's third temptation has Jesus dismissing Satan (Matt 4:10) and Luke, in putting that temptation second, leaves the dismissal out. Doing that shows Luke knew he was not presenting the temptations chronologically. And, since Luke's account ends with Jesus rebuking Satan for testing God (Luke 4:12), it may be he changed the order to stress Christ's deity.

things if you will fall down and worship (προσκυνήσῃς, *proskunēsēs*) me'" (Matt 4:8–9). Jesus responded by quoting God's command only to "worship (עָבַד, *'ābad*) him" (Deut 6:13). But note what Satan demanded. Satan was not seeking a worship vehicle but worship itself. He did not ask Jesus to sing a song. Satan's condition for giving Jesus "all the kingdoms of the world" was that Jesus submit to his (Satan's) ethical authority. Worship is ethics, and the deal was, "Submit to my ethical authority and you can have the world."

Satan asking Jesus to "worship" him shows he wanted Jesus to set his moral compass on Satan rather than God. While that would have destroyed Jesus' mission, there was still more to it. What Satan actually sought was stunningly audacious. Jesus is God himself, and what Satan asked Jesus to do would have demoted God and left Satan in charge. Worship is submitting to, living under, and following ethical authority. Worship is an all or nothing setting of the moral compass we live by. Jesus would not shift his moral compass, and neither should we.

Final Comments

Many implications follow this understanding of ethics and worship being one and the same, and I will mention three. First, ethics and worship being the same is presumed when the Bible says, "The fear of the LORD is the beginning of wisdom" (Ps 111:10; Prov 9:10; also see Prov 1:7; Job 28:28).[16] "Fear of the LORD" refers to setting the ethical compass we live by on God and living to please him. "Beginning of" means what came before is key to what comes next and, even though sequence is involved, the key (to wisdom) referred to is not something that occurs one time and is then irrelevant but rather is something prerequisite that remains necessary forever. And "wisdom" refers not only to ethical insight, but to living an ethically worthy life as well. Wisdom in the Bible is more than head knowledge and always includes aligning ourselves to God and living to please him. So when the Bible says, "The fear of the LORD is the beginning of wisdom," it means, "setting the ethical compass of our lives on God is the

---

[16] The *English Standard Version Study Bible* (*ESVSB*) affirms this interpretation in a comment accompanying Proverbs 1:7 that notes, "The reason that the fear of the Lord is the beginning of both knowledge and wisdom is that the moral life begins with reverence and humility before the Maker and Redeemer . . . . it asserts that submission to the Lord is foundational to the attainment of real understanding." I would add that it is foundational both to understanding ethical truth and to living an ethically worthy life.

key to ethical insight and living an ethically worthy life," which is exactly what Job says when equating "fear of the LORD (i.e., worship)" with "turn from evil (i.e., ethics)" (Job 28:28).

Second, separating the heart attitude controlling how we live from how we conceive worshiping God destroys worshiping him altogether. Participating in a worship service without submitting to God's ethical authority and living to please him is formalism, and God considers formalism totally unacceptable (1 Sam 15:22; Ps 51:16–17; Isa 29:13; Jer 7:21–26; Ezek 33:30–32; Hos 6:6; Matt 15:8–9; Mark 7:6–7). Formalism affects academic work in Christian ethics as well. Teaching and writing in the field apart from submitting to God's ethical authority and living to please him is invalid and dangerous. It is invalid because doing so lacks the voice of God, and it is dangerous because doing so leads away from pleasing God, darkens moral witness in the world, and sends those doing it to eternal judgment (Jude 13).

The third thing worth mentioning concerns the way Evangelicals have changed how we speak of "worship." The good part is we are stressing the importance of worship. But a problem occurs when we do it the wrong way, and I fear that, while it is well intended, the change is giving people the wrong idea. Failing to understand how ethics and worship are the same is leading us to confuse vehicles of worship with what they carry, and doing that makes us vulnerable to formalism. The problem occurs when people speak as if "worship" is limited to music and singing. "Music Ministers" are now called "Worship Leaders" or "Worship Pastors" as if pastors doing other things do not lead worship. Because of this, it is not uncommon to hear singing during a church service introduced by someone saying, "Now let's worship," as if what came before (usually a Scripture reading or prayer) was not "worship" and as if "worship" only occurs when people sing or hear music.

It is true that religious music should convey worship, and ministers leading music should connect it with worshiping God. But, however innocently it occurs, speaking of worship this way conditions people to think (1) that other ministers do not lead worship, (2) that music is the only way worship is expressed, and (3) that music itself is worship itself. Solving this requires better teaching on how worship itself is living lives submitted to God's ethical authority and how vehicles of worship are not what they carry and cannot substitute for worship itself.

Besides better teaching, we might also consider revising how we refer to worship when serving the Church. We should stop using "Worship Leader" or "Worship Pastor" only for people in music ministry and should address all church leaders the same way. Ministers who preach lead worship, ministers leading corporate prayer lead worship, ministers reading

Scripture in a church service lead worship, and even ushers collecting tithes and offerings lead worship. So, to avoid the wrong message, we might use titles such as

- Pastor of Expository Worship (instead of Preaching Pastor),
- Pastor of Musical Worship (instead of Worship Pastor),
- Pastor of Administrative Worship (instead of Administration Pastor),
- Pastor of Financial Worship (instead of Financial Affairs Pastor),
- Pastor of Educational Worship (instead of Education Pastor),
- Pastor of Evangelistic Worship (instead of Evangelism Pastor), and
- Pastor of Counseling Worship (instead of Counseling Pastor).

Then, to help people understand how every part of a church service conveys worship, we might use phrases like "Now let's convey our worship to God by sitting under the teaching of his Word"; "Now let's convey our worship to God by going to him in prayer"; "Now let's convey our worship to God by listening to the reading of his Word"; and "Now let's convey our worship to God by giving our tithes and offerings." And when leading music, we should say, "Now let's convey our worship to God by singing." Furthermore, when conveying worship to God through music, we should consider introducing it in ways that better help people understand what it is about by saying things like "Now let's convey worship by singing gratitude to God for saving us," "by singing how we are in awe of God's majesty, goodness, or power," "by singing how unworthy we are to approach him," "by singing to celebrate his presence," or "by singing our need for God's wisdom, healing, or mercy." Then, when a service closes, the officiating minister might dismiss the congregation by saying, "Go now and worship God by living to please him, so that we can express it back to him when we gather here again next Sunday."

NASHVILLE STATEMENT ON BIBLICAL SEXUALITY

The *Nashville Statement on Biblical Sexuality* was conceived by Denny Burk, Professor of Biblical Studies at the Southern Baptist Seminary in Louisville, Kentucky, and President of the Council on Biblical Manhood and Womanhood. It was drafted under his leadership by a team of Evangelical theologians, pastors, leaders, and scholars in Nashville, Tennessee, and published by the Council on Biblical Manhood and Womanhood on August 25, 2017. I was one of 164 initial signatories when the statement was published, and thousands more have signed it since. The statement with all signers is accessible at: https://cbmw.org/nashville-statement.

Preamble

"Know that the LORD Himself is God;
It is He who has made us, and not we ourselves . . ."
—Psalm 100:3 (NASB)

Evangelical Christians at the dawn of the twenty-first century find themselves living in a period of historic transition. As Western culture has become increasingly post-Christian, it has embarked upon a massive revision of what it means to be a human being. By and large the spirit of our age no longer discerns or delights in the beauty of God's design for human life. Many deny that God created human beings for his glory, and that his good purposes for us include our personal and physical design as male and female. It is common to think that human identity as male and female is not part of God's beautiful plan, but is, rather, an expression of an individual's autonomous preferences. The pathway to full and lasting joy through God's good design for his creatures is thus replaced by the path of shortsighted alternatives that, sooner or later, ruin human life and dishonor God.

This secular spirit of our age presents a great challenge to the Christian Church. Will the Church of the Lord Jesus Christ lose her biblical conviction, clarity, and courage, and blend into the spirit of the age? Or will she hold fast to the Word of Life, draw courage from Jesus, and unashamedly proclaim His way as being the Way of Life? Will she maintain her clear, counter-cultural witness to a world that seems bent on ruin?

We are persuaded that faithfulness in our generation means declaring once again the true story of the world and of our place in it—particularly as male and female. Christian Scripture teaches that there is but one God who alone is Creator and Lord of all. To him alone, every person owes gladhearted thanksgiving, heartfelt praise, and total allegiance. This is the path not only of glorifying God, but of knowing ourselves. To forget our Creator is to forget who we are, for he made us for himself. And we cannot know ourselves truly without truly knowing him who made us. We did not make ourselves. We are not our own. Our true identity, as male and female persons, is given by God. It is not only foolish, but hopeless, to try to make ourselves what God did not create us to be.

We believe that God's design for his creation and his way of salvation serve to bring him the greatest glory and bring us the greatest good. God's good plan provides us with the greatest freedom. Jesus said He came that we might have life and have it in overflowing measure. He is for us and not against us. Therefore, in the hope of serving Christ's Church and witnessing publicly to the good purposes of God for human sexuality revealed in Christian Scripture, we offer the following affirmations and denials.

Article 1

WE AFFIRM that God has designed marriage to be a covenantal, sexual, procreative, lifelong union of one man and one woman, as husband and wife, and is meant to signify the covenant love between Christ and his bride the Church. WE DENY that God has designed marriage to be a homosexual, polygamous, or polyamorous relationship. We also deny that marriage is a mere human contract rather than a covenant made before God.

Article 2

WE AFFIRM that God's revealed will for all people is chastity outside of marriage and fidelity within marriage. WE DENY that any affections, desires, or commitments ever justify sexual intercourse before or outside marriage; nor do they justify any form of sexual immorality.

Article 3

WE AFFIRM that God created Adam and Eve, the first human beings, in his own image, equal before God as persons, and distinct as male and female. WE DENY that the divinely ordained differences between male and female render them unequal in dignity or worth.

Article 4

WE AFFIRM that divinely ordained differences between male and female reflect God's original creation design and are meant for human good and human flourishing. WE DENY that such differences are a result of the Fall or are a tragedy to be overcome.

Article 5

WE AFFIRM that the differences between male and female reproductive structures are integral to God's design for self-conception as male or female. WE DENY that physical anomalies or psychological conditions nullify the God-appointed link between biological sex and self-conception as male or female.

Article 6

WE AFFIRM that those born with a physical disorder of sex development are created in the image of God and have dignity and worth equal to all other image-bearers. They are acknowledged by our Lord Jesus in his words about "eunuchs who were born that way from their mother's womb." With all others they are welcome as faithful followers of Jesus Christ and should embrace their biological sex insofar as it may be known. WE DENY that ambiguities related to a person's biological sex render one incapable of living a fruitful life in joyful obedience to Christ.

Article 7

WE AFFIRM that self-conception as male or female should be defined by God's holy purposes in creation and redemption as revealed in Scripture. WE DENY that adopting a homosexual or transgender self-conception is consistent with God's holy purposes in creation and redemption.

Article 8

WE AFFIRM that people who experience sexual attraction for the same sex may live a rich and fruitful life pleasing to God through faith in Jesus Christ, as they, like all Christians, walk in purity of life. WE DENY that sexual attraction for the same sex is part of the natural goodness of God's original creation, or that it puts a person outside the hope of the gospel.

Article 9

WE AFFIRM that sin distorts sexual desires by directing them away from the marriage covenant and toward sexual immorality—a distortion that includes both heterosexual and homosexual immorality. WE DENY that an enduring pattern of desire for sexual immorality justifies sexually immoral behavior.

Article 10

WE AFFIRM that it is sinful to approve of homosexual immorality or transgenderism and that such approval constitutes an essential departure from Christian faithfulness and witness. WE DENY that the approval of homosexual immorality or transgenderism is a matter of moral indifference about which otherwise faithful Christians should agree to disagree.

Article 11

WE AFFIRM our duty to speak the truth in love at all times, including when we speak to or about one another as male or female. WE DENY any obligation to speak in such ways that dishonor God's design of his image-bearers as male and female.

Article 12

WE AFFIRM that the grace of God in Christ gives both merciful pardon and transforming power, and that this pardon and power enable a follower of Jesus to put to death sinful desires and to walk in a manner worthy of the Lord. WE DENY that the grace of God in Christ is insufficient to forgive all sexual sins and to give power for holiness to every believer who feels drawn into sexual sin.

Article 13

WE AFFIRM that the grace of God in Christ enables sinners to forsake transgender self-conceptions and by divine forbearance to accept the God ordained link between one's biological sex and one's self-conception as male or female. WE DENY that the grace of God in Christ sanctions self-conceptions that are at odds with God's revealed will.

Article 14

WE AFFIRM that Christ Jesus has come into the world to save sinners and that through Christ's death and resurrection forgiveness of sins and eternal life are available to every person who repents of sin and trusts in Christ alone as Savior, Lord, and supreme treasure. WE DENY that the Lord's arm is too short to save or that any sinner is beyond his reach.

Initial Signatories

Institutional affiliation for identification purposes only

Denny Burk President
Council on Biblical Manhood and Womanhood

John Piper
Founder & Teacher, Desiring God
Chancellor, Bethlehem College & Seminary

James Dobson
Founder & President, Family Talk
Founder & Former President, Focus on the Family

Russell Moore
President, Ethics & Religious Liberty Commission

J. I. Packer
Professor of Theology, Regent College

Wayne Grudem
Research Professor of Theology and Biblical Studies, Phoenix Seminary

R. Albert Mohler, Jr.
President, The Southern Baptist Theological Seminary

Tony Perkins
President, Family Research Council

D. A. Carson
President & Co-Founder, The Gospel Coalition
Research Professor of New Testament, Trinity Evangelical Divinity School

John MacArthur
Pastor, Grace Community Church
President, The Master's Seminary & College

Sam Allberry
Editor, The Gospel Coalition

R. C. Sproul
Founder & Chairman, Ligonier Ministries

Rosaria Butterfield
Author of *The Secret Thoughts of an Unlikely Convert*

Francis Chan
Author & Pastor, We Are Church

Marvin Olasky
Editor in Chief, *World Magazine*

Ligon Duncan
Chancellor & CEO, Reformed Theological
Seminary

Steve Gaines
President, The Southern Baptist
Convention
Pastor, Bellevue Baptist Church

Andrew T. Walker
Director of Policy Studies, Ethics &
Religious Liberty Commission

H. B. Charles, Jr.
Pastor, Shiloh Metropolitan Baptist
Church of Jacksonville, Florida

Christopher Yuan
Speaker & Author, Moody Bible Institute

Dennis Rainey
Founder & Former President, FamilyLife

Frank Page
President & CEO, Southern Baptist
Convention Executive Committee
Former President, Southern Baptist
Convention

Nancy DeMoss Wolgemuth
Author & Speaker, Revive Our Hearts

Daniel L. Akin
President, Southeastern Baptist Theological
Seminary

Kevin DeYoung
Senior Pastor, Christ Covenant Church

Alistair Begg
Reverend, Parkside Church

Heath Lambert
Executive Director, Association of Certified
Biblical Counselors

Jerry A. Johnson
President & CEO, National Religious
Broadcasters

Mark Dever
Pastor, Capitol Hill Baptist Church

Randy Alcorn
Director, Eternal Perspectives Ministries

Karen Swallow Prior
Professor of English, Liberty University

Matt Chandler
Pastor, The Village Church

Fred Luter
Senior Pastor, Franklin Avenue Baptist
Church
Former President, Southern Baptist
Convention

James Merritt
Pastor, Cross Pointe Church
Former President, Southern Baptist
Convention

Jack Graham
Pastor, Prestonwood Baptist Church

J. D. Greear
Pastor, The Summit Church

Darryl Delhousaye
President, Phoenix Seminary

Thomas White
President, Cedarville University

Bryant Wright
Senior Pastor, Johnson Ferry Baptist
Church
Former President, Southern Baptist
Convention

Don Sweeting
President, Colorado Christian University

Jeff Purswell
Director of Theology, Sovereign Grace
Churches

Johnny Hunt
Pastor, First Baptist Church of Woodstock
Former President, Southern Baptist
Convention

Jason K. Allen
President, Midwestern Baptist Theological
Seminary

Erick-Woods Erickson
Editor in Chief, *The Resurgent*

Mark L. Bailey
President & Senior Professor of Bible
Exposition, Dallas Theological Seminary

K. Erik Thoennes
Professor & Chair of Theology, Talbot
School of Theology, Biola University

Vaughan Roberts
Rector of St. Ebbe's Church, Oxford, UK

David French
Senior Writer, *National Review*

Paige Patterson
President, Southwestern Baptist
Theological Seminary

R. Kent Hughes
Visiting Professor of Practical Theology,
Evangelism and Culture, Westminster
Theological Seminary

Jeff Iorg
President, Gateway Seminary

Sam Storms
Lead Pastor for Preaching and Vision,
Bridgeway Church

Richard Land
President, Southern Evangelical Seminary

Barbara Rainey
Co-Founder, FamilyLife

Robert A. J. Gagnon
Scholar & Author of *The Bible and Homosexual Practice*

Samuel W. "Dub" Oliver
President, Union University

Ronnie Floyd
Senior Pastor, Cross Church
Former President, Southern Baptist Convention

C. J. Mahaney
Senior Pastor, Sovereign Grace Church of Louisville

Jason G. Duesing
Provost, Midwestern Baptist Theological Seminary & College

Matt Carter
Pastor, The Austin Stone Church

Chuck Kelley
President, New Orleans Baptist Theological Seminary

Burk Parsons
Copastor, St. Andrew's Chapel

Eric Teetsel
President, Family Policy Alliance of Kansas

Alastair Roberts
Scholar & Author of *Heirs Together: A Theology of the Sexes*

Kevin Ezell
President, North American Mission Board, Southern Baptist Convention

Ray Ortlund
Pastor, Immanuel Church

O. S. Hawkins
President, GuideStone, Southern Baptist Convention

Thom S. Rainer
President & CEO, LifeWay Christian Resources

Michael Reeves
President and Professor of Theology, Union School of Theology, UK

Todd Wagner
Pastor, Watermark Community Church

John M. Frame
Professor Emeritus of Systematic Theology & Philosophy, Reformed Theological Seminary

Randy Stinson
Senior VP for Academic Administration & Provost, The Southern Baptist Theological Seminary

Mac Brunson
Senior Pastor, First Baptist Church of Jacksonville

Paul Nyquist
President, Moody Bible Institute

Thomas Schreiner
James Buchanan Harrison Professor
of New Testament Interpretation, The
Southern Baptist Theological Seminary

H. Wayne House
Dean & Distinguished Research Professor
of Theology, Law & Culture, Faith
International University

J. P. Moreland
Distinguished Professor of Philosophy,
Talbot School of Theology, Biola
University & Seminary

Miguel Nunez
Pastor, Iglesia Bautista Internacional

Bruce Ware
Professor of Christian Theology, The
Southern Baptist Theological Seminary

Michael Goeke
Associate Pastor, First Baptist Church of
San Francisco

Joel Belz
Founder, *World Magazine*, World News
Group

Michael Horton
J. Gresham Machen Professor of Theology
& Apologetics, Westminster Seminary
California

Jackie Hill Perry
Speaker, Writer, Humble Beast Recording
Artist

Dick Lucas
Reverend Prebendary, Rector Emeritus, St.
Helen's Bishopsgate, UK

Afshin Ziafat
Lead Pastor, Providence Church

Stephen Strang
Founder & CEO, Charisma Media

Christiana Holcomb
Legal Counsel, Alliance Defending
Freedom

Jimmy Draper
President Emeritus, LifeWay
Former President, Southern Baptist
Convention

Stephen J. Wellum
Professor of Christian Theology, The
Southern Baptist Theological Seminary

Anthony Kidd
Pastor of Preaching, Community of Faith
Bible Church

James M. Hamilton, Jr.
Professor of Biblical Theology, The Southern Baptist Theological Seminary

Bryan Carter
Senior Pastor, Concord Church

Owen Strachan
Associate Professor of Christian Theology, Midwestern Baptist Theological Seminary

Chris Larson
President & CEO, Ligonier Ministries

Bruce Riley Ashford
Provost and Professor of Theology & Culture, Southeastern Baptist Theological Seminary

Candi Finch
Assistant Professor of Theology in Women's Studies, Southwestern Baptist Theological Seminary

Curtis Woods
Associate Executive Director, Kentucky Baptist Convention

Nathan Finn
Dean, School of Theology and Missions, Union University

James Robinson
Founder & President, LIFE Outreach International
Founder & Publisher, *The Stream*

C. Ben Mitchell
Graves Professor of Moral Philosophy, Union University

Darrell Bock
Senior Professor, Dallas Theological Seminary

William Philip
Senior Minister, The Tron Church, Glasgow, UK

David Mathis
Executive Editor, Desiring God

Ken Magnuson
Professor of Christian Ethics, The Southern Baptist Theological Seminary

Daniel Heimbach
Senior Professor of Christian Ethics, Southeastern Baptist Theological Seminary

Hershael W. York
Victor & Louise Lester Professor of Christian Preaching, The Southern Baptist Theological Seminary

Mary Mohler
Director, Seminary Wives Institute

Hunter Baker
Associate Professor, Union University

Dorothy Kelley Patterson
Professor of Theology in Women's Studies,
Southwestern Baptist Theological Seminary

Jim Shaddix
W. A. Criswell Professor of Expository
Preaching, Southeastern Baptist
Theological Seminary

John N. Oswalt
Visiting Distinguished Professor of Old
Testament, Asbury Theological Seminary

Jack Deere
Author & Speaker, Grace Church of St.
Louis

Juan R. Sanchez
Senior Pastor, High Pointe Baptist Church,
Austin, Texas

Malcolm B. Yarnell III
Research Professor of Systematic Theology,
Southwestern Baptist Theological Seminary

Jonathan Leeman
Editorial Director, 9Marks

Mary A. Kassian
Author & Director, Girls Gone Wise

Mark Daniel Liederbach
Vice President & Professor of Theology,
Ethics & Culture, Southeastern Baptist
Theological Seminary

Matthew J. Hall
Dean of Boyce College & Senior VP
of Academic Innovation, The Southern
Baptist Theological Seminary

Micah Fries
Senior Pastor, Brainerd Baptist Church

Nathan Lino
Senior Pastor, Northeast Houston Baptist
Church

Paul Weber
President & CEO, Family Policy Alliance

Bob Lepine
Vice President of Content, FamilyLife

Andy Naselli
Associate Professor of New Testament &
Theology, Bethlehem Collage & Seminary

John Stevens
National Director, Fellowship of
Independent Evangelical Churches

Casey B. Hough
Senior Pastor, First Baptist Church of
Camden

Russell Shubin
Director, Salem Media Group

Allan Coppedge
Retired Professor of Theology, Asbury Theological Seminary

Daniel DeWitt
Director of the Center for Biblical Apologetics & Public Christianity, Cedarville University

Charlotte Akin
Homemaker, Southeastern Baptist Theological Seminary

David Schrock
Pastor for Preaching and Theology, Occoquan Bible Church

Don Buckley
Physician, Spanish Trail Family Physicians

E. Calvin Beisner
Founder & National Spokesman, Cornwall Alliance for the Stewardship of Creation

Donald A. Balasa
Adjunct Faculty, Trinity International University

Donna Thoennes
Adjunct Professor & Homeschool Mom, Biola University

James A. Borland
Professor of New Testament & Theology, Liberty University

Eric C. Redmond
Assistant Professor of Bible, Moody Bible Institute

Grant Castleberry
Pastor of Discipleship, Providence Church of Frisco, Texas

Jose Abella
Lead Pastor, Providence Road Church

Phillip Bethancourt
Executive Vice President, Ethics & Religious Liberty Commission

Adam W. Greenway
Dean, Billy Graham School of Missions, Evangelism, & Ministry, The Southern Baptist Theological Seminary

Joy White
Homemaker & Assistant Professor of Women's Studies, Cedarville University

Gregory Wills
Dean, School of Theology, The Southern Baptist Theological Seminary

Katie McCoy
Assistant Professor of Theology in
Women's Studies, Scarborough College at
Southwestern Baptist Theological Seminary

Rhyne R. Putman
Associate Professor of Theology & Culture,
New Orleans Baptist Theological Seminary

Barry Joslin
Professor of Christian Theology, Boyce
College

Rhonda Kelley
President's Wife, Adjunct Faculty, New
Orleans Baptist Theological Seminary

Peter Jones
Executive Director, TruthXchange

Bryan Baise
Assistant Professor of Philosophy &
Apologetics, Boyce College

Kenneth Keathley
Senior Professor of Theology, Southeastern
Baptist Theological Seminary

Jeff Struecker
Lead Pastor, Calvary Baptist Church

Rebecca Jones
Volunteer, TruthXchange

Evan Lenow
Associate Professor of Ethics, Southwestern
Baptist Theological Seminary

Daniel Patterson
Vice President for Operations & Chief
of Staff, Ethics & Religious Liberty
Commission

David Talley
Professor of Old Testament, Biola
University

Travis Wussow
Vice President for Public Policy, Ethics &
Religious Liberty Commission

Sean Perron
Chief of Staff, Association of Certified
Biblical Counselors

Michael L. Brown
President, FIRE School of Ministry

Keith Whitfield
Assistant Professor & Dean, Southeastern
Baptist Theological Seminary

Jeffrey Riley
Professor of Ethics, New Orleans Baptist
Theological Seminary

Dannah Gresh
Co-founder, Pure Freedom

Matt Damico

Associate Pastor of Worship, Kenwood Baptist Church

Colby Adams

Director of Communications, The Southern Baptist Theological Seminary

Paul Felix

President, Los Angeles Bible Training School

Colin Smothers

Executive Director, Council on Biblical Manhood and Womanhood

APPENDIX C

USING NATURAL LAW
ON SECULAR TERMS[1]

How should Evangelicals seeking to influence the public square respond to atheists who think natural law justifies a naturalistic ethic completely contrary to what we espouse?[2] Should we use the same natural law approach on which such atheists rely, or should we employ something else? I will argue that once the surrounding culture denies the reflected presence of divinely sourced moral standards in nature, relying on nothing more than nature as it is ceases to be a viable strategy for influencing the public square. I will also argue that, until a culture reaches that point, natural law can be a strategy for building moral apologetics with nonbelievers.

My aim is limited. I do not dispute the reflection of supernaturally imposed moral order in nature; I affirm biblical doctrine on the sufficiency of natural evidence justifying God's

---

[1] Previously published as an article in the *Liberty University Law Review*. Daniel R. Heimbach, "Natural Law in the Public Square," *Liberty University Law Review* 2/3 (Spring 2008): 685–702. Used with permission.

[2] For example, one atheist in a letter to the editor of a Raleigh newspaper said, "As an atheist, I respect natural law," and claimed that by contrast he believed "Christians have to deny basic laws of nature and deceive their own common sense in order to maintain their belief." James Sansom, "Letter to the Editor," *News and Observer* (Raleigh), 8 October 2006.

condemnation of fallen humanity; and I believe that creation has an appeal sufficient to lift the mind of nonbelievers to see the reflection of God in nature. I aim only at the viability of employing natural law on atheistic terms for building support for biblically acceptable moral standards in the public square. I mean only to address the utility of employing natural law in nontheistic terms as a strategy for influencing those who refuse to acknowledge anything in or beyond nature to justify restraining natural passions.

Resurgent Interest among Evangelicals

My reason for addressing this issue comes from a surge of recent interest among Evangelicals in using natural law for moral apologetics in secular culture. Catholics have long espoused natural law for engaging the culture, and their proponents today include Robert George, John Finnis, George Weigel, Timothy Fuller, Clarence Thomas, and J. Budziszewski. Other natural law proponents in today's world include various anthropocentric secularists, such as Hugh Hefner (now deceased), who justified sexual indulgence by what he described as "a sense of connection to the humankind and nature on this planet."[3] And there are others, such as Peter Singer, who sees nothing in nature requiring him to think sex with animals offends "our status and dignity as human beings,"[4] and Andrew Sullivan, an LGBTQ+ rights advocate who justifies "a diversity of moral sexual experience and identity" because he thinks nature reveals that humans are "a moderately adulterous species, made up primarily of mildly unfaithful male-female couples with a small minority of same-sex coupling."[5]

Now joining these proponents is a growing number of Evangelicals who are urging fellow Protestants to reject historic skepticism toward natural law in hope of enhancing moral influence in the public square. This development is separating Evangelicals into traditionalists and revivalists. On the traditionalist side, R. Albert Mohler and John Warwick Montgomery agree with the late Carl F. H. Henry, who urged Evangelicals to engage the culture but without

---

[3] Ronald Bruce Meyer, "Hugh M. Hefner and Playboy (1953)," blog *All about Ronald Meyer's world!* (December 10, 2004), accessible at: http://www.ronaldbrucemeyer.com/rants/1210almanac.htm.

[4] Peter Singer, "Heavy Petting," *Nerve* (March 12, 2001), accessible at: www.Nerve.com/Opinions /Singer/heavy Petting.

[5] Andrew Sullivan, *The Conservative Soul* (New York: HarperCollins, 2006), 97.

accommodating "postmodern nihilism" in the guise of natural law.[6] On the revivalist side, R. C. Sproul, Norm Geisler and Frank Turek, Chuck Colson, Stephen Grabill, Craig A. Boyd, and J. Daryl Charles think Evangelicals must either embrace natural law or give up trying to influence the culture on moral issues.[7]

Articles by Alan Johnson and Carl Braaten launched the current interest among some Evangelicals in giving up traditional Protestant refusal to rely on natural law ethics for sustaining moral influence among non-Christians in the wider culture,[8] and their publications moved Carl F. H. Henry to warn that Protestants, and especially Evangelicals, must not succumb to false promises inherent within natural law philosophy.[9] But now a younger generation represented by Grabill, Boyd, and Charles are again trying to shift Evangelical opinion

---

[6] Mohler believes "to revert to natural law reasoning is to retreat from the high ground of the Christian truth claim" and claims "it is not possible for evangelicals to adopt natural law reasoning as a basis for moral argumentation and remain authentically evangelical." R. Albert Mohler, "Homosexuality in Theological Perspective, Part Four," *Albert Mohler* (blog) (October 6, 2005), accessible at: http://www.albertmohler.com/2005/10/06/homosexuality-in-theological-perspective-part-four/. Montgomery says "the Natural Law Theory cannot hold up . . . because in different culture(s) there are different values." John Warwick Montgomery, "Human Rights & Christianity: Why They Are Inseparable," lecture presented at the University of California at Los Angeles (February 1, 2006), quoted in Michelle Vu, "Human Rights, Christianity Inseparable, Says World Renown Apologist," *Christian Post* (February 6, 2006), accessible at http://www.christianpost.com/article/20060206/7824_Human_Rights%2C_Christianity_Inseparable%2C_Says_World_Renown_Apologist.htm. Carl F. H. Henry, "Natural Law and a Nihilistic Culture," *First Things* (January 1995): 54.

[7] I heard Sproul expressing this at the inaugural meeting of the "Faith and Law Group" on Capitol Hill in Washington, DC, about 1988. Also R. C. Sproul, "Natural Theology and Science" in R. C. Sproul, *Defending the Faith* (Wheaton, IL: Crossway, 2003). Norman L. Geisler and Frank Turek, *Legislating Morality* (Minneapolis: Bethany House, 1998). Charles W. Colson, "Self-Evident Truth," *Jubilee* (February 1992). Stephen J. Grabill, *Rediscovering the Natural Law in Reformed Theological Ethics* (Grand Rapids: Eerdmans, 2006), and Stephen J. Grabill, "Evangelicals and the Brave New World: Why Natural Law Can No Longer Be Ignored," blog *Acton Commentary* (September 6, 2006), available at http://acton.org/pub/commentary/2006/09/06/evangelicals-and-brave-new-world-why-natural-law-c. Craig A. Boyd, *A Shared Morality: A Narrative Defense of Natural Law Ethics* (Grand Rapids: Baker, 2007), 11–12. J. Daryl Charles, "Protestants and Natural Law," *First Things* (December 2006), 33, 37.

[8] Alan F. Johnson, "Is There a Biblical Warrant for Natural Law Theories?" *Journal of the Evangelical Theological Society* 25:2 (June 1982), 185. Carl E. Braaten, "Protestants and Natural Law," *First Things* (January 1992), 20.

[9] Henry, "Natural Law and a Nihilistic Culture," 8.

on natural law by claiming luminaries of the past like Carl F. H. Henry, Helmut Thielicke, Herman Dooyeweerd, Cornelius Van Til, and G. C. Berkouwer were all wrong,[10] and unless Evangelicals take a more Catholic approach to natural law philosophy we will have no "basis upon which to build a moral apologetic" in the public square,[11] and will lose moral influence with non-Christians for having no "bridge to connect the Christian faith and culture."[12] I will carry this debate past both positions by arguing that, while historic Protestant skepticism is largely justified, relying on a natural law strategy for moral apologetics can at times be effective, but not when nonbelievers insist on denying recourse to more than nature for distinguishing what is or is not morally normative in nature.

No One Definition

When it comes to evaluating natural law philosophy and tradition, the most critical task is first to explain what one means by *natural law*, and that is never easy. Many have noted the enormous range and consequent difficulty of capturing the entire corpus in one definition. Arthur Harding observes that "concepts of Natural Law are almost as varied as are the philosophical systems which have been evolved in the history of Western civilization"; Daniel O'Connor thinks "various versions of the doctrine differ so much both in their detail and in their philosophical bases that it is very misleading to talk of *the* theory of natural law"; and Carl F. H. Henry notes how natural law means so many different things to so many different people that some are saying the term has no "precise content" and "changes with an evolving society."[13]

---

[10] Henry, 1. Helmut Thielicke, *Theological Ethics*, vol. 1, *Foundations*, ed. William H. Lazareth (Grand Rapids: Eerdmans, 1979), 150, 383–99, 420–33. Herman Dooyeweerd, *Roots of Western Culture: Pagan, Secular, and Christian Options*, trans. John Kraay, ed., Mark Vander Vennen et al. (Toronto: 1979), 111–47. Cornelius Van Til, *Common Grace and the Gospel* (Phillipsburg, NJ: Presbyterian and Reformed, 1974), 23–95. G. C. Berkouwer, *General Revelation* (Grand Rapids: Eerdmans, 1955), 187–214.

[11] Charles, "Protestants and Natural Law," 14, 37.

[12] Stephen J. Grabill, "Protestants and Natural Law: A Forgotten Legacy," Acton Institute *PowerBlog* (August 9, 2006), accessible at http://blog.acton.org/archives/1095-Protestants-and-Natural-Law-A-Forgotten-Legacy.html.

[13] Arthur L. Harding, ed., *Origins of the Natural Law Tradition* (Dallas: Southern Methodist University Press, 1954), v. Daniel John O'Connor, *Aquinas and Natural Law* (London: Macmillan, 1968), 57. Henry, "Natural Law and a Nihilistic Culture," 54.

This is complicated by the fact that natural law involves a range of different conceptions, with no proponent accepting all, and with no principle of coherence—other than referring in some way to *nature* and *law*—uniting all conceptions within a single rubric.

This makes natural law not just difficult, but impossible to define without proposing a definition that either is innocuous or limited to less than everything encompassed by natural law tradition taken as a whole. It means we must either define natural law so broadly as to involve no fixed content—as perhaps *anything referring to nature and morality any way at all*—or must use a definition covering less than everything natural law tradition encompasses as a whole. I will start with a broad yet less than comprehensive definition that Christians will consider familiar, and will proceed then to interact with conceptions extending beyond that less than comprehensive starting point.

Unless stated otherwise, *natural law* as used here means a combination of the following: (1) that some sort of ethical law exists by which human laws and behavior can be evaluated; (2) that this ethical law is in some sense objectively fixed; (3) that this objectively fixed ethical law is in some way present in nature; (4) that what this objectively fixed ethical law demands is accessible in some way (by reason, or intuition, or experience, or sensation) to human beings in their natural state (apart from revelation, regeneration, or indoctrination); and (5) that what this accessible, objectively fixed ethical law requires relates to everyone, everywhere, all the time. Nevertheless, readers should remember this is a working definition that does not fully cover all versions of natural law philosophy, because not every version agrees with all or even any of these defining elements. Indeed, some more recent variations maintain that natural standards are all relative, subjective, and sensual and therefore entail no fixed content.

Divided Streams of Meaning

Using this ostensibly more familiar but admittedly less than comprehensive definition, it is nevertheless clear that the evolution of natural law tradition through history divides into profoundly irreconcilable streams over whether the power by which one determines what is normative in nature is itself part of nature, or is located beyond nature and only reflected in nature; that is, whether the morally normative in nature involves nothing more than what occurs in nature or reflects rationally discernable purposes and plans for how natural things should work even when they do not and in reference to which human beings can evaluate natural occurrences as morally good or bad. In discussing these streams, I will refer to versions deriving norms from nothing but nature as *naturalist* and to those relying on a source beyond nature as *supernaturalist.*

Despite differing on other matters, Protagoras and Socrates both took a naturalist view of natural law. Protagoras is famous for asserting that "man is the measure of all things—of things that are, that they are, and of things that are not, that they are not."[14] He was not sure if gods existed, but did not care because he claimed if gods do exist they are no help when it comes to moral knowledge.[15] While Socrates may have regarded gods with more respect, he did not think their existence made any difference to moral knowledge. From what we know, Socrates taught that all men possess a sense of morality by virtue of human nature and can know what morality requires by consulting their own natural desires. Thus, Plato credits Socrates with arguing: "No one goes willingly toward the bad . . . neither is it in human nature . . . to want to go toward what one believes to be bad instead of to the good."[16] Protagoras and Socrates were naturalists because neither relied on the supernatural authority, and both held that nature as it is, and nature alone, supplied its own standard of moral valuation.

But, while Protagoras and Socrates were naturalists, it appears that many if not most ancient Greeks held some version of a supernaturalist approach to natural law. At least we know from Thucydides that the ancient men of Athens invoked a supernaturalist version of

---

[14] Protagoras, *Truth or Destruction*, fragment 1, quoted in Diogenes Laërtius, *Concerning the Lives, Teachings, and Declarations of the Eminent Philosophers or just Lives of the Eminent Philosophers*, 9.51. Quoted in Bertrand Russell, *A History of Western Philosophy* (New York: Simon and Schuster, 1945), 77. Protagoras was a sophist and an agnostic, living around the same time as Socrates. Although no complete work of his survives, portions of his work and thought have been preserved through citations made by other authors of the time. For more see Robin Waterfield, *The First Philosophers: The Presocratics and Sophists* (Oxford: Oxford University Press, 2000), 210.

[15] Protagoras, *About Gods*, fragment 4, quoted in Laërtius, *Lives*, 9.53, also quoted in Edward Schiappa, *Protagoras and Logos: A Study in Greek Philosophy and Rhetoric* (Columbia, SC: University of South Carolina Press, 2003), 141. The original reads περί μέν θεών ούκ έχω είδέναι, ούθ ώς είσιν ούθ ώς ούκ είσιν όποϊοί τινες ίδέαν πολλά γάρ τά κωλύοντα είδέναι ή τ'άδηλότης καί βραχύς ών ό βίος του άνθρώπου, which Schiappa renders "Concerning the gods I am unable to know, whether they exist or whether they do not exist or what they are like in form" (Schiappa, 141). For more information see Schiappa, *Protagoras and Logos*, 141–154.

[16] Plato, *Protagoras*. In *Plato: Complete Works*, ed. John M. Cooper (Indianapolis, IN: Hackett, 1997), 787.

natural law to justify conquering weak neighbors. When the people of Melos appealed to natural conscience for maintaining independence, the ancient Athenians answered that "of the gods we hold the belief, and of men we know, that by the necessity of their nature, wherever they have power, they always rule."[17]

Seeing the difficulty Socrates had resisting the subjectivity of Protagorean sophistry, Plato rejected naturalism in favor of supernaturalism, but on terms other than the Athenians used to justify conquering weak neighbors. Plato held that morality in nature was a matter of finding happiness by reaching the proper balance between sensual (material) and intellectual (nonmaterial) pleasures. Rather than relying on the subjectivity of human perception, Plato anchored the objectivity of natural morality not in nature itself, but in something beyond nature. He argued that the right balance for human happiness does not come from nature as it is, but from conforming nature to supernatural standards, or forms, that exist independent of nature and are only reflected in the nature we observe and experience. While Plato avoided the problem of moral subjectivity by fixing standards of natural law in supernatural forms, he did not rely on supernatural revelation and developed a view of natural law philosophy that justified totalitarian control of religion, work, education, sex, and the smallest details of family life.[18]

After Plato, Aristotle developed a version of natural law philosophy that reverted once more to naturalism. Aristotle held that what natural law requires does not come from anything beyond nature, but involves nothing more than observing nature as it is. Aristotle thought moral objectivity in natural law depends on assuming everything in nature has just one function regardless of human ingenuity; and because he thought nature shows there are different sorts of human nature, Aristotle justified slavery and argued that freeing slaves was immoral. "It is clear," he said, "that some men are by nature free, and others slaves, and that for these slavery is both expedient and right."[19] Following Aristotle, Epicurus took naturalism a step further, reducing natural law to sensuality because "if you fight against all your sensations, you will have no standard (in nature) to which to refer, and thus no means of judging even those judgments which you pronounce false."[20]

---

[17] Thucydides, Ἱστορίά τῶν Πόλοποννησίων (*History of the Peloponnesian War*), 5.105.2.

[18] For this see Plato, Πολιτεία (*Republic*).

[19] Aristotle, Πολιτικά (*Politics*), 1255.a.1–3.

[20] Laërtius, *Lives*, 10.146.

In the first century BC, the Roman philosopher Cicero resorted to a version of natural law rather similar to that used by the ancient Athenians. Cicero's version of natural law attempted to justify the expansion of the Roman Empire as a *natural* duty to assemble as many as possible into a single civil community "associated by a common acknowledgment of moral right."[21] Augustine criticized Cicero's natural law philosophy mainly for the naïve optimism by which Cicero assumed the possibility of arriving at a common moral basis—equally acceptable to the godly and the ungodly—sufficient for uniting all humanity in a single governing administration responsible for upholding and defending moral right and wrong.

Because "moral right is that which flows from the fountain of justice," and because the one true God is the only source of true moral justice, Augustine questioned how Cicero's presumption of an "assemblage of men associated by a common acknowledgement of moral right" can ever arise to unite those who serve the one true God with those who desert him to worship "impure demons."[22] Augustine argued "it is only when the soul serves God that it exercises a right control over the body," and it is only when reason submits to God that it is able then to "govern as it ought the passions and other vices." As such, there can be no true moral justice in individuals who do not serve God and "there certainly can be none in a community composed of such persons," and if so, there can be no "common acknowledgement of moral right which makes an assemblage of men a people whose affairs we call a republic." Augustine therefore argued that Cicero must be wrong since there can be no valid basis—no natural law case for common moral ground—for believing those who know the one true God could ever agree on moral matters to the degree required for uniting them in a commonly administered society (or republic) with those "who serve not God, but demons."[23]

The early Church mainly followed Augustine's refusal to rely on natural law philosophy to influence the ethical thinking of non-Christians. But that changed in the thirteenth century when Thomas Aquinas rediscovered Aristotle and used some of his ideas to formulate another version of natural law—one based on biblically grounded supernaturalism in place of Aristotle's scientific naturalism.[24] Unlike Aristotle, Aquinas did not think nature was itself the

---

[21] Cicero, *On the Republic*, 1.25. Augustine divided sharply with Cicero on this point (Augustine, *The City of God*, XIX.21).

[22] Augustine, *The City of God*, XIX.21.

[23] Augustine, *The City of God*, for the five preceding quotations.

[24] For more see O'Connor, *Aquinas and Natural Law*, 4–5.

origin of moral truth. He explained that "the light of natural reason, whereby we discern what is good and what is evil, which pertains to the natural law, is nothing else than an imprint on us of the divine light."[25] While Aquinas believed that men see enough of God's moral reason in nature to guide them toward earthly happiness, he also cautioned that "human reason is not itself the rule of things."[26] Rather, human reason was only a capacity for perceiving principles "contained in the eternal law" of God.[27] So, for Thomas, natural human capacity for discerning and interpreting true moral standards reflected in nature is checked, validated, and illuminated by biblical revelation and in that way moral agreement uniting Christians with non-Christians depends on whether and to what extent non-Christians agree to seeing in nature what Christians can verify in relation to Scripture.

In the sixteenth century, John Calvin reaffirmed how Aquinas identified moral law in nature with the everlasting moral law of God.[28] Calvin argued that there is in reality just one moral law, and so "the law of God which we call the moral law is nothing else than a testimony of natural law and of that conscience which God has engraved upon the minds of men."[29] Nonetheless Calvin was not as confident as Aquinas in the sufficiency of fallen humanity to run a morally just civil order relying on natural reason alone. Calvin held that, while "the purpose of natural law . . . is to render men inexcusable,"[30] it did not mean that unregenerate men, left to their own devices, could ever accurately comprehend—much less accept—the sort of moral grounds needed to secure civil happiness. Calvin believed sin so thoroughly obscures the natural exercise of reason that men must have God's "written law to give us a clearer witness to what was too obscure in the natural law."[31]

This led Calvin to conclude that men have by nature enough moral knowledge to justify God's wrath, but not enough on its own to provide a sufficient basis for "the preservation of society." He explained that as fallen beings "we quite fail to take our concupiscence into

---

[25] Thomas Aquinas, *Summa theologica*, q. 91.2.

[26] Aquinas, q. 91.3.

[27] Aquinas, q. 91.3.

[28] For more see William Klempa, "John Calvin on Natural Law," in *John Calvin and the Church: A Prism of Reform*, ed. Timothy George (Louisville: Westminster/John Knox, 1990).

[29] John Calvin, *Institutes of the Christian Religion*, 4.20.16.

[30] Calvin, 2.2.22.

[31] Calvin, 2.8.1.

account, for the natural man refuses to be led to recognize the diseases of his lusts. The light of nature is extinguished before he even enters upon this abyss."[32] Calvin therefore held that by natural reason men never truly discern, never truly desire, and never truly will what is morally good and right apart from supernatural intervention of the Holy Spirit.[33] So, while Calvin maintained a version of natural law, its moral content was supernatural, its standards could not be discerned apart from the Holy Spirit, and therefore appealing to natural law could not be used for defining common moral ground with non-Christians who reject the Holy Spirit and rely on nothing more than natural reason or conscience.

Other than debate among theologians regarding various supernatural approaches to natural law following either Aquinas or Calvin,[34] the history of natural law philosophical tradition since the sixteenth century has been one of steady decline into ever more narrow versions of naturalism and less and less confidence in the possibility of grounding moral objectivity in a common view of nature.[35]

In the early seventeenth century, only two generations following Calvin, the Dutch jurist Hugo Grotius reaffirmed the possibility of employing natural law philosophy on naturalistic, non-supernatural terms.[36] While continuing to hold that moral principles of natural law cannot be *fully* known apart from accepting God's existence, Grotius nevertheless put such faith in non-regenerate reason that he asserted that human capacity to arrive at sound principles of

---

[32] Calvin, 2.22.24.

[33] Calvin, 2.22.25–27.

[34] One notable highlight in this discussion was an exchange between Emil Brunner and Karl Barth published as *Natural Law*, trans. Peter Fraenkel (London: Centenary Press, 1946). Brunner challenged Barth in an essay titled, "Nature and Grace," and Barth responded in a sharply worded essay simply titled, "No!"

[35] It is often said of rationalists of the seventeenth and eighteenth centuries, who severed natural law from supernaturalism, that "far from establishing a new era of human liberty, (they) actually set the stage for a process of deterioration which, if unchecked, will destroy the very liberty which they asserted" (Arthur L. Harding, "The Ghost of Herbert Spencer: A Darwinian Concept of Law," in Harding, *Origins of the Natural Law*, 69–70). See also: Emil Brunner, *Justice and the Social Order*, trans. Mary Hottinger (New York: Harper, 1945), 4–10.

[36] This does not conflict with Oliver O'Donovan's corrective to how Hugo Grotius is sometimes unfairly criticized. The point here pertains even though Grotius also stressed duty to obey God and claimed natural reason requires "that we must obey God without qualification." See Oliver O'Donovan, "The Justice of Assignment and Subjective Rights in Grotius," in Oliver O'Donovan and Joan Lockwood O'Donovan, *Bonds of Imperfection* (Grand Rapids: Eerdmans, 2004).

social justice "would have a place even were we to accept the infamous premise that God did not exist or did not concern himself with human affairs."[37] In so doing, Grotius made natural law a product of autonomous, non-regenerated human reason. He severed reason from needing to affirm the existence of God to the extent that how men think of God has no necessary bearing on their ability to exercise reliable moral judgment.

Following Grotius, others joined in divorcing natural law from supernaturalism. Thomas Hobbes claimed that a law of nature (meaning a moral rule derived from nature) is "the dictate of right reason, conversant about those things which are either to be done or omitted for the constant preservation of life and members, as much as in us lies";[38] and Jean Jacques Rousseau believed that self-love is of itself alone "always good . . . in accordance with the order of nature."[39] This enlightenment version of supernaturally detached natural law philosophy, which venerated reason "as much as in us lies," came to be used during the French Revolution to justify stealing whatever working class people wanted and slaughtering others—not for what they did but for what they had. On this, Jacques Ellul observes "it was not for nothing that the French Revolution inaugurated the cult of the goddess Reason,"[40] meaning that once men believe nothing transcends their own reason, then nothing they think reasonable can ever be criticized as being wrong.

In the nineteenth century, John Stuart Mill and Herbert Spencer developed still more narrow versions of naturalistic natural law philosophy. Severed from the supernatural, these men found it harder than ever to justify fixed moral standards based on nothing but nature as it is. Human reason did not seem as reliable as it had. Mill denied that we should assume nature even requires a unitary principle justified by whatever someone or other considers reasonable. He decided that natural laws are nothing more than regularities observable in nature, that moral judgments based on natural laws are therefore nothing more than descriptions of

---

[37] Hugo Grotius, *On the Right of War and Peace*, trans. F. W. Kelsey et al. (Oxford: Oxford University Press, 1925), 12.

[38] Thomas Hobbes, "Philosophical Rudiments Concerning Government and Society," in *The English Works of Thomas Hobbes*, vol. 1, ed. William Molesworth (London: J. Bohn, 1839), 10.

[39] Jean Jacques Rousseau, *Émile*, trans. Barbara Foxley (New York: Dutton, 1921), IV.174.

[40] Jacques Ellul, *The Theological Foundation of Law*, trans. Marguerite Wieser (Garden City, NJ: Doubleday, 1960), 31–36.

what happens to occur in nature, and that consequently faith in our own non-supernatural "humanity" should replace all "supernatural religions."[41]

At the same time, Herbert Spencer reduced natural law to evolutionary naturalism, and in a way that erased distinctions separating human from animal life, and denied society should assist weaker members. According to Spencer, the only moral law in nature is the "law of natural selection" as defined by Charles Darwin—the law that nature favors "survival of the fittest." For Spencer this meant there is no duty for stronger, more able members of society to aid the survival of anyone less fit. He held that "human justice must be a further development of subhuman justice" and concluded that nature requires the strong and fit to eliminate every less fit member of the human race.[42]

Finally, the twentieth century witnessed the collapse of hope of finding any fixed moral content based on taking a naturalistic (non-supernatural) approach to natural law philosophy. While religious proponents still debate Thomistic versus Reformed versions of natural law theology, atheistic secularists have come to conclude that natural law philosophy provides little or no fixed content, and whatever may be left is certainly not thought sufficient to secure social survival, much less to provide an adequate basis on which to establish reliable social order.

H. L. A. Hart developed what he called a "minimal content" naturalist version of natural law, by which he meant the only truly necessary moral content nature requires of civil law is the absolute minimum without which most people in society will stop voluntary cooperation with a legal system.[43] Similarly, Rudolf Stammler and Georges Renard both argued that with no reference beyond nature, natural law assures no fixed content at all. Stammler proposed a "variable content" version, and Renard a "progressive content" version,[44] with both narrowing natural law philosophy to a form able to convey any moral content at all. Stammler and Renard together reduced natural law to what some have dismissed as "an empty bottle

---

[41] John Stuart Mill, *Three Essays on Religion* (London: Longmans, Green, Reader, and Dyer, 1874), 50.

[42] Herbert Spencer, *The Principles of Ethics* (London: Williams and Norgate, 1892–1893), IV.12.

[43] H. L. A. Hart, *The Concept of Law* (Oxford: Oxford University Press, 1961), 189–95.

[44] For Stammler see Rudolph Stammler, *Economy and Law according to the Materialistic Conception of History* (Leipzig: Verlag Von Veit, 1896). For Renard see Georges Renard, *Law, Order and Reason* (Paris: Recueil Sirey, 1927).

decorated with a nice label." While their versions of natural law philosophy are far from anything recognizable to Christians and are nowhere close to the definition with which we started this survey, they do constitute a segment of what natural law tradition has come to include. In this, they do in fact represent what natural philosophy has come to mean for many if not most secular (nonsupernaturalist) proponents in contemporary Western culture.

Diminishing Prospects for Agreeing with Nonbelievers

Again, my reason for tracking the divided history of natural law tradition is neither to dispute the reflection of God's moral order in creation, nor to reject the sufficiency of natural evidences to justify God's condemnation of fallen humanity, nor to question the reality of moral conscience in all members of the human race. Rather, I have highlighted how natural law philosophy has in fact evolved through history as proponents have divided over supernaturalism and rejecting the relevance of anything more than nature for evaluating nature. I will now treat how this affects prospects for relying on natural law philosophy for influencing nonbelievers in the public square.

From the actual evolution of natural law tradition through time, it is hard to ignore how once proponents reject supernaturalism, they have always found it more and more difficult to agree on any common moral ground with supernaturalists. From Protagoras to Spencer, from Aristotle to Stammler, naturalists have slid from agreeing on basic standards sufficient for assuring civil happiness, to only discovering laws of individual survival, to denying any fixed standards at all. Over this same history, naturalists have also claimed that natural law justifies slavery, slaughtering the innocent, classifying dishonesty as a virtue, and exterminating weak or needy members of the human race. What this history shows is that rejecting the supernatural severs natural law from moral objectivity so that approaching natural law on naturalist (non-supernatural) terms necessarily degenerates into naturalism and subjective reliance on sensuality. From a purely naturalist (non-supernatural) point of view, there is no basis for distinguishing moral laws *in nature* from regularities *of nature*. Without the supernatural, natural law reduces to ethical naturalism because moral judgment based on nothing but nature can never justify anything more or less than whatever we happen to see, feel, or experience in nature.

Noting how natural law philosophy deteriorates apart from supernaturalism does not mean Evangelicals should never use natural law for moral apologetics in the public square. Yet it is helpful to illuminate when and to what degree relying on natural law philosophy is a viable strategy for moral apologetics with naturalists. Jacques Ellul suggests that the utility of natural law apologetics for influencing nonbelievers depends on the state of religious-moral decline in surrounding culture.[45] A limit is reached on the ability of supernaturalists to influence naturalists using natural law apologetics when naturalists start refusing to accept any matter reflecting faith in the supernatural. The possibility of finding common moral ground is finally erased at the point that naturalists refuse to cooperate with those who will not at the outset agree (or pretend to agree) that nothing natural is ever wrong because nothing exists beyond nature as it is.

Ellul discusses how the effectiveness of relying on natural law philosophy for establishing common moral ground with naturalists diminishes with the religious-moral decline of culture. So long as most people believe in the existence of God—or at least believe that moral standards observable in nature depend on some notion of supernatural reality—there is hope of reaching some basic agreement on moral standards justified through appeal to natural law. Nonbelievers and believers will for a while agree on moral standards discoverable in nature without seeming to require faith in anything more than nature. After most members in a culture lose faith in God, however, (not saving faith but belief that God exists) reaching the point of denying that nature depends on anything more than nature as it is, it becomes increasingly difficult for those who believe that way to agree on any objectively fixed morality. At this point, therefore, it becomes increasingly difficult for supernaturalists to find common moral ground with naturalists on nonsupernatural naturalistic terms.

In describing the pathology of legal philosophy and systems of law, Ellul observes several stages by which societies increasingly lose the ability to establish common moral ground based on natural law. First, denying that natural law depends on more than nature makes it more and more difficult for anyone to evaluate law (whether moral or civil) by anything other than itself, and law "becomes purely a combination of technical rules."[46] Second, losing the ability to recognize the reality or relevance of any authority beyond what exists results in juridical technique

---

[45] Ellul, *Theological Foundation*, 31–36.
[46] Ellul, 31.

falling victim to whatever power insists on controlling it.[47] Third, denying accountability to any authority beyond itself, the state starts claiming absolute authority over all aspects of law; and when this happens the state becomes "judge of law" and is no longer "judged in its actions by the law."[48] Fourth, when the state transcends law (presumes absolute power over law), then what law is required by the state "gradually ceases to be observed and respected."[49] More and more citizens begin viewing the law as unworthy and cease to cooperate voluntarily, penalties are then tightened, the police system grows, and society falls into chaos.

At the fifth and final stage, Ellul observes that attempts are often made (by Christians or men of good will) "artificially to revive natural law, with the hope of bringing law back to life." Nevertheless, these attempts are doomed after passing "a point of no return," which occurs when denying the supernatural meets wide-scale failure to agree on a body of commonly respected standards relying on nature.[50] At this final stage, non-supernatural appeals to natural law philosophy are completely ineffective. Nonbelievers can no longer be moved to restrain natural appetites based on appealing to nothing more than nature; and Ellul argues that, once a culture reaches this point, moral order cannot be restored apart from renewing faith in God. He argues that once a culture sinks to this level, no restoration is possible except for replacement by a "new civilization"; and that "can only originate in the will of God."[51]

What Ellul contends is that since the application and influence of moral standards sufficient to secure and maintain social order is essentially connected to supernaturalism, only faith in the moral authority of God is in the end sufficient to check those who think they are of themselves able to create law for themselves. Since creators are superior to what they create, men are in the end immune from criticism based on nothing more than whatever laws they happen to create. What men make can be unmade however it suits their passions, and only authority beyond human manipulation is sufficient to check human manipulation. While most members of society still accept the reflection in nature of something more than nature, it is possible to establish common moral standards on appeal to nature. Nonbelievers and believers will agree on common standards discoverable in nature without seeming to require faith in anything

---

[47] Ellul, 32.
[48] Ellul, 33.
[49] Ellul, 33.
[50] Ellul, 35.
[51] Ellul, 35–36.

beyond nature. However, when a declining culture loses confidence in the reality of moral authority beyond nature reflected in nature, it becomes next to impossible for naturalists and supernaturalists to arrive at common moral ground based on acceptably similar views of nature.

Reducing Evangelical Reliance on Natural Law for Moral Influence

This suggests that Evangelicals must not think natural law philosophy will always offer the best strategy for restraining evil and promoting good in the public square.[52] The unavoidable problem with employing natural law philosophy as an apologetic strategy in atheistic circumstances is that naturalism will never persuade atheistic naturalists to accept what is supernatural. In other words, *those who rely on more-than-nature cannot use nothing-but-nature to persuade those who deny anything-more-than-nature to accept what depends on more-than-nature.* If an atheistic naturalist denies being able to see in nature any reason for restraining natural passions, he will never be persuaded to accept a more restrictive standard by appealing to nothing more than that very nature in which he denies seeing any reason for restriction. Such thinking will not change without referring to something, or someone, greater than nature, an authority by which natural sensations, experiences, and observations can be evaluated as to moral worth and legitimacy.

Without accepting the supernatural and relying on something beyond nature itself, natural law philosophy loses touch with moral objectivity and leads to indulging whatever passions arise from natural sensation and experience. To ground universally fixed moral objectivity independent of human subjectivity, natural law requires more than atheistic naturalism. That is, natural law philosophy must rely on something more than nature as it is. It requires the supernatural. And Evangelicals considering the value of natural law philosophy for moral apologetics must understand that we cannot maintain irreconcilable claims. That is, we cannot use supernaturalism to ground our own knowledge of universal moral objectivity, while at the same time alleging that those we plan to convince require no such thing.

---

[52] I refer to the problem of getting non-Christians, and particularly those opposing all notions of reality beyond the mundane, to embrace standards compatible with Scripture without appealing to something beyond nature by which to distinguish what in nature is morally normative from what is not.

Evangelicals attracted to natural law philosophy on supernatural terms may try limiting its definition to exclude atheistic naturalism. If so, we may not at the same time apply a non-atheistic point of view to arrive at some alleged common moral ground with those who approach natural law on atheistic terms. Further, should we accept a broader view encompassing the entire range of natural law philosophic tradition to increase likelihood of finding common ground with moral atheists, we will find that the only moral standards on which atheistic naturalists agree are those derived from ethical naturalism and no more. Either way Evangelicals operating in the public square are kept from arriving at common moral ground with avowed atheists, because no one in the public square can win the day by misrepresenting what others mean by natural law.

Once nonbelievers in a secular culture reject traditional moral norms as alien to natural passions, it becomes impossible—not just difficult but impossible—to restore their recovery by relying on nothing more than nature as it is. At this point, appealing to natural law philosophy is powerless to restrain moral decline, and moral apologetics by Evangelicals in the public square must look to another approach. An approach not hampered by denying reliance on more than nature for evaluating nature; one not afraid of directing men beyond themselves to their Creator; one that promotes civil happiness, justice, and social order by appealing to Jesus Christ, not theocratic fashion, but in ways respecting the right of anyone to persuade anyone else based on whatever that person considers convincing.

Evangelicals called to influence moral matters in public policy and to argue values in the public square must realize that, in a nihilistic, postmodern context, appealing to nature's supernatural Creator is surely more promising than resorting to natural law philosophy on atheistic terms. Where then does that leave us? On the one hand, Alan Johnson, Carl Braaten, Stephen Grabill, Craig Boyd, and Daryl Charles are surely right about Scripture affirming a universal moral order reflected in nature, so that access to this reflection transcends all races, classes, cultures, and religions. Yet I believe they are wrong where they fail to distinguish between the competing approaches to natural law. They fail to distinguish between taking a supernatural, biblically based approach to natural law that supposes a reality beyond nature for determining what is or is not moral in nature, and the various atheistic approaches to natural law that either require denying there is anything wrong with nature or refuse to allow recourse to more than nature for evaluating nature. Failing to make this distinction leaves their case for reviving natural law as a "bridge category" sitting astride a logical *non sequitur* that supposes the term "natural law" refers to exactly the same thing for naturalists and supernaturalists alike. Failing to realize this distinction, however, involves more than logic, for as long as Evangelicals conflate incompatible notions of natural law, Evangelical moral apologetics in the public square is reduced to no more than arguing over what is acceptable to atheistic naturalism.

On the other hand, Carl F. H. Henry, R. Albert Mohler, and John Warwick Montgomery—to say nothing of earlier giants of Protestant theology such as Thielicke, Dooyeweerd, Van Til, and Berkouwer—are right to insist that Evangelicals must never deny the relevance of supernaturalism for engaging the culture and must not allow the morality of natural reason to be severed from the morality of transcendent revelation. Nevertheless, I believe these also are wrong where their concerns lead to overlooking how the strategic value of using natural law philosophy for moral apologetics varies with cultural degeneration. So while Evangelical traditionalists are right to warn against accommodating "postmodern nihilism" in the guise of natural law, they should not deny the value of natural law for influence in the public square so long as the culture does not insist on reducing natural law to moral atheism.

In the final analysis, I believe we should be neither naively optimistic nor naively pessimistic. We should neither ignore nor exaggerate reasons for historic Protestant skepticism, and we should neither claim that natural law is never more than naturalism nor deny that natural law ever encompasses naturalism. Evangelicals challenging historic Protestant skepticism toward employing natural law philosophy must not confuse biblically refereed knowledge of God's moral standards reflected in nature with atheistic theories that deny there is anything wrong in nature. And those warning that we must not reduce natural law to naturalism should not dismiss natural law arguments where seen by nonbelievers as still persuading them to accept God's standards for securing common life. Of course, God's authority over creation applies whatever men think or say, but the degree to which men deny that truth does directly affect the degree to which natural law philosophy can work as a bridge for identifying and defending moral ground acceptable to nonbelievers in the public square. In the end we must affirm with Carl F. H. Henry that moral power for once more establishing social cohesion and restoring general respect for the governing role of law will not come from "reading the entrails of evolutionary nature" but by "recognizing anew the Divine Valuator and a recovery of the *imago dei*."[53]

---

[53] Henry, "Natural Law and a Nihilistic Culture," 60.

Natural Law Philosophy and Natural Theology

Were Emil Brunner and Karl Barth discussing theology or philosophy in their famous debate over natural law?[54] The answer is a bit of both, but it was mostly theology. And when Thomas Aquinas addressed natural law in his *Summa Theologica*,[55] was it theology or philosophy? Once more the answer is both, and he was intentionally mixing one with the other, which is why what he did is referred to as "syncretistic." It is not possible to be "syncretistic" unless you are mixing different things together. The problem is theology and philosophy are completely different things having completely different starting points with completely different presuppositions about God, reality, human nature, the autonomy of reason, the basic ethical problem, and how to solve it, and it is terribly confusing to use a single term, *natural law*, for these two very different things. So, to avoid mixing things up and confusing one with the other, it makes good sense if we would just agree to use different terms for each, using the term *natural law theology* for what Christians know about moral norms reflected in creation based on the Bible and passages like Romans 1:18–20, and using the term *natural law philosophy* for human theories about finding norms in nature starting with personal experience and trusting only in ourselves without believing in God or the Bible, or even having to presuppose transcendent reality.

This has implications, of course, for how Christians try to influence nonbelievers on moral issues contested in a mixed culture where Christians live on an equal basis with others outside the Christian community. And this matters especially where it concerns Christians engaging others on moral issues affecting civil law and public policy under rulers committed to governing on secular terms without presupposing any particular faith tradition or worldview. In that case, it is important to understand that natural law philosophy is not the same as natural law theology, and agreeing to anthropocentric, naturalistic presuppositions on secular terms will never reach the same norms Christians anticipate based on natural law theology formed by a Biblical worldview. Better then to influence others on moral issues person-to-person based on the Word of God and real-world consequences than pretending faith commitments make no

---

[54] Emil Brunner and Karl Barth, *Natural Law*, trans. Peter Fraenkel (London: Centenary Press, 1946).

[55] Thomas Aquinas, *Summa theologica*, II.I, q. 2, viii.

difference and ethics establishing the common good in public arenas has nothing to do with the Moral Ruler running things.

So is natural law philosophy a "bridge" enabling Christians to have moral influence in a secular culture? Is it the price we must pay for a "seat at the table" to affect ethics in public policy? That depends on how closely the worldview presuppositions we have align with those we are trying to influence. If the worldview presumptions of a target audience aligns closely with ours, then appealing to natural law philosophy seems to work. But if they do not, relying on natural law philosophy can be a bad idea. Practically speaking, natural law philosophy can be a way to explain how the moral thinking of people with different worldviews happens already at some points to agree with what Christians think. But natural law philosophy never persuades others to change their minds on ethical issues over which they disagree with Christians. In other words, natural law philosophy cannot bring people with radically opposed worldviews together and for that reason is not able to help Christians in a secular culture gain support on moral issues that others with opposing worldviews are determined to reject. We must understand that natural law theology and natural law philosophy are not the same thing and that worldview presuppositions make all the difference to how the moral witness of Christians persuades others to agree with us.

CLARIFYING METAETHICAL PHILOSOPHY

This appendix supplements Chapter 7 by covering metaethical philosophy in more depth. In philosophical terms, *metaethics* is the branch of philosophy that explores the status, foundations, and scope of moral values, properties, and words.[1] The word metaethics comes from two Greek words, μετά (*meta*), meaning along with or at the side of (and so perhaps also behind or beyond), and ἠθικός (*ēthikos*), referring to character or morally worthy living. As a branch of philosophy, metaethics is thought to focus on what is above and behind other levels of ethical understanding. Other levels address what is or is not ethically right or wrong, but metaethics is thought to addresses what ethics is in the first place. In theological terms, however, metaethics is human minds attempting to stand above and behind the mind of God. Ethics must start somewhere and, if it does not start with God, it starts with something else. There is no compromise position, no mixing of one with the other, and no halfway point between these two perspectives. One subordinates the other. And, if the mind of God does

---

[1] Kevin M. DeLapp, "Metaethics," *The Internet Encyclopedia of Philosophy*, June 16, 2021. https://www.iep.utm.edu/metaethi/.

not transcend and subordinate what human minds conceive, then human minds presume to transcend and subordinate what the mind of God reveals.

Metaethics claims not to be ethically "normative" and claims rather to focus on what is above and behind ethical right and wrong and as such regards "normative" ethics as a lower level of analysis. But thinking this way is problematic because philosophers doing metaethics never really detach themselves from normative thinking. Thinking itself is impossible without employing a worldview, and the worldview one employs inevitably determines how one thinks about right and wrong.[2] So philosophers doing metaethics either naïvely believe they can do something impossible (believe they can examine what is above and behind normative ethics without affecting normative ethics), or they knowingly pretend to do something different than they are (pretend metaethics has no impact on normative ethics when they know it does).

Metaethics & Theological Ethics

Metaethics is the element in philosophical ethics that most conflicts with the role the Word of God and divine revelation play in defining, framing, and directing ethical insight. For that reason, metaethics also is the element in philosophical ethics that most challenges Christian ethical understanding. But, sadly, this challenge is hardly ever discussed in books introducing Evangelicals to philosophical ethics or in books presenting how Christian ethics interacts with, compares to, or criticizes philosophical ideas about the nature and relevance of ethical understanding.

The irony involved is twofold—first because metaethics disagrees with what God considers most essential to understanding ethical truth, and second because, since the 1950s, philosophers have focused more attention on this element than any other in philosophical ethics. Even though Evangelicals have engaged every other element in philosophical ethics, we have all but ignored the one element on which philosophers disagreeing with us have focused most of their attention. Indeed, the situation has been rather like people in a house guarding the front door while ignoring burglars in the kitchen. That needs to be addressed, and this appendix moves in that direction.

---

[2] On this, see Kai Nelsen, "Ethics, Problems of," 118 (see chap. 7, n. 33); Douma, *Responsible Conduct,* 8 (see chap. 1, n. 16).

Metaethics always clashes with biblically faithful ethics because it presumes human minds have standing to define what most affects ethical truth, meaning it presumes to do what theology does. But, while theology starts with revelation, metaethics does not. Theologians start with what God says, but philosophers doing metaethics start with themselves and so put themselves in God's place. They assume standing to make ultimate claims and, in so doing, demote and relativize everything and everyone, including God. This makes metaethics inherently idolatrous and never exactly true. Or, at least, it means no metaethical position is true in the eyes of God (Isa 45:19) because no metaethical position honors the ethical sovereignty God has over creation (Ps 33:8–9). It is either "Thus says the LORD" or "Thus says a metaethicist." There is only one transcendence and only one can be ultimately right and true.

This is why Barth (1886–1968) considered philosophical ethics, and metaethics in particular, to be inherently "idolatrous."[3] An idol is anything taking the place of God, and claiming to have standing over the Word of God is idolatrous by definition. Put another way, aligning the moral compass we live by to anything viewed as over or behind God constitutes idol worship because it replaces the ultimacy of God with something else. Ramsey once suggested "Christian theological ethics is metaethics," by which he meant moral theology can be viewed as being the only acceptable metaethical position.[4] But this is problematic because philosophers in metaethics do not accept Ramsey's idea, and that means conceiving theological ethics as true metaethics makes no sense to them without first changing how they think.

Barth saw no value in identifying theological ethics with metaethics to get philosophers to accept ethical revelation and instead insisted "nontheological thinking" will never "justify theological thinking," warned not "to justify Christian ethics at the bar of philosophical ethics," and argued that any Christian ethics rendered acceptable to philosophers "is no longer a proper theological ethics."[5] So, despite Ramsey's suggestion, it is best not to mix theology with metaethics. They are mutually exclusive perspectives on what ultimately is above and behind ethical understanding. Both cannot be true at the same time, and reconciling them is not possible without changing what one or the other means. There is only one ultimacy in ethics, and

---

[3] Karl Barth, *Ethics*, 16–17, 19–24 (see chap. 1, n. 26).

[4] O'Donovan, *Resurrection and Moral Order*, 8 (see chap. 1, n. 69). O'Donovan studied with Ramsey, and this appears to be something Ramsey never published but that O'Donovan remembers him saying.

[5] Barth, *Ethics*, 21–22.

Christian ethics must criticize, reject, and subordinate every metaethical position or cease to be properly Christian. There is only one transcendence, only one ultimacy above and behind normative reality, only one starting point for ethical truth. And, if that ultimacy is not God himself, then whatever thinking comes of it is not just inaccurate but idolatrous.

Metaethics & the Rest of Philosophical Ethics

Although metaethics is considered part of philosophical ethics, it also stands apart from philosophy. This difference comes not only from being more abstract, but also from being less philosophical in nature. What distinguishes philosophy from theology is that philosophy speculates and theology declares. Philosophy starts with human reason and experience and asks questions. It starts with "if" and speculates, "if this is the case, that may be the case." And what makes theology different is starting with revelation and declaring, "because God says this, that is the case." Declaring something true to begin with is theological, rather than philosophical, in nature, and nothing declaring something true to begin with is properly philosophical. The most significant thing distinguishing metaethics from the rest of philosophical ethics is that instead of starting with speculation, it starts by declaring. It does not start with "if" but with saying something is the case.

This section uses two terms—*dogma* and *a priori*. *Dogma* refers to beliefs taken as true and bearing authority over what we think, say, and do, and related terms include *dogmatism* and *dogmatics*. Dogma can be analyzed and applied but not questioned because it is believed to be from authority requiring acceptance, submission, and obedience. Questioning dogma doubts the authority it comes from and so questioning a claim denies that it is dogmatic. For Christians, *dogma* refers to revelation from God and is what makes theology "theological." Dogma cannot be treated as if subordinate to another set of starting beliefs without rejecting God or treating the Word of God as if subordinate to other beliefs thought to have more authority than God. *A priori* is a Latin phrase meaning "from what was before," and the phrase is used in English to indicate "something a way of thinking starts with in order to think about other things." An a priori assumption is not something deduced from something else but is a starting belief based on which other things are deduced. An a priori belief is not questioned because questioning a belief claim means it is not a priori. It is not belief accepted to begin with.

Metaethical positions are a priori belief statements every bit as a priori and dogmatic as the Apostle's Creed. In other words, they are like saying, "I believe in God, the Father Almighty, Creator of heaven and earth," which means they are not theories so much as faith statements, and, because of that, they operate more like other dogmas attacking Christian dogmas than just guessing at ethics apart from God. So, it turns out, what distinguishes metaethics from other philosophy is the same as what causes it to clash so much with Christian ethical thinking. It makes dogmatic, a priori assertions against trusting God's moral compass and does so more directly and obviously than the rest of philosophical ethics. Philosophical theories can be respected as guessing at ethics in ways that sometimes get things right even if clouded by finitude and fallenness. But metaethical positions do not act like theories and instead act like assertions of transcendence crossing over from what philosophers do into what theologians do. They do not theorize the way philosophical positions usually do but rather make grand claims every bit as a priori and dogmatic as theology.

Subsections of Metaethics

Metaethics has three subsections. *Epistemological metaethics* focuses on what ethical knowing is, how we gain knowledge used in making moral judgments, and what sort of thing it is when we have it. *Ontological metaethics* focuses on what ethics itself is, what sort of thing moral values and beliefs are, what they cover and to what extent, and where they come from. Are they real apart from people believing them, or are they made up? Are they objective and fixed or subjective and changing? Must they make sense, or does that matter? What makes them obligatory, and must they be grounded? And *linguistic metaethics*, also referred to as *analytic metaethics*, focuses on what ethical speaking is. Are moral statements about facts or about values apart from facts? Are moral utterances about something true or false or just about feelings or opinions of the person speaking? What does it mean to say something is right or wrong, and does it matter other than to the person speaking? And, if moral judgments matter, how is that established? The figure below outlines the three subsections of metaethics along with their initial subdivisions.

SUBSECTIONS OF METAETHICS

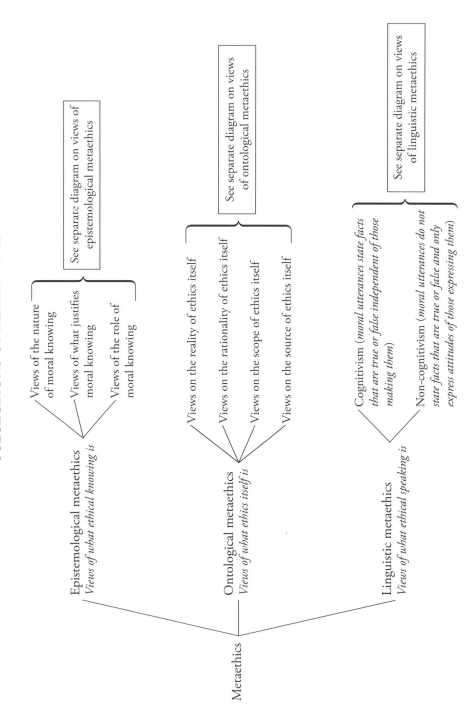

Metaethics

Epistemological metaethics
Views of what ethical knowing is

- Views of the nature of moral knowing
- Views of what justifies moral knowing
- Views of the role of moral knowing

See separate diagram on views of epistemological metaethics

Ontological metaethics
Views of what ethics itself is

- Views on the reality of ethics itself
- Views on the rationality of ethics itself
- Views on the scope of ethics itself
- Views on the source of ethics itself

See separate diagram on views of ontological metaethics

Linguistic metaethics
Views of what ethical speaking is

- Cognitivism (*moral utterances state facts that are true or false independent of those making them*)
- Non-cognitivism (*moral utterances do not state facts that are true or false and only express attitudes of those expressing them*)

See separate diagram on views of linguistic metaethics

While the subsections of metaethics are easy to distinguish conceptually, they interrelate in practice so much that philosophers working in one subsection always affect the rest. This means metaethical positions always have a mix of epistemological, ontological, and linguistic implications. In practice, metaethical positions never affect just one subsection by itself and always affect all three. And, of these subsections, the one attracting the most attention has been linguistic metaethics. In fact, work in linguistic metaethics has spawned so many new positions and terms they are hard to keep up with, and philosophers do not always agree on what they mean. We now will sort through the landscape in a way meant to keep it all straight along with helping readers understand what metaethical philosophers have been doing.

Epistemological Metaethics

Epistemological metaethics considers what ethical knowing is. It claims not to address actual right and wrong and only to focus on what knowing morality entails. The word *epistemology* comes from two Greek words: ἐπιστήμη (*epistēmē*), meaning "understanding" or "knowledge," and λογίζομαι (*logizomai*), meaning "think about" or "study." So, *epistemology* means "the study of knowledge" and, in metaethics, the term refers to positions on what ethical knowing is. Epistemological metaethics, in turn, has three subdivisions, with one considering the nature of moral knowing, one considering what justifies moral knowing, and one considering the role of moral knowing.

The first subdivision in epistemological metaethics considers the nature of moral knowing, and this subdivision, in turn, has two further divisions—one dealing with the "thickness" of moral knowing and one dealing with the scope of moral knowing. Each of these further divisions includes two positions. The "thickness" of moral knowing concerns the degree of concreteness involved in moral knowing. Is moral knowing something vague and hard to apply with confidence? Or is it something clear and applied with confidence? The first "thickness" position is "thin epistemological metaethics" and the second is "thick epistemological metaethics." Gilbert Ryle and Clifford Geertz are associated with discussing this thick-thin distinction, and Bernard Williams and Alasdair MacIntyre are best known for arguing that moral knowledge is "thick."[6]

---

6 Gilbert Ryle, "What Is *Le Penseur* Doing?," in *Collected Papers 2: Collected Essays 1929–1968* (London: Hutchinson, 1971), 480–496; Clifford Geertz, "Thick Description: Toward an Interpretative

The scope of moral knowing has to do with applicability. Does moral knowing pertain to everyone or only to particular people in particular ways? The first scope of ethical knowing position is "metaethical epistemological universalism" and the second is "metaethical epistemological particularism." Philosophers associated with positions on the scope of moral knowing include Brad Hooker, Margaret Little, and Jonathan Dancy.[7]

Besides the nature of ethical knowing, another subdivision in epistemological metaethics considers what justifies moral knowing. Again, what is considered is not actual right and wrong but only how knowing it is justified. Does moral knowing need justifying and, if so, what qualifies? Four approaches are taken, and two of them include different versions. The four approaches in epistemological metaethics are "metaethical epistemological foundationalism," "metaethical epistemological coherentism," "metaethical epistemological contextualism," and "metaethical epistemological intuitionism."

Metaethical epistemological foundationalism is thinking moral knowing is justified by facts or beliefs that themselves need no justifying. This approach assumes moral beliefs are not valid unless justified by something indisputable, and there are different positions on what counts as "indisputable." Metaethical epistemological foundationalism divides into "metaethical epistemological naturalistic foundationalism," which holds that moral knowing is justified by nonmoral facts discoverable in the natural world, and "metaethical epistemological non-naturalistic foundationalism," which holds that moral knowing is justified by "basic beliefs" that are self-evident. In other words, such beliefs are thought to be "basic" because, unlike regular beliefs, they are not inferred from other beliefs and are just obvious. Philosophers associated with metaethical epistemological foundationalism include James Van Cleve, William P. Alston, Ernest Sosa, and David Brink.[8]

Theory of Culture," in *The Interpretation of Cultures: Selected Essays* (New York: Basic Books, 1973), 3–30; Bernard Williams, *Ethics and the Limits of Philosophy* (Cambridge, MA: Harvard, 1985); Alasdair MacIntyre, *After Virtue*, (see chap. 4, n. 1).

[7] Brad Hooker and Margaret Little, eds., *Moral Particularism* (Oxford: Clarendon, 2000); Jonathan Dancy, *Practical Reality* (Oxford: Oxford, 2000).

[8] William P. Alston, "Has Foundationalism Been Refuted?," *Philosophical Studies* 29 (1976): 287–305; James Van Cleve, "Foundationalism, Epistemic Principles, and the Cartesian Circle," *The Philosophical Review* 88/1 (January 1979): 55–91; David Brink, *Moral Realism and the Foundations of Ethics* (Cambridge: Cambridge, 1989); Ernest Sosa, "The Foundations of Foundationalism," *Nous* 14/4 (November 1980): 547–64.

Metaethical epistemological coherentism is thinking moral knowing is justified by inclusion in a coherent belief system. This approach assumes belief systems are self-contained and moral knowing is justified if it fits other beliefs in the system containing them. That is, moral knowing just needs to be part of a network of belief that holds together. But this approach also assumes nothing links moral knowing in one belief system with moral knowing in other systems. To be justified, moral knowing needs only to fit everything else people believe. Philosophers associated with metaethical epistemological coherentism include Geoffrey Sayre-McCord, Sven Hansson, and Erik Olsson.[9]

Metaethical epistemological contextualism is thinking moral knowing is justified by conforming to what people in a context think it requires, and this approach includes two positions—"metaethical epistemological normative contextualism" and "metaethical epistemological structural contextualism." Metaethical epistemological normative contextualism holds that moral knowing is justified by whatever "epistemic practices" people in a context accept, *and metaethical epistemological structural contextualism* holds that moral knowing is justified if it fits beliefs accepted by a group of people. Metaethical epistemological structural contextualism is a lot like metaethical epistemological nonnaturalistic foundationalism with the only difference being that one considers context and the other does not. Philosophers associated with metaethical epistemological contextualism include Mark Timmons and Kai Nielsen.[10]

Finally, metaethical epistemological intuitionism is thinking moral knowing needs no justifying, either because it is impossible or because it is unnecessary. The answer given to "What justifies moral knowing?" is "nothing" because it is "not that sort of thing." It is thought that people know moral properties the same as knowing a tree when they see one. When people see a tree, they just "see a tree" without needing to prove it and, since seeing physical things needs

---

[9] Geoffrey Sayre-McCord, "Coherence and Models for Moral Theorizing," *Pacific Philosophical Quarterly* 66 (1985): 170–90; Geoffrey Sayre-McCord, "Coherentist Epistemology and Moral Theory," in Walter Sinnott-Armstrong and Mark Timmons, ed., *Moral Knowledge? New Readings in Moral Epistemology* (Oxford: Oxford, 1996); Sven Hansson and Erik Olsson, "Providing Foundations for Coherentism," *Erkenntnis* 51 (1999): 243–65.

[10] Mark Timmons, "A Contextualist Moral Epistemology," in *Moral Knowledge? New Readings in Moral Epistemology,* ed. Walter Sinnott-Armstrong and Mark Timmons, (Oxford: Oxford, 1996); Kai Nielsen, *Why Be Moral?* (Buffalo, NY: Prometheus, 1989).

no justifying, neither does "seeing" things by moral intuition. Philosophers associated with metaethical epistemological intuitionism include Robert Audi, Lawrence Blum, and Kevin DeLapp.[11]

The last subdivision in epistemological metaethics considers the role of moral knowing. Does moral knowing have an external role or not? Does it matter to others besides the knower? Or does it matter only to the knower? This approach includes two positions—"metaethical epistemological externalism" and "metaethical epistemological internalism." Metaethical epistemological externalism is thinking moral knowing is externally relevant. What a person knows matters outside the knower and is not merely internal to himself or herself. What is known applies to what others should or should not be or do as well as to what the knower should or should not be or do. It is thinking moral knowing attributes properties of good, bad, or indifferent beyond the knower him- or herself and are more than personal opinions.

Metaethical epistemological internalism is thinking moral knowing has no external relevance and only matters within the knower. By this position, moral knowing does not attribute properties of good, bad, or indifferent beyond the knower himself or herself, and is, therefore, nothing more than personal opinion. Philosophers associated with these positions on the role or relevance of moral knowing are Gilbert Harmon and Nicholas Sturgeon.[12]

---

[11] Robert Audi, "Moral Knowledge and Ethical Pluralism," in *Blackwell Guide to Epistemology*, ed. John Greco and Ernest Sosa (Oxford: Blackwell, 1999), 271–302; Lawrence Blum, "Moral Perception and Particularity," *Ethics* 101/4 (1991): 701–25; Kevin DeLapp, "Moral Perception and Moral Realism: An 'Intuitive' Account of Epistemic Justification," *Review Journal of Political Philosophy* 5 (2007): 43–64.

[12] Gilbert Harmon, *The Nature of Morality* (Oxford: Oxford University Press, 1977); Nicholas Sturgeon, "Moral Explanations," in Geoffrey Sayre-McCord, ed., *Essays on Moral Realism* (Ithaca, NY: Cornell University Press, 1988), 229–55.

VIEWS OF EPISTEMOLOGICAL METAETHICS

Views of what ethical knowing is

Views of the nature of moral knowing

Views on the thickness of moral knowing (Geertz, Ryle)

- Thin metaethical knowing (*moral knowing is generic and not concrete or specific*)
- Thick metaethical knowing (*moral knowing is concrete and specific*) (Williams, MacIntyre)

Views on the scope of moral knowing (Hooker, Little, Dancy)

- Metaethical epistemological universalism (*moral knowing pertains to everyone*)
- Metaethical epistemological particularism (*moral knowing only pertains to particular people in particular ways*)

Views of what justifies moral knowing

Metaethical epistemological foundationalism (*moral knowing is justified by facts or beliefs that themselves need no justifying*) (Alston, Van Cleve, Brink, Sosa)

- Metaethical epistemological naturalistic foundationalism (*moral knowing must be based on non-moral facts about the natural world*)
- Metaethical epistemological non-naturalistic foundationalism (*moral knowing consists of basic beliefs that do not need justifying because they are self-evident*)

Metaethical epistemological coherentism (*moral knowing is justified by being part of a coherent belief system*) (Sayre-McCord, Hansson, Olsson)

Metaethical epistemological contextualism (*moral knowing is justified if it fits what people accept*) (Timmons)

- Metaethical epistemological normative contextualism (*moral knowing is justified by standard knowledge practices followed by people accepting them*)
- Metaethical epistemological structural contextualism (*moral knowing is justified by what an accepted belief system requires*) (Nielsen)

Metaethical epistemological intuitionism (*moral knowing needs no justifying*) (Audi, Blum, DeLapp)

Views of the role of moral knowing

- Metaethical epistemological externalism (*moral knowing is externally relevant*) (Sturgeon)
- Metaethical epistemological internalism (*moral knowing is not externally relevant and only matters to the knower*) (Harmon)

Ontological Metaethics

"Ontological metaethics" addresses what ethics itself is. It claims not to address what is actually good or bad or is actually right or wrong but only to focus on what moral values and beliefs are. The word *ontology* comes from two Greek words: ὤν (*ōn*), which is the present participle of εἰμί (*eimi*, to be) and means "being," and λογίζομαι (*logizomai*), meaning "think about" or "study." So *ontology* means "the study of being" and *ontological metaethics* refers to positions on "the being" of ethics itself. Ontological metaethics has four subdivisions, one considering the reality of ethics itself, one considering the rationality of ethics itself, one considering the scope of ethics itself, and one considering the source of ethics itself. The one considering the scope of ethics itself is close to the subdivision in epistemological metaethics that considers the scope of moral knowing. But the two are different because the epistemological subdivision focuses on what ethical knowing is and the ontological subdivision focuses on what ethics itself is.

The subdivision in ontological metaethics considering the reality of ethics itself includes two approaches—"metaethical ontological realism," sometimes referred to as "ontological objectivism," and "metaethical ontological nonrealism," sometimes referred to as "ontological subjectivism" or "ontological constructivism." These two approaches to the reality of ethics itself each include three positions. Metaethical ontological realism, also known as metaethical ontological objectivism, is thinking moral values exist apart from believing them, and, in turn, includes three positions—"naturalistic metaethical ontological realism," "nonnaturalistic metaethical ontological realism," and "dispositional metaethical ontological realism."

Naturalistic metaethical ontological realism, also known as "concrete metaethical ontological realism," is thinking moral values are realities found scientifically by examining the physical world. It is thinking moral values are "out there" in nature and can be proven by gathering and testing material evidence the way scientists prove the existence of gravity or magnetism. Philosophers associated with naturalistic metaethical ontological realism include Alan Gewirth, Deryck Beyleveld, Michael Boylan, Nicholas Sturgeon, and Paul Bloomfield.[13]

---

[13] Alan Gewirth, *Reason and Morality* (Chicago: University of Chicago, 1980); Deryck Beyleveld, *The Dialectic Necessity of Morality* (Chicago: University of Chicago, 1992); Michael Boylan, *A Just Society* (New York: Rowman & Littlefield, 2004); Nicholas Sturgeon, "Moral Explanations," in *Essays on Moral Realism*, ed. Geoffrey Sayre-McCord (Ithaca, NY: Cornell University, 1988), 229–55; Paul Bloomfield, *Moral Reality* (Oxford: Oxford, 2001).

Nonnaturalistic metaethical ontological realism, also known as "abstract metaethical ontological realism" or "transhuman metaethical ontological realism," is thinking moral values are abstract realities that exist apart from nature. The position agrees with thinking moral values exist apart from believing them and agrees they can be discovered. But the position then says they are not discovered scientifically. Moral values are thought to be facts ascertained by reason or some other faculty apart from material evidence gathered from nature. Philosophers associated with nonnaturalistic metaethical ontological realism include G. E. Moore, W. D. Ross, W. D. Hudson, Iris Murdoch, and Russ Shafer-Landau.[14]

Dispositional metaethical ontological realism is thinking moral values are, in a sense, "real" but also are not completely objective in relation to believing them. This position supposes moral properties are "dispositional," meaning they are latent potentials not actualized unless certain things happen. For example, a drinking glass is "fragile" whether it breaks or not. The property of being "fragile" is latent. It is real but not actualized unless the glass is dropped or hits something causing it to break. In the same way, dispositional metaethical ontological realism claims that moral properties exist the way being "fragile" exists in a drinking glass. They are latently "real" but not "actualized" unless an occurrence manifests their reality. Philosophers associated with dispositional metaethical ontological realism include John McDowell, David Wiggins, Sabina Lovibond, David McNaughton, Mark Platts, Jonathan Dancy, and Kevin DeLapp.[15]

The second approach in ontological metaethics toward the reality of ethics itself is metaethical ontological nonrealism, also known as "metaethical ontological subjectivism" or "metaethical ontological constructivism," which is thinking moral values are not "out there" in

---

[14] G. E. Moore, *Principia Ethica* (Cambridge: Cambridge, 1903); W. D. Ross, *The Right and the Good* (Oxford: Oxford, 1930); William Hudson, *Ethical Intuitionism* (New York: St. Martin's, 1967); Iris Murdoch, *The Sovereignty of Good* (New York: Routledge & Kegan Paul, 1970); Russ Shafer-Landau, *Moral Realism: A Defense* (Oxford: Oxford, 2003).

[15] John McDowell, "Values and Secondary Qualities," in *Morality and Objectivity*, ed. Ted Honderich (New York: Routledge & Kegan Paul, 1985), 110–29; David Wiggins, *Needs, Values, Truth* (Oxford: Oxford, 1976); Sabina Lovibond, *Realism and Imagination in Ethics* (Minneapolis: Minnesota University, 1983); David McNaughton, *Moral Vision* (Oxford: Blackwell, 1988); Mark Platts, *Moral Realities: An Essay in Philosophical Psychology* (New York: Routledge, 1991); Jonathan Dancy, *Practical Reality* (Oxford: Oxford, 2000); Kevin DeLapp, "The Merits of Dispositional Moral Realism," *Journal of Value Inquiry* 43/1 (2009): 1–18.

the world because they are not independently real and are only alleged to be "real" by those believing them. And metaethical ontological nonrealism, in turn, includes three positions, which are "metaethical ontological nonrealist error theory," "metaethical ontological nonrealist fictionalism," and "metaethical ontological nonrealist pluralistic relativism."

Metaethical ontological nonrealist error theory is thinking moral values are not really real and believing they are is mistaken. In fact, thinking moral values to be real is wrong no matter how strongly people believe they are. The philosophers most associated with metaethical ontological nonrealist error theory are J. L. Mackie, Simon Blackburn, and Richard Joyce.[16] Metaethical ontological nonrealist fictionalism agrees with thinking moral values are not really real and agrees that believing them real is mistaken. But the position then adds that people claiming them "real" know they are pretending. They know it is a sham and deceive others on purpose. Philosophers associated with metaethical ontological nonrealist fictionalism include Nadeem Hussain, Mark Kalderon, and Mark Sainsbury.[17] Finally, metaethical ontological nonrealist pluralistic relativism is thinking moral values do not exist apart from believing them, but groups of people make up values suiting social interests. Nonrealist pluralistic relativism restricts the degree of relativity in moral nonrealism by saying that, in order to flourish, groups make up values serving their social interests and these social interests tend to reflect common human characteristics. Philosophers associated with metaethical ontological nonrealist pluralistic relativism include David Wong and Philippa Foot.[18]

The subdivision in ontological metaethics considering the rationality of ethics itself includes two approaches—"metaethical ontological rationalism" and "metaethical ontological nonrationalism." Metaethical ontological rationalism is thinking moral values are inherently rational in the sense of being orderly, possible to analyze, and fitting the way humans think. Rationalism affects ontological as well as epistemological thought, and the difference

---

[16] J. L. Mackie, *Ethics: Inventing Right and Wrong* (London: Penguin, 1977); Simon Blackburn, "Errors in the Phenomenology of Value," in *Essays in Quasi-Realism*, ed. Simon Blackburn (Oxford: Oxford, 1993); Richard Joyce, *The Myth of Morality* (Cambridge: Cambridge, 2001).

[17] Nadeem Hussain, "The Return of Fictionalism," *Philosophical Perspectives* 18/1 (2004): 149–87; Mark Kalderon, *Moral Fictionalism* (Oxford: Clarendon, 2005); Mark Sainsbury, *Fiction and Fictionalism* (London: Routledge, 2010).

[18] David Wong, *Moral Relativity* (Los Angeles: University of California, 1984); David Wong, *Natural Moralities: A Defense of Pluralistic Relativism* (Oxford: Oxford, 2006); Philippa Foot, *Natural Goodness* (Oxford: Clarendon, 2001).

is epistemological rationalism concerns knowing and ontological rationalism concerns the nature of moral values themselves. Philosophers associated with metaethical ontological rationalism include Immanuel Kant, Michael Smith, and Niko Kolodny.[19] Metaethical ontological nonrationalism is thinking moral values are beliefs that function apart from reason because they either are irrational (are just feelings) or are transrational (are beyond human reasoning). Philosophers and thinkers associated with *metaethical ontological nonrationalism* include Terry Horgan, Michael Timmons, and Mark Rogerson et al.[20]

The subdivision in ontological metaethics considering the scope of ethics itself should not be confused with positions regarding scope in epistemological metaethics. Epistemological metaethics considers scope only as to moral knowing and ontological metaethics considers the scope of moral values themselves. As with other subdivisions in ontological metaethics, this one also includes two approaches—"metaethical ontological universalism" and "metaethical ontological relativism." Metaethical ontological universalism is thinking moral values are the same for all, and metaethical ontological relativism, sometimes referred to as "moral nihilism," is thinking universal moral values do not exist and what values people affirm are not the same for everyone. Philosophers associated with the first approach include Immanuel Kant and Sergei Prozorov, and philosophers associated with the second include Gilbert Harmon, Bernard Williams, Hilary Putnam, and Laura Zanotti.[21]

The last subdivision in ontological metaethics considers the source of ethics itself. Where do moral values come from, and what makes them obligatory? Like other subdivisions in

---

[19] Immanuel Kant, *Religion within the Limits of Reason Alone,* trans. Theodore Greene and Hoyt Hudson (New York: Harper & Row, 1960); Michael Smith, *The Moral Problem* (Oxford: Blackwell, 1994); Niko Kolodny, "Why Be Rational?," *Mind* 114/455 (2005): 509–63.

[20] Terry Horgan and Mark Timmons, "Troubles with Michael Smith's Metaethical Rationalism," *Philosophical Papers* 25/3 (1996): 203–31; Mark Rogerson et al., "Nonrational Processes in Ethical Decision Making," *American Psychologist* 66/7 (2011): 614–23.

[21] Immanuel Kant, *Groundwork for the Metaphysics of Morals,* trans. Thomas Abbott, ed. Laura Denis (Peterborough, ON: Broadview, 2005); Sergei Prozorov, *Ontology and World Politics: Void Universalism 1* (New York: Routledge, 2013); Gilbert Harmon, "Moral Relativism Defended," *Philosophical Review* 85/1 (1975): 3–22; Bernard Williams, *Ethics and the Limits of Philosophy* (Cambridge: Harvard, 1985); Hillary Putnam, *Ethic without Ontology* (Cambridge: Harvard, 2004); Laura Zanotti, "Questioning Universalism, Devising an Ethics without Foundations," *Journal of International Political Theory* 11/3 (2015): 277–95.

ontological metaethics, this one, too, includes two approaches—"metaethical ontological naturalism" and "metaethical ontological nonnaturalism." Metaethical ontological naturalism is thinking moral values do not generate themselves and must come from nature. And, since nature consists of material things and only nonmoral facts come from examining material things, metaethical ontological naturalism holds that moral values come from nonmoral material facts. Philosophers associated with metaethical ontological naturalism include Louise Antony, David Copp, and David Enoch.[22]

Metaethical ontological nonnaturalism is thinking moral values cannot come from nonmoral facts in the natural world either because they exist in and of themselves or because they come from a source other than nature. This approach includes two positions—"metaethical ontological nonnatural sui generism" and "metaethical ontological nonnatural supernaturalism." Metaethical ontological nonnatural sui generism is thinking moral values "just are." *Sui generis* is Latin for "of its own kind," and this position holds that moral values are "brute facts" having no source outside themselves. Moral values are thought to exist "because they do" and are thought to be obligatory "because they are." Their existence and obligatory nature depend on nothing. Philosophers associated with defending or criticizing metaethical ontological nonnatural sui generism include W. D. Hudson, Georg Gasser, and Jessica Katz.[23] Metaethical ontological nonnatural supernaturalism is thinking moral values do not come from nature but also are not "brute facts" because their reality and obligatory character come from something transcending nature. It is thinking moral values are real and not imaginary because they come from a supernatural source. Theologians think this way, but some philosophers do as well, and philosophers associated with such thinking include Herbert Spiegelberg and Erik Wielenberg.[24]

---

[22] Louise Antony, "Nature and Norms," *Ethics* 111/1 (2000): 8–36; David Copp, "Why Naturalism?," *Ethical Theory and Moral Practice* 6/2 (2003): 179–2000; David Enoch, *Taking Morality Seriously: A Defense of Robust Realism* (Oxford: Oxford, 2011).

[23] W. D. Hudson, "Moral Facts *Sui Generis*," in *Ethical Intuitionism* (London: St. Martin's, 1967), 12–17; Georg Gasser, "Moral Facts *Sui Generis* For Non-naturalistic Metaphysics of Moral Realism," *Philosophisches Jahrbuch* 118/2 (2011): 232–250; Jessica Katz, "Non-natural Moral Properties: *Sui Generis* or Supernatural?" (PhD dissertation, Bowling Green State University, 2018).

[24] Herbert Spiegelberg, "Supernaturalism or Naturalism: A Study in Meaning and Verifiability," *Philosophy of Science* 18/4 (1951): 339–368; Erik Wielenberg, *Robust Ethics: The Metaphysics and Epistemology of Godless Normative Realism* (Oxford: Oxford, 2014).

VIEWS OF ONTOLOGICAL METAETHICS

Views of what ethical itself is

Views of the reality of ethics itself

Metaethical ontological realism or objectivism (*moral values exist and are true or false independent of those believing them*)

- Naturalistic metaethical ontological realism or concrete realism (*moral values are physically real and exist independently*) (Gewirth, Beyleveld, Boylan, Sturgeon, Bloomfield)
- Non-naturalistic metaethical ontological realism, or abstract metaethical realism, or transhuman metaethical realism (*moral values are abstract realities or ideals that exist apart from the natural world*) (G. E. Moore, W. D. Ross, Hudson, Murdoch, Shafer-Landau)
- Dispositional metaethical ontological realism (*moral values are inherently present in how things are*) (McDowell, Wiggins, Lovibond, McNaughton, Platts, Dancy, DeLapp)

Metaethical ontological nonrealism or subjectivism or constructivism (*moral values do not exist apart from human belief and are not true or false apart from those believing them*)

- Metaethical ontological nonrealist error theory (*moral values do not exist independently and thinking they do is mistaken*) (Mackie, Blackburn, Joyce)
- Metaethical ontological nonrealist fictionalism (*moral values do not exist independently but people pretend they do*) (Hussain, Kalderon, Sainsbury)
- Metaethical ontological nonrealist pluralistic relativism (*moral values do not exist independently but people groups construct values serving their social interests*) (D. Wong, P. Foot)

Views of the rationality of ethics itself

- Metaethical ontological rationalism (*moral values are inherently rational*) (M. Smith, Kolodny)
- Metaethical ontological nonrationalism (*moral values are beliefs that operate independent of human reason*) (Horgan, Timmons, Rogerson et. al.)

Views of the scope of ethics itself

- Metaethical ontological universalism (*moral values apply to or are true for everyone*) (Kant, Prozorov)
- Metaethical ontological relativism (*moral values do not apply to all and are not true for all*) (Harmon, Williams, Putnam, Zanotti)

Views of the source of ethics itself

- Metaethical ontological naturalism (*moral values come from a nonmoral source found in nature*) (Antony, Copp, Enoch)
- Metaethical ontological nonnaturalism (*moral values do not come from a source in the natural world*)
  - Metaethical ontological nonnatural sui generism (*moral values are brute facts that need no explanation*) (Hudson, Gasser, Katz)
  - Metaethical ontological nonnatural supernaturalism (*moral values come from a supernatural source transcending nature*) (Wielenberg, Spiegelberg)

Linguistic Metaethics

Since the middle of the twentieth century, linguistic metaethics, also known as "analytic meta-ethics," has attracted more attention than any other subsection of metaethics, and, for a time, it was thought to be the only thing metaethics considers. Linguistic metaethical analysis was essentially unknown prior to G. E. Moore (1873–1958), and Moore's *Principia Ethica* launched decades of debate over whether moral language is about facts or values and whether moral properties can or cannot be analyzed scientifically.[25] In the 1970s, philosophers in metaethics began addressing more than moral language.[26] Even so, they still focus more on moral language than on other aspects, first, because there is so much now circulating with which to interact and second, because moral language ends up determining how everything else gets treated.

Linguistic metaethics addresses what sort of thing ethical speaking is. Are moral utterances about things "out there in the world," or do they just express attitudes? Are they claims of fact, claims of value, or claims involving facts and values at the same time? Are they about what is true or false, or are they opinions with no bearing on reality? Linguistic metaethics claims not to address what is right and wrong, or is good or bad, and only to address moral utterances themselves. Even though linguistic metaethical positions allege to be nonnormative, all have enormous implications that inevitably determine how people conceive right and wrong and assess what is good and bad.

All positions in linguistic metaethics take one of two approaches, one treating moral utterances as cognitive and the other treating them as noncognitive. "Cognitivism," also called "descriptivism" or "linguistic realism," is thinking moral utterances are about facts that are "truth-apt," meaning they characterize people and actions in ways meant to be taken as true or false. The core element in cognitivism is thinking there either is no difference between facts and values or they are related in a way that allows deriving values from facts. Cognitivism, therefore, maintains that moral utterances say things claimed to be true or false about their subjects. To be cognitive, an utterance does not need to say anything actually true or false about people or actions and needs only to claim something is true or false about them.

---

[25] G. E. Moore, *Principia Ethica* (Cambridge: Cambridge University Press, 1903).

[26] Expanding the focus of metaethics to include epistemological and ontological questions started with John Rawls, *A Theory of Justice* (Cambridge: Harvard University Press, 1971) and Peter Singer, *Practical Ethics* (Cambridge: Cambridge University Press, 1980).

On the other hand, "noncognitivism," also called "nondescriptivism" or "linguistic nonrealism," is thinking moral utterances are not about facts that are "truth-apt," meaning they do not claim anything true or false about people or actions. Instead, noncognitivism thinks moral utterances are only about the person speaking and are just attitudes, opinions, or reactions. It is thought that facts and values are so different nothing connects them, and values cannot be derived from facts. And, therefore, moral utterances cannot be truth claims or even about what someone making them believes to be real or true.

Cognitivism includes three approaches—"cognitive objective realism," "cognitive subjective realism," and "cognitive antirealism." Cognitive objective realism, also called "nonrelative realism," is thinking moral utterances are about facts taken to be true or false regarding things in the real world. Cognitive subjective realism, also called "relative realism" or "contextual realism," is thinking moral utterances are about facts that are relatively true, or "true in a sense," because their reality depends on things that vary. And cognitive antirealism is thinking moral utterances are about alleging facts that do not exist and so claim things that are never true.[27]

Each cognitive approach has variations. Cognitive objective realism includes two positions—"cognitive objective naturalism" and "cognitive objective nonnaturalism." Cognitive objective naturalism, also called "reductivism," is thinking moral utterances are about facts true of the natural world. It is also called "reductionism" because it involves thinking moral utterances are about realities that "reduce" to natural facts. This position denies any real difference between facts and values and holds that moral values are deduced from nonmoral facts in nature. Philosophers associated with cognitive objective naturalism include G. E. Moore, Peter Railton, Richard Boyd, David Brink, Michael Smith, and Frank Jackson.[28]

Cognitive objective nonnaturalism, also called "nonreductivism," is thinking moral utterances are about realities not in nature. It is also called "nonreductionism" because it

---

[27] One philosopher who covers this generally is Hilary Putnam, *Reason, Truth, and History* (Cambridge: Cambridge, 1981).

[28] G. E. Moore, *Principia Ethica* (Cambridge: Cambridge, 1903); Peter Railton, "Moral Realism," *Philosophical Review* 95/2 (1986): 163–207; Richard Boyd, "How to Be a Moral Realist," in *Essays in Moral Realism,* ed. Geoffrey Sayre-McCord (Ithaca, NY: Cornell, 1988), 181–228; David Brink, *Moral Realism and the Foundations of Ethics* (Cambridge: Cambridge, 1989); Michael Smith, *The Moral Problem* (Oxford: Blackwell, 1994); Frank Jackson, *From Metaphysics to Ethics* (Oxford: Oxford, 1998).

involves thinking moral utterances are about facts not "reducible" to nonmoral facts of nature because they are immaterial realities. They are not apprehended by the physical senses but some other way, perhaps by a sixth sense referred to as "conscience" or "intuition." Philosophers associated with cognitive objective nonnaturalism include Nicholas Sturgeon and Judith Jarvis Thompson.[29]

Cognitive subjective realism, also known as "relative realism" or "contextual realism," is thinking moral utterances are about facts that are relatively true because their reality depends on things that vary, and a philosopher associated with developing this approach is Mark Timmons.[30] Cognitive subjective realism in turn includes two positions—"cognitive speaker relativism" and "cognitive situationism." Cognitive speaker relativism is thinking moral utterances are real in reference to the person speaking. It is thinking moral utterances are more than attitudes and say things considered true or false regarding their subjects but only in relation to the speaker's point of view. Philosophers associated with cognitive speaker relativism include John MacFarlane and James Drier.[31] Cognitive situationism, also called "situational relativism," is similar, but instead of thinking the reality of moral utterances depends on a speaker's point of view, cognitive situationism thinks it depends on something larger, like the point of view shared by "people in a culture," "people in a neighborhood," or "people in similar situations." This position denies that moral utterances are just attitudes but then says moral utterances are about subjective realities not true in the same way for all. Philosophers associated with this position include Gilbert Harmon, David Wong, and Stephen Finlay.[32]

---

[29] Nicholas Sturgeon, "Moral Explanations," in *Essays on Moral Realism,* ed. Geoffrey Sayre-McCord (Ithaca, NY: Cornell, 1988), 229–55; Nicholas Surgeon, "Moral Explanations Defended," in *Contemporary Debates in Moral Theory*, ed. James Dreier (Malden, MA: Blackwell, 2006), 241–62; Judith Jarvis Thompson, "Moral Objectivity," in *Moral Relativism and Moral Objectivity*, ed. Gilbert Harmon and Judith Jarvis Thomson (Malden, MA: Blackwell, 1996), 65–68.

[30] Mark Timmons, *Morality without Foundations* (Oxford: Oxford, 1999).

[31] John MacFarlane, "Making Sense of Relative Truth," *Proceedings of the Aristotelian Society* 105/1 (2005): 305–23; John MacFarlane, "Relativism and Disagreement," *Philosophical Studies* 132/1 (2007): 17–31; James Drier, "Internalism and Speaker Relativism," *Ethics* 101/1 (1990): 6–15.

[32] Gilbert Harmon, "Moral Relativism Defended," *Philosophical Review* 84/1 (1975): 3–22; Gilbert Harmon, "Relativistic Ethics: Morality as Politics," *Midwest Studies in Philosophy* 111/3 (1978): 109–21; David Wong, *Moral Relativity* (Berkeley, CA: University of California, 1984); Stephen Finlay, "The Conversational Practicality of Value Judgment," *Journal of Ethics* 8/3 (2004): 205–23; Stephen Finlay, "Oughts and Ends," *Philosophical Studies* 143/3 (2009): 315–40.

Cognitive antirealism is thinking moral utterances claim to be about facts that do not really exist and so are always false and never true. It is "antirealist" because the approach denies that moral utterances are about real facts. But it is "cognitive" because it still says moral utterances are "about facts," even though what is claimed is never really true. Cognitive antirealism, too, includes two positions—"cognitive error theory" and "cognitive fictionalism." The terms *error theory* and *fictionalism* repeat terms used earlier in discussing sorts of ontological nonrealism. These different sets of nonreality positions do interrelate. But they are not the same because one set is ontological, having to do with what ethics itself is, and the other is linguistic, having to do with what ethical speaking is.

Cognitive error theory is thinking moral utterances are about something not really real and thus never true. They are truth claims that must always be wrong, and philosophers associated with cognitive error theory include J. L. Mackie and Richard Joyce.[33] Cognitive fictionalism also thinks moral utterances are about alleging facts not actually true, with the only difference being that cognitive fictionalism adds thinking those making them know they are pretending and do it on purpose. Cognitive fictionalism claims that moral utterances are "a show of moral reality," using deception to discourage or incite others. Philosophers associated with cognitive fictionalism include Nadeem Hussain, Mark Kalderon, James Woodbridge, Richard Joyce, and Mark Sainsbury.[34]

The other approach in linguistic metaethics is noncognitivism, also known as "nondescriptivism" or "linguistic nonrealism," which is thinking moral utterances are just about those speaking. They are not about other people or what they do and are not even meant to be about anything other than the speaker himself or herself. While cognitivism thinks values link with facts, noncognitivism holds that moral values have nothing to do with facts and says thinking so is a "category mistake." But, if moral utterances are not about facts, what are they about? Noncognitivism says the answer is that they can only be about those uttering them. Noncognitivism claims that moral

---

[33] J. L. Mackie, *Ethics: Inventing Right and Wrong* (London: Penguin, 1977); Richard Joyce, *The Myth of Morality* (Cambridge: Cambridge, 2001).

[34] Nadeem Hussain, "The Return of Fictionalism," *Philosophical Perspectives* 18/1 (2004): 149–87; Mark Kalderon, *Moral Fictionalism* (Oxford: Clarendon, 2005); James Woodbridge, "Truth as a Pretense," in *Fictionalism in Metaphysics*, ed. Mark Kalderon (Oxford: Clarendon, 2005), 134–77; Richard Joyce, "Moral Fictionalism," in *Fictionalism in Metaphysics*, ed. Mark Kalderon (Oxford: Clarendon, 2005), 287–313; Mark Sainsbury, *Fiction and Fictionalism* (London: Routledge, 2010).

utterances are not about facts, do not describe anything in the real world, and are not "truth-apt," meaning they are not about anything falsifiable. And noncognitivism includes two related ideas, first, that moral utterances only are about the person speaking and, second, that they are not even about what the person speaking thinks is true or false. *Noncognitivists* vary on how far to go with these ideas, but all agree both are important to linguistic metaethics.[35]

Noncognitivism includes three versions—"noncognitive emotivism," "noncognitive expressivism," and "noncognitive prescriptivism." Noncognitive emotivism is thinking moral utterances are mindless ejaculations of the person speaking. Thus to say, "Murder is bad" just means "Boo murder!" and to say, "Helping poor people is good" just means "Yea helping poor people!" Moral utterances are thought to be about nothing more than how the person speaking feels apart even from what he thinks, and the philosophers most associated with noncognitive emotivism are A. J. Ayer and C. L. Stevenson.[36]

Noncognitive expressivism is thinking moral utterances express attitudes toward norms. Thus, to say, "Murder is bad," just means "Murder is unacceptable," and to say, "Helping poor people is good," just means "Helping poor people is acceptable." The philosopher most associated with *developing noncognitive expressivism* is C. L. Stevenson.[37] This sort of noncognitivism in turn includes two positions—"noncognitive idiosyncratic expressivism" and "noncognitive normative expressivism." Noncognitive idiosyncratic expressivism is thinking moral utterances express a speaker's acceptance of norms. Thus, to say, "Murder is bad," just means "I do not accept murder," and to say, "Helping poor people is good," just means "I accept helping poor people." The philosopher most associated with *noncognitive idiosyncratic expressivism* is Mark Schroader.[38] Noncognitive normative expressivism is thinking moral utterances express shared attitudes toward accepting norms. Thus, to say, "Murder is bad," means "People like

---

[35] Mark van Roojen, "Moral Cognitivism vs. Non-Cognitivism," in *Stanford Encyclopedia of Philosophy*, para. 1.1, published June 23, 2004, revised June 28, 2018, https://plato.stanford.edu/entries/moral-cognitivism/.

[36] A. J. Ayer, *Language, Truth and Logic* (London: Gollancz, 1936; New York: Dover, 1952; London: Penguin, 2001); C. L. Stevenson, "The Emotive Meaning of Ethical Terms," *Mind* 46/18 (1937): 14–31.

[37] C. L. Stevenson, *Ethics and Language* (New Haven, CT: Yale, 1944).

[38] Mark Schroeder, *Being For: Evaluating the Semantic Program of Expressivism* (Oxford: Oxford, 2008); Mark Schroeder, *Noncognitivism in Ethics* (London: Routledge, 2010); March Schroeder, "Ought, Agents, and Actions," *The Philosophical Review* 120/1 (2011): 1–41.

me do not accept murder," and to say, "Helping poor people is good," means "People like me accept helping poor people." The philosopher most associated with noncognitive normative expressivism is Allan Gibbard.[39]

Noncognitive prescriptivism is thinking moral utterances are commands a speaker uses to discourage or incite others. Thus to say, "Murder is bad," is simply issuing "Don't murder!" as an order, and to say, "Helping poor people is good," is simply issuing "Help poor people!" as an order. The position holds that while moral utterances do not describe, recognize, or apply existing moral truth (such as murder being bad or helping poor people being good), their function is to command things be done or not done. But, of course, this also means moral utterances have no authority beyond what is given by whoever issues them. Philosophers most associated with noncognitive prescriptivism are Rudolf Carnap, R. M. Hare, and J. J. C. Smart.[40]

The most recent development in linguistic metaethics is a position known as quasi-realism or mixed theory. As debate between the cognitive and noncognitive camps has evolved, efforts have been made, not only to fine tune the opposing sides, but also to explore a position that could unite them. The term "quasi-realism" indicates "something like realism" that is not completely so, and the term "mixed theory" indicates searching for compatible elements and willingness to drop elements that cannot be reconciled. In sort, some philosophers in metaethics have been thinking moral utterances might be descriptive and attitudinal at the same time. That is, they are thinking moral utterances might be about more than just those speaking and still be expressing something about them. And philosophers associated with this movement include Simon Blackburn, Stephen Barker, David Copp, Michael Ridge, and Daniel Boisvert.[41]

---

[39] Allan Gibbard, *Wise Choices, Apt Feelings* (Cambridge: Harvard, 1990); Allan Gibbard, "Normative Concepts and Recognitional Concepts," *Philosophy and Phenomenological Review* 4/1 (2002): 151–67; Allan Gibbard, *Thinking How to Live* (Cambridge: Harvard, 2003).

[40] Rudolf Carnap, *Philosophy and Logical Syntax* (Bristol, UK: Thoemmes, 1935; New York: Harcourt Brace, 1937); R. M. Hare, *The Language of Morals* (Oxford: Clarendon, 1952); J. J. C. Smart, *Ethics, Persuasion, and Truth* (Oxford: Oxford, 1984).

[41] Simon Blackburn, *Essays on Quasi-Realism* (Oxford: Oxford, 1993); Simon Blackburn, "Quasi-Realism No Fictionalism," in *Fictionalism in Metaphysics*, ed. Mark Kalderon (Oxford: Oxford, 2005), 322–38; Simon Blackburn, "Anti-realist Expressivism and Quasi-realism," in *The Oxford Handbook of Ethical Theory*, ed. David Copp (Oxford: Oxford, 2006), 146–62; Stephen Barker, "Is Value Content a Component of Conventional Implicature?," *Analysis* 60/3 (2000): 268–79; David Copp, "Realist-Expressivism: A Neglected Option for Moral Realism," *Social Philosophy and Policy* 18/2 (2001): 1–43; Michael Ridge, "Ecumenical Expressivism: Finessing Frege," Ethics 116/2 (2006): 302–36; Michael

VIEWS OF LINGUISTIC METAETHICS

Views of what ethical speaking is

Cognitivism, or descriptivism, or linguistic realism (*moral utterances are about facts that are true or false*)

- Cognitive objective realism, or nonrelative realism (*moral utterances are about facts that are true or false in the real world*)
  - Cognitive objective naturalism or reductivism (*moral utterances are about realities reducible to nonmoral physical facts in nature*) (Moore, Boyd, Brink, Railton, Smith, Jackson)
  - Cognitive objective nonnaturalism, or nonreductivism (*moral utterances are about moral realities not reducible to nonmoral physical facts in nature*) (Sturgeon, Thompson)

- Cognitive subjective realism, or relative realism, or contextual realism (*moral utterances are about facts that are relatively true or false*) (Timmons)
  - Cognitive speaker relativism (*moral utterances are about something real in the speaker's point of view*) (MacFarlane, Drier)
  - Cognitive situationism, or situational relativism (*moral utterances are about something real in relation to the situation in which they are made*) (Harmon, Wong, Finlay)

- Cognitive antirealism (*moral utterances are about facts but are always false*) (Putnam)
  - Cognitive error theory (*moral utterances are about something never actually real*) (Mackie, Joyce)
  - Cognitive fictionalism (*moral utterances are about something never actually real but those making them pretend they are about something real*) (Hussain, Kalderon, Woodbridge, Joyce, Sainsbury)

- Quasi-realism, or mixed theory (*moral utterances are both descriptive and attitudinal*) (Blackburn, Barker, Copp, Ridge, Boisvert)

Noncognitivism, or nondescriptivism, or linguistic nonrealism (*moral utterances express attitudes of a speaker and are not about facts that are true or false*)

- Noncognitive emotivism (*moral utterances are emotional ejaculations of the one speaking*) (Ayer, Stevenson)
- Noncognitive expressivism (*moral utterances express attitudes toward accepting norms*) (Stevenson)
  - Noncognitive idiosyncratic expressivism (*utterances express a speaker's acceptance of norms*) (Schroeder)
  - Noncognitive normative expressivism (*utterances express acceptance of norms by people like the speaker*) (Gibbard)
- Noncognitive prescriptivism (*moral utterances are commands used by a speaker to discourage or incite others*) (Carnap, Hare, Smart)

Conclusion

We started this discussion observing that, in philosophical terms, metaethics is the branch of philosophy that explores the status, foundations, and scope of moral values, properties, and words. And we noted that, in theological terms, metaethics is human minds attempting to stand above and behind the mind of God. The difference in these perspectives amounts to whether ethics starts with God or with us and to whether understanding ethics depends on what God says or on what we say. In other words, the difference amounts to whether ethical right and wrong is learned from God or is conceived apart from God.

In closing, I would like to discuss how metaethics relates to the Fall—the biblical doctrine of how we became sinners in the first place. After creating Adam and placing him in the garden of Eden, God issued a command telling Adam (and hence humanity) "you must not eat from the tree of the knowledge of good and evil" adding that "on the day you eat from it, you will certainly die" (Gen 2:16–17). This first ever command of God established the greatest ethical obligation we have, which is learning what ethics is and requires from God, on his terms, in his way, and under his authority.

Adam was only just created and had much to learn. But, before God issued that first ever command, Adam already knew God was good, wise, and in charge. Adam already knew that pleasing and obeying God was morally "good" (טוב, *ṭôḇ*) and that displeasing and disobeying God was morally "evil" (רַע, *rāʿ*). So, when God prohibited eating from "the tree of the knowledge of good and evil" (Gen 2:17), he was not leaving Adam (and later Eve) with no moral compass and, rather, was commanding that they not assert moral independence. Disobeying anything God commanded would have perverted human nature and alienated us from God. But what God focused attention on was defining ethics according to God versus defining ethics apart from God. Eating "from the tree of the knowledge of good and evil" in defiance of God meant rejecting God's moral compass and striking out on their own. It meant not trusting the way God defines "good and evil" and making up something different.

Ridge, "Ecumenical Expressivism: The Best of Both Worlds?," in *Oxford Studies in Metaethics*, vol. 2, ed. Russ Shafer-Landau (Oxford: Oxford, 2007), 51–76; Michael Ridge, *Impassioned Belief* (Oxford: Oxford, 2014); Daniel Boisvert, "Expressive-Assertivism," *Pacific Philosophical Quarterly* 89/2 (2008): 169–203.

This relates to understanding the subject at hand because metaethics does what God ordered our first parents not to do. It does the very thing God prohibited in the garden, which was defining what ethics is and requires for ourselves rather than learning it from him. We cannot follow God's moral compass without learning it from him, and conceiving what ethics is and requires other ways never produces the same thing. In biblical terms, metaethics tempts us the same way the serpent tempted Adam and Eve: "Your eyes will be opened and you will be like God, knowing good and evil" (Gen 3:5). It tempts us to make up what ethics is and requires apart from God. It tempts us to think we control ethics and can define it ourselves, which is to say, metaethics promises what caused humanity to fall in the first place. We cannot trust or use metaethics without dishonoring God. But we can study metaethics to the glory of God because understanding, criticizing, and responding to metaethical thinking based on learning ethics from God is the path God placed us on before the Fall—before Adam and Eve took ethics into their own hands.

Appendix E

OVERCOMING DIVISION
ON THE ETHICS OF TORTURE[1]

Ethicists in the United States were shocked into assessing the ethics of torture starting on April 28, 2004, when shocking accounts filled the news of prisoner abuse at the Abu Ghraib prison in Iraq.[2] In the aftermath, seventeen soldiers and officers were removed, of which eleven were variously convicted in courts-martial, sentenced to military prison, dishonorably discharged, or demoted. And since that time the ethics of torture has been debated in presidential politics and at various conferences, summits, and roundtables, resulting in several books.[3]

---

[1] Previously published as an article in the *Journal of Faith and War*. Daniel R. Heimbach, "The Problem with Assessing Torture," *Journal of Faith and War* 2/2 (Winter 2010), posted December 9, 2010, accessible at https://faithandwar.org/index.php/national-security/44-strategic-leadership/98-the-problem-with-assessing-torture. Used with permission.

[2] The Abu Ghraib story was first reported by Dan Rather on the CBS program, *60 Minutes II*, on April 28, 2004.

[3] Significant books contributing to recent debate concerning the ethics of torture include Mark Danner, *Torture and Truth: America, Abu Ghraib, and the War on Terror* (New York: New York Review of Books, 2004); Sanford Levinson, ed., *Torture: A Collection* (New York: Oxford University Press, 2004); Jennifer K. Harbury, *Truth, Torture, and the American Way* (Boston: Beacon Press, 2005); Karen J. Greenberg, ed., *The Torture Debate in America* (New York: Cambridge, 2006); Alfred W. McCoy, *A Question of Torture: CIA Interrogation, from the Cold War to the War on Terror* (New York: Henry Holt

While no one defends what occurred at Abu Ghraib, the ensuing ethics debate has left the nation deeply divided, or at least confused, as to what moral boundaries apply to the way interrogators go about obtaining vital information from noncooperating prisoners in a war against forces using terror tactics to implement Islamic *sharia* law claiming totalitarian authority over everyone in the world. The division we face now has nothing to do with what occurred at Abu Ghraib, but rather concerns subsequent questions having to do with interrogating confessed or alleged terrorists such as those confined at Guantanamo. In this debate Evangelicals are as deeply divided as others—a situation that leaves us open to suspicion that we could be shaping our ethics to fit political preferences rather than shaping our politics to conform with fixed ethical standards.[4]

I plan here to address this division compromising Evangelical moral witness on torture and will suggest a way forward. In particular, I will argue that there is nothing truly necessary causing this division and will show that what appears to be contrasting positions is mainly a matter of semantics. That is, I believe it comes mainly from using a single word different ways and then supposing those who disagree are favoring positions they do not. But while a semantic problem stands in the way of addressing truly important questions lying beyond, solving this problem is easier said than done.

As a topic, torture is already so highly volatile that all efforts to analyze the ethics of torture are in constant danger of sinking into a swamp of passion. Furthermore, the issue is complex, rendering it susceptible to idealistic simplification, and natural human revulsion toward brutality makes attending other critical aspects extremely difficult. As a result, much of what passes for moral debate on torture is greatly muddied by desires either to attack or defend particular politicians, agencies, or parties. Since I mean to reconcile unnecessary disagreement, I will not criticize or defend specific actions taken by the United States, will not catalog ways in

---

and Company, 2006); Bob Brecher, *Torture and the Ticking Bomb* (Oxford: Blackwell, 2007); David P. Gushee, ed., *Religious Faith, Torture, and Our Soul* (Macon, GA: Mercer University Press, 2010); and Marc A. Thiessen, *Courting Disaster: How the CIA Kept America Safe and How Barak Obama Is Inviting the Next Attack* (Washington, DC: Regnery, 2010).

    [4] For example, David Gushee has wondered if "instinctive political conservatism" was to blame for keeping Evangelicals from joining efforts to condemn the former Bush Administration for espousing torture. David P. Gushee, "What the Torture Debate Reveals about American Christianity," in *Religious Faith*, ed. Gushee, 78.

which prisoners were brutalized, and will not discuss feelings I have had reacting to what others said or did. My purpose, rather, is to produce what both sides might consider a fair assessment of the ethical issue and to propose a framework sufficient to structure and compare what most concerns Evangelicals contributing to contemporary debate regarding the ethics of torture.

Recognizing the Semantic Problem

I first went on record about how failing to define torture hinders moral analysis soon after the current round of public discourse got started,[5] and I have mentioned it again several times since.[6] But I am not the only one to notice how failing to define torture makes it impossible to distinguish allies from opponents, much less engage in constructive moral debate.

Richard Posner says that because "the word *torture* lacks a stable definition," moral evaluation is controlled by whatever "point along a continuum . . . the observer's queasiness turns to revulsion."[7] Jean Bethke Elshtain says that "if everything from a shout to the severing of a body part is *torture*, the category is so indiscriminate as to not permit of those distinctions on which the law and moral philosophy rest."[8] David Gushee acknowledges that, when it

---

[5] Daniel R. Heimbach, "The Truth about Torture?," *A Christian Ethics Symposium* (December 16, 2005), accessible at http://www.evangelicaloutpost.com/torture/archives/001741.html.

[6] Daniel R. Heimbach, "Daniel Heimbach on Torture," *First Things* (posted January 6, 2010), accessible at http://firstthings.com/blogs/evangel/daniel-heimbach-on-torture; Daniel Heimbach with David Gushee and Jonathan Merritt, "Online Bonus: Just War vs. Just Peacemaking," *Relevant Magazine* (April 22, 2009), accessible at http://www.relevantmagazine.com/component/article/118 -mayjune-2009/16702-online-bonus-just-war-vs-just-peacemaking; Daniel Heimbach with David Gushee and Jonathan Merritt, "Just War: Christian Views Clash over War and Peace. Is There Such a Thing?," *Relevant Magazine* 39 (May-June, 2009): 68–72, accessible at http://www.relevantmagazine .com/compoent/article/119-issue-preview/16629-digital-issue-mayjune or at http://www.mygazines .com/issue/759/73; Daniel Heimbach, "A Take on Torture Talk," *The Weekly Standard* (January 2, 2006/January 9, 2006): 6. Also see Erin Roach, "Ethicist: NAE torture declaration 'irrational,'" *Baptist Press* (March 15, 2007), accessible at http://www.bpnews.net/printerfriendly.asp?ID=25190; Ken Camp, "Not all coercive force is torture, Baptist ethicist insists," *Religious Herald* (October 2, 2008), accessible at http://www.religiousherald.org/2736.article.print; and Ken Camp, "Human Rights & Wrongs: Not all coercion is torture, ethicist says," *Associated Baptist Press* (October 2, 2008), accessible at http://www.abpnews.com/content/view/3547/53.

[7] Richard Posner, "Torture, Terrorism, and Interrogation," *Torture*, ed. Levinson, 291.

[8] Jean Bethke Elshtain, "Reflections on the Problem of 'Dirty Hands,'" *Torture*, ed. Levinson, 79.

comes to "the exact kinds of acts that constitute torture, there is no single definition."[9] Tyler Wigg-Stephenson fears that, because assessing torture all depends on first defining what it means, we may be forever "stuck in the same fruitless, frustrated (false) agreement in which we presently find ourselves."[10] David Luban notes that dictionary definitions of torture are all notoriously vague, being nothing more than "a list of equally vague synonyms," and for this reason remarks that any effort "to wring greater specificity . . . out of a dictionary is, by the very terms of the problem, a cheat" serving "only to provide a seemingly-objective source for spinning the meaning of a word" any way at all.[11] Finally Keith Pavlischek and I both criticized the *Declaration on Torture* issued by the National Association of Evangelicals in 2007 on mainly semantic grounds, with Pavlischek saying it failed "to define torture with any degree of precision,"[12] and with me saying it should not have divided Evangelicals "into renouncers and justifiers" without defining the point at issue because no Evangelical anywhere "disagrees with rejecting immorality or defends mistreating fellow human beings made in the image of God."[13]

What is interesting about these statements is how they come from both sides of the moral debate. Everyone truly serious about assessing the ethics of torture understands that we have a semantic problem, and if Evangelicals now seemingly divided into opposing camps can delay charging into moral battle, we may find we have more reason to cooperate than to attack.

Analyzing the Semantic Problem

Following Luban's advice to avoid dictionary definitions, and to focus instead on what is really being said in the torture debate, it is possible to discern four distinctly different senses in which the term is being employed. These I will label (1) *no means ever torture*, (2) *evil means*

---

[9] David P. Gushee, "5 Reasons Torture Is Always Wrong," *Christianity Today* (February 2006): 33.

[10] Tyler Wigg-Stephenson, "Tortured Truth," *Religious Faith*, ed. Gushee, 137.

[11] David Luban, "Liberalism, Torture, and the Ticking Bomb," *The Torture Debate in America*, edited by Karen J. Greenberg (New York: Cambridge, 2006), 58.

[12] Keith Pavlischek, "Human Rights and Justice in an Age of Terror: An Evangelical Critique of *An Evangelical Declaration Against Torture*," *Books & Culture* (December 3, 2008), accessible at http://www.booksandculture.com/articles/webexclusives/2007/september/ept24a.html.

[13] Quoted by Erin Roach in "Ethicist: NAE torture declaration 'irrational,'" *Baptist Press* (March 15, 2007), accessible at http://www. bpnews.net/printerfriendly.asp?ID=25190.

torture, (3) *coercive means torture*, and (4) *any means possible torture*. The first and fourth of these are used by so few they are not worth serious attention. But the second and third are worth examining because all serious efforts to assess the ethics of torture end up using one or the other. I will first survey all four senses and then will show how the second and third, while semantically different, do not necessarily conflict morally.

The first most broadly opposed sense in which torture is being used employs what we may call the *no means ever torture* definition. Used this way, torture refers to rejecting anything that overcomes a person's will to withhold information, no matter how mild. Torture in this sense has no minimal limitation. It has no minimum threshold to what is disallowed. Andrew Sullivan takes this approach where he says, "What defines torture is not this or that technique" but rather is whatever brings prisoners to "the limit of their ability to withhold information." It is anything however mild that causes "captives . . . to confess."[14] In other words, if a prisoner talks, he was by this definition "tortured" no matter what measures were used, however minimal.

The second still very opposed but more discerning sense in which torture is being used employs what may be called the *evil means torture* definition, a definition using torture to reference any never-justifiable form of coercion. This definition assumes coercive force but uses torture as a blanket term for treating fellow human beings in ways that can never be justified. It uses torture to indicate forms of treatment that are in themselves inherently evil and so can never be right no matter what. Torture in this sense is never justifiable because that is what torture means to the person using the term. Impossible-to-justify actions cannot be justified simply because that is what they are, and many participating in current debate are using the term in this sense. That is what Sister Dianna Ortiz means in saying torture is a "crime against humanity"[15]; it is what Douglas Johnson means in saying "torture is a crime against the human spirit"[16]; it is what Tyler Wigg-Stevenson means by saying torture is "to bend toward evil that which God has given for good" or is "to perpetrate the untruth that the nation is more than God has made it to be"[17]; it is what Glen Stassen means in saying "all torture . . .

---

[14] Andrew Sullivan, "Mark Thiessen: It Was Torture," *The Daily Dish*, April 21, 2009, accessible at http://andrew sullivan.theatlantic.com/the_daily_dish/2009/04/mark-thiessen-it-was-torture.

[15] Sister Dianna Ortiz, "What Torture Does to Human Beings," *Religious Faith*, ed. Gushee, 44.

[16] Douglas A. Johnson, "What Torture Does to Human Beings," *Religious Faith*, ed. Gushee, 63.

[17] Tyler Wigg-Stevenson, "Tortured Truth," *Religious Faith*, ed. Gushee, 146–47.

is a fundamental violation of God's primordial will"[18]; it is what David Gushee means in saying "torture is always wrong,"[19] even though he agrees that "interrogators should have some flexibility in applying pressure to encourage prisoners to reveal information that could save lives"[20]; and it is what I meant when I said, "it is always wrong to apply force immorally, and if that is what . . . (is meant) by *torture* then I do indeed strongly oppose torture . . . under any circumstance and urge everyone else to oppose it as well."[21]

Interestingly and to the irritation of their critics,[22] this second sense in which torture refers to never justifiable evil means is the same definition Jay Bybee used in claiming nothing less than pain "akin to that which accompanies serious physical injury such as death or organ failure" truly qualifies as torture,[23] and it is the same sense Marc Thiessen used in denying that President George W. Bush ever authorized torture because for Thiessen only killing a person "would be torture."[24]

The third somewhat less completely opposed, but also more inclusive and most highly nuanced, sense in which the term torture is used employs what may be called the *coercive means torture* definition. In this case torture refers to any sort of coercion employed for the purpose of forcing resistant prisoners to reveal information needed to save lives. Here torture refers to something more than mild persuasion but extends to cover all sorts of coercive treatment. It includes not only forms that may sometimes be justified but also forms that can never be justified. By this definition, torture not only covers ways of treating people that are always

---

[18] Glen Stassen, "The Religious Roots of Human Rights," *Religious Faith*, ed. Gushee, 163.

[19] David P. Gushee, "5 Reasons Torture Is Always Wrong," *Christianity Today* (February 2006), 33–37; Gushee, "What the Torture Debate Reveals," *Religious Faith*, ed. Gushee, 75.

[20] Gushee, "5 Reasons," 33.

[21] Quoted by Ken Camp in "Not all coercive force is torture, Baptist ethicist insists," *Religious Herald* (October 2, 2008), accessible at http://www.religiousherald.org/2736.article.print; and in "Human Rights & Wrongs: Not all coercion is torture, ethicist says," *Associated Baptist Press* (October 2, 2008).

[22] Tyler Wigg-Stevenson is frustrated with how, on the issue of torture, "our opponents have undone us with their agreement, their nonresistance," and with therefore being forever "stuck in the same fruitless, frustrated agreement in which we presently find ourselves." Tyler Wigg-Stevenson, "Tortured Truth," *Religious Faith*, ed. Gushee, 136–37.

[23] Jay S. Bybee, "Memorandum for Alberto Gonzales, Counsel to the President; Subject: Standards of Conduct for Interrogation under 18 USC; §§ 2340–2340A" (August 1, 2002).

[24] Marc Thiessen, *Courting Disaster* (Washington, DC: Regnery, 2010), 2, 18, 131.

evil but also covers ways that are not always evil—or at least are not evil all the time—and can therefore at times be morally justified under limited circumstances. And because this is what torture means to those using the term this way, it means that for them torture includes both never-justifiable as well as sometimes-justifiable sorts of action.

This is what Charles Krauthammer means in saying "torture is not always impermissible" and "there are circumstances in which, by rational moral calculation, torture not only would be permissible but would be required";[25] it is what Richard Posner means in saying that "if torture is the only means by which to save the lives of thousands, perhaps tens or hundreds of thousands, of people . . . (then) it seems to me, torture must be allowed"[26]; it is what Jean Bethke Elshtain means by saying torture includes "extreme forms of physical torment" that are never morally justified but also includes forms of "coercive interrogation" that "may, with regret," be morally justified under very limited circumstances[27]; it is what Albert Mohler means in saying "we cannot deny that there could exist circumstances in which . . . torture might be made necessary"[28]; it is what Wayne Grudem means when saying "government has a right—even a moral obligation—*within specified limits*, to use such compulsion"[29]; and it is what I meant in saying that, if we use Krauthammer's view of *torture* as applying *coercion per se*, then, after setting proper boundaries for moral use, we should without apology defend obligation to exercise justified coercion within proper restraints.[30]

The fourth and least critical sense in which the term appears in current debate is what may be called the *any means possible torture* definition. In this sense torture refers to justifying anything that works no matter how severe, distasteful, or inhumane. This approach like the

---

[25] Charles Krauthammer, "The Truth about Torture," *The Weekly Standard* (December 5, 2005), 22. Also, Charles Krauthammer, "The Truth about Torture," *Torture*, ed. Levinson, 309.

[26] Richard Posner, "Torture, Terrorism, and Interrogation," *Torture*, ed. Levinson, 293.

[27] Jean Bethke Elshtain, "Reflections on the Problem of 'Dirty Hands,'" *Torture*, ed. Levinson, 87.

[28] Albert Mohler, "The Truth about Torture?," *A Christian Ethics Symposium* (December 16, 2005), accessible at http://www.evangelicaloutpost.com/torture/archives/001741.html.

[29] Wayne Grudem, *Politics According to the Bible* (Grand Rapids: Zondervan, 2010), 428.

[30] Daniel R. Heimbach, "The Truth about Torture?," *A Christian Ethics Symposium* (December 16, 2005), accessible at http://www.evangelicaloutpost.com/torture/archives/001741.html; Daniel R. Heimbach, "Daniel Heimbach on Torture," *First Things* (posted January 6, 2010), accessible at http://firstthings.com/blogs/evangel/daniel-heimbach-on-torture; and Daniel Heimbach, "A Take on Torture Talk," *The Weekly Standard* (January 2, 2006/January 9, 2006): 6.

first includes a side to the category with no limitation. But rather than having no minimum to what is disallowed, in this case there is no maximum to what is allowed. Although no one consistently defends this sense of the word, critics of torture fear it is what some defenders may be seeking,[31] and it certainly is true that some arguing in favor of torture have at times said things tantamount to using the term in this fashion. It is evident, for example, in John McCain's notorious remark that "you have to do what you have to do. But you take responsibility for it"[32]; it is suggested in Richard Posner's statement that, "*in extremis*," one must apply "as much pressure as it takes"[33]; and it is suggested in former Vice President Cheney's remark reported by Marc Thiessen that he and former President George W. Bush "were determined (in the aftermath of 9/11) to do everything that we could to avoid and prevent any further attacks on the US. . . . And we were prepared to take whatever heat was generated . . . (in order) to prevail."[34]

Solving the Semantic Problem

At this point I wish to clarify that I know of no Evangelical scholar who assesses the ethics of torture in either of the most radical senses that define torture in ways having no categorical limit. No Evangelical employs either the *no means ever* or *any means possible* definition, which means of course that all Evangelicals assessing the ethics of torture are employing either the *evil means* or *coercive means* definition. We will now look more closely at how these two more sensible definitions relate.

The first important thing to note is how neither sense used by Evangelicals is conceptually limitless, and this means of course that no Evangelical is employing either of the extreme

---

[31] For example, David Gushee warns against "the kind of self-deception . . . characteristic of a descent into sin" that allows us to "deny we are torturing" when we are (Gushee, "5 Reasons," 37); and this leads Gushee to conclude that when it comes to renouncing torture "white evangelicals" have "lost touch with their own tradition and with the broader Christian tradition" (Gushee, "What the Torture Debate Reveals," *Religious Faith*, ed. Gushee, 76–77).

[32] Reported by Evan Thomas and Michael Hirsh in "The Debate Over Torture," *Newsweek* (November 21, 2005).

[33] Posner, "Torture, Terrorism, and Interrogation," *Torture*, ed. Levinson, 293.

[34] Thiessen, *Courting Disaster*, 236.

definitions. This is important to recognize because in the passion of moral battle it is easy to tar opponents with positions they do not truly defend. *Evil means torture* Evangelicals should not associate other Evangelicals of defending *any means possible torture*, and *coercive means torture* Evangelicals should not associate other Evangelicals with defending *no means ever torture*.

Next, I recommend that Evangelicals debating the ethics of torture set aside the passion of moral battle long enough to notice how we are all dealing with much the same thing. I mean here that we are all traversing the same moral landscape. Everyone involved agrees that some coercive actions are inherently evil and can never be justified no matter what, and that other coercive actions while regrettable may be justified under limited circumstances.

If we avoid the word *torture* for a moment and simply focus on what Evangelicals use to frame moral analysis, there really is far more on which we agree than disagree. Every Evangelical assessing the ethics of torture, whether in the *evil means* or *coercive means* sense, shares a common set of convictions that include the following:

1. That techniques of prisoner interrogation range on a continuum from extremely mild to extremely severe.
2. That some forms of coercion qualify as evil means that never can be justified, and these lie toward the severe end of the continuum of interrogative methods.
3. That besides these there are regrettable but not always evil forms of coercion that sometimes may be justified, and these forms lie toward the less severe end of the continuum of interrogative methods.
4. That even not-always-evil forms of coercion should never be used unless truly justified and using them when not justified is terribly bad.
5. That there is a moral boundary distinguishing never-justifiable forms of interrogation from sometimes-justifiable forms of interrogation.
6. That the ethics of torture cannot be measured merely by whether techniques work or not, whether in the *no means ever* sense or in the *any means possible* sense.
7. That we must never cease caring more for morality than politics and must never substitute political expediency for moral scrutiny.
8. That we must never cease guarding ourselves against succumbing to forms of self-deception that justify descending into sin.

9. That legality and morality are not the same thing and, if they differ, legality must give way to morality, not the other way around.

10. That US law and international conventions ratified by our government are both too imprecise and need improving by adding more easily measured boundaries for distinguishing never-justifiable from sometimes-justifiable methods of interrogation.

These points of agreement show that what divides Evangelicals on the ethics of torture is more a matter of semantics than substance. We employ a commonly held moral framework that involves a continuum of interrogative means extending from extremely mild measures (such as delaying a meal or restricting visitors) to measures everyone agrees are never justifiable (such as killing innocent family members or rape). And we all understand that along this continuum, between measures that are never justifiable and those not worth disputing, there is a third category consisting of measures that need to be restricted as far as possible but that are sometimes justified under limited circumstances. Whether and under what circumstances such measures are properly justified requires exercising relative moral judgment, a form of wisdom by which decisions are reached on whether or when to use measures hardly ever allowed and never preferred but also not in the category of means that are never justifiable. What I mean here is nothing more than what David Gushee means when acknowledging that interrogators need "some flexibility in applying pressure to encourage prisoners to reveal information that could save lives,"[35] or than what Wayne Grudem means in saying government has a moral obligation "within specified limits" to use measures "in order to attempt to compel the terrorist to do what is morally right"[36]; or than what I have meant in saying elsewhere that "we should without apology defend obligation to exercise justified coercion within proper restraints."[37]

In diagram form, all Evangelicals are assessing the ethics of torture by dividing the continuum of interrogative means into three moral categories as follows:

---

[35] Gushee, "5 Reasons," 33.
[36] Grudem, *Politics*, 428.
[37] Heimbach, "Truth about Torture," "Heimbach on Torture," and "Take on Torture," 6.

Rarely objectionable mild means	Coercive means that must be avoided as much as possible but are sometimes justified	Never-justifiable, inherently evil means
	←————————————————————————→	

What this shows is that much of what passes for disagreement separating Evangelicals on the ethics of torture is not substance but semantics; and where that is the case, we should clarify terms and work together as allies rather than act like opponents. But, while clarifying semantics solves one problem, it also reveals other, more complex and difficult problems. So, while I do not think Evangelicals are divided on the moral framework used to evaluate torture, I do recognize that we are genuinely divided and need to continue debating how the framework we use applies to particular forms of interrogation.

I mean by this that, while Evangelicals are not really disagreeing on what frames moral analysis, we should not ignore two important further questions revealed by recognizing this fact. These further questions are (1) how to draw the moral boundary separating the never justifiable evil means category from always regrettable but sometimes justifiable category and (2) how to go about making the relative judgments needed to decide whether and when forms of coercion in the sometimes justifiable though regrettable category are truly justified or not. I will now consider these briefly before concluding.

Going beyond the Semantic Problem

No serious effort to assess the ethics of torture can afford to ignore either of the further questions exposed by solving the semantic problem. But of these two further questions, the first is more difficult than the second, and that is because it cannot be answered without settling two things about which people very often disagree—accepting the reality of universally fixed norms, and then identifying what norms apply when drawing the moral boundary beyond which no exceptions are allowed. While Evangelicals agree on the first condition, we are not agreed on the second. When it comes to identifying never-justifiable forms of coercive interrogation, Jean Bethke Elshtain relies on personal intuition, saying "everything in me says no" when confronting "extreme forms of physical torment,"[38] and Marc Thiessen sees no bound-

---

[38] Jean Bethke Elshtain, "Reflections," 85.

ary short of physical death.[39] But Evangelicals must do better because neither of these options provides any real help—Elshtain because feelings cannot be measured in any reliable way, and Thiessen because death limits nothing so far as getting prisoners to talk.

Here I think the five reasons David Gushee gave in *Christianity Today* for rejecting never justifiable actions are very helpful.[40] They should not be used for deciding whether or when regrettable forms of coercion are sometimes justified but can be helpful for knowing when we are dealing with ways of treating people that can never be justified no matter what. It is theologically and biblically sound for Evangelicals to hold that no means of coercion can ever be used that by its very nature either (1) dishonors the image of God, (2) oppresses the innocent, (3) deifies human government, (4) is arbitrary or sadistic, or (5) destroys the moral purpose of civil government. These five characteristics are all rather general and subject to interpretation, but they are also indisputably biblical, which means using them to draw the line on never-justifiable forms of coercion makes much better sense than using nothing more than subjective feeling or stopping at nothing short of death. But in answering this question, I think Evangelicals should also accept and apply the portion of just war tradition that has long eschewed a list of measures judged to be inherently evil and therefore never to be justifiable no matter what, a list usually thought to include acts of rape, pillage, purposely indiscriminate destruction (terrorism), purposely harming or killing innocent third parties, sexual molestation, and desecrating holy places.[41]

---

[39] Thiessen, *Courting Disaster*, 131.

[40] David P. Gushee, "5 Reasons Torture Is Always Wrong," *Christianity Today* (February 2006), 33–37.

[41] References to prohibiting within just war tradition all use of certain means held to be inherently immoral or evil under any circumstance can be found in Roland H. Bainton, *Christian Attitudes Toward War and Peace* (Nashville: Abingdon, 1960), 97 and 166; Thomas E. Murray, *Nuclear Policy for War and Peace* (New York: World, 1960), 43; Paul Ramsey, *War and the Christian Conscience* (Durham, NC: Duke University Press, 1961), 79, 84, 224, et al. References can also be found in Augustine, the Second Lateran Council, and Vitoria. Augustine in the fifth century held that Christian moral influence did not allow soldiers fighting a just war to profane temples, kill persons who fled to temples for refuge, rape women, take plunder or exact revenge. See *The City of God*, I.1–7. In the twelfth century, the Second Lateran Council (1139) held that just war did not allow using crossbows, bow and arrows, or siege weapons. See "Second Lateran Council (1139)," *Catholic Encyclopedia* (New York: Robert Appleton, 1913). Then, in the sixteenth century, Francisco de Vitoria held that just war generally did not allow indiscriminate slaughter, indiscriminate destruction of property, raping virgins, dishonoring matrons, killing women or children, looting temples, taking booty from the property of innocent victims, executing all captured enemy soldiers, executing all surrendering enemy soldiers, selling an enemy

The second question that comes from realizing Evangelicals are all using the same framework for assessing the ethics of torture is how to decide under what circumstances otherwise regrettable forms of interrogation may be warranted. Here the obvious answer is to employ principles of just war restraint that apply to assessing regrettable actions short of those judged to be inherently evil and never justifiable. Interaction between interrogators and captured members of an enemy force is itself a form of war involving actions threatening general or personal welfare, plans or information affecting life or death, which side wins or loses, and need to evaluate if, when, or to what degree using force by one side against the other is justified. The principles of just war have been worked out for making morally responsible decisions where relative judgment is required in just this sort of situation. Thus, applied to evaluating when otherwise regrettable forms of interrogation might be justified, just war tradition offers the following:

No evil means: Morally justified interrogation must never include any means so corrupt in itself as never to be justifiable no matter what. See the discussion above for determining where this moral boundary lies.

Just cause: Morally justified interrogation must always try to correct or prevent some wrong actually done or threatened by a prisoner or forces with which he is aligned. No coercive interrogation is justified only for fear of something never done or threatened, or only to express racial, religious, or cultural prejudice, or only to fish for information with no prior basis in fact.

Competent authority: Morally justified interrogation must be authorized by whatever authority is ultimately responsible for national security. No coercive interrogation is ever allowed by interrogators unaccountable to the higher authority.

Comparative justice: Morally justified interrogation must determine that stakes justifying coercive measures are more worthy than stakes justifying resistance. Justice is sometimes divided, and no coercion is justified for reasons interrogators themselves know are less worthy than reasons justifying a prisoner's refusal to cooperate.

population into slavery, or setting captured cities on fire. See Francisco de Vitoria, *The Indian and the Law of War* (1139), III.

Right intention: Morally justified interrogation must intend to restore properly justified social order and nothing else. No coercion is allowed simply to punish,[42] entertain, do research, send a message, or only to promote the self-interest of interrogators.

Last resort: Morally justified interrogation must never use any regrettable means except as a last resort. No coercion is ever allowed if the same result can be achieved other ways.

Probability of success: Morally justified interrogation must have some basis for believing the one interrogated knows the information sought. Coercive interrogation is more or less justified to the degree that interrogators know a prisoner is withholding information. No coercion is justified on prisoners with no way of knowing the information sought, and little is justified where likelihood of a prisoner knowing desired information is low or uncertain. Concomitantly, much coercion may be justified to obtain information from prisoners who are known to have targeted information.

Proportionality of projected results: Morally justified interrogation must have reasonable hope of achieving a good worth more than whatever harm or loss may be suffered in obtaining it. No coercive means is allowed that intentionally causes more harm than good.

Proportionality in the use of force: Morally justified interrogation must never use more coercion than required to correct or prevent whatever wrong justifies interrogating a prisoner in the first place. No form of coercion is allowed that exceeds what justifies taking someone prisoner.

Discrimination: Morally justified interrogation must only use coercion with combatants serving a power threatening national security and public safety. No coercive

---

[42] While Francisco de Vitoria in the twelfth century argued that punishing a defeated foe is a properly warranted intention (see *The Indian and the Law of War*, III), Vitoria's justification of punishment is not generally accepted as consistent with classical just war tradition, which restricts proper intention only to restoring civil peace by stopping or undoing whatever wrong justified going to war in the first place. Punishing a defeated foe is more typically associated with the crusade ethic of war. But whether punishment is or is not a proper just war intention in the overall sense, it still has no proper place in determining justified forms of prisoner interrogation.

measure may ever be applied to innocent third parties or to parties not themselves responsible for hazarding national security or public safety.

Good faith: Morally justified interrogation must always keep promises made to prisoners and must always treat them as human, not subhuman (i.e., as animals or devils). No coercive measure is ever justified that breaks promises or degrades humanity.

Right spirit: Morally justified interrogation should only be authorized and conducted by those who regret needing to use coercive measures. No coercion can be rightly authorized or applied by persons who relish or enjoy doing so.

Conclusion

I have argued that nearly everything over which Evangelicals seem currently divided in assessing the ethics of torture is semantic, not substantial, and I have proposed that solving this semantic problem will help us avoid rhetorical attacks and free us instead to focus on two subsequent challenges: (1) settling the question of what truly distinguishes the category of *inherently-evil-actions-that-can-never-be-justified-under-any-circumstance* from the category of *regrettable-actions-that-are-sometimes-justified-under-limited-but-morally-definable-circumstances*, and (2) settling the question of by what principles otherwise regrettable actions may sometimes be justified.

I do not think solving the semantic problem will or even should end all Evangelical divisions; and I expect that in some ways solving the semantic problem might even increase the intensity of Evangelical debate. But, if that happens, it will bring a new sort of intensity that produces better results than produced thus far. In fact, I do not think solving the semantic problem even requires that we all agree on a single definition of *torture*, only that we recognize semantic differences well enough to treat each other fairly and to cooperate in assessing the truly important questions that follow. If we ever reach that point, I think Evangelicals should continue challenging each other very strongly on how best to answer the threshold of essential evil question and the justification of regrettable means question. I only hope that solving the semantic problem will allow us to lay aside acrimony, demagogy, prejudice, and politics and to focus instead on pursuing a shared goal—all done in a manner characterized as much by love as by reason, and as much by reason as by love.

NAME INDEX

SUBJECT INDEX

SCRIPTURE INDEX

62:10 *427*
63:11 *298*
64:1 *450*
65:5–13 *475*
65:9–13 *474, 483*
65:13 *474*
68:30 *442–43*
68:34 *508*
72:13 *428*
72:19 *105, 475*
73 *10*
73:3 *429*
73:13 *429*
82:3–4 *441*
84:2 *511*
86:9 *105*
86:11 *14*
89:5 *474*
89:48 *342*
90:14 *370*
91:4 *298*
91:5–6 *474*
91:14–15 *450*
93:3 *474*
96:8 *508*
96:9 *59, 508*
96:11–13 *474*
97:1–6 *474*
97:6 *474*
98:4–6 *511*
98:7–9 *474*
100:1–2 *511*
100:3 *396, 525*
101:7 *298*
102:27 *84, 92, 138, 434–35, 508*
103:19 *60*
104:5 *474*
104:10–13 *474*
104:14 *474*
104:14–15 *359*
104:15 *358*
104:16 *474*
104:17–18 *474*
104:19–22 *474*
104:24 *474*
104:31 *474*
107:23–38 *484*
109:28 *511*
111:2–3 *474*

111:10 *521*
113:9 *331*
115:1 *508*
115:16 *474*
116:17 *508*
117:1–2 *508*
118:1 *508*
118:1–4 *508*
119 *10*
119:2 *498*
119:9 *14, 54*
119:37 *60*
119:72 *60*
119:89 *60, 226*
119:91 *60*
119:96 *60*
119:104 *298*
119:105 *54, 132*
119:127 *60*
119:129 *59*
119:144 *60*
119:160 *60, 298*
119:163 *298*
120:2 *298*
120:6–7 *441–42*
121:6 *474*
121:7 *450*
122:8–9 *437*
127:3 *331, 341*
127:5 *332*
128:2 *356*
128:5–6 *437*
139 *325*
139:7 *410*
139:7–10 *68*
139:13 *341*
144:1 *441, 444*
145:3 *49*
145:19 *370*
146:5–6 *305*
146:6 *298*
147:14 *483*
148:3–10 *474*
148:8 *484*

Proverbs
1:7 *521*
2:7–8 *441*
2:8 *14*

2:17 *275*
2:21 *299*
3:1 *141*
3:2 *138, 143*
3:2–3 *308*
3:3 *11*
3:17 *428, 431*
3:21 *268*
4:8 *97*
4:12 *129*
4:17 *305*
5:6 *298*

2 John

1:6 *265*
1:8 *193*

Jude

3–4 *155*
7 *387, 389*
13 *522*

Revelation

1:13 *396*
2:10 *414, 416, 422*
2:26 *143*
3:17 *427, 429*
3:20 *ix*
4:8 *508*
4:11 *508*
5:9–10 *458*
5:12 *508*
5:13 *474*
7:9 *458*
9:21 *363*
11:18 *476*
12:9 *416*

12:11 *414*
13:1–8 *414*
13:7 *414*
13:8 *485*
14:6 *458*
14:8 *359*
17:1–2 *404*
17:2 *359*
17:14 *414*
18:4 *414*
18:8 *414*
18:15–16 *427*
18:23 *363*
19:11 *309, 441*
19:11–15 *444*
19:11–16 *439*
20:7–8 *416*
20:7–9 *444*
21:1 *137, 146, 148, 496*
21:1–7 *142*
21:2 *144*
21:3 *144*
21:4 *416, 428, 443*
21:5 *496*
21:5–8 *146*
21:8 *299, 363, 399*
21:10–14 *492*
21:10–27 *67*
21:26 *492*
21:27 *386*
22:3 *144, 416*
22:5 *143*
22:12 *11*
22:15 *363, 386, 405*
22:18 *356*
22:18–19 *355*
22:19 *356*